Approaches to Teaching the History of the English Language

APPROACHES TO TEACHING THE HISTORY OF THE ENGLISH LANGUAGE

Pedagogy in Practice

Edited by Mary Hayes

and

Allison Burkette

OXFORD
UNIVERSITY PRESS

For Cherry Lee,
a true language
professional,
with respect,
Michael R Pressman

OXFORD
UNIVERSITY PRESS

Oxford University Press is a department of the University of Oxford. It furthers
the University's objective of excellence in research, scholarship, and education
by publishing worldwide. Oxford is a registered trade mark of Oxford University
Press in the UK and certain other countries.

Published in the United States of America by Oxford University Press
198 Madison Avenue, New York, NY 10016, United States of America.

Library of Congress Cataloging-in-Publication Data
Names: Hayes, Mary, 1972– editor. | Burkette, Allison, editor.
Title: Approaches to teaching the history of the English language :
pedagogy in practice / edited by Mary Hayes and Allison Burkette.
Description: New York, NY : Oxford University Press, [2017] |
"First Edition published in 1996." | "First Edition published in Paperback 2001." |
Includes bibliographical references and index.
Identifiers: LCCN 2016050789 (print) | LCCN 2017014915 (ebook) |
ISBN 9780190611064 (pdf) | ISBN 9780190611071 (online course) |
ISBN 9780190683429 (ebook) | ISBN 9780190611057 (pbk. : alk. paper) |
ISBN 9780190611040 (cloth : alk. paper)
Classification: LCC PE1075 (ebook) | LCC PE1075 .A64 2017 (print) |
DDC 420.9—dc23
LC record available at https://lccn.loc.gov/2016050789

9 8 7 6 5 4 3 2 1

Paperback Printed by Webcom, Inc., Canada
Hardback Printed by Bridgeport National Bindery, Inc., United States of America

This book is dedicated to our children. Anne Paige Tschumper, Kate Tschumper, and Noah Burkette, whose patience and support were ever-present throughout this adventure. And Francis Shackleton Hayes-Lawrence, who was born when this project was and discovered language as it took shape.

And it is dedicated to the memory of Braj B. Kachru (May 15, 1932–July 29, 2016) and Claire Sponsler (January 28, 1954–July 29, 2016), irreplaceable scholars and teachers. We hope this volume speaks to their lasting influence on their fields as well as our own academic work.

CONTENTS

ACKNOWLEDGMENTS

While collaborating on a book project whose subject is so extensive, we have profited from having so many kind and keen-minded colleagues. At our home institution, the University of Mississippi, our department chairs, Ivo Kamps in English and Don Dyer in Modern Languages, have supported this project from its incipience and, more broadly, have encouraged us to craft a History of the English Language curriculum that fits the needs of our undergraduate, graduate, and online students. Additionally, Ivo Kamps provided funding for the "Future of the History of the English Language" panel at the Modern Languages Association meeting in Vancouver (January 2015), one of the seeds from which this project grew. Thanks to his generosity, we were able to hire three extraordinary young scholars to help us dot our i's, cross our t's, and get myriad other diacritical marks just right: Blake Shedd is an omnivorous polyglot and burgeoning medievalist who can spot an italicized period from a thousand years away; Andrew S. Henning is a digital humanities whiz who got our files, sources, and us organized at urgent moments; and Amber Hodge brought to the project a wealth of skills from her "other life," her years spent in the publishing business before starting graduate school. Our editor at Oxford University Press, Hallie Stebbins, was a joy to work with at every phase of the project. She is smart, insightful, and accommodating and was such a great ambassador for the press. In that vein, we hope that Oxford University Press's anonymous reviewers are now reading the finished product so that they can see that we benefited from their comments. In an unofficial capacity, Katherine O'Brien O'Keeffe, herself a well-reputed and expert HEL teacher, gave us substantial advice. Steven Justice is a model professional mentor; he was unstinting in his support and generous with his criticism. We would be remiss if we did not thank our contributors for their infectious enthusiasm for the project. It was a pleasure getting to know such careful and thoughtful fellow educators. Of course we must thank our own students, especially those who "survived" HEL. Little did you realize that when you were enduring difficult material, uninspiring class sessions, and impossible exams, you were teaching us how to make the course better.

In addition to this wonderful professional network, we received unlimited furtherance from our partners and children, who loved us even when we spent more time with the aforementioned colleagues, each other, and the volume than with them. Thank you for making room in your lives for our love for the English language.

LIST OF CONTRIBUTORS

Michael Adams is Provost Professor of English Language and Literature at Indiana University, Bloomington. He is author of *Slayer Slang: A Buffy the Vampire Slayer Lexicon* (Oxford University Press, 2003), *Slang: The People's Poetry* (Oxford University Press, 2009), *In Praise of Profanity* (Oxford University Press, 2016), and lots of articles, as well as editor of *From Elvish to Klingon: Exploring Invented Languages* (Oxford University Press, 2011), and editor, co-editor, or co-author of some other books. For a while, he was Editor of *Dictionaries: Journal of the Dictionary Society of North America* and, for an even longer while, Editor of the quarterly journal *American Speech*.

Leslie K. Arnovick is Professor of English at the University of British Columbia where she teaches the history of the English language and other language studies. The author of *Written Reliquaries and Diachronic Pragmatics*, Arnovick specializes in medieval English, oral tradition, and historical pragmatics. Along with Laurel Brinton, she is the author of *The English Language: A Linguistic History*, 3rd ed. (Oxford University Press, 2017).

Joan Beal is Emeritus Professor of English Language at the University of Sheffield and previously studied and taught at Newcastle University, both in the North of England. She has been teaching the history of English since 1974, and has developed courses on Late Modern English (1700–1900). She is the author of *English in Modern Times 1700–1945*, the first textbook dedicated to Late Modern English.

Rakesh M. Bhatt is a Professor of Linguistics at the University of Illinois at Urbana-Champaign. He has published two books: *World Englishes: The Study of New Linguistic Varieties* (co-authored with R. Mesthrie) and *Verb Movement and the Syntax of Kashmiri*. His forthcoming book is entitled *Language in Diaspora*, which is under contract with Cambridge University Press. He is famous for his works on Migration, Minorities, and Multilingualism, Language Contact and Code-switching, and Language Ideology, Planning, Maintenance and Shift. His work on Code-switching and Optimal Grammar of Bilingual Language Use (co-authored with Agnes Bolonyai) offers a new perspective on the study of motivations for Code-switching.

Allison Burkette is an Associate Professor of Linguistics at the University of Mississippi. Much of her work makes use of Linguistic Atlas Project data, for which she is the Associate Editor. Her research interests include language variation and its connection to cultural factors, which is the subject of her recent book, *Language and Material Culture* (John Benjamins, 2015).

Thomas Cable is the Jane Weinert Blumberg Chair Emeritus in English at the University of Texas at Austin. He is the author and co-author of books and articles on the history of the English language and on prosody. Since 1978 he has been co-author of *A History of the English Language*, originally published by Albert C. Baugh in 1935; the current edition is the 6th (Pearson, 2013). He is also the author of *A Companion to Baugh & Cable's History of the English Language*, 4th ed. (Pearson, 2013) as well as essays on the teaching of the history of the English language. His scholarship on the study of English poetry from its origins to the present is rooted in an analysis of the structures of language and their development through time. He has received prizes for his teaching and scholarship.

David Crystal is honorary professor of Linguistics at the University of Bangor and works from his home in Holyhead, North Wales, as a writer, lecturer, and broadcaster. His general books on the history of English include *The Cambridge Encyclopedia of the English Language*, 2nd ed. (2003), *The Stories of English* (2004), and *Evolving English* (2010). More focused works, which include teaching appendices, are *Spell It Out: The Singular Story of English Spelling* (2012) and *Making a Point: The Pernickety Story of English Punctuation* (2015).

Jonathan Davis-Secord is Associate Professor of English at the University of New Mexico. He earned his doctorate from the University of Notre Dame in 2008. He is an Anglo-Saxonist specializing in the interactions of language and culture. His first book, *Joinings: Compound Words in Old English Literature* (Toronto University Press, 2016), explores the effect of compounds on style, pace, clarity, and genre in Anglo-Saxon vernacular literature. He has also published on Wulfstan's homilies, the Old English *Boethius*, the Latin sequences of Notker Balbulus and of the Winchester Troper, and the concept of race in Laȝamon's *Brut*. He regularly teaches HEL and courses on Old English and Medieval Latin, aiming to excite students with the beauty of ancient languages and literature.

David Denison is Professor Emeritus of English Linguistics at the University of Manchester and has held a number of visiting positions elsewhere. His research interests are mainly in historical syntax including current change, and his recent work has dealt with word classes, gradience in syntax, and problems of tagging. He has been involved in the construction or revision of several historical corpora of English. He was co-editor of the journal *English Language and Linguistics* for its first fourteen years, was the second president of ISLE (International Society for the Linguistics of English), and is one of the current coordinators of the ARCHER corpus project.

Michael R. Dressman is a Professor of English at the University of Houston-Downtown, where he has served in various administrative positions, including Dean of Humanities and Social Sciences for fourteen years. His teaching and research fields include American literature before 1900, the study of the English language, and writing for special purposes. He has published on the poetry of Walt Whitman and English language pedagogy. He earned his bachelor's and master's degree at the University of Detroit-Mercy and earned his doctorate at the University of North Carolina-Chapel Hill.

Natalie Gerber is an Associate Professor of English at the State University of New York at Fredonia, where she teaches a range of courses related to the structure, history, and use of the English language. Her essays on poets' and lyricists' artful uses and abuses of the resources of the English language appear in edited collections and in journals such as *The Wallace Stevens Journal*, where she is an associate editor.

Matthew Giancarlo is Associate Professor of English at the University of Kentucky. He is the author of books and articles on medieval English literature, history, and culture and also on the history and historiography of English language philology.

Mary Hayes is Associate Professor of English at the University of Mississippi, where she founded and now directs the Medieval Studies minor and graduate certificate. She is the sole author of the third edition of the late Celia M. Millward's classic text, *A Biography of the English Language* and its accompanying workbook. She is currently working on two book projects, both of which speak to her sustained interest in the relationship between language and literature. Her textbook, *The History of English from Anglo-Saxon England to the World Wide Web* (under contract with Cambridge University Press) joins historical linguistics with literary studies. Her current project on medieval literature, *Undead: Resurrection, Reanimation, and Artificial Life in English Vernacular Literature 1348–1543*, studies England's burgeoning vernacular tradition informed by the cultural practices of late medieval death culture.

William A. Kretzschmar, Jr. received his doctorate in English from the University of Chicago in 1980. He is the Harry and Jane Willson Professor in Humanities at the University of Georgia, where he teaches in the English Department. His major publications include *Language and Complex Systems* (2015); *The Linguistics of Speech* (2009); the *Oxford Dictionary of Pronunciation for Current English* (with Clive Upton and Rafal Konopka, 2001); *Introduction to Quantitative Analysis of Linguistic Survey Data* (with Edgar Schneider, 1996); and the *Handbook of the Linguistic Atlas of the Middle and South Atlantic States* (with Virginia McDavid, Theodore Lerud, and Ellen Johnson, 1993). He serves as Editor for the Linguistic Atlas Project, the oldest and largest national research project to survey how people speak everyday English differently in different parts of America. He maintains an active community-language field site in Roswell, GA, and currently serves as UGA's institutional representative for the international Text Encoding Initiative (TEI) Consortium.

Sonja L. Lanehart is Professor and Brackenridge Endowed Chair in Literature and the Humanities at the University of Texas at San Antonio. She is author of *Sista, Speak! Black Women Kinfolk Talk about Language and Literacy* (2002) and *Ebonics* (expected 2017); editor of *Sociocultural and Historical Contexts of African American English* (2001), *African American Women's Language: Discourse, Education, and Identity* (2009), and the *Oxford Handbook of African American Language* (2015); and former co-editor of *Educational Researcher: Research News and Comment.* She has organized and hosted several conferences on African American Language and African American Studies. Her research interests include sociolinguistics, African American Language, language and identity, Critical Race Theory, and Intersectionality in addition to the educational implications and applications of sociolinguistic research.

Seth Lerer is Distinguished Professor of Literature and Dean of Arts and Humanities Emeritus at the University of California at San Diego. He has also taught at Princeton, Stanford, Berkeley, and Cornell, and he has been a visiting fellow at Oxford and Cambridge. He has published widely on the History of English and literary pedagogy. His book, *Inventing English: A Portable History of the Language*, appeared in a new expanded and corrected edition in 2015. His most recent book is *Tradition: A Feeling for the Literary Past* (Oxford University Press, 2016).

John McWhorter is Associate Professor of English and Comparative Literature at Columbia University, teaching linguistics, Western Civilization, and music history. He is a regular columnist on language matters and also race issues for *Time* and *CNN*, writes for the *Wall Street Journal* "Taste" page, and writes a regular column on language for the *Atlantic*, and his work also appears in the *Washington Post*, the *Chronicle of Higher Education, Aeon* magazine, *The American Interest*, and other outlets. He was Contributing Editor at *The New Republic* from 2001 until 2014. He earned his doctorate in linguistics from Stanford University in 1993 and is the author of *The Power of Babel, Doing Our Own Thing, Our Magnificent Bastard Tongue, The Language Hoax*, and most recently *Words on the Move* and *Talking Back, Talking Black*. The Teaching Company has released four of his audiovisual lecture courses on linguistics. He spoke at the TED conference in 2013 and guest hosted the Lexicon Valley podcast at Slate during the summer of 2016. Beyond his work in linguistics, he is the author of *Losing the Race* and other books on race. He has appeared regularly on Bloggingheads.TV since 2006, and produces and plays piano for a group cabaret show, New Faces, at the Cornelia Street Cafe in New York City.

Rajend Mesthrie is Professor of Linguistics at the University of Cape Town, where he holds a National Research Foundation (NRF) chair in Migration, Language and Social Change. He is a past head of the Linguistics Section at UCT (1998–2009), a past President of the Linguistics Society of Southern Africa (2001–9), and past co-editor of *English Today*. He is President of the upcoming International Congress of Linguists (Cape Town, 2018). Among his publications are *Language in South Africa* (ed., Cambridge University Press, 2002), *World Englishes* (with Rakesh M. Bhatt, Cambridge University Press, 2008), and *A Dictionary of South African Indian English* (University of Cape Town Press, 1992).

Haruko Momma taught medieval English language and literature at New York University for twenty-four years before taking the position of Cameron Professor of Old English Language and Literature at the University of Toronto, where she also serves as the Chief Editor of the *Dictionary of Old English*. She is the author of *The Composition of Old English Poetry* (1997) and *From Philology to English Studies: Language and Culture in the Nineteenth Century* (2012); she co-edited, with Michael

Matto, *A Companion to the History of the English Language* (2008). She has also co-edited special issues "The History of the English Language: Pedagogy and Research" and "Old English Across the Curriculum: Contexts and Pedagogies" for *Studies in Medieval and Renaissance Teaching* (2007 and 2015), and "Old English Studies in the Nineteenth Century" for *Poetica* (2016).

Salikoko S. Mufwene is the Frank J. McLoraine Distinguished Service Professor of Linguistics and the College, and Professor on the Committee on Evolutionary Biology and on the Committee on the Conceptual and Historical Studies of Science at the University of Chicago. He works in evolutionary linguistics, from an ecological perspective, focusing on the phylogenetic emergence of language and on language indigenization and speciation in colonial settings. His publications include *The Ecology of Language Evolution* (2001), *Créoles, écologie sociale, évolution linguistique* (2005), and *Language Evolution: Contact, Competition and Change* (2008). He is the founding editor of *Cambridge Approaches to Language Contact*.

Rob Penhallurick is the author of the textbooks *Studying the English Language* (Palgrave, 2003, 2010) and *Studying Dialect* (Palgrave, 2017). He edited the collection *Debating Dialect: Essays on the Philosophy of Dialect Study* (University of Wales Press, 2000) and has written two monographs on varieties of Welsh English. He has worked for the Survey of Anglo-Welsh Dialects, the Survey of English Dialects, and the Atlas Linguarum Europae. He has held posts at the Universities of Leeds, Sheffield, and Tampere and is currently Reader in English Language at Swansea University.

Carol Percy is Professor of English at the University of Toronto. Her interdisciplinary work on eighteenth-century prescriptivism has focused especially on book reviewers, women teacher-grammarians, and the linguistic revisions to the journals of Captain James Cook. She has also co-edited *Languages of Nation: Attitudes and Norms* (2012) and *Prescription and Tradition: Language Norms Across Time and Space* (forthcoming) for Multilingual Matters.

Timothy J. Pulju is Senior Lecturer in Linguistics and Classics at Dartmouth College. His interests include Indo-European historical and comparative linguistics, functional approaches to grammar, and the history of linguistics.

Benjamin A. Saltzman is Assistant Professor of English at the University of Chicago. He is finishing a book titled *Bonds of Secrecy: The Cultural and Literary Mechanics of Concealment in Early Medieval England* and is the recipient of several teaching awards from University of California-Berkeley and the California Institute of Technology.

Philip Seargeant is Senior Lecturer in the Department of Applied Linguistics and English Language at The Open University. He is author of *The Idea of English in Japan* (2009, Multilingual Matters), *Exploring World Englishes* (2012, Routledge), and *From Language to Creative Writing* (with Bill Greenwell, 2013, Bloomsbury), and editor of *English in Japan in the Era of Globalization* (2011, Palgrave Macmillan), *English in the World: History, Diversity, Change* (with Joan Swann, 2012, Routledge), and *Futures for English Studies* (with Ann Hewings and Lynda Prescott, 2016, Palgrave Macmillan).

Matthew Sergi is an Assistant Professor of English, specializing in Early English Drama. In 2011, he received his doctorate in English and Medieval Studies from the University of California-Berkeley, where his dissertation work and publications on the biblical plays of the Chester cycle earned him numerous honors, including the Medieval Academy of America's Schallek Award and the Medieval and Renaissance Drama Society's Palmer Award. Before coming to the University of Toronto, he spent two years as an Assistant Professor of English at Wellesley College, where he continued his research on the Chester plays, which will take its final shape as his first book—*Play Texts and Public Practice in the Chester Cycle, c.1421–1607*. The book investigates how the unscripted festive practices of Chester's citizens shaped, and were shaped by, the dramatic scripts they left behind.

Graeme Trousdale works as a Senior Lecturer in English Language at the University of Edinburgh. His primary research interests are in historical linguistics, with a particular focus on variation and change in English. His current research is in the field of diachronic construction grammar and concerns the processes by which established constructions change, new constructions come into being, and certain constructions fall into disuse. He is the co-author, with Elizabeth Closs Traugott, of a book which explores aspects of diachronic construction grammar, *Constructionalization and Constructional Changes* (Oxford University Press, 2013), and is the co-editor, with Thomas Hoffmann, of the *Oxford Handbook of Construction Grammar* (Oxford University Press, 2013).

Jukka Tyrkkö is Visiting Professor of English at Linnaeus University and Docent (Adjunct Professor) of English philology at the University of Helsinki. A graduate of the University of Helsinki and a long-time member of its VARIENG research unit, his main areas of interest include historical linguistics with particular reference to lexis and phraseology, corpus linguistic methodology and digital humanities, and history of the book. He has been a member of several corpus compilation projects, including the Early Modern English Medical Texts corpus and the Corpus of Late Modern English Texts 3. He has taught numerous courses at several universities over the course of more than ten years, frequently using corpus linguistic methods in his teaching.

Approaches to Teaching the History of the English Language

CHAPTER 1

Introduction

MARY HAYES AND ALLISON BURKETTE

1.1. THE CHALLENGES OF TEACHING THE HISTORY OF THE ENGLISH LANGUAGE

Many instructors who teach the History of the English Language (HEL) would well commiserate with Francis A. March, one of its original professors who authored its first textbook, when he predicted that the curriculum he had helped design would make English "as difficult as Greek."[1] English indeed seems foreign terrain when navigating one's way through "HEL," an acronym hospitable to jokes about the course's "punishing nature."[2] Even expert instructors think that the course is difficult to teach, a valid assessment given its sheer ambit. HEL encompasses not only a wide chronological scope but also diverse fields relevant to literary studies and linguistics. Additionally, the course often satisfies several requirements at a single institution, so instructors thus have to consider how much administrative concerns should influence their course's substance. Even though the course is a traditional offering that is in high demand, few instructors claim HEL as their primary research field but rather specialize in one of its subfields or adjacent disciplines.[3] In a related vein, instructors often wonder how to capitalize on their professional strengths while covering the canonical material. Teaching HEL is "awesome" in the word's original sense. And whether you specialize in medieval literature or sociolinguistics, as a HEL teacher you will realize that you have an awful lot to learn.

As our students will assure us, however, we are not alone in finding HEL difficult. Any instructor who's received a student evaluation confirming that HEL "lived up to its name" would be in good (if fiendish) company.[4] Students who take the course come from various departments, so they enter HEL with manifold strengths. Their predominant collective feeling, however, may be one of displacement from their individual academic comfort zones. Some have studied linguistics, while others who do not yet know the IPA (International Phonetic Alphabet) feel "behind already" in just the first few weeks. Some students self-identify as "history buffs" drawn to obsolete forms of their native tongue, while others are still discovering a basic chronological framework for contextualizing HEL's literary or linguistic events. Some know a foreign language well enough to think English's inflectional system simple, while others do not recognize the English language as having one. In addition to these scholastic differences, students come to HEL courses with individual goals and desires. Many HEL students plan to become English teachers, so they approach the course inspired by their own burgeoning pedagogical philosophies and professional plans. English majors may take HEL because it is "something different" from the conventional literary courses narrowly focused on chronological periods. A linguistics student may want to situate his or her synchronic interest in a broader historical context. And crafting a course that engages this heterogeneous student population makes for yet another challenge incumbent on the HEL instructor.

1.2. THE REWARDS OF TEACHING THE HISTORY OF THE ENGLISH LANGUAGE

Given that HEL is often a required class, it is no surprise that it helps some students work toward tangible professional goals. For example, Education majors in the United States need the course to pass the Praxis Exam II for their certification. And, in light of the formidable number of academic job ads that include HEL, graduate students wisely teach or take the course to make themselves more attractive candidates.[5] Although current academic culture promotes the value of metrics and material outcomes, HEL's true rewards are less immediate and more organic. For example, unlike many others on university campuses, the course is not part of a pre-professional curriculum meant to prepare students for their first jobs. The English Education students who need the course for their certification exams in fact reap a less tangible benefit from taking it; they observe their professors thinking about literary language in various registers, a habit of mind that they will model for their own students.[6] HEL courses, especially in English departments, are often outliers in course catalogs. Yet they tacitly reside at the center of professional conversations about "English Studies" that emphasize the role of praxis and the potential for political engagement in academic courses.[7] For the very reasons that HEL demands much of its instructors and students, it epitomizes the intellectual dynamism and integrated knowledge that have been identified among the humanities' most compelling assets in twenty-first-century university curricula.[8]

Though a traditional and conventional offering, HEL's academic progressiveness becomes apparent when considering its own curricular evolution. At its inception in the mid-nineteenth century, HEL entailed philological study of the British literary canon. From comparative philology, linguistics would originate as a related academic field. When integrated into HEL curricula, linguistics supplied apparatus for analyzing the language's spoken forms as well as its general structure. In a related yet different vein, HEL's parameters would change when prescriptive master narratives about the language were fruitfully problematized by descriptive approaches that recognized the value of so-called nonstandard varieties of English as well as the fraught linguistic, historical, and social relationships between World Englishes and their "mother tongue." In the twenty-first century, HEL courses have come to account for the linguistic variety born of English's productive relationship with technology and social media. For example, as every HEL instructor knows, students enjoy getting historical context for their youth sociolects and have ready opinions about what TwitterSpeak betokens for the language's future.

Although the course has changed to accommodate developments in tributary academic fields as well as the language itself, its chronological ambit remains an identifying feature that, ironically, makes this traditional course academically countercultural and thus an uncommon intellectual forum. Evidence for this claim transpires in the trajectory of English literature courses, whose synoptic breadth was abandoned in favor of narrow period studies shortly after they were first offered in the 1830s. As one of the shrinking number of survey courses, HEL can sustain comprehensive questions and extended lines of inquiry.[9] Speaking to HEL's difference from other English department courses, Haruko Momma judges it an "intellectual advantage" that HEL "has never been subject to the compartmentalization that has affected the rest of the discipline."[10] Momma's observation addresses HEL's chronological scope as well as its interdisciplinary reach. Over the course of a single semester, a HEL course may incorporate material from history, geography, lexicography, philology, literature, grammar, and linguistics, the last of which includes the subfields of phonology, morphology, syntax, semantics, pragmatics, and sociolinguistics. As Michael Adams has observed, in HEL "many elements of a liberal education converge."[11]

As the twenty-first-century HEL instructor well knows, the course has become an arena for exploring provocative subjects such as the imperialist politics responsible for English's global stature or the cultural erasure inherent to language standardization. In such conversations, students attend to the ethical concerns resident in a course's curriculum, metadiscursive thinking that an education in the humanities demands. In negotiating HEL's plural subjects and substantial discourse, an instructor may feel extended beyond his or her professional niche just as students feel alienated from their native disciplinary terrain. Perhaps studying HEL does, in a sense, turn English into Greek. But this translation does not render English inscrutable but in fact more intelligible. Students realize that their mother tongue has (and has had) audiences and users other than "us." By apprehending the ramifications of English's diachronic and global influence, students of HEL can develop an allocentric perspective even if—and perhaps because—English is their first and only language.

1.3. THE VOLUME'S PURPOSE: PRACTICAL PEDAGOGY

Approaches to Teaching the History of the English Language comprises commissioned chapters, each of which focuses on a classic pedagogical challenge relevant to teaching HEL in the contemporary university. Predicated on practical pedagogy, these chapters not only theorize but also describe the activities of seasoned HEL instructors. As a more existential meaning of the word "practice" implies, this volume posits teaching as an idiosyncratic and sustained developmental experience. "Practice" may not make "perfect," but it guarantees raising familiar questions ("How can I cover the entire history of English in a single semester?" "How can I design a class suitable for so many different students?" "How can I use my own academic training while addressing HEL's core material?") in a more nuanced register. In *Approaches to Teaching the History of the English Language*, new HEL instructors will discover mentors in its contributors, who have shared anecdotes, sample exercises, and strategies for teaching HEL under multifarious auspices and conditions. For HEL veterans looking to recast, refresh, or rejuvenate their syllabi, this volume will supply them with ideas and resources to introduce into already successful courses.

As editors of this volume—a medievalist and a sociolinguist—we know firsthand that putting together a satisfying and cohesive HEL course is tough. The seed from which this project grew was our professional friendship that developed thanks to our informal conversations about tricky lesson plans and miraculous solutions. Though often born of necessity, the micro-adjustments we made to our courses in fact changed the stories that they told. For fellow instructors who are themselves trying to decide which stories to tell in their HEL courses, we wanted to provide the type of collegial advice and tried-and-true examples from which we ourselves have benefited. In our volume's chapters, our readers will see how other HEL instructors have incorporated fields as diverse as traditional philology to complexity theory to lexicography to dialectology, accounted for various "Englishes" both diachronic and synchronic, and used multimedia resources and online teaching platforms that highlight HEL's embrace of twenty-first-century technology. As a whole, our volume identifies the course's familiar challenges, offers practical solutions, explains feasible pedagogical approaches, and demonstrates how resourceful instructors have negotiated facile connections between the diverse topics that the history of the English language includes. While offering a series of entry points into a vast professional conversation, *Approaches to Teaching the History of the English Language* is likewise animated by informal and supportive exchanges that (we would like to think) happen adventitiously in many departments' copy rooms.

While our volume implies myriad scenes of teaching, it is informed by a brace of abiding questions:

- How should instructors broach the class's central paradox: an English-language class for native speakers?
- How can they engage students from the various departments that require HEL?
- How should instructors intervene to elaborate on or to complicate the "succinct story" offered by conventional HEL textbooks?[12]
- In that vein, how can instructors impress upon students the value of learning HEL without purveying a complacent master narrative of English's innate or cultural superiority?
- How can instructors negotiate the study of the language's conventional "inner history" versus its "outer history," especially when teaching students who have no linguistics training?
- How can instructors account for the current descriptive perspective on language variation?

Each of these is a practical question whose ethical implications evince HEL's inherent utility to the humanities in the twenty-first century. If a HEL instructor's job is challenging, that is because it is important.

1.4. THE VOLUME'S ORGANIZATION AND CHAPTERS

This book's six parts speak to influences, circumstances, and challenges common to teaching HEL: the unique pedagogical relationship between instructors and students fostered by language study; the course's academic origins and significance to current university curricula; instructors' appealing to their particular scholarly strengths while addressing the course's general subject; the course's diachronic scope and concerns about "coverage"; its inclusion of vernacular, dialectical, and World Englishes; and the utility of multimedia. Each chapter balances theory and practice, explaining in detail exercises, activities, assignments, or discussion questions that an instructor could immediately use.

Language is a communicative medium and, in a HEL classroom, it also enables a process of mutual awareness between the student and teacher. The chapters in Part One, "Reflections on Teaching the History of the English Language," consider the unique pedagogical dynamic that transpires in HEL courses, where instructors encourage students to encounter a common tongue from an unusual perspective. John McWhorter describes his first experience teaching HEL after years of writing about it in Chapter 2, "German, Handwriting, and Other Things I Learned to Keep in Mind When Teaching the History of English." McWhorter chronicles how marshaling his own academic strengths, negotiating HEL's formidable scope, and accounting for students' expectations made him critically consider the course as well as what language itself is. Thomas Cable likewise describes the burgeoning of a pedagogical relationship in Chapter 3, "Restoring Rhythm: An Auditory Imagination of the History of English." With special attention to English's rhythms, Cable offers solutions for how "technical studies" can be "adapted to the sound of language in our ears." If an instructor liberates the English language's oral mode from the phonological charts, Cable contends, the HEL classroom emerges as hospitable to cultivating students' "auditory imagination." Sound changes thus serve as a device that lends cohesion: from Old Englishes to World Englishes to hip-hop music. Additionally, the language's history becomes internalized and thus "portable" for students. Rajend Mesthrie (Chapter 4, "Teaching the History of English: A South African Perspective") takes up the timeless pedagogical issue of enlisting students, in this case his teaching HEL to students with no background in Old or Middle English, a circumstance that resulted from curricular changes from historical to applied linguistics. Although Mesthrie's situation is somewhat particular to his teaching HEL in a postcolonial academic environment, many HEL instructors can commiserate with offering a traditional course while weathering changes in departmental curricula. In a related yet different vein, Sonja L. Lanehart (Chapter 5, "How Is HEL Relevant to Me?") describes HEL as an opportunity to introduce students to "self-regulated learning" that is driven by individual interests and goals. In addition to learning the course material, students also attend to their own changing relationships with the English language via the exercises that Lanehart explains.

Part Two, "The Value of Teaching the History of English: Rethinking Curricula," takes a closer look at HEL as a body of knowledge as well as a university course. In Chapter 6, "Philology, Theory, and Critical Thinking Through the History of the English Language," Matthew Giancarlo appeals to HEL's early academic association with philology to explain its perceived removal from literary theory and subsequent lack of critical self-awareness. In a HEL course, theory and philology can fruitfully cooperate, Giancarlo argues, if instructors urge students to "ask simple but fundamental questions about the knowledge-construction of the field that they are studying," including received ideas about the relationship between synchrony and diachrony, measuring change, and center versus periphery. By critically evaluating HEL's own means of knowledge construction, students will thus think more carefully about how language itself is used to make meaning. In a related vein, Seth Lerer (Chapter 7, "The History of the English Language and the Medievalist") calls for a conversation between medievalists, historical linguists, and literary historians to rethink the narrative of a single tradition and a unified dialect created by nineteenth-century philologists. Medievalists, who are often tasked with teaching HEL, can best show "language having meaning in its diachronic life" via the "variety of literary and linguistic forms at any given place and moment" in the language's history. Lerer offers suggestions for checking the dominant narrative by including examples of early vernacular Englishes. In a related yet different vein, Michael R. Dressman accounts for the importance of vernacularity to HEL in Chapter 8, "English and I: Finding the History of the English Language in the Class." Dressman speaks to teaching at an emerging institution where, for example, English is not the first language of many students. Based on advice from William Labov, Dressman explains adapting sociolinguistic practices for eliciting natural speech to interest students in HEL's subject and, in turn, to generate linguistic information a class can use that semester. As Dressman describes it, sociolinguistics is not just a relevant and new field but a heuristic device in the HEL classroom.

Approaches to Teaching the History of the English Language shifts from exploring the metadiscursive significance of HEL's tributary disciplines to their practical use in Part Three, "Research Paradigms and Pedagogical Practices," where scholars model teaching a HEL course from a particular disciplinary perspective without its overtaking the course. Leslie K. Arnovick, in Chapter 9, "Historical Pragmatics in the Teaching of the History of English," addresses teaching HEL informed by historical pragmatics and historical sociolinguistics, both relatively new fields of study. As both locate the English language in its social and cultural context, these approaches appeal to students since they themselves are language users. Sustained attention to usage underlies the approach outlined by Graeme Trousdale (Chapter 10, "Using Principles of Construction Grammar in the History of English Classroom"). Trousdale describes a HEL course based in construction grammar, a view of language as comprised of "form-meaning pairings" that accounts for different registers of use such as slang. In Chapter 11, "Addressing 'Emergence' in a HEL Classroom," William A. Kretzschmar, Jr. explains another innovative scholarly approach to language, complexity theory, which registers the synchronic interplay of various forms—not just those that became part of standard English. With particular attention to lexical varieties culled from LAMSAS (Linguistic Atlas of the Middle and South Atlantic States), Kretzschmar offers examples for instructors looking to complicate the tired master narrative and consider "the contingencies of their history." Offering students a new view of the language's past thanks to tools recently designed to measure it is the subject of Jukka Tyrkkö's "Discovering the Past for Yourself: Corpora, Data-Driven Learning, and the History of English" (Chapter 12), which explains the utility of the "corpus-based approach" to a HEL course. The corpus-based approach informs David Denison's "Word Classes in the History of English" (Chapter 13), which focuses on using corpora in student activities about word classes. Denison explains how to engage students in researching part-of-speech information, a basic element of language whose examples reveal intriguing pragmatic and semantic questions. A traditional approach to tracking the history of English through its words, lexicography, is innovated in Michael Adams's "Dictionaries and the History of English" (Chapter 14). Students may know that dictionaries include information such as etymologies, meanings, and quotations. Adams includes useful assignments that encourage students to recognize the dictionary as full of "facts and judgments" about English. Additionally, Adams calls for students to look in dictionaries yet also "at them"; whether handwritten on vellum or digital, dictionaries are cultural artifacts that can "foster even more interdisciplinary engagement."

Many of these disciplinary approaches consider apparatus for accessing the language's earlier forms and thus its diachronic story. The chapters in Part Four ("Centuries in a Semester: HEL's Chronological Conventions") not only tackle the practical problems presented by the course's chronological scope but also contemplate how chronological conventions influence what "story" HEL courses tell. In Chapter 15, "English Is an Indo-European Language: Linguistic Prehistory in the History of English Classroom," Timothy J. Pulju responds to a familiar question: How much Indo-European linguistics should an instructor include in a HEL course? More important, he asks: "After the class emerges from the murky depths of prehistory into the comparatively well-lit Anglo-Saxon period, is Indo-European still relevant?" Pulju shows that Indo-European not only can serve as a starting point for a chronologically organized course but also can provide a basis for students' understanding grammatical and lexical items of later Englishes. Mary Hayes, in Chapter 16, "Serving Time in 'HELL': Diachronic Exercises for Literature Students," considers how to achieve chronological coverage without completely streamlining HEL's narrative. She appeals to her experience structuring HEL courses around diachronic translations of the "Shepherd Psalm." Using a single textual tradition as a structuring device, she contends, conveys a story that is cohesive yet heterogeneous. Students become aware, for example, of synchronic variants and purposefully dated forms and thus become critical of HEL's general chronological conventions. A literary approach to HEL likewise informs Haruko Momma's "What Has *Beowulf* to Do with English? (Let's Ask Lady Philology!)" (Chapter 17), which revisits the early history and reception of *Beowulf* to show its cognate origins with HEL in nineteenth-century philology. In turn, Momma argues more broadly for the value to HEL of philology, a traditional approach that literary scholars are currently rediscovering. In the final chapter in this unit, Chapter 18, Joan Beal, "Starting from Now: Teaching the Recent History of English," reflects on her early use of Barbara Strang's *History of English* (which is in reverse chronological order) to argue for the general value of beginning with linguistic changes "in living memory" and moving back in 200-year segments of history. Beal explains that students can move from the known to the unknown to learn linguistic concepts in a familiar context rich in textual and extralinguistic resources. She presents two case studies based on her students' use of the *Oxford English Dictionary* (OED), *Eighteenth-Century Collections Online* (ECCO), *Eighteenth-Century English Grammars* (ECEG), and *Oxford Dictionary of National Biography*.

The material that conventionally comprises the later part of the HEL survey is the subject of Part Five, "Including 'Englishes' in the History of English." These chapters speak to covering "more recent" Englishes—World Englishes, American dialects, and British varieties—in a HEL course. In Chapter 19, "From Old English to World Englishes," Benjamin A. Saltzman explains a situation familiar to many HEL instructors: teaching HEL as a medievalist better trained in the "first half." Saltzman thoroughly surveys available resources and offers practical solutions for including World Englishes (WE) as a meaningful culmination of a brisk survey. In Chapter 20, "An Ecological Account of the Emergence and Evolution of English," Salikoko S. Mufwene likewise considers the position of WE in HEL's larger narrative. Although many HEL textbooks insinuate an explosion of recent varieties of World Englishes, Mufwene proposes situating this variety in sustained line of inquiry about English's diachronic pidgins, creoles, and varieties. In Chapter 21, "Researching World Englishes in HEL Courses: Neologisms, Newspapers, and Novels," Carol Percy describes exercises that have students work with WE slang and jargon culled from newspapers or films. By attending to these varieties of vernacular usage, students taking HEL are less likely to regard World Englishes as "exotic abstractions or curious variants of English or American English." In a related vein, Rakesh M. Bhatt (Chapter 22, "Situating World Englishes into a History of English Course") explains how World Englishes can be integrated into a history of standard Englishes and thus encourage students to rethink what "English" is. More than just a "chapter" in the history of the language, World Englishes suggests a paradigm shift from a "monotheistic ethos of linguistic science" to "frameworks that are faithful to multilingualism and language variation." Allison Burkette (Chapter 23, "Incorporating American English into the History of English") likewise attends to the problem of meaningfully integrating English's later varieties into a broad survey. Burkette's materials for teaching American Englishes show students that "American English" is not a homogeneous whole but rather a "fluid and dynamic amalgamation of dialects and sub-varieties." More important, Burkette demonstrates how American English not only is an essential chapter in a HEL course but also "can be viewed as a microcosm of the still-continuing history of English." For Rob Penhallurick (Chapter 24, "Teaching Diversity and Change in the History of English") addressing the language's diachronic changes necessarily involves its diversity. English's dialects and varieties are not eccentricities but rather the matter of the HEL class Penhallurick describes, which inspired his HEL textbook, *Studying the English Language*. Matthew Sergi considers the English language's diversity from a different perspective: the various Englishes used by students taking HEL. In Chapter 25, "Our Subject Is Each Other: Teaching HEL to ESL, EFL, and Non-Standard English Speakers," Sergi describes the HEL classroom as "the ideal point of convergence for university students with diverse experiences of English." It is by demystifying Standard English as an "arbitrary, contingent, class-marked, and situational set of codes" that studying HEL can in fact make the language's rules less intimidating to nonnative users.

In their attention to these linguistic varieties, these chapters reflect how HEL curricula have come to accommodate twenty-first-century forms. The chapters in Part Six, "Using Media and Performance in the History of English Classroom," likewise speak to HEL's contemporary presence as they consider not only how an instructor might use modern media in HEL courses but also how the course can inspire its students to rethink the relationship between language and its media more generally. In Chapter 26, "Approaching the History of English Through Material Culture," Jonathan Davis-Secord gives the reader a peek inside his "language lab," that is, the archive of e-manuscripts that he uses in HEL classes. He focuses in particular on an exercise based on the Old English Hexateuch's presentation of the Abraham and Isaac story. By giving students something concrete to apprehend, manuscripts make students aware that real people produced them and, in turn, used English's obsolete forms. In arguing for the value of the manuscript medium as a heuristic device, Davis-Secord appeals to twentieth-century pedagogical theory to contend that they make HEL's linguistic abstractions seem more real. Although computerized images are modern apparatus, their non-codexical form in fact evokes many medieval texts. A tangible experience of a prior linguistic form is what David Crystal describes in Chapter 27, "Teaching Original Pronunciation," which draws on his experiences working with the Royal Shakespeare Company as a dialect coach. Crystal shows how these reconstructions, in particular Shakespearean OP, have a place in the history of theatrical dialects as well as the history of English. In fact, an introduction to OP will include an introduction to basic linguistics. Although many HEL students may find Early Modern and Present Day English delightfully similar, Crystal's lessons in OP would alert them to subtle and substantial differences. Performances of a different type interest Natalie Gerber in Chapter 28, "Engaging Multimedia in the HEL Classroom." She identifies popular television shows and YouTube segments predicated on linguistic puns that provide grist for teaching assignments and, more broadly, a lesson about the language's dynamic relationship with modern media. In a different vein, Philip Seargeant addresses HEL's web presence in Chapter 29, "Teaching the History of English Online: Open Education and Student Engagement." In discussing Open University's "webucation" video, "The History of English in Ten Minutes," Seargeant explains how condensing such a compendious subject serves as a fable for the course's sleek packaging for online teaching platforms.

While *Approaches to Teaching the History of the English Language* describes manifold pedagogical circumstances and scenarios, it is not meant to account for all of HEL's subfields and tributary disciplines. Rather, it presents a variety of "master classes" that in turn suggest other successful ways to teach the course. This volume will not answer every question relevant to teaching this notoriously complicated class. What it will do is enable its readers to design pedagogies optimal for their particular institutions, departments, classrooms, and scholarly backgrounds. As our use of the term "pedagogies" suggests, one of the challenges in teaching HEL entails recognizing the manifold ways that an instructor can do so. In turn, the diversity of these pedagogical approaches as well as the research profiles of this volume's contributors should suggest how teaching HEL inspires multidisciplinary conversations and innovative scholarship.

PART ONE

Reflections on Teaching the History of the English Language

CHAPTER 2

German, Handwriting, and Other Things I Learned to Keep in Mind When Teaching the History of English

JOHN MCWHORTER

2.1. INTRODUCTION

I write this as someone with training neither in classroom pedagogy nor even in the diachrony of the English language. My training is in linguistics, within which my main area of concentration was originally pidgin and creole languages—although, even then, my focus was on creolization as a process rather than on the study of a single creole language, and to the extent that I have specialized in a single one of those, it has been Saramaccan, whose vocabulary is heavily Portuguese as well as English, whose grammar is as much African as European, and which exists in no gradation of lects converging by steps with English in the fashion of Jamaican and other Caribbean English creoles.

Over time, I have come to know the history of English largely "through the back door." I developed an interest in the fact that the structural reduction manifesting itself in extreme fashion in creoles manifests itself to intermediate degrees in other languages. Within this commitment to a general model of language change and contact, I found that among various languages, English was typical in being less grammatically "busy" than all of its close relatives and having a contact history consonant with that fact. That is, there is a reason English lacks the arbitrary gender, the difference in word order between main and subordinate clauses, the expression of emotions and mental states with a "reflexive" pronoun (*erinnern sich* 'to remember' in German), and so many other things that German and the other Germanic languages have. English was simplified by the Scandinavian Vikings who invaded Britain starting in the eighth century.

Constructing an academic argument for this case required an acquaintance with the history of English which I had never needed before, and after several years I found against my expectation that I was, at least, conversant in the subject because of these studies. Then, I learned a bit more about the history of the language from two other fortuitous forays. In the early aughts I wrote a book about the increasing informality of public speech in America (*Doing Our Own Thing*) which required me to consult sources on how English was used from the nineteenth century onward in the public square. Once again, I realized at the end of this research that again, by accident, I had a handle on aspects of what we might call the sociolinguistics of modern American English. Moreover, as a linguist who writes for the general public, I have often found myself addressing the issue of prescriptivism. To avoid simply recycling the same standard arguments, one must dig in the sources for further examples of language standards of the past and past usages once acceptable that now sound strange, or at least always be on the lookout for such examples when engaged in other pursuits. The result of this frame of mind over the past fifteen years or so has meant, again, having a sense of developments in the language over the past few centuries.

Developing a course on the History of the English Language (HEL), then, required me to fill in some weaknesses of command especially of Middle English, which I had rarely had occasion to engage more than superficially. My aim for the course was to introduce the students to the development of the language from a language-centered point of view: hardly requiring knowledge of formal phonology or syntax, of course, but my training and interest meant that my course could not be one with more than a polite leaning toward literary analysis. My course was more about, say, the development of new vocabulary and the erosion of endings than about the majesty of the King James Bible or language attitudes toward nonstandard speech. Both of the latter were covered, but fundamentally I am a words and grammar person.

My course was moderately successful. Some students would praise it more highly, but I suspect that is in considerable part due to the fact that I treat lecture as a kind of performance. A critical mass of students liked the course but felt, I sense, somewhat shortchanged by things I did not foresee myself, due to the maddeningly intractable fact that one can never completely remove oneself from one's own mind. I am confident that my next edition of the course will be a solider experience for more students, and this is because I will have attended to two main things.

2.2. MAKING HEL MEANINGFUL

First, I fear I did not ever quite make Old English meaningful to the students. Given that Old English is the beginnings of the language itself, that it is associated with majestic old *Beowulf*, and even that it is discussed at the top of the semester when minds and spirits are fresh, I assumed that covering Anglo-Saxon would be one of the heights of the course.

Instead, I found that Old English was, to a degree I had not anticipated, opaque to most of the students beyond any possibility of finding it "cool." Quite simply, Old English to a layman might as well be German, and these days, few students can be assumed to have studied German. I suspect that in a distant day, for many students

Old English would have made a certain sense on the basis of a certain familiarity with Latin or Greek, but again, today very few students have had that kind of training.

As a result, I found that as one might expect, the only students who "got" Old English in any real way were the few who had had German—for them, it was interesting to compare their German with this other highly inflected Germanic language they had never seen before (we can assume that essentially no students will have experienced Icelandic, and beyond this, no living Germanic language other than German itself reproduces the essence of Old English structure). The other students, however, might as well have been seeing Turkish in my slides. I assumed that always providing glosses would help, but glosses are something linguists are used to reading. Laymen are not accustomed to the likes of this from Ælfric's colloquy:

Wē cildra biddaþ þē, ēalā lārēow, þæt þū tǣce ūs sprecan rihte.
'We boys ask you, oh master, that you teach us to speak correctly.'

One student, a smart and committed one, said that the way she could tell Middle English from Old English was, simply, that she could read the Middle English. To her, Old English was just something alien, and my quest to introduce her to the language over a couple of weeks had, to the extent that I was hoping it would, failed. My playing a video of the pop song "Call Me Maybe" in Old English did not seem to make much difference.

The problem continued even with early Middle English. For example, I posed a question on the midterm that assumed the students understood that periphrastic *do* entered English (at least in writing) at the Middle English stage, after devoting half of a class to explaining how English inherited this usage of *do* from the indigenous Celtic language of Britain (in line with my own research on the subject as shared with the public in my *Our Magnificent Bastard Tongue*, I do teach this story of *do* to students as assumed). The question was whether the following sentence was Old or Middle English and which feature allows one to know:

His sclauyn he dude dun legge. ("He laid down his pilgrim's-cloak.")

Almost no student got this right, and anecdotally it was clear that the reason was that the students found the sentence merely opaque. The fronted object, the placement of *dun* before the *legge*, plus the unfamiliar spelling and vowel changes rendered that sentence a bizarreness to all but a few of them.

The next time I teach the course, I will approach Old English with the assumption that students need to be ushered into an awareness from the ground up of a language that works like German. Without Latin or German, a person needs more time than I assumed to wrap their heads around, especially, nouns and their articles being marked for case, and also unfamiliar word order. They need not just brief description, but practice. To someone like me, a verb being at the end of a sentence feels normal, an alternate to the everyday as familiar as going into reverse in the car or undoing one button on a hot day. To the Anglophone layman, a verb at the end of a sentence seems more like a shoe on the wrong foot or being poked in the eye, one senses.

The proper approach, I suspect, is to get the students accustomed, before giving them actual Old English, Modern English passages with verbs at the ends of sentences, objects fronted, and dative and accusative endings pasted on to nouns where appropriate. My idea is to use familiar passages, such as from the Declaration of Independence as well as modern pop song lyrics, and translate them into Old English-style morphology and syntax such that while the vocabulary itself will be transparent, the students can get used to "funny" things which otherwise would confuse them. Encouraging live class participation through giving various "exercises" of this kind will help imprint the frame of mind desired.

A class of this, supplemented by on-line reinforcement, will help the students process Old English as something more than an intimidating word soup. Then, when in classes after this, introducing a bit of *Beowulf* and some other materials, I will retain always in mind that this language, to all but a very few of the students, is in no sense English at all. A small part of me has a visceral yearning, as a lifelong language fan in awe of other languages and bilingual people, that English were still more like Old English with its odd-looking Germanic vocabulary and plethora of suffixes. That yearning, I now know, is not remotely shared by those introduced to this language for the first time and having come to the course thinking more of Shakespeare than the likes of *Hwæt, wē Gār-Dena in ġeārdagum þēodcyninga þrym ġefrūnon*. To most students, at first this might as well be English backward. It needn't be, at least not to the extent that it was by the end of my course.

2.3. WRITING AND SPEECH

A second change I will make involves a crucial difference between how linguists think of language and how the rest of the world does. In this case, the issue is not that linguists are somehow more enlightened. Rather, there is a certain subset of language the linguist is trained to ignore which, to the public, is often thought of as the essence of language itself.

I refer to writing. A central tenet of linguistic science is that our interest is casual speech, which has existed probably since the dawn of our species whereas writing came along only about 6,500 years ago. In my mind, then, writing, whatever its utility and even charm, is an approximation of speech imprinted onto assorted materials and media, a mere shadow of the "real thing"—people talking.

This is an assumption so deeply seated in linguistics that even someone who has written about the differences, fascinating in themselves, between speech and writing for the public and even preached it in a TED (Technology, Entertainment, Design) talk can have a hard time keeping in mind how foreign that view of language is to most people. That is, most people have a "view" of language indeed—a sense that the "real thing" is language's visual representation, writing, in all of its permanence and tidiness. Speech, it is easy to suppose, is the approximation—a "sloppy" rendition of something that exists in Platonic form on paper.

Hence a person will often talk about his or her language having a "letter" for something where the linguist would say his or her language has a sound for it; hence we describe writing as "saying" this or that, as if writing were performing an action just as a speaker is; hence the eternal question as to what texting is doing to "language," when no one supposes that a few acronyms, quirky spellings, and floutings of punctuation rules will have anything significant to do with the way people speak. "Language" in this question refers to writing, the idea being that *language* is shorthand for writing just as "drinking" can be a shorthand for consuming alcoholic beverages rather than any liquid.

What this meant in my experience of teaching the history of English is that my guiding assumption was that I was teaching the history of English as spoken, with the writing used to demonstrate this a mere tool shedding light on what was coming out of people's mouths. However, quite understandably, to my students, the course was supposed to be about the history of English as written down, with speech, until recently at least, mere static now lost. Specifically, this meant that my students were especially interested in the evolution of English writing.

I certainly had one class on orthography and writing systems. However, a disproportionate number of questions starting as early as Old English were about orthography beyond the mere basics I gave at that early point, and then throughout lectures afterward. Any orthographical oddity in a slide occasioned a question or two, clearly of more importance to the questioner than anything about the loss of case endings and the rigidification of word order. And then, during the actual lecture on orthography and writing systems, there were so many questions that I had to postpone the second half of the lecture to the next class meeting.

This was, of course, heartening in itself, but it showed me that a class on the history of English for laymen must include more coverage of writing issues than I had expected. I saved the students' questions on this subject and will address them in my revised version of the lecture, which I will also spread over two classes. In general, I will include more slides of original documents and inscriptions and discuss the writing more closely. To students, spelling and writing are naturally more immediately accessible than issues of grammatical change—they, themselves, have written for all of their lives; almost none of them have spoken German.

2.4. ENJOYABLE BUTTERFLIES

Lest it seem as if I consider my instruction in the class an utter failure, I should also share something that I found students especially enjoyed. Just as the layman understandably thinks most readily of language as writing, the layman supposes that a class about the history of English will hinge considerably on the facet of historical linguistics that any literate person is aware of: etymology.

Just as with writing, it's easy for a linguist to wave away etymology as mere butterfly collecting, since each word's history is subject to any number of fortuitous cultural reinterpretations over time and is often to a large extent uncertain. The linguist is fascinated by pattern, system, not one-offs and "Who'd-a-thunk-it"s.

Yet that dissimulates a bit: linguists are human, and we enjoy the "butterflies" as much as anyone else. It's just that few of us submit academic papers about them. Nevertheless, I decided from the outset that it would be almost puritanical to deny the students some etymologies. Therefore, I warned in the introductory class that those hoping for a class *all about* etymologies would be disappointed. However, I promised to give them one "fun" etymology at the start of end of each class. My idea was to use the etymologies, to a large extent, as a way of inculcating some general tenets of how language change works—semantic narrowing, sound change, and so on. Yet in some cases I just allowed weirdness a space.

Examples included *punch* (from Hindi for "five"), *fast* (with its contronymic meaning as in *hold fast* versus *run fast*, originally meaning "firmly" but now referring also to speed), *Goodbye* (from "God be with you"), *penthouse* (originally meaning the kind of structure Jesus was born in, the Anglo-French word *pentiz* referring to hanging), the expression *It's raining cats and dogs* (from an expression originally referring to metal bolts called catbolts and dogbolts), and *world* (originally a compound, *wer-eld* "man-age"). These etymologies served as a useful *amuse-bouche* at the start of class (and encouraged a few students to be on time) and/or were a useful way to close things out when a topic didn't lend itself to a natural sense of closure. I did not test the students on these etymologies, of course—perhaps I should have!

2.5. FINAL THOUGHTS

I might share one final lesson I learned, one more thing I sensed I was doing right, in a fashion which I suspect might not be obvious to all teachers of the subject. There is a tendency in many textbooks on the history of English to assume that students are especially interested in how English varies around the world. After Middle English and perhaps Early Modern, the trajectory then takes us to Australia, South Africa, India, Singapore, and so on.

I covered all of the above Englishes, to be sure. However, the only other "indigenous" English I discussed was Irish, briefly. Rather, I found pidgins and especially creoles of more interest, not only to myself but to the students. It seemed to me that beyond a certain point, to introduce the students to more than a few dialects of English itself outside the United States and Great Britain would be ineffective pedagogy, in the simple fact that things would get listy, something I try hard to avoid. Lists of "exotic" vocabulary items and expressions are, like etymologies chosen without care, more collections than lessons, and I suspect the students would have gotten bored. In fact, I detected a slight dip in the heartbeat level of the class by the middle of the main lecture on indigenous Englishes, despite ample sound clips, anecdotes, and attempts to show how each variety taught a lesson about language change in addition to just standing as a conglomeration of facts.

To teach the class as one would have 150 years ago, as if English were a "white" language spoken only in the United Kingdom, the Commonwealth, and the United States would be unforgivably parochial today. However, to spend too long a stretch on the diversity of Englishes that exist would have felt unstructured to the students (despite the rich diversity of backgrounds among today's students at Columbia University).

The aims of introducing students to English as it is spoken across the globe are, it would seem, two. One is to inculcate the idea, invaluable in itself, that there is no single "proper" English and that English takes on varying characters in each new place it is established, just as it did when brought to America. A second is to demonstrate the diversity of peoples among whom English is now native. I chose to get these points across as much through examining variation within American English (including Black English) and then showing the creole forms of English, with the "indigenous" Englishes as but one facet amidst this general lesson.

In sum, I think I got History of English right with the etymological *hors d'œuvres* and in not dwelling at length, in a one-semester class in New York City, on the English of Toronto or Kenya. However, I also learned that I should have begun by giving the students an introduction to, basically, German, while also realizing that to the students, "English" summons up an image of writing, not air from people's mouths. I look forward to my next go-round.

CHAPTER 3

Restoring Rhythm

An Auditory Imagination of the History of English*

THOMAS CABLE

3.1. INTERNALIZING THE SOUNDS OF THE LANGUAGE

If students are invited to think about the history of the language, they are apt to visualize old texts on the printed page or on vellum, works that become accessible only through technical charts of sound changes. And those students who do have some knowledge of linguistics, or of language study, might consider the specifics of the history a matter of memorization, not an invitation to performance. However, the encouragement of unabashed performance offers a way to ease into the study and keep it alive. The very point of this chapter is that an element of imagination can play a part in a course on "The History of the English Language" (HEL) and the sounds of the language at its various stages as best as we can reconstruct are the place to start. In the illustration of connections and continuities as well as changes, one element of historical phonology is the verbal music of the language at various periods. The rhythms and intonations of English interact with the consonants and vowels, in ways that are often neglected.[1]

The reason for the neglect is largely the difficulty of reconstructing verbal melody in any way comparable to the methods of comparative and historical phonology as established over the past two centuries. What I find most interesting about the scholarly inroad that has been made—especially as it is transposed to the classroom—is that it depends at certain points on a leap of the imagination. Both scholars and students are given a license to experiment, to consult their own intuitions, and to risk being wrong. At the very least it is more engaging than a series of charts showing sound changes. For the researchers, of course, the intuitive stage has to be followed by the standard methods of evidence and argumentation—or most productively a cycling back and forth between the two.

The concept of sounds and their performance as used here comes partly from Helen Gardner, whose subject was T. S. Eliot and his predecessors. In her classic essay Gardner developed the concept of "auditory imagination" as the discovery of new possibilities of sound patterns within a language.[2] Gardner's concern was poetry, but the idea is relevant to all forms of the English language from its origins to the present. Her essay focused on innovations by certain major poets who in their verse line "revive the very stuff of poetry, the language and speech-rhythms of their day and country."[3] Thus, these innovations involve a productive looking-back at rhythms that have been forgotten but fit surprisingly well into current verse rhythms. In their re-incorporation they also open up new styles of writing. Beyond the always delightful consideration of poetry, so too the consideration of rhythms of ordinary speech across centuries can be a form of auditory imagination that works in the classroom.

There is an instant enlivening when the technical studies are adapted to get the sound of the language in our ears and make it come alive. In practical terms, this can be something as simple as having everyone read passages of Old English aloud, whether or not they understand all the words. (An interlinear glossed text helps.) At the Middle English stage, it can be the memorization of the opening lines of *The Canterbury Tales*. For Renaissance and Jacobean drama, including Shakespeare, there are compelling reasons for experimenting with a variety of rhythms and considering the evidence for each. For Present-Day English, a good exercise in auditory imagination is careful attention to recordings of varieties of British, American, and global Englishes, accompanied by an in-class analysis of the sounds. Despite its legendary status, the tape that accompanies J. C. Wells's *Accents of English* is still an excellent resource, both in its selection of speakers and in the detailed commentary that Wells provides.[4]

3.2. RECONSIDERING RHYTHMS OF ENGLISH, THEN AND NOW

Among the samples on Wells's tape, the speaker of Nigerian English presents features of that variety that may seem subtle and hard to identify on first listening. However, careful attention and a few hints about what to listen for reveal far-reaching implications that extend back to the origins of English and forward to a projection of the future of English world-wide. These patterns involve the changing rhythms of the language, and they bring home to students the realization that the elements of their own linguistic prosody—the stresses, pitch curves, timing, pauses—are not inevitable. Of course, this is something they already know from movies and television series from abroad. Beyond these differences, however, a world of Englishes seems to be unfolding, in which the familiar intonations of the American and British dialects will be used in the future by a minority of English speakers around the world. This is one of the compelling notes on which the typical course ends, modulating what otherwise may have seemed at moments a narrative of the triumph of the standard reference varieties of the language.

To understand why the rhythms and intonations of the standard and the globally areal varieties of English often differ, it is useful to turn to an idea that could stand to receive more attention in a HEL course: indices of linguistic rhythms. The idea of a division of the languages of the world into *stress-timed* and *syllable-timed* languages goes back to Kenneth Pike in 1945.[5] In its simplest form it holds that languages like English and German are stress-timed because they have equal intervals between stressed syllables, whereas languages like French and Spanish are syllable-timed because they have equal intervals between syllables whether stressed or not. Experiments in the decades since Pike's statement have added a third category, *mora-timed languages,* including Japanese.

For a while, especially in the 1980s, these experiments called into question the actual timing of the supposedly equal intervals. However, the most recent research shows widespread agreement among phonologists that the *impressions* of stress-timing and syllable-timing are real, and these impressions require an explanation.[6] There is also agreement that instead of a binary division between the stress-timed and syllable-timed languages, a continuum of possibilities is more accurate. Finally, a supplementary set of terms has become established: *stress-based* and *syllable-based.* These terms address phonological structure rather than perception; they avoid the problem of discrepancies in clocked intervals; and they reverse the original assumptions of cause and effect. Instead of saying that the phonology of a certain language aims for stress-timing and in imposing this temporal aim brings about certain segmental effects—such as reduced vowels (particularly the mid-central vowel [ə], or schwa)—the idea is that reduced vowels (along with consonant clusters and stress patterns in words) *produce* the impression of stress-timing. In contrast, the opposite elements—full vowels, few consonant clusters, lack of word stress—produce the impression of syllable-timing. Thus, both sets of terms can be used consistently in their appropriate contexts.

With these theoretical concepts in mind, we can return to the more tangible matter of the verbal music of English as recited by the instructor and the students: what it has been (or what we reconstruct it to have been) and comparing that with what it is becoming (or what we can reasonably predict). Findings from experimental studies of the production and perception of rhythm in the twenty-first century can be projected back to earlier centuries and vocalized. The same examples from the experiments reveal surprising tendencies of the language in the present century. We will work forward from Old English.

3.3. REVISITING OLD ENGLISH RHYTHMS

Sometimes the classroom illustrations of sounds can become physical. My most recent experience resulted in a whole class of HEL students marching around the room and reciting the opening lines of *Beowulf.* This unlikely finale depended for its intellectual legitimacy on assumptions briefly outlined in the preceding section and a few additional ones.[7] To begin with, Old English did not have reduced vowels. The extensive system of inflectional endings depended on the full values of the short vowels, especially [ɑ], [ɛ], [u], and [ɔ]; and in polysyllabic words these and other short vowels were not reduced to schwa. The surprising effect is that in its lack of reduced vowels Old English can be said to have similarities with the phonological structure of a syllable-based language like Spanish. In this respect, both Old English and Spanish differ from Late Middle English and Modern English. Consequently, Old English can be hypothesized to have more of the suprasegmental structure of syllable-based languages—that is, the impression of syllable-timing—despite our thinking of Old English as thoroughly Germanic and heavily stressed.

These deductions and hypotheses from theoretical and experimental phonology are supported in the most recent studies of the meter of Old English poems. *Beowulf* has never been thought of as a poem in syllabic meter. Yet the most coherent way to imagine Old English meter is as a precisely measured mix of "accentual" elements (as the meter has traditionally been understood), "syllabic" elements (which may seem more appropriate for French verse), and "quantitative" elements (which are most familiar in Greek and Latin).[8] Thus, the HEL students marching around the classroom aimed to take a step on the pronunciation of each syllable, no matter how stressed or unstressed, or how long or short. The only exceptions were for unstressed syllables grouped together for one beat (one footstep) in highly regulated contexts including the typical "stress-timed" pattern of two or more lightly stressed syllables (*Hwæt, wē* and *hū þā*) and "resolution" (*æþelingas* and *fremedon*). These contexts for grouping have been established and agreed upon by Old English prosodists for more than a century. It is the emphasis on eight "syllable equivalents" that is new:

Hwæt, wē Gār-Dena   in ġeārdagum,
    ˇ
  ①   ② ③④ ⑤ ⑥ ⑦ ⑧

þēodcyninga   þrym ġefrūnon.
  ① ② ③④   ⑤ ⑥ ⑦ ⑧

hū þā æþelingas   ellen fremedon.
 ˇ ˇ   ˇ
 ① ②③④ ⑤⑥ ⑦ ⑧

Four steps to the half-line, eight steps to the line. With grammatical paradigms at hand, it becomes clear that full vowels occur in inflectional syllables: -*a* (twice), -*um*, -*on* (twice), -*as*. There are no spellings with –*e* indicating a reduction to schwa. When a dative –*e* occurs seven lines later in *ofer hronrāde* ("over swanroad") we know it has the full vowel [ɛ], not the reduced vowel schwa [ə]. (The five syllables fill the standard four positions of the half-line, the two syllables of the preposition *ofer* occupying the first position. The dative –*e* counts as fully as those two syllables, or *hron*- or –*rād*- in the count of metrical positions.)

3.4. MIDDLE ENGLISH RHYTHMS

Reduced vowels, however, are abundant at the next stage of the language. Here we come to an apparent contradiction that provides material for an interesting discussion: the sound that many would consider the least musical in the language, "uh" (the mid-central reduced vowel, or schwa) is the key to the sound of the best poetry of the period. Without "uh" the verbal music is lost. The exercise of the auditory imagination can continue naturally by trying out passages of poetry with and without [ə], then asking the implications for ordinary language.

If the centuries between 1150 and 1500 are sometimes known as "the Period of the Leveling of Inflections," changes in the grammatical paradigms interacted with changes in the sounds of the language, apparently reinforcing each other. The full vowels noted in inflectional syllables in Old English all reduced to the mid-central vowel, which in turn was eventually lost, and the system of inflections was unsustainable.

Undergraduates in a HEL class may or may not be familiar with final –e in Chaucer. At the University of Texas at Austin some will have had the sophomore literature survey and so will have read the General Prologue to the *Canterbury Tales*. In any event, even those who have no familiarity with Chaucer usually pick up the rhythm easily. This ease of acquisition makes it all the more interesting that for two or three centuries after the sixteenth century it was not understood that Chaucerian final –e should be pronounced. The formidable poet John Dryden could write in 1700:

> The verse of Chaucer, I confess, is not harmonious to us . . . there is the rude sweetness of a Scotch tune in it, which is natural and pleasing, though not perfect. It is true, I cannot go so far as he who published the last edition of him; for he would make us believe the fault is in our ears, and that there were really ten syllables in a verse where we find but nine. But this opinion is not worth confuting; it is so gross and obvious an errour, that common sense (which is rare in everything but matters of faith and revelation) must convince the reader, that equality of numbers in every verse which we call heroic, was either not known, or not always practiced in Chaucer's age.[9]

During the next two centuries philologists set the record straight, at least for London English and Chaucer's poetry. It took much longer for final –e to be recognized in the alliterative poetry of the West Midlands, contemporary with Chaucer. Literary scholars, editors, and prosodists were long misled by statements of older historical grammars to the effect that –e was lost sooner in the North and in the West than in the Southeast, including London English. The irony is that what might seem to be a problem in historical linguistics found its solution, and the correction to an earlier linguistic solution, in the work of literary prosodists. Furthermore, what seems a narrow problem, whether literary or linguistic, has far broader implications, particularly for our students and their contemporary interests.

Extensive attention to Middle English dialects may not be possible in a one-semester course, but this particular problem offers an opportunity to discuss the key concept of *register*. This is an important part of sociolinguistics of the present day as well as historical linguistics. At any time within a locality, or within a family, older and newer forms of the language are simultaneously in use. The grandparents have usages that are different from those of the pre-teens. Any individual will have usages that vary from one situation to another, depending on the formality of the occasion or the speakers involved. Whatever the general trends might have been in the West Midlands of England during the fourteenth and fifteenth centuries, it is clear that the alliterative poems were composed in a register that invoked a certain formality and hearkened back to earlier days. Final *–e* was alive in this register and was an essential part of the meter.[10]

3.5. PRESENT-DAY ENGLISH RHYTHMS

Though it may seem like a joke from an academic novel, the reduction to schwa and the eventual loss of final vowels—the place of lowly "uh"—is arguably the single most important series of changes in the whole history of the English language.[11] It ranks with the series of changes known as the Great Vowel Shift. It is also a crucial point where the concerns of historical linguistics and of literary prosodists intersect.

The reduction of inflections to *–e* and the eventual loss of that reduced vowel, as described in the last two sections, can be attributed in part to two languages in contact, Old English and Old Norse, between the ninth and eleventh centuries. Certainly in the part of England known as the Danelaw, where speakers of the two related languages interacted regularly, the probable abrasive effect on grammatical endings has long been recognized.[12] Scandinavian speakers of English as a second language would have been likely to get the roots of words right but have difficulty with endings that were similar but not identical. This phenomenon is known as linguistic "interference."

Present-Day interference is especially clear if we state the issue in terms of Braj B. Kachru's Three Circles of English, a model that has been challenged and refined in certain aspects but which remains standard. By Kachru's model, the *Inner Circle* consists of the United Kingdom and Ireland, the United States, South Africa, Australia, and New Zealand; the *Outer Circle* of India, Singapore, and countries of Sub-Saharan Africa; and the *Expanding Circle* of Europe, Japan, China, Korea, and many other countries.[13] These circles correspond roughly to "English as a native language," "English as a second language," and "English as a foreign language," with the understanding that significant portions of the populations of all three circles would be classified differently. Finally, they also correspond, respectively, to "norm-providing," "norm-developing," and "norm-dependent" varieties.[14] This may all sound abstract and theoretical, but examples close to the students' own experiences are not hard to find. They can hear in their own experiences and classrooms the richness of the verbal music that results from these so-called inter-fering patterns.

With the right encouragement, students are always eager to demonstrate features of their own variety of English, whether the features are lexical, morphological, syn-tactic, or phonetic. In Texas, this is true among bilingual speakers of English and Spanish for the usual categories of segmental phonology and also for code-switch-ing and suprasegmentals. Phillip M. Carter has found that the rhythm of American English among Spanish bilingual speakers who had moved from Mexico to North Carolina was influenced by the rhythm of Mexican Spanish.[15] Their English is more syllable-timed.

One of the most thoroughly studied varieties of global English is that of the Malaysian peninsula, where a distinction can be drawn between Malaysian and Singapore English, and further between these two varieties and Beijing Chinese English. If Singapore is in the Outer Circle, Malaysia and China are in the Expanding Circle. Both Malaysian and Singapore English are usually considered syllable-timed compared with British English, which is stress-timed. Yet by the best measurements that have been devised (the Pairwise Variability Index), Malaysian English is more syllable-timed than Singapore English, and Beijing Chinese English is more syllable-timed than either.[16]

For Singapore English as a second language and Beijing Chinese English as a for-eign language, the substrate first languages exert influence, including rhythmical influence. This happens increasingly in Englishes around the world. Natalie Gerber has shown the probable influence of Somali on the English rhythms and rhymes of the Somali-born hip-hop artist K'naan.[17] Where British or American English would have reduced vowels, K'naan often has full vowels that rhyme, or a rhyme between a full vowel and a reduced vowel. As a result, some of the rhyme pairs in his work dem-onstrate a tug between stress-timed and mora- or syllable-timed rhythms of global Englishes and the vowel systems they depend on, much like the tug in Singapore English.

3.6. CONCLUSION

Encouraging students to internalize aspects of the sound systems of English at its various stages makes the history to some extent portable. The sounds of Old English may remain only a dim echo for many, but students have approached me years later and spontaneously recited a few lines from Chaucer. Some of these former students have gone on to distinguished careers themselves in teaching and research. Just last month in London I was on a panel with a former student of a former student of mine. Aside from a feeling of pride, I was curious—in the casual role of sociohistorical linguist—to see if fourteenth-century English has changed in the twenty-first cen-tury. I was reassured to find that the Middle English dialect of the academic tribe is stable—probably more so than during a comparable period of two or three decades in Chaucer's lifetime. The history is portable, but it endures the buffetings of our present cacophonous age. (Are all ages perceived as cacophonous?) The history taps into connections through time and across the globe so that as speakers of English we know with some specificity how our varieties of the language diverge and how they come together.

The main task of the teacher of language is to get the students conscious of the languages they use.

RRD

CHAPTER 4

Teaching the History of English

A South African Perspective

RAJEND MESTHRIE

4.1. A PERSONAL INTRODUCTION

In South Africa, as elsewhere in the world, English studies have tended to be over-shadowed by the study of literature, yet language studies from a historical perspective have not been neglected entirely. This chapter reflects my own experiences in teaching such a specific module and related modules which complement the traditional History of the English Language (HEL). A personal background is therefore in order before discussing teaching and other techniques. This background is not entirely egotistical: it is meant to give a flavour of what kind of History of English courses have existed in South Africa.

When I entered university in the 1970s, the classics tended to dominate language history. Schools and universities still taught Latin, which had high status and was touted as the language from which all worthwhile words from English had been derived. English departments usually taught at least a semester of Chaucer, and some taught introductory Old English. My own realisation that the history of English involved more than a debt to the Romans, the French, and the Renaissance came with an undergraduate encounter (at the now defunct University of Durban-Westville) with Frank Palmer's *Grammar*[1] and David Crystal's *Linguistics*,[2] seminal works of 1971 from Pelican, which brought the synchronic linguistic revolution to undergraduates. The paradox that their synchronic approaches should have stimulated a diachronic interest has to do with their delinking of present-day English structure from the clutches of Latin grammar and lexicon. So if English didn't "come" from Latin (as my schoolteachers had averred), where did it come from? And even though Crystal and Palmer had insisted that a historical form like *āgan* 'to owe' was not to be related to modern auxiliary *ought* in a synchronic grammar, the fact that *ought* was once the past tense of *owe* piqued my interest. In 1978 I entered gradu-ate studies at the University of Cape Town, whose courses promised to satisfy that diachronic curiosity. The English department offered an Honours degree in English language or literature, or even a mix of modules from these areas. Taking all five modules from the language side prepared me for a career in Linguistics and English. The five modules were taught once a week for an entire year: Old English, Middle English, Old Icelandic, History of English, and Linguistics and Literature.[3] This detail is not meant purely as a reminiscence; the suite of options that I had chosen offered as cohesive a programme as one could ask for in the history of English. Plus it had a future Nobel Laureate as one of its dedicated teachers (in J. M. Coetzee who taught the Linguistics and Literature module). The Cape Town options were not taught widely in South Africa, though Old and Middle English did feature strongly at some universities—notably Rhodes University and the University of South Africa. Cape Town itself had had some other notable teachers: Leslie Casson, who had taught Old and Middle English in the 1950s and 1960s, was reputed to have an unwrit-ten law after his name on the development of Germanic /æ$_1$/ as /a:/ (spelt <aa>) in Afrikaans, and Roger Lass taught occasional Old English graduate courses from the 1980s on. The dedication in *Old English: A Historical Linguistic Companion*[4] shows that the book is an indirect result of one of these courses.

By the 1990s the language emphasis changed in South African English depart-ments from the historical to the applied, with increasing focus on English as Second Language and changing pedagogies. This is, of course, a natural turn of events in postcolonial contexts. With the retirement of senior personnel from the English department, there were no new recruitments in Old and Middle English (or unsur-prisingly, Icelandic). I therefore introduced a module within Linguistics on the History of English. The difficulty I faced was that students had little or no previ-ous experience in Old and Middle English. Even the Chaucerian texts they read in the English department were now translations. This chapter reflects on the teaching techniques I used to make up for this deficit. I currently offer graduate students a course on "Pidgins, Creoles and World Englishes," reflecting the study of colonial and postcolonial contact varieties from a linguistic perspective. This topic was not on the agenda in the 1970s and early 1980s; standard histories of English stopped with a chapter on English in the United States with a brief mention of other former colonies, but the work of Kachru, Görlach, MacArthur, Crystal, and others has made it difficult to ignore this topic in South Africa.[5] As it would be overambitious to try to do justice to both topics (traditional HEL and contact varieties) in one module, I currently treat these as two sides of a coin tossed over two semesters.

4.2. TEACHING TECHNIQUES IN THE TRADITIONAL HISTORY OF ENGLISH

This section is concerned with the teaching of the history of English to undergraduate students with a background in Linguistics but constrained by no previous knowledge of Old English. The earliest English known to students would be that of Shakespeare, though some may have encountered Chaucer in translation, and possibly even in the original. The second constraint is that of time—how to give a solid, if undetailed, introduction in a mere thirteen lectures (plus five tutorials). My inspiration came from an introductory graduate course in Medieval Welsh at the University of Texas in 1980 by classicist Gareth Morgan, who inculcated in us a reading knowledge of *Pwyll Pendeuic Dyuet,* the first branch of the *Mabinogion,*[6] under similar constraints. The technique involved teaching the rudiments of the grammar with *all* illustrations coming from the set text, initially in truncated fragments of sentences and then in fuller versions. Students would often encounter the same sentence several times, as typically a sentence could contain many points of grammatical interest to be reflected upon at different stages of the grammar lessons. To our amazement we learned to read the first branch of the *Mabinogion* by the end of the module, even though the example sentences were pretty obscure in the initial stages. Piecing them all together at the end in context to reveal a real unfolding story was only a little short of magical. (The magic faded a bit when trying to read new texts or other branches of the *Mabinogion,* but we had certainly gained a quick entry into the grammatical and literary world of the text.) Would this technique work for introducing Anglo-Saxon over a much shorter span of time?

For the overall course, I chose prose material for Old English, poetry for Middle English and prose for Early Modern English. Students were given grammar lessons as we went along, and only when they had gained familiarity with the readings did we focus on a phonological overview and a thumbnail diachronic history of vowels and consonants. Semantic shift was taught incidentally, as examples cropped up. Table 4.1 gives the overall plan for the course of thirteen lectures (and five tutorials on reading texts).

I now turn to the main part of the course, viz., an introduction to Old English grammar.

4.2.1. Old English

The texts for Old English (OE) were four excerpts from the *Anglo-Saxon Chronicle.* Table 4.2 gives the sequence of the grammar lessons covered.

Table 4.1: OUTLINE OF SHORT UNDERGRADUATE HISTORY
OF ENGLISH MODULE

Session 1	Historical overview
Sessions 2 to 7	Old English with main focus on key grammatical elements (plus two tutorials on reading)
Sessions 8 to 10	Middle English with focus on grammar and phonetics, and key (subsequent) semantic shifts (plus two tutorials on reading)
Sessions 11 to 13	Early Modern English, with focus on grammar and Great Vowel Shift (plus one tutorial on reading)

Table 4.2: OUTLINE OF TOPICS COVERED FOR A
BASIC OLD ENGLISH GRAMMAR

1. Weak verbs–present & past tense
2. Strong verbs–present & past tense
3. Nouns–strong declension
4. Definite & indefinite articles
5. Nouns–weak declension
6. Adjectives–weak and strong forms
7. Personal pronouns
8. Some irregular verbs
9. Relative pronouns
10. The passive
11. More prepositions
12. Other clause structures

This skeleton grammar is covered in a mere eight pages of notes and examples. For a longer, more cohesive reading for this section students were pointed to Chapter 3 of Fennel's *A History of English*.[7] The authentic *Chronicle* readings fitted onto one page, followed by a glossary of five pages covering every word in the reading passages. As an illustration of the technique we looked at the first two grammatical lessons which covered weak and strong verbs, present and past tenses via the paradigms for *fremman* 'to do,' *nerian* 'to injure,' and *drīfan* 'to drive.' First, I had to explain all new symbols—<æ>, <Ǣ>, <þ>, and <ð>—in addition to macrons for long vowels. Then, I taught the notion of ablaut for strong verbs. By the end of the first two lessons, I was able to read the following five example sentences with the class, all examples being excerpted from the *Chronicle*:

1. *Wolde drīfan.*
2. *Hē nyste hwæt hīe wæron.*
3. *Gesōhton lōnd.*
4. *He fōr ūt.*
5. *Com Willem eorl upp at Hestingan.*

After these two introductory classes, students were expected to attempt translations of all future examples. They also read the originals out loud before translating. This helped with basic phonology (postvocalic /r/, medial /h/, pre-Great Vowel Shift values for vowels, attention to length, etc.). By grammar lesson 4, they had covered enough to attempt eleven sentences, the first three of which follow:

6. *On his dagum cuōmon ǣrest iii scipu.*
7. *Hīe wolde drīfan tō þæs cyninges tūne.*
8. *Him gefeaht wiþ Ǣþelwulf cyning.*

Note that sentence (7) incorporates *wolde drīfan* of the earlier sentence (1), thus giving reinforcement to earlier learning. By the sixth and last grammar lesson, students were expected to grapple with longer original sentences like the following, illustrating the basic range of grammatical properties needed for the course:

9. *and þy gēare þe hē cyng wæs he fōr ūt mid sciphere.*
10. *Harold fēng to cynerice swā swā se cyng hit him geūðe.*
11. *Hie wolde drīfan tō þæs cyninges tūne þy he nyste hwaet hie wæron.*

Again, earlier phrases recur in these longer sentences: (4) in (9), while (1), (2), and (7) are components of (11). There were fifty-eight such excerpted sentence fragments (including repetitions), which prepared students well for the eighty-four sentences they would encounter in the *Chronicle* passages. All Old English teachers grasp at any modern connection (in grammatical form or semantics) to resurrect the ancient words, and this was a feature of our classes that was well received in an age when grammar drills are obsolete and grammar lessons have to be endured. At the conclusion of the OE grammar classes, there were two reading tutorials, during which students were asked to translate the *Chronicle* excerpts for 787 (appearance of the first Viking ships), 851 (the first winter stayover by the Viking invaders), 878 (Alfred's victory and coronation), and, of course, 1066 (defeat at the hands of the Normans). These passages comprised roughly eighty-four sentences (taking the OE sentence boundary mark in the *Chronicle* as authentic and not counting some anomalies which involve short phrases rather than sentences). That students could read these passages in the original by lessons 8 and 9 is a minor success story. A historian-colleague at a former university of mine who taught the *Chronicle* in translation to History students was impressed.

Side by side with the grammar focus was the issue of the unfamiliarity of some vocabulary and some of the grammatical and phonetic elements. Fortunately, most of our students are familiar with Afrikaans, a South African offshoot of Dutch. Although showing partial restructuring and a fairly large number of borrowings under contact with languages of the Cape, Afrikaans is probably still best described as a Germanic language for the purposes of historical linguistics. Afrikaans proved a useful point of comparison and aid in the following respects:

(a) Grammatical items retained in Afrikaans but lost in English: There is a wealth of West Germanic features which are retained in Afrikaans (in modified form) but not in modern English, which help South African students read the texts with some degree of familiarity. These are listed below with examples from the *Anglo-Saxon Chronicle* sentences chosen in the grammar lessons:

    (i) Verb-second position after temporal adverbs and the like: *þa salde sē here him micle āþās.*

    (ii) Verb-final position in main clauses if an auxiliary is in verb-second position (after a subject or temporal adverb etc.): *Her wæs Paulus gehwierfed, sanctus Stephanus oftorfod.*

    (iii) Verb-final position in subordinate clauses: *þæt wǣron þā ǣrestan scipu Deniscra monna þe Angelcynnes lond gesōhton.*

(iv) Auxiliary in final position in subordinate clauses: *him eac geheton þæt hiera kyning fulwihte onfon* wolde.

(v) Perfective *ge-*: Afrikaans has retained the Germanic perfective prefix *ge-*, using it as an unmarked past marker: *ix scipu gefengun.*

(vi) Prefixation of particles to verbs: *ofsloh, bestæl, adræfdon, forðferde.*

Note that the word orders of OE and Afrikaans do not always coincide. In particular, the *Chronicle* texts cited have occasional verb final in main clauses without any auxiliary (*Willelm þis land geode*). Still, students in class were better able to cope with word order flexibility, given their knowledge of Afrikaans.

(b) Phonetic elements retained in Afrikaans but lost in English: Most noteworthy here is the presence of a (voiceless) velar fricative [x] after vowels, or vowel + /r/. This still applies to cognates like OE *feohtan*, Afrik *veg* ([fɛx]) 'to fight'; OE *beorg/ beorh*, Afrik *berg* ([bɛrx]) 'mountain.' Also relevant are phonotactic rules like the presence of postvocalic /r/ (OE *norðan*, Afrik *noorde* ([nuərdə]) 'north') and the presence of /l/ before consonants (OE *folces*, Afrik *volk* ([fɔːlk]) 'people').

(c) Vocabulary items remaining in Afrikaans that make Old English base forms more familiar. Compare OE *niman*, Afrik *neem* 'to take'; OE *feng*, Afrik *vang* 'to catch, grasp'; OE *gan*, Afrik *gaan* 'to go'; OE *witan*, Afrik *weet* 'to know'; OE *worden*, Afrik *word* 'to become.'

The Afrikaans affinities with Old English are treated in Branford,[8] who provides an Afrikaans poetic version of the *Wanderer* (lines 19–29). This annotated text with commentary shows the affinities via the large number of cognates and semantic and syntactic compatibility very effectively. Table 4.3 provides a small selection showing ten cognates.

4.2.2. The Middle English Section

This section consisted of four lectures focussed on reading Middle English, without any formal grammar lessons. After the complexity of Old English grammar (or at least its initial unfamiliarity), I felt that points of grammatical interest in Middle English could be taught incidentally from the texts themselves. The same applied to semantics, with latter-day semantic shifts of meaning being discussed as they arose. As all mediaevalists know, semantic shifts help enliven classes and teach etymology at a practical level. The background reading assigned was the chapter on Middle English in Fennel.[9] The readings were from the *General Prologue* to *The Canterbury Tales*, concentrating on the introduction and the portraits of the Knight, Prioress, and Clerk. The reason for choosing a poetic text over prose was that if students had to gain familiarity with only one text, then it had to be this Chaucerian favourite. Furthermore, the narrative style of the *Prologue* makes for easy reading, as if it were prose.

Table 4.3: A SELECTION OF TERMS FROM THE
WANDERER AND THEIR AFRIKAANS COGNATES
(BASED ON BRANFORD 1971)

Old English	Afrikaans	Modern English
ærest	eerste	'first'
earm	arm	'poor'
biddan	bid	'pray'
faran	vaar	'journey, sail'
forlætan	verlaat	'leave, forsake'
geleafa	geloof	'faith'
lof	lof	'praise'
ofermod	oormoed	'over-confidence'
ræd	raad	'counsel, advice'
sælida	seeliede	'seaman'

After students had gained familiarity with the texts through pre-class translation and reading aloud in class, it was time to return to diachronic linguistics, with emphasis on the transition from Old to Middle English. Since this was a Linguistics class, we focussed on the phonetic system of Old English, with emphasis on the vowels and consonants, as laid out in Fennel.[10] We then compared this system with that of the East Midlands of Chaucer. The assignment for this part of the course was based on Cable.[11] Students had to turn in an assignment based on the following: sections 7.2 and 7.3 of Cable covering: (a) vowel development from Old to Middle English; (b) formation of new diphthongs in Middle English; (c) lengthening and shortening of vowels; and (d) consonant development from Old to Middle English.[12] I recommend Cable to all students as a classic tutorial book that, like its prototype, Algeo and Pyles,[13] teaches and at the same time examines students' understanding of the history of English. In modern education-speak its assessment is both formative and summative.

4.2.3. Early Modern English

Two classes were devoted to early Modern English with a quick reading of excerpts from Caxton[14] (1490) and a 1551 translation of Thomas More's *Utopia* (original Latin version of 1516). Thereafter, we turned to the changes from Middle to Early Modern English, with a lecture on the Great Vowel Shift and another on developments in phonetics, grammar, and vocabulary. Again an assignment from Cable[15] proved invaluable in helping students consolidate the lectures and readings. This assignment comprised sub-questions on (a) the Great Vowel Shift (§177); (b) pronouns, with a question on Romeo and Juliet's reciprocal pronouns of address (§182); (c) strong and weak verbs, with variants from Shakespeare's plays and other examples from the likes of Marlowe, Donne, and Spenser (§183); and (d) prepositions with examples from Shakespeare which require a different preposition today (§184).

With this, the course usually drew to a close; students interested in pursuing the history further back in time were pointed to vacation reading from Fennel's (2001) chapter on the pre-history of English in relation to proto-Germanic. The course was thus somewhat compressed but made manageable with greater input from the lecturer for the Old English readings, balanced by greater participation from the students on Middle and Early Modern English, and the exercises on Early Modern English. In wrapping up, passing mention was made of the modern age of colonisation, postcolonisation, and globalisation. Students interested in further work on the history of English had two options if they embarked on graduate studies: Old English taught in detail by Roger Lass as a full semester course and "Pidgins, Creoles and New Englishes," taught by myself. It is to the latter that I briefly turn in the last section of this chapter.

4.3. TEACHING TECHNIQUES IN "CREOLISTICS AND WORLD ENGLISHES"

The postcolonial era and subsequent rampant globalisation has revitalised the story of English. It is no longer appropriate to follow a linear history of English, and even that earlier genealogy of the standard language has been called into question. David Crystal (2004), Ray Hickey (2012), Mesthrie (2003), and others have critiqued the traditional account of the history of English. As Crystal puts it: "'The' story of English, as it has been presented in the mainstream tradition, is the story of a single variety."[16] His book engagingly demonstrates there are many stories of English. Told from the Celtic side, for example, that history looks a little different. Ray Hickey (2012), Hildegard Tristram (2004), and others have argued that the role of the Celtic substrates is not negligible. Research into first language L1 varieties in former "Dominion" territories (Australia, New Zealand, South Africa, United States, and Canada) has also taken on a life of its own in the areas of sociophonetics, lexicography, and the like. It is fair to say that, thanks to the Labovian thrust in English sociolinguistics, the United States leads other countries in characterising the vowel systems of English today. What all this means is that the modern (and postmodern) history of English is a very diffuse topic. For a while it looked like the triad of ENL (English as a Native language), ESL (English as a Second Language), and EFL (English as a Foreign Language) would afford a plausible and manageable typology of the spread of the language in the colonial period. However, many factors complicate and challenge that typology. English creoles are testimony to the colonial contexts of English caught up in forced labour migrations and slavery, which have engendered new codes that only partially fit the traditional typology. Within the global metropolises, code-switching between English and a local code have also produced another kind of hybridity that can be used to express a modern, urban (but not necessarily displaced) identity. The next two sections detail a graduate course (equivalent to fourth-year undergraduate studies at northern universities) on "Pidgins, Creoles and New Englishes." This course is not directly tied to the history of English, as it could equally be construed as a follow-up course to the foundations of language contact. It can, however, very nicely be positioned as a history of English as a contact language.[17]

4.3.1. Approaches to Pidgin and Creole Studies

Contact Languages: Pidgins and Creoles formed the first half of the course with six two-hour seminars devoted to the material in it.[18] The topics covered an overview of the field: origins and features of pidgins; origins and features of creoles; substrata, superstrata, and universals (two sessions); and decreolisation. This graduate course offers much scope for discussion, and the richness of terms, concepts, histories, debates, and controversies led to every seminar being pressed for time. Key approaches include the life-cycle theory, substrate-based theories, universalist theories, gradualist theories, and "anti-exceptionalist" theories that take a somewhat superstratist view. A key aim of the course was to show the structural complexity of extended pidgins and creoles. As a result, theory was always complemented with numerous examples. The three short assignments also addressed this focus of structural analysis. The first assignment was based on identifying major structural features of Tok Pisin from a written text; the second was on overlaps and differences between pidgin and foreigner talk. These were taken from the Sebba textbook. But it was the third one that really engaged, challenged, and impressed the students, dispelling once and for all the notion of pidgins as necessarily simple, derivative, or marginal. Students were given a passage from Cameroon Pidgin English (part of the West African Pidgin English continuum), the *Di Gud Nyus Hawe*, a biblical passage taken from *Modern Englishes: Pidgins and Creoles*.[19] They were asked to render the passage into standard English, while keeping as closely as possible to the idiom and semantics of the pidgin text. They also had to answer short but specific grammatical questions on the text. This seemingly simple assignment would not have been possible without supplying the students with a modern standard version of the passage (*The Holy Bible*, from *Modern Englishes*),[20] which was meant as a guide. Even so, the students found it difficult to come to terms with all the complexities of the pidgin text. A particular area of difficulty was in 'tense—aspect—modality,' especially coming to grips with pre-verbal particles (*di, a, don*). Polysemy of items also afforded difficulty: *di* was both a continuative pre-verbal element as well as a definite article. The excerpt, provided in Table 4.4, showed the dual ontology of extended pidgins. In some ways, they appear to be English varieties (with the help of a large number of English lexical items), but in other ways they seem to be autonomous systems (in syntax, idiom, and the phonological form of words).

4.3.2. Approaches to World Englishes

The second half of the course comprised six two-hour seminars on New Englishes or World Englishes, based on the textbook *World Englishes: The Study of New Linguistic Varieties* by Mesthrie and Bhatt.[21] The focus of this part of the course was on the history of colonisation and the consequent spread of English from the sixteenth century onward; the characteristic features of the L2 varieties of English that ensued; issues pertaining to indigenisation and nativisation; and practical ramifications of the field. As far as theories were concerned, the Three Circles model of Kachru[22] featured

Table 4.4: *EXCERPT FROM* DI GUD NYUS HAWE (SOURCE: TODD 1984: 263)

1. Di fos tok fo di gud nyus fo Jesus Christ God yi Pikin. 2. I bi sem as i di tok fo di buk fo Isaiah, God yi nchinda (Prophet), "Lukam, mi a di sen ma nchinda fo bifo yoa fes weh yi go fix yoa rud fan." 3. Di vos fo som man di krai fo bush: "Fix di ples weh Papa God di go, mek yi rud tret." 4. John di Baptist bi de fo bush, an yi bi di tok sey baptas bi som nomba fo shu sey God dong chus di bad fo di man wey yi dong chen yi hat. 5. Ol pipu fo Judea weti ol di pipu fo Jerusalem bi go fo yi, an yi bi baptas dem fo Jordan wata, an dem bi di gri sey dem bi bad pipu. 6. Fo dat tam John yi krus bi bi biabia fo camel weti nkanda wey yi di di taiam fo yi wes, den yi chop bi bi lukos weti honi. 7. Den yi bi tok fo demo ol sey, "Som man di kam fo ma bak weh yi pas mi, weh yi shus mi a no koret fan fo ben daun an lusinam. 8. Mi a dong baptas wuna weti wata, bot yi go baptas wuna weti di Holy Spirit."

strongly, with suggestions of modification by Schneider,[23] and Mesthrie and Bhatt[24] on the growth of English in Europe today. Strong links were also made with the fields of second language acquisition, language contact (borrowing, switching, and new typological diversities), and pidgin and creole studies of the first half of the course. Retentions from local languages (mistermed "borrowings") and retentions from earlier forms of L1 English (mistermed "colonial lag") also featured in discussions. Once again linguistic structure formed an important element of the course, with stress on both widely recurrent features (so-called New Englishisms or Angloversals) as well as idiosyncratic features pertaining to specific varieties. The notion of "language shift varieties" was also dissected, with brief case studies of Ireland, Singapore, and South African Indian English. As far as exercises went, this section also included short review questions of key concepts and constructions, drawn from the end of each chapter of Mesthrie and Bhatt's *World Englishes*.

The end-of-term essay gave students a chance to write on either part of the course or on a bridge between them. One option was to "adopt a pidgin, creole, or New English" and write an essay on its history, sociolinguistics, and structure in relation to some of the salient themes of the course. Another (the bridging option) was to consider the history of African American Vernacular English and to see where it fitted into the course. This variety did not feature much in either part of the course—as it is not considered prototypical Creole by Sebba[25] or prototypical "New English" by Mesthrie and Bhatt.[26] Students were invited to consider why it fell between the cracks, and to delve into Anglicist versus Creolist positions on the topic.

For reasons of time, colonial/postcolonial L1 varieties of English (or "Settler Varieties") do not make an appearance in either of the courses mentioned in this chapter. South African English is extensively covered in an undergraduate module "Language in South Africa." The first part of this course covers salient topics concerning languages other than English in twelve lectures (overviews of Khoe-San and Bantu language history and sociolinguistics; the history of Afrikaans; contact and variation in present-day varieties). The second part covers twelve lectures on English in South Africa. As far as L1 varieties historically connected to Britain are concerned, the focus is on lexicography, grammatical innovation, and phonetics. The main emphasis is on the development of South African English accents. Commonalities with the antipodeal Englishes of Australia and New Zealand are covered (especially the raising of short front vowels), and specific South African developments like the KIT split,[27] and glide weakening in the PRICE and MOUTH lexical sets. A more modern feature is the reversal of the short front vowel shift,[28] which middle-class L1 speakers participate in, following global trends. This section doubles up as an applied phonetics class, with the students' own accents forming part of the data for analysis. For the first time, middle-class speakers of the prestige variety of South African English discover that they "have an accent too." Of equal interest are the varieties that historically arose as L2s and are to a fairly large extent correlatable with different ethnicities (Black, 'Coloured,' Afrikaner, and Indian). These show large-scale contact effects. Again, students provide data in class, though lecturers have to tread sensitively in a historically divided society. One caveat is to avoid picking on students in a manner that suggests ethnic stereotyping (e.g., "all Black people speak in this way"). A second is to pay heed to psychosociological matters since speakers of a minority or dominated variety might not be aware of their speech habits and unconsciously relate their phonetics to that of more dominant or prestige varieties. A third is to expect style shifting—that is, students at university are likely to give prestige citation forms rather than usual vernacular realisations. Finally, in the new postapartheid society there are students of diverse backgrounds who speak middle-class "deracialising" varieties, more closely aligned with what used to be called "White South African English." They do this largely via having attended desegregated schools in which the prestige variety of White South African English was most influential. Such students run the risk of being stereotyped as *coconuts*, who are alleged by their working-class counterparts to be "dark on the outside, white on the inside." Accents thus carry a heavy cultural load in terms of expected forms of behaviour versus innovations. This set of lectures thus links the HEL course with questions of identity and belonging. These are important questions in a country currently grappling with its colonial and apartheid pasts and the search for a decolonial order. A South African HEL cannot afford to ignore these burning questions.

CHAPTER 5

How Is HEL Relevant to Me?

SONJA L. LANEHART

5.1. INTRODUCTION

While I will admit that I have always been fascinated by language, such is not the case for many of our students who are non-majors. I changed my major to English Language and Linguistics in part because I was interested in trying to make sense of the ancestry and grammar of African American Language. A few, like me, take it because they love language. Others take it because it is an intriguing elective. Still others take it because they believe it will help them write better or "speak correctly" somehow. As teachers, we should be aware of the reasons students take our classes and try to teach it with those reasons in mind and how they connect to our own teaching and learning goals for the course.

The History of the English Language, or HEL as it is affectionately called, is a popular English Language and Linguistics course on college campuses because, in part, it is perceived to be one of the easier classes and also because it is one of the few English Language and Linguistics classes taught on most campuses even when they do not have a Linguistics Department. HEL is often taught in an English Department because it is a good blend of Medieval Studies and Linguistics, which means it is appealing to English and English Education students and those who "like to read" and/or "like to write." HEL does not have so much Linguistics that it becomes intimidating or overwhelming, but it contains just enough special-ized knowledge about language and linguistics that it can fulfill core and elective requirements for several disciplines, particularly Teacher Education. So, although many Linguistics majors may not take HEL, instead opting to take more theoreti-cal classes like syntax and phonology, English majors and Education majors (both, obviously, non-majors with respect to Linguistics) often take HEL. Ironically, the same thing that makes HEL a more appealing class to non-majors than say Sociolinguistics is also what makes it more difficult to teach: HEL is really a hybrid class that requires a wide range of specialty knowledge. As such, those teaching a

HEL class can range from a medievalist to a dialectologist to a theoretical linguist. Instructor interest and training, then, often directs how much depth a particular aspect of HEL will receive. For example, a medievalist or literature instructor might use Thomas Cable and Albert C. Baugh's *History of the English Language* (2012; originally Baugh 1935) because of its almost poetic quality while a linguist might be more interested in John Algeo and Carmen A. Butcher's *Origins and Development of the English Language* (2013; originally Thomas Pyles 1964) and a sociolinguist might be more interested in Celia M. Millward and Mary Hayes's *A Biography of the English Language* (2011; originally Millward 1996). All are good HEL texts, but each appeals more to one audience than another and one instructor than another.

In this chapter, I address teaching HEL as a sociolinguist and being guided by two areas in learning sciences: goals and interest, particularly situational interest and personal (or individual) interest as part of self-regulated learning. In other words, this chapter addresses the age-old student question, "How is this relevant to me?" Part of our job as college teachers involves getting students to realize the practicality of a course for their needs (e.g., "I need to take this class in order to graduate") and another part is to acknowledge, or awaken in some cases, their intellectual curiosity (e.g., "I've always wondered why 'knight' is spelled with letters that aren't even pronounced"). I provide examples of instruction and assignments that correspond to research literature on goals and interest with respect to teaching and learning more broadly and teaching HEL from the perspective of a sociolinguist more specifically.

5.2. FACILITATING GOAL DEVELOPMENT AND INTEREST FOR SELF-REGULATED LEARNING

One dilemma for teachers is whether we should teach only the content of our subject areas like linguistics and history or should we teach both the content and the skills necessary to direct one's own learning? Obviously, students need both content knowledge and skills for self-directed learning because the usefulness of the knowledge they acquire today will be dependent on the skills they develop to regulate and continue their learning tomorrow. In today's society, the content of some aspects of what we teach may be obsolete in a few short years, but the skills we equip our students with for developing content knowledge can last a lifetime.

Self-regulated learning is a multidimensional skill that is exemplified by students who are metacognitively, motivationally, and behaviorally active participants in their own learning.[1] In other words, as students develop their self-regulatory skills they become active controlling participants who direct what they learn and how they go about learning. Although there are different approaches to self-regulated learning, they do have at least one thing in common: the importance of goals in self-regulation. In fact, for most researchers, the term "self-regulation" implies that something is being used as a reference point to guide one's behavior.[2] Simply put, you cannot regulate without something to compare where you are with where you want to be. Goals are seen as those points of comparison.

With the importance of goals for self-regulation in mind, it becomes clear that in order to facilitate self-regulation in the classroom, students need opportunities to develop their own goals and regulate their learning in relationship to those goals. If we want students to regulate their learning when they leave college they need the opportunity to regulate their learning while they are in college. In addition, instructors should be aware of students' personal, or individual, interests and take advantage of students' situational interest in an effective manner.

According to Woolfolk, *personal* or *individual interests* are more enduring aspects of the person, such as being attracted to or enjoying subjects such as languages, history, and sciences or activities such as soccer, music, and gaming.[3] *Situational interests* are more short-lived aspects of an activity, text, or materials that catch and keep the student's attention. Since interests increase when students feel competent, where students start in the class may be different from where they end up.[4] You may notice that in several introductory texts, they start with interesting facts or observations as a way to capture the situational interest of students and then move more gradually into mastering content to better mimic the development of personal interests. So, accordingly, texts with lots of examples that provide real-world context or those with judicious use of appropriate humor for learning the content may help students develop personal interests from these situational interest instances. For today's tech-savvy students, publishers are relying more on interactional, multimodal texts with use of online materials, mobile apps, sound, 3-D images, and more based on the interest in and success of gaming and instructional technology.

Goals are an important part of the self-regulation process and of understanding the personal interests of students and a good place to begin facilitating the development of self-regulated learning skills. There are three steps that can be used to begin this process. First, create activities that provide students the opportunity to develop their skills at setting "useful" goals. For example, at the beginning of the semester, ask students about their short-term and long-term or life goals and have them develop goals for the course that connect to their own personal goals and interests (see 5.6: Appendix A). The information collected will also help instructors to get to know their students and begin the process of developing involvement with the students. This is important because if you intend to relate the content of the course to your students' lives you need to know something about their lives. One way to begin that process is by asking them about their goals and interests.

Once you have an idea of what their goals and interests are, the second step is to provide the opportunity for training in the strategies the students will need to reach their goals. For example, if their goals involve improving their writing skills, then they will need the opportunity to practice and learn the strategies and skills required to achieve those goals. This process begins with pre-testing for their knowledge (see 5.7: Appendix B) and strategies important for the class, and then spending class time teaching the strategies needed for the students to be successful in the class. It is the responsibility of the instructor to teach not only the content of the course but also the strategies and skills that will facilitate learning in the course. It is the responsibility of the student to use effective strategies for his or her own learning and understanding. To monitor both the student and myself, I do a Midterm Feedback Evaluation (see 5.8: Appendix C) that makes this point for both the students and me. I can pool responses that move students closer to their course goals by compiling their responses and sharing with them in an open discussion to make any course corrections for themselves and for me.

In terms of helping students with strategies to master the material, practice in concept mapping is useful. If concept mapping is a required component of the course, practice using the strategies needed to be successful at this component is also required. Such practice could involve breaking down the tasks necessary to complete a concept map (see 5.11: Appendix F) with a concept sorting group activity (see 5.9: Appendix D). For example, the first task in concept mapping is to define the terms using one's own words. Students need to understand the terms before they can be expected to interrelate them. Next, students need to be able to see basic similarities and differences between the terms. Part of what makes concept mapping challenging is that there is more than one way to map the terms because the mapping is connected to students' learning and understanding and their individual interests. The map itself unfolds in the same way the student's knowledge of the content unfolds. In other words, since we all see things differently even though we may share starting points, our differences provide unique ways of seeing the same things.

The third step in using goal-setting to facilitate the development of self-regulated learning skills is to create activities that provide the opportunity for students to make connections between the course content, their interests, and their goals. One of the major complaints of many students revolves around their belief that what they are learning is not relevant and, therefore, they develop little personal interest and motivation to learn and engage the content. By creating activities whose purpose is to develop connections between the students' goals and course content, the instructor can increase the potential that students will choose to be interested and motivated. One way to accomplish this is by tying the goals they set to the information collected during pre-testing about their skills and their short-term and long-term goals. By helping them set goals that deal with the weaknesses they identified during the pre-testing, they can make connections between their goals and the content of the course which, in most cases, involves earning a "good" grade for the course (short-term goal) so, for example, they can graduate and begin their career (long-term goal).

For example, in HEL classrooms, students often have a goal and/or expectation of improving their language and writing skills. By doing a Usage Survey (see 5.10: Appendix E), students are learning about course content (i.e., HEL usage and the misconceptions about HEL) and meeting one of their goals (i.e., learning about language use to address their speaking and writing). This activity also provides an opportunity for the instructor to teach students where to find information (e.g., a HEL textbook) and how to analyze and use such informational resources now and in the future.

5.3. CHARACTERISTICS OF ACTIVITIES USED TO DEVELOP SELF-REGULATED LEARNING SKILLS

The types of activities that are developed and used in the classroom have the potential to influence students' abilities to develop their self-regulated learning skills. Researchers who have investigated the structure of classroom activities have identified at least three areas that instructors can use.[5] First, activities should be developed that provide students the opportunity to make meaningful choices that match their level of knowledge and skill at making choices.[6] This is important because, as indicated previously, self-regulation involves, among other things, setting goals and monitoring progress toward those goals. This requires making choices about learning. In order for students to learn how to make those decisions they need opportunities to make choices. This could include giving students a say in how the class will be managed, what will be discussed, or the specific area students can research (all of which can be initiated with something like the Student Information Sheet in Appendix A). Again, if we want students to be able to make meaningful choices, they need to be given the opportunity to make those choices.

A second aspect of the structure of classroom activities that can facilitate self-regulated learning is the creation of challenging tasks that match the students' skill levels with the level of task difficulty and, when needed, provide scaffolding for success.[7] As with goals, activities need to be challenging yet realistic. Activities that are too easy result in boredom. Those that are far beyond the skill level of the student can, without proper scaffolding, result in frustration, anxiety, and possibly withdrawal from the activity.[8] It is important that students be challenged so they are put into a position to use the self-regulation skills they possess in order to be successful. Concept mapping (see 5.9: Appendix D) is a good way to get students to learn course content while also challenging them to find ways to connect the concepts in the course and to their interests. Such an activity also gives the instructor as well as other students a way to scaffold and build meaningful participation.

A third area relates to evaluation and recognition in the classroom.[9] Research indicates that students who use learning standards (which involve concerns with mastery, challenge, learning, or curiosity) as opposed to performance standards (which involve concerns with grades, rewards, or approval from others) when judging themselves are more likely to develop the skills needed for effective self-regulated learning. For example, students with learning standards are more likely to use effort attributions for success as well as prefer challenging work and risk taking.[10] In addition, these students tend to use deeper-level cognitive processing and self-monitoring strategies.[11]

On the other hand, students who use performance standards to judge themselves tend to focus on their own ability and self-worth.[12] The performance focus tends to be on comparisons with others with one's self-worth as the trophy. This tends to result in ability-type attributions and a motivational pattern to avoid challenging tasks because of a fear of losing self-worth.[13] In addition, students who tend to be more performance oriented are more likely to use shallow cognitive processing strategies, such as rehearsal.[14] With concept mapping, for example, rehearsal is shown to be ineffective early on to the student since concept mapping is introduced early in the course and since memorizing does not equal understanding—a necessary component of concept mapping. Although knowing the definitions of terms as elicited in pre-testing and initial preparation for concept mapping is important, deeper-level processing is necessary to understand intricate relationships between concepts and one's reality of the course—a reality influenced by one's understanding, interests in the course, and goals.

5.4. I LOVE IT WHEN A PLAN COMES TOGETHER

As a sociolinguist whose focus is on English Language and Linguistics and specifically African American Language, I incorporate those interests in my HEL courses in content and in assignments. While the Student Information Sheet helps to introduce the students and their interests to me and a little of me and my interests to them, it also sets the tone for the collaborative and vibrant teaching and learning to come as well as how you can intertwine various aspects of your identity and interests in a classroom context. For example, many of my examples and assignments incorporate *Doctor Who* and *Star Trek* and other fantasy and science fiction (see the sample sentences in Appendix E: A Brief Survey of Usage). At the beginning of class when we do icebreakers (name, where from, favorite book/movie/song or most memorable moment or weirdest thing, etc.), I use what students say to better connect the material to them personally.

In addition to connecting to students' interests and goals, I also move to expand their consciousness. Students come to HEL with at least a vague notion about language and linguistics courses. Some may think HEL is outdated and not relevant to their current lives. But as with most linguistics courses, HEL can become personal for them. HEL answers many whys for them about why English looks and sounds the way it does. One way we address the weirdness is with Gallagher's comedic skit about the English language.[15] (Why do they call a statue a bust when it stops right before what it's named after? Why do they call them buildings when they're already built? Why is it called a TV set when you only get one? Why do they call a woman's prison a penile colony?). More specifically, Gallagher's skit gets at sounds and spellings that most people struggled to learn because of the seeming inconsistency: bomb does not have the same pronunciation as tomb, tomb does not have the same pronunciation as comb, and comb's pronunciation is the same as that for poem.

To build on Gallagher's skit and students' interest in and questions about words, I have them do a Word History Paper. In this assignment, students select a word that intrigues them (I have a list of words they can choose from or they can petition to use one of their own, which I prefer) and then trace its history in English. The final product should be organized around a primary theme about the word's (socio)linguistic history and it should clearly highlight their main observations and points of interest. The students are encouraged to use multimodal texts and tools to explore, present, and complete their Word History.

Gallagher, unwittingly, also brings to light dialectal differences not only in pronunciation, or accent but also in grammar. That provides a good connection to exposing that students know language, but they often do not know about language. That is, they acquire their native language(s), but they are taught the specifics about structure—or, at least, they used to be. Since some students come to HEL because of their interest in improving their writing and/or their speaking, I can use Gallagher to get me to the Modern English Grammar Paper. In this assignment, students investigate the history and current status of a Present-Day English grammatical rule or "problematic point" of usage (e.g., "Do not split infinitives" or "Can one use *different than* as well as *different from*?"). The Modern English Grammar Paper should discuss the historical invention and development of the rule or usage point, and it should survey the treatment of the topic in grammar and rhetoric books from the seventeenth century through the present. In the process, students should also compare prescriptive and descriptive practice with regard to the linguistic feature; in other words, students determine whether or not usage has followed and/or continues to follow the prescriptive rule. For a class that many students take as a required elective, these projects, Word History Paper and Modern English Grammar Paper (both of which were originally suggested by my former graduate schoolmate, Professor Ann Curzan, University of Michigan at Ann Arbor), make the connection between past and present and demonstrate how language is alive. I believe a sociolinguistic bent to a HEL course helps to make this connection even more because using social and historical contexts situates the content with their interests (i.e., they make many choices in what and how they learn and engage) as well as develop skills for lifelong learning (i.e., seeing past the forest and looking at the trees) and critical thinking about everyday occurrences.

With the final class project, I often have students complete an assignment I call "From Old English to Post-Colonial English" (see 5.12: Appendix G) or something similar. The idea is to have them utilize all they have done over the course of the semester. That means students summon their learning and understanding about linguistics, language variation, medieval studies, literature, the English language in general, and HEL in particular. They have learned over the course of the semester to find connections between content and ideas, personal and situational interests, goals and interests, the significance of sociocultural and historical contexts, and how the past informs the present and the future. At this point in the course, the students know what HEL is, why it is important in general and to them personally, and, if I've done my job well, how all we did comes together.

5.5. CONCLUSION

Research seems to indicate that instructors can facilitate the development of self-regulated learning skills. In terms of implementing the strategies suggested, it will be important to keep in mind that a single strategy may not have a significant influence on students' self-regulated learning skills. Facilitating the development of self-regulated, lifelong learners involves a comprehensive involvement on the part of the instructors (in terms of what goes on in their classrooms and support of each other) and the school system.[16] Even though total support is not always possible, it must, as indicated by McKeachie,[17] be kept in mind that:

> . . . the knowledge we communicate to our students is always incomplete, and much is superseded by new research findings so that continued learning is essential for effective functioning. . . . This has a profound implication for teaching. It means that the importance of learning specific facts largely depends on the extent to which these facts are helpful in building networks of conceptual relations that can provide a framework for continual learning. It means that an important aspect of teaching is helping students develop skills and strategies for further learning, rather than simply communicating the results of the teacher's learning. It means that nurturing student motivation for further learning is equally as important as the development of student knowledge and cognition. (129)

I do not always get everything right in a course, but I do know that my students and I always leave the course different from how we entered it. That is how we move closer to where we want to be.

5.6. APPENDIX A: HISTORY OF THE ENGLISH LANGUAGE (HEL) STUDENT INFORMATION SHEET

PREFERRED First Name: _____ Last Name: _____

Best phone number for contact: _____

Best e-mail address for contact: _____

Classification (circle one): FR   SOPH   JR   SR   other (please explain)

Major(s):

Minor(s)/Certificate(s):

Where did you grow up? Where did your parents grow up?

What is your native language(s)? What other language(s) do you speak or write?

What Language or Linguistics courses have you taken (*including courses this semester*)?

Please briefly explain what you think this class is about or should be about.

How do your academic, personal, career, and/or semester goals intersect with your interest in this course? In other words, *what made you choose to take this class this semester*?

What are *you* going to do to contribute to your successful learning and understanding in this course this semester?

Circle the HEL topics you're MOST interested in learning about, *cross out* the ones you have no interest in, and place a *question mark* by the ones you're wary of or unsure about.

> Language Families, Orthography/Writing, Lexicon/Vocabulary, Literature/History, Semantic (Meaning), Morphology (Word Structure), Spelling and Pronunciation, Phonology (Sounds), Syntax (Word Order), Old English (449–1100), Middle English (1100–1500), Early Modern English (1500–1800), Modern (or Present-Day) English (1800–), Variation in the U.S., Global English

What do you see yourself doing 5 years from now?

What excites you most about the syllabus?

What concerns you most about the syllabus?

What would you like to see changed (added or deleted or modified) in the syllabus?

What would you like to accomplish in this class this semester? What are your goals for this class?

What can Dr. Lanehart do to contribute to your successful learning and understanding in this course this semester?

5.7. APPENDIX B: PRE-TEST ON TERMS IN LINGUISTICS

Directions: Define the terms below and provide your own example for each where applicable.

1. Accent

2. Affix

3. Consonant

4. Creole

5. Dialect

6. Etymology

7. Gender

8. Grammar

9. Language

10. Lexicon

11. Linguistics

12. Mood

13. Morphology

14. Phonetics

15. Phonology

16. Pidgin

17. Semantics

18. Syntax

19. Tense

20. Vowel

5.8. APPENDIX C: MIDTERM EVALUATION FEEDBACK

What has *Dr. Lanehart* done that has been helpful in promotion learning and understanding in this class?

What could Dr. Lanehart do differently to promote learning and understanding in this class?

What have *you* done that has been helpful in promoting *your own* learning and understanding in this class?

What could *you* do differently to help promote *your own* learning and understanding in this class?

5.9. APPENDIX D: HEL CONCEPT SORTING

Your group has 20 concepts.

Come up with 6 additional concepts to add to your pile of 20 concepts. Write them down on the slips of paper provided.

Your group is to sort the 26 concepts based on similarities or likenesses—in other words, group concepts that are similar to one another.

There is no specific number of sorted piles you should have. The number of groups you have will depend on the concepts you have and how you see those concepts. However, your group should have more than 1 sorted pile and less than 26 sorted piles.

After your group has sorted the 20 concepts into piles, explain what makes the concepts in a pile similar. So, if you have 7 piles you will have 7 titles or statements that explain your rationale for each pile. The pile titles can be other concepts that fit as titles or use additional slips of paper to write titles for the piles you created.

You are done with this activity when you have completed sorting, naming, and explaining your piles.

If you have any questions, ASK THEM! Have fun.

20 Concepts to sort PLUS your group's additional 6 concepts:

Anglo-Saxon, Caxton, Creole, Dialect, Early Modern English, Etymology, Germanic, Grammatical Gender, Great Vowel Shift, Grimm's Law, Indo-European, Inner History, Lexicon, Linguistic Invasion, Middle English, Norman Conquest, Old English, Outer History, Spelling, Standard English

5.10. APPENDIX E: A BRIEF SURVEY OF USAGE

Directions: The following sentences and clauses contain a grammatical item of dispute or confusion. For each sentence, circle the word you feel should complete the sentence. In the space provided, explain your answer and the dispute or confusion.

1. Although Amy is anxious to learn baseball, River forces lessons on her *disinterested/uninterested* brother.

2. The only discordant note now is the bar conducted perfunctorily by ignorant or *disinterested/uninterested* maestros.

3. In Washington we encounter *to prioritize* all the time; it is one of those things that *make/makes* Washington unbearable.

4. A particular lady of quality is meant here; but every lady of quality, or not quality, *are/is* welcome to apply the character to themselves.

5. Nobody will miss the Tenth Doctor *as/like* I shall.

6. We are overrun by Cybermen, *as/like* the Australians were by rabbits.

7. bring, carry, fetch: Discriminate carefully *among/between* these words.

8. Overeating *affects/effects* one's health.

9. Overuse of antibiotics has an *affect/effect* on our ability to combat deadly bacteria.

10. I used to swim, but I haven't *swam/swum* in a while now.

11. The Master should have been *hanged/hung* for his crimes.

12. Isaac had to come with Paul and *I/me* because school was closed.

13. Between you and *I/me*, they have been friends for many years.

14. To *who/whom* did she give the screwdriver?

15. *Who/whom* do you say is the best companion?

16. *Regardless/irregardless* of what you may believe, I am a doctor.

Awesome-Sauce Bonus: The Star Trek Enterprise has a five-year mission to boldly go where no man has gone before.

5.11. APPENDIX F: HEL CONCEPT MAP

To do a concept map, you record the patterns of associations you make in connection to a specific topic. Your task is to interrelate some of the concepts we have discussed in "History of the English Language." Draw one concept map to show the inter-relationships of all the concepts. Everyone is to have all 22 concepts listed below as part of their concept map. You are to include *8 additional concepts* to reflect your learning and knowledge in this class.

Below are the instructions for doing the concept map. Read the instructions carefully. If you have any questions, ask me for help. REMEMBER: There is *no one right way* to diagram a concept map. Its form is up to you and is dependent on *your* learning, understanding, and knowledge.

1. Use "HISTORY OF THE ENGLISH LANGUAGE" as the concept important to understanding the course and rich in conceptual connections.

2. Think about the topic, HISTORY OF THE ENGLISH LANGUAGE, then write down 8 additional concepts or terms relating to HEL in the spaces provided below.

3. *Define* all 30 concepts (i.e., the 22 below + your 8) *in your own words*. (60 points)

4. *Describe a unique example* (one not used in class or the readings but of your own creation *based on your understanding*) for each concept and list the reading and page number(s) where the concept came from for your 8 concepts only. (60 points)

5. Identify ways the terms and concepts are associated with each other. *Diagram* how the 30 concepts are inter-related based on your thinking. Your diagram should fit on a sheet of paper or poster board between 8.5" x 11" and 15" x 18". (5 points)

6. *Label every association* (e.g., if you draw a line between two concepts, indicate the nature and direction of the relationship. (25 points)

   1. analytic language
   2. borrowing
   3. external history
   4. Germanic
   5. grammar
   6. Great Vowel Shift

   7. Grimm's Law
   8. *History of the English Language*
   9. Indo-Europrean
   10. inflection
   11. internal history
   12. King Alfred

13. levelling

22. word formation

14. lexicon (vocabulary)

23.

15. linguistic invasion

24.

16. morphology

25.

17. Norman Invasion

26.

18. phonology

27.

19. printing press

28.

20. syntax

29.

21. synthetic language

30.

5.12. APPENDIX G: FROM OLD ENGLISH TO POST-COLONIAL ENGLISH

In *A Biography of the English Language* (1996), Millward provides translations of Boethius's *Consolation of Philosophy*, a Latin text, into Old English by King Alfred (page 120), into Middle English by Geoffrey Chaucer (page 188), into Early Modern English by Queen Elizabeth (page 246), and into Present-day English by Richard Green (page 332). In addition to the translations, Millward provides comments on the linguistic aspects of each translation (pages 121, 189, 246–247, and 333, respectively). (I have photocopied and attached the Millward texts cited.) She does, for the most part, what you were asked to do on the Midterm Celebration of Knowledge (Test 1) in the textual identification section. Since she provides a discussion section of the linguistic features for each translation, you will not be asked to do so here.

Instead you are to produce a Post-Colonial English (PCE) translation of the same selection from *Consolation of Philosophy* that each of the translators mentioned earlier did. Because I am asking you for a postcolonial vision of English, keep in mind the definition of colonialism, the variation in the English language as discussed in class special topic presentations (i.e., Angela's presentation on Victorian English, Trudy's and Dan's presentations on Hip-Hop, Matt's presentation on Appalachian English, Marty's presentation on Colonial English) and the last three chapters of Fennell's *A History of English*: chapters 6 (Present-day English), 7 (English in the United States), and 8 (World-Wide English).

Considering what we know and what we think we know about the internal and external history of the historical periods of the English language thus far, what do you believe the English language will or could possibly look like in 400–700 years from now? However you envision the form of the language several hundred years from now, you should have a vision that is logical and informed.

You are to annotate the text you create, identifying, explaining, and validating the linguistic characteristics and conventions of your text with respect to syntax, morphology, phonology, lexicon, semantics, punctuation, and graphics as well as the sociocultural characteristics. So, this is the place where you will do what Millward has already done for the other historical periods of the English language—and then some. Explain and support your PCE text with the materials at your disposal for the course (Fennell, Millward, Baugh/Cable, Algeo, Freeborn, class discussions, class presentations, handouts, guest lectures, etc.). The workbook exercises we did should prove useful in preparing and annotating your futuristic text. You should find the preparation of your concept map helpful as well.

Also, as you prepare your text, keep in mind the following statement and integrate your interpretation of it and its relevance to the inspiration of this assignment and the commentary about the text you produce:

"For such as Chaucer is shall Dryden be."

Be sure to submit your PCE translation *AND* the essay commentary and justification. Have fun!

PART TWO

The Value of Teaching the History of English

Rethinking Curricula

CHAPTER 6

Philology, Theory, and Critical Thinking Through the History of the English Language

MATTHEW GIANCARLO

6.1. INTRODUCTION: "UNDER THE PRESSURE OF THIS NECESSITY"

When considered in the institutional settings of college-level teaching, particularly in North America and Britain, the History of the English Language (HEL) course holds a unique position. It sits at the intersection of a number of disciplines: traditional literary study, with connection to rhetoric and composition programs and occasionally to teaching certification requirements; linguistics and formal language study, often straddling departments of English and departments or programs of Linguistics; and history and cultural studies, as well as related subject studies (e.g., regional studies, national and international studies, studies of ethnicities and communities). HEL often retains the broad interconnections and discipline-crossing foci of what we might call old-style "philology" while boldly moving into the creative terrains of new-style "English Studies" and now, in the twenty-first century, the beckoning and expansive vistas of Global English Studies. The history of these developments has been well documented and critically assessed in recent scholarship.[1] Where the origins and practices of philology were for a time occluded in the professional memory of our broad field, the calls for a "return to philology" have given rise, if not necessarily to an enhanced philological practice (whatever that might mean), then certainly to a greater self-awareness of the paths and investments of literary, linguistic, and textual studies.

But what of "theory"? Those calls to return to philology were famously made most vocally from the quarters of high literary theory (by Paul de Man and Edward Said), and literary theory, now as deeply and variously entrenched in the institutions of English Studies as HEL, can trace a similar genealogy to the homelands of philology.[2]

Indeed the simple term "theory" can evoke a great deal more for the instructor of HEL than it might for other teachers in other contexts. There is the history of philology itself which was, in a real sense, the practical field of early literary theory (as critical textual studies and hermeneutics), which it is enormously helpful to know either as the broad history of philology and language study or as the more specific history of literary study in the Anglo-American academy.[3] There is modern "literary theory" proper, the post-Saussurean study of language and literature from formalisms to structuralism to post-structuralisms, to the various post-post-structuralisms of today (historicisms, identity studies, postcolonialisms and subaltern studies, etc.)—that is, the "after theory" of theory itself.[4] And particularly for HEL, there is linguistic theory at the various levels of language study (phonetics and phonology, morphology, syntax, semantics and pragmatics), from the rudiments of neogrammarian approaches to Chomskyan and post-Chomskyan modern linguistics, cognitive and sociolinguistic approaches, pragmatic questions, lexicography, critical discourse analysis, and more.

Viewed this way, on the subject of theory it might fairly be said that for the teacher of HEL, the cup runneth over. It is simply impossible for any teacher to cover it all, nor should that be the goal. But for "literary theory" and HEL in particular, what can result is a sort of curious stalemate. Instructors of HEL (usually literature teachers, sometimes linguists, frequently medievalists with significant linguistic training) might look askance at theory's pretensions to, but lack of, "real" philology, and teachers of literary theory can be troubled by HEL's proximity to, but lack of direct engagement with, the tools and questions of "real" theory and by HEL's potentially vitiating lack of critical self-awareness. A small but telling example is the recent, comprehensive, and very praiseworthy collection *A Companion to The History of the English Language*, which includes a smorgasbord of topics and approaches to HEL across fifty-nine chapters, ranging from philology and history to literature and linguistics and beyond, but none that explicitly engages with developments in theory.[5] This lacuna is notable even as theoretical issues and questions implicitly subtend a great number of those topics. What is a teacher to do if one wants to bring the connections of HEL and theory to light? And is there any use to it?

As I will suggest here, a productive rapprochement can be achieved between HEL and critical theory in the actual practice of teaching. It is worth recalling, as Utz does from no less a figure than the philologist and ur-theorist Nietzsche, that philology had its motivating impetus in teaching because "philology has always also been a form of pedagogical practice. This pedagogical practice demanded that a selection of the pedagogically and educationally valuable elements be made. Thus, under the pressure of this necessity, has evolved the academic temper we call Philology."[6] The same could be said of theory, and for similar reasons. As a particularized "post-philological" engagement with a world language, HEL can cultivate educationally intimate lessons at the propadeutic and heuristic levels, that is, as a means to introduce and to develop core competencies and skills in critical inquiry. This has been a recent focus of the new critical philology as well as increasingly evident in HEL writings.[7] But HEL needs, I would contend, an explicit and deliberate theoretical component to achieve this educational end.

As with most textbooks on the subject, HEL courses are generally organized temporally, "old" to new/contemporary, with a smattering of technical chapters on historical and linguistic issues. This is unlikely to change, and with good reason. At the same time, by organizing a course along more than a single temporal axis, one that asks theoretical questions orthogonal to linear linguistic history, an instructor can widen its purview and guide students to an understanding of the subject as more than just content-knowledge. With the aid of theory HEL can act as an organon as well as an historical content-field. Again, the historiography of philology—that originary, critical, and self-critical practice—provides guidance for how critical theory can promote this additional intellectual trajectory. For the teacher it is essential to recognize that the material will not do this by itself. Critical engagement must emerge from theoretically informed pedagogical strategies and questions, and so the success of this aspect of HEL is very instructor-dependent.

6.2. ORGANIZING CONTRASTS

What then are some aspects of the connection between HEL and critical theory that can aid student inquiry and understanding? In addition to a straightforward temporal organization, the inquisitive scaffolding of a class can draw from, and be regularly punctuated by, a set of contrasts and conceptual tensions that it is the instructor's job to present as productive antinomies. They are the differential perspectives by which HEL (and, in effect, language study in general) is cognized. These contrasts are familiar from outside the domain of "theory," and indeed any linguistically competent instructor will already be making use of them, implicitly or explicitly. To a large extent, the point in highlighting them is to foreground the overlap of theory and practical philology and to provoke students to ask simple but fundamental questions about the knowledge-construction of the field they are studying. Some of these constitutive contrasts can also be approached as Derridean binaries—for investigation and problematization, if not necessarily for strict deconstruction—deriving from the Saussurean traditions at the heart of linguistic, literary, and social inquiry.[8] They include:

- *Synchrony vs. diachrony*: students need to be aware of the differences in looking at the language at "points of time" versus "through time" or "across time," a contrast inherent in the very structure of the HEL class, but also fundamental to the theoretical awareness of the conditions of critical understanding and intellectual frameworks, and for much of the inquiry into related issues (e.g., lexical developments, usage changes, and controversies over standards and variation, historical identity, and difference);
- *HEL as "content" vs. "structure"*: students will naturally tend to have a lexicon-centric view of the language, that is, the presupposition that English is the "words" of the language (and to a lesser extent the sounds); inadvertently, this can lead to a triumphal "banking model" of the language (to borrow from Paolo Frière), with English being "rich" because so many glittering and different words

have been poured into it, waiting for our withdrawal. Of course, languages are constituted by words and sounds, but this content-focus needs to be contrasted dialectically with the more subtle linguistic notion of language as structure(s), including lexical and lexicon structures that shift over time, syntactic structures, usage structures, and more, reflecting at every level the changing structures of knowledge-organizations in HEL which also differ markedly across time and among communities;

- *HEL as displaying levels of change*: with a differential focus on synchrony versus diachrony and content versus structure, there is a commensurate need to make explicit how change occurs at different levels of linguistic operation and awareness and to different degrees. HEL is the ideal place to showcase not only phonetic/phonemic change but also semantic changes, changes in usage and syntax, changes in social lingual patterns, and changes in social lingual ideology (how the language itself is viewed). Foregrounding the facts of dynamic change in HEL can promote a sort of "readerly awareness" for students of the horizon of potential change inherent in all linguistic practice, making clearer the fundamental Saussurean proposition that language *is* difference and that its identity emerges not in spite of, but because of, its changes;

- *Conscious vs. unconscious variation and change in HEL*: teaching HEL is a premier forum for presenting what we might call "the philological unconscious": not only that language/English changes and adapts without our being aware of it as "we" change and adapt it (and to it), thus reflecting certain tendencies and biases, but also that English is consciously deployed as well, as choices, usages, and interactions enact social codes of communication. Hence, HEL is an excellent field for introducing students to historical questions and issues of semiotics, acts of meaning-making, which are both linguistic and cultural, intended and unintended, and culturally determined. These grounding contrasts, simple but challenging and conceptually powerful, can provide further scaffolding for several more. The historical aspects of HEL lend themselves well to further questions of theoretical inquiry that are, in essence, meta-questions about the nature of language and symbolization;

- *Stability vs. instability in language, hence identity vs. difference*: given the facts of language change over the long historical horizon and across large geographical spaces (time-depth and space-width), how can we identify "English" as a stable and positive object of knowledge? To raise this question is not to assert that we cannot but simply to inquire into the grounds and assumptions of that knowledge-production. From Old English to Middle English to Modern English to Global Englishes; and from within supposedly unitary-but-varied English-language communities (e.g., Old English dialect regions; Southern English and Scots; and SBE to U.S. English to various national and world regional Englishes): in what ways do we model our thinking about "the" language that can account for both its variability and also its continuity?

- *Standard vs. nonstandard, center vs. periphery*: these contrasts are closely related to the former, and much outstanding scholarship has investigated the "standard vs. nonstandard" divide in HEL in recent years. Especially with the advent of digital technologies and resources, HEL has developed into a very good place for introducing students to the diversity of linguistic practices of more than one tradition, community, standard, or set of assumptions. As with the contrast of stability vs. instability, the tension between standard/nonstandard and center/periphery matches the post-structuralist "decentering of the canon" in literary and cultural study. Even as traditional/canonical and standard works still play a very important part in inquiry (in both HEL and literature), there is now more dialectical awareness, in both senses: an appreciation for non-standard dialects of expression, and a greater sense of the give-and-take, the dialectics, among various expressive communities;

- *Language difference and identity*: this last topic is not an antinomy or opposed contrast but a paired and dually reinforcing binary. The current climate of literary and cultural studies emphasizes an awareness of the determinate constructedness of all claims to identity: personal, sexual, ethnic, communal.[9] But this critical awareness is *not*, therefore, an assertion of their insubstantiality, or their insincerity/unauthenticity, or of mere relativism. Teaching HEL can help students to understand this critical and dialectical binarism of self and language, speech and identity, without being either too reductive or too abstract. As the study of the language that is for most students both self and other—that is, "my" recognizable and authentic language yet also the potentially unrecognizable and even estranged language of other peoples, nations, histories, and identities—HEL can foster inquiry into how language performs identities. It also highlights how English pressures identities, even in native-speaking contexts.

6.3. TEACHING PRAXIS

Doubtless more topics and contrasts could be added to this list. We can note a few things from it as a preliminary inventory of theoretical concerns. First, to reemphasize what was said at the beginning, these issues are not unique to literary or critical theory either in origin or application. But they are "theoretically reflective" ways of leading both teachers and students to think about how they are thinking. Insofar as they are familiar, it shows how instructors of HEL are—to repeat the unavoidable phrase—"always already" engaged in acts of theory when teaching the historical and philological parameters of Englishes. What is suggested here is a framework for raising these theoretical issues to pedagogical salience in ways that could fruitfully connect them to student experience in other courses and contexts. Organized in this or a similar manner, these topics also point to the now-familiar shared philological genealogy of literary theory and linguistics: from (late) philology to structuralist linguistics and semiology, to its destabilization, to its productive pluralization. So-called "returns to philology" and "post-philology" in literary and theoretical fields have retraced part or all of this trajectory, not really to bring us back to Grimm or Jespersen or Sweet or even to the early philological Saussure but to lay explicit claim to a tradition of self-critical inquiry that has given birth to a number of distinct and co-equal disciplines.[10] Viewed in this light, it can be the role of the HEL instructor to let ontogeny recapitulate phylogeny by emphasizing, at least at points, the self-critical and quasi-Hegelian dialectics of the field, the way language study and HEL have proceeded in large part by reflecting on their own capacities and shortcomings as a mode of knowledge-creation.

That is to say, the instructor must push and pull both with and against the disposition of the course material and, in doing so, help students to see how it has been shaped as a field. A few suggestions can be made for how such a meta-perspective can be put into actual practice in the classroom to inform lessons, exercises, and assessments. These practices are not as distant from the "factual content" of the course as they might first seem, although again it must be stressed that critical-theoretical awareness about HEL simply will not emerge for students without clear guidance and fostering by the instructor. With that in mind, instructional points can be raised around such questions as:

- *How does model making and metaphorization influence our understanding of what language is and what HEL has been or meant*? For example, what difference does it make to think of languages, and the English language, as residing in "families" with "trees" (as in familiar *Stammbaum* or tree diagrams) versus "areas" experiencing "waves" (as in *Wellentheorie* or wave-model diagrams)? How have certain ways of thinking about HEL, even at its most technical, influenced its perception? A recent example is Gupta's critique of Kachru's "concentric circles" model of World Englishes; and Giancarlo's historicization of the model of the "Great Vowel Shift."[11] Even simple or popular metaphors (e.g., English as a "word-sponge," English as colonial invader or pathogen, English as "evolving in competition," English as medium or coin of exchange, even "the story of English") invite reflection and commentary.[12] Models and metaphors are as necessary as they are potentially limiting. It is worth recalling that Saussure's innovations in the *Cours de linguistique générale* began by critiquing the conceptual limitations of prior philological models, from which he went on to offer models and metaphors of his own, including the epochal "signifier/signified" dyad.[13] While it would be unreasonable to ask most students to engage in quite that high a level of second-order critique, it is nonetheless pedagogically very useful to draw attention to how the synchronic and diachronic dimensions of English language history have been symbolically recognized over time.
- *What changes, what doesn't, and how*? Today it is very easy to engage students in "close reading" exercises with the aid of HEL resource books and increasingly available digital materials. As an augment to synchronically focused content (e.g., learning those Old English paradigms), students can get a greater sense of intellectual autonomy and critical agency through direct encounters with the diachronic contrasts of content and structure across different levels of change. It can also be productively disorienting. Given, for example, the kinds of changes words have experienced or the shifts in syntax that English displays historically, what can students make of it as indicative of the nature of English language practice? Dictionary exercises in the semantic shifts of nouns or exercises in the changing

patterns of adjectival modifications (e.g., the rise of the expanded possessive from French) can be investigated not just for their own sake but also for offering perspective on how languages adjust and change in different contexts. Even details such as the historical extent of "h-dropping," derhoticization, be-verb paradigm variations, regional pronunciation variants that have found their way into de-regionalized standard pronunciations, and others, all can be deployed to demonstrate to students the "stable instabilities" of English, not as exceptions to the rules but as the normal and fluxional state of affairs, and then to encourage them to be able to critically identify such variations on their own.

- *What are significant levels of difference and modes of difference?* The facts of differential language performance and language stratification invite particular attention, which can be rewarded with strong student engagement. This focus encourages critical reflection on *how* English is deployed in different contexts. There are also sensitive issues to be negotiated. Textual and historical examples can be drawn from the stratification of English vocabulary into familiar Germanic-Latinate-Greek lexical clusters, which can also be stretched into the basilectal part of the spectrum with slang and popular or ephemeral forms. The matter can also be pushed sideways, that is, into the English language forms of other nations, regions, and alternate Englishes and English hybrids. Such exercises can make students as aware of the significance of everyday word choices and expressive variations as they are (or should be) in literary or other contexts. One successful exercise in this mode is to assign students to interview a fellow student whose English is in some way different and interesting from their own: second-language speakers, different regional speakers, different national standards. Such an exercise should come with clear assignment guidance and the strong (and grade enforced) caveat to the interviewer that the speaker is expressly *not* to be stigmatized or pathologized ("Your English is interesting because it is wrong") but rather explored and better understood because it offers a diverse contrast ("Your English is interesting because it is different, and unique, and worth understanding.") In addition to inquiry into technical levels of analysis and background, such interviews can and should solicit reflective responses from the speaker to questions such as, *How does English act in your community? Are you regularly aware, or have you been made aware, of differences between your English and other people's English? How? How do you feel about it? What differences seem to you most prominent? In what contexts do you find other people's speaking most different from your own? Does media affect your perception of English?* Such quasi-sociolinguistic inquiries, even at a rudimentary level, can bring home the prevalence and significance of differences in ways that are not very distant from learning to read the differences of Middle English or Shakespearean English. It can also give students experience talking about language difference without (or bracketing) prescriptive judgment. If Chaucer and Hamlet spoke English differently, so does your neighbor. With help from the teacher of HEL, students can see how those differences are related and reflect on them.
- *What counts as "real" English, and why?* This last question, which may seem obtuse to students at the beginning of an HEL course, can be productively developed

throughout and at the end. From the striking differences of Old English and Middle English, through the more familiar territories of Early Modern and Modern Englishes, to the disseminating expansiveness of World Englishes, creoles, and hybrids: students who might be indignant at the centripetal assumptions of earlier writers about "proper" or "standard" English may have their own assumptions challenged in the face of modern developments. As noted, a critical attention to modelling can help, both for comprehending the diversity of English and for drawing attention to the choices and occlusions that are made under the pressure of necessity. This critical perspective can be extended to traditional materials. What, for example, is the real representative value of the speech practices of Shakespeare, or Austen, or the "Chancery standard" of the late fourteenth and early fifteenth centuries, or the Late West Saxon literary standard of the tenth and eleventh centuries, or the lexical choices of the great age of English dictionary making from the eighteenth and nineteenth centuries? Students can be made aware of the constructedness of the object of study by determinate choices, without (it must be stressed) thereby crudely asserting the delegitimization of that same field. Rather, it brings to attention the critical fact that "real" English is, like "real" literature, to a large extent, what we have made it out to be, and what we will continue to make it to be, in perception and practice.[14]

From the foregoing topics and questions, it should be clear that I am suggesting an engagement between theory and HEL that is not simply an exercise in assigning some traditional theory readings to students and then trying to connect the dots, as it were, between the language and the paradigms. Articles and studies from Roman Jakobsen, for example, or the work of Emile Benveniste, or Geoffrey Leech on English stylistics and linguistics, among others, retain their perennial value, especially for advanced students.[15] Particular studies of authors and the English language (e.g., Fishkin's work on Twain and the chapters of various authors in the Blackwell guide), also provide ground-level examples of theoretically informed praxis.[16] In contrast to this, an approach both more organic and more productive for a comprehensive HEL course is to use the concepts of theory to establish an overall pattern of self-reflexive critical engagement.

In doing so, the HEL instructor can thereby respond to certain pressing professional issues as well. Gupta identifies what he calls "four nodes of convergence" in the historiographical development of philology which carry over, often tacitly, to theoretical and linguistic praxis: the fixing of texts/objects of study, a normative emphasis on origins and genesis, an aspiration to the apprehension of unity, and an explicit grounding in institutional settings.[17] One could note that these "nodes" characterize practically any intellectual pursuit that aspires to the status of a science in the modern academy. HEL both presumes, and can critically engage with, all four: the "text"/objects of English; the desire for (or romance of) origins so characteristic of HEL; the drive for comprehensive understanding and unity in the face of English diversity; and its often dominant presence in institutional settings (English-language institutes, global English-language standards, and education in commerce, travel, diplomacy, and more). But in these instances it is not necessarily the case that

HEL "doesn't encourage engagement with its own political economy," as Gupta says of the history of philology. Like the current re-envisionings of the new philologies, HEL can promote the "contrary drift which unpicks the presumptions around the four nodes"—that is, it can be properly dialectical in teaching as well as research.[18] Indeed, it would seem crucial that teaching be included in this critical circle or cycle, as the classroom is the most common and meaningful forum where provisionally stable knowledge-claims can be both transmitted and interrogated and modified.

Germane to this educational process are Sheldon Pollock's requirements for a truly "modern" philology, which all gesture in the direction of critical self-awareness. In addition to its particular virtues of attention to linguistic and literary detail and historical embeddedness, Pollock calls for a philology (which he defines expansively as the "critical self-reflection of language") characterized by "historical self-awareness," non-provinciality, and methodological and conceptual pluralism.[19] As a hegemonic example of an expansive world language (and even this could be contested), English study and HEL are poised to engage with and contribute to such a revitalized and theoretically self-aware philological trajectory. And as Utz has argued, "English Studies" needs to revitalize and diversify its own conceptual purview if the traditional aspects of literary and language study are to adapt to changing institutional and intellectual climates.[20] This is to say, our jobs can no longer and will no longer be just—or even mainly—teaching great (English) books and the great (Standard English) language, even if the canon has been diversified. HEL and English Studies in general need to get more comfortable crossing intellectual, methodological, and institutional boundaries, for their own sakes and the sakes of our students, at the same time avoiding a wholesale reorientation (or rebranding) as merely instrumental training for marketplace employment. Doing so will require a theoretical adroitness on the part of its practitioners at two levels at least, primary and reflective.

6.4. PROVISIONAL CONCLUSIONS

This last point about the institutional settings of our practice raises important questions that go beyond the scope of HEL proper. We can ask (as others will), "What's the pedagogical upshot or takeaway from theorizing HEL?" In an era of metrics and assessments, it is necessary to ask precisely these questions about ends and goals, even as it is simultaneously necessary to question the questions; to interrogate the utility of utility, as it were. It would be naïve to deny the past instrumentality and committedness of philology and HEL in ideologies both laudable and deeply troubling, given their histories. If anything, this checkered history should prompt contemporary philologians to be cautious of making any grand claims for the power of philological language study as liberatory, antihegemonic, or otherwise. [21] At the same time, theory-study should offer more than just a navel-gazing genealogy of a discipline (or disciplines) from antiquarianism to philology to linguistics, or from philosophy and philology to theory, or from enlightenment to modern to postmodern. These trajectories are relevant and even helpful, but they do not actually enact critical thinking.

As should be clear from the preceding sections, what is desired is not just new instrumental knowledge or a framework for committed action or just broader professional self-awareness but *a shift in episteme*, in both the Platonic and Foucauldian senses: an awareness of what constitutes "justified true belief" about the history of our language, its origins and developments; and an awareness of the founding assumptions/*a priori* at the base of the knowledge and discourses about our language that represent the conditions of the "possible truths" about English for a period or epoch.[22] From this perspective, different eras have had vastly different Englishes as conceptual constructs and fields of discourse, especially since the eighteenth century: from an aspirant (but failed) neo-classical and statuesque language in the era of Pope and Swift to a daughter-language of Indo-Germanic antiquity in the great age of Anglo-Germanic philology to the language of burgeoning colonial presence and power to "English triumphant"—a narrative implicit still in many of the HEL textbooks in use today—to "World English" to "Global English" to its pluralization and "globalized Englishes." Each has carried with it certain metaphors, assumptions, and entailments that beg examination.

We stand now, it may seem, on the border of a new epoch where the characterization of English(es) is best understood by an entirely new set of discursive formations, the "networks" and "transmissions" of globalized exchange and conflict. Exemplary is Pennycook's *Global English and Transcultural Flows* for reconceiving English through "the ways in which the flows of cultural forms produce new forms of localization, and the use of global Englishes produces new forms of globalization."[23] This is a neatly chiastic scheme analogizing the dynamics of English with "the flows of cultural forms" in a systolic-diastolic pulse between the local and global. Not monuments, then, or spreads or invasions, or trees, waves, or circles, or evolutions, but "flows" "paths" and "networks": the point is not the truth or untruth of such newly minted metaphors but the truths they make possible to be seen. For instructors as well as students, it is certainly useful to have critical purchase on the various backgrounds of such a view, drawing as it does from the dialogism and polyvocality of Bakhtinian theory, the critical reappraisal of arguments about cultural hegemony in the Frankfurt School, and others. Simple models of bilingualism and polylingualism give way to even greater complexity as code-switching becomes code-meshing, a means of creating "identity" as the product of rhizomatic fluidity.[24] A similar example drawn from a more strictly critical-theoretical context would be (and here I can only suggest its relevance) an approach to HEL from the paradigm of Actor-Network Theory (ANT) and material-semiotic analysis.[25] To view English from a constructivist and non-foundationalist perspective is to grant "the" language, and different versions of the language, different kinds of agency. How does it change our understanding of English, for example, to think of its role as the lingua franca of the global transportation network as a kind of quasi-object, as a "translation" of "assemblages" with agency and material effects all its own, outside the intention or agency of any one community of users? This would be a different approach to the social aspects of English, one to which the philological-theoretical legacy of HEL might be able to offer valuable insight or qualification.

Be that as it may, the many potential theoretical inflections of HEL thus share in the general goal of *greater discourse awareness,* within its traditional field and beyond it, as the particular exigencies and contexts of teaching may invite or require. What makes HEL particularly useful is its close attention to the particulars of actual linguistic practice, and the undeniable historical importance of its object, however defined. Practitioners can be aware, and perhaps wary, of what Gupta has called (speaking specifically of the developments of theory and literary study) "a desire to render the discipline a site for social and political responsiveness and intervention," even as we can acknowledge, via theory and the history of philology, that it has ever been thus.[26] Viewing such awareness as a provisional pedagogical and teaching outcome, rather than as a committed yet unattainable critical ideal, relieves some of the pressure of grandiose expectations that have also tended to accompany both philology and theory. As any teacher of the history of the English language will attest, when it comes to encountering English in the world, our reach always exceeds our grasp. With the help of theory, we can better understand why, and what it might mean for the future.

CHAPTER 7

The History of the English Language and the Medievalist

SETH LERER

7.1. INTRODUCTION

"The rise of English," aver the authors of the popular television history *The Story of English*, "is a remarkable success story." Writing in the 1980s, but in an idiom still current in our popular historiography, the PBS presenters stand in awe of a language "more widely spoken and written than any other language has ever been," a language that "emerged" from early Germanic dialects and a panoply of local forms to become a global means of communication. Whatever forms it may have taken in past times and whatever varieties sprouted in various locations, "English" remains as much a legend as much as a language.[1]

This television series was far from unique in giving voice to such a legend. For throughout the history of the "History of the English Language," it has been the narrative of origin, establishment, challenge, and triumph that has shaped its telling. Almost unique is the account of English that does not recount this story that favors, in Tim Machan's words, "not [a] chronological but [a] topical, . . .thematic" account of the vernacular. Textbooks continue to sing something of a romance of the language, a tale of travail and transmission, of birth shrouded in mystery and of afterlife, now, evanescing in the ether of the digital expanse.[2]

Like all good romances, the tale of English has a medieval feel to it, and the medievalist has long been valued (or victimized) as the curator of the vernacular's deep past. Historical linguistics has remained the purview of the medieval scholar, and the bulk of undergraduate instruction in the History of the English Language (HEL) remains assigned to the Anglo-Saxonist or the Chaucerian in a department. Of course, one would expect such literary historians to have linguistic command. Old English poetry and prose lives, in the classroom, with the glossary and paradigm almost as much as with the pulpit or the harp. You need a knowledge of the verb form and the sound change to make sense of early English writing, much as you require an awareness of the manuscript environments and material cultures of the text. You need, as well, not just a basic sense of Middle English to teach Chaucer, but a broad linguistic sensitivity: a sense of how Chaucer self-consciously presented himself as an innovator in vocabulary, an ear for the regional humor of the "Reeve's Tale," and, more broadly, the realization of just how and why Chaucer's lithe, French-veneered pentameters differ from his London compatriot William Langland's alliterative lines.[3]

Few students, however, of Shakespeare or of Dickens would be similarly expected to master the nuances of historical pronunciation, or the habits of the print shop, or the details of the lives of compositors and typesetters. Shakespeare in the "original pronunciation" is still looked upon, by many, as a stunt.[4] Milton's idiosyncratic spelling is effaced in paperbacks of *Paradise Lost*.[5] Dickens's fascinations with regional and class dialect, George Eliot's engagement with Victorian philology, or Henry James's preference for the sound of a particular typewriter as he dictated—these are the subjects for the scholarly panel rather than the schoolroom discussion.[6] In a similar fashion, few students of American literature would be expected to have competence in the dialect origins of New England, New York, or New Mexico writers. The history of the "American Language" is often relegated to collections of strange words or assemblies of sharp aperçus by Webster, Twain, and Mencken.[7] And while scholarship and teaching in the African-American traditions has increasingly included an attention to the lived vernacular of both rural and urban descendants of enslaved groups, few literary scholars have seen linguistic attentions to "Black English" as central to their professional identity.[8]

HEL largely remains the purview of medievalists, and my chapter seeks to interrogate the history of this professional association in our purposes and pedagogy. I'd like to argue that precisely because HEL remains a narrative of origin and change, it has been left to those who specialize in origins to be its overseers. To make this argument, I need to tell some stories of my own, some personal and some institutional. In the process, I will make some claims not only for what medievalists can do for the teaching and study of the History of the Language, but what the History of the Language can do for the non-medievalist. My overarching goal—here, as in a professional lifetime of teaching, writing, and lecturing on the subject—is to urge a broader conversation among medievalists, historical linguists, and literary historians generally. In the end, I argue that our literary history remains inseparable from our linguistic history, and that a medievalist's perspective can illuminate that tie.

7.2. PHILOLOGY AND THE HISTORICAL OBJECT

With the discovery of phonological and semantic relationships among the languages of Europe, India, and Iran, the Indo-European family of languages took shape as the object of empirical study. No longer were the etymologies of words to be thought of as "metaphysical" or "essential."[9] Country-house antiquarians like the Englishman Horne Tooke (and his fictional descendant, Mr. Casaubon of George Eliot's *Middlemarch*) came to be replaced by German-trained, university-sited scholars of linguistic history. Instead of what Will Ladislaw, in Eliot's novel, called "broken-legged theories about Chus and Misraim," there emerged the scholarship of Sir William Jones, Rasmus Rask, the Grimm Brothers, and Franz Bopp—all creating a discipline of comparative philology. By looking at the sounds of cognate words in surviving languages, philologists could construct their antecedent forms. After such reconstruction, the semantic values of the lexicon emerged, the grammatical patterns of sentences surfaced, and the cultural and social lives of the Indo-Europeans came alive in the hands of historical linguists. As Holger Pedersen put it, "It was the establishment of this fundamental principle in method which pulled etymological scholarship out of the bog where it had been stuck fast since classical times."[10]

Pulling scholarship out of the bog was thus the job of academic philologists, and part of that job was to create, in essence, both the bog and the thing to pull from it. If there was an antiquity to language, there had to be a continuity to change. Vernaculars had to be traceable back to their origins, and in the process, there had to be a linear progression from one state to another. In the case of English, this meant that there had to be, a way of understanding the language as something of a story: as a narrative of change over time, during which both internal and external forces altered forms and sounds and meanings, and yet where, in spite of those alterations, there still remained an entity we could call "English."

What nineteenth-century philology created was this idea of a narrative to both a literary and a linguistic history. The linearity of sound change and semantic shift broadly paralleled the linearity of English literature itself. To understand the one was to understand the other, and it is no accident that such phenomena as the Great Vowel Shift originally took their form as ways of distinguishing the vernaculars of major English writers. As Matthew Giancarlo illustrated, it was the notion of a "language of Chaucer" or a "language of Shakespeare" that framed the scholarly attempts at codifying systems of pronunciation over time.[11] Indeed, historical sound changes have come to be recognized less as the historical representations of "laws" than as the later, scholarly reconstructions of evidence to create a linear teleology. Nineteenth-century scholars, Giancarlo argued, "tacitly reduce[d] the English language to a single tradition and a unified dialect that implies a standard language uniting not only the literary tradition but also the entire language itself."[12] Such a reduction makes the Great Vowel Shift less a story of diachronic and systemic change than a retrospective "recasting of data into intuitable forms." Lengthening in open syllables too, it has been argued, may be less a change in phonology than a series of "compensatory processes." Are changes such as these truly sound "laws" or are they legacies? As Ricardo Bermudez-Otero put it, in a long review of these traditions of philological revisionism, "traditional handbook formulations" may reflect neither the evidence nor the arguments, but instead, may sustain claims now a century old. The Austrian philologist Karl Luick may, in the end, deserve "the credit of having single-handedly manufactured the two most important 'objects' of English historical phonology: the Great Vowel Shift and the ME Length Adjustment."[13]

Such manufacturing of historical "objects" was a feature of much nineteenth-century historical linguistics. The *Oxford English Dictionary* has been long appreciated as a story more than history. Sir James A. H. Murray, the first editor of what was then dubbed the *New English Dictionary* had called himself and his associates, in his address to the Philological Society in 1884, "simply pioneers, pushing our way experimentally through an untrodden forest, where no white man's axe has been before us."[14] Murray and his men become a kind of philological colonial army; their forest of words recalls much less a wood of error than an African jungle—what the character of Dr. Lydgate, in *Middlemarch* would call the "dark territories" of a discipline. Sometimes, however, as Murray himself had noted, "the quest seems hopeless."[15] Now, he is less some Livingston of lexicography than a knight errant on a sacred journey. And if we read the *OED* itself as something of a record of this pioneering push or hopeless quest, we may well find ourselves responding much as the novelist Arnold Bennett responded in the 1920s, calling the *Dictionary* "the longest sensational serial ever written."[16]

It is this deep impress of pioneering, questing, novelistic narrative, and personal engagement that, I believe, has made HEL into something of a sensational serial. Certainly, this is the rhetoric of *The Story of English* with which I began, and it is a rhetoric that links the medievalist with HEL inseparably today. Thus, to begin a History of English with a bow to Indo-European, to Grimm's Law, and to the earliest Germanic texts is to begin with a fundamental claim about language as having meaning in its historical descent and its diachronic life. To begin with literary texts such as Caedmon's *Hymn* or the Alfredian prose prefaces and translations is to affirm that the content of that linguistic history will remain both spiritual and political. Caedmon is an allegorist of vernacular bequeathal. To retell his story of the "first" English poem as an angelic gift is, wittingly or unwittingly, to sustain an imagined heavenly origin for English. Similarly, by teaching a document such as Alfred's *Preface to the Pastoral Care*, we inscribe a political and social claim for bequeathal— here, monarchical rather than divine, but a bequeathal nonetheless. To privilege this text is to privilege another version of a top-down history, another gift of vernacularity designed to bring harmony and understanding to a fractured world.

I think we want to hold on to these stories because they give to the History of English a sustaining social purpose. They frame each subsequent example we may choose along the axes of divine and human power, and they make clear that the teaching and study of the History of the Language is, itself, a process of continual reaffirmation—of looking for sites of social harmony in the face of threat or terror. Each act of teaching, in effect, reinscribes Alfred's own imagination of his task.[17] It is as if they had said: "Our ancestors, who formerly maintained these places, loved wisdom, and through it they obtained wealth and passed it on to us. Here one can still see their track, but we cannot follow it." Therefore, we have now lost the wealth as well as the wisdom, because we did not wish to set our minds to the track.

When I arrived in Oxford in the fall of 1976 to read for a second BA in the Course II English Honours School (Medieval Literature and Historical Linguistics), this was the first text opened at my first tutorial. Just following the story of Cynewulf and Cyneheard in *Sweet's Anglo-Saxon Reader in Prose and Verse* (an excerpt that the head note calls a "tragic narrative"), Alfred's preface appeared with the title, "On the State of Learning in England," and it became clear to me, even on that first day, that my tutorials—for all their superficial emphasis on aesh one and aesh two, or on the question of whether there really had been an "Early West Saxon"—would really be about the state of learning in England and the creation of a set of books (again in Alfred's words) "most necessary for all men to know."

7.3. BECOMING A MEDIEVALIST

Some things have changed, and some have not. Perhaps the biggest shift in medieval English literary studies since my time at Oxford has been the curricular and pedagogic split between Old and Middle English and, in turn, a powerful reconception of vernacularity in the post-Conquest British Isles. These changes have had some, but maybe not enough, impact on the teaching of HEL, and I want to offer an account of them here.

There was a time when being a "medievalist" in an English department brought with it expectations of both scholarly and pedagogical facility with pre- and post-Conquest languages and literatures. There was a time when literary history was written as a feature of the Old and Middle. My sense is that the split between them came with the assertion of a historically defined, culturally driven study of Middle English literature, keyed to the awareness of political and religious dissent in the fourteenth century, the fascination with "vernacular theology" in the fourteenth and fifteenth century, and the rejection of the old verities of idealistic, formalist new criticism.

In the 1990s, these developments crystallized in a set of highly influential collections and anthologies. *The Cambridge History of Medieval English Literature* begins not with a sustained treatment of the Anglo-Saxon age but with a chapter "Old English and its Afterlife": a chapter I was assigned to write, I vividly remember, to offer a bow to the pre-Conquest but to make clear that the idea of the "medieval" in the English literary tradition really begins with shifts and interplays between the Insular and Continental and with the rise of certain forms of writing (lyric, romance, chronicle) and the decline of others (epic, riddle, elegy). There remains, by and large, very little traditional philology in that volume: few explorations of linguistic change, almost no chapters on single authors, and at times even, a depriviledging of the "literary" over the historical and social.[18]

The project of what came to be known as vernacular theology may, too, have grown out of this professional matrix. A group of scholars recognized the ways in which the English language (often in its regional varieties) had become the medium for personal devotion, speculation on the nature of authorship and intention, and reflection on the place of linguistic variety and change in an emerging sense of history itself. The publication of *The Idea of the Vernacular* made it possible to see a great landscape of writers and readers in a variety of Englishes from the twelfth through the fifteenth centuries. The whole idea of spiritual devotion and social reform had become a vernacular project, from the Rising of 1381 through the making of the Wycliffite bible.[19]

These energies in Middle English tended, I believe, to displace Anglo-Saxon as the constitutive field of medieval studies in the American English department (one could well make the argument that Anglo-Saxonists themselves were partially complicit in this process, as Old English continued to retreat into lexicography and paleography). If this is now the purview of the "medievalist," then what being such a medievalist teaches is the variety of literary and linguistic forms at any given place and moment in the history of the language. For what post-Conquest studies of the past three decades have stressed is the idea of vernacularity itself as a social condition of variety rather than of standard. Standards, much like canons, remain based on values rather than essentials. They are creations of social groups and have their meaning only in relationship to those behaviors deemed non-standard: linguistic behaviors characterized by such terms as "regional," "archaic," and "colloquial."

Embedded in this project and its legacy, as well, has been a focus on the history of ideas rather than the history of language. True, a volume such as *The Idea of the Vernacular* constitutes a chrestomathy of linguistic forms, but it embeds, as well, an argument about displacing study of those forms over the study of ideas. This is a book about an "Idea," and no finer statement of this principle could be found in a text printed in the middle of the book, a preface to an English biblical translation prepared around the year 1400 and now surviving in a manuscript in Trinity College, Cambridge.[20] Arguing that Latin should not necessarily remain the sole language of spiritual narrative, this writer avers: "And to hem that seien that the gospel on Engliche wolde make men to erre, wyte wele that we fynden in Latyne mo heretikes than of ale other langagis."[21] The writer goes on, making the case that mere attentions to grammatical correctness cannot substitute for a true intellectual engagement with God's word:

> Witte thei that, though a clerke or another man thus lerned can sette his wordis on
>   Engliche better than a rewde man, it foloweth not herof that our langage schuld be
>   destried. It were al on to sei this, and to kitte oute the tunges of hem that can not speke
>   thus curiosly. But thei schulde understande that 'grammaticaliche' is not ellis but abite of
>   right spekyng and right pronounsyng and right wrytynge.[22]

To rear a student on such excerpts is to raise a sensibility far different from one generated by King Alfred's *Preface to the Pastoral Care*. For this is not an argument for canonicity and power but a claim for individual ability. This offers not a lament for lost skills or virtues but a recognition that the local and the present can bear as much meaning as the past. This is a history of an idea of the vernacular not from the top down but from the bottom up. It is an idea that, potentially, places the student above the master.

7.4. THE MEDIEVALIST AND LANGUAGE HISTORY

For the past twenty years, medieval literary study in America has grappled with the implications of such arguments.[23] Have they had equal impact on the teaching of

HEL? I am not sure. One version of such a reformed curriculum might displace the canonical and the authorial traditions. Instead of figuring Middle English as the language of Chaucer—or, in turn, by arguing that a knowledge of Middle English gives us an access to Chaucer—we might imagine a curriculum framed along different lines. A "Middle English" section of HEL might look at the struggles for prose style above poetic fluency. It might envision the late-fourteenth century less as the purview of a clutch of London poets than the panorama of East Anglian mystics, Northern Biblicists, and Midlands romancers. It might argue, for example, that Julian of Norwich is as much an innovator in linguistic use as Chaucer was, or that Margery Kempe drew on the resources of a colloquial vernacular to create narratives of power equal to those of the Wife of Bath or the Prioress.

And it might argue, too, for the sustained use of discursive modes far from the purview of a London poet. What would it mean, for example, to teach medieval English poetry in a HEL course as a story of the alliterative tradition: not just of its literary survival but of its lexical omnivorousness? Any prosody that demands verbal variation of this kind demands a large vocabulary. The poems of the *Gawain*-Manuscript are full of words of Scandinavian, French, Celtic, and Old English origin. Some of these words survive; many do not. What does it mean, we well might ask, to read a poetry that relishes its vast vocabulary, even if that vocabulary lives largely, or solely, within the textual world of that poem? We argue, still, that Chaucer brought new words into the English language. What would it mean to argue that a poem such as *Gawain* brought far more words into a vernacular poetic—except that fewer of them stuck?

By contrast, what would it imply to teach a History of English as a history of documents rather than dreams? The development of a powerful official vernacular has long been seen as happening only in the early fifteenth century. Traditional histories of the language present a "triumph" or a "return" to English with, say, Henry V's English will of 1422 or of the records of the London Guilds from the same decade. There remains a vivid and rich tradition of the documentary in the vernacular that our notions of Conquest and Gallicization have effaced. The Old English prose traditions of the charter, will, and chronicle remain familiar. Less familiar are the twelfth- and thirteenth-century prose texts emerging from the abbeys and the monasteries. Richard Rolle and Julian of Norwich did not come out of nowhere. Prayer and meditation are constitutive discourses of vernacularity. So, too, are letters, and the rise of the personal epistle in the fourteenth century bears eloquent testimony to men and women of a variety of skills and social classes trying to come to terms with how the English language can mark family relationships.

This is my point: the medievalist teaching HEL has had an all-too-familiar and confining role. On the one hand, he or she has been the curator of a deep past, a figure in a literature department charged less with sensibility than with knowledge, a person who may give the modern student a taste of the early forms of English. On the other hand, he or she has been charged with providing access to an otherwise opaque part of the literary canon. Often the history of English is invoked to make Chaucer or Shakespeare accessible. In turn, examples from Chaucer or Shakespeare come easily to hand in illustrating changes in pronunciation, grammar, and vocabulary.

Given the changes in medieval literary study of the past two decades, I believe our teaching of the History of the Language should not just respond to but also deeply engage with such changes. We should move past great kings or fathers of English poetry to recognize that English was (and of course still remains) a wildly varied and contested form of social expression. What the current medievalist knows is the profoundly ideological and social basis behind verbal choice and textual performance. I think the teacher of HEL should know this as well.

What the medievalist also knows is that the "Middle Ages" in the British Isles did not end firmly with the coming of the printing press, or the ascension of Henry VIII, or the visits of Erasmus to Queens College, Cambridge. Debates about the very nature of historical periodization and, in particular, religious periodization, have flared off and on for the past twenty-five years—ever since Eamon Duffy's *Stripping of the Altars* challenged the hegemonies of institutional history by arguing for a sustained, vivid, and versatile popular Catholicism throughout the first decades of the sixteenth century. Not only had Duffy's work questioned old narratives about the Reformation displacing a moribund Catholic Church, but it also questioned a growing narrative among literary medievalists about the importance of Lollardy in late-medieval dissent and, in turn, about relationships of power and vernacularity in the late fifteenth and early sixteenth centuries. In the process, it brought a generation of medievalists into the ambit of the Early Modern: James Simpson, for example, sussing out the nature of indoctrination and control in his *Burning to Read*; or Sarah Beckwith, searching for sacramental rituals in her *Shakespeare and the Grammar of Forgiveness*.[24]

If these, and many other scholars, have seen something of a "long fifteenth century" in literature and culture, few have seen it in the history of language. We make a great effort to teach and read Chaucer in Middle English, yet we assume that poetry from Wyatt through Shakespeare can live, at least in the classroom, on a continuum of modern sound and sense. Poetry from the late fourteenth and the fifteenth century circulated widely, especially in manuscript anthologies and commonplace books, throughout the Tudor period. It was clearly understood (if recognized as somewhat old-fashioned). Reading Wyatt and Surrey in, for example, the Devonshire Manuscript of the 1530s—with its almost nonexistent punctuation, its irregular spellings, and its lapses of scansion—reveals how alien their language really is to us. A poem such as Wyatt's "They flee from me" has, we want to believe, all the hallmarks of literary modernity: a smoldering subjectivity, a careful monitoring of the verse line and the sentence, a sureness of rhyme and assonance. And yet, such features may well be the result of editorial ministrations from Richard Tottel onward. To read a Wyatt poem such as the one that begins "Absence absenting causithe me to complain," in its manuscript environment is to see something far more similar to Lydgate, Hawes, and post-Chaucerian aureate poetics than it is to see it as the lament of an English Petrarch[25]:

> Absens absenting causithe me to complaine
> my sorowfull complaints abiding in distresse
> and departing most pryvie increasithe my paine
> thus lyve I vncomfortid wrappid all in hevines.

In short, if we wish to find the line between the medieval and the early modern blurred in literary history, religious life, social reflection, and the wiles of court-iership, we should similarly find the lines of language equally unclear. Documents from well into the Reformation reveal old words and phrases. When did "medieval English" end? Or for that matter, the "Middle Ages?"

Taking an approach from the History of the Language, we may answer such ques-tions in new and potentially rich ways. For what the medievalist knows now, almost above all else, is the variety of sounds and spellings, the habits of scribes, and the tantalizing relationships the look of language on the written page and the old ech-oes of a human voice. Scribes spelled as they spoke—not absolutely true for every scribe, but largely true throughout the fourteenth and the fifteenth century. English changed in pronunciation and in grammar, and some of these changes are recorded in the spellings of the Paston Letters. But English gradually was being standardized on the page: William Caxton's adoption of "Chancery English" rewrote the look of the vernacular in print.[26] Originating in the household of the medieval English Kings, Chancery emerged out of the mix of domestic administration to come to control the production of official documents by the middle of the fourteenth century. From the 1380s to the 1450s, Chancery taught a house style of spelling, grammar, lexis, and idiom. Caxton's publications of the English authors Chaucer, Gower, Lydgate, Malory, and others calibrated themselves not to the older spelling habits of the scribes but to the newer conventions of Chancery. As John Hurt Fisher argued years ago, Caxton's achievement was to take a standard of official writing for a literary standard. In the process, he contributed to the modernization of English.

The role of Chancery has been more subtly nuanced, if not challenged, since Fisher advanced his claims over three decades ago. And yet, what seems to me to remain uncontestable (whatever the details) is Fisher's point that "the most impor-tant development of the [fifteenth] century was the emergence of writing as a sys-tem coordinate with, but independent from, speech."[27] This split between the voice and hand (or type) had grown so great that by 1569 the scholar John Hart could write in his *Orthographie*:

> In the modern and present manner of writing there is such confusion and disorder, as it may be accounted rather a kind of ciphering, or such a darke kinde of writing, as the best and readiest wit that euer hath bene could, or that is or shal be, can or may, by the only gift of reason, attaine to the ready and perfite reading thereof, without a long and tedious labour.[28]

One year after Hart's book appeared, Roger Ascham published his *Scolemaster*, in which he recalled his "forefather's time, when papistry as a standing pool covered and overflowed all England [when] few books were read in our tonge, saving cer-tain books of chivalry, as they said, for pastime and pleasure, which, as some say, were made in monasteries by idle monks or wanton canons."[29] With such a sentence, Ascham puts to rest the old traditions of the Middle English poets: John Lydgate, known as the "Monk of Bury," and Stephen Hawes, whose *Pastime of Pleasure* remained his most famous work. Such writers had a brief resurgence in the middle

1550s, when the Catholic Mary Tudor was the Queen and printers rushed back into print the old books of romance, chivalry, and sacramental allegory. But by the second decade of Elizabeth's rule, they were long gone.

It may be fair to say, then, that the end of medieval literature and language came late: with the growing split between the written and the spoken, with the suppression of old books, and with a recognition that the past now was the past. By the end of the century, Edmund Spenser could write an English self-consciously archaic in feel and flavor, and Thomas Speght would have to print his Chaucer with a glossary.

My own story of English may have wandered more widely than some of the companion chapters in this volume. But what I have wished to illustrate are a variety of ways in which the medieval literary teacher/scholar can put pressure on the History of English to teach new and unexpected texts, to see the medieval as much longer and much blurrier than it had seemed, and to see literary and linguistic histories in dialogue about their institutional inheritances.

CHAPTER 8

English and I

Finding the History of the English Language in the Class

MICHAEL R. DRESSMAN

When a class section of History of the English Language (HEL) first meets, it is important for the instructor to acknowledge that the students are not subject-specific blank slates, with no language history of their own. Each one comes to the learning encounter with a unique and quite personal relationship to the English language. It is highly unlikely that the students have reflected on their experiences with English, or any other language, in the linguistic way that the instructor will introduce to them in the class. An opportunity will be missed, however, if the instructor does not mine and employ the language histories of the students to further the learning goals of the HEL class.

I have spent most of my teaching career at "emerging" universities, that is, institutions that began as branch campuses of major state systems and that have evolved into regional, relatively free-standing schools, with largely commuter students. Such universities have student populations that are highly diverse in age, race, ethnicity, and life experience, including many military veterans. These universities also have a great number of students who did not begin as freshmen at those particular institutions. The student body comprises some who have transferred from community colleges, others who have attended faraway schools but are now returning to live at home (for a host of reasons), and still others who are getting back into higher education after a lapse of years—sometimes decades. Furthermore, many of them are reenrolled as part-time students while caring for families and holding down jobs, full-time or part-time. The range of background and ability level may vary enormously in any given class, but the one thing going for the instructor at a university such as mine is that the students, in nearly every case, are in school "on purpose." Very few are attending because it just seemed to be the next thing to do or because the family is footing the bill. Their education is part of their career and life goals.

There is, therefore, an intellectual curiosity that makes it possible to expect goodwill on the part of the learners.

The HEL class at many U.S. universities is taught at the "upper division," that is, during junior or senior year. In a perfect world, one in which the emerging university does not exist, the HEL class would have a prerequisite of some relevant sort, perhaps, an introduction to linguistics or studies in grammar, at least something that introduces concepts of phonology, morphology, syntax, and semantics. As it happens, HEL often has as a prerequisite only English composition or "junior standing." Therefore, the HEL instructor will have the additional responsibility of introducing the class to linguistic concepts that are utterly new to most in the class, as well as grammatical matters that were last visited by this group of students in high school, if ever.

So far, I have been totaling up the deficiencies of the students in regard to their preparation to attack HEL as a subject within the scope of linguistics. There are other ways in which students come to the HEL class underprepared for things that, perhaps, at a conventional college or university in the past, could be presumed by the instructor. Examples would be a general knowledge of U.S. or world history or, even, a smattering of literary history. It would be reckless, in my case, to take such background for granted.

Typically, most HEL instructors have known that their responsibility is to convey to students the distinctions between Old, Middle, and Modern English; the consequences of the repeated invasions of Britain by Romans, Saxons, Vikings, and Normans; the Indo-European language family; sound changes; the loss of inflections and the consequent importance of word order and prepositions; the growth of spelling conventions; the emergence of printing; and the spread of English through colonialism. However, the instructor today, at emerging universities and, I am fairly sure, at most U.S. universities must also be prepared to supply background material on the Roman Empire, the rise of Christianity in Europe, the Renaissance (or Early Modern Period, if you will), the Reformation, the Enlightenment, the African slave trade, and world geography.

Having listed what I, as the instructor, must bring to the HEL course to allow the students make any sense of what they are studying, I intend to digress now and consider what the point of the course is for this particular audience of students. The students who take the HEL course at my university have various motives. They may be fulfilling an area requirement or elective in any number of degree programs. It could be that they are laying the foundation for some future educational or certification prerequisite. For those students who had a choice to take this class rather than another, they may simply be hoping to learn something new. Since HEL, at my university, is not a "required course" for any degree plan, it does not bear that burden or stigma. Still, the educational pride of the department and the instructor are on the line. We want those who complete our HEL course to have had a fair version of the genre, especially if they intend to go forward with their studies in a field that presumes concepts and facts usually obtained in HEL. Still, the course must be engaging and possible for students who approach it with goodwill, even though with little direct preparation. Again, that mention of *goodwill* is not used casually.

I return now to what I said at the outset about the fact that the students themselves bring some potential benefits to the course setting. Since the language of instruction is English, they have all gone through the process of learning the language, either as a first language, a second language, or a foreign language. A way for the instructor to dive into the subject of language is to exploit that language learning experience. For this purpose, I use a diagnostic essay called "English and I." My original use of this type of essay was in composition classes, which is why I refer to it as "diagnostic," but it also serves that function in HEL. My developing the idea for this early-in-the-term essay came from my desire to find a way to get first-year writing students to give me a good sample of their writing without their having to struggle with what they had to say. The inspiration for this topic came from adopting an honored linguist's proven method for natural speech elicitation.

Many years ago, when we were both much younger, I had the opportunity of going to dinner with sociolinguist and dialectologist William Labov. I was part of a group of faculty members hoping to learn lessons from him about linguistic scholarship. As it turns out, the main thing I took from that encounter was something that I have used ever since in my teaching. Labov had said that the secret to getting a really good sample of someone's natural speech is to put the informant at ease. Then the researcher should ask the person something that is personal, but not rude, and is easy to answer spontaneously. The topic I remember Labov saying he had used is, "Tell me about the time you almost died." He said that he had never run into anyone who could not begin talking and go on for several minutes in response to that prompt.

In my composition classes I began to use Labov's topic to get students writing in a continuous stream and it worked well. My most memorable essay was by a former Vietnamese military pilot who described what it was like to have his transport aircraft be hit by ground fire and nearly crash while an airplane full of men behind him in the cabin reacted in horror. I kept the "Tell me about the time you almost died" diagnostic prompt for a few years, but I was looking for something similar that could be more easily adapted to the course material. At the time, I was using readings about language in my composition classes. Also, the number of non-native speakers of English surged in our classes, so I shifted the diagnostic essay topic to "English and I."

Students were asked to compose an essay that described their individual and personal relationship with the English language. Realizing that some students might be reluctant to reveal personal life details to a professor, I tried to follow Labov's injunction to work to make the informants feel at ease. I told them my own story of the English language in my life by giving them the kind of background information a fieldworker in the Linguistic Atlas Project might elicit. Here is a sample of how I begin:

> My father was a salesman, and we moved rather often as he was transferred to a new territory or looked to work for a new company. My parents met working at an airplane factory during World War II. My father had a brief career as a milkman, driving a horse cart through the streets of Covington, Kentucky, and he went to college for a year before the war. My mother was a student at a music conservatory. Both

my parents' families had roots in the Cincinnati, Ohio/Northern Kentucky area, but my mother's parents moved to West Virginia before she was born. My father's family were mostly of German descent. My father's grandparents spoke German, and his parents spoke enough German to use it when trying to keep secrets from the children. (My Dad told me that he and his brothers and sisters usually guessed that his mother was pregnant when she and his father spoke a lot of German.) My mother's family was Irish and German, with one of my great grandmothers coming from Canada. Both families were Catholic.

I was born in Cincinnati, but when my father got a new sales job, my family moved to Charleston, West Virginia, my mother's hometown, while I was quite small. My earliest memories are of an apartment building in Charleston. Just before I turned five we moved to Pittsburgh, Pennsylvania. This is when and where I was first informed by others that I "talked funny." Although Pittsburgh is not that far from Charleston, the local speech in those places is very different in accent and vocabulary. There are even grammatical or syntactic differences.

I then offer my students some examples of words I used and how I pronounced them, and I offer the contrasting Pittsburgh approach to those words. As a West Virginian, I would say "winda" (window) and "pella" (pillow). I would say "chimly" (chimney), and my pronunciation of the word "how" sounded more like "hal." The Pittsburghers, on the other hand, pronounced "downtown" like "dahntahn." They called telephone poles "telly poles," and their pronunciation of "o" was far different from mine. My friends' mothers would tell the children to "redd up your room," a local term for "straighten up" or "tidy up."

As you can guess, this is now a storytelling session. Some students in the class offer, with almost no encouragement needed, their own experiences as the new kid in school or the new employee at work who was perceived as linguistically different.

My story continues, as my family (there are now five children) moves from Pittsburgh to Cleveland, Ohio. There I am again in a new local language area that is very different from the one to which I had spent the previous six years attempting to conform. Once again, I am told I "talk funny." This is around the time I started to become interested in linguistics, although I did not know the term at the time. I find that the words, pronunciations, and expressions that I was accustomed to were the source of mirth or puzzlement for others. When we made return visits to see relatives in Cincinnati and Charleston, I began to notice differences in their speech, too. People in Cleveland sounded a lot more like the people on television shows. My Cincinnati relatives were clearly more Southern. My first name was "Mahkl." They also had the habit of asking you to repeat what you had just said, if they had not quite heard it, by saying, "Please?" My West Virginia relatives would say "you all." In Pittsburgh, people had said "yinz" or "yunz." People in Cleveland said "you guys."

When the family moved back to Pittsburgh just before my senior year in high school, I was ready for the assault that eventually came. When I was again told that I "talked funny," I had a ready answer: "No, you talk funny. Listen to yourself!" This was not always well received, but it did eventually lead to a brief discussion on regional differences in American English. I made good friends in my high school class with a boy from New Orleans. We enjoyed swapping language stories. Again, as I tell my language history, students chime in. They recount times when they are visiting relatives or going back to places they had lived before and being told that their language had changed so much.

I wind up the preliminary session for the diagnostic essay by telling the class that my experiences have made me very interested in language and, because they and I will be working on language together for this semester, I would like to gain a greater insight into their own language history. This is the prompt I give them:

Short Essay: English and I

Write a short essay in which you tell me about your personal history and relationship with the English language. Describe how, when, and where you learned the language; and let me know how English has figured into your life as a means of communication and as a school subject.

Write for about half an hour. Use standard written English conventions, but do not make a rough draft or recopy. This is a narrative–a story–so it does not have to prove a point. However, I would like to know whether you have any concerns about English that you want to be sure that I include in the course, if possible.

Many of the students at our university are the first in their families to go beyond secondary education. Some were not born in the United States. Often a majority of my class will be made up of students who learned another language before learning English. Most often the language is Spanish, but we have large numbers of students with Asian, African, Arabic, and Eastern European language backgrounds. Some of these students have learned English in school in their home countries, but they are now having to use it practically. The native English speakers in the class include people who have moved to Houston from other states or English-speaking countries, often because the family moved here for work. There are, of course, native Texans–African American, European American, Mexican American, and, increasingly, Vietnamese Americans–with their own quirks of language, such as "fixin' to" and the inability to hear the difference between "then" and "than." Some of the African American students identify as *Creoles*, black, or mixed race people from Louisiana with a French language background.

This first essay in the composition classes that I taught worked very well. I learned about the students' language backgrounds, and I used the experiences that they related in those early essays during the term to help them contrast rules or practices in their native language or home varieties of English with the expectations in written English of the type expected at a university. Although the first-year writing course is generally called "rhetoric and composition," a focus on fundamental language features makes the study more personal. Furthermore, the approach of investigating *general grammar* is a step in the classical trivium that comes before logic and rhetoric. So, accidentally, I found myself well grounded, pedagogically.

It was not long before I started to use this same essay, "English and I," as an early-in-the-term exercise in my upper-division writing classes and linguistically oriented classes, such as Studies in Grammar, Introduction to Linguistics, and HEL. In one grammar class, populated with twenty teacher education students, I learned that I was one of three native speakers of English in the room. Most of the students had Spanish as their first language, having come to English in pre-school, elementary school, or more recently as adult learners. In that class, there was also a student who was trilingual in Arabic, Spanish, and English and a bilingual student with a background in Greek and English.

As in the composition classes, "English and I" produced remarkable and very useful results. I gained insight into the language-learning backgrounds of my students and had the opportunity to talk with them about questions on language acquisition and things they had been told by family members or teachers about language and grammar. So I have made the "English and I" essay an essential part of my HEL classes.

Drawing on the "English and I" essays, the instructor can lead the class to the study of phonology while dealing with concepts such as regional or ethnic accent, as well as language acquisition and first-language influence on pronunciation in English. Morphology and spelling can be related more easily to students' own experience in the light of contrastive analysis with other languages. For example, children who speak English or French need to learn spelling conventions that are not reflected grapheme by grapheme in their written languages. By contrast, Spanish is much closer to alphabetic/phonemic correspondence. On the other hand, English rules of capitalization mystify native speakers and writers of Spanish. English's ability to make instant compound phrases that function as words is similar to German's more formal allowance for that kind of compounding; this ability in spoken English, however, can sometimes confuse or frighten even the native speaker when it comes to writing down a phrase such as "the little boy who lives down the street's dog."

There are many topics that arise in the student essays that result in fruitful and course-supportive discussion topics. Some are technical or grammatical, but most are sociolinguistic in nature, such as attitudes on language and family rules about which language is permitted or encouraged when. These rules can vary widely from household to household. Some fathers (and it is usually fathers) forbid English in their house or at the dinner table. In other families, children are encouraged or required to speak English as much as possible. Students share stories of the immigrant experience of children, who pick up the language quickly from friends or in school, serving as translators and representatives of parents and older relatives who have not yet mastered English or may never do so.

For the Spanish-speaking students, there may be self-consciousness in certain circumstances, anywhere from ordering at a Mexican restaurant to applying for a job that calls for the applicant to be bilingual. Many of my students fear that their "kitchen Spanish," spoken at home but without the polish of the full repertoire of sophisticated Spanish grammar and vocabulary, will embarrass them if they claim to be bilingual. Naturally, Spanglish as practiced among students and heard on local radio is discussed, which is quite helpful when introducing pidgin and creole dialects. This consciousness of Tex-Mex Spanish is reinforced by the local broadcast media that regularly import reporters rather than risk having someone considered of questionable dialect on the air.

In parallel to the non-English speakers' concerns, students who have African American Vernacular English as one of their varieties (or their principal out-of-the-classroom variety) are curious, and sometimes defensive, about their own language and its place in the language spectrum. The Ebonics controversy from the 1990s is still an alive and troubling episode for black students and their families. Again, family rules and attitudes have a chance to be aired, and the instructor has the chance to talk about the rule-governed bounds of what the students have heard called "broken English." One might question whether time spent on such a scattershot series of topics can create a coherent course on what is a defined traditional subject, such as HEL. However, my experience has been that making the course about language first can, as in the composition class, enhance the focus, especially for the students before me, on what they are studying and why.

The point of such a general language emphasis and contrastive instruction is to attempt to break the stranglehold that afflicts many students—even, or especially, non-native speakers of English—that the rules are the rules and anything against "the rules" is not English. The instructor's hope is that the students will come to experience the rightness of saying that language is arbitrary but conventional. Rules in linguistics are matters of appropriateness to context. There are rules for writing and speaking the language; they are just not always the same rules in every situation. Nor should we expect them to be. There are always questions of competence and performance. Some non-native English speakers are ahead on some topics. The experiences of Spanish-speaking students, or students from other languages with strong grammatical gender, are valuable assets in the analysis of the loss of grammatical gender in English. This topic also lends itself to a review of how useful, though stigmatized still by some, the agreement of "they/their/them" with singular antecedents, such as "everyone," has become in contemporary English, while Spanish struggles for inclusiveness with terms such as "Latino/a." Students who struggle with a noticeable accent or have an unusually hard time learning writing conventions may need to have it acknowledged that, like any skill, some people have a greater automatic fluency than others. Such is the nature of human language. We cannot always will ourselves into competence as easily as we would like. Circumstances may have had a lot of influence. I point out that Henry Kissinger, a university professor and a former U.S. Secretary of State, came to the United States at age fifteen, and he always had a detectable German accent when speaking English, but Henry had a younger brother, named Walter, who came to America at a younger age, and Walter grew up without a German accent. Christine Lagarde, the head of the International Monetary Fund, has a French accent in English, but no one in the public arena dismisses her as less intelligent because of that.

At every stage of studying the history of English, I reinforce the reality that the language was on the tongues of people who were using it and not just on the tips of the pens of the monks who were recording it. Poets can import new words, but the people have to start using them if they are to last. Once they are engaged in the process of the language's development, the students like the stories of Caedmon, the Abbess Hilda of Whitby, Bede's concern for the history of his Church and his people, and Alfred's intention that priests be able to teach their parishioners. For some students, it is oddly freeing to realize that variation in spelling or spelling as one spoke was the norm until relatively recently. So the story of William Caxton's worry about what version of English to use for his printing business and the rise of London English and Chancery English as standards give some context as to how we have arrived at some of current practices. Until recently, who could have foreseen that printed books themselves might be experienced as just an historical phase, as velum manuscripts were before them?

Besides the "English and I" essay, in order to tap into already existing student interests and experiences, I have tried two kinds of assignments that allow students to use the course material and possibly expand ways that they see the topics of the course in context. Most students do not find being asked to watch a movie of their choosing a chore. One assignment is that a student must review a movie that is performed in English, but not North American English. The focus of this review is broader than plot, theme, characters, setting, and special effects, although the reviewers must comment on those to create background for the real heart of this review: a chart and commentary on the English variety or varieties used in the film. The chart and commentary are developed in contrast with the reviewer's own variety of English. The James Bond films are favorites, but Guy Ritchie's action films are also well represented. The students are asked to select a number of vocabulary examples that are not common in their own language, cite contrastive pronunciation for words that they use but that are heard pronounced differently in the film, and search for expressions or syntactic variants from their own language. The English use of "she must have done" rather than the American "she must have" or "she must have done so" often grabs attention.

With video downloads so easy to come by these days, this assignment is easier to require than it was in years past when obtaining a videotape cartridge was necessary. Films from England, Scotland, Ireland, and Australia are plentiful. There are also possibilities from South Africa, West Africa, and the Caribbean. And, of course, there are the films of Bollywood or their tamer mainstream equivalents such as *Slumdog Millionaire* or the Marigold Hotel films. I caution students to stick with contemporary films or, at least, recent films set in the twentieth or twenty-first century. Historical dramas and movie versions of classic plays yield less useful results, for the purpose I am hoping to achieve—the students' realization of English operating elsewhere in the world by a different set of rules.

The other assignment that attempts to tap student interest or experience is the five-minute talk on a language subject about which the student has become an expert, even if only superficially. The topic of the talk can be anything related to the course, preferably on a subject in which the speaker has a more than passing level of interest or expertise. I give the students a list of possible topics from which to choose, but they are free to propose other topics for approval. Depending on the students' interests, in one class we might have talks on "The Irish Contribution to English," "What Bill Cosby Had to Say About Ebonics," "Who Were the Vikings?" "Jargon of Texas Law Enforcement Agencies," "How French Was Chaucer's English?" "Language Acquisition in Deaf Children," "What Johnson's Dictionary Did Not Have," "'Making Groceries' in Louisiana," "English in Ghana," "Dual Language Education in Houston

Schools," "The Historical Pronunciation Movement in Shakespearian Theater," or "Anglicization of Native American Place Names." Of course, these topics are so wide that a five-minute talk may seem like a ludicrously short space to explore the subject, but the point is for the student to become familiar with the broad outlines of the subject and know enough to speak for five minutes, with minimal notes (a small note card with bullets), no handouts, and no power point slides, to a roomful of their peers. The speaker may illustrate some point with a few drawings or symbols on a whiteboard, and each speaker also submits to the instructor a portfolio of the research done to prepare for the talk.

This assignment takes the place of a research paper. There is, however, other writing in the course; all the exams include short answers or essays, in which participants can demonstrate "linguistic reasoning," the flag under which critical thinking flies in HEL. The idea here is to expose the speaker and the other members of the class to some kind of course-topic enrichment, enlarging the scope.

The instructional materials available to the HEL instructor are many and varied, but the challenges facing the HEL instructor go beyond the mountains of available teaching aids and the razzle-dazzle of multimedia. Those challenges include the students' lack of preparation for such a course and, furthermore, the students' lack of motivation to see how this course has any relationship to them. Some instructors use primary research. Professor Connie Eble at the University of North Carolina-Chapel Hill has for years has had students collecting examples of campus slang as a means to making the HEL class and other courses more about the students themselves. Using, where possible, the students' own background in language, their existing academic or personal interests, and their curiosity about cultural or scientific topics can motivate a more engaging and enriched learning experience in the HEL class.

PART THREE

Research Paradigms and Pedagogical Practices

CHAPTER 9

Historical Pragmatics in the Teaching of the History of English

LESLIE K. ARNOVICK

9.1. INTRODUCTION

What does it mean to explore the historical dimensions of pragmatics? This chapter introduces historical pragmatics as an arena for assessing historic form, context, and meaning in use. My purpose here is to equip those tasked with teaching the history of English with (1) a summary of historical-pragmatic theory and methodology, (2) a set of exemplary studies that can be adapted for classroom use, and (3) citations of work with exercises appropriate for class or homework. The overview presented in what follows should provide instructors with sufficient background to incorporate a unit on historical pragmatics into a course on the history of the English language.

Because historical pragmatics represents the marriage of historical linguistics and pragmatics, this chapter begins by defining "pragmatics" and "historical pragmatics" and situating them in historical-linguistic scholarship. After relating the background of the discipline and its aims, the discussion moves to the range and scope of data targeted by historical pragmatics. Considerable attention is devoted to the electronic corpora available for historical-pragmatic research. Various kinds of historical-pragmatic processes are then presented with cross-references to case studies explicated in the third revised edition of *The English Language: A Linguistic History*.[1] Three expanded case studies follow, highlighting the productivity of historical-pragmatic analyses. The chapter concludes with a cautionary anecdote about the observer's paradox. Given its emphasis on past contexts for language use, historical-pragmatics may offer appreciably detailed accounts of linguistic change in English.

9.2. LOCATING HISTORICAL PRAGMATICS IN HISTORICAL-LINGUISTIC SCHOLARSHIP

Historical pragmatics is the study of "language use in its social, cultural and above all historical context. It investigates patterns of language use in earlier periods and examines how such patterns changed over time."[2] Both social and linguistic matters lie at the heart of historical pragmatics. Although language contact and language-internal factors—phonological, morphological, lexical, syntactic, semantic—promote language change, cultural factors also effect change to these systems. Today we know as well that sociolinguistic factors influence the pragmatic realm of the grammar. Discursive structures may be introduced, altered, or eliminated. Such phenomena as discourse markers, politeness principles, text production, discourse types, speech acts, orality, and literacy fall under the aegis of historical pragmatics, although historical pragmatics is not alone in its attention to these subjects. Two other, related methodologies partly coincide with historical pragmatics. They warrant mention in order to clarify terminology. A field called "historical discourse analysis" has emerged in the new century; corpus-based, it departs from the textually based historical pragmatics. According to Brinton (2003),[3] historical discourse analysis may be subdivided according to its methodologies into (1) historical discourse analysis proper (which is essentially synchronic in the analysis of pragmatic factors during a particular stage of a language), (2) diachronically oriented discourse analysis (which traces the evolution of forms or functions having a discourse function), and (3) discourse-oriented historical linguistics (which seeks the origins and motivations for changes in discourse).[4] Despite these distinctions, Elizabeth Traugott questions the significance of differentiating historical discourse analysis from historical pragmatics.[5] Brinton herself finally places historical discourse analysis in apposition to historical pragmatics.[6] Such is the congruence that we may subsume their endeavors and locate historical dialogue analysis within historical pragmatics for the purposes of this chapter.

Historical pragmatics also overlaps with the new field of "historical sociolinguistics" (also known as "sociohistorical linguistics"). Historical sociolinguistics applies the methods of sociolinguistics to the study of language change.[7] The foci of this method are extralinguistic determinants such as ethnicity, class, gender, age, or group identification. Historical sociolinguistics asks how such factors influence a speaker's choice of a linguistic variant, subsequently leading to change.[8] Examples of historical sociolinguistics reveal two approaches: (1) "apparent-time," or contemporaneous, studies, most notably William Labov's fieldwork in Martha's Vineyard and New York, during which he observed differences between younger and older speakers, extrapolating from their variation directions of language change[9] and (2) "real-time studies" (i.e., studies of actual historical contexts in which social variables underlie language change over time). Practitioners of historical sociolinguistics have looked, for instance, at the use of second-person pronouns as polite (*you*) and familiar forms (*thou*) in the Early Modern period.[10] Although historical sociolinguistics and historical pragmatics may complement one another in explaining language change, this chapter concentrates on historical pragmatics.

9.3. WHAT IS PRAGMATICS?

To define historical pragmatics it is first necessary to define pragmatics. Pragmatics focuses on non-literal meanings. It examines the use of English relative to its grammar and it analyzes the relationship between language structures and their functions.[11] The practice of pragmatics manifests itself in discourse analysis, speech-act theory, relevance theory, and evaluation of cognitive communicative principles.[12] Whereas pragmatics denotes a kind of linguistic analysis, it also represents a kind of competence that language users possess. In this sense, pragmatics is the "ability of language users to pair sentences with the contexts in which they would be appropriate."[13] The contexts for linguistic performance are social, and they are as broad and deep as society itself, for social context, "presupposes the existence of a particular society, with its implicit and explicit values, norms, rules, and laws, and with all its particular conditions of life: economic, social, political, and cultural."[14] Pragmatics thus comprehends "any background knowledge assumed to be shared by both speaker and hearer and which contributes to the hearer's interpretation of what the speaker means by his or her utterance."[15] In short, pragmatics is at once the "linguistic dimension of social interaction" and the linguistic description of that dimension.[16]

9.4. WHAT IS HISTORICAL PRAGMATICS?

Toward the end of the twentieth century, historical linguists embarked on research founded in a newly articulated assumption:

> In the case of pragmatics, it is reasonable to assume that communication in earlier periods can also be described in terms of pragmatic phenomena such as speech acts, implicature, politeness phenomena, or discourse markers.[17]

On the basis of this principle, they began to apply pragmatic methodology to language from the past. As a result, historical linguistics, the scientific study of language change over time, was rendered more sophisticated.

Historical pragmatics is a relatively young field, which is to say that changes over time in the pragmatic realm have only been studied through its particular lens in the last twenty-five years or so.[18] In 1995 Andreas Jucker edited a landmark volume of articles on varying aspects of the nascent field. Just as important as the essays contained in that volume was the introductory matter making it clear that a new theoretical framework, encompassing both disciplines, was being established.[19] Pragmatics, which studies spoken language, had, up to the 1990s, primarily restricted itself to the contemporary language of Late Modern English. Similarly, historical linguistics studies the language of historical texts, but linguistic forms rather than contexts were most often its priority. If pragmatics did not treat written language from the past, neither did historical linguistics yield a full and satisfying picture of it. Speaking to the necessity of supplementing non-pragmatic historical explanations—here she talks about semantic processes—Elizabeth Closs Traugott concludes that "additional ingredients" are necessary in order to account for semantic change.[20] Emerging as a hybrid field, historical pragmatics has come to proffer extra, if not secret, ingredients for addressing semantic as well as other kinds of language change. Altogether, historical pragmatics considers "changes in the linguistic structure resulting from altered communicative needs which are due to changes in the social structure."[21]

The discipline has two schools as it is practiced, "pragmaphilology" and "diachronic pragmatics."[22] Pragmaphilology represents primarily a macro approach. In pragmaphilology, "sociohistorical and pragmatic linguistic aspects of historical texts are measured."[23] Pragmaphilology enfolds the "contextual aspects of historical texts, including the addressees and addressers, their social and personal relationship, the physical and social setting of text production and text reception, and the goal(s) of the text."[24] Diachronic pragmatics represents, in contrast, a micro approach that asks another set of questions about early texts. It focuses on the linguistic inventory and its communicative use across different historical stages of the same language. Andreas Jacobs and Andreas Jucker distinguish two subtypes within this second category of research. "Diachronic form-to-function mapping" takes a linguistic form as a starting point in order to trace its changing discourse meanings. The complementary " 'diachronic function-to-form' mapping takes a speech function as a starting point in order to trace its changing realizations across time."[25] The former, form-to-function mapping, considers lexical items, syntactic structures, prepositional phrases, verbal constructions, deictic elements, discourse markers, and interjections. Once mapped, form-to-function change may be attributed to pragmatic causes. Alternatively, function-to-form mapping investigates phenomena such as the constraints on "recruitment of extant terms to express a semantic category."[26] This latter form of mapping might, for instance, illuminate constraints on the development of lexical resources for expressing epistemic possibility.[27]

As historical pragmatics has matured into a discipline it has gained a handbook, *Historical Pragmatics*,[28] and a journal, the *Journal of Historical Pragmatics* (2000–). Historical pragmatics has also extended its range and scope to delineate pragmatic forms, interactional or interlocutory dynamics, and discursive domains:

Pragmatic forms: discourse markers, terms of address, connectives, and interjections;
Interactional pragmatics: speech acts, politeness, impoliteness;
Discursive domains: scientific and medical discourse, journalism, religious and political discourse, courtroom discourse, literary discourse, and public and private correspondence.[29]

9.5. THE DATA

In the early days of historical pragmatics, diachronic explorations were often constrained by the nature of the data available. If pragmatics concerns the use of language by speakers to achieve communicative ends, then it follows that detecting speech in the past, especially in the absence of sound recordings, is problematical.[30] Moreover, given that speech is the ultimate source of linguistic change over time, we are hampered in seeking its evidence in the first place. Confronting the possibility that data is inherently flawed, or "bad," as it has been called, we may be tempted to give up. Yet written documents from the past do give us inklings of the way people spoke in previous eras.

Through the evolution of historical pragmatics as a discipline and the access to historic texts possible in the information age, scholars have made inroads in the study of communication from the past. One basis for advancement is theoretical. There is now consensus that written texts from the past can and should be understood as communicative acts in their own right. This recognition has granted them legitimacy as objects of historical-pragmatic analysis.[31] The second foundation on which historical pragmatics rests is the relatively recent availability of speech-like data from earlier periods, along with electronic tools for searching them.[32]

Only one generation ago (roughly thirty years), evidence of "authentic" spoken language was limited to documents such as letters, wills, and plays found in print thanks to late nineteenth- and early twentieth-century editors (e.g., publications of the Early English Text Society). Other documents (like newspapers) could be found on microfilm. Just as data was limited, so too was their retrieval. Mindful of human error, scholars surveyed texts for linguistic data manually, reading word for word.

Technology changed all this: both the body of texts and the means of surveying them have expanded. Medieval manuscripts have been transcribed or copied in facsimile into electronic form. Previously unavailable manuscripts and early printed books have now been scanned, by way of such resources as *Early English Books Online* (*EEBO*). Other documents, formerly difficult to obtain, have been digitalized. Historic newspapers and political pamphlets, diaries, and commonplace books have been gathered together. Trial records and transcripts of witness depositions have also been published electronically, as have transcriptions and recordings of spoken language in the form of actual and scripted conversations (e.g., radio and television). Materials available today cover a spectrum of spoken and written evidence.[33] A methodology called corpus linguistics (outlined next) enables scholars to retrieve—very precisely—linguistic data from the past.

9.6. HISTORICAL CORPORA

Electronic corpora, with their rich data, have revolutionized historical linguistics, in general, and historical pragmatics, in particular. Let me use a bibliographic sketch to highlight the most useful of these collections, suggesting along the way potential directions for corpus-based research. Digital corpora constitute a difference in kind from early, manual corpora. As a construct, the corpus is not a recent innovation. Ancient corpora took the form of concordances to religious texts like the Hindu Vedas and the Hebrew Bible. Such indices were followed by concordances to literary canons of major authors. Concordances to Chaucer and Shakespeare

are characteristic, but there are others.[34] Laurence Sterne, for example, composed a concordance to Milton's prose. Then there are concordances to Dryden's poetry and to Joyce's *Ulysses*.[35] One used to have to go to the reference room to consult concordances.

The first electronically searchable corpus was produced in 1961 at Brown University (the *Standard Corpus of Present-Day American English*, also known as the *Brown Corpus*) by Henry Kučera and W. Nelson Francis for the purpose of computational analysis. Over the course of six years, Kučera and Francis computed the frequency of approximately one million words collected from 500 different samples of U.S. English. After assessing the sociolinguistic significance of these words, they published the seminal work in corpus linguistics, *Computational Analysis of Present-Day American English,* in 1967.

Subsequently, the publishing house Houghton-Mifflin commissioned Kučera and Francis to compile a corpus of one million words, all accompanied by citations, to form the basis of its new *American Heritage Dictionary*. While this development would change the nature of modern lexicography, it also lent another tool in the form of searchable dictionary corpora to the historical linguist. Let me pause to mention the benchmarks published online or on CD-ROM. The *Dictionary of Old English*, which holds all extant Old English texts, issued the corpus at its base as the *Dictionary of Old English Web Corpus*. Also searchable electronically is the *Middle English Dictionary*, based upon 3 million citation slips and covering the period between 1100 and 1500. Then again, the *Oxford English Dictionary (OED)* with its constituent *Historical Thesaurus to the OED* can be used as a database by virtue of the quotations it contains. The *Brown Corpus* was followed in the 1970s by the *Lancaster-Oslo/Bergen Corpus (LOB Corpus)*, a collaboration between British and Norwegian universities, as a British English companion to the *Brown Corpus*. Like *Brown*, the *LOB Corpus* contained sample texts.

The next event in the development of corpus linguistics was to make entire texts machine readable. In 1977 a group of linguists and engineers working in Norway assembled a growing archive of digital texts from different genres, varieties, and time periods, which eventually took the form of the *International Computer Archive of Modern and Medieval English (ICAME)*. The second edition of *ICAME* saw the addition of the *Helsinki Corpus of English Texts (HC)*.

The *HC* represented a turning point in corpus linguistics with its substantial collection of texts dating from 750 to 1710. Eventually surpassed by larger and broader corpora, *HC* nevertheless proves practical today as a place to begin research on English material. Often it facilitates a good overview of the kind of genres and registers that may be productive for study. Results may similarly suggest the time period and text type that seem promising. Databases which hold more specific collections or which are larger than the *HC*'s 1.5 million words can then be consulted.[36] The *Corpus of English Dialogues* (1560–1760), for instance, was created especially for historical-pragmatic research: it accommodates both "authentic dialogue" (trial records and witness depositions) and "constructed dialogue" (drama, didactic tracks, and prose fiction).[37] Scholars and students wishing additional samples of authentic dialogue might consult the legal records found in *English Witness Dispositions 1560–1760* and

The Proceedings of the Old Bailey; both supplement the *Corpus of English Dialogues*. The *Proceedings* corpus integrates almost 200,000 trials held between 1763 and 1913 at London's central criminal court. Direct speech that occurs in the *Proceedings* has been located, tagged for part-of-speech, and annotated with historical and cultural information in *The Old Bailey Corpus* (ca. 113 million words). The *Old Bailey Corpus* proves valuable for recording the words of "non-elite people."[38] Digital editions of letters (business and personal correspondence) allow insight into another kind of authentic dialogue. Annotated with background information about correspondents, the *Corpus of Early English Correspondence* (1418–1680) was created to illuminate socio-linguistic matters, especially with regard to change over time.

Collections of other specialized genres correct a traditional imbalance in the kind of materials available for linguistic research. The three-part *Corpus of Early English Medical Writing 1375–1800* offers medical writing in the vernacular from the medieval to the modern periods: *Middle English Medical Texts* (ca. 1375 to ca. 1500), *Early Modern Medical Texts* (1500–1700), and *Corpus of Early English Medical Writing* (1640–1740). With this corpus it is possible to trace the emergence of the medical register out of Latin and the classical tradition into vernacular theory and practice. The corpus encompasses a range of materials in a variety of styles and forms, from folk remedies to academic medicine.

Corpora also make it possible to concentrate on the language of a particular historical period. Already mentioned is the *Old English Dictionary Corpus*. The *Corpus of Middle English Prose and Verse* adds to the texts used in the *Middle English Dictionary*, "the largest and most significant monuments of Middle English": for example, the Middle English Bible, Higden's *Polychronicon*, *Cursor Mundi*, the chronicles of Robert Mannyng and Robert of Gloucester, Mandeville's *Travels*, Hoccleve's *Regiment of Princes*, the A, B, and C texts of *Piers Plowman*, *Prick of Conscience*, the *Ormulum*, and *South English Legendary*. Updates will incorporate the complete six-text, Chaucer Society edition of the *Canterbury Tales*.[39] Moving beyond the Middle Ages, we find the *Lampeter Corpus of Early Modern English Tracts* (1640–1740). With 1.2 million words, the *Lampeter Corpus* presents political, religious, economic, legal, and other treatises from the early modern period.

Resources for the modern period permit the study of national varieties. I have already referred to the *LOB Corpus* of British English as well as specialized collections of authentic dialogue and medical writing. *ICAME* now includes collections of regional Englishes (e.g., Australian English, New Zealand English, Indian English, and East-African English). Like the *Brown Corpus*, another asset for those pursuing U.S. English is the *Corpus of Historical American English* (*COHA*). *COHA* assembles material dating from the early nineteenth century through to Present-Day English in the twenty-first century (1810–2009). With *COHA*, contributing around 400 million words, we arrive at sources of mega data, the potential of which is still being realized. The *American English Google Books Corpus* exceeds *COHA* and other corpora with 155 billion words.[40]

For scholars interested in mapping later Modern English, especially for constructed dialogues, there are television and literary collections. The *Corpus of American Soap Operas* (*SOAP*) is useful for scrutinizing informal language and language variation in Present-Day English. *SOAP* "contains 100 million words of data from 22,000 transcripts from American soap operas from the early 2000s."[41] Literary genres such as African-American poetry, Canadian poetry, English drama, or versions of the English Bible appear in *Literature Online* (*LION*), the Chadwyck-Healey repository now owned by ProQuest. ProQuest produces a range of databases for further consultation (e.g., the previously mentioned *EEBO*) as well as an archive of historic English newspapers from the nineteenth to twenty-first centuries.

9.7. CORPUS LINGUISTICS AND BRIEF CORPUS SEARCHES AS EXERCISES

A methodology called corpus linguistics has emerged in order to help scholars search and construct electronic corpora. This system presents an intricate tool for analyzing data that has been structured and stored digitally. To create a corpus, content specialists work hand in hand with software engineers to sort linguistic forms and design a database. Algorithms allow identification and annotation of certain words or phrases: sentences may be parsed, parts of speech tagged, or contextual information inserted. Recent corpora like the *Old Bailey Corpus* have already done much of the work a scholar (trained in the complex methodology) would otherwise be obliged to conduct. It therefore behooves the individual researcher to choose a database on the basis of its annotations as well as its content. At that point, phrases and combinations of words can be searched or mapped in a corpus. When a search generates adequate results, analysis—aided by statistics as necessary—follows. Grammatical structures, usage, meaning, and discursive strategies may be evaluated according to historical-pragmatic principles.[42]

For a brief introduction to corpus linguistics, see the *COHA* website which features a five-minute tour of its corpus and web interface.[43] Because it demonstrates various ways of searching for and comparing linguistic forms, phrases, and other collocations, its guided searches may be followed in the classroom. Innovative instructors might experiment further with corpus studies in class.[44] Instructors could convene class in a computer lab to give students practice performing basic corpus searches.

9.8. CASE STUDIES

The standard textbooks on the history of the English language (e.g., Algeo 2009; Baugh and Cable 2012; Millward and Hayes 2011; van Gelderen 2014) do not treat historical pragmatics, though they may do so in future editions. The third revised edition of Brinton and Arnovick (2017) has enhanced its discussions of historical-pragmatic (and historical-sociolinguistic) insights, presenting numerous cases of historical-pragmatic change for instructors to sample.

1. *invited inferences*: the development of causal from temporal *since* or the use of *while* to mean 'although' instead of 'during'[45];

2. *social change*: the development of slang and in-group re-appropriation of deroga-tory or offensive terms like *girl, lady, gay*, and *half-breed* (88), the use of second-person pronouns in dialogues (e.g., trial transcripts, depositions, handbooks);

3. *politeness*: the absence of "positive" or "negative" face in OE, the emergence of *you* as a polite form and *thou* as a familiar form, change from the polite formula *pray/prithee* to *please* (90–91, 112–113), the change from *excuse me/pardon me/ forgive me* (which ask for the forgiveness, imposing on the hearer) to *sorry*, which is purely deferential;[46]

4. *discourse markers*: the use of OE *þa* 'then' to mark narrative climax, the use of ME *gan* 'began' to mark episodes, and of ModE *well* to indicate a "dispreferred response," the reduction of full imperative clauses to form discourse markers like *look*, as in *Look, I don't want any trouble*,[47] the changing pragmatic inference that promotes pragmatic markers like OE *hwæt* 'what' and comment clauses like ModE *I say* and *(as) you say*;

5. *grammaticalization*: the development of the *to* that marks the infinitive of the verb (e.g., *to eat*) from an OE full preposition that took a (verbal) noun object (77), the grammaticalization of a future marker in the construction *be going to* (as in *I am going to be rich someday*) which no longer carries any sense of direction or motion, the conversion of prepositions like *of* meaning 'off, from' into the possessive case markers, e.g., *the leg of the table*, the conversion of the adverbs *more* and *most* into degree markers, the conversion of the preposition *by* to mark the agent in a passive sentence, the appropriation of the OE demonstrative *that* as the definite article *the* and of the OE numeral *one* as the indefinite article *a/an*[48];

6. *figurative shifts*: a shift from concrete to abstract meaning, often from physical to mental, in metaphor, e.g., *translate* first meant 'to carry across', a shift from spa-tial to temporal meaning, as in *days gone by*, a shift from an internal psychological state to an external object evoking that state or vice versa, e.g., *dreadful* 'full of dread' (a subjective experience) comes to mean an objective situation 'causing dread or fear;' the death of metaphor or its becoming a denotation of a word, e.g., *mouth of the river*, synecdoche, metonymy, synesthesia.[49]

Let me now offer three in-depth examples of historical-pragmatic analysis.[50] Because of their significance as historical-pragmatic processes, "grammaticalization" accompanied by "subjectification" in the development of Modern English *shall* and *will* concern the first case study. The second, a look at the development of *Good-bye*, pursues a story of increased politeness while introducing another significant discur-sive process called "pragmaticalization." The third case, on directives in Old English, illustrates the range of insights which are possible from a series of synchronic surveys.

9.9. CASE STUDY: GRAMMATICALIZATION AND SUBJECTIFICATION OF *SHALL* AND *WILL*

Elizabeth Traugott's work on grammaticalization and its pragmatic-seman-tic motivation represents form-to-function mapping at its most productive.[51]

Grammaticalization is a morphological and syntactic process though which a word with a full lexical meaning becomes a lexically-empty grammatical marker.[52] The rise of the Present-Day English markers of future time, *shall* and *will*, from full lexical verbs (OE preterite-presents) represents a clear example. In Old English, *sculan* and *willan* possessed deontic (necessity-based) meaning (modality) as they signified obligation and intention, respectively. By the end of the Middle English period these forms conveyed, for the most part, predictions about the future based in belief (i.e., epistemic, possibility-based meaning). Their syntax was also altered as these full verbs became auxiliary verbs. Over time, through grammaticalization, the auxiliaries *shall* and *will* become temporal (i.e. grammatical) markers.[53]

While *shall* and *will* display a clear weakening and decrease of deontic meanings, their epistemic meanings strengthen and increase. As Traugott has established, the increase of epistemic meaning witnessed here is metonymic; increased epistemicity represents the increased coding of informativeness about the speakers's attitude toward the proposition. This increase proves consistent with subjectification. In fact, the effect of the semantic change underlying the development of these temporal markers is clearly pragmatic because, "there is strengthening of focus on knowledge . . . and belief."[54] Furthermore, the pragmatic factor is probably causal: "the principle of informativeness and relevance presumably drives speakers to attempt to be more and more specific through grammatical coding."[55] Subjectification, the movement exhibited here, favors an orientation internal to the speaker at the expense of an external orientation: "meanings become increasingly based in the speaker's subjective belief state, or attitude, toward what is said."[56]

9.10. CASE STUDY: *GOOD-BYE*

It has been argued that pragmatic markers develop through grammaticalization or a more specialized progress of "pragmaticalization."[57] What we observe in the history of *Good-bye* is a pragmatic movement, to which clear pragmatic motivations can be surmised. To ascertain the development of *Good-bye*, I surveyed all entries in the English Drama collection of the Chadwyck-Healey electronic database.[58]

The form is first found in Early Modern English as a blessing, *God be with you*. The phrase underwent contraction, becoming an unanalyzable single word: *god be wy you, god-b'w'y, godbwye, god buy'ye*. Further formal change occurs through analogy with forms such as *Good Day: good-b'wy, goodby*. Contemporary orthography yields Present-Day English *Good-bye*. Concurrent with formal change is a pragmatic shift. When *Good-bye* appears in dialogue dating from the late seventeenth century onward, a greeting close alone survives. However automatically it is said, *Good-bye* has affective value for the partners in the discourse. Because the conversational routine of closing represents a device for polite social interaction, saying *Good-bye* reduces the risk of face threat.

When the blessing is re-analyzed as a polite closing greeting, the religious institution of blessing is lost or "de-institutionalized." In the late nineteenth century, however, well after the formal and pragmatic transformation is complete, the original blessing reemerges in a fully analytic form. *God be with you* fails to work as a parting greeting in its resurrected state, behaving instead as any other independent blessing. When a present-day speaker intends to deliver a blessing on taking leave, a separate blessing must be added to mark that distinct illocutionary act:

> Closing Section:
> Explicit Blessing followed by Closing Sequence:
> A: Go with God.
> B: Thank you.
> A: Bye.
> B: Bye.

Overall, the derivation of *Good-bye* from *God be with you*, yielding a change in salutation act and form, can be seen to serve a pragmatic function. A process identified by Karin Aijmer may bring us closer to descriptive adequacy. She applies the term "pragmaticalization" to the diachronic derivation of pragmatic markers from lexical material.[59] Pragmaticized forms "involve the speaker's attitude to the hearer." Pragmaticalization, like grammaticalization, is associated with an apparent bleaching or loss of meaning in its initial stages, which on further inspection, can be seen to represent such pragmatic gains as the development of new pragmatic meanings and the strengthening of conversational implicatures.[60] Over time, pragmaticalization leads to the conventionalization of pragmatic meanings in these ways. In the case of *Good-bye*, increased organizational clarity can be supposed to motivate the pragmaticalization of *God be with you*.[61] Saying *Good-bye*, the speaker participates in the organization of the discourse and the closing of the conversation rather than participating in an earlier, ritualized event of blessing. Correspondingly, when the speaker does intend to deliver a blessing on parting, an explicit utterance emphasizes its declarative force. Pragmatic function is clarified as discursive and illocutionary function are distinguished through the use of distinct formal utterances.

9.11. CASE STUDY: DIRECTIVE SPEECH ACTS

An exercise in pragmaphilology can be seen in Thomas Kohnen's studies of performative or directive speech acts in Old English.[62] Kohnen surveyed "ask" and "order" verbs (e.g., *biddan* 'ask', 'beg', *halsian* 'implore', *(be)beodan* 'command', and *læran* 'instruct') in the *Helsinki Corpus* according to text type and function, comparing his data with the frequency of directives in Modern English. He observes that directive performatives were "much more frequent in Old English," than in Modern English where he finds "suggest" verbs (e.g., *suggest* and *recommend*), verbs that reflect "a clear tendency to avoid face-threatening performatives."[63] Kohnen concludes that Old English has "a significantly larger proportion of (apparently) face-threatening acts," because "ask" performatives, which appear in speech situations in which the addressor is subordinate to the addressee, and "order" verbs, in which the addressor is superordinate, are more common than in Modern English. With the "suggest" verbs apparent in Present-Day English, in contrast, the relative status of the inter-locutors appears to be equivalent. Thus today, in lieu of ordering someone to close the window, a speaker might ask if the hearer is able or willing to close it.[64] The difference between Old English and Present-Day English conversational strategies, as manifest in verb use, mirrors the strict maintenance of Anglo-Saxon social structure, in which rank and status is hierarchal.

By continuing to explore parallels among usage, politeness strategies, and society, Kohnen refined his hypotheses. He discovered that while hierarchal relationships seem to manifest themselves in speech acts that threaten face in Old English, explicit performatives and second-person imperatives (e.g., commands) nevertheless play a relatively small role in the language. More often, the early English tend to rely on first- and third-person modals to indicate common ground in the conversation. Similarly constructions like *(neod) þearf* 'it is necessary' (an impersonal) and *uton we* 'let's + infinitive' seemed to lessen the threat to face.[65] A nuanced image comes to light when additional data is taken into account.

9.12. EXERCISES FOR CLASSROOM USE

Within its broader mandate, Brinton's textbook on historical linguistics covers historical-pragmatic phenomena and research (e.g., inferential- and discourse-based approaches, grammaticalization, and lexicalization). Each chapter concludes with exercises that instructors can look at in class. Let me mention two from Brinton's own chapter on historical-pragmatic approaches to language change: (1) an exercise (using data she provides) for students to analyze the development of *after all*, and (2) an exercise asking students to analyze speech acts in a passage (printed in the textbook) from *Pride and Prejudice*.[66]

9.13. CONCLUSION

When we approach the language of the past from the vantage point of the present, we must proceed carefully and cautiously. Above all, we must proceed with humility. When I teach Old English, I remind my students that the pronunciation they learn is ultimately a scholarly reconstruction. Phonology is not my subject here, of course, but the reconstruction of Old English sounds affords a larger object lesson. Certainly there is good evidence for our historical reconstructions. Our linguistic description is based in knowledge of the larger phonological system (e.g., the vowel system of Germanic), in puns and rhyme, in poetry, in Anglo-Saxon orthography, in later pronunciation in the language (e.g., Middle English), and in the phonology of cognate languages (e.g., Old Icelandic). Still, it is possible that Caedmon or Cynewulf might cringe if a time machine transported either poet to Vancouver and he were to hear us read Old English out loud in my class. To urge humility in approaching language from the past in general, I relate an anecdote taken from David Macaulay's, *Motel of the Mysteries* (1979). In that illustrated children's book, archaeologists from the year

4022 discover a motel located in what was once Usa (USA), a country buried in detritus when a catastrophic event occurred in the twentieth century. Human remains are discovered in the motel room (with ensuite tub and toilet) they excavate, leading to an interpretation they find obvious, namely, that the room is one of many burial vaults belonging to a vast funerary complex on the site.[67] When the archaeologists unseal the "inner burial chamber" reachable from the main part of the "tomb," they find a "highly polished white sarcophagus" and a "Sacred Urn." Attached to the wall opposite the urn is a scroll of sacred parchment.[68] On top of the urn itself rests a hat and "Sacred Collar" which the celebrant wears when performing the ritual chant into the Sacred Urn during the final burial ceremony .[69] Lying on top of the urn, the paper strip used to secure the hat to the celebrant's head bears an inscription, the "atonal" pronunciation of which the archaeologists reconstruct as:

Sān-i-ti-zëd föřyō-ŭr p´-rŏt-ëcti-ŏñ.[70]

In the funny failure of Macaulay's archaeologists we find a pericope not only about humility but also about the obligations we face as historical linguists (and medievalists).

Historians of the English language must acknowledge an observer's paradox when we analyze the past. Attempts to examine historic language preserved in written form should begin with the recognitions that first of all, we may never hear with our ears what was actually said or written at the time. Second, what we see with our eyes we will inevitably misinterpret. Because we are not members of the culture or speakers of the language (stage) which produced these texts, our efforts are compromised. While we can never be certain about the language we reconstruct for earlier periods of English, we may indeed be more confident about our gains when we incorporate historical-pragmatic methods into our analyses.

CHAPTER 10

Using Principles of Construction Grammar in the History of English Classroom

GRAEME TROUSDALE

10.1. INTRODUCTION

Teaching a History of English Language (HEL) class is a daunting task, in terms of both the scope (what do you leave out?) and the method (what skills do you want your students to have at the end of the class?); it is further complicated by the fact that it sits at the intersection of a range of traditions (e.g., classical philological approaches, the literary connection, and developments in modern linguistics). In this chapter, I suggest some of the ways in which the principles and methods of construction grammar can help to elucidate some of the issues that students encounter when studying the history of the language. The approach is consistent with that of the historical linguist as a detective: how do we uncover the clues to the patterns and systems in the data that we observe at earlier stages of the language, and how do those patterns and systems change over time?

In order to do this, it is necessary to think about some of the principles of construction grammar (e.g., what is a construction?) and how these relate to (English) historical linguistics (e.g., how did that construction come into being? Why do speakers of English no longer use that construction?); in addition we need to consider the methods that can be used to uncover constructions in a language (e.g., the use of corpora, the relevance of etymological dictionaries, and the students' own experience of variation in their speech community). Some of these concerns are of course shared with other theoretical approaches to language structure and language change, but given the pedagogical focus of the volume, this chapter will not go into theory comparison. Instead, the focus is on laying out some of the ways in which work on construction grammar may be of relevance to the teaching of language change (especially with reference to English). This is contextualised within the framework of the

HEL classroom, so the chapter also provides some general suggestions for work that might be carried out by students.

The chapter is organised as follows. In section 10.2, I lay out some of the principles of construction grammar and make connections with diachronic linguistics. In 10.2.1 I briefly consider the relationship between idioms and constructions. Section 10.3 provides a brief discussion of how work on constructional change might fit into the broader remits of an HEL class. In Section 10.4, I focus on exploring concrete examples of constructional changes, with some discussion of collostructional analysis (10.4.1), change in lexical constructions using etymological dictionaries (10.4.2), and ways of thinking about grammatical change (10.4.3). Section 10.5 is the conclusion.

10.2. WHAT IS CONSTRUCTION GRAMMAR?

Various chapters of Hoffmann and Trousdale's *The Oxford Handbook of Construction Grammar* provide detailed summaries of various aspects of construction grammar.[1] In this model of knowledge of language:

- the construction (an entrenched, conventional association of form and meaning) is the basic unit of language, characterising both lexical and syntactic items;
- constructions are associated in a network: phonologically specified constructions inherit properties from more general schemas, while similarly behaving micro-constructions are associated via lateral, extension links;
- constructions do not involve derivation or transformation.

Goldberg recognises that constructions characterise linguistic items that vary in their degree of complexity and abstractness. At one end of the continuum are monomorphemic lexical items such as *car* and *speak*; at the other, abstract grammatical structures such as the English Passive, which associates a particular syntactic configuration $[NP_i \{BE/GET\} V_{PPart} (NP_j)]$ with a particular meaning, in which links exist between particular aspects of form and grammatical function/argument structure (e.g., NP_i in the English Passive constructions is associated with the grammatical role of Subject, and the thematic role of Patient). Between these two extremes are:

- morphologically complex forms, like the deverbal agent noun morphological construction, with the form [V.er], as in *player* and *singer*
- fixed idioms like *by and large* and phatic expressions like *How do you do?*
- schematic idioms like *pull* NP_i's *leg* 'tease SEM_i'
- snowclones[2] like XP *is the new* XP as in *grey is the new black,* or *Uber is the new Google.*

In all of these cases, there is a particular formal configuration that is conventionally associated with a given function, and most frequently a coded meaning.

By way of illustration of the network relation, Goldberg discusses the particular meanings associated with [P N]$_{pp}$ patterns in English. Typically, prepositions take NP complements, not just bare count nouns (e.g. *in the pub*, not **in pub*). However, there is a subset of PPs in which such [P NP] sequences are conventionally used by speakers of English. These include expressions like *in hospital*, *at* work, and *in prison*. In such cases, the meaning of the [P N]$_{pp}$ sequence concerns some sort of salient activity associated with the referent of the noun, e.g. in the case of *hospital*, the activity is the treatment of those who are ill. This explains the difference in meaning between (1) and (2):

(1)   The doctor is in the hospital

(2)   The doctor is in hospital

In (1), the doctor could either be working or be undergoing treatment, with the wider discourse context presumably supplying the most likely interpretation; in (2), only the "treatment" interpretation is possible. Thus the [P N]$_{pp}$ sequence inherits certain properties from the more general PP construction in English (e.g., that the adposition precedes the noun) but must be specified as a separate construction because of its specific meaning.

10.2.1. Idioms and Constructions

The [P N]$_{pp}$ sequence described previously is a useful example to illustrate some of the ways in which idioms and constructions are related to one another. Indeed, the problem of the correct analysis of idioms was fundamental to the development of construction grammar as a linguistic theory.[3]

In many cases, idioms can be characterised as syntactic sequences that are conventionally associated with a particular semantic meaning, or pragmatic function.[4] In some cases, it is possible to see a link between the meaning of an idiom and the lexical semantics of a monomorphemic word (e.g., between *saw logs* and *sleep*, and *kick the bucket* and *die*). In other cases, the idiomatic expressions appear to have a more grammatical function. For instance, the expression *be on the verge of* Ving has a meaning associated with imminent futurity; the expression *as long as* serves as a conditional perfective in utterances such as *I'll go as long as you promise to come with me*. Idiomatic expressions can thus have a grammatical and a lexical function, and one aspect of (diachronic) construction grammar is to attempt to see how these grammatical and lexical constructions come into being.

10.2.2. Changing Constructions

As conventional pairings of form and meaning, both "sides" of a construction are subject to change. For example, lexical constructions may undergo formal phonological changes with no change in conventional meaning (e.g., OE *hring* > ModE *ring*);

conversely, forms may remain constant while undergoing semantic change (ModE *hot* 'at an elevated temperature' > 'trendy'). The application of this to syntactic constructions is more complex, but nevertheless there is evidence of similar patterns. For example, Colleman and De Clerck demonstrated that in Late Modern English, the Double Object construction (e.g., *John baked Sarah a cake*) underwent semantic specialisation, in that certain subgroups of verbs are no longer licensed.[5] Verbs of banishment, like *forbid*, are attested in earlier stages of English (see example 3) but this is no longer possible in the contemporary language.

(3)   I therefore for the present dismiss'd him the Quarter deck

          (1771, Cook, *Journal*)[6]

The important issue here is that this is a change affecting the more general schema, and it underscores the idea that words and argument structure constructions can undergo similar kinds of meaning change.

In the cases of *ring, hot*, and the Double Object construction, the focus is on changes to constructions that are already part of the system of English (i.e., to established constructions). But another important area of enquiry in English historical linguistics is the coming into being of new constructions. For instance, *all*-cleft constructions (e.g., *all I did was call her the wrong name*) are not attested in the Old or Middle English periods but come to be established in the modern period.[7] Much work in diachronic construction grammar is concerned with how new constructions emerge, and how this relates to mechanisms of change such as reanalysis and analogy, and more general processes such as grammaticalization.

10.3. PLANNING A CURRICULUM

It is unlikely that a constructional approach would be appropriate for an entire history of English course. One of the reasons for this relates to one of the issues mentioned earlier, namely, that construction grammar has had little to say about phonology, and phonological changes are typically central in a history of English class. There are other areas of enquiry which do not immediately lend themselves to a constructional analysis (or indeed to any formal linguistic analysis), such as the use of different writing systems, or the influence of various "external" factors, like the changing status of English in relation to French following the ascension of William I, or the effects of the printing press on the standardisation of English spelling. It would be difficult, therefore, to give a comprehensive account of the evolution of English simply using construction grammar alone.

However, many courses on the history of English touch on the following areas of enquiry, all of which are amenable to a constructional analysis:

• comparative reconstruction. Usually reconstruction is associated with establishing properties of earlier lexical, morphological or phonological systems, but

recent research in diachronic construction grammar has illustrated how constructions may be helpful in syntactic comparative reconstruction.[8]

- semantic change. As noted previously, some work on the diachrony of argument
  structure constructions has illustrated ways in which the kinds of changes associated with the meanings of words may be applicable to other kinds of constructions, including clause types.
- syntactic change. A number of studies which have drawn on principles of construction grammar have elucidated particular changes in English syntax.[9]
- cross-componential changes, such as grammaticalization, lexicalization, and
  degrammaticalization. Some work in diachronic construction grammar has
  attempted to account for similarities and differences between these processes.[10]
- the spread of English as a global language. Some recent work in construction
  grammar has explored the way in which synchronic variation may be a reflection of diachronic processes involved in the establishment of new varieties of
  English.[11]

Thus it would be possible to conceive of a course entitled "Constructional approaches
to the history of English," and such a course could involve the development of particular transferrable skills, including the processing and quantificational analysis of
large data sets. The focus, however, would be on the non-phonological history of
the language, and would have less to say about the contextual and external factors
that have had a role to play in the shaping of English over time. As a result, in my
own practice, I have found it more useful to make reference to constructions and
construction grammar as a way of unifying what may appear to be rather disparate
changes, as will be explored in section 4, "Using Construction Grammar in Teaching
the History of English."

A final point to bear in mind is that while it is possible to make use of construction grammar in order to explain patterns of change in English, the reverse is also
true. In other words, it can also be illuminating to draw on data from the history of
English to explain properties of constructions and how they relate to one another.

10.4. USING CONSTRUCTION GRAMMAR IN TEACHING THE HISTORY OF ENGLISH

10.4.1. Collostructions

There are a number of different ways in which historical linguists have made use
of construction grammar in particular, and usage-based frameworks in general. For
example, quantitative approaches to corpus data have shone a light on how particular constructional patterns have changed over time.[12] Martin Hilpert, for example,
looks at what nouns typically appear in the frame *many a noun* in the late Modern
English period.[13] This is clearly a construction in the Goldberg sense of the term,
given the mismatch between form and meaning ([many a N_i] ↔ ['many instances of
SEM_i']). Hilpert carries out a diachronic collostructional analysis of the pattern, in
order to establish whether there are changes to the kind of noun that fills the N slot

in the construction over time.[14] This enables the researcher to uncover particular patterns of meaning change. Using the COHA corpus, Hilpert first identified which were the most typical collocates per subperiod (from 1810–2000), and then considered whether changes to the collocational patterns may have some semantic motivation. Hilpert's findings show that in the first period (1820–1860), nouns that "relate to the domain of human emotion"[15] are the distinctive collexemes; subsequently, nouns denoting periods of time (*day*, *hour*), then human beings (*citizen*, *reader*) come to be preferred. Overall, the construction becomes less frequent over time. Hilpert also observes a stylistic shift in the period, from literary texts to newspaper and other journalistic writing.[16]

While research of this kind does not focus on large-scale changes in the history of English, it nevertheless reveals interesting relationships between words and the constructions in which they appear, and how this may change over time. It is also extendable to other constructions, including grammatical constructions.[17] Students who are familiar with linguistic corpora could use this method to explore other possible collostructional changes (e.g. between *be-* and *get*-passives).

10.4.2. Lexical Changes

My experience of teaching HEL classes has suggested that one thing that students find accessible and intuitive is exploring the ways in which words whose meanings used to be transparent come over time to lose that transparency. (An example of such a change is the history of the word *nickname* < *eke-name* 'additional name', with the initial consonant supplied by a reanalysis of the sequence with the indefinite article, i.e., *an eke-name*.) Investigating the history of words is fairly accessible and engaging and can also be used to demonstrate some of the ideas inherent in constructional approaches to language. Here I outline a technique to show how atomic constructions (i.e., form-meaning pairings which cannot be further analysed into meaningful subcomponents) can develop from complex ones.

One approach for this is to begin with sets of words that used to be compounds but have over time become monomorphemic. Traugott and Trousdale provide some examples of words which have shown a decrease in analysability from the Old English (OE) period onwards.[18] These include *daisy* (< OE *dægesege* 'day's eye'), *nostril* (OE *nosþyrl* 'nose opening'), and *barn* (OE *bere-ern* 'barley place'). In addition to reinforcing understanding about general linguistic issues (the differences between compound, complex, and simplex lexical items), it encourages students to think about reanalysis and analyzability. Furthermore, these examples allow students to think about whether form change and meaning change are related. In the case of *daisy*, the metonymic associations are clear for the OE form but are not recoverable for the Modern English form, so that the formal reanalysis precludes a metonymic interpretation.

The second stage is to introduce examples which are partly analysable—where one part of the word is still recognisable but the other part is obsolete or restricted diatopically or in some other way. Traugott and Trousdale provide examples such as *werewolf* (< OE *werewulf*, lit. 'man-wolf'), *bonfire* (< ME *bonefire*, lit. 'fire of bones') and *cobweb* (< ME *coppeweb*, lit. 'spider-web').[19] These cases are complex for a number of reasons. For example, on a more general level, they show how analysability is a gradient phenomenon. Unlike examples like *daisy* and *barn*, it is clear that with these examples, contemporary speakers will be able to associate the second part of the word with an extant lexeme but are unlikely to be able to do so for the first part of the word.

The final stage is to introduce examples which suggest that a historical pattern of word-formation (however weakly entrenched) has fallen into disuse. A possible case study from Traugott and Trousdale concerns the development of the earlier suffixes Old English-*lian*/Middle English -*le*, which have become reanalysed as part of verb stems, rather than as suffixes.[20] Examples include OE *handlian* 'touch repeatedly' > *handle, twinclian* 'shine intermittently' > *twinkle*, and *nestlian* 'make a nest' > *nestle* (178). In this set, we have clearly historically morphologically related items (cf. the *barn/werewolf* sets earlier) which are now no longer seen to be related to one another.

By using different sets of examples in this way, it is possible to demonstrate some important aspects about the nature of lexical change. For instance, we can use this data to show to students how the loss of a morphological boundary over time may have phonological reduction effects, and that that this combination of formal changes means that a previously analysable sequence is no longer transparent to the modern language user. This loss of transparency on the formal side is related to increased opaqueness in terms of the meanings of certain expressions. This can sometimes result in particular kinds of semantic change (e.g., loss of figuration in the case of *daisy*, generalisation in the case of *barn*, since barns are no longer expressly used to store barley). In addition, by using sets of examples that are "graded" in their degree of analysability, it is possible to show how these processes are not an all-or-nothing affair but rather show degrees of opaqueness in meaning change. Finally, by including an earlier morphological pattern in the set, it is possible to show how this kind of change does not only affect random lexical items but may also apply to morphological subpatterns in the language.

In addition, these data sets illustrate something about the nature of constructions in language, and of constructional change. The focus is on change in both the form and meaning poles of a sign (or in the case of the third data set mentioned previously, a set of signs, or a schema) and demonstrates one particular kind of lexicalization pattern that is relevant to diachronic construction morphology. Such data also underscore the difference between constructions of different degrees of complexity (i.e., between atomic and complex constructions) and the relationship between micro-constructions that are more specified phonologically and the abstract schemas that sanction them.

Thus a study of lexical changes of the kind outlined in this section reveals some of the ways in which work on the history of English can inform our understanding of the shape of constructions as they change, and vice versa. The next section extends this discussion to the development of grammatical constructions.

10.4.3. Grammatical Changes

The study of grammatical changes often proves more conceptually difficult for students than changes in the lexicon. Nevertheless, it is possible to introduce some basic ideas in the area of constructional change, depending on the degree of complexity the instructor wishes to introduce. I consider three possible topics here, and relate these to issues in diachronic construction grammar. The first strikes me as feasible for beginning students, while the second and third are topics which perhaps are more suited to advanced students.

The first topic concerns changes in word class.[21] Denison's recent research has shown a number of instances in which, in the recent history of English, nouns appear to have been recategorised as adjectives. Examples include common nouns like *fun*, *key, genius*, and *pants*, as well as proper nouns, as illustrated by examples (4) and (5):

(4)   she insisted on sharing with me, which was so pants (Jilly Cooper, *Wicked!*, 2006)

(5)   A 'very London' response to Leytonstone Tube terror attack (*The Telegraph*, 6 December 2015)

Examples such as these allow students to consider issues such as grammaticality and how this relates to change, as well as developing an understanding of the properties of word classes. From a constructional perspective, it can also shed light on the nature of underspecification in categorisation. This relates to a debate about the proper treatment of linguistic primitives.[22]

The second topic concerns changes in information structuring constructions. It builds on the issues of grammaticality associated with word classes (as earlier) but extends this to the issue of syntactic structures. The pattern here has to do with copula reduplication and is exemplified by example (6):

(6)   the problem is is that it takes a while to change the fleet (COCA)

Perhaps paradoxically, a good way in to this from a diachronic perspective is to think about it purely synchronically, by encouraging the students to explore the question as to whether this reduplication of *is* is a disfluency or a productive pattern in the contemporary language; in other words, the exercise could begin with introspection and an exploration of the students' views on grammaticality before corpus data is explored. Anne Curzan provides a useful data set which could be used as part of such an exercise, demonstrating which constructions are more established as "hosts" for the reduplicative copula, and which constructions are relative newcomers (based on frequency in the COCA corpus).[23] As Curzan has shown, there is evidence from corpus data that some constructions (e.g., *wh*-pseudoclefts) more frequently serve as hosts for the reduplicative copula than others (e.g., declarative clauses with a simple NP subject). In particular, research has sought to establish what links might be involved between the development of this construction and the development of pseudocleft constructions more generally, especially in terms of cleft constructions as discourse management devices.[24] Thus, a particularly important aspect of this is the relationship between syntactic structure and information structure, and how this might be expressed in constructional terms: it is clear that there is an association between the formal properties of the construction and its discourse function. Using this data to explore how construction grammar could be used as a tool for accounting for the variation and the changing associations between form and function would be a challenging but insightful exercise. It also allows students to think about change as "on-going," and helps to show the links between earlier stages of the language and the ways in which English is developing today.

The last example concerns changes to the transitive construction in the history of the language. Trousdale considers the loss of impersonal constructions like (7) in the history of English[25]:

(7) Him   ofhreow   þæs   mannes
     3SM.dat   pity-1/3S.past   def.s.gen   man.s.gen
     'He pitied the man'

The argument proposed is that the impersonal construction is a subtype of the English Transitive construction, and has a number of subconstructional variants (e.g. those where the Source is coded as genitive and the Experiencer as dative, vs. those where the Source is nominative and the Experiencer dative). Different verbs could appear in the different subconstructions: some verbs (like *sceamian* 'be ashamed') could appear in more than one type, and different verbs persist in impersonal-type patterns for longer than others. For instance, even as late as the sixteenth century, *like* could appear with a source subject and an experiencer object, as shown in (8):

(8) the lykor liked them so well that they had pot vpon pot
     (1567 Hartman [HC cefict1a])[26]

This gradual loss of a constructional schema is related to other changes in the history of English, such as the reduction in case marking of verbal arguments and the increased obligatoriness of a morphosyntactic subject in a finite clause. One possible study to explore this in more depth would be to carry out a collostructional analysis of verbs in OE and ME corpora, to see which verbs were most strongly attracted to the Impersonal construction in the OE period, and to see how this changes over time. This would be more appropriate as a dissertation topic, given the necessary research involved.

10.5. CONCLUSIONS

This brief account of some aspects of construction grammar and its application to the history of English has attempted to show ways in which changes in the grammar of English (including aspects of morphology) can be explained using some of the features of constructional approaches to language. Any HEL course which was based entirely around constructions would be able to provide only a limited account of the development of the language, for reasons stated previously, but this is true of all linguistic theories. One potential benefit of exploring aspects of the history of English from the construction grammar perspective is that this can help to explain recurrent patterns across a number of subareas of the grammar, from the loss of transparency in compounds to the loss of argument structure constructions. Another area of interest is in the interface between corpus linguistics and historical linguistics: much work in diachronic construction grammar is also concerned with the changes in frequency of a given construction, and this is best investigated using large computerised corpora. Finally, construction grammar has also been concerned with sociolinguistic variation,[27] and therefore with on-going changes in a language. Exploring students' own perceptions of grammaticality and acceptability of particular constructional patterns can give an insight into how the grammar of English continues to evolve, especially when this complements a more robust corpus-based approach.

CHAPTER 11
Addressing "Emergence" in a HEL Classroom

WILLIAM A. KRETZSCHMAR, JR.

"Emergence" is a word from the study of complex systems, a relatively new kind of science currently useful in physics, genetics, evolutionary biology, and economics, but also a perfect fit for the humanities. The science of complexity describes how massive numbers of random interactions can give rise to order, regularities that "emerge" from the interactions without specific causes. I have previously made the case that human speech is a complex system:[1] massive numbers of interactions between speakers give rise to patterns in language and the emergence of regularities that we perceive in language use around us. In this chapter, I want to discuss how to present emergence as a continual theme in English. Emergence offers us a new option for presentation of the story of the language, one centered on the continual emergence and re-emergence of patterns of lexical, phonological, and grammatical forms of English out of the interaction of its speakers and the contingencies of their history. As will become clear, this marks a major change in how we understand the history of the English language, and following from that, how we might teach it.

The History of the English Language (HEL) is a venerable course in the English curriculum. All major universities in Britain and America (by this term I mean North America, and so include Canada) teach a HEL course, and many other universities worldwide teach general courses on the English language, most of which include an introductory and a historical component. The introductory part of the course trains students to use the technical terms of linguistics, like the International Phonetic Alphabet (IPA) for phonetics, and emic words like phoneme and morpheme for more advanced elements in the linguistic hierarchy. The traditional organizational pattern of the historical part of the course covers periods in HEL from Indo-European up to the present day. These courses are typically meant for undergraduates who lack training in English-language studies, often the early university student with minimal prior training in linguistics. In my state, and in many other states across America, the HEL course or one of its alternatives like "Structure of English"—such courses all teach about the same thing—are required for Education students who want to teach Language Arts in primary and secondary schools. The idea of the requirement is that students will learn about Standard English, the kind of English that American schools must teach, and a historical treatment will justify the status of Standard English for the students. Of course, in many English Departments the HEL course is taught by medievalists who never get past Chaucer and the Great Vowel Shift and so do not offer comprehensive coverage of world and modern English. Thus, HEL can be an unpopular course, either because it is a requirement or because it does not quite accomplish all of its goals. On the other hand, the HEL course has a perennial attraction for students who want to know more about their language. In the version of it I taught recently, I had students not just from English and from Education but from five different colleges across the university.

The traditional pattern of the HEL course divides the subject matter into two parts, the internal history of the language and the external history of the language. External history is cultural history, who did what to whom over the centuries, like the coming of Germanic mercenaries to defend the Romanized British population of Britain but who instead defeated them and established England (to them "Angleland," or land of the Angles, one of the Germanic ethnic groups). HEL external history also talks about the Norman invasion by William the Conqueror, whose people historically had been Vikings but who brought the Norman French language to Britain. HEL teachers have recognized that this kind of external history somehow changes the language, but they have not often been able to say exactly *how* events changed the language. Still, HEL students must hear about such history, to the extent that students sometimes wonder whether they are taking an English history class instead of history of the language.

The other part of HEL, internal history, is just about the language itself, not events affecting the population of speakers. The idea that a language can have an internal history arose in the nineteenth century, as the modern science of linguistics was developed out of earlier, more spiritual notions. As the apostle John writes, "In the beginning was the Word" and later "the Word became flesh." The power of words also used to be part of speculations about Egyptian hieroglyphs, and it appears prominently in the practice of magicians, as recently in the Harry Potter books and movies, and even more recently in the popular Lev Grossman novels and the current TV series based on them, aptly called "The Magicians." In magic words have the power to accomplish physical actions. Harry Potter used Latinate words that had the power to light things or to move things or, in the worst case, to kill people with the "Avada Kedavra" curse, which is also a play on the words of the traditional magical incantation "Abracadabra" with the modern word *cadaver*. Lev Grossman talks about magicians intoning complex spells in ancient languages like Old Church Slavonic. But the nineteenth-century Neogrammarians, as they called themselves, changed all that. They were interested in sound changes which, the Neogrammarians argued, took place mechanically in languages, without exceptions. Their classic theories of comparative and historical linguistics led to the creation of the Indo-European family tree of languages, where all the branches of the tree can be described in terms of such regular sound changes (Figure 11.1).

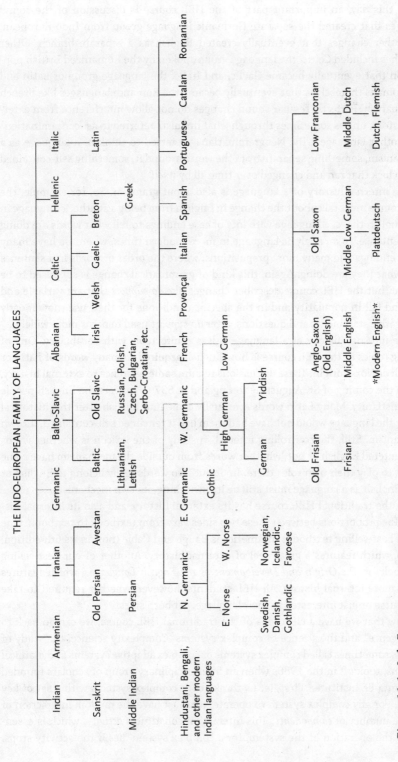

Figure 11.1. Indo-European stemma
(adapted from http://www.linguatics.com/indoeuropean_languages.htm)

To this day, an important part of the HEL course is discussion of the sound changes that created the separate Germanic language group from Indo-European, and other changes that eventually created English as a separate branch. Other branches included Celtic, the language group spoken by the Romanized British population that eventually became Gaelic, and Italic, the language group of Latin and the Romans themselves that eventually became the Romance languages like French and Spanish. Perfectly regular sound changes do not allow interference from external history, unless sometimes through what linguists referred to as "contamination" from other languages. The Neogrammarians preferred to think of a language as a mechanism, something separate from the world around it, something self-contained like a clock that ran and changed over time all by itself.

The internal history of a language is also about grammar. So, for example, the HEL course must talk about the change in English from being a synthetic language in Old English times, a language with lots of case endings to tell what words are doing in a sentence, to an analytic language in more modern times, where we have many fewer endings and many more prepositions, where the order of words in a sentence tells what they are doing. Again, this kind of grammatical change is supposed to be regular, but the HEL course describes changes like *do-support* that are variable and rise and fall in popularity and in the specific conditions for their use (now mostly in negative statements and questions, after *do-support* used to occur more widely).

The internal history of a language is less comfortable with vocabulary. One of the big topics in the HEL course is how English acquired so many words of Latin or French or Norse origin. These discussions require some reference to external history, say to the coming of St. Augustine to England in 597 to convert the English people to Christianity. Many Latin words eventually came into English after this historical event: the language would not have had them had it remained self-contained, its own mechanism. Still, the controlling interest in study of the lexicon is whether words have entered English or not, whether words from outside the mechanism have come into it to play their own roles there. In or out? Do words really belong to English or not? English as a language must still be its own thing, its own mechanism.

So, the traditional HEL course has its external history, and also its internal history. The proportions between these two sides vary from textbook to textbook. One of the best-selling textbooks in America is Baugh and Cable (now in its 6th edition, 2012), which features a great deal of external history. Another of our best-selling textbooks is *The Origin and Development of the English Language*,[2] which features much more internal history. All HEL students, however, whether required to take the course or just interested in their language, get both sides.

Now that we have a clear idea of the traditional HEL course, we can go back to "emergence" and the science of complex systems. Complexity science, the study of what is sometimes called complex systems or complex adaptive systems or dynamical systems, took off in the 1980s when an interdisciplinary group of scholars founded the Santa Fe Institute.[3] First, let us think about complex systems with a set of key terms. For any complex system to operate, we must have the random interaction of a large number of *components*. This interaction constitutes *activity*, which is essential to the operation of the system, for a complex system dies if the activity stops.

As the interactions continue the components affect each other in what might be called an *exchange* of information, which leads to *reinforcement* of behaviors among the components, and thus to the *emergence* of stable patterns in the complex system, all without any central control. What do these stable patterns look like? Really, any number of things. The human body is a complex system, with many subsystems, like your immune system, that are also complex systems in themselves. An ant colony or a beehive is also a complex system in how the insects behave. The ecology of a forest or wetland is a complex system, also with many interrelated subsystems. Our economic markets are also complex systems, whether we are talking about the national market or any local market. For each one of these examples, you can imagine what the components, activity, exchange, reinforcement, and emergence might be. For speech, the randomly interacting "components" in the complex system are all of the possible variant realizations of linguistic features as they are deployed by human agents, us speakers. The activity in the system consists of all of our writing and conversations. The exchange of information is not the same as sharing the meaningful content of what we say and write (which is exchange in a different sense), but instead the implicit comparison of the use of different components by different speakers and writers, in different situations. So, we notice if somebody says *you guys* or *y'all* or just *you* for the second-person plural pronoun. Feedback from exchange of information causes reinforcement, so speakers and writers are more likely to use particular components in future occurrences of particular circumstances for speech—say, to be more likely to say *you guys* or *y'all* or *you*. Human agents can think about and choose what linguistic variants to use, but that does not change the fact that we make choices in relation to the system. The order that emerges in speech is simply the configuration of components, whether words, pronunciations, or grammatical constructions, that come to occur in all of the circumstances in which we actually communicate. The process operating in complex systems just explains better what we already knew: we tend to talk like the people nearby, either physically or socially near, and we tend to use the same linguistic tools that others do when we are writing or saying the same kind of thing. We know, for example, when to use *you guys* or *y'all* or *you*. Language change in HEL, then, is the result of the ongoing process. All living languages continue to change in response to changing conditions. When we talk about emergence in the HEL course, then, we should be talking about the historical process.

This is not what HEL instructors have been doing. James Milroy has argued persuasively that our common practice as historians of the language funnels historically varied sources of English into the unified, monolithic language we so often describe today.[4] Milroy did not say so, but we can identify this modern language as Standard English, the language that the schools are teaching and that state and national exams are testing. When HEL instructors funnel their discussion toward the school Standard, we get the historical process exactly backward. We might rather consider that the natural tendency of a language, as of many another aspect of the natural world, is to become more diverse, and as we shall see, that is what complex systems predict. Milroy has suggested that we ought to be more interested in the maintenance of features in the language, since maintenance runs counter to such a tendency for diversification, and he has further suggested that we need to look at social factors as the mechanism that can encourage maintenance of features in the language. Milroy is thus asking us to put the external history of the language more fully in play, so that we can connect social factors to language. An awareness of complex systems, too, suggests that we should do so. Any complex system must account for *contingency*, another key term: a good example is what happened to world ecology when that huge asteroid struck earth, and mammals outsurvived the dinosaurs. Or, what happens when an infectious agent enters your body and your immune system changes in order to fight it (and leaves antibodies behind in case the same infection should come again). So, for the HEL course, if we only look forward to those elements that appear in modern Standard English, we are missing out on the process of change that adapts the language to all of the contingencies from external history of the speakers of the language.

Let us continue by looking more closely at the complex system of speech. Table 11.1 shows the thirty most common terms for that most iconic of American dialect terms, *dragonfly*, as they were collected from the 1,162 speakers in the Linguistic Atlas Project survey of speech in the Eastern States (the Linguistic Atlas of the Middle and South Atlantic States).[5] There are many more terms for the same thing than we would ever have believed. For *dragonfly*, there are 119. Seven different terms occurred more than 100 times each in the survey.

Table 11.2 shows the rest of the list. Eighty-three of the 119 different terms only occurred once or twice. Even if we take out things that we think may be mistakes or simple morphological variants, we still have a huge number of different terms. And this degree of diversity in expression is not limited to dragonflies: we see it for every item in the lexicon we survey. Variation is the norm in language, not the more limited set of forms that we assume people use in correct Standard English. If you thought *dragonfly* was the right word for the insect, now you know that it is normal for people to call it by many names.

Again, this is not what the language looks like in the HEL course. The focus on vocabulary there is about loan words, about when words from Latin or French or Norse came into English. The textbooks never talk about all the different ways to say the same thing. English is massively redundant in how we can use words to achieve our meaning. Our HEL course just picks out one way to look at the language, what nineteenth-century linguists would call "contamination" of English from other languages. Our HEL students should know that there have always been rich resources in the language for expression of even common concepts; we have never all agreed to call one thing by a single name, not the dragonfly or anything else, either. A good question, not now asked in HEL courses, is how many different ways we can talk about the same thing at any given time, in any given place. So, for example, if we notice how many names for God occur in *Caedmon's Hymn*, or how many words for a soldier occur in *Beowulf*, we might not attribute them just to the poet's creativity but say that they illustrate the richness of the Old English vocabulary.

If we look at all the *dragonfly* data from a complexity perspective, we not only see variation, we also see that the variation is patterned in two different ways, in a particular frequency profile and with scaling of that profile in every size group and

Table 11.1: THIRTY MOST COMMON TERMS FOR *DRAGONFLY* IN LAMSAS

Variant Term	Count
snake doctor	536
snake feeder	413
mosquito hawk	360
darning needle	294
dragonfly	196
skeeter hawk	175
devil's darning needle	158
mosquito hawks	89
snake doctors	77
dragonflies	42
snake feeders	35
darning needles	28
spindle	23
snake waiter	19
skeeter hawks	17
devil's darning needles	14
devil's horse	13
mosquito	12
devil's riding horse	8
mosquitoes	8
devil horse	6
devil's needle	6
snake servant	6
skeeters	5
gnat hawk	4
gnats	4
june bug	4
mosquitos	4
needle	4
snake flies	4

subgroup we look at. When all the variant types of a linguistic feature are graphed according to their token frequency, the chart will have a small number of highly frequent responses and a much larger number of less frequently occurring responses. We call this an A-curve, short for asymptotic hyperbolic curve. Figure 11.2 shows the A-curve for the *dragonfly* responses.

The distributions in our Atlas data always have this shape. Just to prove that it is not just a chart from *dragonfly*, Figure 11.3 shows the A-curve for all of the different realizations of the [æ] vowel in the word *half*, as elicited in the Eastern

Table 11.2: REMAINING EIGHTY-NINE TERMS FOR *DRAGONFLY* IN LAMSAS

Variant Term	Count
snake guarder	4
snake master	4
snake spindle	4
galli nipper	3
girl nipper	3
skeeter	3
bottlefly	2
busy bug	2
darning bug	2
darning fly	2
devil riding horse	2
devil's bug	2
devils' horse	2
devil's horses	2
devil's knitting needle	2
devil's needles	2
donnel feathers	2
dragon fly	2
drum hawk	2
galley nipper	2
galli nippers	2
gally nippers	2
gnat bug	2
gnat catchers	2
jar fly	2
johnny crowhorse	2
knit needle	2
needles	2
partridge	2
praying mantis	2
saltpeter fly	2
snake bugs	2
snake charmer	2
snake cure	2
snake doctor fly	2
snake eaters	2
snake feed	2
snake fly	2
snake leaders	2
snake peters	2

Variant Term	Count
snake skeeter	2
snake weeder	2
snake worm	2
stinging bee	2
bedbug	1
big mosquito	1
big mosquitoes	1
bull bats	1
bull haver	1
chulabama	1
covered up her ears	1
dobson fly	1
dragon flies	1
flea	1
flies	1
gadfly	1
gally nipper	1
girlie nipper	1
girlie nippers	1
granddaddies	1
guinea fowl	1
harmony birds	1
humming bird	1
humming birds	1
July flies	1
July fly	1
june bugs	1
katydid	1
locust	1
mosquito hood	1
niggers	1
niggers call them	1
quail	1
sand flies	1
sand fly gnat	1
schlange geeder	1
schlange heeder	1
sew up your ears	1
sew up your eyes	1

(continued)

Variant Term	Count
shite poke	1
sing-gaily	1
snake tender	1
snake tenders	1
snake waiters	1
spider	1
spidle	1
spinners	1
they catch skeeter	1
yard flies	1

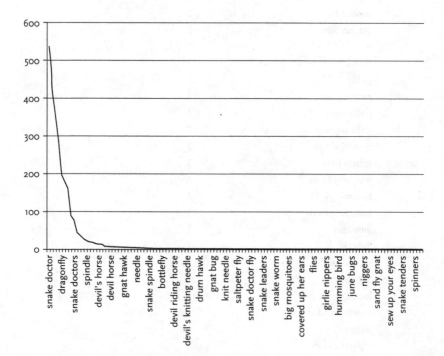

Figure 11.2. A-curve of *dragonfly* responses

States: thirty-four different ways to represent the pronunciation of the vowel in *half* in the IPA transcriptions used for the Atlas.

The best way to think of this is with a term taken from economics, the so-called 80/20 Rule, which expresses the fact that 80% of the wealth in many societies is owned by about 20% of the people, although sometimes the actual proportions

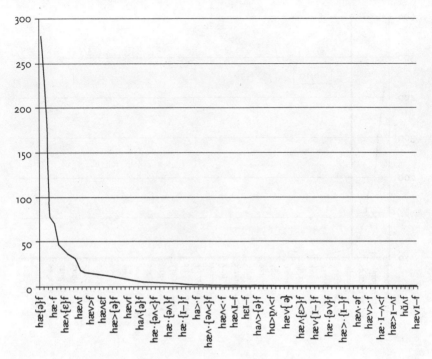

Figure 11.3. Realizations of the vowel in *half*, all LAMSAS speakers

might be 90/10 or 70/30. In Figure 11.4, we see that the top twelve terms for *drag-onfly*, about 10% of the 119 variants, account for 89% of all the responses to the question.

Finally, we observe that this distributional pattern scales to different levels of analysis. In Figure 11.3 we saw the A-curve for *half* for the whole Eastern States survey, and in Figure 11.5, using the same data, we see the same curve for just the women on the left and just the most educated speakers on the right. The shape appears clearly in each graph, overall and in both subsamples—and in every subsample in survey data. To take the point a bit further, Figure 11.6 shows the different pronunciations of the /i/ vowel in the word *three* for twelve different subsamples of our LAMSAS survey.

The A-curve is obviously present for all the groups until you get to the smallest groups at the right side. Even there, for very small groups of speakers, we still see a version of the A-curve, now a bit sketchy and abstract but still with one or two forms that occurred more often than other forms that occurred less. So, we see the A-curve in every group, and we see it more clearly in groups that have at least, say, 100 people in them.

The reason that it is important to look at all the different groups, even knowing that they will have the same distributional pattern, is that they do not have their entries in the same order. Table 11.3 shows a set of charts for the top variants of what term you might use for a heavy rainstorm, also from LAMSAS, in six categories.

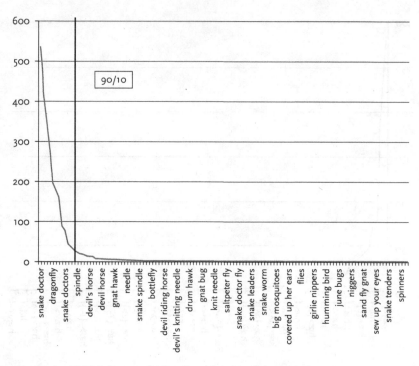

Figure 11.4. 80/20 Rule as applied to *dragonfly* terms (here, 90/10)

Each of these categories would have the A-curve if plotted, but the thing to see here is that each category has roughly the same set of terms but no two categories share the same order of terms. So, when we look at the whole set of speakers at the top left, we see that the top four terms are "cloudburst," "downpour," "heavy rain," and "hard rain." The older speakers at bottom right have the same terms but the order changes to "cloudburst," "heavy rain," "downpour," and "hard rain." Women have the same terms, but change the order to "downpour," "cloudburst," "hard rain," and "heavy rain." These differences in order, really differences in frequencies of terms as they are used in the different groups, are how we perceive that different groups of people talk differently. It is not that women use words that men do not use, or Southerners use words that Northerners do not use—common words unique to a single place or group are quite rare—but rather that women and men use the same words but at different frequencies, and Southerners and Northerners use the same words but at different frequencies. The scaling property of the complex system of speech accounts for our perception that there are regional and social dialects.

So, this is the order that emerges from massive numbers of random interactions among the components in the complex system of speech, rather than from a simple cause or a set of rules or any controlling agent. What comes out of the process of the complex system is not the grammar that we usually talk about, but instead a series of frequency patterns. Grammar comes from our perception of these regularities in frequency in language, not from any inborn or learned set of rules.[6] The emergent

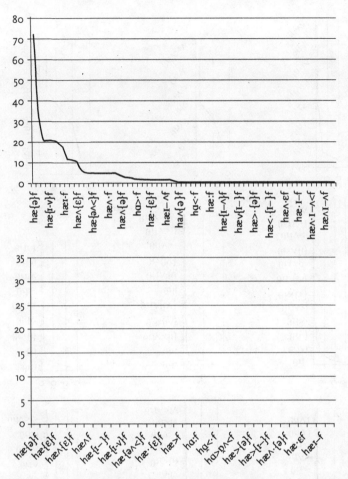

Figure 11.5. A-curve for the vowel in *half* for just women (360) and just educated speakers (138)

pattern opens the door to a different view of language change as well. The emergence of English, then, does not happen just once, in the way that the traditional HEL course focuses on Standard English, but instead happens all around us all the time. Emergence has happened and keeps happening in an infinite number of groups of people, whether the groups are defined by regional or social criteria. We can choose to observe English at any level of scale, whether at the highest level of English as a world language or at lower levels like national languages in Britain or America, or at still lower levels in regions like the American North or South, and at even smaller levels like the groups of students and faculty at a university (such as those in different fields of study). This is the natural diversity of language that Milroy talked about.

The key challenge for students and instructors in HEL courses will be the incorporation of complex systems into the traditional coverage of HEL. The drive of nineteenth-century linguistics to make the study of language more scientific by

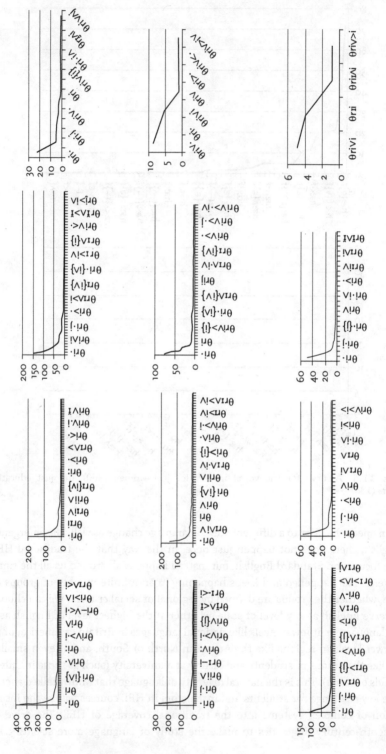

Figure 11.6. Pronunciation of /i/ in *three*, twelve groups of LAMSAS speakers

means of grammatical and exceptionless phonological "rules" has never been as successful as linguists might have hoped, whether the original Neogrammarians or more recent generativists. The reason is that our idea for such rules comes from frequency patterns in the complex system of speech, and the complex system has different patterns for every different group of speakers, however such groups are defined. Emergence in English is not once-and-done; it continues in every place where the language is spoken or written, in every locality, and in every kind of conversation or text. It will always be possible to notice exceptions to the patterns we see at the largest level of scale, like English as a world language, when we consider English at a different level of scale, like English as a national language in Britain or America, or English in smaller groups like those in regions or social groups. Thus, while we can still apply the common terms and concepts of contemporary language study and linguistics in order to create an accurate description of periods in HEL, the real story of the language will be about continual emergence and re-emergence of lexical, phonological, and grammatical patterns of English out of the interaction of its speakers and the contingencies of their history. HEL from a complex systems perspective cannot leave out the people in favor of paradigms and rules, and that casts the important facts of the language as regularities that always exist within a matrix of variation, subject to continual change both in the past, as we know has already occurred, and in the future.

What can we do to incorporate emergence into the HEL course? Complex systems can describe the process by which we perceive our language behavior to be associated with our communities and practices; thus, the study of speech as a complex system addresses language as an aspect of culture that emerges from human interaction. The nonlinear A-curve and the property of scaling, signs that a complex system has operated in a speech community, are teachable on a conceptual basis, so that students and their teachers will not have to engage at all with the more technical aspects of complexity science.[7] All students and their instructors have to see is the shape of the A-curve pattern, and appreciate the fact that there is always going to be wide variation in how people pronounce and convey the meaning of things. The complex systems approach cannot replace normal linguistic terminology because of emergence, but these linguistic terms should be used to describe what has emerged in the language. We do not want to throw the baby out with the bath water by abandoning the genuine progress that linguistics has made. We should cover the same historical and linguistic ground as traditional HEL textbooks do, but through emergence we will be able to do a much better job than those texts of talking about natural and inevitable change in the language, and about the fact that English is different in different places and social situations even while we can still talk about it as one language.

Let us take a familiar example. The Indo-European stemma in Figure 11.1 emphasizes the differences between language groups and, eventually, modern languages. We can take the same facts and turn them around to a complex systems point of view, as in Figure 11.7.

We can say that the various branches of the Indo-European language family, including our Germanic group with English in it, emerged with different language patterns as a result of differential language change as people moved to settle new

Table 11.3: SIX CATEGORIES FOR "HEAVY RAIN"
TERMS, FROM LAMSAS

All	2052
cloudburst	345
downpour	332
heavy rain	171
hard rain	146
gully washer	120
big rain	84
flood	84
pourdown	61
hard shower	57
heavy shower	47
Younger	678
downpour	172
cloudburst	162
heavy rain	55
hard rain	42
gully washer	36
hard shower	20
big rain	17
pourdown	16
flood	14
heavy shower	14
Men	1441
cloudburst	260
downpour	180
heavy rain	132
hard rain	103
gully washer	83
flood	68
big rain	56
pourdown	43
heavy shower	38
hard shower	33
Middle	739
downpour	103
cloudburst	95
heavy rain	57
hard rain	56
gully washer	48
flood	39
big rain	33

All	2052
pourdown	25
hard shower	23
trash mover	19
<u>Women</u>	<u>611</u>
downpour	151
cloudburst	85
hard rain	43
heavy rain	39
gully washer	37
big rain	28
hard shower	24
pourdown	18
flood	16
shower	10
<u>Older</u>	<u>624</u>
cloudburst	86
heavy rain	59
downpour	56
hard rain	48
gully washer	35
big rain	33
flood	30
pourdown	20
heavy shower	15
hard shower	14

areas. That is, when groups of Indo-Europeans moved away from their original homeland, the members within each group would interact more, talk more to each other than they would to members of other groups. Thus the habits of speech that developed over time within any one of the groups would be different from the habits that developed in any of the other groups. In other words, the frequency profile of the linguistic choices that people made in one group became different from the frequency profile of the choices people made in another group. This daisy model of the Indo-European language family does not just focus on differences but also on the potential overlap of the petals, of the language families that emerged near each other. The groups were never entirely separate, and people at the edges of the daisy petals could understand each other, as suggested by their overlapping edges. Of course, the daisy is another kind of tree in that it has a branching structure, but this model suggests how the emergence of different varieties of speech in different groups can have continuities, not just separation.

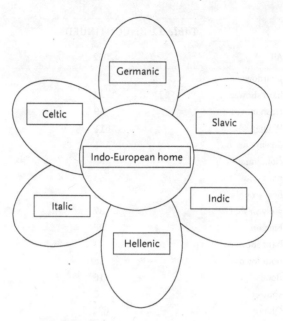

Figure 11.7. The daisy model for Indo-European expansion

We can show the same thing with words, as in Table 11.4. It is most often the case that the words for the modern languages grouped together in the same branch are more similar to each other than they are to the words in other branches of Indo-European. This of course is what the comparative and historical linguists in the nineteenth century looked for. The words for "blood," for example, pattern nicely by language branch according to the initial sound of the words, as do the words for "flower." English, however, has borrowed the Romance word "flower" as well as keeping the Germanic word "bloom." There is a little more variation within the branches for "father" and "eye." Gothic, the easternmost language of the Germanic branch, has the word "atta" for "father," influenced by the Slavic words to the east.

Correspondences and differences like those in Table 11.4 led the early twentieth-century linguist Jules Gilliéron to proclaim that "each word has its own history," just the opposite position from the Neogrammarians but a theory equally subject to scientific study and description. Gilliéron described all of the variants of terms for common objects in France (as presented here for "dragonfly" in LAMSAS), such as in his entire book on terms for "*saw*."[8] Neither way of thinking can be ignored: there are important systematic correspondences between languages and language branches, at the same time that word histories sometimes take their own way and need to be addressed outside any regular system of correspondences. While lists like those in Table 11.4 from Carl Darling Buck do permit us to talk about regular sound changes, they also testify to the mutual influence of adjoining groups of speakers. This influence is not a bad thing, as the traditional word "contamination" may imply, or a chaotic process as Gilliéron's position might suggest, but rather a normal occurrence in the complex system of speech. We should say so in the HEL course.

Table 11.4: COMPARISON OF WORDS IN INDO-EUROPEAN
BRANCHES. FROM BUCK (1949)

Italic/Romance		Celtic		Germanic		Slavic	
Blood (Buck 4.15)							
Latin	sangue	Irish	fuil, cru	Gothic	bloþ	Slavonic	kruvi
French	sang	Welsh	gwaed, crau	Swedish	blod	Russian	krov
Spanish	sangre			**English**	**blood**	Polish	krew
Father (Buck 2.35)							
Latin	pater	Irish	athir	Gothic	atta	Slavonic	otici
French	pere	Welsh	tad	Swedish	fader	Russian	otec
Spanish	padre			**English**	**father**	Polish	ojciec
Eye (Buck 4.21)							
Latin	oculus	Irish	suil, rosc	Gothic	augo	Slavonic	oko
French	oeil	Welsh	llygad	Swedish	oga	Russian	glaz
Spanish	ojo			**English**	**eye**	Polish	oko
Flower (Buck 8.57)							
Latin	flos	Irish	blath	Gothic	bloma	Slavonic	cvetu
French	fleur	Welsh	blodyn	Swedish	blomma	Russian	cvetok
Spanish	flor			**English**	**flower, bloom**	Polish	kwiat

We can also take example from the greatest change of all that occurred in English pronunciation, the Great Vowel Shift (GVS), which made the vowels of English differ from those of continental European languages. The story of the GVS as it is traditionally told in the HEL course is that the long vowels were subject to raising in both the front and the back. This version of the GVS gives the impression of regularity, in line with nineteenth-century perfection of sound change. However, we know that this version of the shift did not happen everywhere in England. Figure 11.8 shows what happened to the long vowels in Scotland and parts of Northern Britain, as suggested by Jeremy Smith.

The back vowels did not undergo raising, and an additional front vowel in Scottish English was raised. In Scotland in 1700, a *cow* was still a [ku]. In Glasgow today, one of the subway stops is called *Cowcaddens*, and only the tourists pronounce the first syllable as [kaʊ]; the locals are variable, but a common pronunciation is [kɪkædnz] where the historical /u/ vowel has been fronted and unrounded. The sound change is just not as neat and regular as the Neogrammarians would have liked. That is how the complex system of speech works, with the emergence of particular habits of pronunciation or word usage in local and regional communities throughout the English-speaking world. Top-level generalizations like the GVS are still useful as long as we know that they are broad abstractions, and that we can expect linguistic life to be much messier on the ground among actual speech communities. In the HEL course,

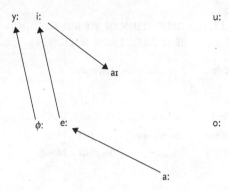

Figure 11.8. Northern Great Vowel Shift. From Jeremy Smith, *An Historical Study of English* (London: Routledge, 1996)

we need to tell the story of what happened to English on the ground, as change happened differently in different places, and the complex systems model allows us to do that without giving up the top-level generalization.

Once we get to the modern period, emergence tells us that we need to do two things. First of all, we need to acknowledge the fact that World English is very diverse. The largest number of users of English do not speak it as a native language, or even speak it very well at all. Following World War II, English has become a lingua franca, a language used for trade or other communication between people who do not speak the same language. Airline pilots worldwide, for instance, are supposed to use English to communicate with the airport tower. As Figure 11.9 shows, English is used as a first or native language, in a few countries like the United States, the United Kingdom, and Canada. In many other countries, especially in the European Union, English is taught as a second language in primary schools so that a very high percentage of the population, especially younger speakers, can speak English moderately well. In other countries around the world English is not universally taught, but some bits of English occur widely for trade.

If we change our viewpoint from percentages and go by the number of speakers, India, Pakistan, and Nigeria each has more English speakers than Britain does, and together these countries have as many English speakers as America. In places like China or India (both in the 0–20% group) a very large number of people may not speak English but still use some part of the language in their daily lives, from isolated words on up to set phrases or sentences. In the HEL course, we need to recognize that English is no longer the sole property of the English and the Americans: the historical course of the language has spread it worldwide, with somewhat different habits of speech emerging in each place.

We need to talk about the diversity of English in the HEL course as it occurs in Britain and America, too. The complex systems approach tells us that, contrary to the expectations of many educated people, accents and dialects are never going away. Americans and the English will continue to form regional and social groups of speakers with somewhat different habits, different pronunciations, and terms

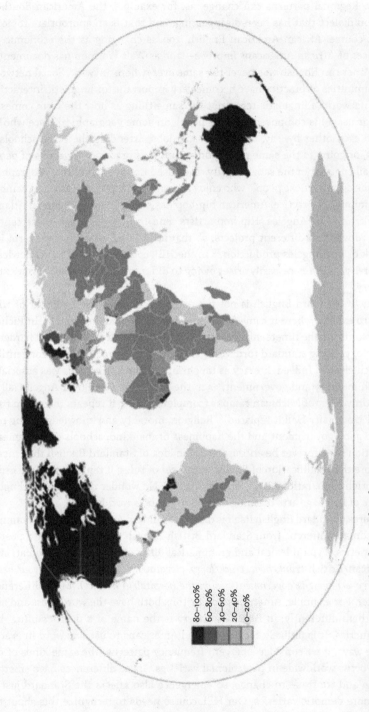

Figure 11.9. Percentage of English speakers by country

80–100%
60–80%
40–60%
20–40%
0–20%

and constructions that are used more frequently than they are in other groups of speakers. Regional patterns can change, as, for example, the American Southern Plantation dialect that has been disappearing, and that is an appropriate topic for the HEL course. African American English, too, is changing as the economic circumstances of African Americans improve—and as Walt Wolfram has documented, African American English was never the same everywhere anyway.[9] Social networks and communities of practice have become very important for linguistic interaction. A social network (a linguistic term, not the same thing as how the term comes up in popular usage) is composed of those people in some geographical place who are linked to each other by, say, doing the same jobs, attending the same schools or churches, or going to the same pubs. Communities of practice are groups of people who are all engaged in the same activity. They need not be in the same geographical place. For example, those people who enjoy and perform hip-hop music are members of a community of practice. American hip-hop has several regional centers: Atlanta, New York, and Los Angeles. Hip-hop artists tend to move between these centers in order to work on different projects, so that an Atlanta artist may perform in a New York or Los Angeles production.[10] In the HEL course, we need to acknowledge this diversity, which necessarily arises owing to different contingencies of our external history.

Finally, If Standard English is not the natural and inevitable endpoint of HEL, we have to explain where it came from and what we should do about it. In Richard Bailey's words, by the nineteenth century "attitudes toward grammar had hardened into ideology. Using standard forms of the language was a requirement for gentility (and much else)."[11] Indeed, literacy as taught in the growing schools was associated with both morality and government, as in the motto inscribed over Angell Hall on Bailey's University of Michigan campus (completed 1924, it repeats the motto from the 1871 University Hall it replaced): "Religion, morality and knowledge being necessary to good government and the happiness of mankind, schools and the means of education shall forever be encouraged." The idea of Standard English thus means much more than codification of English into a set of rules; it represents social order, moral uprightness, rationality, even nationalism. No wonder that Standard English is a staple of language arts teaching in primary schools worldwide.

Of course, Standard English itself is diverse. Standard American English grammar and lexicon are different from Standard British English (RP) and standard postcolonial varieties. Typical lexical and grammatical differences are quite familiar, such as American/British *trunk/boot, truck/lorry, elevator/lift, toilet/loo, Mind your head/ Caution, government is/government are, in the hospital/in hospital*. Most differences are subtler. For example, Americans and Britons both have the words *post* and *mail* but use them differently; in Britain a *surgery* is the name of a doctor's office, but not in America. It is unlikely for Britons and Americans to use *any* word in exactly the same ways, if we consider emergent frequency patterns. The same kinds of differences occur worldwide in postcolonial varieties. These differences have emerged over time and continue to change, so emergence also affects the Standard just as it does more demotic varieties. Our HEL course needs to recognize this about the Standard, and to tell the story of the creation of Standard ideology in the eighteenth and nineteenth centuries by entrepreneurs like Noah Webster. It is not an attack on Standard English to show that it had its own path to creation, and is now subject to emergence like other varieties. To do so will allow students and teachers to understand better how the school Standard is related to their own home varieties, and to the varieties they use in social networks and communities of practice.

Emergence, then, as a property of the science of complex systems, allows us to tell a better story about HEL. We do not have to get rid of most traditional elements of the HEL course, but now we can put those elements in an environment that makes more scientific sense. Emergence gives us a way to show how external history, which we have always insisted on telling without really knowing why, really does change the language by describing the contingencies that formed and reformed groups of speakers. Emergence gives us a way to talk about internal history without cutting it off from the speakers. The cost is replacement of the logical perfection of change that nineteenth-century linguists developed as a reaction to spiritual interpretations of language. In return, we get to align ourselves with a twenty-first-century science that we can share with economists, ecological and evolutionary biologists, physicists, and others of our colleagues all across campus. In so doing, we can show that linguistics and HEL deserve the status as real science that the Neogrammarians wished to confer on them.

CHAPTER 12

Discovering the Past for Yourself

Corpora, Data-Driven Learning, and the History of English

JUKKA TYRKKÖ

12.1. INTRODUCTION

Although the history of corpus linguistics can be traced back to the 1960s, the discipline emerged as one of the dominant approaches to linguistic inquiry during the 1990s. As a research paradigm based on the use of representative samples of authentic data, frequency-based quantitative arguments, and context-sensitive qualitative analysis, corpus methods are used in virtually every field of linguistics. In English historical linguistics, corpus methods became a viable option following the release of the *Helsinki Corpus of English Texts*, the first carefully stratified historical corpus of English, in 1991. Covering a time span of nearly 1,000 years from the Old English period to the end of the Early Modern period, the corpus opened the door to a new way of approaching language history.[1] Over the three decades since then, numerous historical corpora—large and small, generic and specialised—have been compiled and made available to the research community. In addition to corpora developed specifically for linguistic studies, a wide variety of digital archives have also appeared on the scene, affording us access to diachronic datasets that sometimes span many billions of words. As a result, new theoretical approaches, such as variationist historical linguistics, have emerged largely as a result of corpus evidence.[2] Importantly, the use of large and richly annotated corpora has not only made it possible to search and analyse these ever-increasing amounts of data with great efficiency but also to perform analyses that help us uncover patterns and co-occurrences in the data in a bottom-up manner and explain the effects of individual predictors in complex multifactorial models.[3] Here, perhaps, we have a rare occasion to justifiably use the term "paradigm shift."

"Digital pedagogy" is an umbrella term that refers to a wide variety of approaches to teaching where computers and digital resources are used, and the use of corpora is one such method. From the perspective of digital teaching environments, online courses and e-learning platforms, the point of departure for corpus linguistics is that rather than being a type of teaching material to be specially produced, corpora and corpus tools are what real scholars use in their work. This point was already made a more than thirty years ago by Tim Johns, one of the great pioneers of digital pedagogy, when he wrote that there is "nothing novel in the use of the concordancer to examine large quantities of text for the purpose of discovering patternings in the use of language: it is a computing tool that has been used by linguistic and literary researchers for over 25 years."[4] However, as Johns went on to argue, despite their long and successful history of use in research, the same tools had not made much of a dent in the classroom.

Since the early 1990s, the usefulness of corpora in language education has been recognised more widely and discussed quite extensively in literature.[5] Many textbooks, grammars and dictionaries are now corpus-based, and corpus resources and methods of *data-driven learning* have enjoyed increasing popularity in EFL (English as a Foreign Language) and ESL (English as a Second Language) classrooms as well as in the teaching of academic English and other specialised registers.[6] However, despite the importance of corpus evidence to research, when it comes to teaching the History of English most textbooks do not as a rule provide quantitative corpus evidence and many teachers prefer assigning canonical set texts rather than making corpora available to students directly—even when such resources are now readily available.[7]

In this chapter, I will discuss some of the key benefits of using corpora and corpus linguistic methods in the History of English classroom and as material for student assignments. Specifically, I will argue that the corpus linguistic approach to the History of English is ideally suited to impressing upon students two important facts about language change, namely, that diachronic variation is a never-ending and complex process rather than a succession of stages and that awareness of changes over time does not override the need to consider synchronic variation at the same time.

12.2. CORPUS LINGUISTICS AND THE HISTORY OF ENGLISH

When considering the use of corpus methods in the classroom, it is important to emphasise just how central corpora have become to historical linguistics. Over the last two decades, corpus linguistics has become one of the most influential methodological approaches to language history. For example, Tony McEnery and Andrew Wilson describe corpus linguistics as "the *sine qua non* of historical linguistics,"[8] and Andreas Jucker and Irma Taavitsainen, the two foundational figures in historical pragmatics, claim that "the advent of corpora and corpus linguistics has changed the whole research paradigm of linguistics."[9] It therefore seems self-evident that students should be exposed to the contemporary methods and tools of the field they are studying, and all the more so if the methodologies in question are considered fundamental to the core practices within the discipline.

Corpora are regularly put to many valuable uses in historical linguistics, and the large historical megacorpora and even larger historical text repositories available today facilitate entirely new approaches to historical lexicology and lexicography, such as the findings of first attestations and the evidence-based analysis of lexical emergence and obsolescence.[10] Indeed, the most fundamental innovation brought about by corpus-based approaches has been the introduction of quantitative data into the analysis of language variation and change. Corpora allow us to study representative samples of a language or some specialised registers thereof and to identify not only what the language was like at a given time, but also to pinpoint crucial moments when periods of rapid change were taking place and to identify the social groups, text types, and regions that either led such changes or lagged behind them. Although data-driven analysis can mean genuine bottom-up analyses with few *a priori* assumptions, in most cases the usefulness of corpus methods is realised in the way corpora can inform us about the frequencies, patterns, and contexts of pre-determined phenomena. Whereas only a decade or two ago a historical linguist studying a relatively infrequent word, phrase, structure, or pattern would need to ask colleagues to share any examples they came across, today all the extant examples in a corpus of millions or even billions of words can be retrieved within seconds, read in context and then analysed further. This not only means that the amount of evidence is greater than before but also that the evidence at hand is exhaustive as far as that specific corpus is concerned. Unless mistakes were made in the formulation of the query, such as not accounting for spelling variation or unexpected variants of a syntactic structure, the researcher can be confident that the examples found and, therefore, the frequencies they indicate, really include every single occurrence in the present dataset. Findings from corpora can either validate or invalidate the researcher's intuitions about the topic at hand, and while this is already very useful when the research concerns present-day language, it is absolutely invaluable when the object of inquiry is historical.

Finally, although the convenience of accessing millions or even billions of words of data with virtually no delay, the ability to perform complex queries, to form statistically well-argued inferences and to link linguistic evidence with textual and sociolinguistic metadata are all recognised benefits of corpus methods, it is important to note that there are also some aspects of corpus linguistics that have affected the research paradigm at a deeper level. The discipline of historical linguistics has always been more comprehensively materials-based than the study of present-day language use, but the use of large computer-readable corpora has ushered in significant changes in the way linguistic data is handled. Because corpus linguistic research relies on the precise retrieval of items of interest from clearly defined datasets, much more emphasis is placed on *transparency* and *verifiability* than what was normal a few decades ago. Rather than resting on the authority of the individual scholar, today's corpus-based historical linguistics relies on the open discussion and dissemination of the primary data, open discussion of the methods of analysis and retrieval, open discussion of the statistical approaches taken, and so on. At the same time, as the discovery of raw evidence has become much easier and quicker, the task of the researcher has shifted from simply collecting interesting examples of historical language use toward explaining the phenomena in a theoretical framework. As Merja Kytö notes,

> Access to computerised data has also meant an increase in the awareness of the importance of language-theoretical considerations in linguistic research: it has become much less acceptable to simply collect examples and present them without paying attention to language theory or generalisation than it was in the days of pre-electronic historical language study.[11]

Thus, and this seems worth emphasising to students especially, the use of corpus methods in the research or teaching of the History of English does not diminish the need for a linguist's conventional understanding of language; evidence-based scholarship is not an alternative to good old-fashioned linguistic sensitivity but rather an invaluable addition to it. It is also important to recognise that corpus methods, too, have their limitations, and that the proper understanding of these limitations requires traditional linguistic scholarship. Matti Rissanen, the project leader behind the *Helsinki Corpus*, identified three potential challenges in historical corpus linguistics and gave them the memorable names of the "philologist's dilemma," "God's truth fallacy," and "mystery of vanishing reliability."[12] The first fallacy refers to the danger of interpreting corpus data out of context, both historical and linguistic; the second warns against making overreaching generalisations based on inadequate data; and the third reminds us that as the number of contextual variables increases, the less possible it is to compile a corpus that would be representative in terms of each variable. Although Rissanen's article was published two years before the public release of the *Helsinki Corpus* and thus in many ways the beginning of historical corpus linguistics, the three problems have stood the test of time.

12.3. CORPUS METHODS IN HEL TEACHING

Considering the wide range of linguistic topics that are today studied using corpora and corpus methods, there can be no doubt that virtually any specific aspect or phenomenon of language history can be introduced to students with the help of the similar resources. As Anne Curzan notes in her discussion of HEL teaching with corpus methods, "corpora open the possibility of providing students with an individual, interactive way to investigate larger historical changes, be they syntactic, morphological, semantic, or orthographic."[13] In the simplest case, making historical corpora available to students will mean exposing them to a much greater volume of authentic evidence of historical English than would ever be possible through the pages of a textbook or even an anthology. Not only do large corpora contain more data *per se*, but through corpus methods it is possible to find (most) items of interest almost immediately and to review them all at the same time. The opportunity to see dozens or hundreds of examples, rather than one or two, will foster the sense that the historic variants were an actual living language.

Referring back to Leech's "Teaching and Language Corpora: A Convergence,"[14] Ute Römer divides the use of corpora in language teaching into two primary types: *indirect* and *direct applications*.[15] The former concerns the way corpora and corpus methods can affect the teaching syllabus or have an effect on the development of teaching materials, and the latter concerns data-driven learning, either in the form of teacher-corpus interaction or learner-corpus interaction.[16] I shall focus on the latter in the present discussion. As a general rule, data-driven or corpus-based learning can be either *teacher-mediated* or *research-focused*,[17] that is, learning in which the teacher guides students through carefully prepared exercises and well-punctuated teachable moments, or learning through personal initiative of the students, either individually or in groups. Both methods have considerable merit. Ideally, in my view, the teacher should point the way with carefully designed tasks that are guaranteed to produce suitably pedagogical findings, but students should, whenever possible, be given the opportunity to elaborate on the initial task by replicating the analysis on a different corpus, by expanding or refocusing the queries, by exploring the metadata, and generally engaging with the issue on their own.

As already noted previously, perhaps the greatest benefit of corpus methods comes from the way corpora allow us to make visible and observe processes of language change as continua or, more accurately, as numerous parallel continua. Although beginning students will undoubtedly benefit from a more traditional, period-based introduction to language history, from the intermediate level onward students should understand that language is a gradually changing entity and that linguistic changes come about as a result of complex overlapping and interacting mechanisms. Sufficiently large corpora, as well as the use of several different corpora, will allow students to make first-hand observations not only about the dominant trends but also about the early adopters and the laggards and, moreover, allow them to compare evidence from different registers, genres, regions and sociolinguistic strata.

It goes without saying that the successful integration of corpora and corpus methods into the HEL teaching classroom requires careful thought and planning. As wonderful as corpora can be in providing students with first-hand access to endless examples of language-in-use, that same wealth of data can quickly become overwhelming and serve only to confuse rather than to enlighten. In the following discussion, I take as a premise that HEL students generally have no previous experience with corpus linguistic methods, and that the course plan affords little time for a thorough introduction to more sophisticated corpus methods, particularly quantitative methods that require statistics. It is therefore important to distinguish between those concepts and methods that are crucial to the correct interpretation of corpus data and consequently should always be discussed prior to using corpora, and those that can be safely left for later.

The key considerations when planning corpus-based HEL teaching are *resources, time*, and the *students' skill level*. The availability of the *appropriate corpora, corpus tools*, and *other resources* is naturally a major consideration. In general, there is a great wealth of available datasets,[18] corpus tools,[19] and supplementary digital archives available today,[20] which makes it entirely realistic to assign tasks to students which only a decade or two ago would have formed the core of an entire research project. Because corpus linguistic research relies so fundamentally on the quality of the corpus, HEL teachers should always review the corpora in advance to know the language varieties it represents and to ascertain that the corpus has been compiled diligently. Likewise, the teacher should have an understanding of what each query tool can and cannot do, know the formats in which data can be exported for further analysis, and so on.

The availability of *time* is an important factor in determining whether or not corpus methods can be used for teaching a specific topic. Although corpora make it easy to access vast amounts of data, it is important to budget time both for preparing the lesson and any corpora and other digital sources in advance and to plan ahead exactly how much time the students will need for completing the tasks given to them. For the teacher, this means checking the corpus or corpora ahead of time to make sure that the relevant linguistic features can be found and to get a sense of the potential challenges and teachable issues. While it is possible to carry out exploratory analysis of new datasets without much preparation, doing so is rarely very successful in the classroom because students rightly expect the exercises to lead to a payoff in the form of an enlightening realisation, and usually finding something is more satisfying than not doing so. Likewise, the teacher should know ahead of time if the dispersion of the feature of interest is very strongly skewed within the corpus. It is not a problem if it is, but the fact should be reflected in how the task is set to the students. Dividing the classroom into small groups and asking each group to work with a different corpus (or part of a large corpus) will only be effective if at least most of the groups can actually find something to analyse. The more analysis the exercise requires, the more time will be needed. Running queries is usually relatively quick, but if the students need to prune unwanted hits, classify the concordance lines into semantic or syntactic categories, or perform some of the other typical corpus linguistic tasks, more time will be required. One way of circumventing some of the time issues is to present the students with pre-collected data or partially analysed data, but doing so naturally takes up more of the teacher's—or his or her teaching assistant's—time.

Finally, the students' *skill set* in terms of both HEL knowledge and corpus methods plays a crucial role in planning the lesson plan. Although corpus methods can be wonderfully engaging and at best turn regular lessons into real explorations of new topics, it is absolutely crucial that students have been taught the fundamentals before corpus methods are brought into the picture. This means not only understanding the basic concepts of corpus linguistics (see section 12.3.1) but also having the opportunity to discuss and review the choices made in a constructive environment. A factor crucial to the successful use of corpus methods is that students have a good understanding of the fundamental concepts of corpus linguistics.

12.3.1. Corpus Fundamentals for the HEL Classroom

Like all corpus linguistic work, the corpus-based teaching of language history relies on a set of core concepts which every researcher, teacher, and student should master. Corpora can be deceptively easy to use, but if the concepts of *representativeness, sampling, frequency*, and *dispersion* are not understood correctly, the researcher or student may easily come to entirely false conclusions. The most important concept in corpus linguistics is arguably *representativeness*, because the entire discipline rests on the understanding that corpora are reliable samples that can be used as the basis of meaningful observations about language at large or, quite often, about a specific variety of language. It is therefore of paramount importance that before corpora are used in the classroom, some time is spent on discussing what a corpus is, how corpora come to be, and what were the compilation principles of the individual corpora used. In short, to use corpora and interpret corpus findings appropriately, students should understand how the corpora they use were compiled. Visualisations can also be helpful when the nature of corpus evidence is discussed. As an example, Figure 12.1 gives the number of books per year in the Early English Books Online (EEBO) corpus with the diameter of the marker denoting the word count. As the figure demonstrates, the amount of available data increases dramatically from approximately the middle of the seventeenth century.

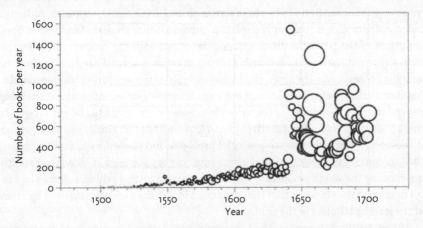

Figure 12.1. Number of books per year in the Early English Books Online corpus

Sampling, or the process of selecting the texts that make up the corpus, is a concept closely related to representativeness. In order to satisfy ourselves about the suitability of a given corpus to a particular research task, we should know how the population was defined by the compilers of the corpus and we should have a reasonably good sense of how the sampling was carried out. *Random sampling* is generally preferred in statistics because randomness is the assumption behind many statistical equations, but it is rarely possible with historical language data because extant data from the time period or the specific registers under investigation may be scarce or the quality of the primary data may mandate excessive amounts of processing and editing—for example, transcription and annotation of manuscripts or manual correction of poorly photographed printed texts. Instead, the practical concerns of corpus compiling, and in particular the compiling of historical corpora, typically force the compilers to rely on other approaches to sampling. Consequently, corpus compilers have typically had to resort to *opportunistic sampling*, defined as sampling where the sampling frame exerts a considerable influence on the composition of the corpus. For example, the researchers may have available to them a previously collected archive of texts and in an effort to save time the decision is made to use the archive or a part thereof instead of looking for more sources and then preparing the new data for corpus use. Although often unavoidable, opportunistic sampling is problematic because it may introduce a strong selection bias, that is, a significant skewing of the data because the sampling favours some sources of data over others. These problems can often be alleviated to some extent by correctly identifying the biases involved and by reporting the findings accurately instead of generalising too broadly. Additionally, the compiling of historical corpora often involves *judgment sampling*,[21] where texts are selected on the basis of the compilers' or external authorities expert knowledge of the historical circumstances. For example, when our research team in Helsinki was compiling the *Early Modern English Medical Texts* corpus,[22] we worked closely with Peter Murray Jones, Librarian of King's College, Cambridge, and renowned medical book historian, to ensure that the texts selected for the corpus represented the most important medical works of the sixteenth and seventeenth centuries. Although judgment sampling is frequently used, it is important that students (and researchers) are aware of the potential disadvantages associated with the method. Most important, any results obtained from such a corpus must be evaluated carefully against the selection criteria and the researcher must exercise extreme caution when generalising their findings, especially when it comes to frequency-based inferences concerning general trends in language. At the same time, while students should be encouraged to think about issues of representatives and to look into the texts included in the corpus, it is easy to overemphasise the potential problems and challenges to such an extent that students walk away confused about why corpora are used at all and constantly questioning the validity of all findings obtained using corpus evidence. It may be useful to remind the students that the corpora and tools they use are also used by many of the leading scholars in the field.

Understanding the concepts of *frequency, standardised frequency*, and *dispersion* is likewise fundamental to using quantitative corpus evidence and the HEL teacher should make sure that every student understands these concepts before using corpora independently. In general, students find *frequency* and *standardised frequency* fairly straightforward concepts to master, but it is generally safest to avoid hasty introductions to more sophisticated concepts such as the reliability of point estimates which, while important, tends to confuse students at first. For beginning students, it is probably enough that occasional reminders are given to take the observed frequencies with a grain of salt. When it comes to *dispersion*, a much less frequently discussed concept than frequency in corpus linguistic literature, there are again wide-ranging implications when it comes to the correct interpretation of corpus findings. Although statistical measures for discussing dispersion generally go beyond the HEL teaching classroom, students should be encouraged to pay attention to how widely a given linguistic feature is used across the different texts in the corpus. Is the feature used in most texts, in a small number of them, or perhaps in only one? Dispersion is particularly important to consider when using small corpora, where a high frequency of occurrence in one or two texts can lead to a false impression of a given linguistic feature's usage. If suitable metadata is available, students can be asked to analyse the frequencies by register or sociolinguistic parameter. Tasks like this are generally interesting to students, who will enjoy discovering tendencies within the corpus.

It is worth mentioning here that many corpus tools only provide so-called pooled point estimates or bag-of-words frequencies—that is, single mean frequencies and/or standardised frequencies for the entire corpus or for sections thereof. For example, although the widely used corpora made available through the Brigham Young server, such as the *Corpus of Historical American English* (COHA), give raw and standardised frequencies for diachronic sections, there is no convenient way to access text-specific frequencies or to see dispersion statistics.

12.4. A PRACTICAL EXAMPLE

In this author's experience, a particularly fruitful approach to designing a corpus-based session is to create a fluid flow in which students are encouraged to explore the topic in progressive stages. The experience of discovering the past for oneself can be a memorable one, and it almost certainly leaves a more lasting memory for most than simply reading a fact from a book or hearing it in a lecture. Stepping into the role of a researcher turns the discoveries into much more personal and hence memorable experiences. The students can work alone, or the classroom can be divided into several small research teams, each of which is tasked with extracting the relevant information from a different corpus. All groups can be given the first initial task, but after that the groups can be encouraged to come up with new questions based on their findings, to find answers to the follow-up questions using the corpora available, and so on, until at the end of the session, or the beginning of the next session, each group presents their work.

For a practical example, I shall use an old favourite, the history of the past participle *gotten*. While *gotten* stands today as perhaps the most salient distinguishing feature between American and British English, students are usually surprised to learn that *gotten* was in fact reasonably common in Early Modern English and started disappearing toward the end of the seventeenth century. Described by Marianne Hundt as an example of "post-colonial revival" rather than of colonial lag, *gotten* has become increasingly popular in American English especially since World War II while remaining one of the most staunchly opposed "Americanisms" in the Commonwealth Englishes.[23] There is no clear understanding of why *gotten* went into a decline at the end of the Early Modern period or re-emerged two centuries later; Anderwald, for example, rules out simple prescriptivist explanations using evidence from grammars.[24]

As the topic is introduced to the class, evidence from a suitable corpus, such as the 400-million-word COHA, can be presented (Figure 12.2). In my view it is always preferable to visualise quantitative evidence rather than presenting it only as a table. Scatter plots showing individual data points are preferable to bar charts, because they highlight dispersion and give the students an immediate sense of the amount

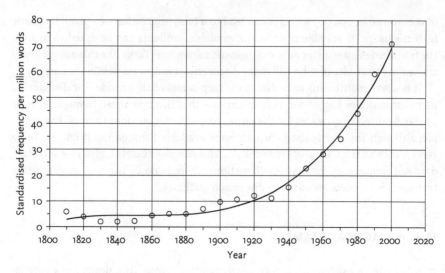

Figure 12.2. Frequency of *gotten* in the Corpus of Historical American English

of evidence. When lines are fitted to scatter plots, it is generally a good idea to use polynomial or LOESS curves because they highlight the non-linear nature of dia-chronic trends. More sophisticated visualisations, such as box-and-whisker plots, violin plots, and bean plots are generally best left for actual corpus linguistics classes, because many students find them difficult to read and there is often not enough time for discussing them in detail in HEL courses.

Although a trend like this can be communicated to the students during a lecture, it is much more memorable if the students discover the trend for themselves using a variety of large historical corpora, such as the EEBO corpus. Gotten is a particularly suitable feature to use when introducing students to quantitative historical analysis because the word form is simple and the quantitative evidence shows a clear trend. Thus, for example, students might run a query using the UCREL's CQPweb tool and the EEBO corpus to find the standardised frequencies from 1500 to 1700 (see Figure 12.3).[25]

The evidence looks quite compelling and there is not much doubt about the general direction of the trend: the frequency of *gotten* remained stable until approximately the beginning of the seventeenth century, at which point a steady and reasonably rapid decline began. A similar trend can be observed when it comes to dispersion, calculated here as the percentage of books that include at least one occurrence of *gotten* (Figure 12.4). The apparent positive cline at the beginning of the timeline also makes an interesting talking point, giving the students some food for thought when it comes to the composition of the corpus and the impact it has on the quantitative results.

Having explored the frequency of the participle alone, the students might be encouraged to compare the *have got* and *have gotten* structures (Figure 12.5). The EEBO data will show that while the former is clearly less frequent than the latter in

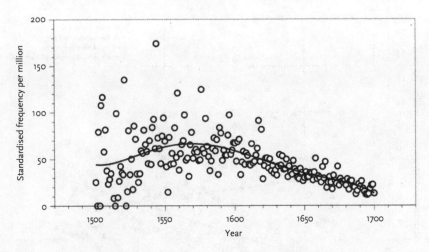

Figure 12.3. Frequency of *gotten* in the Early English Books Online corpus

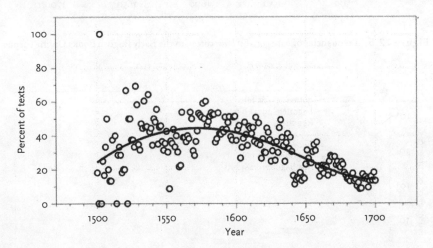

Figure 12.4. Dispersion by book of *gotten* in the Early English Books Online corpus

the sixteenth century, the two trajectories intersect around the middle of the seventeenth century.

The students may be encouraged to explore the early history of the stative, or possessive, participle *got* and the dynamic, or recipient, participle *gotten*. Did the distinction, current in PDE (Present-Day English) American English, already exist in the Early Modern period? Given the amount of evidence—6,558 occurrences of *have got* and 6,288 items of *have gotten*—and the ambiguities involved in the analysis it is not feasible to analyse the concordance lines in class, but if each student in a class of thirty was assigned 200 examples to analyse as homework, half of dataset could be analysed in a week. Another example of a follow-up that students may come up with concerns prefixed participle forms such as *forgotten* and *begotten*. The

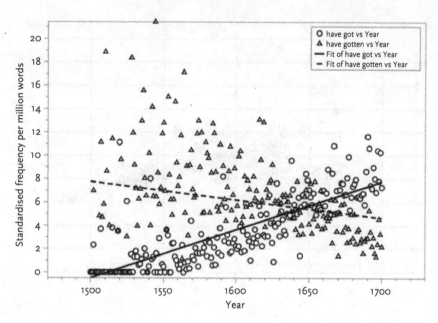

Figure 12.5. Frequencies of *have got* and *have gotten* in the Early English Books Online corpus

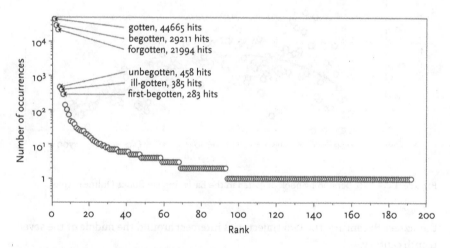

Figure 12.6. Frequency curve of types of -gotten

students may know either intuitively or through literature that while *gotten* is a very low-frequency variant in PDE British English, *forgotten* is in fact quite widely used. Running a wildcard search on the EEBO corpus, students will discover that there are a total of 192 types and that, ordered by rank, their frequencies follow the familiar non-linear frequency profile with more than half of the occurrences being hapax legomena (Figure 12.6).[26]

With corpora it is trivial to retrieve large numbers of authentic examples in context, and thus students can be asked to do independent study of a word like *begotten*—and perhaps of *beget* as well—to determine how it was used in Early Modern writing. The concordance lines can be sorted or filtered by collocate positions, or a collocation analysis can be carried out to determine word associations; if the option is available, n-grams can be retrieved to identify frequently occurring word sequences. Here, for example, the students can discover that *begotten* was primarily used in the concrete sense of procreation, especially in the Biblical context, while the abstract causative sense appears to have been quite rare. Further investigation of the collocates will reveal that in addition to words like *Son, only, child, children* and *God*, there appears to be a strong association between *begotten* and the legal domain, with some of the common collocates being *illegitimately, unbegotten, adulterously, lawfully, incestuously*, and so on. Depending on the focus of the course, the semantics and pragmatics of individual words and phraseologies may be explored in more detail using corpus evidence.

Returning to the frequency profiles, the students might be given the task of comparing the diachronic frequency development of *gotten* and the two highest-frequency prefixed forms *begotten* and *forgotten*. The results will show that while the use of *gotten* declines, both *begotten* and *forgotten* appear to reach a plateau around 1550 and to undergo no further change over the Early Modern period. Seeing the three frequencies more or less come together at the end of the timeline naturally invites the follow-up question of what happens later? If the students are asked to calculate a mean frequency for each word over the last twenty-five years of the seventeenth century, they will get the frequencies of 20.44 per million words for *gotten*, 20.01 for *begotten*, and 15.33 for *forgotten*. Some suitable PDE corpora can now be used to assess the situation 300 years later: the British National Corpus gives the corresponding frequencies as 1.12, 0.2 and 39.39, and the Corpus of Contemporary American English gives 65.22, 0.21, and 27.72 (see Figure 12.7). Three different trajectories can thus be identified: the frequency of *begotten* has plummeted in both variants, the frequency of *forgotten* has increased somewhat in both variants (but more in British English), and the frequency of *gotten* shows the by-now-familiar differentiation between the two variants, having become nearly extinct in British English and quite ubiquitous in American English.

It goes without saying that the more corpora available, the more flexibility the teacher will have in designing corpus-based sessions and assignments, and the more fluidity can be built into the session. The teacher can make a practical distinction between corpora and tasks that are to be the focus of a particular session and resources that can be quickly consulted if a question comes up in class. As a general rule, if something can be demonstrated in practice using a quick corpus query, the opportunity is probably worth taking.

As evidence from more corpora is introduced, the students will be drawn into a realistic research scenario and new questions can be explored. What caused these trends? Are they equally apparent in all genres and registers, or could we use corpora to identify early adopters and stragglers? Circling back to the COHA corpus, the students could be asked to explore register variation by highlighting the frequency differences between PDE registers. In Figure 12.8, I have added the register-specific

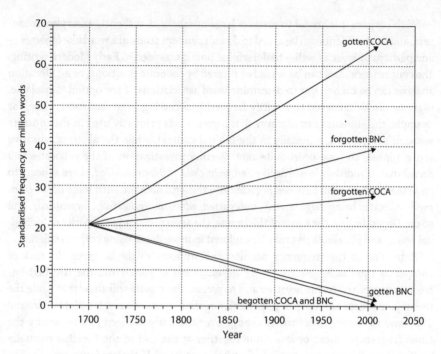

Figure 12.7. Developments of *gotten*, *forgotten*, and *begotten* in British and American Englishes

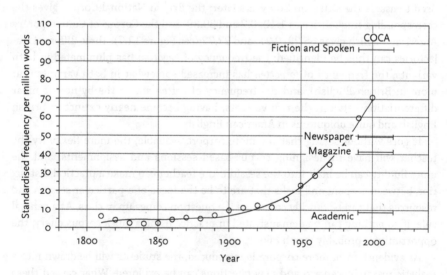

Figure 12.8. Later register of differences of *gotten* in American English

frequencies of *gotten* from the *Corpus of Contemporary American English*. Students can be asked to come up with explanations for the differences: is the use of *gotten* context-specific in the sense that, for example, academic authors simply do not have much need for the expression, or is it a case of active stylistic avoidance? Are all the articles in American academic journal written by American authors? Questions like this, and countless others, can encourage students to actively think about the linguistic data we use as evidence and the complexity that lies behind linguistic phenomena.

12.5. CONCLUSION

The use of corpora has the potential of enhancing the HEL teaching classroom in a wide variety of ways. From expanding the choice of examples to opening up the concepts of variation and change to students, corpora can be put to many different uses both in the classroom and as the primary material of activities and research tasks. What makes corpora and corpus methods particularly exciting is that they encourage exploration and careful consideration of the evidence. By giving students the opportunity to use the same methods and materials that scholars use in their professional research, we also afford them the opportunity to experience the same excitement we feel when making new discoveries.

CHAPTER 13
Word Classes in the History of English

DAVID DENISON

13.1. INTRODUCTION

Word classes or parts of speech (POS) may seem a rather banal aspect of language, but they lead us into some intriguing aspects of language history. It is probably an advantage of this topic that most people will have at least some idea of which words are nouns, which adjectives, and so on, though there may be some haziness about how we arrive at such identifications. If verbs are "doing words," how come *demolition* is a noun? If adjectives are "describing words," how come *very* in *the very idea* is an adjective?—to which the answer, of course, is that notional definitions like those are no longer linguistically respectable. Most modern linguistic approaches privilege form over semantics. We determine word classes primarily by distributional properties—that is, the kinds of syntactic environment a word can fit into—and, where appropriate, the potential for inflectional endings.

Any respectable introduction to language will discuss suitable tests for word class, though we should be aware that semantic properties have a way of sneaking back in when we look more closely at how language works. Most research in the various formal grammatical frameworks, just like most school-level analysis, assumes that every single word in every grammatical sentence belongs to one and only one part of speech. Even if (like me) you don't accept this assumption, it is still a useful abstraction that allows us to make generalisations about whole classes of words.

In this chapter we will look at research that students can carry out with the aid of, or sometimes actually in search of, POS information. And students *should* be carrying out research. In the history of the English language, just as with scholarship generally, what teachers or textbooks say should not be taken for granted. Experts can be wrong, or their facts out of date. Even with valid assertions, it is unrewarding for students simply to parrot back to their teacher the examples they have been given. Where possible, students should be finding their own data to help make sense of—and test critically—the surveys or generalisations or hypotheses on offer. If they can do this from time to time, it is more fun all round, and everyone (instructors too!) learns more.

13.2. TAGGED CORPORA

What data sources can students use? Certainly conversations, newspapers, film and TV dialogue, novels, emails, texts—any of these can provide useful examples, as appropriate, of change in progress or change in the past. It is surely a good idea to be alert to language around us, and there is always the chance of discovering something useful or even a usage previously unnoticed. But the language we encounter casually is usually too haphazard to help with a specific research question. Incidentally, quite apart from problems of inefficiency, there are other risks in relying on casually observed data, as Arnold Zwicky has observed:

> [. . .] the Recency Illusion, the belief that things YOU have noticed only recently are in fact recent. This is a selective attention effect. Your impressions are simply not to be trusted; you have to check the facts. Again and again—retro *not*, double *is*, speaker-oriented *hopefully*, split infinitives, etc.—the phenomena turn out to have been around, with some frequency, for very much longer than you think. It's not just Kids These Days. Professional linguists can be as subject to the Recency Illusion as anyone else. [. . .] Another selective attention effect, which tends to accompany the Recency Illusion, is the Frequency Illusion: once you've noticed a phenomenon, you think it happens a whole lot, even "all the time." Your estimates of frequency are likely to be skewed by your noticing nearly every occurrence that comes past you. People who are reflective about language—professional linguists, people who set themselves up as authorities on language, and ordinary people who are simply interested in language—are especially prone to the Frequency Illusion.[1]

We needn't stop listening and looking, but it is well to bear Zwicky's warnings in mind.

A standard way of garnering data is to search a *corpus* (plural *corpora*), a systematic collection of linguistic material, usually, these days, in electronic form. In principle, a corpus search allows us to make factual statements about the relative frequency of a particular usage at a particular time and provides genuine rather than invented examples of relevant usage. There are a number of corpora of English available over the web, some of which are freely available, possibly after registration, others requiring a paid individual or institutional subscription.

Corpora differ in the linguistic *mark-up* they offer. It is common for words to be *POS-tagged*, where each word is associated with a tag that identifies its word class (and perhaps more). The set of classes used, the *tagset*, may be akin to the conventional parts of speech but usually reflects a rather more fine-grained classification. For example, the CLAWS-5 tagset used in the British National Corpus (BNC) has fifty-seven simple word class tags, and some others have many more still. Thus four kinds of noun words are differentiated in the CLAWS-5 tagset, as shown in Table 13.1.

Even this short extract from the tagset illustrates some items of interest. The word *data* may be singular or plural ("The data is . . ." or "The data are . . ."), a fair representation of usage in a 100-million-word corpus but not to the liking of purists conscious of its etymology in a Latin plural. A collective noun like *committee* may take

Table 13.1. KINDS OF NOUNS IN THE CLAWS-5 TAGSET

NN0	Common noun, neutral for number (e.g., *aircraft, data, committee*)
NN1	Singular common noun (e.g., *pencil, goose, time, revelation*)
NN2	Plural common noun (e.g., *pencils, geese, times, revelations*)
NP0	Proper noun (e.g., *London, Michael, Mars, IBM*)

either singular or plural agreement in British English ("A committee which is . . ." vs. "A committee who are . . .," the latter less likely in American English). Concrete and abstract nouns are not distinguished, as the tagging is distributional rather than meaning-based. On a practical note, tags for subclasses of a particular part of speech are usually grouped together alphabetically so that a wildcard such as the asterisk (= "any 0 or more characters") can be used to capture related tags in a single search, for example, in the list in Table 13.1, *N** for all nouns or *NN** for all common nouns.

Tagged corpora make searching much more efficient. If you are interested in the modal verbs *can* and *may*, you can exclude the noun and verb *can* associated with food preservation and the noun *May* 'fifth month,' or vice versa. If you are interested in *impact* as a verb rather than a noun, you can search more efficiently with tags, and for *impact* as a transitive verb you can search for it followed directly by a pronoun, determiner, or noun. Note that such a rough-and-ready search strategy will give you some false positives on the one hand (the so-called *precision* of the search is sub-optimal) and will miss some valid data on the other (sub-optimal *recall*). Ideally, both recall and precision should be as close to 100% as possible, but compromises are normal.

A corpus that is not just tagged but also *parsed*—that is, with each sentence given a structural analysis—would allow us to look for structures rather than just strings of words and/or tags. Then we could look directly for verbs that take direct objects. Depending on the parsing adopted, we could search for relative clauses, say, or pronoun subjects. Note that nominative forms of pronouns—which can be searched for without parsing—are not the same as subjects, as the following examples from the Corpus of Contemporary American English (COCA) and its Historical counterpart (COHA) show. In (1), accusative *me* is subject of a verb; in (2), nominative *I* is not subject.

(1)   a.   And then maybe you and <u>me</u> could go to Hawaii or something (2006, COCA)

       b.   So what do you want <u>me</u> to do? (2015, COCA)

(2)   and [they] presently guessed that it was <u>I</u> (1832, COHA)

For reasons of practicality, however, this chapter will not discuss parsed corpora further. Much useful work can be accomplished simply by searching for text strings, and more still with the possibility of using POS tags as well.

Some corpora have a rudimentary semantic tagging, but even if not, if you were interested, say, in synonyms for telling a joke, you could try searching for a verb before a phrase like *a joke* to get such verbs as *attempt, crack, make, play, repeat, share, tell* (and/or you could search the definitions of the online *Oxford English Dictionary*). Furthermore, most tagged corpora are *lemmatised*, so that all forms of a single lexical item can be picked up in a single lemma search, *cat/cats* or *good/better/best* or *buy/buys/buying/bought*. Be aware of lemmatisation in the way a corpus is set out. Usually, for example, the contracted negative *n't* is separated from its verb, contrary to conventional spelling. This allows one to search for both forms of negative particle, *not* and *n't*, with the same tag. Thus in COHA, a search for "would n't" or more generally "*_vm* *_xx*" (any modal verb followed by any negative) will produce thousands of hits, but "wouldn't" finds none.

There is much more to be said about corpus searching if you want to take it further, for example with more complex searches involving alternatives or wildcards or regular expressions. Details vary with corpus and search engine—the interface through which you put your queries. There are many textbooks (Hoffmann et al. 2008 is excellent, of general utility even though designed for work with a particular corpus.)[2]

Note that tagging of large corpora is done by software programs ("taggers"), and a proportion of tags, typically 4–6% or so, will inevitably be incorrect. Where and how tagging goes wrong is also of interest, as we shall see.

13.3. SOME CORPORA AND OTHER DATA SOURCES

If at all possible, students should have access to the online *Oxford English Dictionary* (*OED*). I will also illustrate this chapter from corpora made conveniently available by Mark Davies of Brigham Young University (BYU), especially his Corpus of Historical American English (COHA) and Corpus of Contemporary American English (COCA). The same search engine is used for a number of corpora stored at BYU, present-day and historical, including some really huge ones. The British National Corpus (BNC) is one of those put out by BYU, and also, in a more up-to-date edition and with arguably a more manageable search engine, at Lancaster University.

Another source is the web, good for up-to-the-minute usage but presenting various challenges: unknown size of "corpus," which makes statistics difficult; ever-changing material, so that results are irreproducible; often unknown provenance, leaving doubt as to the variety of English in question. There is much literature with a discussion of the problems of internet source material and how to mitigate them.[3] A convenient search engine for internet material is WebCorp, which is better than using an ordinary content-oriented search engine like Google or Bing.

Other BYU corpora include Google Books, Global Web-Based English from 20 different countries (GloWbE), a Time Magazine archive, and Hansard (records of UK parliamentary proceedings). Here are some other suggestions, by no means a complete list, some of them referenced at the end of the chapter. From the Survey of English Usage at University College London you can purchase ICE-GB (1 million words of current British English, written and spoken) and the Diachronic Corpus of Parsed Spoken English (DCPSE, two matched corpora of spoken English from the 1960s and the 1990s, nearly 900,000 words). These are very carefully produced corpora with a lot of spoken material, fully tagged and parsed. The search engine is comprehensive but idiosyncratic, and the corpora are not free.

The Corpus of Late Modern English Texts (CLMET3.0) includes 34 million words from 1710 to 1920, divided into three subperiods of seventy years each, tagged. Four carefully produced corpora from the Universities of Pennsylvania and York totalling over 7 million words cover the periods from Old English through to 1914 (YCOE, PPCME2, PPCEME, PPCMBE2). They are fully tagged and consistently parsed, but the search engine, CorpusSearch, takes serious training to master and is probably not suitable for any but the most advanced classes. A Representative Corpus of Historical English Registers 3.2 (ARCHER) is a multi-genre corpus of 3.3 million words from 1600 to 1999. The project is coordinated from Manchester and will be available in a tagged version at Lancaster and a tagged and parsed version at Zurich. The Old Bailey Corpus (OBC) is some 134 million words of transcribed London court proceedings from 1720 to 1913, a remarkable resource.

13.4. SEARCHING A CORPUS

To make good use of a corpus you should have some idea of its coverage of material— periods, genres, media, and so on—and of the tagset used. A good corpus will offer documentation that explains the procedures followed in collecting, transcribing and marking it up. Online search engines differ in features and screen interface. Some corpora are available for use on your own computer rather than online, whether with their own search engine or by means of a general-purpose concordance program.

The online search engine for the BYU corpora has its idiosyncrasies. For COHA you enter a search word or string, optionally specifying word classes or periods or genres, and click "Find Matching Strings." The "List" search tabulates in decreasing order of frequency up to 100 forms that satisfy your search, with detailed numbers by decade between 1810–1819 and 2000–2009. All or a selection of the hits can be displayed, a screenful at a time. (Note that the collections for the first couple of decades are rather patchy and unreliable.) The "Chart" search produces a decade-by-decade histogram with absolute frequencies and counts per million words. The "KWIC" (key word in context) search shows the number of hits and displays them in context with a handful of words on either side of the search item colour-coded to indicate POS: nouns in turquoise highlighting; verbs, magenta; adjectives, green; prepositions, yellow; adverbs, brown; function words, grey. A "Compare" search tabulates the collocates (words in the contexts of the hits) of two different search strings, allowing you to assess the differing behaviour of each item, or compares two periods.

13.5. DERIVATION

One way that new words get made is by *derivation*, the addition of an affix. The usual effect of a *suffix* (an affix attached at the end) is to change the word class, as in *sketch*$_N$ > *sketchy*$_{Adj}$ or *tender*$_{Adj}$ > *tenderise*$_V$ but not always, as in

$rocket_N$ > $rocketry_N$ (different *kinds* of noun, however, in this case). Via derivation we get families of words like $abstain_N$—$abstinent_{Adj}$—$abstention_N$, $permit_V$—$permission_N$—$permissive_{Adj}$, $strong_{Adj}$—$strongly_{Adv}$—$strength_N$—$strengthen_V$, $invite_V$—$inviting_{Adj}$—$invitation_N$, $attend_V$—$attendance_N$—$attention_N$—$attentive_{Adj}$, and so on.

Semantic change may affect whole families of words, as when the *strong* family is extended from describing human muscle-power to, say, the force of an argument, or coffee. Sometimes, though, different members of the family go different ways. Thus the verb *abstain* is most typically used in two senses: to forego something (usually pleasurable) and later, to refrain specifically from voting. The noun *abstention* eventually follows the verb in both of these contexts, but the adjective *abstinent* has apparently never been used of someone who doesn't vote. There is endless scope for research in the *OED* into the semantic histories of word families. For two examples of relevance here, see my discussion of the negative connotations of recent senses of *sketchy* in American English versus the entirely neutral *sketch* (noun or verb) and on the frequently negative connotations of *discrimination* and *discriminate* versus the positive connotations of the adjective *discriminating*.[4]

To return to word-formation, an interesting exercise is to look for trends in the use of different suffixes. For example, choose some suffixes that form abstract nouns, whether general ones like *-ment* and *-ity* or more specialised ones like *-age*, *-ance/-ence*, *-ation*, *-hood*, *-ism*, *-ship*, etc. For each such suffix, use the *OED Online* to find new formations, with dates of first use from which you can calculate numbers in a given decade or half-century. To do this, try the "Advanced search" facility, specifying

- Search in   *Entries*\
- search string   *???*age*   (wildcards followed by the suffix in question; a minimum of 6 letters should avoid monosyllables like *phage*)
- in   *Headword*
- Part of speech   *Noun*
- Date of entry   *1800–* or *1950–1999*   (don't shorten ranges as 1950–99)

If you choose a longish timespan or leave the date filter blank, you can then click *Timeline* to see a convenient graphic representation (histogram) in numbers by fifty-year periods, though more careful work would discount irrelevant hits which come up in the sample search described previously, such as the entries *road rage* or *monophage*, as well as borrowings like *ménage à quatre*.

In addition to the dictionary, you can use a large corpus to get a better idea of frequency of use at a given time: COHA or CLMET3.0 or EEBO or (with more caution) *Google Books*, or even the quotation database of the *OED* treated as a corpus. For example, there have been student fads in recent decades in the United States and Britain where non-standard words in *-age* have been coined humorously despite the prior existence of words which should have blocked them.[5] Something similar is illustrated in (3):

(3)   He makes up words out of his head. At lunchtime, he says it's time for
        eatage. When we get head call, it's time for pissage. Lights-out, and it's time
        for sleepage. (2003, COCA)

Here, collected from the *OED* (s.v. *-age* suffix), are some recent *-age* words (i) first
found on or after 1900; (ii) consisting of a single word; (iii) not obviously French
borrowings; (iv) which happen to occur in COCA:

*coverage | creepage | ecotage | footage | gallonage | megatonnage | narratage | ohmage |
plottage | plussage | signage | wordage*

An upright bar " | " in a search string separates alternatives, though unfortunately
this option is incompatible with POS limitation to nouns (by adding "_nn*"), lemma
search to capture plurals as well as singulars (by adding square brackets), or wild
cards. The search string indicated above gives the chart shown in Figure 13.1. Sadly,
the recent word *flamage* 'vitriolic argument or ranting [online]' does not occur in
COHA or COCA, though there are seven examples in GloWbE.

If students are aware of derivational innovations in their own circles, get them to
investigate the distribution or history of similar patterns or try plotting the spread of
the *-gate* suffix (from *Watergate*, 1972–3) for scandals and cover-ups more generally.

13.6. CONVERSION

One property that somewhat distinguishes English from "Standard Average
European" is the ease of *conversion* from one word class to another without any overt
change of form, allowing the word to be used in either class. Viewing conversion (a
technical term) as the addition of an affix which happens to be zero explains the
alternative term, *zero-derivation*. The commonest case is transfer between noun and
verb in either direction (historically, that is). The words *bottle, fashion,* and *hammer,*
which intuition says must have started as nouns, may be used as verbs. The verbs *dive*
and *fling* may be used as nouns.[6] Alteration of stress (compare $import_V$ and $import_N$)
can be included in "zero."

1890	1900	1910	1920	1930	1940	1950	1960	1970	1980	1990	2000	
0	2	0	14	95	143	252	434	476	658	1113	1148	SECTION
0.00	0.09	0.00	0.55	3.86	5.87	10.27	18.10	19.99	25.99	39.83	38.83	2000

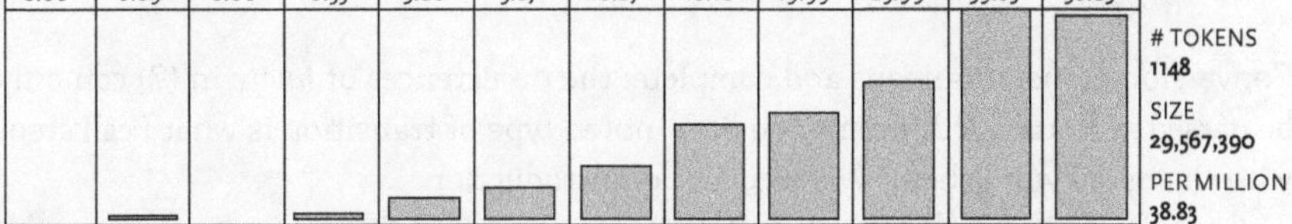

TOKENS
1148

SIZE
29,567,390

PER MILLION
38.83

Figure 13.1. Twelve nouns in with *-age* suffix in COHA

An obvious contributor to the ease of conversion in English is the loss of much inflectional marking in the language, especially in the centuries between late Old English and early Modern English, since one sure-fire way of distinguishing parts of speech in, say, the classical languages is the different inflectional paradigms associated with verbs, nouns, and adjectives. Our intuitions on which word class has historical priority must always be checked, for example, in the *OED*; sometimes the first appearances are more or less simultaneous. Other conversions include adverbial particle to noun (*ups and downs*), adjective to noun (*musical, uniform*), adjective to verb (*big up, gross out*), and particle to verb (*to out someone*).

Recent denominal verbs—or at least, conversions *thought* to be recent—arouse particular ire from prescriptivists. Business and computer Englishes favour such usages as *action* as a verb, *progress* as a transitive verb, and so on.

(4) Air Force Space Command is <u>transitioning</u> its current mix of medium and heavy lift expendable boosters to the new Evolved Expendable Launch Vehicle for space launch. (2003, COHA)

(5) Put your request into an email and I will <u>action</u> it. (2012, GloWbE)

(6) "We still want people to take risks and <u>progress</u> the sport," says Gaffney. (2012, COCA)

Rather than use the suffixed derivative *invitation*, many speakers use the zero-derived noun *invite*, a usage that invites much criticism.[7] The *OED* shows that *invite*$_N$ goes back to the seventeenth century and was used in the eighteenth, for example, by the socially elevated writer Fanny Burney:

(7) Every body Bowed, & accepted the <u>invite</u> but me ... for I have no Notion of snapping at <u>invites</u> from the Great. (1778, *OED* s.v. *invite* n. 1)

A tagged corpus like COHA should allow students to find examples for discussion, but care is needed. Why does "[invite]_nn*" (= the lexeme *invite* tagged with POS noun) get so many hits that are verbs? Conversely, when we search for "[action]_vv*" (= the lexeme *action* with POS tag lexical verb), why are almost all the hits actually nouns? It is instructive to try to work out why the tagger may have gone wrong in particular cases.[8]

13.7. STEPWISE CHANGE

Conversion is instantaneous and complete: the occurrences of *invite* in (7) can only be parsed as nouns. A different and little-noted type of transition is what I call stepwise change of word class.[9] We need a brief introduction.

Consider nouns and adjectives. Both can occur as modifiers of a head noun; the nouns *drug* and *health* in (8) and the adjective *serious* in (9) are all modifiers of the head noun *problem*:

(8)   These individuals mask an increasing <u>drug</u> problem and claim that it is necessary to solve the problem of drugs as a <u>health</u> problem. (2007, COHA)

(9)   It became a <u>serious</u> problem. (2000, COHA)

Both word classes can occur as head of a predicative complement, and either a mass noun like *nonsense* or an adjective like *worthless* can occupy that position by itself:

(10)   The claim is <u>nonsense</u> (1982, COHA)

(11)   The claim is <u>worthless</u> (2002, COHA)

The underlined words in (10) and (11) are distinguishable in other contexts that show they are respectively noun and adjective, for example, the asterisk here is a notational convention for something ungrammatical:

(12)   a.   They sent us some nonsense/*worthless. (only N possible)
        b.   The claim is very/so *nonsense/worthless. (only Adj possible)

The fact that nouns and adjectives share certain parts of their distributions, as illustrated in (8) through (11), means that those contexts leave the word class of their filler underdetermined or vague if there isn't clear evidence of the correct class elsewhere (as there was with (12)). And with certain words the external evidence is conflicting. A number of nouns in the last few decades have been gaining the possibility of functioning as full-fledged adjectives in addition to their earlier status (e.g., *ace, amateur, apricot, bandaid, cardboard, champion, core, corker, cowboy, designer, dinosaur, draft, freak, fun, genius, key, killer, landmark, luxury, niche, pants, powerhouse, rubbish, surprise, toy, Velcro*).[10] They don't become adjectives instantaneously. There is a period of transition, during which some evidence points to them not yet being adjectives and other evidence suggests that they are. And they retain the option of being used as nouns.

Early in the process, the word can be coordinated with items that are definitely adjectives, which suggests but certainly does not prove that it has become an adjective itself:

(13)   There's the expectation that it's this <u>fun</u> and easy thing that takes a few days. (2015, COCA)

Or the word occurs to the left of another modifier which is definitely an adjective:

(14)   <u>Key</u> new evidence comes from two directions. (2005, COCA)

Even stronger evidence that a word has achieved adjectival status is when it can itself be modified by intensifiers like *so, very, too*, and the like:

(15)   They both knew that Molly was thinking about Fred's scars, which looked too <u>amateur</u> to be from surgery (1995, COCA)

Likewise the ability to occur as a post-modifier:

(16)　["]What'd he say to her?" "Probably said something <u>genius</u>, like 'Pardon me.'"
　　　(2014, COCA)

And the clincher is when the transitioning word occurs as a comparative or superlative, an inflectional property unavailable to nouns:

(17)　For many of the country's <u>nichest</u> and most powerful, a recession might be
　　　preferable to what it takes to get the economy moving again (1994, COCA)

Even a syntactic comparative or superlative will do:

(18)　Organizational services are moving from the realm of being discretionary to
　　　being more <u>key</u>, more critical to an improved quality of life (1995, COCA)

Adjectival properties are added at different speeds and different periods for different words, and speakers at any one time may be more or less conservative. Thus most speakers would accept *something fun*; younger speakers would probably accept *so fun* where their older relatives would say *such fun*; but so far, relatively few would accept the attested comparative *funner*. The previous examples have not been selected to reflect the chronology of particular changes. The process for a given word can sometimes be tracked in dictionaries and especially historical corpora.

I suggest the word *key* in senses like "essential, crucial" for an exercise of this kind. The process by which it develops an adjectival use has been discussed from several points of view.[11] The usage is frequent enough and the transition close enough to completion among younger speakers for data to be easily found. Students can search for suitable diagnostic contexts, perhaps cautiously using the POS tags assigned to *key* to help them find pertinent examples. An additional exercise that will teach them a lot is to get them to explain why they think the tagger might have gone wrong in cases where they judge a sentence to have been mistagged. Examples will quickly appear if you search COHA for "[key]" as, respectively, noun, adjective, or verb. The menu to the right of the search window allows you to specify POS, while the square brackets ensure that *key* is treated as a lemma and all inflectional forms are included. The BNC at Lancaster with its BNCweb interface allows you to see not just the simple tags but the so-called *ambiguity tags* used when the tagger is unable to decide on an analysis with reasonable certainty. For example, out of 2,280 occurrences of the form *keys* in BNC, 134 are tagged "NN2-VVZ" (= either plural of a common noun or 3 sg. pres. of a verb, but more likely the former), while 37 are tagged "VVZ-NN2."

Another possibly stepwise change is seen in the past participles of verbs of mental disposition. They can behave either as adjectives or as verbs. Compare

(19) Jim was frightened by a spider.
(20) Jim was frightened of spiders.
(21) Jim was frightened.

In (19), *frightened* is a verb. The sentence is the passive of *A spider frightened Jim*, and the likely interpretation is of an instantaneous event; we could say *What happened to Jim was that he was frightened by a spider*. That would not be an appropriate transformation of (20), which describes a state. In (20), *frightened* is an adjective; it can be modified readily by *so* or *very*. Sentence (21) is ambiguous. This area of the language has seen a gradual change over the last four centuries. In Shakespeare's time it was normal to write *much interested, much concerned*, and so on, the modifier *much* being appropriate for a verb. Over time it became increasingly acceptable, and nowadays more or less obligatory, to use modifiers like *very* that are appropriate to adjectives.[12] This kind of change could be tracked in COHA or ARCHER or PPCMBE2, and students could be encouraged to think of other evidence that would show whether a participle was verbal or adjectival.

13.8. CLITICISATION/GRAMMATICALISATION/UNCONVENTIONAL SPELLINGS

Unstressed function words are often combined as *clitics* with the preceding word. Thus, the strings *have to* and *has to* are typically pronounced [hæftə, hæstə] with devoicing of the final consonant of the verb, but only when they mean 'must':

(22) a. the crops they have to [hæv tə] sell 'the crops for sale that they possess'

      b. the crops they have to [hæftə] sell 'the crops that they must sell'

Now, there is usually no sign in writing of the devoicing, though in fact *haf(f) to* (106×), *haf t* (4×), *haf ter* (2×) and *haf tuh* (2×) do occur in COHA, some no doubt representing dialect or foreign speech. However, informal pseudo-phonetic spellings like *gonna* for *going to*, *gotta* for *got to*, *kinda* for *kind of*, and so on are increasingly common as representations of colloquial speech and/or a non-standard speaker. All are interesting topics for research.

The informal spelling *gonna* is lemmatised as two "words" separated by a space in COHA, *gon na*. Figure 13.2 shows its rise.

(Incidentally, the infinitive marker with POS tag *TO* lemmatised as *na* occurs in both *gonna* and *wanna*; search for "na_to" in the current COHA interface.) Students can compare the frequencies of standard and informal spellings by date or genre; they can see whether particular subjects or lexical verbs promote the use of the non-standard spellings. To make a fair comparison with standard *going to* as an auxiliary of the future, it would make sense to ensure that the following word is a verb. In COHA one could search for "going to *_vv*" or perhaps "going to_to" (= the infinitive marker *to* as opposed to the preposition), in order to avoid irrelevant verb phrases like *going to bed* or *going to London* which do not have equivalents with *gonna*. Then improve the search to catch split infinitives like (23) as well:

(23)　a.　She thought he was <u>going to</u> really hurt her (1978, COHA)

　　　b.　It's not too sharp, so it's probably <u>gon na</u> really hurt when it hits you (1999, COHA)

　　Another good topic is the strings *sort of*, *kind of*, and *type of*, sometimes known as SKT constructions. What is of interest here it is not so much the phonetically similar contraction to *kind a/kinda/sorta*, and so on, as the word classes involved, originally noun and preposition, respectively, "kind_nn1 of_io." Such a tagging is fully justified in a sentence like (24), less obviously appropriate in (25), but it would be completely inappropriate in (26) (where in fact the two words are "ditto-tagged" as an adverb in COHA).

(24)　in making a particular kind of wine (1834, COHA)

(25)　"I don't generally do those kind of things," answered Randal (1839, COHA)

(26)　"Didn't you kind of hate to give it up?" (1918, COHA)

　　The pattern of (25), where the number of the determiner *these* or *those* agrees not with the SKT noun but with the noun after *of*, is surprisingly old—and a prescriptivist bugbear. The pattern of (26), where the word after *of* is not a noun but a verb, adverb, or adjective, has been seen with *sort* and *kind* for quite a long time and is just starting to appear with *type* as well; SKT-word + *of* seems to be lexicalised as a kind of adverb or hedge. British and American Englishes differ in their rates of use and perhaps their formality judgements of *sort of*.[13] Exercises here could include seeing just how frequent SKT constructions are and have been in the past, finding examples of the main kinds of use, discussing how taggers have (or have not) coped with them,

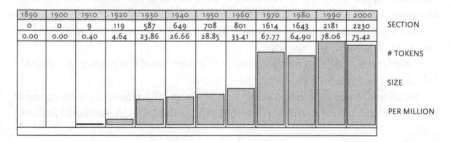

1890	1900	1910	1920	1930	1940	1950	1960	1970	1980	1990	2000
0	0	9	119	587	649	708	801	1614	1643	2181	2230
0.00	0.00	0.40	4.64	23.86	26.66	28.85	33.41	67.77	64.90	78.06	75.42

SECTION

\# TOKENS

SIZE

PER MILLION

Figure 13.2. The form *gonna* (gon na) in COHA

and comparing frequencies of *sort of* and *kind of* in British and American English or in different genres.

Finally in this section, consider the unreal conditional sentence in (27). Contracted versions, (28), would also be standard English, especially in fast speech.

(27)   If I had known sooner, I would have gone to see you. (1834, COHA)

(28) a. If I'd known sooner, I would've gone to see you.

      b. If I'd known sooner, I'd've gone to see you.

In colloquial usage, separate developments have been taking place in both clauses over a long period.[14] In the *if*-clause, many speakers insert an extra *have*, nearly always unstressed:

(29) If I'd've known sooner, I'd've gone to see you.

This can make for parallel verb strings in each clause. The apparently superfluous morpheme also appears in various other guises in writing, as in (30), with or without apostrophes. The spelling *of* arouses particular prescriptive ire. For some speakers, apparently, the first contracted verb *'d* can be expanded, as in (31), though others (a majority?) find both *would* and *had* ungrammatical here even—remarkably—if they're happy with the contraction *'d*.

(30) a. If I'd of known sooner, . . . (pronounced [əv] with schwa, the same as (29))

      b. If I'd'a known sooner, . . . (pronounced [ə] with schwa and loss of [v])

(31) a. If I had've known sooner, . . .

      b. If I would've known sooner, . . .

The second morpheme can also be written or spoken in full as *have*, though less commonly than the reduced forms, and there is even corpus evidence that some speakers can pronounce it as stressed *of*, with the vowel of *hot* rather than a schwa. There are other permutations of these variants.

In the second, main clause of (28), what is historically the infinitive of the auxiliary verb *have* is perceived by many speakers not just phonetically but also lexically and syntactically as the preposition *of* and can appear as such in writing. Whether or not it has been reanalysed as *of*, once again the [v] can disappear under lack of stress

(32) a. . . . I would of gone to see you.

      b. . . . I woulda gone to see you.

The same possibilities arise after *could*, *should*, *might*, and the infinitive marker *to*.

This maelstrom of possibilities is a good topic for student investigation and discussion. It raises questions of "correctness" and the role of prescriptive and proscriptive grammar. It is something that students can question in their own experience and usage. Linguistically speaking, it is a classic example of grammaticalisation. It is also a nightmare for the lemmatisation and tagging of corpora!

This perhaps is the most elaborate test case given in this chapter, suitable for classes with a good knowledge of English grammar and a willingness to tangle with variation. Other groups will be able to find more modest projects to expand their knowledge of the history of English.

13.9. DATA SOURCES AND ABBREVIATIONS

ARCHER   A Representative Corpus of Historical English Registers version x. 1990–1993/2002/2007/2010/2013. Originally compiled under the supervision of Douglas Biber and Edward Finegan at Northern Arizona University and University of Southern California; modified and expanded by subsequent members of a consortium of universities. Current member universities are Bamberg, Freiburg, Heidelberg, Helsinki, Lancaster, Leicester, Manchester, Michigan, Northern Arizona, Santiago de Compostela, Southern California, Trier, Uppsala, Zurich. Information available from http://www.projects.alc.manchester.ac.uk/archer/.

BNC   The British National Corpus, version 3 (BNC XML Edition). 2007. Oxford University Computing Services on behalf of the BNC Consortium. Available online at http://bncweb.lancs.ac.uk/ and at http://corpus.byu.edu/bnc/.

CLMET3.0   De Smet, Hendrik, Hans-Jürgen Diller & Jukka Tyrkkö. 2013. The Corpus of Late Modern English Texts, version 3.0, Available at https://perswww.kuleuven.be/~u0044428/

COCA   Davies, Mark. (2008–) *The Corpus of Contemporary American English: 520 million words, 1990-present*. Available online at http://corpus.byu.edu/coca/.

COHA   Davies, Mark. (2010–) *The Corpus of Historical American English: 400 million words, 1810–2009*. Available online at http://corpus.byu.edu/coha/.

ECCO   Eighteenth Century Collections Online. Available online at http://find.galegroup.com/ecco/.

EEBO   Early English Books Online. Available online at http://eebo.chadwyck.com/home and soon from BYU and see now http://www.textcreation-partnership.org/tcp-eebo/.

GloWbE   Davies, Mark. (2013) *Corpus of Global Web-Based English: 1.9 billion words from speakers in 20 countries*. Available online at http://corpus.byu.edu/glowbe/.

OBC   Huber, Magnus, Magnus Nissel, Patrick Maiwald & Bianca Widlitzki. 2012. The Old Bailey Corpus. Spoken English in the eighteenth and nineteenth centuries. Available at www.uni-giessen.de/oldbaileycorpus.

OED   Simpson, J. A. & E. S. C. Weiner (eds.). 2000–. *The Oxford English Dictionary Online*. Available at www.oed.com/.

PPCEME   Kroch, Anthony, Beatrice Santorini & Lauren Delfs. 2004. Penn-Helsinki Parsed Corpus of Early Modern English. http://www.ling.upenn.edu/hist-corpora/PPCEME-RELEASE-3/index.html.

PPCMBE2   Kroch, Anthony, Beatrice Santorini & Ariel Diertani. 2016. Penn Parsed Corpus of Modern British English, 2nd edition. http://www.ling.upenn.edu/hist-corpora/PPCMBE2-RELEASE-1/index.html.

PPCME2   Kroch, Anthony & Ann Taylor. 2000. Penn-Helsinki Parsed Corpus of Middle English, 2nd edition. http://www.ling.upenn.edu/hist-corpora/PPCME2-RELEASE-4/index.html

WebCorp   WebCorp: Linguist's search engine. Birmingham City University. Available at http://www.webcorp.org.uk/.

YCOE   Taylor, Ann, Anthony Warner, Susan Pintzuk & Frank Beths. 2003. The York-Toronto-Helsinki Parsed Corpus of Old English Prose. http://www-users.york.ac.uk/~lang22/YCOE/YcoeHome.htm.

CHAPTER 14

Dictionaries and the History of English

MICHAEL ADAMS

14.1. INTRODUCTION

Dictionaries are largely misunderstood, even by literature professors and linguists working in English departments, the very people most likely to teach courses on the history of the English language. Nevertheless, in various ways, they are potentially useful resources for such courses. Obviously, dictionaries—especially historical dictionaries—are full of historical facts and judgments about English. In their etymologies, they tie English to other languages within the Proto-Indo-European group; in their sense analysis, they reveal not just different meanings but often implicitly the cultural basis for those meanings. Their quotations amplify voices from the past into the present day, allowing students to think about the relationships between meaning and register, both of them historically situated. The quotations also illustrate syntax and can include metalinguistic commentary. Usage labels also reflect language attitudes, and while some dictionaries account for standard or at least mainstream English, variety from slang to regionalism is also well represented in the dictionary record of English. Students can find out a lot about English by looking *in* dictionaries, and my treatment will include some useful assignments that draw on the dictionary as a work of reference.

But there's more. Students can learn things about the history of English by looking *at* dictionaries, too. As cultural artifacts, dictionaries help to bridge so-called inner and outer histories of English, which at times seem almost to be competitive concerns in the history of English classroom. Dictionaries and glossaries are made by people to codify English at different times (from Old English on) for different reasons, most of which aren't as simple as "so that people can look words up and find their meanings." Whether a dictionary is handwritten on vellum or mechanically typeset or presented as a digital text matters historically and tells us about the audience one or another codification is meant to serve. Outer history informs language ideology; language ideology drives codification; dictionaries express and challenge language ideologies. Whereas dictionary-as-reference connects the history of English and linguistics, dictionary-as-artifact leads to even more broadly interdisciplinary engagement.

Finally, students can make glossaries and dictionaries, individually or in groups, even groups as large as a whole class. They can participate self-consciously in linguistic description and codification. In doing so, they learn language facts of various kinds, identify protocols of description, and orient the glossary culturally in its apparatus and the essay that introduces it. At its best, writing such glossaries isn't just another assignment, not just intellectual make-work; when they're done well, students' glossaries can add to the sum of human knowledge and communicate knowledge about the English language effectively, even compellingly, to both professional and popular audiences. In writing such a glossary, a student isn't just writing *about* the history of English but is actually *being* a historian of English, and the experience, as well as the knowledge it produces, is likely to stay with the student for a long time.

14.2. LOOKING *IN* DICTIONARIES

Look it up. That's what we're told to do if we have questions about English words and their histories, and it's the obvious point at which to start with dictionaries in a history of English course. Useful historical information is hard to find in most dictionaries. College and pocket dictionaries serve immediate needs—spellings and definitions—and etymological problems are rarely emergencies. Etymologies in dictionaries are often cursory and not infrequently wrong, partially wrong, or inconclusive—don't assume that "unknown" is a final verdict, and a supposedly Latin etymology might actually be Anglo-French, or vice versa.[1] Etymologies in the *Oxford English Dictionary* (*OED*) are generally more accurate, and in the third edition—the one we use online—they are increasingly thoughtful, complex, discursive, and reliable. Some general-purpose dictionaries have valuable approaches to etymology, especially the *American Heritage Dictionary of the English Language* (*AHD*), now in its fifth edition (2011), which includes an appendix of Proto-Indo-European (PIE) roots, to which relevant etymologies within the main dictionary text are cross-referred. One irresistible feature of the appendix is that Modern English reflexes of quite different meanings are grouped under their common PIE etymon, an interesting way to plumb the historical depths of English polysemy.

There are several notable dictionaries of etymology, including Onions's *Oxford Dictionary of English Etymology* (1966),[2] Skeat's *Etymological Dictionary of the English Language, Fourth Edition* (1909),[3] and Barnhart and Steinmetz's *Barnhart Dictionary of Etymology* (1987),[4] which summarize the etymologies of words more thoroughly than most general dictionaries can afford to do. As one of America's great commercial lexicographers, Clarence Barnhart, once observed, "From a practical standpoint, few if any dictionaries are prepared to yield precious space to . . . thorough etymologizing, as most dictionary users have little interest in or use for etymologies."[5] Among the few who do, of course, are students in courses on the history of English.

In contrast with these standard works, Liberman's *Analytic Dictionary of English Etymology*[6]—which sets a new and very high standard—is unusual because rather than pronouncing briefly and definitively on the origins of words, it assesses a massive amount of writing relevant to etymologies in article length entries. It considers etymologies as problematic rather than catering to the idea that each etymology is a crux with a one-sentence solution. The first volume of this multivolume work, subtitled *An Introduction*,[7] has been followed by the compendious *Bibliography of English Etymology: Sources and Word List* (2010)—students can look up words in which they are interested in the word list and find a list of all works Liberman has found that discuss the etymologies of those words arranged alphabetically. An advanced undergraduate or graduate student with the right library in support could write an etymological article on the basis of material listed in the bibliography and quite possibly supersede some formulaic etymologies in standard dictionaries, but the *Bibliography* is pedagogically useful in various ways.[8]

One useful application of all these resources—besides just looking things up—is that they represent different methods, different assumptions about how to find and report what's important about the history of words. That is, they don't share the same historiographical assumptions—they operate subtly different theories of history. It's unusual for courses on the history of English to question what "history" means, but they probably ought to, and instructors looking for an opening to do so find one here. Dictionaries also represent the history of words in different modes. For instance, the American Heritage Dictionaries, Merriam-Webster Dictionaries, and the New Oxford American Dictionaries all intersperse "word history notes" among their entries. These tell a word's story rather than account formulaically for its historical derivation, as in traditional etymologies. Undoubtedly, some users of dictionaries—including students in our courses—find stories easier to read and more memorable than cryptically abbreviated accounts of etymology.

These etymological resources support a number of exercises useful in history of English courses. The easiest and most obvious of these is to have students write a word history on the American Heritage model. At times, I have used the American Heritage book *Word Histories and Mysteries: From Abracadabra to Zeus* (2004) as a supplementary text to support this and the next likely exercise, in which students explore word-formative processes by working through the entries in that book and finding as many processes as possible, reporting the processes with examples, of course.[9] Students respond well to words because they're more familiar than other linguistic items and looking at them structurally can in fact cross over into matters of phonology and syntax.[10] I strongly advise that this exercise precede the writing of any word histories.

It is not obvious to students that English is fundamentally Germanic, nor is it obvious that the Germanic-ness of vocabulary in use would vary according to text type. I sometimes cull 100-word passages from texts of various types: prose fiction, prose nonfiction, academic writing, web text, poetry, journalism, and so on. I hand them out to a class at random and students figure out the proportions of Germanic, Romance, and other word origins in their texts. In class, we share the results and average all of the poetry samples, all of the web text samples, and so on, and compare them—which types of texts are more Germanic and which less so? The answers are not revelations to those who study English professionally, but students are often surprised that poetry tends to be more Germanic and academic writing proportionally less so. Similarly surprising is the amount of English ultimately derived from PIE, which can be exposed in a similar exercise. Students need only a good dictionary to perform well on these last two exercises, and, if nothing else, they will become adept at interpreting etymologies in dictionary entries.

The very idea of "looking up" obscures the fact that dictionaries are readable texts. You can read general dictionaries—people certainly have, though it takes some practice at figuring out how to read them[11]—but the historical ones are better for reading and we know that lovers of language have taken considerable pleasure in reading them,[12] partly because they invite readers to construct various sorts of narrative while evaluating the quotations among themselves and in relation to other types of entry-level information, like etymology.[13] The quotations are full of cultural information tagged with a date, and some include metalinguistic commentary; each quotation is culled from a text, and text types are relevant to evaluating the information but are themselves metalinguistic information that, along with the rest, bridges the inner and outer histories of English. To put it more forcefully: in its mixture of linguistic and metalinguistic information, every substantial entry in a historical dictionary infuses inner with outer history and vice versa.

You can practice this sort of reading with students in the classroom if you have digital access. You can put a recent installment of "Among the New Words" (ATNW), a quarterly feature of *American Speech*, and read through it together. The cultural information there is easier for students to read than that in the *Middle English Dictionary* or the *Dictionary of the Older Scottish Tongue*, and so the technique and value of reading a historical dictionary/glossary makes sense more immediately. Some historical dictionaries raise the interesting question of whether they can enregister regional lexis or niche vocabularies, like occupational jargons. For instance, how can the *Dictionary of Prince Edward Island English*[14] *not* be enregistering Prince Edward Island English (PEI)?[15]

Digital formats require that we learn to read dictionaries in new ways—reading the *OED* online is not the same as reading it in print. Yet it's certainly worth reading in both versions—different media are likely to lead to different experiences of the histories of English words.

14.3. LOOKING *AT* DICTIONARIES

According to the *OED*, *material culture* means "the physical objects, such as tools, domestic articles, or religious objects, which give evidence of the type of culture developed by a society or group." Sidney Landau, an accomplished lexicographer and author of a leading text on lexicography, writes, "Dictionaries do not spring into being. People must plan them, collect information, and write them. . . . No other form of writing is at once so quixotic and so intensely practical."[16] In the interest of "correctness," some treat dictionaries—which they tend to call *the* dictionary—as quasi-religious objects, and in their intensely practical effects, they are taken as tools, too. It is easy to forget, concerned with dictionary texts as we are, that dictionaries are physical objects, or, at least they were until the advent of the digital age, and thus part of material culture—they are material as well as intellectual artifacts and are often most informative about language history along the wavering line between those two artefactual states. People plan dictionaries, and what they plan is manifest not merely in the words and treatment of them but in the very books they fill.

What people buy, shelve, give, use, and annotate similarly says something, not about the lexicographer's plan but rather about the language attitudes and ideologies the lexicographer accommodates or challenges. Imagine a distant future in which digital dictionaries—no doubt implanted in our brains—have erased the *OED* from memory. An archeologist of that time might dig up an improbably preserved copy of the printed first edition of *OED*—perhaps my copy!—in thirteen volumes. What does it mean that such a big dictionary originating apparently—given the front matter—in nineteenth-century Britain was reprinted in 1961 and owned and obviously thumbed by an American born in that very year. What do we expect of a dictionary that big, and what does it represent about any number of imagined communities, in which a people's bonds were their words?

Of course, not all dictionaries are as big as the *OED*. Even historical dictionaries can be much smaller. So the archaeologist who excavates my library would perhaps wonder what it means about the history of English and its varieties—as well as about attitudes toward those varieties—that the *Dictionary of Prince Edward Island English* records a smallish distinct vocabulary in a single volume of 192 pages,[17] and the *Dictionary of American English*[18] (*DAE*; 1938–1944) runs to only four large volumes— where do these Englishes figure in the whole story of English? *DAE* did not enter twentieth-century words, meanings, and quotations, which is revealing about attitudes toward old and new in a language's history. But it also didn't include regionalisms or slang, which is why we have since had a *Dictionary of American Regional English*[19] (1985–2013) considerably larger than *DAE* and the first two volumes of a *Historical Dictionary of American Slang*.[20] What does the segregation of these lexicographical artifacts imply about attitudes toward certain types of speech and texts? What does it imply methodologically about historicizing English that broad swathes of English vocabulary don't keep company in a super-dictionary? Eventually, perhaps, digital historical lexicography will answer such questions.

In the pre-digital age, people not only turned to dictionaries for answers about all things lexical but also consumed them as objects. You can carry a paperback dictionary—quite possibly a knock-off of one of the deservedly reputable ones—in your pocket, portable knowledge of English, though not in itself mostly historical, nonetheless historical evidence of the price some people put on the knowledge. In those paper days, dictionaries were used to mark special occasions, like high school graduation or admission into college. So, the *American Heritage College Dictionary* (2002) appeared in a deluxe edition, with a deep red linen binding and gold lettering to distinguish it from the everyday edition mass produced for the masses—it was an attractive book, and books do furnish a room. The deluxe edition was also thumb-indexed so that look-ups were easier. If one urgently needed the spelling of a word beginning with the letter P, one could find it fast, but really, thumb-indexing was less about emergency knowledge and more about the middle-class owner, the dictionary user who pays—or whose Aunt Sophie pays—for convenience and design.

The material and the textual aspects of dictionaries converge in features of dictionary-as-book, like dust jackets. Jackets add color and sheen, figures, and icons to the otherwise solid, nondescript binding of anything but a linen-covered book. They're the covers by which you do judge the book. The jacket for the third edition of Bryan A. Garner's *Garner's Modern American Usage* includes, on the back along the spine, an alphabetical list of topics—nonwords, plurals, punctuation, sexism, word-swapping—covered in some of the entries.[21] Our archaeologist concludes that these subjects especially concerned at least some twenty-first-century Americans. There are ten blurbs, front and back, which say that it's a notable book—famous writers and newspapers of record recommend it. Most important, the front tells us, in small white letters under the big blue-lettered title, that it's "The Authority on Grammar, Usage, and Style," emphasis, I suspect, on the "The." *The American Heritage Dictionary, Second College Edition* (1982) announces at the top front of its dustcover, "The single source for people who need to be right," whether that need is merely visceral or required on the job.[22] Our archeologist might speculate that publishers in late-twentieth- and early-twentieth-century America could rely on certain language ideologies to sell dictionaries, implications to be worked out after the dig. The back of the *Dictionary of Prince Edward Island English*'s jacket reproduces the entry for *catawampus* which includes quotations from works by L. M. Montgomery, the quintessential PEI author; so, the jacket commodifies and markets PEI linguistic and literary identity in a perfect act of enregisterment.

While they are textual, dictionary structure and design are elements distinct from entry text and just as expressive of language attitudes and ideologies. If you open up *AHD4* (2000) and look for types of information, you'll notice the appendix of PIE roots, as well as Usage Notes and Word History Notes, Regional Notes, and Living Language Notes, inserted at points among the entries. The array of notes is quite different from *AHD1*'s (1969) exclusive focus on usage notes that drew on the supposed expertise of supposed usage experts, a deliberately prescriptivist response to the arch-descriptivist *Webster's Third* (1961), which had variously disappointed and antagonized many—though far from all—dictionary users of the era. Structure and design can promote language attitudes, and they also register changes in them, as between *AHD1* and *AHD5*.[23]

All of these considerations, the material and macrotextual, may seem only obliquely relevant to the history of English, but that undervalues both the metalinguistic evidence and book historical methodologies. As Deborah Cameron reminds us, until recently "metalinguistic practices have been more sneered at than studied: they have been relegated to the margins and separated from issues considered more central to the study of language, even language 'in use,'"[24] indeed, even language in history. Now, though, we have come to value "talk about talk," as we have come to call it, because, as Cameron puts it, how people understand and evaluate language, and what they actually do with it . . . may not be so easily separated. Studying the discourse in which people reflect on language, and the practices whereby they attempt to intervene in language, is not only of sociological interest; it may also add something to our infinitely complex phenomenon that human language is.[25]

Dictionaries are talk about talk about talk about talk, and they figure in the discourse Cameron has in mind.

This quasi-material perspective provides instructors with new ways to explore the history of English in lectures and discussions, but students can act on it, too. For instance, in an undergraduate seminar titled "English and the Culture of Correctness," focused on the histories and operations of ideologies and attitudes about English, I have students in groups of three or four investigate sets of usage books. Some sets go wide—Follett's *Modern American Usage* (1966),[26] *Merriam-Webster's Concise Dictionary of English Usage* (2002),[27] *Wired Style*,[28] and *The American Heritage Book of English Usage* (1996)[29]—and some go deep, as in all four Fowlers or the four editions of *Garner's Modern American Usage*. In what rhetoric of correctness is each of these books written? How are the metalinguistic issues framed? Differently, one observes, from guiding texts of earlier centuries, but how? Why is the original Fowler small (19 x 12.5 cm) and the most recent Garner big (26 x 18.5 cm)? Why are Fowler and Garner in double columns, and why does Fowler have a line running the height of the page to separate them? Why is the *American Heritage Book of English Usage* not in double columns, and how do such elements of book design argue for various types of authority over language use? Students compare entries across guides or editions to get at differences in the substance of advice, of course, but they draw some historical conclusions simply from looking at the books.

This mode of inquiry translates easily into comparison of dictionaries proper, for the respective make-ups of Cawdrey's *Table Alphabeticall* (1604)[30] and Richardson's *Dictionary of the English Language* (1837)[31] speak volumes about the history of English and of attitudes toward English from Stuart to Victorian England. While few university libraries nowadays own a copy of Richardson and fewer still a copy of Cawdrey, many have Cawdrey via the Scholar's Facsimiles and Reprints series, and, of course, both through various images online. The *Australian National Dictionary*[32] and Jauncey's *Bardi Grubs and Frog Cakes: South Australian Words*[33] are ostensibly about this history of Australian words, but, in their structures and designs, they propose different notions of language history, different emphases, and different values. Comparisons of works like these provoke students to consider the very enterprise assumed in a course on "the history" of English language.

14.4. DOING DICTIONARIES

The term paper is a staple assignment in upper-level history of English courses, and students can look stuff up in dictionaries while writing one. But let me suggest construction of a historical glossary as a plausible, perhaps even preferable, alternative to the term paper. One motivation for taking it up is essay fatigue. Of course, we want all university graduates to write cogently, and practice makes perfect. Nevertheless, the essay over and over can dig an intellectual rut. After all, an essay is only one way to organize phenomena we encounter, only one way to think through phenomena to knowledge about them. Writing a glossary can be an intellectual release from school habits and provide a view of language, word by word, unlikely in other, more usual forms of inquiry.

Some lexicographers may resist this proposition, but dictionaries are not, or at least need not be, doggedly scientific descriptions of big, general vocabularies. Lexicography need not describe a profession, though, obviously, there are professional lexicographers whose work is stored in books or digital works we call dictionaries. Museums display the works of professional painters, but there are plenty of amateur painters, too, whose eyes are sharpened, expression deepened, and lives enhanced by the practice of painting. We can usefully uncouple the less familiar category *lexicography* from *dictionary*, the all-too-familiar one. Lexicography is a practice that is complicated, rich, analytical, creative, historically and publicly engaged, yet also perhaps personal, and it can be an aesthetic or political practice, as well as a method of accounting for the history of English lexis and related linguistic phenomena. Lexicography nudges the history of English from a curricular margin towards the very center of the humanities.

Here are some ideas for course-sized historical glossaries. A student could write a glossary of libfixes[34]; the jargon of a game and the slang of that game's play[35]; hashtags formed on Black Lives Matter; the jargon of an occupation, indeed, any occupation in which a student participates, such as restaurant, retail, or recreational work; family words; local food words; the jargon of an activity[36]; words of war[37]; regional New World forms from contact with Pennsylvania, Texas, or Wisconsin German, or New England or Louisiana French, and so on; or lexis associated with a favorite television show. There is no end to lexical experience—or to experience mediated lexically—and one advantage to promoting a lexicographical point of view is that students can explore things that matter to them, the language in which they themselves live. Yet if they are examining the historical basis of vocabulary they know, they have to exceed themselves into history, as well.

There are many examples of amateur lexicography on the Web, and most of them treat the lexicon superficially—that is not meant as criticism, for the lexicographers in question are doing the job they wanted to do, for themselves and their presumed audiences. But their glossaries aren't good models for historically and culturally engaged coursework. In terms of concept, here are some good examples: Grant Barrett's *Double-Tongued Dictionary*, much of which ended up in Barrett (2006)[38]; Mark Peters's excellent early entries celebrating word formative patterns at *Wordlustitude*[39]; and ATNW. In terms of entry structure, Barrett's work and ATNW are excellent models, and students can variously adopt and adapt their formats, as well as their operational protocols—indeed, at one time, ATNW was a class-based lexicographical project.[40]

In the context of a course on the history of English, constructing a glossary may present some problems of scale. Obviously, students can't compile anything as comprehensive as a small dictionary, let alone the typically long historical dictionary. It's also unlikely that beginning students can construct entries as dense as those found in historical dictionaries—in the course of a term, they haven't time to amass the data required to do so, nor have they developed the requisite skills. Perhaps the biggest problem of scale is our expectation of what counts as history. We expect to account for English over long arcs of time, marking changes from Old to Middle to Early Modern English, for instance, partly because of the bad data problem[41]; we can rarely document language change decade by decade in early periods. Thus, though they cannot give dense or representative accounts of word history, historical dictionaries describe long arcs of use for words with long lives.

In the *OED*, citations mark out twenty- to fifty-year spans.[42] Documenting more frequent intervals would require too much research and too much editorial time. Also, conventional wisdom has it that a finer account reveals little of historical significance. Mainly, though, the scope of the *OED* and other historical dictionaries—their long lists of lemmata and senses—requires restraint. Otherwise, the dictionary in question could go on forever, not alphabetically, but denser word by word and sense by sense. That's not what we want—a dictionary entry is an abstract of lexical data. If we adjust our sense of historical scale, however, students can research and then write the micro-histories of words,[43] demonstrating thereby what dictionaries like the *OED* miss—variation and development in usage and form from year to year and month to month rather than decade by decade or century by century. Micro-history of recent English is no less history than the macro-kind, and the density of description one can achieve in a micro-history is likely to connect lexis to culture in ways that bring inner and outer histories of English into revealing contact. Usually, what can be accounted for recently in micro-history nonetheless develops from old elements of English, so while quotations reflect a short history in some subcultural sphere of usage, etymologizing leads students back to earlier historical periods.

Work on a historical glossary of the kind I am advocating fulfills the philological program. As Cecily Clark explains,

> If one sees life as a continuum, synchronically as well as diachronically, as a seamless fabric in which language is woven together with politics, religion, economic developments and socio-cultural relationships, then all linguistic manifestations are—if rightly understood—capable of illuminating these other spheres, in the same measure as language is enriched, impoverished, reshaped by the contexts in which it is used.[44]

The student who writes this kind of glossary is not reading about philology but rather doing it, which all sorts of educational theory tells us is better both for the grip of learning on the individual student and promoting the human spirit.

The best student research in this vein is "real" research, adding to the sum of human knowledge about the history of English in ways that traditional lexicography cannot.

Glossaries can be significant in ways that term papers cannot. Students engage in the work partly because they are doing something "real" and partly because, again, it asserts a meaningful relationship between history as conventionally understood and their own cultural and lexical experiences. If the glossary is historical on any scale, and if it is a quotations glossary, that is, an iteration of the tradition established by Samuel Johnson and perfected in historical lexicography since the nineteenth century, then the quotations can register historical facts but also cultural ones, language-in-use but also talk about talk, taking a meta-linguistic turn most don't expect from dictionaries.

The first thing a student must do in order to compile a twenty-or-so-page glossary is to identify a limited, coherent vocabulary. It might be coherent because of historical or structural or cultural relationships among certain lexical items, or it might be coherent insofar as it represents a certain sort of experience or expresses a point of view. Once a student has identified a vocabulary worth treating and treatable in some fashion within the scope of a term-paper-length work, she must research that vocabulary as thoroughly as possible. The ease of research depends on the type of college or university in which she studies. There are many more historical dictionaries, dictionaries of regionalisms, and slang dictionaries standing on library shelves than students and even their teachers realize, and many glossaries and word lists in journals. There are also historical corpora worth consulting, though marginal forms—regional, local, socially dispreferred—are less likely to appear in them, though the Linguistic Atlas Project captures many historical American regionalisms and localisms. Obviously, one can find a lot of data through web searches. Nothing replaces wide and dogged reading, but nowadays reading is often overlooked. Reading with a philological eye serves lexicography but also changes the textual experience.[45]

Anyone familiar with historical dictionaries grasps the work underlying a project of this kind. A student constructs a word list and determines the entry forms; she itemizes variants and figures out whether they are significant; she determines etymologies whenever possible and learns to practice restraint when an etymology cannot responsibly be proposed; she writes definitions; and she constructs quotation paragraphs from evidence that might extend beyond the print record, if local rules about human subject research allow students to explore speech in its living contexts. The choice of quotations can illustrate everything from variant forms of a word to syntactic and pragmatic features beyond the reach of definitions, to variation among text types and registers, and into the metalinguistic. The glossary represents historical facts, among which are facts about language attitudes and ideologies.[46]

So much for the student's perspective—what of the teacher's? I usually structure term paper assignments, including historical glossaries, as a staged process, in three drafts. A typical first draft won't be long, perhaps eight pages, but it provides me with a sample of what the student thinks entries in her glossary should look like, given exigencies of the particular vocabulary and the glossary's proposed purposes. At this stage, students and I come to agreement about matters of entry structure and entry style—what's in bold, what's in italics, where does the etymology appear?—and the teacher pushes the student to look further for quotations from different text types, to antedate an item, or to split an entry into different sub-senses with different histories. Usually, I will ask students to include a list of all of the words they intend to treat in their glossaries at this stage, though they will have attempted entries for less than half of them.

Besides the entries, I expect the finished product to include a brief introductory note of about four or five double-spaced pages that explains the vocabulary under investigation, what the glossary contributes to understanding that vocabulary, and the structure of entries. I prefer to see the introduction as well as an expanded and improved glossary as a second draft, but I negotiate with students on this point— some prefer to work out the glossary as completely as possible, and if I know they're up to the challenge, I let them write the introductory note fresh for the third and final draft. It is possible to write twenty pages of glossary about a single word, but most students (wisely) avoid the obligations that sort of treatment entails. Each glossary is evaluated on its scope and coverage, its treatments of words, the extent to which it manages to account for relevant variation, the intelligence with which quotations are chosen and quotation paragraphs shaped, and careful application of whatever entry style and structure the glossarist adopts.

While colleges and universities usually offer surveys of the history of English, topical courses in which the history of English enters through back or side doors are useful in appealing to a wide variety of students—on an elective basis, not everyone will choose a survey, but almost everyone is somehow interested in language history.[47] I have taught courses on slang in which students have often opted to compile glossaries of slang or jargon that matters to them in lieu of writing an essay. But the lexicographical products of history of English courses need not be individual research; indeed, professional lexicography is usually a cooperative venture. Whole courses can be devoted to compiling a glossary, as Pamela Munro has demonstrated several times at UCLA[48]; and Don McCreary has documented his courses on lexicography at the University of Georgia—which have centered on construction and revision of a slang dictionary called *Dawgspeak*, now in at least its sixth edition—in some detail, as has Wayne Glowka.[49] While Munro and McCreary do not teach history of English courses per se, their methods are portable to such courses, and they have demonstrated that students can produce dictionaries of value, contribute to the literature of English lexis, and gain public attention for the discipline.

14.5. CONCLUSION

In two luminous books, John Considine proves that dictionaries are central to the "Making of Heritage" in Early Modern Europe, in part to the extent that language academies set out to glorify the languages they represent. Dictionaries are literature—they are works of the imagination—as well as documents toward histories of their languages, English among them.[50] Dictionaries are part of history, but they also make history, and historical dictionaries, especially, bring social and cultural history into immediate and mutually significant contact with language history. Students in courses on the history of English need to learn how to use them in research but also how to appreciate them as works that integrate much human knowledge with our knowledge of English language. Dictionaries prove that "the history of English is a naturally interdisciplinary subject, one in which many elements of a liberal education converge—if professors and students (and administrators) keep that in mind, it can be the most significant intellectual experience of a student's career."[51]

PART FOUR

Centuries in a Semester

HEL's Chronological Conventions

CHAPTER 15

English Is an Indo-European Language

Linguistic Prehistory in the History of English Classroom

TIMOTHY J. PULJU

15.1. INTRODUCTION

How much Indo-European linguistics should an instructor include in a history of English course? After the class emerges from the murky depths of prehistory into the comparatively well-lit Anglo-Saxon period, is Indo-European still relevant?

To answer the second question first: yes, Indo-European is relevant throughout the history of English, up to the present day. However, that doesn't mean that the answer to the first question has to be "a lot." There are many topics that are important for the history of English, but there is limited time in any college course. Including a lot of Indo-European linguistics necessarily decreases the time available for reading Old English (OE) and Middle English (ME) texts, for tracing the development of modern World Englishes, or for other equally worthwhile activities. Different instructors will legitimately choose to emphasize different material.

Therefore, what follows should not be read as an argument that a history of English course must include a substantial Indo-European component. Rather, it's a set of suggestions for an instructor who wants to include Indo-European but isn't quite sure how or how much. For such an instructor, I hope to show that Indo-European is not just a subject for the beginning of a chronologically organized course, but it can provide a basis for understanding key points of the grammar and lexicon of present-day English. I'll focus on three main topics: Grimm's Law and Verner's Law, ablaut, and preterite-present verbs, all of which, in my experience, can profitably be incorporated in an introductory undergraduate-level history of English class. After that, I'll give practical suggestions as to what sort of materials—textbooks, reference works, homework assignments, etc.—are best suited to teaching these or other Indo-European topics.

Since Grimm's Law is explained and exemplified in most history of English text-books,[1] I won't go through it in detail, but some readers may find the summary chart in Table 15.1 useful for reference purposes.

Grimm's Law is a crucial diagnostic for recognizing an Indo-European (IE) language as belonging to the Germanic branch of the family. Thus, for any course in which the IE family tree is introduced, Grimm's Law is useful for demonstrating the linguistic kinship of Old English, Old Norse, Gothic, etc. But—and here is where Grimm's Law continues to be relevant up to the present day—we don't have to stop with Old English. Rather, since Modern English is full of words borrowed from Greek and Latin, Grimm's Law can help us recognize cognates and non-cognates in the present-day lexicon. Accordingly, the final exam for my course usually includes questions about pairs of English words—a native word paired with a word borrowed from a non-Germanic IE language—asking if they're cognates or not and how we can tell. Examples include *day~diurnal, thin~tenuous, bid~petition, raw~crude*.

The pair *raw~crude* makes clear that my course has a heavy focus on internal history, including sound changes from Old through Middle to Modern English. Recognizing that *raw* and *crude* are cognates (like *thin~tenuous*, but unlike non-cognates *day~diurnal* and *bid~petition*) requires students to have learned not just Grimm's Law (PIE *k > OE h), but also the later change of OE *hr, hl, hn* > ME *r, l, n*. Many instructors, though, will not want to teach as many sound changes as I do. In that case, *raw~crude* could be omitted, but the other pairs I've listed would still be fair game.

Similarly, instructors will have to decide which of the details of Grimm's Law itself should be omitted in an introductory course. For example, the developments of the labiovelar sounds *k^w, *g^w, *g^wh are tricky (especially *g^wh),[2] and I don't teach them to my students. On the other hand, I do include the fact that voiced aspirated *bh, *dh, *gh became the fricatives *β, *ð, *γ before later becoming, in some circumstances, the stops *b, d, g*. Including the fricative stage makes it easier to fit Verner's Law into the sequence of consonant changes from Proto-Indo-European (PIE) to Old English, a sequence I teach to my students. However, Verner's Law—Proto-Germanic voiceless fricatives became voiced in voiced environments when not immediately preceded by the Indo-European accented syllable[3]—is hard to learn. True, students who learn

Table 15.1. GRIMM'S LAW

PIE > Gmc.		PIE > Gmc.		PIE > Gmc.	
p	> *f*	*b*	> *p*	*bh*	> β (> *b*)
t	> þ	*d*	> *t*	*dh*	> ð (> *d*)
k	> *x* (> *h*)	*g*	> *k*	*gh*	> γ (> *g*)
k^w	> *x^w* (> *h^w*)	*g^w*	> *k^w*	*g^wh*	> *$γ^w$* > *g^w/w/b*

it, and who learn later sound changes such as West Germanic *z* > *r* and *ð* > *d*, can account for certain Modern English consonant alternations (e.g., those of *was~were* and *seethe~sodden*). But the payoff for learning Verner's Law is smaller than for Grimm's Law, and for many instructors, Verner's Law may be worth mentioning, but not worth memorizing. In that case, students can probably also simply learn that PIE **bh*, **dh*, **gh* became Old English *b, d, g*, and contrary developments, such as [v] < **bh* in Modern English (ModE) *love*, can be ignored.

For readers whose eyes are glazing over at this point—who find details of sound changes even duller than faculty meetings—I'll add one more way that Grimm's Law can be of interest. Namely, it can provide a useful lead-in to a discussion of the relationship between language and ethnic identity. We identify languages as Germanic in part because of Grimm's Law, and we identify ancient people as Germanic largely because of their languages. To what degree, over the centuries, did the speakers of older Germanic languages share this belief in a common ethnicity? I won't explore this question here; the point is that sound changes (Grimm's Law, Southern Middle English voicing of word-initial fricatives, the California vowel shift in contemporary American English) help to create language varieties that serve as markers of social identity, and thus may interest even those who plan never to take a course in phonetics.

15.3. ABLAUT

Ablaut (or apophony, or gradation) is the name given to a synchronic alternation of vowels in related word-forms in PIE. It's not a sound change. Many languages have synchronic alternations of sounds. For example, in ModE, [u] and [i] alternate in the related word-forms *food~feed, tooth~teeth, goose~geese*, while [aɪ] and [ɪ] alternate in *hide~hid, thrive~thrifty, white~Whitman*. The [ɪ] of *hid* is not a transmogrified offspring of the [aɪ] of *hide*; rather, in synchronic terms, *hide* and *hid* are two related word-forms that have different vowels.

It's worth stating the above explicitly, because the concept of synchronic alternation often gives students fits. Recognizing that English has its own synchronic vowel alternations makes it easier to see ablaut as a synchronic alternation, in PIE, of the vowels **e*, **o*, **ē*, **ō*, and **Ø* (i.e., zero). If students understand alternations in principle, they can then understand how a single PIE root, such as **sed-* 'sit', could have up to five different related forms in the proto-language itself; in this case, **sed-*, **sod-*, **sēd-*, **sōd-*, **sd-*.[4]

Of course, as most readers of this essay are already aware, the ModE alternations exemplified previously, though synchronic in their own terms, nevertheless have their origins in Pre-ModE sound changes: early OE umlaut for [u]~[i], ME vowel shortening for [aɪ]~[ɪ]. All the same, whatever their diachronic origins, the synchronic alternations are synchronic. Similarly, ablaut was a synchronic alternation in Proto-Indo-European, irrespective of its origins. As it happens, specialists disagree about exactly what Pre-IE sound changes led to PIE ablaut,[5] so for a history of English course, it's probably best to begin with the PIE system, and not worry about Pre-IE.

For the history of English, what's most important is that ablaut is the source of numerous interesting alternations in Old, Middle, and Modern English. This is most obvious in the strong verb system, where the vowels of the principal parts of OE Classes I–V can mostly be traced back to original *e, *o, or *Ø.[6] But ablaut is not limited to strong verbs, nor, for that matter, to Germanic. In fact, it's often easier to recognize ablaut in words borrowed into English from other IE languages. For example, from Latin, we have e-grade protect, etymologically 'to cover', and o-grade toga, etymologically 'a covering', both from the PIE root *(s)teg-. Recognizing the native cognate thatch 'covering for a house' as another descendant of the PIE o-grade form is a bit harder. Grimm's Law accounts for the initial consonant, but recognizing the vowel requires knowing the sound changes PIE *o > Gmc. *a > OE [æ] > ME [a] > ModE [æ].

The payoff here is that it's fun for students to discover that protect, toga, and thatch are cognates (along with stegosaurus, a dinosaur whose spine was roofed with bony plates).[7] Ablaut, along with knowledge of vowel changes from PIE to ModE, reveals these connections. Or, to return to the root *sed- 'sit', ablaut and vowel changes account for the present stem sit (e-grade), the preterite stem sat (o-grade), the noun soot 'stuff which has settled' (ō-grade), and the noun nest 'place where a bird sits down' (prefix *ni- 'down' plus Ø-grade *sd-). The e-grade is also apparent in the borrowed words sedentary and supersede (note, too, that including the latter word might incidentally help students to remember to spell it with an <s> instead of a <c>).[8]

Unfortunately, learning 5,000 years of vowel changes, from PIE up to Modern English, is probably even harder than learning consonant changes, simply because there are so many vowel changes in the history of English. So, for instructors who aren't planning to test students on the details of, for example, Middle English vowel lengthenings and shortenings, it might not be worthwhile to go into all the details of ablaut. But it's still worth mentioning it as a phenomenon, if only so that students will know that strong verbs, which are so important to the grammar of Old, Middle, and Modern English, can be traced back to a pattern that already existed in the earliest reconstructible ancestor of English.

15.4. PRETERITE-PRESENT VERBS

A question that, in my experience, gets short shrift in most history of English textbooks is, why did Old English have preterite-present verbs? Luckily, this doesn't seem to be a question that occurs to very many students, and thus an instructor can usually safely ignore it. If the question does get asked, it's always possible to answer, "These things happen in language. We can't expect it to make sense all the time."

Yet now that I've raised the question, I hope that it piques the interest of at least some readers of this chapter. Upon reflection, it does seem odd that a small set of verbs should assign present meaning to preterite forms. Interestingly, a few such verbs are also found in other Indo-European languages—for example, Latin *nōvī* 'know,' *ōdī* 'hate,' *meminī* 'remember,' Greek *oîda* 'know.' To be certain, multiple examples of the same curiosity don't make it any less curious, but they do suggest that there's something more going on than mere linguistic randomness.

In this case, the meanings of the Latin and Greek verbs, along with those of the Germanic preterite-presents, help us to see the answer. Cross-linguistically, many verbs, like 'throw' and 'stand up,' denote actions or events. However, some, such as 'know' (OE *cann*), 'be obligated' (OE *sceal*), 'be able' (OE *mæg*), and so on, denote states of being. Verbs of the second type, in PIE, had distinct person/number suffixes that marked the verb as stative; the same basic pattern can be found in many non-IE languages spoken today.[9] But the PIE stative endings were not restricted to verbs with inherently stative meaning. Rather, many verbs that were construable as both events and states could take either the eventive or the stative endings, depending on which meaning was intended. For some words, this pattern persisted from PIE into some of the daughter languages—for example, Greek *tʰnḗskei* 'dies' (active), *tétʰnēke* 'is dead' (stative).

However, already in late PIE, and increasingly over the centuries in the daughter languages, the PIE stative came to be reinterpreted as a perfect tense. For many verbs, the difference between the stative and the perfect is slight; thus, 'is dead' can easily be reinterpreted as 'has died' and 'is awake' as 'has awakened.' The perfect interpretation of the stative form, once it was introduced, eventually became the standard meaning, and thus a new perfect tense was born. The new perfect tense could now be used with verbs which would have made little sense as statives—for example, 'I am in the state of kicking' is semantically bizarre, but 'I have kicked' is perfectly sensible. Being widely used, the perfect persisted as a tense into most of the IE languages, including Germanic.[10]

In Germanic, the perfect tense was eventually conflated with the aorist, the simple past tense inherited from PIE, yielding the Germanic preterite.[11] This conflation makes sense given that both tenses referred to events in past time, and it was possible to let context, rather than word forms, make the distinction between 'I VERBed' and 'I have VERBed.' (A similar conflation occurred independently in the prehistory of Latin, and then again, many centuries later, in spoken French, where the *passé composé*, originally a perfect tense, has subsumed the functions of the *passé simple*.)[12] However, a relatively small set of verbs in Germanic had maintained the old stative meaning from PIE onward. These were verbs whose meanings were inherently stative (e.g., 'fear,' 'owe,' and 'be able.' They were therefore less likely to be reinterpreted as perfect tense forms, and so, never having developed perfect meaning, they didn't go on to change from perfect to preterite meaning. Instead, they kept their old stative form—a form that now, synchronically speaking, was the preterite form in Germanic—along with their old meaning: stative, not past tense.

To return to the question which began this section—why did Old English have preterite-present verbs—the answer is that, diachronically speaking, the preterite-present verbs were never preterites in meaning. They were stative forms with stative meaning. Like all stative forms, including those that developed perfect and/or preterite meanings, they had different endings from those of active/eventive verb forms. Thus, they didn't have the active third singular present indicative ending -*þ*.

Moreover, they had the expected root vowel grades of PIE stative/perfect forms: *o*-grade in the singular, Ø-grade in the plural. Thus, for example:

OE *wāt* 'I know' < PIE *woid- (cf. Gk. *oîda* 'I know')

OE *witon* 'we know' < PIE *wid- (cf. Gk. *ísmen* 'we know')

The present-day relevance of all this is that it explains various facts about Modern English. For example, the modal verbs *can, may,* and *shall,* because they descend from stative singular forms, all have vowels descending from the PIE *o*-grade, and they all lack the third sg. *-s* that has replaced the earlier eventive third sg. *-þ.* The vowel of *will,* on the other hand, shows that it was originally not a stative, but that it has joined the class of English modals because its meaning fit in with the semantics of the OE preterite-presents. *Could, might, should,* etc., are recognizable by their dental suffixes as not being of PIE date, but rather, as weak preterite forms whose original preterite meaning is sometimes still seen in Modern English: "Mom says that I can" versus "Mom said that I could." In sum, without going into everything that we could say about the modal verbs, the point is that here, as elsewhere, much of the structure of Modern English can only be fully understood if we recognize that English is an Indo-European language.

15.5. PRACTICAL SUGGESTIONS

Having, I hope, made the case for the continuing relevance of Indo-European, I now move on to practical advice for how to include it in a class. First, though, it's worth noting again that much depends on how much internal history, especially details of sound changes, the instructor wants to include. The recommendations that follow are based on my own predilection for a course heavy on language structure, but I hope that they will be useful even for those who have not drunk deep from the well of historical linguistics.[13]

I'll begin with textbooks. I don't pretend to have examined every available option, but I can recommend two that have worked for me: Algeo and Butcher's *The Origins and Development of the English Language* and Millward and Hayes's *A Biography of the English Language,*[14] both of which come accompanied by excellent workbooks. Both books lay out key sound changes in careful detail, and both workbooks include numerous exercises that will enable students to learn the sound changes by applying them rather than simply learning about them.

Even these textbooks, though, include less Indo-European material than I want. For instructors who either want to provide an extra-heavy dose of Indo-European to students or simply want more detail about linguistic prehistory for their own enlightenment, the following reference works may come in handy. Fortson's *Indo-European Language and Culture*[15] gives good overviews of major topics; Sihler's *New Comparative Grammar of Greek and Latin*[16] is informative about Indo-European even for those who don't know the classical languages. Prokosch's

Comparative Germanic Grammar[17] is outdated in some regards but remains a very valuable reference work. Wright and Wright's *Old English Grammar*,[18] though old, is clear, concise, and still very useful. More up to date is Hogg and Fulk's excellent two-volume *Grammar of Old English*[19]; more challenging for non-specialists, but well worth assaying, is Ringe and Taylor's *Linguistic History of English* (two volumes so far, with more to come).[20] Finally, for those interested in the Indo-European origins of the Modern English lexicon, Watkins's *The American Heritage Dictionary of Indo-European Roots*[21] is invaluable, a worthy complement to the *Oxford English Dictionary*.

Turning to assignments: historical linguistic knowledge comes out of the point of a pencil. Reading about sound changes, or watching someone write word histories on the board, isn't enough; students need to practice the material themselves. Accordingly, the last time I taught history of English, there were thirteen quizzes and ten graded homework assignments in a ten-week course, along with numerous ungraded exercises. My quizzes normally focus on a single concept; homework assignments cover more ground. Following are some examples: first, some questions from an early-term quiz; second, a few questions from an early-term homework; third, a question from an end-of-term homework.

(1) Give the specified forms of the PIE ablauting root *reidh-* 'ride'.
> *e*-grade
> *o*-grade
> zero grade

Give the specified form of the PIE ablauting root *bher-* 'carry'.
> lengthened *ē*-grade

(2) Fill in the blanks with the correct phonetic symbol.
> Lat. *pécu* 'sheep', Goth. [___e___u] 'money'
> Gk. *agrós* 'field', Goth. [a___rs]
> Skt. bh*árase* 'you are carried', Goth. [___era___a]

(3) When your *tooth* hurts, you go to see the *dent*ist. When you want your *teeth* straightened, you go to the ortho*dont*ist.
> (a) Describe the *origins* and *development* of the difference in VOWELS between *tooth* and *teeth*.
> (b) State the *origin* of the difference in VOWELS between *dent* and *dont*.
> (c) State the *origin* of the differences in CONSONANTS between *tooth/teeth* and *dent/dont* (apart from the presence/absence of <n>, which you can ignore).

For those instructors who don't want to make many exercises of their own, I repeat my recommendation for a textbook, such as Algeo and Butcher or Millward and Hayes, that comes accompanied by an extensive workbook. An ideal workbook, like the two in question, will include more exercises than can reasonably be assigned in a single term, thus allowing instructors to choose the exercises that fit best with their individual courses.

15.6. CONCLUSION

There are many possible goals for a course in the history of English. One that I emphasize, alongside things like getting students to read *Beowulf* aloud, is "relief from puzzlement."[22] Specifically, I mean the puzzlement that yields questions such as, how come the plural of *mouse* is *mice*, or why do *fox* and *vixen* start with different consonants? The answers to such questions, of course, do not always involve Proto-Indo-European, or even prehistory: *mice* is due to umlaut, *vixen* to borrowing from Southern dialect. But some other questions can only be answered with reference to Indo-European—for example, how come the past tense of *drive* is *drove*, or why do poets sometimes write third singular indicative *dare* instead of *dares*? If students, by the end of my course, can answer such questions, and thus avoid being puzzled by them in the future, I'm satisfied. If, in addition, they can recite the first eleven lines of *Beowulf* in Old English, they'll be set for life.

CHAPTER 16

Serving Time in "HELL"

Diachronic Exercises for Literature Students

MARY HAYES

16.1. INTRODUCTION

Teaching a course that covers a broad chronological ambit affords instructors the opportunity (though perhaps not the time) to think about time. Many chapters in this volume address topics orthogonal to HEL's chronology, which itself presents formidable challenges. A History of the English Language (HEL) course might well begin with some phase of English's prehistory and culminate with the language's transformative relationship with twenty-first-century social media. Even if an instructor starts relatively "late" with the arrival of the Germanic tribes to Britain in the fifth century, he or she must cover fifteen centuries in as many weeks. A different yet related problem transpires in HEL's traditional historical periodization, a convenient device that is notoriously approximate. Furthermore, in dutifully "covering" HEL's chronological periods, an instructor may wonder whether the course still presents a coherent yet complicated story or a complacent retrospective.[1]

In this chapter, I speak to how an instructor could engage students in thinking critically about HEL's chronological conventions by framing the course around a diachronic textual tradition. My example involves a sequence of vernacular translations of Psalm 22 (23), the "Shepherd Psalm," which an instructor could easily personalize and diversify given that the psalms were translated into English more than any other biblical book. Practically speaking, organizing a HEL course around a textual tradition makes its sprawling chronology more manageable. In the example that I discuss, each traditional chronological unit culminates with an exercise focused on a certain vernacular translation of the Shepherd Psalm. Each exercise is a finite task yet part of an extended project, pedagogical activity that enlists students in a sustained line of inquiry. In addition to promoting this valuable intellectual habit, this sequence encourages students to examine the chronological conventions used to organize HEL curricula. The Shepherd Psalm's textual tradition presents in miniature the language's general idiosyncrasies—older forms competing with newer ones, synchronic variants, and nonstandard orthography—that problematize streamlined narratives offered in HEL textbooks, which tend to focus more on linguistic ancestors of standard English. More broadly, this sequence encourages students to apprehend the constructed nature of the conventional chronological periods. As my own students develop a more sophisticated take on the retrospective construction of the past, they realize that translation practices and, by extension, their studying the History of the English Language entail more than making "old books" legible to contemporary users.

This textual tradition's general use to HEL students suggests its particular value to English and Education majors, students whose curricula focus on literature. When HEL originated in the nineteenth century under the aegis of "English Language and Literature," it was informed by classical philology, a practice that had an early influence on the textual studies that underpins today's curricula in English departments.[2] Thus, the dearth of teaching materials geared toward teaching HEL to literature students or, more broadly, including literature in HEL curricula, is surprising.[3] Furthermore, despite their shared origins in philology, historical linguistics and literary studies are often seen as competing rather than cooperating elements in a HEL course.[4] Of the two HEL courses that I teach, one is offered through the English department, and the other is cross-listed with Linguistics. Incorporating literature into language study and encouraging students to see literature as language are long-standing pedagogical goals of mine. So although students might object to my prolonging their "HEL" into a "HELL," I contend that a "HELL" course would not only be more legible to literature students but also help unify historical linguistics and literary studies.

16.2. TRANSLATION INTO HELL

Literature scholars teaching HEL in English departments should recognize two key features that make it different from other English courses: its broad scope and its study of language from a linguistic rather than a literary perspective. HEL's scope is uncommon because shortly after English literature became an academic field in the 1830s, surveys were replaced by courses narrowly focused on literary periods.[5] For nearly two centuries, literary study has been "durably bound up with its ability to define cultural moments and contrast them against each other."[6] As Ted Underwood argues in his evaluation of this curricular convention, narratives of historical contrast, fraught with "fateful turns," have come to be privileged over those predicated on continuity.[7] For its synoptic ambit, HEL affords the instructors the opportunity to inform the course with an animating question or intellectual problem, a pedagogical endeavor that does not fit well into a "contrastive framework."[8] For example, my students have benefited simply from tracking diachronically the changing definitions of "literate" and "vernacular," an exercise that suggests to them how contemporary attitudes about "standard English" are likewise culturally contingent. As every HEL instructor knows, however, students often have a hard time understanding that "continuous change" does not imply teleology. Many of us have witnessed class discussions where a student roundly asserts that English has progressed beyond its primitive beginnings in order to correct another student's diagnosis of the language's current depravity evident in social media. As with any historical narrative, the language's story will not always produce a tidy moral meant to accommodate its preceding fateful turns.[9]

Addressing the teleological thinking engendered in studying HEL is in fact easier than denaturalizing HEL's chronological periodization, a heuristic device stubborn for its utility to the course's administration.[10] As Haruko Momma points out in her essay in this volume, George Hickes's treatise *Institutiones Anglo-Saxonicæ, & Mœso-Gothicæ* (1705), which has been identified as the "first history of the English language,"[11] called the language spoken after the Conquest "Old English" and the one before it "Saxon" or "Anglo-Saxon." In the 1870s, Henry Sweet introduced the familiar tripartite division of HEL into Old English, Middle English, and Modern English. Informed largely by Sweet's paradigm, scholars have debated the number and names of the periods as well as the criteria used to define them.[12] Though periodization is perhaps a fiction necessary to administering the "history of English" as an academic course, it may imply to inexperienced students the homogeneity of its historical stages. "Old English" was of course losing its inflections before the Norman Conquest. And at any moment in Early Modern English, the rise of periphrastic *do* and the Great Vowel Shift did not coincide chronologically and in fact transpired at different rates in different dialects.[13] Furthermore, HEL courses mostly focus on the history of dialects that were the ancestors of Standard English, thus sacrificing variety for cohesion.

The diachronic exercise that I will describe offers some subtle antidotes to problems germane to HEL's chronological scope. First, the assignments are each named according to their relevant text rather than a historical period. This small detail will convey to students that the text's variety of English, for example, King Alfred's English in the Paris Psalter, is a specific rather than a general form. In turn, students will apprehend the existence of other synchronic varieties as well as the idealized nature of a textbook's "Englishes." Additionally, the sequence corrects conventional notions of linear chronology since textual traditions do not always evince genealogical transmission so much as influence. For example, although the fourteenth-century Wycliffite translators saw their project as a popular vernacular enterprise, they did not use preceding English versions but rather the Latin Vulgate. Of the two Wycliffite versions, the early ("EV") and late ("LV"), the King James translators chose to work with the earlier, less polished one for its greater fidelity to the Greek. While the King James Version (KJV) has been recognized as a venue by which King James consolidated his power,[14] it drew heavily on the translation of William Tyndale (1494–1536), who had been executed as a heretic for composing this very work. And although King Alfred's translation is not a known source for any Middle English version, Richard Rolle's Psalter reflects the influence of Old English forms, perhaps via Old English glosses included in an earlier Middle English glossed psalter.[15] This psalm's textual tradition does not chart a history of a certain variety per se. But, as do exercises that have students track lexical or morphological items, the texts in this diachronic sequence provide tangible examples of the complex nature of diachronic change.

Additionally, individual texts will have atypical forms that suggest to students the artificiality of smooth chronological narratives. For example, the KJV used two purposefully archaic forms to imbue the work with a timeless quality: the third person singular inflection "-eth" (instead of the emerging standard, "-s") and "thou" (instead of the current "you") to address God. The latter is an interesting choice given that "thou" and its declension had been the less formal variety. Furthermore, synchronic variants evince the prior existence of "Englishes," not just the variety that would inform the standard. When comparing the two Wycliffite versions, students can apprehend stylistic as well as dialectical differences; the LV reflects an East Midlands dialect that influenced the burgeoning standard, while the EV includes forms from several dialects. In its diachronic scheme that encompasses synchronic examples, this exercise accommodates yet problematizes a conventional chronological narrative.

Given that the criteria for demarcating English's diachronic variants is approximate and artificial if not arbitrary,[16] this convention evokes the academic debate about the extent to which historical periods generally are just a convenient device. For example, Anglo-Saxon speakers did not think of themselves as speaking "Old English." King Alfred, however, would identify his vernacular as "English" in his translation of Gregory's *Cura Pastoralis*.[17] Yet Alfred's variety of Old English was in fact a literary language used in texts centuries after it was no longer spoken. Although these chronological boundaries are far from perfect, any HEL instructor who has had a student allege that Shakespeare wrote in Old English understands their purpose. Victorian philologists would have known King Alfred's language as "Anglo-Saxon," and Old English today is taught much like foreign languages are.

A second way that HEL differs from other English courses is for its study of English *as a language*. When HEL originated in the nineteenth century, English literature curricula were more closely affiliated with those in Modern Languages departments. As James Turner observes, "pioneers of English literature rarely separated study of literature from study of language."[18] Although English majors often have to take a foreign language as part of their programs, many of them do not come to HEL with an understanding of how inflections work. And in their English literature courses, this "monolingualism" is reinforced since students are not encouraged to consider the English language in a linguistic register. For students of English literature, Momma argues, HEL can lure them out of their "'English' box" and thus encourage them to regard English "from outside in the light of 'non-English': foreign languages, historical varieties, 'substandard' variation, dialects, idiolects, creoles, pidgins, and more."[19] A HEL instructor need not make English "as hard as Greek."[20] Yet I find myself disturbed rather than comforted by my own students' collective relief when we get to Early Modern English; because its texts are legible, they equate it with their own variety and are less keen to examine its distinctive features. Although many HEL instructors encourage students' familiarity with and ownership of their language, I advocate the (less sympathetic) view that there is value in students' sense of estrangement from prior phases of English. And although some instructors favor working through the chronology in reverse,[21] I like to start with the earlier periods precisely because they are not immediately legible. After working through Old English, Middle English, and Early Modern English texts with attention to linguistic items, students will read Present Day English text—even "literary" works—differently. And as students analyze exemplary texts from English's earlier phases, they will recognize that even though these texts are in English, "we" are not the target culture.

The sequence of exercises that I describe is predicated on translation, which could work against cultivating this allocentric sensibility. Many readers understand "translation" in terms of replacement and substitution. Yet a savvy HEL instructor can use the notion of "translation" as a premise for a productive conversation about why native speakers would study the history of the English language. A point of entry into this conversation presents itself in Francis March's remark that "[t]he chief use of study of English before Chaucer is better understanding and mastery of English in Chaucer and since Chaucer."[22] In this comment, two worrying ideas emerge. First, the language's history should not be interpreted as a series of centers of gravity. For example, many HEL instructors are familiar with Christopher Cannon's reevaluation of Chaucer's monumental influence on the English lexicon. According to Cannon, the OED overestimates the number of words that Chaucer newly introduced to English because the dictionary's contributors expected to find them in his works rather than in lesser known sources.[23] The Shepherd Psalm sequence works against this retrospective interpretation of linguistic history; although the text itself is famous, the translators usually are not. Furthermore, this sampling of vernacular translations should imply to students myriad more with a countless variety of forms. Second, March's remark that the value of "English before Chaucer" is its utility to understanding later Englishes (including Chaucer's) makes HEL curricula a matter of demystification. This idea might resonate with today's students, who have easy access to translation software. In foreign language courses, it's an open secret that students use "google translate" to figure out what a text means. In English literature courses, they may not appreciate the nuances of the translator's "invisible hand" and thus why a professor would insist on a certain translation of a literary text.

As I have designed it, the sequence of translation exercises works against the easy recuperation of a text's single meaning. In my upper-level HEL class cross-listed between English and Linguistics, I have my students complete their own translations, which I find more beneficial than their memorizing paradigms. In both my upper-level class and the undergraduate one intended for English and Education majors, students answer questions about linguistic items. In linguistic analysis, HEL instructors have ready apparatus for encouraging students to understand how the Old English language works rather than just what an Old English text "says." Additionally, some of my assignments include historical meta-commentary about translation. Ælfric's Preface to his translation of Genesis, for example, comments on what a risky endeavor it is. Anglo-Saxon translators imagined themselves working with old materials yet creating something new, a conceit that offers a nice analogy for language change. In these translations, students can see English's transformation, and that English is *still* changing. They don't get a fixed perspective on language but rather a rocky (but much more interesting) ride on a moving walkway.

The grist for similar diachronic exercises organized around a textual tradition is found in several HEL textbooks, which use passages from the Bible and Boethius.[24] Recently many scholars have addressed the "philological turn" in English Studies, which revisits how philological practices were the source of many modern university disciplines. In his *Philology: The Forgotten Origins of the Modern Humanities*, Turner explains philology's use for biblical exegesis throughout the Middle Ages and beyond.[25] Indeed, innovations in philological practices were often responses to the religious climate generally and the Bible's position in it. The practical reasons why the Bible is a fit object for traditional philological study make it well-suited for use in HEL courses. It is available in myriad translations from the Anglo-Saxon period through the present day. The history of English vernacular Bibles is particularly interesting. Romance languages had descended from Latin; English vernacular worship was more vexed. In the first HEL textbook, *Method of Philological Study of the English Language* (1868), Francis March said that he wished space limitations did not preclude his inclusion of comparative biblical translations.[26]

Yet the Bible's importance to philology changed in the nineteenth century. As Turner explains, "When the fluid diversity of philology fragmented into specific new disciplines in the later nineteenth century, the 'divinity' of biblical philology looked odd among the 'humanities.'"[27] Indeed, HEL instructors might wonder whether the Bible suits medieval exegetes or nineteenth-century philologists more than twenty-first-century students. This question occurs to me often because I teach in the Bible Belt, the "buckle" of the Bible Belt in fact. For religious students, I risk their thinking the assignment irreligious. Many of these students are surprised to learn of the Bible's various vernacular translations and that the King James Bible (KJB) was not the first, yet students who would not self-identify as pious have similar knowledge gaps. For all students, our sustained focus on the same passage conveys the constructed nature of the exercise. This extended assignment, however, could cultivate unintended sentiments in students: burnout and boredom. Yet the successive translations suggest a textual dynamism; the same text "recreating" itself provides a nice conceit for language generally. Furthermore, the Bible's provocative translation history gets students thinking more broadly about how its textual tradition suggests in miniature how complicated the English language's story is.

Later I explain some exercises focused on Psalm 22 (23), the "Shepherd Psalm," whose long-standing popularity suggests many more translations than I could include or even account for in this chapter. I have made use of diachronic sequences in several forms in the two versions of HEL that I teach. One course is cross-listed between English and Linguistics, and it includes graduate and undergraduate students. As an option for the "pre-1800" requirement for English graduate students, the course has a relatively modest scope, "Old to Standard English." For our textbook, we use Millward and Hayes's *A Biography of the English Language*, which I supplement generously with language drills and textual examples. The other HEL course is comprised solely of undergraduates and is offered in the English department. In it, I use Seth Lerer's *Inventing English: A Portable History of the Language* and David Burnley's *The History of the English Language: A Source Book*. In the following sections I include and describe exercises used in each class.

16.3. *THE PARIS PSALTER* (NINTH CENTURY)

For the Anglo-Saxons, the psalter was itself a classroom text. To learn how to read and write Latin, clerical students memorized psalms.[28] More generally, their vernacular translations of the psalms distinguished the Anglo-Saxons from other Western European cultures. They were aware of the Bible's translation history, from Hebrew into Greek and then from Greek into Latin, which, according to Patrick O'Neill, "may well have encouraged them to embark on the hazardous undertaking of translating it yet again from Latin into Old English."[29] For the "Old English" version of the psalm, I have used the *Paris Psalter*, whose prose paraphrase of the first fifty psalms has been attributed to King Alfred. The text that follows is taken from O'Neill's *Old English Psalms* (2016), which is also available online.[30]

16.3.1. *Paris Psalter* Exercise for Historical Linguistics Students

As I explained earlier, in the upper-level class the students not only study the Old English translation but also do their own. Here is a condensed version of that assignment's rubric:

1) For every noun, give its case and number. If the noun is modified by an adjective and/or a demonstrative pronoun, please identify these with your noun. (That is, in these cases, what you have is a noun phrase that you'll translate as a unit.)
2) Provide an interlinear translation of the OE text. That is, show me how you translated the passage word-for-word. Note: you must show that your nouns, pronouns, adjectives, and demonstrative pronouns are in the right case.
3) Provide a "smooth" translation that straightens out the syntax of your interlinear translation. You can make a few lexical changes for the sake of semantics, but in this portion of the assignment you should be working with the raw materials from question #1.
4) a) Morphology: What case is "feohland" (line 1) in? Why is it in this case?
   b) Syntax: In line 4, explain the syntax of "ne ondræde ic."
   c) Phonology: In line 4, how do we get our PDE reflex of "yfel" (phonologically speaking)?
   d) Morphology: In line 6, what is the tense, person, and number of "hatedon"? What is its subject?
   e) Graphics: In line 9, why is the "i" doubled in "tiid"?

Given how quickly a HEL course moves, the students do not become proficient in Old English per se. A manageable alternative would be having them memorize paradigms, but I do not do that since I put greater value on their being chart-literate. Perhaps more important is their understanding the language in a literary context. For most students, this HEL course represents their first exposure to Old English, so I annotate thorny items such as adjectives that take the genitive. In these annotations, I also give the infinitives for irregular verbs, tell students what class the verb is in, and offer hints to account for variations (i.e., the form we would expect to see were this word declined or conjugated according to the textbook standard). My annotations also refer them to an online beginners' Old English dictionary, which is handy for giving the genitive singular and nominative plural for each noun; students can then easily identify the type of noun they are working with.

16.3.2. *Paris Psalter* Exercise for Undergraduate Literature Students

The lower-level version of HEL includes less linguistics, and students do not study Old English even for chart-literacy. I have adjusted this assignment by giving them my own clumsy translation whose stilted wording retains the linguistic information that we have covered. O'Neill's translation in *Old English Psalms* would work fine with the basic questions:

1) In present-day usage, "mildheortnes" (line 8) connotes "mercy."
   a) In the *Romanum* psalter on which this translation was based, the Latin word is "misericordia." Using the Oxford English Dictionary, find the Present-Day English reflexes of this word. What are they, and what do they mean?
   b) Given that Present-Day English has words derived from the Latin "misericordia," explain Alfred's choice of "mildheortnes." Use the Old English Dictionary if it enriches your answer.
   c) Look up "mercy" in the Oxford English Dictionary. Why didn't Alfred use this word?
2) For Alfred's "feohland" (1) the Latin Vulgate uses an etymon for the word "pasture."
   a) Consult with the Old English dictionary, and explain what "feohland" literally means. (Hint: It's a compound word.)
   b) Look "pasture" up in the Oxford English Dictionary. Informed by the word's etymology and history, explain how the meaning of "pasture" differs from "feohland."
3) In line 7, Alfred uses the word "folc." His other choices would have been "lēode" or "mǣgð."
   a) In light of what you know about the Old English vocabulary, explain why Alfred had (at least) 3 words to choose from.
   b) Look these 3 words up in the Old English Dictionary and explain how "folc" best fits the purpose behind Alfred's translation.

4) Informed by Lerer's discussion of Old English literature's characteristic syntax,[31] explain this sentence's structure: "And he establishes me in exceedingly fine pastureland, and has fed me by the water's edge, and turned my mind from sadness to joy" (lines 1–2).

Compared with the upper-level exercise, this one treats language from a philological standpoint. Simply put, students do not analyze words for their linguistic information but rather locate them in their textual and cultural context. The questions direct them to consider linguistic items in terms of a writer's choices.

In this exercise for the lower-level class, students also examine Ælfric's famous Preface to Genesis, where he himself comments on how translation is "dangerous" ("pleolic"). To keep students' attention to the philological aspects of translation, I ask them the following question: "The homilist Ælfric (955–c. 1010) translated parts of the Book of Genesis. In his *Preface to Genesis*, he gives reasons why he was reluctant to do so. Explain three (3) of his reasons in terms of what you know about Anglo-Saxon literacy and textual practices." An instructor interested in pursuing this line of inquiry might include Alfred's famous preface to his translation of Gregory's *Cura Pastorialis*. In it, Alfred explains his educational initiative, which includes translating "those books most necessary for men to know" from Latin into English. According to Alfred, this translation campaign stems from a dire decline of learning in his culture. Although scholars had once traveled from abroad to England due to its reputation for learning, very few men in England at the time could read Latin texts. While registering Alfred's bleak assessment of current learning, the Preface also intimates how his translation campaign functioned a means of consolidating his own reign, evident in Alfred's original use of the word "Englisc" to define his people's language. Given Alfred's role in creating a vernacular written standard, this preface could open up a conversation about the construction of "Old English" by its users as well as those of us studying it retrospectively.

16.4. *WYCLIFFE'S BIBLE* (LATE FOURTEENTH CENTURY)

Though originally associated with John Wycliffe (c. 1320–84), the Wycliffe Bible now suggests a collection of translations composed and edited by his followers.

16.4.1. Wycliffe's Bible Exercise for Historical Linguistics Students

For the upper-level class, their Old English translations are now a valuable resource. This exercise asks them to describe briefly the change that did or *did not* take place between Old and Middle English. The line numbers refer to those in the later Wycliffite version (LV); the EV and LV are available in a dual-column edition online.[32]

Phonology (Consonants): yuels (4)

Phonology (Vowels): Y (4), Thou (4), hows (6), daies (6)

Graphics: gouerneth (1), whi (4), ʒerde (4), schadewe (4), siʒt (5), thi (6), heed (5), lijf (line 6; I'm looking for 2 items)

Morphology: refreischyng (3), ledde (3), art (4), pathis (4), hem (5), myn (5, and comment on why it is "myn" as opposed to "my" as we see immediately above it), coumfortid (5), that (5), troublen (5)

Syntax: Of riʒtfulnesse (4), Y schal not drede yuels (4), hast maad (5)

Lexicon: gouerneth (1), pasture (2), nurschide (2), aʒens (5), merci (6)

These Wycliffite translations were not based on Old English versions but rather the Latin Vulgate. Additionally, Alfred's prose psalms are themselves recognized as paraphrases rather than translations from the Latin *Romanum* psalter, which was probably introduced to England by Augustine of Canterbury in the late sixth century.[33] My students know that they are not tracking a genealogical relationship between Alfred's psalm and the Wycliffite psalm. Yet the texts' similarities provide my students with some basis for observing general diachronic changes. Additionally, in this upper-level class they consider this text in its synchronic dimension by analyzing its dialectical features. I adapt this question from the chart "Features of ME Dialects" in the workbook for *A Biography of the English Language* (Millward and Hayes).[34]

16.4.2. Wycliffe's Bible Exercise for Undergraduate Literature Students

In the lower-level class, I ask them to compare King Alfred's translation with the Wycliffite version, attending to lexical choices, which are the easiest to notice and explain for students less familiar with Old English. I give the Present-Day English reflex of the Old English word and then the Wycliffite translator's choice. They consult with the *Oxford English Dictionary* and comment on the Middle English lexeme.

1) "feed" (Paris Psalter, line 2) becomes "nourish" ("*nurschide*," line 2 in Wycliffite text)
2) "mind" (Paris Psalter, line 2) becomes "soul" ("*soule*," line 3 in Wycliffite text)
3) "shadow" (Paris Psalter, line 4) becomes "shadow" ("*schadewe*," line 4 in Wycliffite text)
4) "evil" (Paris Psalter, line 4) becomes "evils" ("*yuels*," line 4 in Wycliffite text)
5) "gyrd" (Paris Psalter, line 5) becomes "yard" ("*ʒerde*," line 4 in Wycliffite text) (n.b. Consult the second definition of "yard" as a noun. Though the Middle English translator retains the Old English word, this usage is now obsolete).

I have never asked my students to compare the two Wycliffite translations, but I suspect that even undergraduate students would be able to identity and explain lexical and graphic differences at least. To introduce more synchronic variants, an instructor might include Richard Rolle's Psalter (1340), which reflects Old English influence transmitted via a Middle English text familiar to Rolle.[35] In turn, for its Northern dialect, Rolle's Psalter will differ from the contemporary West Midlands Psalter (ca. 1350). By these examples, I mean to show that even in the class focused on literature, an instructor could easily introduce students to Middle English dialectical variants.

While I have not yet had my lower-level class examine Middle English dialects, I did have them consider variation more generally in essay questions relevant to the Wycliffe Bible. They read the Preface to a Wycliffite Concordance, whose anonymous author is concerned with "diverse manners of writing."[36] Indeed, this text offers a user's perspective on the diversity of and novelties in written Middle English. Students answered the following essay question: "Identify and explain an example of each of the following: 1) changing graphics in the written alphabet; 2) variant spellings of the same word; 3) various words that have the same meaning; and 4) a single word that can have totally different meanings." The single time I assigned that text, I provided a Modern English translation of it, but for various reasons I can understand why an instructor might not want to do so. Even students new to Middle English could work through the text using the Middle English compendium. It is difficult for a beginner to use, however, precisely because of the nonstandard orthography about which the writer complains.

In a related yet different vein, another essay in the Middle English exercise had students consider the variety entailed in translation. In his Prologue to a Wycliffite Bible,[37] John Purvey speaks to the choices the Wycliffite translators made when turning the Latin Bible into the vernacular. I asked students to do the following: "Identify three of Purvey's concerns about this English translation and explain how they relate to Ælfric's." In Purvey's explanations of the reasons for and conventions of vernacular translation, students will see that "plain English" is itself a contingent ideal and, by extension, that the linguistic variety of "standard English" is itself a cultural construct.

16.5. EARLY PRINTED BIBLES

For Early Modern English translations, there is a useful resource. It is a commercial website that sells printed facsimiles of bibles. My students have enjoyed the turning-page editions, though an instructor would be wise to supplement the site's editorial apparatus. For some students, just seeing the King James Bible alongside many other translations adjusts their preconceptions of its generic innovation.

16.5.1. Early Printed Bibles Exercise for Historical Linguistics Students

In the exercise that I gave to the upper-level class, the students worked with the King James Bible (1611) as well as the Great Bible (1539), which was the first authorized English Bible. Although the texts' genealogical relationships are largely beyond the scope of the class, some of the questions culminated or reviewed general changes to the language evident in these diachronic translations. Since this course satisfies the "pre-1800 requirement" in my department, it ends with Early Modern English. So for these students this was the last exercise of this type.

Phonology

1. The words "Shepheard" (KJB verse 1) and "sheep" have the same root. When and why did their vowels start sounding different?

2. In the KJB version verse 2, the speaker lies down in "greene" pastures. In OE (line 2), this resting place is "good." How would <good> have been pronounced in OE?

3. In PDE, a common pronunciation of "path" is /pæθ/, and "paths" is often /pæðz/. Comment on these different pronunciations of the singular and plural forms. (Hint: The spelling of "pathes" in KJB verse 3 suggests how OE morphology had a lasting influence on phonology).

Graphics

4. Consider the KJB verse 2, and explain the spelling of the word "mee" in terms of historical linguistics.

5. In the facsimile edition, how does the word "righteousness" (KJB, verse 3) reflect on Early Modern graphic conventions?

6. Look at the facsimile version of the Great Bible. It has no verse or line numbers. In the phrase "Yea, though I walke thorow the valley" (KJB, verse 4), why is the word "the" printed as it is?

7. In KJB verse 4, in what word do we see <u> used as an allograph of <v>?

8. The word "house" appears in KJB line 6. The corresponding word in the OE version is hūse (line 9; inflected for case).
   a. When did the vowel sound start being represented with a digraph?
   b. Why did the vowel sound start being represented with a digraph?

Morphology

9. Regarding "Names" (KJB, verse 3). The word appears in the OE version (line 3) but in a different construction. What is the case and number of this word *in the OE version*?

10. Say we were going to translate the KJB version word-for-word *back into OE*. What would be the case, number, and form (i.e. spell it out) of the OE word *in our new translation*?
    a. case:
    b. number:
    c. form:

11. The form of "Names" seen in the KJB version actually comes from an Old English convention. What is it?

12. As it is used in KJB verse 5, why is the form "mine" unusual for an Early Modern text? Why is it perhaps used here?

13. Regarding "runneth" (KJB, verse 5)
    a. What is the tense and number of this verb?
    b. What ME dialect(s) would have favored this form?
    c. Why did the KJB author(s) use this form?

Syntax
14. In KJB (verse 4), the line "I will feare no euill" shows two striking changes in syntax when compared to the OE version (line 4). What are they? (Hint: One is listed on the OE syntax chart, and the other is a very common OE convention that is considered "nonstandard" in PDE).

Lexicon
15. Why is the use of the word "thou" in the Early Modern versions interesting?

    Bonus question: From a phonological standpoint, one of the words in the KJB version has something in common with "steak," "great," and "break." What is the word? What is does it have in common with those other words?

16.5.2. Early Printed Bibles Exercise for Undergraduate Literature Students

In the lower-level class offered to undergraduates, they attended to fewer and less difficult linguistic items in the Great Bible and KJV. Their prompt read: "Below are words selected from the facsimile of the King James Bible. Explain the significance of each to the history of the English language":

Morphology: leadeth (5); names (9); thou (12); mine (15; Hint: Compare "mine" with other uses of the first person possessive.)
Graphics: beside (5); euill (12); the (6).
In the Great Bible, observe how the word "the" is written. Explain its significance to the history of the English Language.
Phonology: In the KJB psalm, the word "me" is spelled two different ways. What phonological phenomenon is evident in this graphic difference?

In various versions of this assignment, I have some sort of question that asks students to compare the Early Modern versions' lexical items, which are easy for them to pick out. Although I have not yet included the Douay-Rheims version in an assignment, students will readily recognize the higher number of Latinate words and, in turn, the cultural significance of this lexical fact.[38] Additionally, if an instructor were to define the criteria well, he or she could have students unpack why the KJV was meant for oral performances and the Douay-Rheims as a clerical study bible meant for private reading.

In the assignment intended for undergraduates studying literature, the Bible questions were included with others on Early Modern English language commentary. In these essays, I have asked students to examine short excerpts by Thomas Wilson, George Puttenham, Alexander Gil, John Hart, and others and to explain their central claims. In some variations, I have included a prompt: "What would X (writer) say to Y (writer) about Z (language issue)?" Given that many students excel when they are encouraged to use their imagination, in the future I will include an essay assignment that situates the KJV in its linguistic context by asking students what advice selected sixteenth- and seventeenth-century commentators would have offered the biblical translators in 1604.

16.6. PSALM 23 AND PRESENT-DAY ENGLISHES

After the students examined these diachronic examples, I had them consider the relationship between English and new technology. This "new technology" was text messaging, which (speaking of broad chronologies) should suggest how long I have been teaching HEL. In 2005 Australian evangelists had finished translating the Bible's 31,173 verses into SMS. They sent subscribers a verse at a time. In text message speak, the first lines of our psalm were rendered thus: "U, Lord, r my shepherd. I will neva be in need. U let me rest in fields of green grass. U lead me 2 streams of peaceful water." Although my upper-level class technically concludes with the year 1800, in both classes, I have used the following prompt in a culminating essay: "Discuss how (at least) one Old English writer, (at least) one Middle English writer, (at least) one Early Modern writer, and (at least) one post-1800 writer would respond to the Bible's translation into SMS. Specifically, how would these writers interpret the SMS Bible as a comment on the state of the English language in the 21st century?" The service still exists, but this assignment is now obsolete since the verses are abbreviation-free. But students write in idiosyncratic forms of textspeak, and they have strong opinions about text messaging's effects on the English language. So the prompt above is based on the hypothetic that the psalm is written in some kind of textspeak. While my essay prompt's preservation of the SMS form ("U, Lord, r my shepherd") is artificial, it is thus not unlike King Alfred's vernacular retained in writing centuries for centuries after it had become obsolete as a spoken variety. Given the wide use of autocorrect, SMS is perhaps not the timeliest social media patois. But it does afford instructors a ready example of the difference between Englishes written and spoken varieties, a topic generally important to the language's diachronic varieties. And the entire semester, students have been immersed in dated forms of the language. Why not SMS?

16.7. RESOURCES FOR TEACHING

Following are some easily accessible resources for instructors interested in adapting the diachronic sequence I have explained.

1. Early Modern Bibles
   http://www.bibles-online.net/
   This commercial website for "The Bible Museum, Inc." includes turning-page facsimiles.

2. Old English Dictionary (for beginners)
   http://www.old-engli.sh/dictionary.php
   This online dictionary is perfect for beginners since it provides information about noun declensions and verb conjugations.
3. Eadwine Psalter, Trinity College, Cambridge (MS R.17.1)
   http://sites.trin.cam.ac.uk/manuscripts/r_17_1/manuscript.php?fullpage=1
   For HEL instructors who account for material culture in their courses, this twelfth-century psalter is available online. (The Shepherd Psalm is at f.039v.) The Eadwine Psalter includes three versions in Latin as well as one in Old English and one in Anglo-Norman. The mistakes in the Old English suggest that literary variety of Old English was no longer in use.[39] Thus organizing the course according to conservative "periods" can undercut neat periodization.
4. The Vespasian Psalter, British Library (Cotton Vespasian A I)
   bl.uk/manuscripts/viewer.aspx?ref=Cotton_ms_Vespasian_a_i_f002r
   The Vespasian Psalter dates from the eighth century and is the oldest surviving translation of part of the Bible into English. The Vespasian Psalter is a glossed manuscript; the complicated relationship between Latin and the English vernacular is evident in the page layouts. Additionally, glossed manuscripts were often teaching devices, so the Vespasian Psalter perhaps gives witness to the process of language learning.

CHAPTER 17

What Has *Beowulf* to Do with English? (Let's Ask Lady Philology!)

HARUKO MOMMA

17.1. BEOWULF THE FOREIGNER

In the "Heroes and Demons" episode of *Star Trek: Voyager*, one of the crew members has a favorite interactive computer program based on *Beowulf*. Another crew member, hearing the title, refers to the original piece as "an ancient English epic." That this information is meant to be accurate may be inferred from what he says next: the poem is "set in sixth-century Denmark." Medieval historians would agree on this general time frame of the poem, for the protagonist's maternal uncle Hygelac has been identified as Chlochilaichus, who died in a Frankish raid sometime between 516 and 531.[1] Yet the idea of *Beowulf* as an English epic, though common, is not without a problem. To begin with, the poem is not an epic, at least in the classical sense (*in medias res* and all that). Nor does it conform to M. M. Bakhtin's idea of the genre as a representation of "'peak times' in the national history."[2] The poem instead begins with the rise of one realm, with an infant growing to become a good king, and ends with the fall of another, with an old king dying without an heir. Perhaps more immediate to our concern, *Beowulf* is set not in England but in Scandinavia, with no insular characters involved in the plot. And even more important still, the language of *Beowulf* does not exactly look like English.

Editors of *Beowulf*, like those of other Old English verse texts, have tried to make the poem look more familiar by using the Roman alphabet (rather than English Vernacular minuscule and Square minuscule used by the Anglo-Saxon scribes), with the exception of the runic letters eth < ð > and thorn < þ > (both representing the *th* sound, that is, /ð/ and /θ/), together with the letter ash < æ > (originally a Latin ligature, here representing the low front vowel /æ/).[3] Even then, the strangeness of *Beowulf* is flagrant, as can be seen from the presentation of its opening sentence in one of the standard editions[4]:

Hwæt! We Gardena   in geardagum,

þeodcyninga,   þrym gefrunon,

hu ða æþelingas   ellen fremedon. (*Beowulf*, ll:1–3)

Here only a few words are immediately recognizable: *we* ('we'), *in* ('in'), and per-haps *hu* ('how'). The first word *hwæt* is a false friend, for it is not a pronoun (i.e., 'what') but an interjection, which has been rendered by modern translators as diversely as 'lo!' (e.g., Tolkien 2014), 'listen!' (e.g., Liuzza 2000), and 'so' (Heaney 2000).[5] Observant readers may also note that the compound elements *-dena* (1a) and *-cyninga* (2a) remotely resemble the modern English words "Dane" and "king," respectively. But they need to study the paradigm for strong masculine nouns to fig-ure out that these compound elements here mean "of the Danes" and "of the kings," respectively, because their ending *–a* denotes genitive plural.[6] Yet even observant readers may not realize that *geardagum* (1b) is a compound consisting of 'year' and 'day' (to mean 'days of yore'), unless they are aware that the first letter *g*, because it is followed by a front vowel, has undergone a sound change called palatalization and is therefore pronounced as [j] or like the letter *y* in, well, the word *year*.[7] The conjugation system of Old English verbs is richer than that of modern English verbs. The last word *fremedon*, for instance, is an inflected form of *fremman* ('to do, to perform'), with the ending *–ed–* denoting past tense, and *–on*, indicative plural (i.e., '[they] performed').[8] In order to decipher *Beowulf*, therefore, students of Old English must first parse each word in the text and then piece them together like a jigsaw puzzle. It is only after this laborious process that the first three lines of the poem may be rendered to a relatively straightforward sentence, like the one found in Tolkien's prose translation:

> Lo! the glory of the kings of the people of the Spear-Danes in days of old we have heard tell, how those princes did deeds of valour.

It should be noted, however, that not all Old English compositions look as foreign as this passage. In fact, *Beowulf* is one of the most challenging works of Old English, whereas many other Anglo-Saxon texts have a more familiar look. *Apollonius of Tyre*, for instance, is a translation from a prose Latin narrative most likely of Greek ori-gin, and as such this first so-called English romance depicts a world more familiar to modern readers.[9] In the concluding sentence of the text, for instance, the narrator tells how the protagonist, having completed his adventures, lived happily ever after by spending his old age on something far more sensible than fighting a dragon:

> and he leofode on stilnesse and on blisse ealle þa tid his lifes. . . . And twa bec he silf gesette be his fare; and ane asette on ðam temple Diane, oðre on bibliotheca.[10]

> [and he lived in peace and in bliss for all the time of his life. . . . And he himself made two books about his journey and placed one in the temple of Diana and the other in a library. (My translation)]

17.2. *BEOWULF* AND HEL

Despite its foreign appearance, *Beowulf* has a special place in the history of English—a discursive subject that draws its substance if not its matter from our collective notion of the language, its speakers, and the culture constructed by them. While our subject (HEL) is fundamentally a product of the modern university, this does not mean that no one prior to that time took interest in the subject. To the contrary, the study of historical aspects of English has its beginnings in the Reformation; hence by the time Samuel Johnson (1709–84) wrote an essay entitled "The History of the English Language," the accumulation of scholarship conducted by generations of antiquaries served as a rich depository for him. While his substantial treatise provides many specimens from "the age of *Alfred* to that of *Elizabeth*," it does not mention *Beowulf* even once. To be fair, Johnson acknowledges that he was able to illustrate the language "in some parts imperfectly for want of materials." In fact, very few antiquaries prior to his time had paid attention to what was going to be popularly known as an ancient English epic. But the absence of *Beowulf* in Johnson's "History of the English Language" is still symbolic, especially since the poem was to attract an inordinate amount of attention in the following century.[11]

What made the study of historical English in the nineteenth century distinct from the one in the previous centuries was an intellectual movement known as the new philology, which began in Scandinavia and Germany during the 1810s, and which reached the English shore in the early 1830s, thanks to the efforts of innovative scholars including John Mitchell Kemble (1807–57). Kemble is known for publishing the first English edition of the entire text of *Beowulf* (1833) as well as the first English translation of that text (1837). His work from this period also includes a pamphlet entitled the *History of the English Language*. This 1834 publication was intended as a syllabus of a lecture series dedicated to the "first, or Anglo-Saxon period." Of the twenty lectures outlined here, six are solely dedicated to *Beowulf*. In the rest of this chapter, I will compare the approaches taken by Johnson and Kemble to the history of English in order to consider how the new philology of the nineteenth century has altered the contour of the subject. Frequent references will be made to *Beowulf* as a touchstone to highlight some of the most prominent characteristics of the new philology.

Differences between Johnson and Kemble are observed in many areas including the occasion for the publication of their respective pieces under the title "history of the English language." Kemble wrote his *History* as part of his efforts to have a permanent professorship established for the study of English at his Alma Mater, Cambridge.[12] Johnson's treatise was made for his *Dictionary of the English Language* and placed between its "Preface" and a section called "A Grammar of the English Tongue." As such, Johnson's "History" is a prolegomenon to his synchronic lexicon, whose corpus mostly covered a period from the time of Sidney onward, because of his desire not to "croud my book with words now no longer understood."[13]

Before we consider other differences between Johnson and Kemble, I would like to point out one criterion in which they were more or less in agreement: namely, periodization. For both authors, "Old English" was a language spoken in post-Conquest England, whereas the language of England prior to that time was not English but "Saxon" or "Anglo-Saxon." This periodization goes back to George Hickes's treatise *Institutiones Anglo-Saxonicæ, & Mœso-Gothicæ* (included in his monumental *Thesaurus* of 1705), which has been described as "the first history of the English language."[14] The more familiar division of Old, Middle, and Modern English was introduced in the 1870s by Henry Sweet to underline "the unbroken development of our language."[15] This tripartite model provided a convenient framework for the study of English language and literature, which at the time was on the rise as an academic discipline. In the process, however, Sweet inadvertently created a major break between Old and Early Middle English, which had earlier been treated as one period, despite the major political break in between. More recently, scholars use "early" and "late" to divide medieval English into two portions, with a transitional phase falling in the post-Conquest era. This is a welcome restoration of the empirical periodization in the tradition of Hickes, especially since it acknowledges the continuity of linguistic form as well as literary tradition from the late Anglo-Saxon period to the early post-Conquest era.[16]

17.3. GENEALOGY OF *BEOWULF*

Johnson's "History of the English Language" begins with a genealogy, according to which "[t]he whole fabrick and scheme of the English language is *Gothick* or *Teutonick*." In other words, English belongs to "that tongue, which prevails over all the northern countries of *Europe*." Johnson further provides a diagram (Figure 17.1), adapted from Hickes, to visualize the relationship among the individual Teutonic (i.e., Germanic) languages [italics in the original].[17]

While Kemble would not have been opposed to the classification of English as a Teutonic tongue, his *History of the English Language* places the language in a much broader context: it belongs to "one of a large class of connected tongues which pass beyond the narrow limits of Germany, and reach into the remotest parts of Asia; binding together in one great Sisterhood, the Upper Indian, the Sclavonic, Greek and Latin languages."[18] By this, Kemble, of course, refers to what we call today the Indo-European family of languages. The idea was still very new at the time, and Kemble seems to have been informed by the work of scholars abroad, since the outline of his first lecture commends the work of Rasmus Rask and Jacob Grimm.[19]

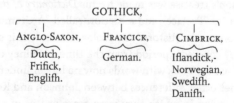

Figure 17.1. Relationship among the individual Teutonic languages

The idea of a generic connection among the languages of Asia and Europe goes back, however, to William Jones, a one-time president of Johnson's Literary Club and judge of the Bengal Supreme Court, who, in 1786, speculated that Latin, Greek, and Sanskrit must "have sprung from some common source, which, perhaps, no longer exists: there is a similar reason . . . for supposing that both the *Gothick* and the *Celtick*, though blended with a very different idiom, had the same origin with the *Sanscrit*."[20] Jones's observation triggered a new type of language studies characterized by two principles: (1) it uses comparative methods of analysis; and (2) it treats all historical languages on equal footing, rather than privileging Greek and Latin. These underlying principles may explain why the new philology of the nineteenth century evolved into two seemingly opposite directions: on one hand, it gave rise to comparative studies of multiple languages, with Sanskrit at its center; on the other, it gave rise to many different branches of national philology. For Kemble, his mother tongue had inherent value, not only because of its grander genealogy but also because of its singularity within that genealogy; and it was the case with other national philologists elsewhere both in England and in the rest of Europe. For Johnson and other men of letters who had been fed on the honey-dew of neoclassicism, however, English was no more than a Gothic dialect spoken by those Saxons who "about the year 450 . . . first entred *Britain*." These were, Johnson adds, "a people without learning, and very probably without an alphabet." In placing literacy over oral culture, Johnson imagined the speech of the unlettered Saxons to have been "always cursory and extemporaneous."[21]

There is little doubt that Johnson and Kemble both valued English and desired to prove its excellence by examining an early part of its history; but they made use of the diachronic trajectory of the language to tell a very different story. For Johnson, who saw the origin of English in the tongue of the unlettered people, the history of the language was by necessity teleological, "advance[ing] from its first rudeness to its present elegance."[22] He contends that the insular Saxons took their first step forward through conversion in the late sixth century, for Christianity "always implies or produces a certain degree of civility and learning." Yet the real catalyst for Johnson was the language of this religion, for it allowed the *gens Anglorum* access to the civilization of Rome. Thus the Saxons of England began "by degrees acquainted with the *Roman* language, and so gained, from time to time, some knowledge and elegance, till in three centuries they had formed a language capable of expressing all the sentiments of a civilized people." Johnson seems to have regarded King Alfred of Wessex (r. 871–99) as the first and foremost of such cultivated Anglo-Saxons, for the very first specimen that he provides in his "History" is the Anglo-Saxon "paraphrase or imitation" of Boethius's *Consolation of Philosophy*, which is generally attributed to Alfred.[23]

Kemble, on the other hand, refers to the titles of several Old English prose texts in the outline of his first lecture, but the outline of his subsequent lectures scrutinizes verse alone. Behind this predilection lies Kemble's conviction that poetry was "the only representation of the Saxon mind."[24] Yet he does not seem to have placed an equal amount of value in individual Old English poems; in fact, the only one he discusses in his *History* is *Beowulf*, or to be more precise, its opening section, the hero's crossing of the ocean, and his victory over Grendel and Grendel's mother.

Once having covered "the first and most interesting portion of Beowulf," he felt it "not necessary to examine at present any other purely Saxon Poem."[25] The only other text Kemble discusses in detail is Lawman's *Brut*, an Early Middle English alliterative poem narrating the history of Britain in the time of the Anglo-Saxon invasion.[26]

But why does *Beowulf* take center stage in Kemble's *History of the English Language*? In his opinion, *Beowulf* is "not an Epic Poem in the sense in which we call the *Iliad*" as such; nor should it be seen as an "Origin of Romantic fiction in England." Rather, the poem should be "considered as a History" in that it reflects the Anglo-Saxon memory of the migration period.[27] Kemble elaborates this point in the preface to his 1833 edition of *Beowulf*, according to which the protagonist was probably "an Angle of Jutland." Hence the poem "records the exploits of one of our own forefathers, not far removed in point of time from the coming of Hengest and Hors[a] into Britain: and . . . the poem was probably brought hither by some of those Anglo-Saxons who, in A.D. 495, accompanied Cedric and Cyneríc."[28] Today we are aware that *Beowulf* is set in a slightly later period, and that the protagonist was, in all likelihood, not an Angle like Horsa and Hengest. But Kemble was not alone in claiming *Beowulf* as a monument for his own nation. In the early phase of the new philology, one historical language might be claimed for more than one nation; thus *Beowulf* could be a heritage text for any linguistic community in Scandinavia, the North Sea region, or Germany. For example, five years after Kemble's *History*, an eminent German scholar published a book bearing the title *Beowulf: The Oldest German Heroic Poem Preserved in the Anglo-Saxon Dialect*.[29]

17.4. VALUE OF ENGLISH

The difference between Johnson and Kemble may also be detected from the type of linguistic features they privileged. In his "History," Johnson cites only one other Old English text after the *Boethius*: a relatively close rendition of the Gospel. In other words, the two texts that he uses to illustrate Old English literature are both prose based on the Latin. Although Johnson was aware that translations by force "retain the phraseology and structure of the original tongue," he seems to have believed that such an exercise was useful for those insular Saxons whose ancestral tongue "must have been artless and unconnected, without any modes of transition or involution of clauses." This statement makes it reasonably clear that the lexicographer considered syntax, rather than vocabulary, to be the most important criterion for measuring the level of sophistication for English. For instance, he describes the Old English *Boethius* as "a specimen of the *Saxon* in its highest state of purity," in that there are "scarcely any words borrowed from the *Roman* dialects." Johnson nonetheless considered the language of this Alfredian text to be capable of expressing "all sentiment of civilized people," because of its use, I believe, of hypotactic constructions or, to borrow Johnson's expression, "modes of transition or involution of clauses."[30] The specimen that Johnson gives from the Old English *Boethius* includes its opening section, in which the Anglo-Saxon author provides historical backgrounds to this philosophical dialogue. This original composition, as can be seen from its opening portion which follows, is characterized by intricate syntax:

> On ðære tide ðe Gotan of Sciððiu mægðe wið Romana rice gewin up ahofon, and mid heora cyningum, Rædgota and Eallerica wæron hatne, Romane burig abræcon, and eall Italia rice þæt is betwux þam muntum and Sicilia þam ealonde in anwald gerehton, þa æfter þam foresprecenan cyningum Þeodric feng to þam ilcan rice.[31]

> [At the time when the Goths of the Scythian nation raised up war against the kingdom of the Romans, and with their kings, who were called Rædgota and Alaric, captured the city of the Romans and brought under their control the whole kingdom of Italy which lies between the mountains and the island of Sicily, then, after those kings we have mentioned, Theoderic succeeded to that same kingdom.][32]

According to Johnson's story of progress, English prose developed to the state of elegance over several centuries and culminated in Thomas More (1478–1535). In fact, Johnson devotes the largest amount of illustration to this early modern author.

For Kemble, the value of English, or at least the value of the earliest phase of the language, does not lie in syntax but, rather, in morphology. According to the syllabus, his lecture series was to alternate commentary on poetry and analysis of grammar: Lecture VI, for instance, was to analyze Beowulf's voyage, followed by a lecture on the "Theory of the Cases." Kemble explains that there are "[t]wo methods of declension": one is to use morphological endings to register grammatical relationship; the other is to use prepositions for the same purpose. Historically, Kemble points out, the former method was "adopted by early languages" in the Germanic family, whereas the latter method was more prominent in later languages. Of the two, he clearly privileged the former, as he stipulated that "[d]eclension is not arbitrary but a necessary consequence of our reasoning power."[33] Given Kemble's principle, almost philosophical in nature, the history of English shows how the language has lost its original method of expressing relations more rapidly and more drastically than many other Germanic languages: for instance, English has long disposed of adjectival endings for case, number, and gender as well as strong and weak forms, whereas many of its sister languages, including German, have retained them to this day.[34]

17.5. THE METER OF *BEOWULF* AND THE STUDY OF SOUNDS

In his *History of the English Language*, Kemble cites from two poems—*Beowulf* and Lawman's *Brut*—to demonstrate "the Saxon mind" yet to be corrupted by "conquest, commerce and international communion."[35] Johnson on the other hand presents an entirely different history of English verse. To begin with, he does not provide even a single example from Old English poetry, or alliterative verse for that matter. The first two specimens of verse that he prints are both from *Poema Morale*. Johnson seems to have chosen this twelfth-century devotional poem on the basis of its form, for this is one of the earliest known syllabic poems, with regular rhymes, to have been composed in English. While he considered *Poema Morale* to be an ancestor of English verse, "the history of our poetry" proper did not begin until "the time of the illustrious *Geoffrey Chaucer*, who may perhaps, with great justice, be stiled the first of our versifyers who wrote poetically."[36]

One of the reasons Johnson did not quote from Anglo-Saxon poets was, to use his expression, "our ignorance of the laws of their metre and the quantities of their syllables," because the lack of this knowledge "excludes us from that pleasure which the old bards undoubtedly gave to their contemporaries." Johnson was rather pessimistic about the prospect of ever figuring out the craft of "the old bards," as he considered it "very difficult, perhaps impossible, to recover" the quantities of Old English syllables.[37] When we turn to Kemble's *History*, we find a completely different outlook on the native form of English verse, for he was convinced that he understood Anglo-Saxon poetry better than any English scholar from earlier generations. One of the areas of linguistic investigation on which the new philologists made remarkable progress during the nineteenth century was phonology, and their achievement in turn expanded possibilities for the study of Old English poetry. In Kemble's *History*, the first lecture on grammar concerns elucidation of the "mechanism of the Anglo-Saxon vowels." His methodology was once again comparative or "[e]tymological," as he shows in the outline Gothic and Anglo-Saxon vowels placed side by side. It was precisely "the Law of Relation" thus formulated that enabled the new philologists to discern the length of each Germanic vowel.[38] In editing *Beowulf*, Kemble followed the insular practice of lineating Old English verse according to half lines (rather than long lines), but he differed from earlier British editors in his use of the accent mark to indicate long vowels. Thus, for example, he presents the opening sentence of the poem as: *HWÆT We Gár-Dena / in gear-dagum. / þeód-cýninga, /þrým ge-frunon / hú ða æþelingas / ellen fremedon.*[39] From our vantage point, Kemble's edition does not always catch long vowels in the poem (e.g., Klaeber's edition additionally has *wē, ģeār-, ģefrūnon*, and *ðā* for the same passage).[40] But what was important at the time was the conviction held by Kemble and other new philologists that their methods were sound and capable of advancing linguistic knowledge. The study of Germanic vowels continued to develop for the remainder of the nineteenth century. It was the fruit of this investigation that enabled the neogrammarian Eduard Sievers to publish *Altgermanische Metrik* in 1893. His theory of five metrical types could not have been formulated without the understanding of vowel and syllable length in Germanic languages.

17.6. CONCLUSIONS

In this chapter, I have compared Johnson's and Kemble's publications on the history of the English language as a case study to show how the approach to the subject changed after the introduction of the new philology in the early nineteenth century. Both authors endeavored to promote the subject, and in each case, the endeavor met with partial success. Kemble's lecture series was not an official one, and despite its auspicious beginning, it attracted fewer and fewer people, until he was apparently forced to leave it off without completing.[41] Cambridge never established a professorship for him; but his scholarship laid the foundation for the study of historical English, which was to occupy a significant place in English studies when the subject began to develop as an academic discipline in the second half of the nineteenth century. Johnson's *Dictionary of the English Language* was so successful that it has since served as a model for synchronic lexicons, while his method of using a choice of literary texts as a source for citations reinforced the idea of canon for English literature. The philology of the nineteenth century, on the other hand, brought about a new lexicographical model, whose foremost example, the *Oxford English Dictionary*, is compiled on "historical principles," with its citations drawn from a much greater corpus.[42]

So what has *Beowulf* to do with English? This title question was inspired by the famous letter written by Alcuin of York (ca. 740–804) after hearing of the sacking of Lindisfarne. Writing from the continent, where he served as adviser at the court of Charlemagne, Alcuin saw the Viking attack of 793 as a divine retribution for morally questionable behaviors among English clerics, such as taking meals while oral poets performed vernacular songs about pagan heroes like Ingeld:

> Let God's words be read at the episcopal dinner-table. It is right that a reader should be heard, not a harpist, patristic discourse, not pagan song. What has Hinield [Ingeld] to do with Christ? The house is narrow and has no room for both. The Heavenly King does not wish to have communion with pagan and forgotten kings listed name by name.[43]

For Alcuin, who was "a major figure in the revival of learning and letters," *Quid Hinieldus cum Christo?* ("What has Ingeld to do with Christ?") was a rhetorical question, for he no doubt placed book learning over oral tradition, and Latin over the vernacular.[44] But in our case, "What has *Beowulf* to do with English?" is a genuine question, the answer to which may be either "nothing" or "a lot," depending on whom we ask: for Johnson and the antiquaries before him, the poem hardly had any place in the history of English; for Kemble, it represented the spirit of the language itself. And for us, the poem may symbolize the vitality and versatility of the English language: *Beowulf* takes place in the heroic age, and yet the poet himself was a Christian; the poem depicts a pagan world from a Christian perspective, presenting, for instance, the local monster Grendel as Cain's descendant.[45] *Beowulf* is a treasure hoard of poetic vocabulary filled with kennings and other traditional expressions; as Kemble states, Germanic speakers' power of coining new words was "one of their most remarkable advantages."[46] Yet the *Beowulf* poet was also versed in Latin language culture; hence he may measure time by using the word *non* (1660a), a loanword from the Latin *nona*, signifying the liturgical ninth hour ('noon' in modern English, but here 3 P.M.). *Beowulf* is not an epic the way Alcuin, who definitely knew Vergil, would have understood the genre[47]; nor does the poem sing about peak times in the national history. Instead, the poet tells of one disaster after another that took place in days of yore: Ingeld, for instance, marries Hrothgar's daughter to end the feud between his people and the Danes (hence Kemble's epithet "woman lover,"[48] but his love toward the bride soon turns sour because of the pre-Christian culture of perpetual vengeance. *Beowulf* is a work of synthesis, mixing many—and often opposing—elements to tell an intricate story about people whose deeds of valor were invariably followed by epic failures. The world of *Beowulf*, in other words, is always already fallen, and yet it is the constant breakdown of an existing order that keeps the poem new. And this is why *Beowulf*, allegedly the first English-language epic, has held a symbolic place in the history of English—a language that has met with many challenges, but which has somehow managed to emerge from them, each time having been made ever so slightly more resilient, more expressive and more capacious.

17.7. APPENDIX: SAMPLE EXERCISES

1. In Image 17.1, you will see the first sentence of *Beowulf* as it appears in the sole-surviving manuscript[49]:

Image 17.1. British Library, Cotton Vitellius, A. xv, 132r: The Opening Sentence of *Beowulf*

   Transcribe the passage by using Dobbie's text given on page 3 as a guide, and consider how the Anglo-Saxon scribe's text differs from that of the modern edition.

2. Take at least three translations of *Beowulf* and compare the way they render the first sentence of the poem (or any other part of the poem).[50] For the Old English texts with glosses, Jack (1994) or Alexander (1995) may be consulted.[51]

3. The following is an Old English medical recipe for dizziness (*ad vertiginem*); first, translate it (a suggested translation is provided at the end of the appendix), and then consider why so many of the words used here have survived into modern English[52]:

   Nim betonica & wæll swyðe on win oþþa on ald ealað &
   take   boil well   or
   wæsc þæt heafod mid þam wose & leg siððen þæt wyrt swa wærm abutan
   infusion   since
   þæt heafod & wrið mid claðe & læt swa beon ealla niht.
   wrap[53]

4. Johnson speculates that the original speech of the insular Saxons was characterized by "abruptness and inconnection," and maintains that such features "may be observed even in their later writings."[54] In making such a statement, Johnson may have had in mind such texts as the *Anglo-Saxon Chronicle*. The following passage comes from the entry for 495 CE in this first vernacular English historiography:

Her cuomon twegen aldormen on Bretene, Cerdic & Cynric his sunu, mid .v. scipum · in þone stede þe is gecueden Cerdicesora & þy ilcan dæge gefuhtun wiþ Walum.[55]

[In this year two chieftains came to Britain, Cerdic and his son Cynric, with five ships, at a place that is called Cerdicesora ['Cerdic's Shore'], and on the same they fought against the Welsh. (My translation)]

Analyze this passage and discuss its syntactic characteristics. The *Anglo-Saxon Chronicle* is believed to have its origin in Alfred's Wessex. Compare this excerpt with the one from the Old English *Boethius* provided on page 217. How do these passages differ from each other? Why should the two texts roughly from the same period and area look so different?

5. According to Johnson's "History of the English Language," already in the early seventeenth century, Thomas More's "works were considered as models of pure and elegant style."[56] The following passage comes from More's *History of King Richard III*, a text from which Johnson offers a large excerpt:

[Richard] slewe with his owne handes king Henry the sixt, being prisoner in the Tower, as menne constantly saye, and that without commaundemente or knowledge of the king, which woulde vndoubtedly yf he had entended that thinge, haue appointed that boocherly office, to some other then his owne borne brother.[57]

What are the formal characteristics of this passage? Do you agree that his style is "pure and elegant"? Johnson argues that More's writing holds an important place in the history of English, in part because "our language was then in a great degree formed and settled," and in part because his "works are carefully and correctly printed, and may therefore be better trusted than any other edition of the *English* books of that, or the preceding ages."[58] Does Johnson's observation shed light on More and his age, which experienced the rise of print culture?

CHAPTER 18

Starting from Now

Teaching the Recent History of English

JOAN BEAL

18.1. INTRODUCTION

In the undergraduate programme in English Language and Literature that I took at the University of Newcastle upon Tyne between 1971 and 1974, a compulsory first-year course on the History and Structure of English could be followed up with one or both of two optional courses: The History of English up to 1450 and the History of English from 1450 to the Present Day. Naturally, I took both, but what might appear strange to readers accustomed to the "Time's arrow" approach to the history of English is that the "1450 to the Present Day" course was taken in the second year of the programme and the "up to 1450" in the final year. This was consistent with the stance taken in the textbook published by the then Professor and Head of Department, the late Barbara M. H. Strang, in which part one of the introduction covers principles of linguistic change, and part two is headed "Changes within living memory." Following this, the book is arranged in chapters covering 200-year blocks of time in reverse chronological order, starting with Chapter I: 1970–1770. In the preface, Strang discusses her motivation for this bold choice:

> Over some twenty years of personal involvement in this teaching [the history of English] I have been struck by the fairy-tale—not to say nightmare—quality the subject has for some students. Grimm's Law, Verner's Law and the Great Vowel Shift seem to operate in a world strangely mutated from that in which they converse.[1]

Of course, as other chapters in this volume demonstrate, Grimm's Law need not be a nightmare, and, as the current fashion for medievalism in popular culture shows, distance and difference have their attractions. However, since taking over the "from 1450 to the Present Day" course as a very young lecturer in 1977, and having later developed courses (or modules, as they are now termed in the UK) on Late Modern English,[2] it has been my experience that learning about the recent history of English strikes a chord with students who recognise the operation of sociolinguistic forces still evident today and find connections with other courses in linguistics and literature. The wealth of primary and secondary sources available for the study of this period also provides ample opportunity for student-led investigations.

One anecdote from my lecturing experience illustrates the first of these points. In a lecture on changes in English pronunciation in the late modern period, I referred to a cartoon from *Punch* reproduced in Bailey's *Nineteenth-Century English*.[3] The cartoon shows young Lord Reginald, with his governess in a café. Lord Reginald says, " 'Ain't yer goin' to have some Puddin', Miss Richards? It's so jolly!" When Miss Richards replies: "*There* again Reginald! '*Puddin*'!—*Goin*'!—*Ain't yer*! That's the way Jim Bates and Dolly Maple speak—and Jim's a Stable-Boy and Dolly's a *Laundry-Maid*!' the boy's retort is "Ah! But that's the way Father and Mother speak, too—and Father's a *Duke* and Mother's a *Duchess*!! So *there*!'" I then showed the students Labov's famous "crossover" graph,[4] illustrating the linguistic insecurity of the lower middle class, who style-shift in using pre-consonantal /r/ more in more formal styles, whilst the higher and lower classes shift much less. Both illustrations showed the same phenomenon of the upper and lower classes behaving in a similar way, whilst the middle class (represented by the nanny/governess in the cartoon) insist on linguistic "correctness." This has been quite a lengthy explanation, but in the classroom jaws dropped. The students were, to use a British slang term, gobsmacked.[5] They instantly understood the meaning of "linguistic change from above" and witnessed the same sociolinguistic processes taking place in nineteenth-century Britain and twentieth-century New York. They also appreciated the connection between their studies in sociolinguistics and the history of English.

18.2. CURRICULUM DESIGN

In the late 1980s, when I began to teach eighteenth- and nineteenth-century English in distinct modules there was no textbook to guide me. It was at exactly this time that Charles Jones described the eighteenth and nineteenth centuries as "the Cinderellas of English historical linguistic study."[6] Not until the late 1990s did textbooks dedicated to these centuries appear. First to appear in 1996 was the book by the late Richard Bailey referred to earlier, and then Manfred Görlach straddled the millennium with his texts on nineteenth-century and eighteenth-century English in 1999 and 2001 respectively,[7] whilst my own book on eighteenth-century English pronunciation also appeared in 1999.[8] When my textbook *English in Modern Times* was published in 2004,[9] it was the first volume to cover all and only the late modern period, although volume IV of the *Cambridge History*[10] deals with the period from 1776 onward. Since then, Ingrid Tieken has produced *An Introduction to Late Modern English*[11] so teachers and students now have a choice of textbooks.

In designing a curriculum for the study of Late Modern English, I set out to teach students about structural changes in the language in the context of the external history of the Anglophone world during this period, so the first week was dedicated to a survey of political, social, and scientific events with an emphasis on the emergence of "modernity" in all these spheres. Following this, changes in the lexicon, morpho-syntax, and phonology were covered. In each case, a session devoted to the structural changes involved was followed by one dealing with attempts to regulate change in the relevant areas. Thus, a session on lexical innovation was followed by one on lexicography; discussion of morphosyntactic change by that of grammars; and of phonological change by that of pronouncing dictionaries and the elocution movement. This was intended to counteract what had hitherto been the received view that few structural changes had taken place in the language after 1700 and that the eighteenth century in particular was characterised by prescriptivism. The pairing of sessions on linguistic change with those on attempts at regulation enabled students to learn that changes did occur in this period, and, by examining the so-called prescriptive texts firsthand, to discover for themselves the principles behind texts such as Johnson's *Dictionary*,[12] Lowth's *Short Introduction to English Grammar*,[13] and Walker's *Critical Pronouncing Dictionary*.[14] Although these sessions concentrated on the evolution and codification of Standard British English, albeit with some discussion of American English, the two final sessions provided a more diversified account of British dialects and the emerging World Englishes of the period.

This curriculum and the content of the lectures and workshops were developed and modified over several years in response to feedback from students at the universities of Newcastle and Sheffield (both in the north of England) and taking account both of new scholarship in the emerging field of Late Modern English studies and also of new resources such as corpora and digital collections. *English in Modern Times* was designed as a textbook to support this curriculum as well as a general introduction to Late Modern English. The chapters in this book give a good idea of the content of lectures on my Late Modern English course, so the following sections concentrate on the activities carried out in workshops and the assignments carried out by students. These sections take the form of case studies on teaching and learning in two areas: lexical innovation and codification of grammar.

18.3. CASE STUDY 1: LEXICAL INNOVATION

The first area of language dealt with in my Late Modern English course was the lexicon because it is at this level that the connection between the internal and external histories of the language is most transparent. We are also very fortunate in having the online *OED* as a teaching resource. In the UK, all institutions of higher education and many schools and public libraries have access to this resource, and I have made full use of it since the days when the second edition of the *OED* was only available on CD-ROM. Indeed, I have used the *OED* as a resource for teaching lexical innovation and change to first-year undergraduates as it enables them to conduct small-scale research projects at an early stage and to experience the satisfaction of finding out something new for themselves.

In a lecture entitled "Fun with the OED," I took first-year students through a demonstration of the various searches that can be performed with the Advanced Search facility in the online *OED*. The first thing I did was to show them a search for words first cited in 1999 by entering '1999' in the first search box and choosing 'first quotation' from the drop-down menu. I did this search 'live' so that the students could see how this worked and then asked if they were surprised at the number of results (this varies as the *OED* is constantly updated, but a search in March 2016 yielded thirty-three). We then looked at a selection of the words identified in this search and discussed the semantic fields represented. It was easy to see that the lexical innovation reflected in the search results was dominated by the vocabulary of information technology and online communication: *blog* (noun and verb), *blogger*, *blogging, blogosphere, e-edition, net-book, weblogger,* and *wi-fi* all had first citations in this year. This immediately resonated with students who had grown up taking these developments for granted and demonstrated the connection between lexical innovation and external history. The inclusion in the result list of still-current slang terms such as *bling, chavvy,* and *munter* also provided amusement. I then went on to demonstrate how the advanced search facility could be used to discover the extent of borrowing from specific languages at different times, and the number of first citations from specific authors. Following the lecture, students were given an assignment involving similar searches, the results of which were discussed in workshop sessions.

The students taking my third-year Late Modern English course had already taken the compulsory first-year history of English course and so had completed the assignment described in the previous paragraph. I was therefore able to assume a familiarity with the Advanced Search facility and could set an assignment which required them to consider the context of lexical innovation and to investigate the sources used by the *OED*. Since the first edition of the *OED* was to be discussed in the following week's lecture as an example of nineteenth-century lexicography, this exercise also helped them to critique the principles and methods behind the dictionary.

The instructions presented to the students are set out below. One of the intended learning outcomes of the Late Modern English course was that students should learn how to work together as a team, negotiating the division of tasks and taking collective responsibility for the final presentation.

GROUP TASK 1: LEXICAL INNOVATION

This task is to be completed as a team assignment: you will be put into small groups.

Each group should research lexical innovation, in the sense of words first cited in *OED* online, for a particular year, as assigned (1729, 1789, 1829, or 1889).

You should find the following:
- How many words are first cited in this year?
- Where do they come from? (to do this, search for "French," "Latin," "Greek," etc. under "Language Name" and "Your Year" under "First Citation." This should give you the number of words from each major source. Then look for any unusual etymologies (use your judgement on this). Where words are

clearly English in origin, find how many are compounds, prefixed, suffixed, and so on.

- Look at the history of Britain in that year (historical encyclopaedias, time-lines, etc., are useful for this). Was anything special happening that might influence lexical innovation (war, politics, new inventions, etc.)?
- Look at the sources of citations. Are any particular sources prominent?

In the first instance, you should produce a presentation of ten minutes, which you will give in Week 4. You should either produce printed handouts, OHP slides, or PowerPoint (laptop and data projector will be available).

You should organise the tasks as a team: probably the best way to do this is to arrange to meet, delegate tasks, and then meet again before the presentation and/or contact each other by email.

The groups were assigned different years so that, when the presentations were given, the class would see results from over the whole of the late modern period. One slight drawback was that the groups assigned dates from the nineteenth century had a lot more data to deal with than those researching 1729 and 1789. However, it was explained to these groups that, rather than giving overall statistics for numbers of citations, they should instead select examples for discussion.

Students performed well on this task though there was a certain amount of fire-fighting to be done when team dynamics were difficult. However, with a little encouragement and emphasising that the lessons learnt from these difficulties would be invaluable in most workplaces, the students appreciated the opportunities provided for individual and group research. They particularly enjoyed finding interesting examples, their "own" words, and proved adept at illustrating their presentations with suitable images.

Figures 18.1 through 18.4 replicate slides presented by Katherine Austin, Natalie Dent, Heather Hardy, Katherine Rutherford, and Jamie Wroe, who as a group were assigned the year 1889. Figure 18.1 shows how the team presented the overall picture of first citations from 1889. The pie chart effectively represents the major sources of borrowing, and later slides discussed the importance of Latin and Greek etymologies in scientific vocabulary first cited in this year.

Later Modern English – 1889

- 955 words were first cited in 1889.
- Their origins vary greatly with many words being 'borrowed' from other languages, particularly Latin (150), Greek (95) and French (92).

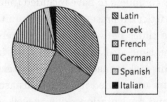

Latin
Greek
French
German
Spanish
Italian

Figure 18.1. Overall statistics 1889

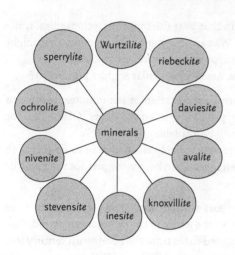

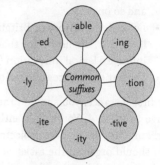

- " ...newly discovered or freshly classified natural objects, particularly minerals and fossils, gave great productivity to the suffix–*ite*." (Bailey 1996: 146-7)

- This can clearly be seen in 1889 as a vast amount of words for minerals were coined, often using the name of the founder or the place the mineral was found followed by the –*ite* suffix.

Figure 18.2. Suffixes: 1889

Figure 18.2 highlights the importance of suffixes in lexical innovation, illustrating with examples from 1889 the citation from Bailey about the use of the -*ite* suffix to coin words for newly discovered minerals.

Figure 18.3 is an example of how the students matched trends that they noticed in the first citations with events in the external history of the Anglophone world. They had been advised that first citations from a particular year would reflect events in the years leading up to it, thus their choice of events from the 1850s. Although words from Australia were not numerically dominant amongst the first citations from 1889, the student here has clearly followed up his or her interest and taken ownership of this topic.

Figure 18.4 is a good example of what the students can discover by searching for the sources of citations. This student has noticed the dependence of the *OED* on other dictionaries and has learnt something about the *Century Dictionary* in the process. In class, we discussed how this demonstrated that words first cited in the *OED* under the date 1889 had actually been in use earlier in order for the *Century Dictionary* compilers to have included them.

This particular presentation was quite ambitious: the five students produced thirty-one slides between them and were challenged to complete their presentation in the time available. This in itself is a testimony to how much the students enjoyed this task, as each student had taken responsibility for his or her part of the assignment and carried it out enthusiastically. In doing so they acquired valuable research and presentation skills as well as learning about historical lexicology and lexicography.

• In 1889 a total of 9 words were first cited which were of Australian origin...

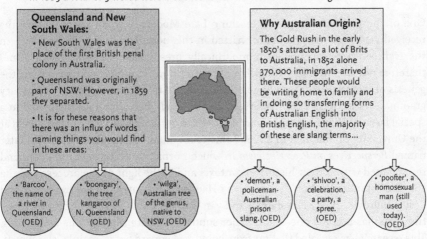

Queensland and New South Wales:

• New South Wales was the place of the first British penal colony in Australia.

• Queensland was originally part of NSW. However, in 1859 they separated.

• It is for these reasons that there was an influx of words naming things you would find in these areas:

Why Australian Origin?

The Gold Rush in the early 1850's attracted a lot of Brits to Australia, in 1852 alone 370,000 immigrants arrived there. These people would be writing home to family and in doing so transferring forms of Australian English into British English, the majority of these are slang terms...

• 'Barcoo', the name of a river in Queensland. (OED)

• 'boongary', the tree kangaroo of N. Queensland (OED)

• 'wilga', Australian tree of the genus, native to NSW. (OED)

• 'demon', a policeman- Australian prison slang. (OED)

• 'shivoo', a celebration, a party, a spree. (OED)

• 'poofter', a homosexual man (still used today). (OED)

Figure 18.3. Australia

Later Modern English- sources of citation

• Of the 955 words that were first cited in the Oxford English dictionary in 1889, **158** were cited from the *Century Dictionary* (The Century Dictionary Online)
• The first edition was published from 1889-1891
• This very first edition of the dictionary, was an expansion of the smaller *Imperial Dictionary*.

The *Century Dictionary* aimed to:
❖ Create a general dictionary of the English language, which could be serviceable for every literary and practical use.
❖ Be a more complete collection of the technical terms of the various sciences, arts, and professions than had yet to be attempted.

• The *Century Dictionary* and its aims, help to explain the high number of technical terms which were first cited in the OED in 1889.
• Its publication in 1889 helps to explain the high number of words which were first cited from this source, as it was a new source.

Figure 18.4. Citations from the *Century Dictionary*

18.4. CASE STUDY 2: EIGHTEENTH-CENTURY GRAMMARS AND GRAMMARIANS

One of the main challenges in teaching Late Modern English is to counter the received view that the grammars written in this period, and, more specifically, in the eighteenth century, were monolithically prescriptive and conservative and therefore not worthy of a serious linguist's attention. Jane Hodson writes that "the genesis of twentieth-century linguistics lies in the rejection of eighteenth-century grammar."[15] Hodson's 2006 paper was one of a number of studies published in a special issue of *Historiographia Linguistica* which resulted from a colloquium held at the University of Sheffield in 2003.[16] This colloquium was the first in a series later named *Perspectives on Prescriptivism* in which normative texts were discussed and re-evaluated within their historical contexts and in the light of the process and the stages of standardisation as set out by Haugen[17] and later refined by James and Lesley Milroy[18] and by Nevalainen and van Ostade.[19] This re-evaluation of normative texts has become one of the major subfields of Late Modern English studies. This research has revealed that far from being, as Leonard put it, mainly "clergymen, retired gentlemen, and amateur philosophers"[20] who "were writing for the edification and use of gentlemen, to warn them against inadvertent contamination with the language of the vulgar,"[21] eighteenth-century grammarians came from various social classes, were female as well as male, and had different motives for compiling their works.

Eighteenth-century grammars have been made much more accessible to researchers than they were in Leonard's time. In particular, the *Eighteenth-Century Collections Online* (ECCO) database has made it possible to search and download a wide range of texts and to examine the contents of works which, as Geoffrey K. Pullum noted with regard to Lowth, have tended to be "more mentioned than read."[22] More recently, the *Eighteenth-Century English Grammars* (ECEG) database has greatly facilitated teaching about these grammars since it is freely available (after registration) and enables searches in fields such as birthplace, gender and occupation of author, intended audience, and so on. This allows students to discover (usually to their surprise) that several eighteenth-century grammars were written by women, that they were written with various readers in mind, and that the normative rules attributed to these grammars in some linguistic textbooks were either less prescriptive than they had been led to believe or did not exist at all.

The assignment on eighteenth-century grammars required students to work in groups (usually of four, but in some cases three or five) to produce a poster about a grammarian of their choice. Prior to being given this assignment, the students had a lecture on eighteenth-century grammars and a workshop held in an IT (information technology) suite in which they were introduced to ECEG, ECCO, and the online *Oxford Dictionary of National Biography*.

In producing their posters, students were asked to address the following points:

1. Give a brief biography of the grammarian, suggesting, if possible, why he or she wrote the grammar (motivation, background, etc.)

2. Look at the title page and preface of the grammar. What kinds of reader did the author have in mind?
3. Do you think the grammar would be suitable for its target readership?
4. What sections does the grammar have (syntax, orthography, etc.)?
5. How many "parts of speech" are named in the grammar, and what names do they have (noun, verb, adjective, etc.)?
6. How does the author illustrate his or her "rules"?
7. To what extent is this grammar "prescriptive"? Take a well-known "rule," such as the proscription against ending sentences with prepositions, and discuss the way in which this is presented by the grammarian.

The students presented their posters at a conference-style session in the foyer of the building in which the School of English is housed. Staff and postgraduates were invited to the session, which also attracted "passing trade," as the foyer is situated between the teaching and administrative areas and the café. As the building also houses the History department, the posters were viewed by several professors of eighteenth-century history, who gave constructive and encouraging comments. Figure 18.5 is a photograph of a poster on display at one of these sessions and gives a good idea of the standard of presentation achieved by the students, who took great pride in displaying their posters and answering questions about them. Some of these posters were subsequently re-used in displays on open days for high school students considering applying for programmes in English at Sheffield, as an example of the innovative teaching and learning methods used.

The poster presentation not only encouraged students to discover for themselves the diversity of eighteenth-century grammars but also gave them the opportunity to practise a kind of presentation widely used in postgraduate conferences and in other professional contexts. Students in the Late Modern English course were often in their final semester of the programme and appreciated the opportunity to acquire skills that would be useful in their future careers. Most of all, they worked hard and enjoyed doing so. Since many graduates of our English programmes go on to teach English, I considered it particularly important to counteract widespread false information about grammarians, such as the assertion that Lowth invented the rule prohibiting split infinitives.[23]

18.5. CONCLUSION

I have attempted in this chapter to give a flavour of the experience of teaching and learning Late Modern English, along with practical suggestions for teaching and learning activities. Over the years in which I have taught these courses, the increasing availability of electronic resources has made it possible for students to explore for themselves the texts and contexts of this period. Of course, such resources are also available for the study of earlier periods in the history of English, and the assignments described in the two case studies here could be replicated in courses on Early Modern or Middle English. What is particularly striking in my experience of teaching

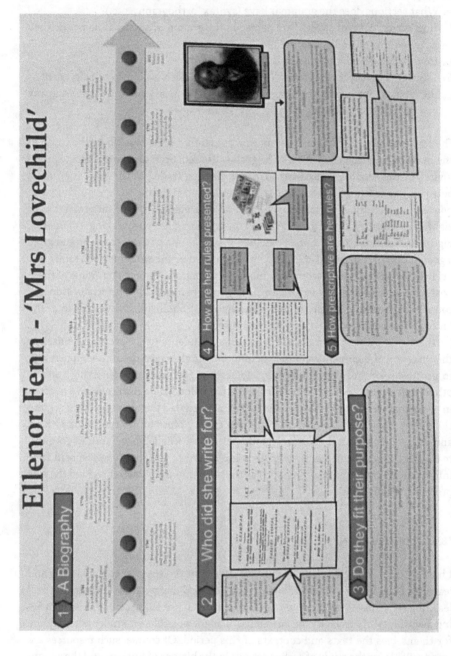

Figure 18.5. Poster display (photograph by Joan Beal)

Late Modern English is the extent to which students relate the issues discussed in class to their own experience: the awareness of the link between linguistic variation and social class in the cartoon from *Punch*; the discovery that familiar slang words had their origins in nineteenth-century Australia (Figure 18.3); or the "grammar grumbles" of today's pedants aired in much less prescriptive terms by eighteenth-century grammarians. When teaching the History of English, it might well be worth following Strang's example and starting the course with Late Modern English before moving into less familiar territory.

PART FIVE

Including "Englishes" in the History of English

CHAPTER 19

From Old English to World Englishes

BENJAMIN A. SALTZMAN

19.1. INTRODUCTION

As medievalists, we often say (and sometimes even boast) to our students—not just to those in the History of the English Language (HEL) classroom, but also to freshmen who might be lured into our Old English classes, or even to accountants at dinner parties—that Old English looks scarcely like the Modern English we know today, that there is an intriguing foreignness to the earliest stage of our language, indeed that it must even be taught as a kind of foreign language.[1] These are claims for how far the language has come, how much it has changed over the past thousand-odd years, and implicitly therefore one of the reasons why it is worth studying in the first place, both as an integral part of an HEL curriculum and as a language in itself. As Haruko Momma has pointed out, this view of Old English is hardly new: not only does Old English look "foreign" today, but until the 1870s, when scholars referred to the language as Saxon or Anglo-Saxon, they were emphasizing its Germanic origins over its affiliation to the English of the day.[2] In part, it is this remarkable difference between Old and Modern English that justifies teaching the linguistic history of English as a stand-alone undergraduate course, inspiring student curiosity and interest along the way. And the same is true at the other end of the historical spectrum: as the varieties of English unfold around the world today, it is precisely their diversity and their difference—often problematically stated in terms of nativeness and foreignness—from some semblance of a "standard English" that makes the study and thus the teaching of those Englishes so compelling and rewarding. Yet even positing "the Modern English we know today," as I have just done and against which a linguistic history of the language is often drawn, assumes a relatively stable entity knowable to a certain *we* that is nevertheless class-marked by virtue of regularly being in a position to enjoy such off-hand conversations about linguistic change—academics, in other words, who attend dinner parties with accountants.

I think for many of us who teach the history of the language from a scholarly background in Old or Middle English literature, these World Englishes pose a daunting pedagogical challenge. And as Seth Lerer reminds us, Anglo-Saxonists and Chaucerians at American universities are typically an English department's first defense against this piece of the curriculum. In Chapter 7, Lerer argues that "precisely because HEL remains a narrative of origin and change, it has been left to those who specialize in origins to be its overseers."[3] Regardless of medievalists' own increasingly diverse cultural experiences of English, a hard-won diversity that has already benefited the field of Medieval Studies, medievalists' exposure to World Englishes as a field of study is necessarily more limited than those scholars of later periods, during which English first began to spread across the world. How then are such medievalists to grapple with the task of teaching precisely that which is most distant and most different from the origins of the language that we study, especially given that the scholarship on World Englishes now comprises an established and thriving field far outside the scholarly comfort zone of most medievalists? How, in other words, can we do justice to the global phenomenon and the particularities of English in today's world?

19.2. THE HISTORY OF TEACHING THE HISTORY OF WORLD ENGLISHES

The model for HEL courses is still, as Lerer's chapter (7) in this volume demonstrates, very much an origin story, and accordingly the standard textbooks still opt for a chronological narrative of development from PIE (Proto-Indo-European) to PDE (Present Day English). As an alternative, some instructors prefer a reversed model, such as the ingenious and highly effective plans Joan Beal (Chapter 18) and Matthew Sergi (Chapter 25) propose, which works its way backward from PDE and invites students to contribute to the class's understanding of the diversity of Englishes from the start.[4] However, if the standard approach to teaching HEL is a chronological narrative—an approach that has been used since the first histories of the language were written (e.g., by Samuel Johnson in 1755) and one that I think many instructors, including myself, hesitate to abandon because it feels intuitively right—then it makes sense that our textbooks and syllabi and students arrive at PDE and particularly World Englishes at the end of the course, though it is a shame that the arrival must make do with what little steam is left in the term to explore the widespread and complex, rapidly proliferating, and infinitely changing landscape of English as it is spoken around the world today.[5] Doing so entails opening a new door (and it's one thing to point to the door as something that can be opened, but it's another to open it fully and thoroughly explore the other side) that involves material more complicated and amorphous than anything that has come before, precisely at the point in the term when the instructor and the students might secretly prefer mere summary and review. At the end of this chapter, I will propose a slight alteration to the order of the material presented in the course in order to allow for a deeper engagement with World Englishes on the part of the students.

But first, it is worth considering how part of this challenge arises from the sudden addition of a third dimension into the pedagogical narrative. We use models, of course, to translate messy reality into a neat and comprehensible scheme, whether we are talking about the Great Vowel Shift or, in this case, the spread of English around the globe. But even the simplest and most traditional model of the history of English, which diachronically charts the development of English from OE (Old English) to ME (Middle English) to ModE (Modern English), leaves room for addressing synchronic variation in, for instance, register or regional dialect. We might say then that the traditional and most basic HEL model operates on a two-dimensional plane on which internal or external variables (e.g., matters of phonology and politics) can be plotted along diachronic and synchronic axes.

World Englishes break this model. But to be sure, the break is productive: it happens when the models used for representing HEL are fused with those used for representing the diversity of World Englishes. For example, it is common to rely directly or indirectly on Braj B. Kachru's concentric circles model (see Figure 19.1), which—although it is not without its problems and although there are certainly others to choose from—is still the dominant one even as it undergoes revision and critique.[6] Though few HEL textbooks print Kachru's diagram, its logic often informs and organizes their accounts of World Englishes, just as it does much of the scholarship in the field.[7] The model consists of three circles: the inner circle includes countries where English is spoken as a first language (United Kingdom, United States, Canada, Australia, etc.), the outer circle includes countries where English is spoken as a second language (often where English is an official or semi-official language and a remnant of colonial rule), and the expanding circle includes countries where English is being acquired and learned as a nonnative or foreign language (e.g., China, Russia, and other places where learning English gives individuals access to new opportunities). Pidgins and creoles are not included in the model, but HEL courses and textbooks will now typically address them in the context of World Englishes. There are numerous other models as well, but these only further demonstrate the complexity of adding this dimension at the end of an HEL course. One such model proposed by Yasukata Yano, for example, even adds a third dimension to Kachru's two-dimensional circles in order to account for the level of proficiency and functional nativeness of some outer and expanding circle English users (Figure 19.2).[8]

Once we introduce World Englishes into an HEL course and whichever model we adopt in doing so, the temporal plane that has grounded the path from OE through ModE explodes into dozens of new geographical and geopolitical planes (consisting of not only Kachru's three circles but also each of the countries and regions represented within those circles and now even the levels of proficiency). On each of these new planes, a particular variety of English requires consideration not only in terms of its diachronic formation but also in terms of the cultural context in which it is being acquired, its autonomy, its relation to other languages, the converging effects of globalization (e.g., the way the entertainment industry and commerce shape local languages from the outside), and the fact that all of these variables (and numerous others) are responsible for creating a form of English that is both related to and quite

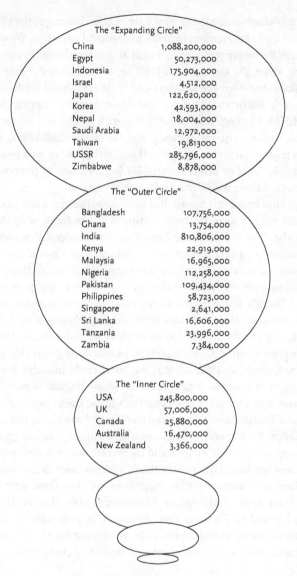

The "Expanding Circle"

China	1,088,200,000
Egypt	50,273,000
Indonesia	175,904,000
Israel	4,512,000
Japan	122,620,000
Korea	42,593,000
Nepal	18,004,000
Saudi Arabia	12,972,000
Taiwan	19,813000
USSR	285,796,000
Zimbabwe	8,878,000

The "Outer Circle"

Bangladesh	107,756,000
Ghana	13,754,000
India	810,806,000
Kenya	22,919,000
Malaysia	16,965,000
Nigeria	112,258,000
Pakistan	109,434,000
Philippines	58,723,000
Singapore	2,641,000
Sri Lanka	16,606,000
Tanzania	23,996,000
Zambia	7,384,000

The "Inner Circle"

USA	245,800,000
UK	57,006,000
Canada	25,880,000
Australia	16,470,000
New Zealand	3,366,000

Figure 19.1. Kachru's three concentric circles

distinct from the model of Standard English that has oriented the HEL course up to that point.

The available textbooks are typically one's first line of defense in approaching this complex conclusion to the course. If we look at a sample of four current HEL textbooks, we will notice that although many have revised and added to their chapters on World Englishes, their approaches and material on the topic have remained fairly consistent. In general, they tend to push World Englishes to the end of the course with disproportionally light coverage[9]:

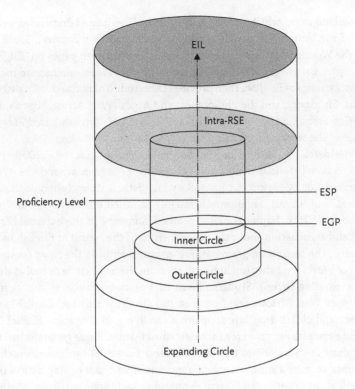

Figure 19.2. Yano's three-dimensional model

- Baugh and Cable, *A History of the English Language*[10] (1st ed., 1935; 6th ed., 2013): The antepenultimate chapter on the "Nineteenth and Twentieth Centuries" includes twelve pages on "English World-wide" (covering Australia and New Zealand, South Africa, West and East Africa, South Asia, Singapore, Malaysia, Hong Kong, the Caribbean, and Canada—all former British colonies), followed by one page on "Pidgins and Creoles." The eleven-page final chapter, "The Twenty-first Century," was newly added for the sixth edition and discusses, among other things, Kachru's three circles, cross linguistic influence, and the growing importance of the Chinese language.
- Pyles and Algeo, *The Origins and Development of the English Language* (1st ed., 1964; 6th ed., 2010)[11]: A three-page section on "World English" at the end of the chapter on Late Modern English (1800–present) offers two brief case studies (Irish English and Indian English) and concludes with a paragraph on the "essential oneness of all English" (originally from the first edition). Pidgin and creoles are discussed in the context of AAVE (African American Vernacular English) inside the brief section on "Ethnic and Social Dialects."
- Millward and Hayes, *A Biography of the English Language* (1st ed., 1989; 3rd ed., 2011)[12]: Following a forty-five-page chapter devoted to PDE, the final chapter, entitled "English around the World," includes fifty-three pages on "English as a

Native Language," which covers the dialects of America and England as well as the rest of the United Kingdom, Canada, Australia and New Zealand, South Africa, and the Western Atlantic. The chapter ends with fourteen pages on "English as a Nonnative Language," which begins with a list of features common to most non-native varieties of English, then provides case studies of nonnative English in Asia (India, Singapore, and the Philippines) and Africa (West Africa, Nigeria, Liberia, and Cameroon), and concludes with a discussion of "English-based Pidgins and Creoles." The workbook contains samples of various World Englishes.

- Van Gelderen, *A History of the English Language* (1st ed., 2006; rev. ed. 2014)[13]: A substantial penultimate chapter on "English around the World" is organized not by region but instead by linguistic features (phonological, grammatical, and lexical), an approach roughly modeled on recent World Englishes textbooks.[14] This chapter contains a broad summary of the external history to start and a discussion about the consequences of the spread of English to end. In between, the section on grammar, for instance, outlines the most common features of World Englishes (including those from the inner circle as well as the outer and expanding circles). Students learn that pronoun doubling "occurs in many Englishes: West African, and Romance and Slavic (non-native) English" and that subject and object drop "are frequent as well, e.g. in Singapore English" (260). Useful examples are given for each described feature. These generalizations helpfully draw out similarities between a diverse variety of Englishes, which allows students to gain a broad sense of representative types of linguistic variation, though at the expense of a deep understanding of any one particular English variety. An appendix provides samples of several World Englishes.

It makes sense that these textbooks take similar approaches to introducing World Englishes (with the partial exception of van Gelderen) and that they tend to place World Englishes at the end of the course. In part, the placement of World Englishes toward the end corresponds to their vital role in PDE, but it is also a gesture that conveys an uncertain, though optimistic, future for English, one in which the linear development charted thus far explodes in countless directions, one in which the diversity of the language will continue to change and perhaps expand. But these approaches also look backward, drawing on a long tradition of teaching the history of the language. Baugh's *History* has been around for more than eighty years and is now in its sixth edition. Pyles's *Origins* has gone through the same number of editions over the course of more than fifty years. Both of these classic textbooks—the former by a Chaucerian and the latter by a linguist of American English and onomastics—were first written well before World Englishes became a scholarly concept and discipline in the 1980s, but their organization and methods have left an enduring impression on the way we teach HEL.[15]

Each revised edition of Baugh's *History*, for example, retains the basic structure of the first, even as each edition becomes more attentive to the diversity of Englishes around the world. The first and second editions thus ask early in the course: "Will English Become a World Language?" This question taps into popular curiosity: people wonder whether English will become the one "language of all the world, or at least its civilized portions"; it is a wish that "springs partly from considerations of national pride, partly from a consciousness of the many disadvantages that result from a multiplicity of tongues"; it is a dream of "how much pleasanter travel would be if we did not have to contend with the inconveniences of a foreign language"; and English seems a plausible alternative to all of the artificial universal languages that were being proposed at the end of the nineteenth century.[16] This question is asked, in other words, from a highly ethnocentric perspective. The third edition, re-edited by Thomas Cable in 1978, retains Baugh's original question ("Will English Become a World Language?") and the initial statements about the desirability of English as an international language, but it then points to the expansion of English in the years after World War II and hints at several colonial examples where the relationship between the official language of English and the local vernacular complicates the answer.[17] In the fourth edition (1993), the section becomes more definitive ("English as a World Language"), and the implicit desire for English to become a universal language is replaced with a brief reflection on the global success of English supported by a quotation from Kachru.[18] By the sixth edition, Cable has cut this introductory section, and moved the discussion of English around the world to a brief survey in the final chapter on the twenty-first century.[19]

Similar changes are evident elsewhere in the book. Baugh's first edition (1935), for instance, contains a brief section on "English in the Colonies," which primarily discusses lexical features of English in Australia, South Africa, and Canada; bear in mind that by the 1930s the power and expansiveness of the British Empire was just beginning to come down from its peak, though it would still be fifteen years before India would become a republic.[20] The second edition (1957) leaves this section intact but renames it "English in the Empire" (a curious change).[21] The third edition (1978) adds discussions about South African English grammar as well as the role of English in other former colonies in sub-Saharan Africa and India, which "have a choice of retaining their colonial linguistic inheritance or rejecting it."[22] The fourth edition (1993) substantially expands the section (still entitled "English in the Empire") and divides it into subsections on each major region of British colonization (e.g., Australasia, South Asia, the Caribbean); it also adds a lengthy new section on pidgins and creoles.[23] By the sixth edition, Cable has retitled the section "English World-wide," but includes the same outer-circle examples as the previous two editions.

It is easy to draw attention to dated attitudes found in early textbooks. But we should bear in mind that when Baugh was at work on his first edition, "World Englishes" lacked scholarly attention, perhaps due in part to the technological limitations of researching the phenomenon already underway with, say, AAVE or the varieties of English in colonies prior to independence (e.g., Jamaica). Yet the earliest organization of textbooks like Baugh's History has significantly influenced the shape of most current books on the history of the language and therefore the way many of us tend to teach the course today.[24] The field has changed, of course, and we must appreciate the revisions that have been made to these pioneering works. Thomas Cable had to work within the constraints established by his predecessor, updating the book where possible, elsewhere framing views as intellectual history rather than linguistic fact, and most recently altering the organization by adding a new chapter.

We can see that the revisions and updates correspond to advancements in the study of World Englishes, yet they are still bound by the framework established by Baugh almost ninety years earlier.

The 1960s began to see greater interest in the uses of English around the world. In 1962, Randolph Quirk, for example, called for linguistic tolerance of other forms of English and the ceding of British control over a correct and standard form of the language (a position he would later retract in favor of an international standard).[25] But it was the instrumental work of Braj B. Kachru and two conferences held in 1978 (the same year Cable published the third edition of Baugh's *History*) that introduced World Englishes as a field of study in its own right. In the 1980s, the field took off. The beginning of the decade saw the first issues of the journal *World Englishes* (at the time titled *World Language English*), and the end of the decade saw the publication of Millward's *Biography*.

Millward's first edition (1989) strikes a balance between a broad survey of "English as a Nonnative Language" and an introduction to the particularities (external history, phonology, syntax, lexicon, etc.) of a small selection of "nonnative" Englishes (all from the outer circle).[26] Millward was a medievalist, but it is interesting to note that during the publisher's review process she received feedback from Kachru himself (one of fifteen readers listed in her acknowledgements).[27] The first edition of the *Biography* might very well be a product of its generation, informed by the decade's worth of developments in the then emerging field of World Englishes, even though a rhetoric of deficiency is sprinkled throughout the list of features common to many nonnative varieties of English: "Erratically incorrect stress placement," "Mistakes in the use of verb tenses," "Extensive misuse of prepositions."[28] The chapter is divided between native and nonnative varieties, where the same number of pages are devoted to the dialects of English in the United States (Millward's secondary area of research) as to the varieties of nonnative English around the world: though the coverage of nonnative varieties seems disproportionately light, Millward could very well have been aiming for balance (especially compared to other contemporary textbooks). Still, Millward's *Biography* owes its general structure to the tradition set by Baugh in the 1930s and Pyles in the 1960s, in which the global aspects of the language fall at the end of the course and are somewhat downplayed with priority given to English varieties from the inner circle.[29] When I teach HEL, I use the most recent edition, now revised by Mary Hayes, which largely retains the original structure, necessitated by the need to keep it a reasonable length, but brings important details (e.g., in the section on Indian English).

Finally, van Gelderen's *History* is a new textbook, freed from some of the constraints faced by revised editions of older ones. Although van Gelderen still opts to place World Englishes at the end (again, a justifiable decision), her approach stands out from the others in the way it prioritizes dominant linguistic features and general similarities across World Englishes rather than highlighting the individuality and autonomy of a selection of Englishes. If World Englishes adds a third dimension to the history of the language (as I have suggested earlier), then van Gelderen shows us what is pedagogically at stake in designing an HEL course that tries to fit this third dimension within the two-dimensional framework established by the bulk of the course. Van Gelderen gives students an up-to-date introduction to World Englishes that is concise and comprehensible. However, by orienting World Englishes linguistically rather than geopolitically, the textbook becomes approachable only by flattening out that third dimension and reducing World Englishes to a single plane comprised of their most homogeneous and dominant features. Minor or rare particularities of a given variety of English must be passed over in order for the material to be presented in coherent and easily absorbed paradigms. At the same time, van Gelderen is keenly sensitive to the ethical dynamics of this material, noting for instance that the terminology of superstratum and substratum (applied to the languages that combine to form a creole) is "not appropriate since it seems to imply one is 'higher' than the other."[30] And students learn that consequences of the spread of English include the marginalization of non-English speakers and the loss of linguistic diversity. These are important insights, which we will consider in more detail later.

What a review of these textbooks makes readily apparent is the fact that the trade-offs and decisions involved in teaching World Englishes to an HEL class—inevitable decisions about whether, for instance, to survey dominant and general linguistic features or to select one or two Englishes as exemplary; if the latter, on what basis and in what order?—carry complex ethical weight.

19.3. WORLD ENGLISHES, PEDAGOGY, AND THE ETHICS OF ALTERITY

The history of World Englishes is bound up with a history of colonialism and imperialism, oppression and hegemony. We cannot ignore the fact that where English has arisen as a second or official language in the so-called outer circle (indeed, even in the US and Australia), it has arisen often in direct connection to periods of colonial rule. Where English pidgins and creoles have developed, they have done so often in the context of slavery and subjugation. And where English becomes a dominant language, vernacular languages and the cultural heritage of which they are an integral part are often at risk of being wiped out. In many areas of the world, however, creoles and Englishes also become a site of local identity in their own right, used as a medium for empowerment and sooner or later for literary creativity. Elsewhere, English acquisition—especially in the expanding circle, but also in the outer circle—becomes associated with global opportunities, bringing with it a perception of prestige and new possibilities for cross-cultural communication.

On the one hand, then, we find Salman Rushdie saying that "those people who were once colonized by the language are now rapidly remaking it, domesticating it, becoming more and more relaxed about the way they use it. . . . Today the children of independent India seem not to think of English as being irredeemably tainted by its colonial provenance. They use it as an Indian language, as one of the tools they have to hand."[31] On the other hand, even if English in India, for instance, has started to move beyond its colonial past, it is still corrupted by another hierarchy— as Arundhati Roy has written about and experienced—one where its prestige and usefulness is primarily associated with the elitism of the upper castes, new forms of Indian nationalism, and global capitalism.[32] No matter how one approaches it, therefore, on the most local and the most global levels, English can be viewed as severely disempowering and oppressive or deeply empowering and liberating—but more often than not it is a knotty entwinement of the two.[33]

When the academic field of World Englishes was first being formed in the late 1970s and into the 1980s, one of its primary goals (as represented by journals like *World Englishes* and organizations like IAWE [International Association for World Englishes] and TESOL [Teachers of English to Speakers of Other Languages]) was to advance English language teaching. In many respects, this goal has remained central—but it has also made the ethics of studying World Englishes more pressing and critical. Research into local varieties of English and New Englishes, as one facet of the TESOL mission, for instance, thus aids the development and application of strategies for teaching English more effectively and ethically around the world, particularly in ways that take local Englishes into account.[34] These practical concerns have been at the center of some of the field's fiercest and most important debates, such as the one between Randolph Quirk (arguing against the "tolerant pluralism" of a liberation or deficit model of linguistics in favor of language policies that teach and promote a standard form of English abroad) and Braj B. Kachru (who responds to Quirk's ideological assumptions by drawing attention to, *inter alia*, the linguistic and sociolinguistic realities of multilingual cultures, the ineffectiveness of language policies, and the nature of language spread).[35] And still other debates have emerged around topics such as linguistic imperialism.[36] What makes these debates so heated and important is the shared sense on both sides that the stakes are high: that the way we think about English around the world involves the lives of real people, whose identities, cultures, and languages are vulnerable in the face of a dominant, powerful, and growing language; and more important, that the perspective of the "we" doing the thinking can influence the nature of that vulnerability.

These ideological and ethical debates highlight a second and even greater challenge that HEL instructors face when introducing students to World Englishes. To an outsider like me—someone who specializes in the oldest forms of the language—these debates feel unnerving, particularly because they take place in a fast-paced academic field concerned with immediate and contemporary circumstances: World Englishes are shifting under our very feet. Nevertheless, the ethical questions that motivate these debates do belong in the HEL classroom. In fact, I have noticed that many HEL students are eager to engage with them, and that is a good thing. For they can bring to life the current relevance of the seventeenth-century debates about, say, standardization and spelling reform: the students can experience history unfolding before their eyes.

Recent HEL textbooks tend to be sensitive to the precarious ethics surrounding the history and diversity of Englishes around the world, though they avoid bringing the ideological debates to the forefront (van Gelderen is an exception). And although it is hard to avoid hints of triumphalism in a history of the language (it has come so far and against all odds!),[37] these textbooks largely do so by continuing the descriptivist tone set earlier in the course. Sometimes, however, this descriptivist tone can flatten the sociolinguistic reality, which on the upside provides an excellent teaching opportunity. Millward's first edition, for example, was published six years after Salman Rushdie first wrote the passage quoted earlier, and yet she claims that "the Indians themselves . . . have been unable to agree whether the standard for Indian English should remain British English or whether a separate Indian Standard should be established that would openly accept widely used Indianisms."[38] Students will notice that Millward's statement represents the authoritative position on Indian English, whereas Rushdie's is describing the movements from the ground up. Elsewhere, Millward's description of imperial language imposition is overly tidy: "In the mid-nineteenth century, the British promulgated an official policy of training natives in English and established a number of universities. By the early twentieth century, English was the official language of India."[39] By the third edition, Hayes has made the force of colonial imposition more apparent and has clarified that English is only the "associate official language" alongside the official language of Hindi. I think students benefit immensely from seeing how the scholarly views on these issues change over time and are not as simple as either Rushdie and Millward would suggest.

The lesson, then, is that care must be taken not to gloss over the often bloody messiness of history. This means continuing the same kind of descriptivist mode from earlier in the course that is just as attuned to sound changes and semantic weakening as it is, for instance, to socioeconomic and technological factors. For medievalists like me, this might be an intuitive approach facilitated by the temporal distance that separates us from the objects of our study. For how else can one convey the linguistic (and sociolinguistic) material with the sensitivity it deserves? How does one then avoid speaking for those on the periphery? Indeed, how does one speak of a "periphery" without reinforcing it? How do we teach students, moreover, to critique the ideological orientation of the scholars and sources that we rely upon for the course, when we ourselves might be employing similarly dangerous ideologies without even knowing it?

The anxieties at the core of these questions reflect a notion of foreignness and periphery that is deeply engrained in the way scholars conceptualize World Englishes and exemplified by the models and technical language of the field. Even if there is now resistance to notions like "native" and "non-native" or "English as a foreign language" (replacing nativeness, for instance, with proficiency), these concepts are still unavoidable. But nativeness and foreignness are always a matter of perspective. Whether we are talking about endocentric or exocentric influences on a language, the influence can flow in any direction depending on where one stands—it does not just flow from the inner circle to the outer circle. The acrolectal and official English of Singapore, for instance, persists alongside the basilectal Singlish, which is rejected by policymakers, yet used in much creative writing: "Experience," we might say, "thogh noon auctoritee."[40] Moreover, what constitutes World Englishes, it is important to remember (though our textbooks make it hard to forget), is not just the New Englishes of the outer and expanding circles or the creoles and pidgins that sound all the more distinct, but also the variety of Englishes spoken in the inner circle, ranging from Scots English to AAVE.

The English language is a language of perpetual otherness within itself. No matter where you stand and no matter what variety of English you hear or speak—whether Old English or Received Pronunciation or Jamaican Creole—the view is always one of difference and otherness, combined with a peculiar sense of familiarity and affiliation: what I hear is different from the English I speak, and yet I recognize or know it *as* English at some fundamental level. The fact that Old English arouses such similar sentiments about its apparent foreignness should alert us to be historically wary of notions of nativeness (whether functional or geopolitical) and should defamiliarize any comfort we might have over what English is as a language.

19.4. ON MOVING BETWEEN WORLD ENGLISHES AND OLD ENGLISH, OR POSSIBLE STRATEGIES

There are obvious limits to what can be included and taught in an HEL survey course. But at a minimum, a course in the history of the language should spark the students' curiosity about the diversity of English around the globe; it should strongly problematize the assumption that there is or can be a standard English or even a set of standard Englishes; and it should engage the students with some of the ethical stakes involved in the spread of English, both historically and contemporarily. The course, moreover, should give the students the tools and inspiration to interrogate the notions of a standard and explore the varieties of English (whether Old or New) on their own or perhaps in future independent tutorials.

In practice, I see two possible strategies for incorporating World Englishes into an HEL course, aimed at doing justice to the particularities and autonomy of given varieties of English while introducing students to some of the broader historical and ethical complexity. There are certainly a multitude of different approaches to be taken (some more effective than others), and to many readers my first suggestion will probably seem familiar and intuitive, maybe even already with a place in their courses. Rather than attempting a broad and cursory survey of World Englishes, I like to focus a lecture or two on one or two particular varieties of English, say, AAVE and Jamaican Englishes. The idea is to delve into the English just as one would delve into Middle English, covering the external history, social and cultural influences, linguistic features (phonology, grammar, etc.), lectal relations (acrolect, mesolect, basilect, pidgins, and creoles), pressures from other languages, and of course diachronic changes. This approach has the advantage of giving students an in-depth understanding of one particular variety and introduces them to methods that they can then apply to other varieties or use to contemplate general theories about English as a global language.

This method can be combined with a second strategy, which involves handing the research and even some of the teaching over to the students. As Matthew Sergi has shown, student-based research into linguistic communities can be incredibly successful. My approach is slightly different, but has similar goals. I assign my students to select, research, and present to the class one variety of English. This not only gives each student an in-depth look at a particular English but also gives the other students a broader overview of several varieties and the dynamics of their histories. The core of the assignment consists of writing an essay that covers the salient features of a variety of English (including its "outer" and "inner" histories) and conducts indepth research into one aspect of complexity (e.g., lexical borrowings or grammatical influences from a local language or the effect of a political event on the use of English in the region). Students are first directed to general resources, such as David Crystal's *English as a Global Language* or Tom McArthur's "English World-wide in the Twentieth Century."[41]And once they have selected a variety of English and written a prospectus, they can be directed to more specific and detailed resources, such as the journal *World Englishes*, the book series *Varieties of English Around the World*, and volume 5 of *The Cambridge History of the English Language*, as well as databases for more advanced research, such as the *Electronic World Atlas of Varieties of English* (eWAVE) and the *International Corpus of English* (ICE).

The one major obstacle to this assignment, however, is that if the course follows the plan laid out by most textbooks, then by the time World Englishes are introduced, the term has all but come to an end. The students will have gained the technical knowledge to approach their research with rigor but will lack the time to do so. To make this strategy work, therefore, one might instead begin the course with an introduction to World Englishes and follow it up immediately with Old English and the subsequent historical stages of the language in chronological order.[42] As the students write their chapters over the course of the term, they perform individually on a separate plane what the class as a whole is simultaneously absorbing about the language as it develops from Old English to Modern English. By the end of the term, the class can then return to World Englishes for brief student presentations of their research.

There are a few other practical reasons for starting with World Englishes and then jumping immediately back to Old English: first, it allows us to ask big questions from the start, which get the students engaged and help them to frame their understanding of the historical stages of the language: How do new languages form? How are languages shaped by interactions with other languages? What kinds of cultural, sociological, and political events influence language changes? How do we determine the discreteness of languages?

Second, the proximity between the lessons on World Englishes and Old English gives students a contemporary inroad to understanding the diversity of Indo-European languages back in the mists of time. And it invites related discussions about whether, for instance, what we are currently witnessing in World Englishes is akin to the process by which the Romance languages emerged from Latin, as Robert Burchfield surmised, or slipping into the "barbarous diversity" that characterized Germanic and the earliest stages of the language, as Tom McArthur has suggested.[43] Likewise, it allows students to consider, from the start, how other languages and multilingual situations have shaped and continue to shape the English language, along the lines of the compelling case made by Rajend Mesthrie.[44]

Third, and relatedly, it begins the course with an expansive sense of inclusiveness and invites students to think about their own diverse relations to the English language, a pedagogical desideratum addressed by Michael R. Dressman (Chapter 8) and Matthew Sergi (Chapter 25) in their contributions to this volume.

Fourth, it helps to problematize the foreignness associated with Old English, which as McWhorter (Chapter 2) suggests, is often the sole or primary basis for distinguishing Old English from other forms of English: if it looks odd or difficult or different, it is Old English. But by addressing World Englishes, and especially creoles, first, students can learn to challenge this paradigm from the start and become more attuned to the particular and salient differences between varieties of English. Ultimately, we can begin to think about the meaning of otherness and difference through the lens of language: for every encounter with English—whether an encounter with Old English or Singlish or Nigerian English—is an encounter with a peculiar paradox of foreignness and familiarity.

Finally, by addressing the role of imperialism in the formation of many current Englishes, the instructor can lay the groundwork for the class to contemplate the very real experiences and often violent forces of colonialism and colonization that have shaped the language from its earliest stages, whether we are thinking of the Jutes or the Vikings, the Normans or the East India Trading Company. In other words, once attuned to the messy—at once individual and global, sometimes oppressive, sometimes empowering—diversity of today, one can perform better histories of the past.

19.5. FINAL THOUGHTS

I was asked to write this chapter as a reflection on the experience of teaching World Englishes from the perspective of someone who works far afield on the opposite end of the historical spectrum, and as someone who nevertheless intuitively feels that it is an important, indeed essential component of the course. This is, admittedly, not a unique experience: almost everyone who teaches HEL, I imagine, will have a specialty in one or several areas and corresponding weaknesses in others. This is as true for the nineteenth-century literary scholar who must confront Old English as it is for the Chaucerian who must confront AAVE. In some ways, it is the defining pedagogical challenge of this course.

Those of us who specialize in Old or Middle English and who, faced with developing an HEL syllabus, feel we can only scratch the surface of contemporary Englishes, might find reassurance in the realization that English really is always foreign and its history is always disorienting, that the orientation of foreignness and familiarity is determined by one's perspective, and that no one, no matter how linguistically talented, is qualified to speak from a perspective within every English, or even from an intimate knowledge of most Englishes. Anglo-Saxonists know these limitations well, as the language continues to surprise us despite its largely fixed, finite, and distant corpus. This humbling realization is nevertheless very welcome in our globalized world where it is so easy to take for granted the dominance of the English language and the privileges of, say, "native proficiency."

As a medievalist, I see a virtue in precisely this discomfort produced by pedagogical encounters with World Englishes, discomfort which alters our status as HEL's "overseers" (to use Lerer's term) and which can be productively turned back on the way we teach and think about the medieval. It reminds us not to simplify the earlier history of the language into a series of natural and smooth developments, and instead invites us and our students to grapple with the much more violent, disorganized, and disruptive reality of language, not only as its history unfolds today, but also as it did in the distant past.

CHAPTER 20

An Ecological Account of the Emergence and Evolution of English

SALIKOKO S. MUFWENE

20.1. INTRODUCTION

Traditional accounts of the history of the English language have focused more on the changes that have marked the transitions from Old English to Middle English and from the latter to Modern English than on the specific language contact ecologies and dynamics that produced the changes.[1] This is more striking regarding the emergence of English during apparently the seventh century, almost two centuries after the Germanic tribes consisting mainly of the Angles, Jutes, and Saxons crossed the Channel in the fifth century to colonize England in the wake of the collapse of the Western Roman Empire, a form of colonization. None of these tribes spoke a language called English; yet historical attestations show that by the seventh century a new language indigenous to England had emerged that historians of the language call Old English.

In the tradition of Indo-European studies, which rely on lexical and morphosyntactic correspondences to establish genetic classifications, the language is considered Germanic, thus as having little if any connection with the indigenous Celtic languages that its demographic expansion would gradually replace or marginalize. This genetic classification has not been disputed, despite the fact that a great deal of Modern English vocabulary is from Latin and French, and the latter putatively actuated the Great Vowel Shift.

One must thus wonder why English creoles, which on average have inherited more than 90% of their vocabularies and large proportions of their grammars from their nonstandard English lexifiers, have been stipulated as separate non-Germanic languages. Have linguists convincingly articulated what make(s) the language contact ecologies in which English creoles emerged different from those that produced not only Old English but also varieties such as Scots and Irish Englishes, American,

Australian, and New Zealand Englishes, and those lumped in the category of "indigenized Englishes," spoken in former British exploitation colonies of Africa and Asia?

By underscoring the role of language contact as the actuator of the emergence of Old English and its subsequent evolution that produced so many different varieties, I invite the reader to ponder over whether the same research methods and standards have been applied for all offspring of Old English, older and recent ones, including English creoles, which have typically been treated as "children out of wedlock."[2] I use the term *emergence* for cases when the first attestation of a language (variety) is recognized. The term *evolution* stands for transmission with modification of something that exists already. The modification, which involves changes in form/structure and/or use, may of course culminate in the emergence of a new phenomenon, as in the case of the previously mentioned varieties. Such emergence amounts to speciation.

I will simply describe my evidence or just present it in abridged form because it may be found in the rest of this book. As a creolist who assumes that the emergence of creoles tells us a great deal about how the modern European languages from which they have evolved emerged, my primary goal is to show that one develops a different, if not a more accurate, understanding of the history of the English language if the subject matter is approached in a way similar to that of the emergence of creoles.

English historians make a distinction between, on the one hand, the "internal history," which is focused primarily on the evolution of its structures, and, on the other, its "external history," which deals with "migrations, wars, colonization, economies," among other factors that I consider "ecological."[3] These factors are the actuators of change, in the sense that they influence the behaviors of the speakers who introduce modifications that culminate in phonological, morphosyntactic, semantic, and pragmatic changes, as well as in the emergence of new language varieties.

20.2. THE BIRTH OF THE ENGLISH LANGUAGE: AN EXTERNAL HISTORY

In the fifth century, the Roman colonists had abandoned their Western Empire, including Britannia (now known as England) to protect Rome against the Germanic invasion. This is an indication that, although the Romans allowed the indigenous rulers in the provinces to run for important offices anywhere in the Empire, they did not colonize these territories on a model of the effective European settlement colonization of the New World since the sixteenth century. In the latter case, the Europeans sought to settle new homes away from Europe.[4] Also, the Romans did not practice the same kind of exploitation colonization that the Europeans implemented in most of Africa and Asia during the nineteenth and twentieth centuries, because the local rulers were Romanized and participated in the government of the Empire. Some emperors, such as Publius Aelius Hadrianus Augustus, who built Hadrian's Wall, were not from Rome.

In the administrative and military void the Romans left behind, the Britannic Celts engaged in wars with each other. According to one version of the controversial history of the Anglo-Saxon settlement in England, the Brythonic Celts actually called on the Germanics across the Channel for protection from the Picts and Scoti in today's Scotland. However, the Germanics, consisting of the Angles, the Jutes, and the Saxons, found their hosts so weak they decided to settle and rule the land.[5] About two centuries later, a new language identified by its historians as *Old English* was born from the contacts of the continental European languages brought to England.

Although it has traditionally been claimed that the Celts did not contribute to the evolution of the invaders' new language (because the invaders and the conquered populations apparently did not mix), scholars of Celtic Englishes claim otherwise.[6] According to them, some Celts who worked for or with the Germanics must have learned it, although the masses of the populations did not practice, let alone shift to, the new languages brought to their land. That is, the situation would have been comparable to that of the Roman colonization of parts of Europe, although the Germanic invasion was settlement colonization and the administration of the land must not have been any more inclusive than when Europeans settled the New World from the sixteenth century onward, marginalizing rather than assimilating the Natives.

The Germanic colonists did not speak the same language. Nor is it evident that these continental European languages were more mutually intelligible than modern Danish, Dutch, and German, for instance, although they all belong to the West-Germanic family. They actually settled different places in southern and eastern England, corresponding to the following kingdoms: Northumbria, Mercia, East Anglia, Wessex, Essex, Sussex, and Kent (see Figure 20.1). It is only a couple of centuries later that they merged into the same kingdom. Old English was then born too, with various regional dialects. Why or how did these different dialects emerge if the settlers were converging toward a common language?

Old English is actually a name attributed to the language not by its speakers but retrospectively by and for the convenience of scholars of the history of the English language. An important relevant question is whether it emerged by koinéization and thus in a way similar to the emergence of new forms of English in the early stages of England's colonies in the New World. The difference between koinéization and what has traditionally been characterized as "creolization"[7] is that the former involved the contact of dialects of the same language and/or of languages that are genetically related,[8] whereas the emergence of creoles involved the additional factor of the contact of the lexifier with other languages. From the point of view of the mechanisms involved, no difference is obvious because the same kinds of competition obtain among, for example, variants for similar communicative functions and the same kinds of selection processes apply to competing variants. Out of the contact of competing languages and/or dialects, a new variety emerges, regardless of whether it is considered a new variant of the competing dialects or genetically related languages or a separate language altogether, as in the case of creoles.[9]

Because the term *English creole* suggests some genetic connection to the English language, I am prompted to ask what the terms *English* and *England* may tell us about the origins of English. They are etymologically related to *Angle* and *Anglia*, and they suggest the following etymological meanings: *England*, 'land of the Angles,' and *English*, 'way/language of the Angles,' 'typical of the Angles.' This is actually consistent with the folk definitions of languages around the world.[10] For example, French is

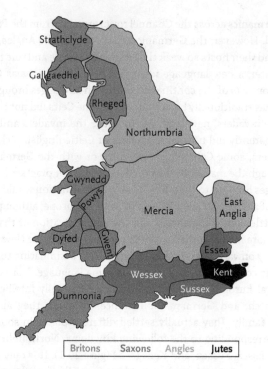

Figure 20.1. Britannia, A.D. 660

etymologically the language of the French people, and German is that of the German population.[11] One is easily tempted to conclude that the language of the Angles, north of Wessex and Essex, prevailed over those of other Germanic invaders.

However, the word *Ænglisc > Anglisc > Englisc*, whose earliest attestations appear in the twelfth century, was also synonymous with *Anglo-Saxon*, the alternative name for *Old English*. History also tells us the unifier of England as a kingdom was from Wessex and not from the North. Although this does not preclude the speculation articulated earlier, especially if (the descendants of) the Angles may have been more numerous, it appears that there are still things to be sorted out. As a matter of fact, some scholars argue that English is a Scandinavian language, an " 'Anglicized' Norse."[12]

If the foregoing speculation is correct, it is tempting to argue that Old English emerged in the same way as English creoles in the eighteenth century, from one language that won a Pyrrhic victory over its competitors but was influenced and modified by the latter.[13] The question remains whether or not Celtic substrate influence contributed to its structures. Features typically invoked in support of this hypothesis, such as the auxiliary *do* for negation and questions and the "internal-possessor construction" (as in *John wiped his face*), appear to have emerged later than during the Old English phase. Such issues must be addressed by scholars of Celtic Englishes.

These issues do not deny the role of language contact in shaping English. Thus, a related question arises: is there a convincing reason other than the non-European ancestry of the creators of English creoles for stipulating that they are separate, non-Germanic languages but English is still Germanic? The question becomes more critical if it is indeed the case that the Celtic languages exerted significant substrate influence in shaping English as a separate Germanic language from those spoken by the Angles, the Saxons, and the Jutes.

Less commonly discussed is the fact that the contacts between the invading Germanic populations and those between them and the indigenous Celts were not really of the same kind as those that produced creoles. In the latter case, populations speaking different languages were brought together in settings in which they had to resort to the language of the master to establish communication among themselves. Although the Celts certainly did not speak the same language, nor can we claim that their languages were mutually intelligible, so far no evidence has been adduced to show that they had been brought together to work for the Germanic invaders in the same way that the enslaved Africans were. Nor were they under pressure to shift vernaculars. Thus, the Celts may have been no more involved in the emergence of Old English than Native Americans and Australian Aborigines in the emergence of, respectively, North American and Australian Englishes.

Therefore, can we not stick to the question of whether the language of the Angles, for whatever reason, was appealing to the other Germanic invaders, who gradually shifted to it and in the process influenced it with their own adstrate features? This may also explain the emergence of the different dialects of Old English, which may be correlated with the features of the other relevant Germanic languages and their dialects.

20.3. THE SPREAD OF ENGLISH IN THE BRITISH ISLES

Regardless of whether or not the Brythonic Celts influenced the emergence of Old English, this language remained the mother tongue of predominantly the "Anglo-Saxons." The situation was apparently comparable to that of Native Americans seeing the European colonists take away their lands,[14] develop a new socioeconomic and political world order, and operate in new languages from which they were generally marginalized.

Interestingly, even the westward territorial expansions of the invaders on both sides of the Atlantic are similar except for the formation of the reservations to which Native Americans were driven in Anglophone North America, as opposed to the gradual cultural and genetic assimilation of the Celts in England. Now most of the Britannic Celtic languages are dead, just like a few remaining Native American languages appear to be merely buying time. In both cases, the surviving languages are spoken by minority populations, although in the case of North America, this situation is the consequence of the fact that large numbers of the indigenous peoples were exterminated by germs and associated illnesses from the Old World and by wars against them, whereas in the case of England the majority of the Celts have mixed with the Germanic invaders and shifted to the new indigenous language: English. The new indigenous culture that emerged is also English, reflecting the new socioeconomic world order, just like North America has seen the emergence of new indigenous cultures, viz., American, Canadian, and Québécois, which are different from European cultures.

To be sure, the original plan or course of action may have been the Germanicization of England and the Europeanization of the American and Australian colonies, consistent with the observation that the European colonists wanted to build better Europes than what they had left behind.[15] However, there is an indigenization process that ultimately has produced new indigenous cultures, namely, English, American, Canadian, and Australian Anglophones, from these territorial expansions of the colonizing populations.[16]

The foregoing comparisons raise interesting questions from an ecological perspective not only regarding the impact of the Norse and Norman French invasions on the evolution of English but also about the role of Celtic languages in the emergence of Middle English and the timing of that influence. Thus, the observation that "hardly any English vocabulary is Celtic" bears as much on this discussion as the fact that the lexical contribution of Native American languages to American English is negligible, being limited to cultural loans.[17] It may reflect the possibility that, for several centuries, the Anglo-Saxons did not generally socialize any more with the Brythonic Celts than the European settlers with Native Americans. Although the Europeans traded with Native Americans, not every European settler, nor every Native American, was a merchant. Nor were trade encounters daily events. Thus, the Celtic contributions to the grammar of English invoked by scholars of Celtic Englishes may be due to later influence, when the Celts could mix with the Anglo-Saxons and communicate with them in the latter's language. We need some documentation of when the mix of populations occurred.

The Danes and Norwegians conquered the northern and Eastern parts of England (corresponding to Northumbria, Mercia, and East Anglia) in the ninth century, established the Danelaw, and prevailed over the Anglo-Saxons until the time of the Norman Conquest in 1066.[18] Old Norse then became the prestigious and more attractive language, thus providing a basis for the argument that Old English and Old Norse subsequently hybridized into Middle English.[19] The hybridization was allegedly the outcome of Anglo-Saxons shifting from Old English to Old Norse and modifying it with vocabulary and grammar from their substrate language. However, 50% of the Germanic vocabulary of Middle English is shared by both Old English and Old Norse; 33% is from Old English only and 17% from Old Norse only.[20] This would support the traditional hypothesis of language shift from Old Norse to Old English with significant superstrate influence on English grammar.

Joseph Embley Emonds and Jan Terje Faarlund identify Middle English as a creole.[21] The process is more comparable to the indigenization of English in Africa and Asia, consistent with the scholarship on World Englishes, though one must wonder whether the lexical and grammatical divergences are as extensive in the latter case as in the former. Mutual intelligibility, which has frequently been invoked to justify the stipulation that English creoles are separate languages altogether and "indigenized

Englishes" are "non-native," is not a reliable factor. Familiarity with the othered variety or accent is a significant factor, independent of the extent of (dis)similarities between its characteristics with those of one's own.[22]

The Norman Conquest in 1066 was a real game-changer, with French becoming the new superstrate, at least for part of England's population, and the language of government and high social functions. Both Old English and Old Norse were demoted, while the Celtic languages were apparently still marginalized by all invaders. However, there was apparently no general shift to French, although those who worked in the Norman administration and other superstrate institutions learned it, as must have those who served them as cooks, gardeners, and in similar housekeeping functions.

God knows whether the servants produced French varieties comparable to those that have recently been derided as Butler and Pidgin Englishes, outside Europe. Since this chapter is about the evolution of English, we need not speculate further on this beyond pointing out that the linguascape of England at the time must have been more complex than has usually been reported. We must also assume that if the Normans were wise rulers, they must have learned some Old English and/or Old Norse before they gave up French for English as their vernacular in the thirteenth century. Bilingualism in French and English within the Norman aristocracy must have been the gradual transition to the language shift, making phenomena such as the Great Vowel Shift, attributed to French influence, a more gradual process than has usually been reported in the literature.

The Norman French rule also brought the Anglo-Saxons and Scandinavians to mingle presumably as equals, which facilitated the evolution (discussed above) that culminated into Middle English, notwithstanding the influence attributed to French.[23] To be sure, French influence is more lexical than grammatical.[24] For instance, the temptation to interpret pied-piping in relative clauses and questions as French and/or Latin influence appears to be a case of congruence because the pied-piping alternative to preposition-stranding was also available in Old English.[25] As a matter of fact, some ethnography of pied-piping in English today also suggests that French influence did not spread throughout the whole English-speaking population in England. In Modern English, it has remained contained in the standard varieties and, as a matter of fact, mostly in the written ones. Even the genitive form *whose* is seldom used in spoken nonstandard English relative constructions. Nonstandard speakers prefer two separate clauses, with the possessive pronoun *his, her, its,* or *their* used in the one with the possessive construction. This shows that population structure is a critical ecological factor even in the history of English.[26]

By the time of the Norman Conquest, English must also have spread further west than the original Germanic settlements in northeastern and southern England, concurrently with the territorial expansion of the Anglo-Saxons. There is not much information about the extent to which the Celts acquired it either as a second language or as a vernacular. It would take up to the twelfth century before English reached eastern Ireland, where it would be contained in urban, trade centers until the seventeenth century and would be little known by the majority of Irish populations.[27]

In the meantime, escaping the Norman French invasion, the Anglo-Saxon monarchy sought refuge in Scotland, where the local rulers also would adopt the refugees' language as the political and social superstrate. The spread of English in Scotland produced not only Scots English, under the influence of the indigenous Celtic languages, but also caused the gradual demise of the latter, which is made more evident now by the moribund condition of Scottish Gaelic.[28] Scots English appears to be the first indigenized, non-Anglo-Saxon English variety in the mouths of Celts. It may represent the first incontrovertible attestation of lasting Celtic influence on English. It also underscores the significance of population structure as an ecological factor, as most of this influence has remained contained in Scotland, although some of it has been exported to the colonies of the New World, Australia, and New Zealand, among other important settlement and exploitation colonies.

The spread of English in Ireland since the seventeenth century, under the Cromwellian promotion of the development of potato plantations by English planters, coincided with its exportation to New World colonies. On account of the preceding discussion, this suggests that the Irish who went to the colonies as indentured servants either did not speak English natively or learned English in the colonies, alongside the enslaved Africans with whom they worked. They would have played a non-negligible role in shaping the features of the English creoles that would emerge in the plantation settlement colonies, notwithstanding the critical role of the enslaved Africans as agents of their emergence.

There are similarities between features of Irish and Scots Englishes and those of English creoles, such as in the pronunciation of *family* as /fambli/, *little* as /liʔl/ or /likl/, and *goat* as /gwot/, and in the use of *dis ya* 'this here,' *too* + Adjective 'very,' *never* + Verb 'didn't,' and *I/Me know him for a long time* 'I've known him for a long time.' They suggest that it is misguided to focus almost exclusively on the role of African substrate languages in their divergence from especially the acrolectal English varieties in the United Kingdom and in North America.[29] One must also pay attention to features of the lexifier, which was typically nonstandard and included xenolectal features of non-native European speakers.[30] However, we must first discuss the emergence of Irish English as contact-induced and associated with language shift.

The first significant presence of English in Ireland was in urban centers of the southeast and the east, all the way to Dublin, where the "Anglo-Norman adventurers" remained a minority and learned Irish too.[31] English was learned by the few Irish who interacted with the Anglo-Saxon colonists, while the Irish generally continued to speak Irish. This is comparable to the spread of English in African and Asian exploitation colonies. A turning point in this history was the seventeenth century with "the arrival of large numbers of settlers from Lowland Scotland" in especially northeastern Ireland. They "were non-aristocratic settlers who farmed the land and established towns as their bases[;] their linguistic influence on the local population was far greater than that of earlier settlers in the south."[32] The Irish who went to work on the farms of the English planters, a small proportion relative to those who came from the Scottish Lowlands and the English Midlands, learned their language.

A greater catalyst to the emergence of Irish English was the development of the linen industry in the eighteenth century, which brought masses of Irish to the emergent industrial centers[33] and gave them economic motivation to learn English.[34] The language was then learned primarily naturalistically, which made substrate influence easier, especially if the workers learned it from other workers with more experience rather than directly from native speakers from England. The condition of homogeneity of the substrate favored Irish influence,[35] as in the case of Melanesian English pidgins.[36]

One must remember that until the eighteenth century, formal education was the privilege of children in the affluent and powerful socioeconomic classes, even in Europe. Many, if not most, of the European indentured servants in the settlement colonies were indeed illiterate.[37] England and Wales passed its Elementary Education Act in 1880, and the American Commonwealth of Massachusetts was the first state to pass a compulsory education law, which occurred in 1852.[38] These historical facts shed some light on how English spread in the rest of the world, in which form (standard or nonstandard), through which kinds of speakers (native or non-native), and through or independent of schooling.

20.4. THE SPREAD OF ENGLISH OUTSIDE THE BRITISH ISLES

It is English colonization that spread English around the world. However, one must distinguish between different styles of colonization in language history because the commitment of the English colonizers to their language varied depending on whether they were engaged in trade, settlement, or exploitation colonization.[39] For instance, during their trade ventures along the African coast all the way to Canton and in the hinterlands of North America, the English relied on interpreters.[40] English pidgins emerged late in the eighteenth century, the earliest perhaps in Canton, where the term *pidgin* (English) emerged in the early nineteenth century.[41] Nigerian and Cameroon Pidgin Englishes are offshoots of Sierra Leone Krio, an early nineteenth-century phenomenon whose ancestry lies in Jamaican Creole.[42] The English pidgins of the Pacific all emerged in the mid-nineteenth century,[43] as the English had traded with the indigenous populations through interpreters using Maritime Polynesian Pidgin.[44] The English also traded with Native Americans in their languages through interpreters. American Indian English is a late nineteenth-century phenomenon, reflecting the late engagement of Native Americans in the kinds of occasional interactions with the European colonizers that could produce a pidginized variety.[45]

The English insisted on communicating among themselves and with other people in their settlement colonies in English. This condition forced the enslaved people and indentured servants living with and working for them to shift early to English as their vernaculars, owing to a variety of reasons: (1) During the homestead phase, the enslaved people were in the minority and had nobody else with whom to speak their ancestral languages. (2) Although there was statutory discrimination, the very small size of homesteads during the onset of the colonies did not favor residential segregation. Thus, all the locally born children of the European colonists and of the enslaved Africans, called Creoles, spoke the European colonial language, typically a non-standard koiné, as their mother tongue. (3) As the settlements grew bigger, the foreign-born Africans and the later-indentured servants had the White and non-White Creoles as model speakers, by the Founder Principle.[46] (4) When the homesteads that grew into sugarcane or rice plantations instituted residential seg-regation, there were enough non-White Creole models, often monolingual speakers of the European colonial language, for the European colonial vernacular to continue as the dominant language among the enslaved people. (5) When the Anglo economic system prevailed among the European colonists, the change eroded national segre-gation among them. With the ensuing gradual social integration of Whites, in oppo-sition to other populations, English spread as the dominant vernacular of the United States, Canada, and Australia, among other former British settlement colonies. (6) During this process of language shift, while adults spoke the new vernacular with nonnative accents, their children did not or selected fewer and fewer of the non-native features into their speech. After a couple of generations, the selection oper-ated by the children led to the disappearance of Italian, German, and Scandinavian Englishes, among other varieties. (7) On the other hand, continued social or geo-graphical segregation maintained varieties such as Gullah (the American English creole on the coast of South Carolina and Georgia), African American Vernacular English, Amish English, Appalachian English, and the like as distinct from the main-stream varieties. Among other factors, (8) regional segregation also fostered differ-ences between not only national varieties (e.g., British, American, and Australian Englishes) but also regional varieties within each polity (e.g., Midwestern versus Southern Englishes in the United States).

Overall, naturalistic language learning through socialization or regular inter-actions with others produced the aforementioned English varieties, subject to substrate influence.[47] The extent of the latter varies depending on the timing and rigidity of segregation in the case of varieties spoken predominantly by populations of non-European descent and that of massive shift to English as the vernacular in the case populations of European descent. It also depends on whether or not the nonna-tive speakers were the majority and interacted mostly among themselves, as in the case of segregated (descendants of) Africans (similarly to the Irish outnumbering the English in Ireland), as opposed to continental European Americans assimilating incrementally with the Anglophone majority in North America and Australia. Note that the children always increased the proportion of native speakers relative to non-native speakers among the free immigrants.[48]

The scenario of the spread of English in the exploitation colonies of Africa and Asia was different, with the language being transmitted primarily through the school system. The English colonizers, the majority of whom did not intend to settle new homes but worked only for a few years in the service of the East India Company and, later on, of other British companies or colonial administration, did not socialize with the Natives. In the exploitation colonies, the British did not intend to share their language with the Natives either. As clearly articulated in Lord Macaulay's *Minute on Indian Education* (1835),[49] English had to be taught only to a small elite class of aux-iliaries who would work in the service of British colonization by interfacing between the Natives and the colonizers, many of whom did not bother to learn the indig-enous languages. The Native colonial auxiliaries who learned English used it as a lingua franca for communication with the colonizers and among themselves when they did not share an indigenous language. Few are those who spoke it at home, especially since formal education favored boys and the latter often married un- or less-schooled wives, who did not speak English.

After independence, as the former Native colonial auxiliaries replaced the colonizers as rulers of their countries and adopted English as the/an official language of their new nation-states, the former colonial language became an emblem of socioeconomic accomplishment. As its non-native speakers interacted more among themselves and as more and more of them served as model speakers to new learners, a situation similar to that in Ireland arose. This process, which allowed extensive substrate influence, led to the emergence of "indigenized Englishes," through "indigenization" as adaptation to the communicative habits and needs of the new speakers.[50] These new "postcolonial Englishes"[51] have usually been treated as less legitimate by speakers of what Kachru identifies as the Inner Circle,[52] consisting of polities where English is the mother tongue of the majority, which typically consists of populations of European descent. It is opposed to the Outer Circle, consisting essentially of the former exploitation colonies discussed previously, where English serves as an official language and prestigious lingua franca.[53]

20.5. CONCLUSIONS: THE BIG PICTURE

The spread and speciation of English into diverse varieties have been actuated by its external history.[54] Like any other language, English is a kind of parasitic species symbiotically attached to those who speak it and who foster its ecological niche. It is through their communicative practices that it undergoes various changes that can eventually produce the various stages of speciation discussed in the preceding sections. Within the approach adopted in the present chapter, whether the resulting varieties are lumped in the Inner or Outer Circle or whether they are treated as new dialects or separate languages is a matter of politics. The restructuring processes that have produced the relevant structural divergences from their proto-varieties are of the same kind, regardless of whether the agents are native and non-native speakers.

I chose a narrative that often raises issues about the received doctrine. The goal was to get the reader to think harder about whether that received doctrine makes sense, whether the suggestions sketched above provide more adequate explanations, albeit incomplete ones, and whether a more accurate account of the history of English lies elsewhere. The exercise will involve interpreting the structural data presented in the rest of the book against the history outlined in the preceding sections.

CHAPTER 21

Researching World Englishes in HEL Courses

Neologisms, Newspapers, and Novels

CAROL PERCY

21.1. INTRODUCTION: CONTEXTS AND OVERVIEW

I'm fortunate to be able to teach topics involving "World Englishes" in the context of a large department of English in a university in a very multicultural city, and my colleague Matt Sergi and I are fortunate to have a variety of contexts in which to teach them. The University of Toronto's undergraduate program includes two relevant courses: a second-year one-semester course focused on "The English Language in the World" as well as a third-year (also single-semester) course on "The History of the English Language" (HEL). Our graduate program has also included at least one HEL course a year: among these is "Diasporic Englishes," which I have taught in alternate years. As a result of being able to teach World Englishes relatively often to often-excellent students, I've had useful opportunities to devise (and revise) assignments. In particular, I've learned a lot from colleagues and from my students, graduate and undergraduate. While in class we apply transferable skills to specific texts and periods, and in their essays students can apply those newly learned skills to material that interests them whether it's linguistic or literary. I routinely ask authors of the very best essays to donate them to posterity: model HEL papers help students in courses that bridge disciplines and of course signal my interest in students' work. These papers also have been a useful memory aid to me as I write this chapter.

How can World Englishes fit into a HEL course? As we all do, I try to rise to the challenge of teaching HEL in a particularly short semester (twelve weeks) by structuring the course thematically. While my current course schedule is basically chronological, its explicit structure highlights linguistic subtopics and how to apply them. For instance, I currently begin the course by emphasizing vocabulary—word formation, loanwords, and semantics. I illustrate this with Early Modern English, using search results from the *OED (Oxford English Dictionary) Online*, excerpts from Burnley's sourcebook, and an extract from a Shakespeare play in facsimile from the First Folio. While I also cover all other aspects of Early Modern English, including aspects of its standardization, I give particular attention to describing and analyzing grammatical variation in the eighteenth-century unit; to accents and dialects in the nineteenth-century unit; and to spelling and medium generally in a section on contemporary English. I currently introduce Language Classification and "Creoles" at this point in the syllabus. Since I can make broad contrasts through time with parallel biblical translations (as one of the texts illustrating spelling), I supplement the translations of Mark 6: 18–30 in Burnley with one from the Jamaican New Testament by the Bible Society of the West Indies.[1] And following Creoles is the unit on "World Englishes." Here I emphasize language policies in a few countries representative of larger categories (currently, Kachru's convenient but contentious "Circles," which, students will realize, do not easily encompass Creoles).

The regrettable brevity of the HEL course and each unit in it inevitably homogenizes the diversity of World Englishes, but I hope that the unit's place in my course schedule serves some useful rhetorical functions. As the chronological culmination of the course, World Englishes highlights diversity and variation, and as the last topic discussed before we begin the course's second chronological cycle starting with Proto-Indo European, language policies involving World Englishes relate to the standardization of Englishes more generally. I highlight the topics of standards and standardization while teaching HEL, exploiting if not extenuating the definite articles in the course title. As the course (currently) ends with Middle English, it's useful for students already to have considered the status of other varieties of English in multilingual contexts.

In this chapter I'll be showing how in my HEL course schedule I emphasize methods in class, so that in their research essays my students can apply a method illustrated from one period and region of English to primary sources from another. Although most of our HEL students are majors or specialists in literature, others take it as a breadth requirement, and of course all of them have diverse interests—literary, linguistic, historical, scientific. Acknowledging and exploiting this diversity, I can craft research paper prompts that (like the schedule) highlight a range of methods that can be applied to World Englishes. Although we learn about neologisms and using the *OED Online* in the Early Modern English unit, students can write a research paper about neologisms in any variety of English or period, and many choose contemporary topics. We learn about dialects and style-shifting in the nineteenth- and twentieth-century unit, currently using the D. H. Lawrence short story "Fanny and Annie" that is excerpted in David Burnley's anthology.[2] In their research papers, students can choose their literary text, and most choose postcolonial or Victorian fiction from their other courses. Finally, we learn terms connected with standardization and with language policy in the World English unit, and students have the opportunity to use online newspapers as both primary and secondary sources in their research on issues relating to English in a particular country. This topic is more (and very) popular in the "English in the World" course, but model papers produced for that course have sometimes inspired students in the HEL course. Analyzing the jargon and slang of a particular activity is also a popular research topic for students and can of course be applied to World Englishes material. Indeed, in the days when our HEL course ran for a year rather than a term, all of the students had to both write and present on jargon and slang, and I recall a particularly dynamic presentation on Singapore army slang given by a student and some of his friends from outside the class. Toronto and its university are usefully diverse. Indeed, many varieties of "World Englishes" are present in our undergraduate classrooms; in this volume (Chapter 25) my colleague Matt Sergi describes how his students are trained to describe each other's dialects.

21.2. THE *OED ONLINE* AND NEOLOGISMS IN WORLD ENGLISHES

All of my HEL students use (and critique) the *OED Online* to describe and interpret trends in neologisms, including lexical borrowing. At the end of the term some students might choose to write research essays on neologisms in a variety of World Englishes. Earlier in the term all of my students complete repeatable multiple choice "e-xercises" (adapted from Blackboard's Test function) to understand the structure and the limitations of the *OED*. These e-xercises encourage students not only to interpret entries and to find new words and/or senses from particular languages, regions, authors, and texts but also, and especially, to regard the *OED* critically. Currently, I introduce this skill in the Early Modern English unit. For my own preparation, I draw on sources including Nevalainen's overview of neologisms recorded in the *Chronological English Dictionary* (*CED*) for the year 1604, when the first monolingual dictionary of English appeared.[3] Every year I compare Nevalainen's analysis of the *CED* to results from the *OED Online*: differences in the results from year to year show the students how the ongoing editing process affects the content of the dictionary. In class (as well as in the e-xercise) I emphasize critical skills as well as skills of synthesis. We're reminded that the publication of a particular book in a particular year will affect the statistics for that year: for instance, there are many words of Spanish origin (direct or indirect) because it was in 1604 that Edward Grimeston published his translation of José de Acosta's *Naturall and Morall Historie of the East and West Indies*. Grimeston's translation includes the first citation of words like *chocolate*, *criollo* 'creole,' *guano*, and *zero*. We consider the nature of the sources that the editors draw on: to what extent would a translation of a Spanish Jesuit missionary's work reflect English usage more generally? We spend a lot of time analyzing early quotations from a few entries: (how) do sources and glosses and figurative extensions indicate that a word like *chocolate* might be in more general use? We analyze the language and the labels used by the editors themselves: a later sense of *chocolate* designates "a black or dark-skinned person," with further editorial labels that generate much discussion.[4] Finally, we compare an entry or two from the third and second editions of the *OED*, observing extensions of meaning and changes of attitude: the words *criollo* and (in *OED2*) *creole* are useful to focus on here since we will later touch on *creoles* and the politics of language categorization. Students are rightly interested by the biases of lexicographers, past and present. For exemplifying ethnocentrism in the *OED2*, Benson has identified many entries connected with China that today's students can compare with the *OED Online*. (And although users of the *OED Online* have no access to the *OED1*, students might enjoy material from Mugglestone's article about changes in editors' attitudes to what in the first edition might be described as "savage" or not "civilized," and Ogilvie's accessible arguments about editorial attitudes to *Words of the World*.[5]) By using a small selection of entries to emphasize lexicographers' methods, I hope to encourage and prepare my students critically to use the *OED* as a tool for their own research.

A sharply defined "World Englishes" topic is among the infinite possibilities for a final research paper, and beginning with the "Advanced Search" function of the *OED*, over the years students have explored a variety of perspectives and regions. Since our university is in North America, many of the students are interested in "Inner Circle" topics, including the history of cultural and linguistic contact between Europeans and First Nations. Particularly memorable topics include a critique of the *OED* as a source of information on Inuit loanwords in North American English and an analysis of established and new Algonquin loanwords in the journal of an explorer of North America, Alexander Henry the Younger (d. 1814). Students also supplement the *OED* with a variety of resources. Thanks to our university's extensive and expensive e-subscriptions, our students have access to background chapters by Romaine and Rice.[6] In recent years, thanks to the efforts of Stefan Dollinger and others, our students have also been able to draw on the online edition of the *Dictionary of Canadianisms on Historical Principles*.[7] Other students have focused on immigrant borrowings into Inner Circle Englishes: a splendid student paper on Yiddish loanwords in U.S. English (written by a speaker of Mandarin) is available to later students (like the Algonquin paper mentioned earlier). I find these sample papers invaluable as inspirations for other work. Other research topics in the HEL course have used (and critiqued) the *OED Online* as a source of information on the vocabulary of "Outer" and "Expanding Circle" Englishes. Recently one student, born in Hong Kong, assessed the *OED Online* as a source of information about the British occupiers' English and attitudes in the nineteenth and twentieth centuries, and an Indian-born science major wrote about the historical and global distribution of so-called Indian food and words denoting it. Food words seem particularly appealing, as food can be borrowed and changed across cultures very easily. This student found the *Corpus of Global Web-Based English* (*GloWbE*) particularly useful as a quick index of the global distribution of a word or spelling: to what extent is *tikka masala* a British rather than an Indian dish?[8]

21.3. ONLINE NEWSPAPERS: LANGUAGE POLICIES AND LANGUAGE STRUCTURES

For identifying and appreciating the difficulties of implementing language policies involving English around the world, I have found online newspapers invaluable resources for me and my students. Although we use these more extensively in the undergraduate and graduate courses devoted to World English, student work from these courses has illustrated my World Englishes unit in the HEL course and inspired some HEL students' research papers. In past undergraduate courses I picked a single "Outer Circle" country and required all the students to write a short report on "English in the news" that drew only on online English-language newspapers and some reference works that I had selected. Assigned Nigeria, most students wrote about issues relating to English in primary, secondary, and/or further education; a few others discussed the use of English (or not) in "Nollywood" film or in other cultural genres. A particularly perceptive student—the same student speaker of Mandarin who wrote on Yiddish loanwords in U.S. English—used the newspapers as a corpus to analyze how Nigerian English-language journalists represented pidgin and its speakers, including criminals and politicians. These assignments drew undergraduate students' attention to the often subtly distinctive properties of English in the newspapers. Indeed, my graduate students were given a second assignment, to identify and categorize what they felt were distinctive properties of a particular variety of an "Outer Circle" English. My graduate students of Diasporic Englishes can choose their countries freely. In the fall of 2015, I gave the forty undergraduate students in my very multicultural classroom similar free choice, for a series of assignments starting with a few sentences explaining a newspaper article, including a group panel discussion on similar topics, and culminating in a research paper. Students in future classes—HEL included—can now be inspired by excellent papers on topics which include the marketing of English to Indian "housewives," the problems in teaching English in the francophone regions of Cameroon, the significance of English in a multilingual multimedia firestorm in the Philippines, the status of English acronyms like *NBA* in Chinese-language media, and the use of English by winners of the Eurovision song contest. I've realized that an essential resource in courses that encourage such student-driven research is a textbook that provides theoretical approaches to language ideologies as well as language categorizations and structures. A recent one that seems to fit the bill is Mario Saraceni's 2015 *World Englishes*.[9]

Ultimately such student-driven and peer-reviewed projects gave all of us even more satisfaction not only because they were topical and original but also because the process was initially administratively chaotic and intellectually challenging (for me and for them). It is essential to make available a select list of reputable and accessible reference works covering such topics as the language situation and policy, history, and economy of any country. For the many students writing on single-country issues, the sources freely (if often confusingly) available through *onlinenewspapers.com* were adequate although we usually had to use a source (like Wikipedia) to identify the status and bias of the available newspapers. Other students found subscription databases like *Factiva* helpful; they could search for a phrase like *Eurovision* or *Oxford Dictionary of English* or *spelling bee* and (with some work) view it in newspapers from many different countries.[10] The assignment also had its pedagogical benefits. Using (and critiquing) current newspapers as primary and secondary sources seems to deter plagiarism, and, at least in some cases, to encourage a relatively critical attitude about the bias of the sources. For some of the topics, many of the students acquired other transferable skills—identifying and interpreting trends in metalanguage, whether by journalists or in online comments. These assignments certainly encouraged student and instructor engagement. Although the course ended three months ago, as further news articles appear about, for instance, the position of English in Switzerland, I am still exchanging emails with students.

21.4. LITERATURE: STYLE-SHIFTING AND CODE-SWITCHING IN FICTION OR FILM

In all of my HEL courses, I incorporate a unit on style-shifting and code-switching, in both life and in literature. Because some of my students are multilingual or bidialectal and because many of them are majoring in literature, it is pleasing to teach them methods of analysis that give them a more abstract understanding of material they're already familiar with. It is equally pleasing for my students to be able to share interesting content with me, whether anecdotes about their family's code-switching in restaurants or examples of literary texts that are particularly rich with style-shifting. Clips from films or TV shows can be used in class and for research projects; indeed, in my most recent undergraduate and graduate classes, two students independently chose to focus on the 2012 Bollywood comedy *English Vinglish*. Indeed, when I have teaching assistants, they often choose to guest lecture in the dialect and/or World Englishes unit and can select particularly topical or popular video clips. In the HEL course, in the context of the introductory unit on pronunciation and social "indexing" of linguistic varieties, I use a short story excerpted in the Burnley anthology. While literary dialect does not reflect usage in real life, linguistic stereotypes can be useful for introducing some of the basics of phonology and sociolinguistic analysis. Discussing D. H. Lawrence's "Fanny and Annie" allows us to identify some of the salient sociolinguistic variants in this Midlands dialect, including features important elsewhere in the course such as 'h-dropping' and 'g-dropping' and the second-person pronoun: Fanny's prospective mother-in-law, Mrs. Goodall, "fairly hated the sound of correct English. She *thee'd* and *tha'd* her prospective daughter-in law."[11] I have ultimately not found it easy or fruitful to spend time discussing particular dialect words or other distinctive details of the text, but our more abstract discussions of the techniques and effects of style-shifting have encouraged some students to interpret style-shifting in other literary texts, usually chosen from their Victorian or postcolonial courses.

In class, applying methods demonstrated by Ferguson and by Hodson, I ask students a series of questions about style-shifting in the story at hand. What are some effects of restricting dialect to dialogue and of relaying narration mostly in standard English? What are some effects of relaying a character's thoughts in standard English even if they speak in dialect? What are the implications of representing characters with identical backgrounds as speaking in different ways? Ferguson emphasizes how style-shifting has structural as well as representational functions, for instance, by contrasting characters. In *Wuthering Heights*, because the foundling Heathcliff does not speak dialect and of the two local servants only the pious Joseph does, readers are guided to see Heathcliff's development not as social but psychological and explicitly contrasted with Joseph's traditional morality.[12] So, when discussing "Fanny and Annie" in class we spend particular time using Hodson to classify some of the shifts in an individual's speech, as reflecting some combination of interpersonal factors (often but not necessarily accommodation), emotion, or transformation.[13] The story concludes with Mrs. Goodall represented as speaking in more "standard" English. In our class discussion (and in their essays), our interpretations of specific style-shifting are integrated into a literary argument about the text. While I encourage my English majors to write literary arguments about style-shifting in postcolonial fiction, in class we also discuss the relationship between literary stereotypes and life. Writing about "Received Pronunciation," Agha provides a seminal (if lengthy) account of how representations of speakers—exemplary or not—construct as well as reflect cultural ideologies and practices.[14] Although some of my students choose essay topics that encourage them to subordinate linguistic description to literary interpretation, all of my students write one short linguistic essay, many repeatable online e-xercises, and a final—and very linguistic—test.

If the course structure permits, it's of course possible to include other assignments combining linguistic observation with literary analysis. In past sections of "The English Language in the World," my students have explored how the literary impact of poetry and short prose texts can be affected by a range of linguistic techniques, style-shifting or code-switching being just one of these. Indeed, when I can, I will usually incorporate some traditional close reading using phonetic and grammatical terminology, and any "World English" literary text can of course benefit from this traditional approach. In the fall 2015 section of "The English Language in the World," one of the three weekly class hours was devoted to a text (or two) from the postcolonial *Concert of Voices* anthology and an applied linguistic feature. In addition to style-shifting and code-switching, we analyzed the jargon of postcolonial studies in the "Introduction to the First Edition, the specific speech act of cursing in Pauline Johnson's "The Cattle Thief," lexical borrowing in Mulk Raj Anand's "Duty" and Leslie Marmon Silko's "Yellow Woman," metalanguage in Lee Maracle's "Charlie," and slang and profanity in Nalo Hopkinson's "A Habit of Waste." In the first week of the course, in class discussion we inferred some connections between names and identities; the students had been asked to introduce themselves on the course blog by reflecting on any connections between their names and identities, and in class discussion we added the function of names in Kamala Das's poem "An Introduction."[15] Toward the end of the course, the students had an in-class close reading test, in which they were asked to construct literary arguments about the given extracts using the specified (and expected) linguistic details. Assessing these tests, I found this component of this English course satisfyingly fruitful for training my students in focused close literary reading, while helping them develop a vocabulary of linguistic description and analysis. It can of course be adapted to other anthologies: Ahmad's *Rotten English* is even cheaper and contains more essays and more texts that are not specifically postcolonial.[16] For these activities, I found the principal challenge was finding secondary sources that were succinct and accessible; while I will continue to do something like this in future courses, I will make the resources available for the student in a hard-copy anthology as well as electronically.

21.5. MODELS OF METHODS: STUDENT PAPERS ON WORLD ENGLISHES

Especially when a HEL course lasts only one semester and the semester is short, it is challenging to give every potential subtopic all the time it could occupy. After I emphasize a "method" for each "period," I hope that my students will be able to combine them in their further research. By getting permission to make some of the best papers available for posterity, I hope not only to encourage past students but also and especially to encourage future students to apply some of the required methods to material that they've chosen. Currently, I post a selection of the most inspiring undergraduate papers in the Blackboard course management platform for my HEL course; these presently include a paper on language policy (analyzing evidence from Nigerian newspapers about the state of the education system), one on code-switching and style-shifting (representations of pidgin in Nigerian English newspapers; Yiddish and Yiddish English in Cahan's *Yekl: A Tale of the Ghetto*); and several on loanwords (Algonquin in an English explorer's journal; Yiddish in American English; English in German). Because we have so many international students in University of Toronto classrooms, there is no shortage of topics, and because we have graduate courses in HEL and Diasporic Englishes, over time our excellent graduate students have provided more papers for posterity. In the early days of the internet many contributed to my online encyclopedia of the cultural history of English: random diasporic topics in *The English Language(s): Cultural and Linguistic Perspectives* include Robert Burns, the functions of English in the Arabian/Persian Gulf, and the reception of Jamaican dub poetry in Toronto. The first volume of my open-source journal *The English Languages: History, Diaspora, Culture* (2010–13) contains papers on topics including Newfoundland dialect in poetry, Jamaican Creole in Jamaican education, and English language teaching in contemporary Turkey. The latter paper, by David Zok, has been cited ten times on Google Scholar as of March 2016. Alexander Eastwood subsequently developed his paper on the translation into American English of the first of the Harry Potter novels for publication in the *Papers of the Bibliographical Society of Canada*.[17] It is a pleasure to elicit good work from engaged students; for scholars from many disciplines and at all stages of their careers, World Englishes provide compelling topics for analysis.

CHAPTER 22

Situating World Englishes into a History of English Course

RAKESH M. BHATT

22.1. THE SECOND DIASPORA OF ENGLISH

The spread of English beyond the British Isles, as part of the colonization experience—the second diaspora[1]—brought profound changes in the structure and functions of English. The second diaspora, in geographic terms, covers a vast territory: mainly all of British (and American) colonies in Africa (e.g., Ghana, Kenya, Nigeria, South Africa, and Tanzania), South Asia (e.g., India, Pakistan, Sri Lanka, and Bangladesh), Southeast Asia (e.g., Singapore, Hong Kong, Malaysia, Indonesia, and the Philippines), the Caribbean (e.g., Jamaica, Bahamas, and the Virgin Islands), and other regions in West Asia, the Americas, and Oceania.[2] The global spread of English, from "Inner Circle" (Native speakers) to "Outer" (English as a Second Language speakers) and "Expanding" (English as a Foreign Language speakers) Circles, is conceptualized by Kachru in terms of three concentric circles (see Figure 22.1).[3]

This chapter deals mainly with the "Outer Circle" varieties of English: the spread that introduced English to sociocultural and historical contexts traditionally not associated with it, and in the process, of course, acquiring new—nonnative—speakers. Today, according to some conservative estimates, the ratio of native speakers of English to nonnative speakers is 1:3.[4] It is in fact in the second diaspora that we now find users of English placed in diverse contexts of use. Schneider sums it up rather well: "Black South African soccer-playing youth, Nigerian market women, Singaporean taxi drivers, Indian tourist guides, Japanese hip-hoppers, Hong Kong businessmen, and Philippine call center agents use it or struggle with it, for different reasons, in widely different forms, in all shapes and sizes, as it were."[5] So, while the Sun did finally set on the British empire, English language kept, and keeps, shining throughout the empire, in nonnative sociolinguistic contexts.

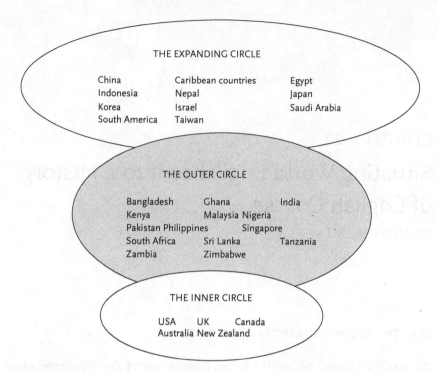

Figure 22.1. Kachru's concentric circle model

The second diaspora was different from the first as this second instance of spread resulted in a new codification of English, World Englishes.[6] The pluralization, EnglishES, as Kachru noted in *The Alchemy of English*,[7] disables a monolithic vision of English and replaces it with a pluricentric vision, which brings into clear focus variation and change in English in distinctive sociocultural contexts and language contact situations. The pluralization also has an ideological function: it represents among scholars of English studies an awareness of the sociolinguistic differentiation in the form, function, and use of English; it legitimizes different voices English represents now; and it shows, *par excellence*, the effects of cross-pollination—code-switching/mixing and other sociolinguistic forms of hybridity—with local linguistic forms in new cultural ecologies that English populates now. In other words, there is now a growing consensus among scholars that there is not one English language anymore; rather, there are many English languages.[8]

The different English languages, studied within the framework of World Englishes, represent diverse linguistic, cultural, and ideological voices. World Englishes represents a paradigm shift in research, teaching, and application of sociolinguistic realities to the forms and functions of English. It rejects the dichotomy of US (the native speakers) vs. THEM (the nonnative speakers) and emphasizes instead WE-ness.[9] The pluralism is an integral part of World Englishes and the field has, especially in the last four decades, critically examined theoretical and methodological frameworks that are based on monotheistic ethos of linguistic science and replaced them with frameworks that are faithful to multilingualism and language variation.[10] This conceptual-theoretical shift has in fact extended the empirical domain of the study of English: English is regarded less as a European language and an exclusive exponent of Judeo-Christian traditions, and more as a pluricentric language, representing diverse sociolinguistic histories, multi-cultural identities, multiple norms of use and acquisition, and distinct contexts of function.

The success of the paradigm shift, from the English language to World Englishes, was largely made possible by a certain politics of language variation and change, termed "Liberation Linguistics," that focused on the forms of linguistic beliefs and practices that accent the socio-political dimensions of language variation rooted in contexts of social injustice—and attempt to transform these contexts radically in the interest of the speakers of the "other tongue": the "nonnative" varieties of English.[11] It is from this liberation linguistic-theoretic perspective that we are able to capture, understand, and discuss the creative linguistic potential of English language use worldwide. In the next section, I discuss precisely the different dimensions of creativity—in form-meaning pairings—that is betrayed in routine linguistic interactions in nonnative contexts.

22.2. DIMENSIONS OF CREATIVITY

In this section, I present data of various linguistic processes of nativization (indigenization) as evidence of transformations, noteworthy in at least four dimensions of creative language use: grammatical, discoursal, sociolinguistic, and literary. Taken together, these dimensions reveal how local "cultural grammars"[12] displace standard English norms establishing local (Indian, Singaporean, Nigerian, etc.) Englishes as the new norm in nonnative interactional contexts.

22.2.1. Grammatical Creativity

I begin by discussing some standard set of data that seem to exemplify nonnative grammars. Consider the following set of English sentences:

(1) *Progressive aspectual forms with stative verbs*
    I was knowing your face.

(2) *Variable use of definite article*
    Oh the maths, the maths nowadays seems to be complicated.

(3) *Clefting, for marking prominence/focusing*
    It's looking for more land a lot of them are.

(4) *Inversion in embedded questions*
    McCloskey does not consider precisely what is the difference between standard English and Hiberno-English . . .

The data in (1)–(4) are paradigm examples of Belfast English;[13] these syntactic innovations also characterize the grammar of Indian English.[14] These innovations, (1)–(4) in Irish (and Indian) Englishes, are understood as part of the parameterized differences in the English grammar; however, there are other innovations that seem to belong to the syntax-pragmatics interface. I discuss one such instance next: the use of "only" in Indian English.

One of the most innovative diacritic, that makes English audibly Indian, is the use of the pragmatic particle "only" that asserts the pre-suppositional structure of an utterance.[15] "Only" in Indian English (only) appears immediately to the right of the presentationally (non-contrastively) focused constituent, carries a specific semantic reading of "least likely," and performs the pragmatic function of indexical assertion, drawing the attention of the hearer to a particular part of the speaker's utterance. In (5), the particle "only" appears after the object phrase, marking presentational focus: "only" (a) expresses the unexpectedness, the "least likely" component of the meaning, and (b) makes salient a part of A's utterance.

(5)

A: Why are these women dressed like that?

B: These women wear everyday expensive clothes only.

Other World Englishes speakers have also introduced similar innovations as part of their English repertoire. The particle "la" is the most common discourse-pragmatic particle used mainly by speakers of local Singapore English,[16] which occurs with a range of interactional functions such as requests, invitations, promises, suggestions, and so on, as long as the interlocutors share an element of solidarity.

I close this subsection with a discussion of a particular type of grammatical innovation in World Englishes that has emerged in deference to the grammar of local culture: the use of undifferentiated tag questions. I turn to those data now.

The use of undifferentiated tag questions in World Englishes demonstrates how local English-language users subvert the standard form of tag to honor the grammar of local culture.[17] In standard varieties of English, tag questions are formed by a rule that inserts a pronominal copy of the subject after an appropriate modal auxiliary. A typical example is given in (6).

(6)   John said he'll work today, didn't he?

Tags express certain attitudes of the speaker toward what is being said in the main clause and in terms of speech acts and/or performatives. Functionally, tags in English generally behave like epistemic adverbials such as "probably," "presumably," and the like–as shown in (7).

(7a)   It's still dark outside, isn't it?

(7b)   It's still probably dark outside.

On the other hand, undifferentiated tag questions, such as in (8a) and (8b) subvert the colonial codifications of use to express local identities.[18]

(8a)   You are going home soon, isn't it?

(8b)   You have taken my book, isn't it?

The meaning of the tags in (8) is not the one appended to the meaning of the main proposition; it is usually constrained by cultural constraints of politeness, by the politeness principle of non-imposition. In other words, such tags serve positive politeness functions,[19] signaling deference and acquiescence. The evidence for functional difference can be found in the contrast between Indian English tags in (9) and British English tags in (10).

(9)   *Unassertive/Mitigated*

(9a)   You said you'll do the job, isn't it?

(9b)   They said they will be here, isn't it?

(10)   *Assertive/Intensified*

(10a)   You said you'll do the job, didn't you?

(10b)   They said they will be here, didn't they?

The perceptual–interpretational contrast between (9) and (10) is revealing: Indian English speakers find the undifferentiated tag expressions in (9) as non-impositional and mitigating, while tags in (10) appear to them as assertive, direct, and intensified.[20] This claim is more clearly established when an adverb of intensification/assertion is used in conjunction with the undifferentiated tag; the result is, predictably, unacceptable (shown in the starred sentences below) to the speakers of different varieties of Indian English.

(9a*)   Of course you said you'll do the job, isn't it?

(9b*)   Of course they said they'll be here, isn't it?

In a culture where verbal behavior is severely constrained, to a large extent, by politeness regulations, where non-imposition is the essence of polite behavior, it is noteworthy that Indian English speakers replace English canonical tags with undifferentiated tags. Variants of this undifferentiated tag are common in other World Englishes. In Hong Kong English, they are often used when seeking confirmation and involvement,[21] in mainly local positive politeness functions. Similarly, speakers of colloquial Singapore English (Singlish) use either the tag 'isn't it' or the tag 'is it' mainly to signal local solidarity.[22] Bamiro and Bokamba have discussed the case of West African English speakers using undifferentiated tags ("isn't it," "not," "no") to express deference in local interactional contexts.[23]

Undifferentiated tags are not exclusive instances of innovations in the linguistic grammar of World Englishes that reflect a local linguistic identity of the users. The linguistic expression of agency and identity can be seen elsewhere in the grammar, as in the use of the modal auxiliary "may." The data in (11), from speakers of Indian English, show that the use of the modal auxiliary "may" to express obligation politely in local cultural contexts.[24]

(11)   *Indian English*

(11a)   This furniture may be removed tomorrow.

(11b)   These mistakes may please be corrected.

Similar uses of the modal auxiliary are attested elsewhere in World Englishes: a polite softener "may" replaces "could" among Black South African English speakers;[25] Singaporean English speakers use "would" as a polite form, as a tentativeness marker, and as a marker of irrealis aspect.[26]

22.2.2. Discoursal Creativity

The grammar of local culture has not only affected the linguistic grammar, as discussed earlier, but has also transformed the discourse structures of Englishes across cultures. The creativity at the discoursal level in World Englishes is best exemplified by the now often cited Chinua Achebe's example, (12) from *Arrow of God*, where the chief priest is telling one of his sons why it is necessary to send him to church:

(12)

I want one of my sons to join these people and be my eyes there. If there is nothing in it you will come back. But if there is something then you will bring back my share. The world is like a Mask, dancing. If you want to see it well, you do not stand in one place. My spirit tells me that those who do not befriend the white man today will be saying 'had we known' tomorrow.[27]

Achebe, then speculates, "supposing I had put it another way. Like this for instance:"

(13)

I am sending you as my representative among those people—just to be on the safe side in case the new religion develops. One has to move with the times or one is left behind. I have a hunch that those who fail to come to terms with the white man may well regret the lack of foresight.

The first passage, (12), expresses the local rural sensibilities—the use of local proverbs and other culture-bound speech patterns—expressing a local Nigerian discoursal identity. Achebe concludes that though the material is the same, "the form of the one (12) is in character, and the other (13) is not."[28]

The difference, ultimately, between the two contrastive samples above, (12) and (13), has more to do, as Kachru pointed out,[29] with the use of native similes and metaphors, the transfer of rhetorical devices, the translation ("transcreation") of proverbs and idioms, the use of culturally dependent speech styles, and the use of syntactic devices. These rhetorical structures and stylistic devices are also employed in contemporary, non-literary texts, as evidenced in (14): the text of an email sent to me requesting advice on a specific issue (the text is reproduced as is, with the exception of deleting possible identifiers).

(14)

> *Respected Sir,*
>
> *Handfolded Namaskar!*
>
> Hope this e-mail of mine will find you in a good mood and sound health.
>
> We met in Delhi at the Press Club of India some time back and I hope you will recollect that meeting with Kashmiri writers and scholars.
>
> To me as a student of literature interacting with you was a fascinating and memorable experience. I am sure you also must have enjoyed that interaction. I believe you must have concluded your research by now and must be preparing to compile the findings.
>
> I and all other writers whom you met send you *AAHI* and wish you good luck.
>
> Sir, I have *a little* request. I am to speak at a seminar at Delhi on Wednesday next and my topic is '[xxxxxxx.]' In my paper I am certainly to argue against certain points raised by Sh. X, in favour of his claim that '[xxxx].' I do not agree with him.
>
> Sir my request to you is just to kindly let me know, if you may, whether you also think and believe as Dr. X believes or you have a contrary view after touring the 'Language region.'
>
> Sir, you as a professional Linguist have very deep understanding of the subject and your opinion is certainly more considered, valid and authentic and it is definitely going to add a new dimension and authenticity to this subject of great importance.
>
> Sir, This is a scholarly urge which I hope you will respond to in a positive manner.
>
> With very warm regards.
>
> [XXX]

The structure of this email-letter follows a rather standard pattern in World Englishes[30]: The salutations initiate the discourse, followed by what Rom Scollon and Susan Wong Scollon have called "facework,"[31] followed by the reasons and justifications for the "request," and finally the actual request. From the perspective of World Englishes discourse, several points are noteworthy here. First, one notices the transfer of discoursal and rhetorical norms of the first language, Kashmiri, in the use of the "greeting," *Handfolded Namaskar*, and conveys "blessings" from others using the culturally appropriate Kashmiri form, *AAHI*. The capitalization of *AAHI* is presumably a textual cue to the reader of its special status, a Kashmiri word code-mixed for the special purpose of conveying 'blessing' at once establishing solidarity in an English text. Second, the use of the form *Respected Sir* in the salutation section presents an asymmetric relationship between the writer and the intended reader. This strategy is often used in local cultural contexts to minimize threat to face and to express polite behavior, as noticed elsewhere in Nigerian English by Ayo Bamgbose.[32] Furthermore, the "no-naming" strategy is part of a structured system of "expressing respect" in the South Asian context.[33] Third, the actual "request" is made after considerable facework is done, and reasons and justification for the request are presented. Finally, the palliative forms, *a little* and *just*, are used precisely when a request is mentioned in a bid to minimize the illocutionary force of the speech act.

In sum, World Englishes discourse provides evidence of a new linguistic etiquette, one in which the linguistic interactional norms faithfully follow—are shaped by— the grammar of local culture; and in doing so, we notice an extension and expansion of the indexical potential of English.

22.2.3. Sociolinguistic Creativity

Finally, I discuss the dimension of sociolinguistic creativity in World Englishes, which is also observed in "native" contexts but rarely highlighted in discussion of English language variation. Let me illustrate this dimension by using an example from the native context to foreground my discussion of sociolinguistic creativity in World Englishes. In the exchange that follows, (15), PBS show host Tavis Smiley interviews Pam Grier and asks her about her controversial role as a lesbian in the show *The L Word,* eliciting her response to those in the black community critical of her role in that show:[34]

(15)   Code-switching from Standard to African American English
      Smiley: You know as well as I do that gayness, homosexuality, lesbianism, still very much a taboo subject—not as much as it used to be, but still very much a taboo subject inside of black America specifically
      Grier: Oh, espe- yeah.
      Smiley: And black folk love Pam Grier. Everybody loves Pam Grier, but black folk especially love Pam Grier. What do you say to black folk who say, *Now, Pam Grier you done got caught up in it. Now you done gone too far.*

What is surprising about this excerpt is that precisely at the moment where Smiley brings up the concern to Grier about the black community's negative response to the show, he switches from his normal method of speech (Standard English) to the dialect of the critical group (African American Vernacular English) to distance himself from them, in much the same way that an author switches to a speaker's specific vocal patterns to make a clear division between the *narrator* and the *character*. In other words, Smiley singles out that group, people to whom that dialect is specific, so that Grier understands that it is only the one group saying these things. The switch, in voicing, is thus strategic in its sociolinguistic function: distancing the narrator from any responsibility of ownership of the message.

Speakers of World Englishes also switch between different English identities available to them to perform different sociolinguistic functions. Mesthrie, for example, discusses the case of downshifting in the use of the mesolectal variety of South African Indian English by a young Indian attendant at airport security in South Africa to a passenger of the same ethnic background, as shown in (16).[35]

(16)   You haven' got anything to declare?

The unmarked choice in this context would normally be the formal acrolectal equivalent, "Do you have anything to declare?," which closely approximates the standard. As Mesthrie notes, although the security guard and the passenger were strangers, the speaker was tacitly defusing the syntax of power (acrolect) in favor of mesolectal, ethnic solidarity, while still doing his duty.

Such switching and mixing often result in the development of a new, hybrid code offering multilingual experiences of cultural difference as well as a sense of the entanglement of different cultural traditions. Bhatt presents the following evidence of this linguistic hybridity:[36]

(17)
There have been several analyses of this phenomenon. First, there is the "religious angle" which is to do with Indian society. In India a man feels guilty when fantasising about another man's wife, unlike in the west. The *saat pheras* around the *agni* serves as a *lakshman rekha*.[37]

In this bilingual English-Hindi mode of news-feature presentation, the Hindi idiom is left untranslated.[38] Such untranslated words "do have an important function in inscribing difference. They signify a certain cultural experience, which they cannot hope to reproduce but whose difference is validated by the new situation. In this sense they are directly metonymic of that cultural difference which is imputed by the linguistic variation."[39] The code-mixed Hindi items in (15), rooted in the most important historical narratives (Vedas) and the great Hindu epic (the *Ramayana*) of India, realizes an important sociolinguistic function: these words serve as vehicles of cultural memory, animating simultaneously with the global-colonial a local-indigenous identity. Code-switching between English and Hindi thus yields a hybridity that makes the semantic possibilities more flexible, movement between global-colonial and local-indigenous identities more manageable, and the goal of decolonization and democratization of English more realizable.

We find recognition and acceptance of this sociolinguistic hybridity, the new Englishes, in other genres as well; particularly, popular—hip-hop—culture. The linguistic choices in hip-hop relate to the issues of identity politics and power struggles within the local contexts of the use of this global cultural product.[40] Pennycook's discussion of Japanese rappers Rip Slyme's rap "Bring Your Style," for instance, investigates questions of agency, identity, and the politics of representation.[41] Blending African American speech styles with Japanese language, these rap artists not only manage to organize a genre that is simultaneously global and local but also employ the language-blend locally as a form of "resistance vernacular."[42] Similar trends appear in creative articulations of World Englishes genre of hip hop: in East African hip-hop,[43] in West African (and diaspora) hip hop,[44] and in East Asian hip hop.[45] In these local genres of hip hop, one notices a semiotic process of the social production of difference: local hip hop departs from the "core" in its rejection of features that characterize the mainstream gangsta rap norms such as heavy sexualization, misogyny, politics, and monolingualism.[46] The linguistic production of difference in this genre relies heavily on the specific sociolinguistic choices that the artists make. The most dominant paradigm of difference is serviced by code-switching: the use of local languages in the global medium, English, extends the meaning potential of this genre to produce local indexicalities.[47]

The subtle code-switching in everyday interactions, as discussed earlier, exemplifies the capacity of World Englishes speakers to mobilize various complexes of nuances of meaning possible only through hybridity; we find recognition and acceptance of this linguistic hybridity in local, popular print-news media. Das, for instance, opined about Indian English in the following manner:

(18)

We are more comfortable and accepting of English today, I think, partly because we are more relaxed and confident. Our minds have become decolonised and "Hinglish" increasingly pervades our lives. For a hundred years the upper middle classes have mixed English words in their everyday talk, but the present media argot is the creature of the new satellite and cable channels. Zee, Sony and Star, supported by their advertisers, have created this uninhibited hybrid of Hindi and English. Avidly embraced by the newly-emerging middle classes, this new popular idiom of the bazaar is rushing down the socio-economic ladder.[48]

The sociolinguistic creativity in World Englishes also helps to subvert the symbolic domination of standard English, as it creatively indexes local indigenous identity, yielding a polyphony of voices. Remarking about this polyphony, Green notes that English remains varied and wonderful, and concludes, quoting Anthony Burgess, that English is:

(19)

[A] whole language, complete with the colloquialisms of Calcutta and London, Shakespearian archaisms, bazaar whinings, references to the Hindu pantheon, the jargon of Indian litigation and shrill Babu irritability all together. It's not pure English, but . . . the language of Shakespeare, Joyce and Kipling—*gloriously impure.* (emphasis added)[49]

22.3. TEACHING WORLD ENGLISHES

The "gloriously impure" World Englishes present the possibility of understanding the limitations of our disciplinary discourse that has so far produced incomplete, and oftentimes misleading, understandings of the phenomena of the spread, functions, and acquisition of Englishes worldwide. To capture the complexity of linguistic hybridities associated with plural identities, as discussed above, our disciplinary discourses of the global use and acquisition of English must bring into focus local forms shaped by the local logics of practice. This shift in the disciplinary focus, as I have discussed elsewhere,[50] has larger theoretical aims: on the one hand to enable a more nuanced analysis of the globalization and localization dialectic and, on the other, to invert the tyrannical imposition of the universal.[51] With this shift, we begin to see how local communities have been appropriating global norms, adopting various strategies (such as the linguistic, discoursal, and sociolinguistic hybridization analyzed above), even as the global produces progressively subtler discourses to control the local.[52]

This process of inversion requires, in the context of the observations of hybridity in World Englishes, a reevaluation of disciplinary discourses of standard language, native speakers, and intelligibility. The evidence of hybridity—linguistic, discoursal, and sociolinguistic—confronts the limited and entrenched knowledge these constructs offer and demands that they be replaced with a knowledge that is faithful to linguistic difference and to the global realities in which the difference obtains. The evidence presents the urgency with which we need to redefine the disciplinary discourses of abstract and theoretical dichotomies (language-interlanguage, standard-nonstandard, native-nonnative, target-fossilized) to validate and incorporate the local hybridities. As we move toward reconfiguring our disciplinary discourses, we have to consider the following[53]:

- "Standard language" has to be treated as endonormatively evolving from within each community according to its own histories and cultures of usage. Standards can't be imposed exonormatively from outside one community.
- Appropriated forms of local English are not transitory and incomplete "interlanguages." Since they manifest a stable system with a rule-governed usage in the local community, as discussed earlier, they have to be treated as legitimate languages. Similarly, the term "fossilization" should be reserved for individual manifestations of idiolects of speakers who are new to a language. It shouldn't be used to label sociolects which display collectively accepted norms of usage in a community.
- We have to abandon the use of the label "non-native speaker" for multilingual subjects from World Englishes contexts. In the case of communities that have appropriated English and localized its usage, the members should be treated as "native speakers." We have to explore new terms to classify speakers based purely on relative levels of proficiency, without employing markers of ethnicity, nationality, or race, and overtones of ownership over the language.

- We have to encourage a mutual negotiation of dialectal differences by communities in interpersonal linguistic communication, without judging intelligibility purely according to "native" speaker norms. Both parties in a communicative situation have to adopt strategies of speech accommodation and negotiation to achieve intelligibility.

To conclude, an inquiry into World Englishes invites theoretical approaches to the study of English that are interdisciplinary in its orientation, methodologies that are sensitive to multilingual and multicultural realities of language-contact situation, and pedagogies that respond to both *intra*-national as well as *inter*-national functions of English. The beginnings of such a socially realistic linguistic framework will find a place in a model of English Language Teaching (ELT) that is based on the assumptions of plurality and multiple standards.[54] The guiding principle for ELT should be local standards for local contexts. The norms for learning and teaching in such a plural model must be endonormative, as argued in Kachru,[55] so that the learning content is in communicative and sociolinguistic harmony with the new contexts of use. This pedagogical shift carries the empirical advantage of making the "available" Englishes "accessible" to the potential consumers, enabling expressions of local identities in the use of these norms. The creative use of language variation, representing plural identities, must find a space in the local pedagogical practices, in the English teaching curriculum generally, and more specifically in the construction of instructional materials.

CHAPTER 23

Incorporating American English into the History of English

ALLISON BURKETTE

23.1. INTRODUCTION

With a course as chronologically broad and topically deep as the History of the English Language (HEL), it's often handy to have a theme or two that can be used to underpin a larger narrative. What I would like to do here is to take two themes—those of contact and persistence—and show how they could be used to connect the history and diversity of American English to a greater HEL narrative. I've chosen to use the concepts of contact and persistence for a couple of reasons, the most immediate being that they appeal to me as a sociolinguist interested in language variation and change. Another reason that contact and persistence work well in a HEL context is that together they represent a contemporary understanding of biological evolution as a combination of gradual, small-scale changes punctuated by sudden large-scale (or "catastrophic") changes. This perspective casts evolution as a series of jerks that break up relative stability (as opposed continual change that occurs at a slow and steady creep). A brief "jerk" versus "creep" discussion can thus complement the presentation of a model of language change that focuses on contact and persistence.[1]

Before setting aside the comparison of biological evolution to language change, I've also found it helpful to point out to HEL classes that, in the same way that human evolution didn't come to a screeching halt when *homo sapiens* appeared, the English language did not cease its development with the appearance of Present Day English. A quick look at American English can help drive home to students the fact that *English isn't finished yet*. The idea that, as long as there are people speaking it, the English language will not stand still (so to speak) is common sense to those of us who have spent time studying HEL, but to students this can be a novel concept. An often equally novel concept is the idea that the variation that we see in the English language now reflects both changes that are brought about through contact with other speakers/languages as well as changes that are continuations of processes found throughout the history of English.

The goal of this chapter is to provide a brief general narrative of the history of American English and then pull out a series of teaching foci, suggestions that can be used as touchstones for discussions of American English, potentially reflective of a number of course narratives, including that of "contact and persistence." Following each focus description is an exercise, assignment, or list of additional resources that complements that focus. The additional resources are readings or online videos that look deeper into the topic introduced by the teaching focus, while the exercises are hands-on illustrations of a main point. Many of the exercises and assignments center on lexical borrowing, which I find appeals to undergraduates who are looking for a comfortable way to connect to the more linguistics-oriented HEL material. These foci represent specific topics within the study of American English that could be expanded on or used to illustrate a running theme in the history of English.

23.2. GENERAL NARRATIVE

The story of American English dialects is best told, in my opinion, by Raven McDavid in *Structure of American English*. In this chapter, McDavid outlines the seven forces that contribute to dialect formation: settlement history, colonial cultural centers, migration routes, geography, political/ecclesiastical boundaries, social structure, and the influx of new populations. Of these forces, McDavid cites settlement patterns as the most important.[2] The settlement history of a particular area can explain much about the nature of the dialect(s) that develop there. Each of the early American cultural centers had its own settlement history, a unique mixture of people from different places that resulted in the linguistic characteristics associated with cities such as Boston, New York, Philadelphia, Richmond, Charleston, and Savannah. When the colonial settlers migrated from the big cultural centers westward, they took the speech of their cultural center with them, carrying a city's particular brand of American English to the west and/or to the south, often following the turns of a river valley, sometimes stopping at the foot of a towering mountain range. For example, the dialect boundary between the Northern and Midland dialect regions (proposed by Hans Kurath in 1949,[3] see Figure 23.1) runs along one of the major migration routes in early America (from Philadelphia, the route runs southwest, down the Shenandoah River Valley). In some cases, the force of a political or ecclesiastical boundary shapes a dialect, as such boundaries that work to keep outside influences at bay (e.g., the Pennsylvania Deutsch). Other factors are not as easily mapped, such as the flexibility (or inflexibility) of a location's social structure, which impacts how (in)frequently speakers of different classes or ethnicities interact. A more recent impact on American English has been the movement of new populations into already established areas, most notably the influence of Spanish on the English spoken in states such as Florida and Texas.

As was the case for Old English, dialectal variation has been a part of American English since its beginning and continues to be part of this variety today. Despite mass communication and the spread of communication technology, contemporary sociolinguists (including William Labov and Walt Wolfram) have stated time and again that American English dialects are alive and well. Labov, in fact, has maintained that American English dialects are more different today than they were seventy years ago.

One of the best teaching tools that we have at our disposal for talking about these forces and the resulting dialects is the Linguistic Atlas Project (LAP). The LAP began under the direction of Hans Kurath, who was tapped by the American Dialect Society in 1929 to undertake a large-scale survey of American English. Using a modified version of the methods employed by European dialectologists, Kurath and his fieldworkers began their systematic investigation of regional variation in American English with the Linguistic Atlas of New England (LANE), followed by the Linguistic Atlas of the Middle and South Atlantic States (LAMSAS).[4] The LAP data represent speakers' answers to over 800 targeted questions, aimed at eliciting variation in vocabulary, pronunciation, and grammar. The LAP is still active and much of the data collected for its regional surveys can be accessed and manipulated online at www.lap.uga.edu. Students generally enjoy poking around the LAP website, where they can look at response lists and make maps of where people said what in the 1930s and 1940s. The LAP data are not only interesting, but they represent an academic landmark as well, as Kurath used LAP data from interviews conducted in New England, the mid-Atlantic, and southeast—along with information about colonial settlement and migration—to create the first dialect map of American English (see Figure 23.1).[5]

The thin, dark lines on the map represent isoglosses, limits of occurrence of linguistic features. When a number of features demonstrated similar distributions (i.e., where a number of isoglosses appear to run together), Kurath drew a darker line to indicate a dialect boundary. Figure 23.1 shows us that Kurath divided American English into the Northern, Southern, and Midland dialect regions, demarcations that have held up as research on American dialects has expanded, in terms of linguistic scope and in terms of geography. These three main areas are historically anchored by the colonial hearths of Boston, Philadelphia, and Charleston, whose spreading influence set the tone for the Northern, Midland, and Southern regions, respectively, culturally and linguistically. As European settlement moved westward, the basic divisions of North, Midland, and South were carried across the Midwestern United States. What emerges later is one additional large dialect region, that of the West, a development noted by the American dialect map found in Labov, Ash, and Boberg.[6] Kurath's original boundaries hold up fairly well, which is interesting given the fact that Kurath's map was made "the old-fashioned way" (i.e., drawn by hand) and was based mainly on lexical items, while the map drawn by Labov, Ash, and Boberg is based on digitally recorded pronunciation data collected by a country-wide telephone survey conducted in the 2000s.

23.3. TEACHING FOCUS: EARLY AMERICAN ENGLISH

Contact with the native inhabitants of the New World resulted in lexical borrowings for the names of indigenous animals and plants, as well names for Native American

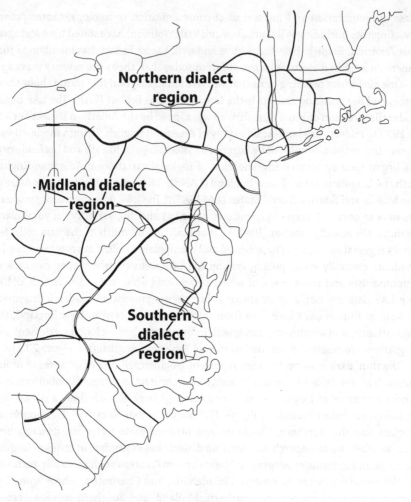

Figure 23.1. Kurath's 1949 dialect boundary map
(map adapted from Kurath, *The Word Geography of the Eastern United States*)

foods and material culture. Many of these represent the introduction of vocabulary to go along with cultural items that would have been new to the European colonists, flora, fauna, and foodways whose entrance into colonists' culture brought the new terms with them.

Animals and Plants	Food and Material culture
caribou (Mikmaq)	hominy (Powhatan)
chipmunk (Odawa)	squash (Narragansett)
moose (Algonquin)	succotash (Narragansett)
opossum (Algonquin)	pone (Algonquin)

quahog (Narragansett)

raccoon (Powhatan)

skunk (Massachusetts)

terrapin (Algonquin, likely Powhatan)

woodchuck (Algonquin)

hickory (Powhatan)

pecan (Illinois)

persimmon (Powhatan)

moccasin (Algonquin, likely Powhatan)

papoose (Narragansett)

toboggan (Mikmaq)

tomahawk (Powhatan)

totem (Ojibwe)

wampum (Massachusett)

wigwam (Eastern Abenaki)

23.3.1 Additional Resources

To put Native American borrowings in geographic context, students can look at an online map of Native American tribal lands (pre-colonization): https://commons. wikimedia.org/wiki/File:Early_Localization_Native_Americans_USA.jpg#/media/ File:Early_Localization_Native_Americans_USA.jpg

Not only does the map underscore the loss of Native American tribes (and their languages) brought about by European colonizers, it also highlights the number and location of place-names that reflect their native residents.

23.4. TEACHING FOCUS: R-LESSNESS

To complement the newness of contact with Native American cultures and languages, you can look at the persistence of a particular phonological feature, r-lessness (non-rhoticity), brought to early New World settlements by English colonists. R-lessness in these earliest-settled areas perseveres, as can be seen in Figure 23.2. The lack of postvocalic [r] in the speech of New Englanders is well documented, though the LANE data show that there is a great deal of variation in the appearance of this feature, which manifests as both no [r] and vocalized [r] in the same environments, not to mention the fact that there are LANE speakers who are r-full, even in areas presumed to be overwhelmingly non-rhotic. This region's leaning toward r-lessness, however, can be traced back to colonists from southwestern England; this non-rhoticity has persisted in the speech of many New Englanders for hundreds of years.

Southern cities such as Charleston and Savannah were also settled by speakers of non-rhotic English and r-lessness has persisted in the speech of these cities as well. For Charleston and Savannah specifically, this persistence was likely aided by the fact that the upper-class residents of these cities retained ties to England (especially to London) longer than their Northern counterparts. John McWhorter, whose 2015 Language Log post addresses American r-lessness[7] posits that the influence of African slaves, whose non-native English would not have contained syllable-final [r], could also have contributed to the spread and perseverance of non-rhotic speech in the South.

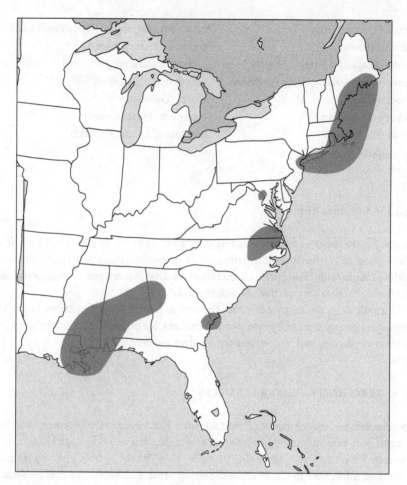

Figure 23.2. R-less areas of American English (map can be found at h9p://en.wikipedia.org/wiki/Rho7c_and_non-.-rho7c_accents)

McWhorter's view of r-lessness in the cities of Boston and New York is interesting as well, as he suggests that we need not look for a "founding population" reason for their non-rhoticity. McWhorter writes that Boston and New York could be r-less for the same reason that some British English speakers are r-less, due to "natural processes of sound change."[8] McWhorter explains that "R's are delicate after vowels at the end of syllables, like l's, and there is no reason that the r-less[sic] that developed in Britain could only have happened there—one might even wonder why it would not happen on its own in places elsewhere such as the United States."[9] The point that r-lessness could be caused by (or simply supported by) a natural linguistic process suggests that there are a number of processes that continue throughout the history of English.

23.4.1 Exercise: Early Am E pronunciation

This exercise, which can be done as a class or as an individual assignment, asks students to use colonial wills and estate inventories to look for variation in early American English (Am E) spelling in order to make some (educated) guesses about what colonial AmE sounded like. Reliable sources for early American estate inventories are available online, including one from Plymouth, Massachusetts, and one from York County, Virginia. The Plymouth colony set ranges in date from 1628 to 1687 and the York County set is comparable, ranging from 1637 to 1679. Working individually or in teams, students can go through transcribed estate inventories, looking for spellings that seem to indicate pronunciation. For example, the following spellings are from Plymouth colony inventories (left) and from York County, Virginia inventories (right).[10]

Plymouth spelling	York County spelling
broadhoos for *broadhouse*	westcoat for *waistcoat*
cubbert for *cupboard*	indico for *indigo*
galloone for *gallon*	cullander for *collandar*
glace for *glass*	chayers for *chairs*
homespoon for *homespun*	huswifes for *housewife's*
marchant for *merchant*	drawes for *drawers*

Pooling examples such as these offers the class an opportunity to reinforce some terms and concepts from phonology. For example, we see consonant devoicing in both the Plymouth and the York County inventories: [g] to [k] in "indico" and [d] to [t] in "cubbert." The inventories also provide orthographic evidence of vowel alternations. The spelling of "broadhouse" with the "oo," for example, suggests that one aspect of the Great Vowel Shift, the shift from [u] to [aʊ], was not present for this speaker. On the other hand, the spelling of "waistcoat" suggests lowering of [e] to [ɛ]. The different directions of vowel movement could be indicative of differences in the dialects of English colonists. Variation within the colonists' speech sows the seeds for what later comes to be perceived as regional or subregional differences (such as the r-lessness in coastal Virginia and North Carolina). Given the previous inventory examples, one might surmise that the spelling of "chayers," for instance, might indicate a pronunciation along the lines of [tʃeˈjɚz], which foreshadows (perhaps) the tendency to diphthongize vowels in contemporary Southern American English. Even though a handful of examples isn't adequate evidence of a large-scale regional trend, colonial writings still afford students the opportunity to gather data and make generalizations that tie together historical evidence with contemporary descriptions of Am E dialects.

23.5. TEACHING FOCUS: AMERICAN ENGLISH SPELLING

The colonial inventories provide a nice bridge to a discussion of Am E spelling, as the colonial wills and inventories were penned prior to Noah Webster's campaign for reform. Colonial writings are full of words spelled with a silent "e" (e.g., "olde" and "corne"), with double consonants (e.g., "towells," "bulletts," and "gunn"), as well as words that include a final "k" (e.g., "arithmetick"), all of which were on Webster's list of spelling superfluities. Though these three reforms in particular were success-ful, as was the move to eliminate the "u" from "honour" and the like, Webster had a fairly long list of suggestions that he felt would make (American) English simpler. It is important to note, as does H. L. Mencken in his chapter on Webster's reforms in *The American Language*,[11] that there has always been variation in English spelling historically, as seen in Shakespeare's use of both *-or* and *-our* throughout the first three folios.

Webster's attempts at reform are not grounded solely in the idea that spelling should be more straightforward. Webster's arguments about fixing American English spelling were also aimed at creating a specifically American system, one that he felt needed to be differentiated from its British origins. Webster writes in his Preface to his 1828 *American Dictionary of the English Language*[12]:

> It is not only important, but, in a degree necessary, that the people of this coun-try, should have an American Dictionary of the English Language; for, although the body of the language is the same as in England, and it is desirable to perpetuate that sameness, yet some differences must exist. Language is the expression of ideas; and if the people of one country cannot preserve an identity of ideas, they cannot retain an identity of language.

Here Webster emphasizes that despite the obvious familial relationship between British and American English, there are differences in culture and environment that must inevitably be reflected by differences in language.

Webster's linkage of an American language with an American identity solidified another, slightly more subtle, connection: that between patriotism and "proper" grammar. What may have begun as a desire for a national language to symbolize the unity of a new country morphed over time into the belief that being "American" meant using a particular kind of language in a particular way. This belief, which rep-resents the American brand of prescriptivism, is the root of present-day "English Only" laws that crop up in federal and state legislatures from time to time.

23.5.1. Additional Resources

a) Mencken's chapter on "The Influence of Webster" from *The American Language* (pp. 247–55) can be found online: http://www.bartleby.com/185/32.html. This chapter outlines the spelling changes that Webster was able to effect, along with a series of more radical (yet not nonsensical) reforms that were never implemented (e.g. eliminating the silent letters in *thumb, island,* and *leopard*).

b) For an accessible, student-friendly piece on spelling reform see "The American Spelling Reform Movement" by Richard Whelan.[13]

23.6. TEACHING FOCUS: LANGUAGE CONTACT

Language contact can be defined as a situation of contact between groups of speakers who do not share a common language. The results of language contact range from lexical borrowing to something more complicated, such as the creation of a pidgin (and then perhaps a creole). In any case, the topic of language contact represents a point of intersection at which there is some coalescence between contact and persistence since language contact offers speakers the choice of new linguistic features to use alongside of features that persist. Talking about language contact also gives you another way to go back over HEL: contact between the Germanic tribes and the Celts (in some ways mirrored by European contact with Native Americans), contact with French during Middle English (ME), persistent contact with Latin, and so on. In the context of Am E, we talk about contact between English speakers and speakers of other languages, as well as the persistence of features that immigrating groups brought with them.

Present-day American vocabulary reflects not only colonial settlement but also borrowings from the waves of European immigrants who followed. Looking at areas that were settled by high concentrations of one particular group, such as the German settlers of Pennsylvania (the Pennsylvania Deutsch, whose German was subsequently affected by contact with English), the Scotch-Irish of the Appalachian Mountain region, or the early Dutch settlement of the Hudson River Valley is another way to contextualize the language contact that informed American English.

23.6.1 Assignment: Using Linguistic Atlas Data

LAP regional survey data are available online at lap.uga.edu. The data are grouped by speakers' responses to targeted interview questions. An assignment I have used many times asks students to look at one database (one set of responses) and, using the *Oxford English Dictionary* (OED) and the *Dictionary of American Regional English* (DARE), have them track down the origins of responses with the goal of trying to put together a story of how those words entered (American) English. Good LAP databases for this assignment are ones that have terms that reflect the settling populations of different regions: "andirons," "bacon," "blood pudding," "bureau," "cornbread," "cottage cheese," "doughnut," "pancakes," and "porch." Students will uncover relationships between colonial (and later) settlement and terms found within American English dialects (e.g., the distinctive use of the term "smearcase" for cottage cheese in areas of heavy German settlement and "bonny clabber" for sour milk in areas settled by the Irish)—along with a little bit of historical backup (i.e., information about waves of immigration throughout the seventeenth and eighteenth centuries).

As an example, take a quick look at the data set that contains words for "porch":

porch	back piazza	balcony
piazza	shed	front stoop(s)
stoop	gallery	patio
veranda	side porch	breezeway
back porch	steps	front shed
front porch	front piazza	terrace(s)
portico	back stoop(s)	back shed
platform	entry	

Even within this (relatively) small data set, we have terms that reflect the influence of Dutch (*stoop*), Italian (*piazza, portico*), and Hindi (*veranda*). OED entries can also be used to date these terms' entrance into English, allowing students to think about whether the terms were already in the English brought to the American colonies or if they are more recent, American adoptions—so, whether in terms of American English they represent contact or persistence. I have my students write up their findings as they come up with historical explanations for the variation in American vocabulary, but it would be easy enough to call up a database online and have students use laptops/tablets to check the online versions of the *OED* and *DARE* and come up with plausible historical explanations for the variation in terms as part of class discussion.

23.6.2. Assignment: Using the *OED*

Another assignment that asks students to look at the borrowing of cultural items and the names that go with them employs the "advanced search" option of the *OED* online. Using the *OED* online, students can undertake an advanced search to look for borrowings from a specific language (Italian, German, French, Hindi, etc.) that made their way into American English specifically. Filling out the "language of origin" field pulls up loanwords that came into English at any point, but indicating a preference for the United States in the "Region" field of the advanced search will narrow the results to terms that entered English as "American" vocabulary. For example, when you look for Italian words used chiefly in the United States, the results include food names such as *arugula, calzone, muffuletta, parmagiana* (as a postmodifier), *spaghetti*, and *zeppole*. The results also contain a lot of terms that seem *Godfather*-esque, terms like *mafia, capiche*, and *paisan* (which is an interesting commentary on Italian contributions to both American English and American culture).

23.6.3. Additional Resources

a) Salmons, Joseph and Thomas Purnell. "Contact and the Development of American English." In *Handbook of Language Contact*, edited by Ray Hickey, 454–78. London: Blackwell, 2012.
b) Sankoff, Gillian. "Linguistic Outcomes of Language Contact." In *The Handbook of Language Variation and Change*, edited by J. K. Chambers, Peter Trudgill, and Natalie Schilling-Estes, 638–68. Oxford: Wiley-Blackwell, 2004.

23.7. TEACHING FOCUS: ENGLISH-BASED CREOLES IN THE UNITED STATES

Gullah is the only agreed-on English-based creole found in the contiguous United States. As part of the LAP surveys of the 1930s, Lorenzo Dow Turner did fieldwork in the Gullah Islands, which are located off the coasts of South Carolina and Georgia. The Gullah Islands were used to house rice and indigo plantations prior to the American Civil War and were thus populated by a large number of slaves from West Africa and a small number of white slave owners. After the Civil War, the majority of the white families left the Islands, which then remained (relatively) socially, economically, and geographically isolated for several generations. The Gullah language has many of the same features found in other slave trade-based English creoles. The origins of Gullah are outlined in Turner's book, *Africanisms in the Gullah Dialect*, in which he lists many familiar terms (familiar, at least, to the American South) that can be traced back to West African languages, including *yam, gumbo, okra, banjo, cooter, goober, pinder* (peanut), *chigger, zombie*, and *to tote* (for "to carry").

In addition to the items of African vocabulary, Turner lists several Gullah grammatical and phonological features that reflect West African heritage. Grammatical features include copula deletion (as in "She pretty") and the use of *done* and *been* as aspectual markers (as in "He done finished" to emphasize completion of an action and "She *been* married" to indicate that she has been married a long time), while phonological features including syllable initial fricative stopping ([d] and [t] for /ð/ and /θ/, respectively), an alternation reflective of West African phonological systems.

23.7.1 Additional Resources

a) Turner, Lorenzo Dow, with an introduction by Katherine Wyly Mille and Michael Montgomery. *Africanisms in the Gullah Dialect*. Columbia: University of South Carolina Press, 2002. The Introduction to this 2002 edition includes good information about Gullah and about Turner, the first African American to earn a PhD in Linguistics.
b) Mufwene, Salikoko and Charles Gillman. "How African is Gullah and Why?" *American Speech* 62 (1987): 120–39.

23.8. TEACHING FOCUS: AFRICAN AMERICAN ENGLISH

Touching on the origins and features of Gullah provides a nice bridge to a discussion of African American English (AAE) and the controversy surrounding theories of its origin: Did AAE begin as a creole? There are three basic viewpoints on AAE origins: the Anglicist position; the creolist position, and the neo-Anglicist position.[14] The Anglicist position of 1960s dialectologists holds that the features of AAE—including those of habitual *be* and third person singular-*s* deletion—have their origins in various dialects of British English. The creolist position posits that, during the slave trade, a creole developed (probably among slaves held on Africa's west coast) and traveled with the slave trade through the Caribbean and then to the American South. The neo-Anglicists of more recent decades argue that, though AAE has its origins in British English dialects, as a dialect it diverged radically from white varieties of English as time went on. This debate sparks a number of high-stakes questions: What is its relationship to other English-based creoles that developed because of the slave trade (Jamaican Creole English, Barbadian Creole English, Gold Coast Creole English, etc.)? If AAE does have creole origins, has it since decreolized? In other words, has it become less creole-like over time due to continued influence from General American English? If AAE is creole-based and, being a creole, then deserves to be recognized as a language, how might this affect the American education system? If AAE developed as a dialect of American English informed by British varieties, what social situation(s) caused it to diverge from other versions of Southern (white) speech? How does this kind of divergence work linguistically?

During the Great Migration (1916–30), African Americans moved out of the American south, carrying their language to northern metropolitan areas. African Americans from Florida, Georgia, the Carolinas, and western Virginia moved to northern cultural centers such as Boston. Mississippi African Americans moved northward to Chicago, Detroit, Milwaukee, and Cleveland, while many African American residents of Texas, Louisiana, and Arkansas moved north to St. Louis and then to Minneapolis as well as west to California cities such as Oakland, San Francisco and Los Angeles. This pattern of migration, shown in Figure 23.3, explains why different regional varieties of AAE have features in common and why the AAE spoken in northern cities have features that people may perceive as "sounding" Southern (e.g., the use of *y'all* as a second person plural pronoun). Whether it is of creole or Anglicist origin, AAE is an American variety borne out of a contact situation which, by sudden change and/or by persistence, developed into a distinctive language that has informed not only the language (and culture) of the South but the entire country.

Before running through some features of African American English, it is important to note that just because a person is African American doesn't mean she speaks AAE. Even if a person does speak AAE, she may not use all of the features associated with the variety and may not employ the features that she does use all of the time. Because of historical relationship between African slaves and Southern white slave owners, it should come as no surprise that AAE has much in common with Southern American English (SAE). In fact, there are only a handful of phonological and grammatical features that are typically cited as differentiating AAE from SAE, including those listed here.

Feature	Example
Consonant cluster reduction	[fæs] fast
Syllable-initial [skr] for [str]	[skrit] street
[f] for final [θ]	[bof] both
Copula deletion	She pretty.
Stressed *been* [to express ongoing action]	They been married.
Habitual *be* [to express repeated action]	He be late to class.
Third person singular –s absence	She need a ride.
Plural –s absence	Two dog walk down the street.
Possessive –s absence	That Mary car.

These are just a few examples of characteristic AAE features, several of which are found in other varieties of American English (not to mention across World Englishes). Consonant cluster reduction, for example, is found across dialects and informal registers of American English, though it is found in AAE to a greater extent than in conversational American English or SAE. A feature list, however, falls short of describing this variety; prosody and rhythm are also part of AAE, as is an ever-changing lexicon.

When dealing with a language variety that is considered to be "non-standard," students may react to features of AAE in a manner that highlights the fact that AAE

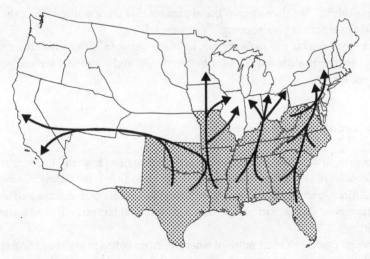

Figure 23.3. The Great Migration
(map available at bld.us/us-map.html)

is still a stigmatized variety of English. As a descriptivist, this is not only a good time to point out the intimate connection between language and identity, but also a good time to point out that, in several ways, AAE is "ahead of the curve" in regard to the ongoing reduction of English inflectional morphology. I'm thinking here specifically of third person singular -s, plural –s, and possessive –s, all of which are superfluous in terms of their function, and, to that end, the deletion of these inflectional morphemes in AAE reflects what Walt Wolfram refers to as the "transparency principle," the idea that deletions can be made only when meaning is preserved in their absence (and who reasonably does not understand the meaning of "He walk down the street," "She has two dog," or "I like Mary car"?). There is other inflectional reduction occurring in American English; for example, younger speakers are more likely to use "more" or "most" when making comparisons, while speakers forty and over (like myself) are likelier to use comparative and superlative morphemes, -er and –est. It's just that this kind of inflectional loss isn't wound up in people's opinions and prejudices about ethnicity and class. As Rosina Lippi-Green suggests in her work *English With An Accent*,[15] if you have a problem with AAE, your problem isn't with language.

23.8.1. Assignment: Comparing LAP Data from Gullah and AAE

How similar is AAE to Gullah? This assignment asks students to find out. All of the data from Turner's Gullah interviews as well as data collected later from African Americans living in North Carolina, South Carolina, and Georgia are available online as part of the Linguistic Atlas Project.[16] Among the LAP questions are ones that target pronunciation and grammar, and it is these specifically that can be used to find similarities (and differences) between Gullah and mainland African American speakers' use of language. Good LAP targets to use for this comparison are: verb forms ("blew," "gave," "knew"), pronouns ("himself," "themselves"), subject-verb agreement ("people thinks," "he doesn't care"), and phrases that allow you to look at the presence/absence of *to be* ("we're going," "you were talking").

Note that similar comparisons can be made between African American speakers and southern white speakers (or between men and women, older and younger speakers, etc.).

23.8.2. Additional Resources

a) Thomas, Erik. "Prosodic Features of African American English." In Jennifer Bloomquist, Lisa J. Green, and Sonja L. Lanehart (eds.). *The Oxford Handbook of African American Language*. Oxford: OUP, 2015. This OUP volume also has chapters on Gullah, variation within AAE, and chapters on AAE in educational settings.

b) Though I wouldn't trust much of what the internet has to say about AAE (or "Black English" or heaven forbid "Ebonics"), I do trust the mini-documentaries put out by the North Carolina Language and Life Project (NCLLP), including a nine-minute piece on African American English: https://www.youtube.com/watch?v=RTt07IVDeww.

c) Smitherman, Geneva. *Black Talk: Words and Phrases from the Hood to the Amen Corner*. (rev. ed.) New York: Mariner Books, 2000. Smitherman's book focuses on AAE lexicon, contextualizing vocabulary use in the African American community in terms of history and culture. Smitherman also addresses the reappropriation of AAE vocabulary by the greater U.S. culture and has said many times at conferences that, be assured, when you see a piece of AAE vocabulary used in a news headline, the black community stopped using it two years ago (e.g. *bling*).

23.9. TEACHING FOCUS: CHICANO ENGLISH AND SPANGLISH

The "influx of new populations" was one of McDavid's dialect-driving forces; when large numbers of speakers who share a cultural or linguistic background move or immigrate to a new area, the language(s) they bring with them have an impact on the speech of that area. Famed dialectologist Lee Pederson once explained to a small gathering of graduate students (myself included) that he felt it would be the influx of Spanish and its continued influence on English that would, eventually, be the factor to divide "American" from "English."

Think of cities in southern California or of Miami, Florida in terms of the contact between English and Spanish—the continued and increasing presence of Spanish in these states is bound to influence the dialects spoken there. The presence of Spanish has already impacted the development of a "new" American dialect, referred to as Chicano English (CE). Chicano English is a *native* form of American English; CE speakers are *not* non-native English speakers and are not necessarily fluent in Spanish. CE speakers are second- or third-generation Americans whose dialect is influenced by their Spanish-speaking parents and/or community. Like AAE, Chicano English is not a unified way of speaking; there is no one way to speak Chicano dialect. Another point made about AAE is also relevant here: one should refrain from making assumptions about a person's language use based on his or her appearance or presumed cultural background. Not every person of Hispanic origin speaks Chicano English (or Spanish). Features of Chicano English include:

Feature	Example
Consonant cluster reduction	[lis] least, [lɛf] left
"sh" [ʃ] as "ch" [tʃ]	[ʃɛck] check
"ch" [tʃ] as "sh" [ʃ]	[tʃeʲk] shake
Devoicing of [z]	[su] zoo, [isi] easy
Devoicing of [v]	[seʲf] save
Substitution of [t] for [θ]	[tri] three
[j] for [dʒ] word initially	[jɛlo] yellow
Copula deletion	This a story about dog.

Multiple negation	We don't want no help or nothing.
More + -er as a comparative	I can't think of a more clearer example.

And, as with AAE, there are also particular prosodic and rhythmic patterns associated with CE, likely due to the influence of regional Spanish varieties, such as Mexican Spanish, and of indigenous languages of Náhuatl (an indigenous language of Mexico).

Linguists consider Spanglish a "hybrid," the product of English and Spanish code-switching, which in this case includes both lexical and grammatical shifting. One feature of Spanglish is the presence of calques (loan translations) such as *correr para officina*, a word-for-word translation of "run for office," and semantic extensions such as *carpeta* for "carpet" (instead of the Spanish *moqueta* or *alfombra*) and *parquear* meaning "to park" (instead of the Spanish verbs *estacionar* or *aparcar*). Spanglish is not a pidgin (it has native speakers, is grammatically and phonologically complex, and has a culture associated with it) nor is it a creole (the mixing of Spanish and English does not reflect the demographics or socio-political relationships one usually finds in creole situations). Like Chicano English, Spanglish is not an example of non-native English speaking; it's an indicator of identity. Both CE and Spanglish represent recent and important developments in American English that are the direct result of contact between English and Spanish—within communities and within the minds of individual speakers.

23.9.1. Additional Resources

a) Fought, Carmen. *Chicano English in Context*. Palgrave: New York, 2003.
b) The North Carolina Language and Life Program (NCLLP) has produced a series of videos about dialects spoken in the United States, including a video on Spanglish: https://www.youtube.com/watch?v=nYMnNlfSMC0. The Spanglish video is just over four minutes long and contains examples of Spanglish, information about language and identity and the importance of that relationship, as well as a brief interview with Walt Wolfram, who talks about what linguists see when they look at Spanglish.
c) The Public Radio International (PRI) story "The Hidden History of Spanglish in California" is available online to read or listen to.[17] This story provides historical evidence of the code-mixing (so to speak) of Spanish and English in the 1830s. The online story has images of letters written in the 1830s as well as signage that reflects present-day mixing of English and Spanish in Los Angeles.
d) Otheguy, Ricardo and Nancy Stern. "On So-Called Spanglish." *International Journal of Bilingualism* 15 (1): 85–100, 2011.

23.10. CHARACTERIZING PRESENT DAY AMERICAN ENGLISH

There is a great deal of variation within American English (which is in itself a persistent feature of the English language). Research conducted by contemporary sociolinguists looks at present-day regional varieties of American English in terms of their vowel systems, which appear to be changing in different ways. The Northern Cities Shift (NCS) is characterized by long, low vowels [ɔ] and [ɑ] moving forward and then upward, while short vowels /ɪ/ and /ɛ/ move down and back (see Figure 23.4, left). Southern Shift (SS) is characterized by the merger of /ɪ/ and /ɛ/ (the "pen/pin merger"), accompanied by front long vowels [i] and [e] moving back and down and back vowels [u] and [o] moving forward. In terms of general direction, the SS represents persistence, as the vowels appear to be moving in the same direction as the Great Vowel Shift. The Western dialect region is characterized by its non-participation in either the NCS or the SS; instead the Western region evidences a merger of [ɔ] and [ɑ] (the "caught/cot merger").

It is important to remember that, when we're looking at vowel shifts (often referred to as chain shifts), we're looking at something that is more of a general tendency than an absolute rule. There are, for example, non-shifted speakers in northern cities. Even speakers whose speech seems to participate in the NCS will use non-shifted vowels and shifted ones.[18]

23.11. SOUTHERN ENGLISH

Southern American English (SAE) has been found to be the most-identified dialect of American English in perceptual studies conducted by Dennis Preston with American speakers[19] and trust me when I say that the "Southern accent" is widely identifiable outside of the United States. SAE is lauded, criticized, imitated, and mocked. Even its own speakers are ambivalent; in an attitudinal study, Preston found that Southerners themselves judged their own language use to be "pleasant" yet "incorrect."[20] And so, what follows is a brief sketch of SAE phonological and grammatical features. The lists are not intended to be exhaustive but instead contain some of the most salient SAE features, the things that people perceive as sounding "Southern."

Phonological feature	Example
Consonant cluster reduction	Ole Miss
Intrusive /r/	wash [warʃ], sort of [sortər]
Deletion of unstressed syllable	'mergency
G-dropping (/n/ for /ŋ/)	huntin' and fishin'
Metathesis	ask [aks]
Merger of /ɪ/ and /ɛ/ before nasals (pen/pin merger)	[pɪn]
Monophthongization of /aɪ/	night [na:t]
Diphthongization	bed [bɛɪd], half [hæɪf]

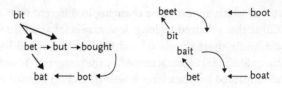

Figure 23.4. The northern cities shift (left) and the southern shift (right)

Many of these phonological features are found in dialects spoken outside the South and their use in SAE is more a matter of the extent to which they are used. Both consonant cluster reduction and g-dropping are common features of conversational American English, though they occur with greater frequency in SAE. The SAE feature intrusive /r/ is characteristic of another dialect as well, but whereas in SAE it is associated more with "rural" or "mountain" speakers, in the northeast, the added /r/ is associated with upper-class Bostonian speech (e.g., John F. Kennedy's famous pronunciation of "Cuba" as [kjubɚ]). In addition, metathesis, especially found in the pronunciation of "ask" as [aks] is highly stigmatized and is probably more commonly associated with AAE, though you do hear it from older, white speakers in Appalachia. Note that metathesis is a feature found throughout the history of English, as we see in Old English "brid" (now "bird") and "hros" (now "horse") and even in the word "ask" itself which metathesized for the first time in Middle English.

Grammatical Feature	Example
A-prefixing	He was a-laughing so hard he fell over.
Was-leveling	They was asking for it.
Don't for *doesn't*	She don't care about that.
Fixin' to	I'm fixing to leave.
[expresses immediacy of action]	
Completive *done*	I done finished my chores.
Y'all	What are all y'all doing later on?
[second person plural pronoun]	
Double modals	We might should help them.
	We might could go with you.
	We may can help.
Multiple negation	He ain't seen nothing like that before.
[often with *ain't*]	
Nonstandard past tense (3 kinds):	
present form = past tense	He give me that yesterday.
regularized form	We knowed you wouldn't care.
past participle = past tense	If I done something wrong, tell me.
	They've tore that down.
Absence of plural *-s*	four year, two gallon, five mile

Irregular prepositions	He lived at High Point.
	The cat crawled on up in the bush.
They for there	They's no way I can do that.

Again, we find that many of these features are found in dialects spoken both outside of the American South and outside of the United States. *Was*-leveling, non-standard past tense, and multiple negation, particularly, are common enough to be described by Jack Chambers as "universals" within the English language as they are used widely, both in present-day and historical varieties of English.[21] The regularization of past tense forms (e.g., *knowed* for *knew*, *drinked* for *drank*, and *telled* for *told*) indicate that the historical shift from strong to weak verbs is ongoing. Instead of viewing these verbs as "nonstandard," we really should talk about them as evidence of the persistence of past tense choices available to speakers since Middle English, ME being an era described by Algeo and Pyles as one in which "some verbs could be conjugated either way."[22] While the General American use of *dived/dove*, *strived/strove*, *sneaked/snuck*, *waked/woke*, and *weave/wove* is somewhat ambiguous in that speakers use both forms without drawing too much prescriptive ire, the SAE forms listed previously and others like them are stigmatized and often used as an indictment against its speakers.

23.11.1. Assignment

a) Watch two NCLLP videos in order to discuss the differences between urban and rural Southern English. The NCLLP video clip on Appalachian English ("Mountain Talk"), https://www.youtube.com/watch?v=03iwAY4KlIU, is about eight minutes long and has longer excerpts of Appalachian speech that students can listen to and use to identify the features named above. Another NCLLP video highlights the use of SAE of a large Southern city, that of Charlotte, North Carolina: https://www.youtube.com/watch?v=MFfM2GMr3lI. Interviews with people from Charlotte contain interesting statements about SAE as it is perceived by its speakers, about SAE in contrast to other varieties of American English, and about the relationship between language and identity. One of the points made in the video is that cities like Charlotte, North Carolina, are populated by a lot of people not originally from there and that this contact is having an effect on the city/language/culture.

23.12. CONCLUSION

Change in language can be brought about through interaction with speakers of other languages; the history of American English contains several examples of contact-based changes, from the early lexical impact of Native American languages to the present-day lexical and grammatical impact of Spanish. Language contact has also resulted in the birth of a creole, Gullah, and the development (via the creole process or not) of a major dialect, African American English. Dialects of American English have also been informed by the continuation of processes or features found throughout the history of English, such as r-lessness, the transition of strong to weak verbs, and the loss of inflectional morphology.

Although you can find descriptions of "American English" that make generalizations about the character of the language spoken in the United States, the approach presented here treats Am E not as a homogenous whole but as a fluid and dynamic amalgamation of dialects and subvarieties that have developed (and continue to develop) from the interplay of the complementary forces of contact and persistence. From this standpoint, American English can be viewed as a microcosm of the still-continuing history of English.

CHAPTER 24

Teaching Diversity and Change in the History of English

ROB PENHALLURICK

In April 1966, at the Symposium on Directions for Historical Linguistics, University of Texas, the formidable team of Uriel Weinreich, William Labov, and Marvin I. Herzog presented a paper on "Empirical Foundations for a Theory of Language Change" (published in 1968).[1] The paper became a significant statement of intent for certain areas of modern linguistics, including variationist sociolinguistics, dialectology, and historical linguistics. It was written at a time when two apparently new and opposing approaches to language study were rising to prominence: generative linguistics (led by Noam Chomsky) and sociolinguistics (with William Labov as figurehead). I say "apparently" because both approaches had their antecedents and one can argue that, to an extent, elements of the two are, with some effort, reconcilable. The paper by Weinreich et al. reviewed the two schools of thought and their antecedents insofar as they affected the study of language change, and it also made a case for the sociolinguistic approach to researching and explaining language change, stating that, "Linguistic and social factors are closely interrelated in the development of language change."[2] That is, the study of language change requires linguistic and social data gleaned from members of speech communities as they go about their everyday lives. Explanations which, on the other hand, confine themselves only to linguistic factors or only to social factors "will fail to account for the rich body of regularities that can be observed in empirical studies of language behavior." The Chomskyan, generative approach is deemed inadequate by the authors owing to its neglect of social factors and owing to its concomitant prerequisite that language be studied as a homogeneous object, its geographical and social diversity rendered of merely superficial interest. Weinreich, Labov, and Herzog conclude their argument with a list of seven general statements central to their thinking about the nature of language change, including the following, to which I have added my own italics: "Not all variability and heterogeneity in language structure involves change; but *all change involves variability and heterogeneity.*" One can draw out the implication of this statement quite easily: the explanation of language change entails consideration of the inherent diversity of language and of linguistic features. For the purposes of the present chapter, one might take this further: teaching the history of the English language (HEL) leads one naturally to talking about its diversity—its dialects and varieties and their features.

Having recently finished writing a history of the study of English dialects, I now know better than I did previously that, from the earliest works to the present day, scholars have been interested in the connection between change and diversity in the English language, the connection between the language's history and its dialects. This is something of a relief to me, because this connection is a basic premise of my university teaching, including the first-year course that I gradually developed, eventually leading to the textbook *Studying the English Language*.[3] It is the design, rationale, content, and delivery of this course that will be the focus of this chapter.

Awareness of the diversity of the language is probably universal among speakers of English. My own perspective has been shaped by being a native speaker of a non-standard, "non-English" dialect of English, that is, Welsh English, a perspective modified by experiencing a Standard-English-promoting education and by living outside Wales in a variety of places, and by an academic interest that began with an introductory course in Linguistics in 1975 at the University College of Swansea, taught by David Parry. Parry was (and is) a philologist and a dialectologist. During his time as a lecturer at Swansea he taught Old Norse, Old English, Middle English, Dialectology, and Linguistics. He also taught many of his students (me included) Phonetics and trained them as dialect fieldworkers, supervising their contributions to his Survey of Anglo-Welsh Dialects, which ran from 1968 to his retirement in 1995, and which was conceived as a counterpart in Wales to the Survey of English Dialects, directed between the 1940s and 1970s from Leeds University by Harold Orton. In the first, typewritten, xeroxed handout of that 1975–6 Introduction to Linguistics course, Parry said: "If the course offered here does have a discernible bias, it is most likely to be a bias towards the study of present-day spoken English (including dialects and slang), this being one of the lecturer's chief interests."[4] In addition to providing a guide to structuralist linguistics, the course concentrated on the history of English as far back as its Indo-European ancestry, including phonological, grammatical, lexical, and semantic change, as well as classes on slang, place names, surnames, regional and class dialects, and "the lore and language of schoolchildren." I got my first full-time teaching post in 1987, and during the years following I regularly taught first-year courses that were introductions either to linguistics or to the history of the English language. At some point during this time, I began my first attempts at designing a course that would be a combined introduction to linguistics, to the contemporary character of English, and to the history of the language. No doubt influenced by my Parry-training, it seemed to me a natural mixture, and the view that the essential diversity of English was central to the course's content also seemed a given. Early versions had the awkward title "English Language Debates," which I never liked, although it was in keeping with the principles of the course. Then Palgrave Macmillan showed an interest in my ideas, which led to my writing a textbook based on the course, and both course and book settled into the much better title *Studying the English Language*. The first edition of the book came out in 2003, the second in 2010. The idea was that we would learn about the English language, its history, and its makeup, and we would learn about how we know what we know about the English language. It was an introduction to knowledge about English and to how scholars theorise and gather evidence about English and language in general—how that knowledge is the ongoing outcome of a process that involves shifting, evolving methods, a range of approaches and perspectives, and debate.

In its writing, the textbook was formed on what I was doing in class as well as on the logic of its own format and scope. For example, it consists of short chapters, which can be read in any order, each dealing with a different theme, each initiated by an example or idea, each chapter possible to read at one sitting, with no cross-references between chapters, but nevertheless many interconnections apparent between them, building into a bigger picture as one progresses through the book. The first edition contained fifteen chapters, to which another three were added for the second edition, which also has revised versions of the original fifteen. A third edition, should it happen, will have twenty chapters. The point here is that the book offers a smorgasbord of topics that are carefully but surreptitiously (one might say) linked together. For any course that uses it, the book provides a choice of topics to concentrate on in class and essential information, explanation, and guides to further reading and resources on these and other associated topics. Just as the book evolved out of what I was doing in class, so now what I do in class has developed in response to what the book does. With the book in place I am freed up with regard to class content, which can be more illustrative and relaxed in the knowledge that the rudiments are covered in the coursebook. In order to illustrate this, and in order to return to the focus of the present chapter, that is, teaching diversity and change in the history of English, I will talk now about the first classes and the first chapter of *Studying the English Language*. I don't intend to write here some kind of promotional piece for my textbook, but it is an integral part of the year-one course, which itself acts as a springboard for courses in subsequent years of the programme, so it would not make sense to exclude it from the discussion. The year-one course in its current configuration consists of two lecture hours per week for eleven weeks, plus a number of smaller-group meetings about once a fortnight. The niceties of the structure (amount and types of contact hours, length of the course, and the like) have fluctuated over the years in response to the bureaucratic and managerial whims of the institution, but the pedagogical aims have been safeguarded and constant.

In addition to housekeeping information about course structure, content, assessment, teachers, and so on, the first lectures aim to introduce the course's philosophy on studying the English language, including fundamental themes and terms, and consist of several hours under the heading "Diversity and Change." Here follow the main points.

The geographical diversity of language is one of its most basic and conspicuous characteristics. This diversity presents us with separate languages, and within each language we encounter regional dialects. That is, language changes in space. English is an especially diverse language, so diverse that the plural term *World Englishes* has emerged since the early 1980s out of scholarly work on varieties of English across the world. But the regional diversity of English is nothing new. English was a diverse language from its very beginnings. At its beginning, the English language was less a language and more an assortment of related dialects. English is a flourishing language whose beginnings can be located in the fifth century A.D. The elements of any living language will be exposed to alteration through time simply because they perpetuate themselves, which entails exposure to social forces. To follow the thinking of one of the founders of modern linguistics, Ferdinand de Saussure, linguistic continuity involves change and linguistic change involves continuity.[5] Linguistic change is never absolute in Saussure's view, but based in "the persistence of the old substance."[6] Languages change through time. And, to follow Weinreich, Labov, and Herzog, "all change involves variability and heterogeneity,"[7] a point which is illustrated often during the course.

All of this leads us to the recognition that the difference between a *dialect* and a *language* is not a rigid division but a matter of degree, for this becomes clear as we explore linguistic change and diversity as a united theme. To some extent, the notions of separate languages and of separate dialects within languages are just that—notions. Notions which help us organize our thoughts about the nature of language and our own identity, notions which do have a clear relation to the linguistic facts as they appear to us, but also abstractions which can readily smooth out important details. Over time the dialects of a language can diverge until they are perceived as separate languages. In contrast, a group of related dialects can over time be subject to social pressures and can appear to coalesce into a unified language. As a result of contact, trade, and migration, languages and dialects can leak into each other, "borrowing" words, sounds, and grammar from each other, for their boundaries (if that is the right word) are highly permeable.

These then are the broader main points, or some of them, that can be made under the heading "Diversity and Change." However, while it is probably good practice in the classroom to begin with a summary of major points, I prefer to begin the narrative (and I like a narrative) with an example or two. I like to move from example to theory and explanation, rather than to present a theory or approach or finding or method and then exemplify it. I see the opening example, if chosen well, as functioning like the intro of a catchy pop song, grabbing the attention. Ideally, one needs a few other hooks as one proceeds. It can also at times help make the material that follows feel more relevant, and one of the aims of the course and textbook is quietly to encourage participants and readers to observe and reflect on their and others' language use.

Chapter 1 of *Studying the English Language* is structured around its own form of a device that I have used in the first class of the course for some time. I present half-a-dozen-or-so short texts, each one accompanied by the question: Is it English? The short texts are as follows:

1. a sentence from a news article in my local newspaper, the *South Wales Evening Post*;
2. a sentence from an item on college football from *The Ann Arbor News*;
3. a transcribed extract from a tape-recorded interview with a retired slate-maker and county roadman in Talysarn, Gwynedd, North Wales;

4. a version of the eighth-century poem *Cædmon's Hymn* written in the Northumbrian dialect of Old English, followed by a word-for-word translation into present-day Standard English;
5. a version of *Cædmon's Hymn* written in the West Saxon dialect of Old English;
6. a poem for children written in Frisian taken from Boelens[8];
7. a sentence from a transcription of a recording of Gullah by Salikoko S. Mufwene,[9] followed by its equivalent in Standard English.

The first three texts facilitate preparatory definitions and comparison of *Standard English* and *non-standard English*, as well as some commentary on differences between written and spoken English. The first two texts also show us that the standard variety of English can incorporate local linguistic colour, in the form of words from another language (such as Welsh) or in the form of local and specialized English words and meanings, and that Standard English, apparently the most core variety of English, possesses a considerable integrated foreign element—for example, there are five loanwords from French in the first text, all borrowed during the late Middle English period. This enables introduction of the terms *loanword, borrowing, foreignism, Middle English*, and *Old English*, brings in the change-through-time theme and language contact, and connects with later discussions in the course and book about the history of British Standard English and the development of other Standard Englishes in other English-speaking territories. Text three draws attention to the *phonological, grammatical (morphological, syntactic)*, and *lexical* ways in which a non-standard English can be distinguished, and to the fact that the geographical diversity of English is related to its spreading out of England into territories where it picked up features from other languages and cultures. This divergence was also aided in some cases by an immigrant English going through a period of comparative isolation (e.g., in North America and Australasia) from its mother dialects or varieties in Britain. Text three also contains recognizable standard features, and the point can be made that standard features can link differing non-standard dialects of English to each other, helping *mutual intelligibility*. Also there can be non-standard links between dialects, for example, there are dialects or varieties of North American and Australasian English which have been influenced historically by the regional dialects of British English, and some of the non-standard vocabulary and grammar that my Welsh-English *informant* (text three) used during our conversations came from dialectal English. Naturally, there is no practical limit to the choice of texts that could be used in these first three slots. Those used in Chapter 1 of *StEL* also tie in with the later narrative about the spread of English from its homeland into other territories in the British Isles and across the globe.

The next bunch of texts (numbers four to six) take the diversity theme chronologically backwards. Even in modern print form there are obvious spelling, grammatical, and lexical differences between Old English *Cædmon's Hymn* and its present-day translation, which can be summarized immediately and then returned to in more depth later (in particular the story of the transition of English from a *synthetic* to an *analytic* language, a story which has contact and dialectal aspects). But also there are clear differences between the Northumbrian and West Saxon versions of the poem.

This corroborates the point that English has always been a geographically diverse language, allows one to say a little about the main dialects of Old English, opens into some historical background on the Germanic tribes who settled in Britain from the fifth century onward, and introduces the terms *Germanic* and *Englisc*. Text six is a sample from the language that is the closest relative of English, Frisian, which in its Old Frisian form was probably to a large extent mutually intelligible with Old English. Now we can add more detail to discussing the continuum of difference that separates (and connects) dialects and languages, and to the interplay of the passage of time and social forces. As de Saussure put it, "languages and dialects differ quantitatively, not by nature."[10] Text six also introduces us to the concept of the *language family*, to *Indo-European* (IE), and to the story of divergence and convergence in the IE family over time, together with the story of theoretical models (such as the *family-tree* and *wave models*) in the philological research that was stimulated by William Jones's (1786) postulation of a "common source" for Sanskrit, Greek, Latin, Gothic, Celtic, Persian, and many other languages, including English.

The final short text, a sample of Gullah, ushers in *creole, pidgin*, and the impact of the slave trade on English. It adds more detail to the discussion of contact, the spread of English, and the development of new varieties, and more detail to the discussion of the distinction between *dialect* and *language*, and the theme of diversity and change. Mufwene says, "A reason commonly invoked to set Gullah apart from other North American English varieties is that it is not intelligible to speakers of other English varieties,"[11] adding, "However, mutual intelligibility is not a reliable criterion for determining whether a particular language variety is a dialect of a language or a separate language." Mufwene argues in favour of strong non-standard English influence on Gullah, alongside influence from West African languages. Gullah illustrates the blurriness of the distinction between *dialect* and *language*. The creole example sums up the creative haziness produced by the enduring diversity of English: so-called *English-based* creoles are on the edge of English, either dialect or language, and they show new diversity evolving out of existing diversity.

As I said earlier, this introductory device in Chapter 1 of the *StEL* textbook is a print version of what I have done in the first class of the course for a while. I still do the class version, because it varies from the print version (as well as relying on it to an extent), and because the classroom offers some benefits over a print book (though not so much, potentially, over an e-book). In class one can play audio, one can withhold the series of answers to the one question "Is it English?" and allow everyone a chance to work it out themselves and to contribute their suggestions, and in the ensuing discussion one can draw from the wealth of visual and audio material that is now available electronically. These are the audio texts that I use currently, in the following order:

1. a speaker of Received Pronunciation (Susan Ramsaran), short extract from the cassette accompanying *Accents of English* (1982) by J. C. Wells—now available online;[12]
2. extract from one of the original audio recordings of my Northern Welsh-English informant;

3. extract from an unpublished recording of David Parry reading *Sir Gawain and the Green Knight*;
4. an audio sample of Western Frisian, available at the Global Recordings Network website;[13]
5. extract from a recording of a Gullah speaker from the cassette accompanying *Regionale und soziale Erscheinungsformen des britischen und amerikanischen Englisch* (1975), compiled by Wolfgang Viereck.[14]

This choice leads to the same themes and details as the print choice, but the audio and visual materials give the discussion a quite different style, and having the textbook in the background means that there can be more emphasis on exemplification in class. Since I first starting using my "is-it-English?" audio choice, the Internet has produced an abundance of resources which can be used to supplement or replace the selections above. See, for example, the British Library's online dialect and accent archive at *Sounds*;[15] or the field recordings available via the websites of the Linguistic Atlas Project of the United States and Canada. John Wells's webpage of his *Accents of English* audio also includes brief commentary on phonetic characteristics of each accent; there are more examples of Gullah online;[16] and the British Library's marvellous Evolving English Timeline includes video and text commentaries, audio, and fantastic images of manuscripts of Old and Middle English.[17]

Similarly, once one touches on the scholarly work which has investigated, collected, revealed, analysed, interpreted, and constructed the knowledge that shapes the themes and narratives of diversity and change in the English language then one can access plenty of excellent online resources. For example: the Linguistics Research Center of the University of Texas at Austin[18] includes rich information from and lessons on early Indo-European languages plus an online edition (2006) of Winfred P. Lehmann's most useful *A Reader in Nineteenth Century Historical Indo-European Linguistics* (1967), and the online reprint of Weinreich, Labov, and Herzog (1968); An Atlas of Alexander J. Ellis's (1889) *The Existing Phonology of English Dialects* (Æ) developed by Warren Maguire;[19] the Leeds Archive of Vernacular Culture (LAVC) based on the collections of the Survey of English dialects;[20] the three websites of the Linguistic Atlas Project of the United States and Canada; and, for an insight into one of the major pioneering works of linguistic geography, *DiWA*, the *Digitaler [Georg] Wenker-Atlas*.[21] The aim here is quickly to follow the information about the dialectal multiplicity and history of English with an evaluative introduction to the history of scholarly work which has produced that information, by such means as mentioning very simple but revealing details, like the development of the modern sense of the term *Old English* by the philologists A. J. Ellis and Henry Sweet in the nineteenth century, which takes us to a brief description of the differences between *comparative philology* and modern *linguistics*, which can lead to a few words on the advent of *dialectology* in the late nineteenth century, the entrance of *sociolinguistics* in the 1960s, and the arrival of *geolinguistics* in the 1970s—each of these last three approaches being stages in the investigation of diversity and change. In a wide-ranging first-year course, such prolific areas can only be touched on, again via careful selection of illustrations, but this sows the seeds for building a more thorough a cquaintance with the work in later courses of the degree programme. For example, at Swansea I teach a second-year course called *Studying Dialect*, very much an in-depth "studying-diversity-and-change" module.

More immediately, the smaller-group seminar meetings of the course provide participants with opportunities to discuss and explore the material presented in the lectures. Different teachers have their different styles for leading these meetings. Participants can be encouraged to use their mobile devices, and quick and efficient access to the Internet is, I think, a good aid to discussion and exploration. But simple old-fashioned worksheets have a place too. Participants can work singly, in pairs, or in groups, responding to questions like the following:

1. List the first five things that come into your head when you think about the history of the English language.
2. List the general time periods of the English language.
3. List three factors things that have contributed to linguistic change in the British Isles over the years.
4. List at least three words that occur in your (regional) vocabulary that you think might not be common in other dialects.
5. List some lexical items from another dialect that you are aware of but do not necessarily use in your variety of English. Is there a reason you choose not to?
6. What is your view on the meanings of these terms?—*dialect, language, accent, Standard English, Received Pronunciation.*
7. List some types of mass media output (tv, radio, online, social media) where you can find (i) Standard English and (ii) non-standard English being used.

These are some of the initial discussion points devised by my co-teachers Alexia Bowler and Ben Jones, with the odd addition from me, in response to the ground covered in the opening lecture hours of the course. The aims are to encourage further engagement and reflection, to provide more opportunity for discussion, questions, and clarification. These discussion-based classes also offer a chance to introduce more material on the history and study of social attitudes toward dialectal diversity in English, from John of Trevisa to perceptual dialectology.

Studying the English Language as a whole (course and textbook) aims to equip its participants/readers with the knowledge to embark on a voyage toward an understanding of the nature of English, how its speakers have shaped it, and how it has shaped its speakers. Its other topic areas, such as language planning, language and gender, semiotics, discourse analysis, the origins of language, and the ideas of de Saussure and Chomsky, help participants navigate through their language-saturated lives, even including dealing with the insidious effects of terms like *employability* and *the student experience* on their education. The ever-present involvement of the variability of English in the language's history is an essential theme in the project.

CHAPTER 25

Our Subject Is Each Other

Teaching HEL to ESL, EFL, and Non-Standard

English Speakers

MATTHEW SERGI

25.1. INTRODUCTION

For any course to make its students more conscious of the English language as a sub-ject of study, it must first make those students less familiar with English—to better understand those language rules that "everyone knows intuitively."[1] A student in an HEL class will excel only as far as she is able to resist mundane familiarity with "what we think we already know," enough to "think consciously about" the language itself.[2] In theory, it follows that significant advantages should be enjoyed by HEL students who enter the classroom *lacking* a native familiarity with classroom English: that is, those students whose first experience with English was as a second language (ESL) or as a foreign language (EFL) or those students who feel most comfortable with a variety of English that differs significantly from the perceived classroom stand-ard (henceforth I'll use NSHV, for "non-standard home variety"). Often deft code-switchers by necessity, those students are more likely to have spent time thinking critically, if informally so, about the social and political markers attached to differ-ent varieties and features; such markers are likely to have been crucial to their daily experience of and success at university. ESL and EFL students are also more likely than other undergraduates to have already spent years parsing and learning English by means of grammatical terms similar to those that must be drilled in HEL classes. In practice, however, the social and cultural disadvantages that challenge ESL, EFL, and NSHV students at North American universities are formidable enough that the HEL instructor cannot simply rely on the course material's inherent emphasis on diversity and defamiliarization to get a fruitful conversation started.

That conversation is especially urgent now. As Paul Stephens and Karin Fischer have observed, the enrollment of international students at North American universities has shown "record-breaking growth" in the last five years; Stephens demonstrates that universities have generally failed to provide an adequate pedagogical or social apparatus to support these students, especially in "humanities and social studies classes that often push the limits of their English-language abilities."[3] I propose that HEL, if it can effectively reframe ESL, EFL, and NSHV students as the uniquely privileged observers and essential contributors that they should be in any discussion about the English language's capacity for variation, might provide that much needed support, acting as a point of entry for those students to engage more actively in the humanities. A retooled HEL could give ESL, EFL, and NSHV students the opportunity to decode—and think critically about—the university language standards that might otherwise exclude or confuse them, including the extra-departmental training programs in basic language skills that can sometimes alienate them.[4] As for those ESL, EFL, and NSHV students who can code-switch into academic English with ease, a retooled HEL would combat the tendency of university culture to devalue or delegitimize discourses in non-standard English, inviting previously hidden or muffled voices into class discussion. Ideally, that reframing would not only shift these students' conception of their own contributions, but it could also help train other students to welcome culturally diverse perspectives in broader university discourse, a benefit that might enrich university culture well beyond the HEL classroom.

This chapter introduces a set of exercises, assignments, lecture topics, and syllabus adjustments that have helped me attune my HEL pedagogy to undergraduates' increasingly diverse prior experiences of English, prompting in-class contributions from ESL, EFL, and NSHV students. I focus on one diversity-oriented exercise in particular, a "fieldwork" assignment that has formed the keystone of all of my HEL and HEL-based courses, with a detailed description of various iterations of the exercise that I have tested at the very diverse campuses of the University of California-Berkeley and the University of Toronto.[5] Then I provide examples of curricular adjustments I have made—examples drawn, for brevity's sake, primarily from my PDE and ME units—that encourage ESL, EFL, and NSHV students to make use of the inherent advantages and valuable perspectives that they can bring to HEL. The methods I present here, while I have not been an HEL instructor for long enough to conduct any sustained study of their efficacy, do effect a visible cultural shift in my classrooms, at least by shaping the course material around the diversity of Englishes represented by the students themselves, and by celebrating instances when that diversity is made visible.[6] Rather than shining a spotlight on student diversity from above, I encourage students to speak up about and talk back to HEL through three basic objectives:

a) to establish, through strategically chosen demonstrative examples for HEL concepts (especially the concept of varieties), a multi-vocal English-language cultural background to which no one in the classroom, not even the professor, has uniformly privileged access;

b) to draw attention, humbly, to the inadequacies and contingencies of the sociolinguistic methods underlying HEL, emphasizing inconsistencies and contradictions in class readings and lectures, as points where a diverse range of student perspectives is required to critique or reshape the course to be more accurate;

c) to present the history of English as a history of conflict and power, a continual oscillation between forcible unity and resistant diversity—and thus to include students' diverse experiences of the sociopolitical dominance of English-language standards as a manifestation of, and as relevant to, that historical pattern.

Undergirding all the ideas I present here is my conviction that HEL instructors can be most effective when they yield some authority, enough to allow the increasingly varied range of native expertises held by their students to continually augment the instructor's perspective on, and mastery of, our radically variegated subject.

25.2. KEYSTONE EXERCISE: FIELDWORK ASSIGNMENT AND MINI-LECTURES

At the beginning of term, preferably attached to a pre-circulated syllabus, I assign the keystone exercise for all of my HEL and HEL-based courses:

EXERCISE I: FIELDWORK ASSIGNMENT

Any single authority's point of view (including your professor's choices for what to focus on in our class!) will inevitably distort or skew our understanding of what's really out there, forcing it into a reductive and largely inaccurate narrative structured around an arbitrary center. Thus, the only way to get the most accurate sociolinguistic picture possible of present-day English and to ensure that our data is up to date, thorough, and at least somewhat resistant to individual bias is to *multiply our central "starting points"* and *our number of authoritative perspectives*. To adequately multiply our perspectives, each of us will have to gather our own data in, become expert in, and present our findings from one present-day variety. Luckily, each of us also *exemplifies* at least one present-day variety.

To complete this assignment, *you must seek out an interview subject from among your classmates*. We will take a social "get to know you" break in the middle of our first class; after that, you'll need to form two-person partnerships (in which each partner is studying the other). In other words, our primary research subject is *each other*. You will have a much easier time with this assignment if you choose someone you do not already know—someone who is a member of a linguistic community in which you do not consider yourself a member. If your partner is willing, you may also choose to interview fellow members of your partner's linguistic community (i.e., if you wish, you can use your partner's friends or family as an alternate case study or to otherwise contextualize your findings).

Having conducted *and audio-recorded* interviews, outside class, with your subject[s], you will generate an *interlinear transcription* that presents about 250 words of your subject's speech in both PDE (Present-Day English) and IPA (International Phonetic Alphabet). After that, you must provide a *summary of the salient features* of your sample, followed by an *in-depth analysis, informed by research into similar varieties,* of *one specific feature or set of features.* Deadlines for this assignment are staggered, extending across the semester, so we will be introduced to a new set of varieties each week.

We can only approach the vast breadth of present-day Englishes through a collaborative effort. Your presentation is not only an exercise, but also a real contribution to class material! So pay close attention: *the research presented by your fellow students (about your fellow students) will be included on the final exam* for our course.

Above all, the presentation of this assignment must allow students to choose among options of what they consider their "linguistic community," giving them the freedom to identify publicly in whatever way they wish, and as creatively as they wish. I take care to explain that concepts like "present-day variety" and "linguistic community" can be interpreted in multiple ways—just as linguists interpret them—according to regional or ethnic origin, identity group, social group or situation, profession, shared expertise or interest, or channel of communication. A HEL instructor who intends to reach out to ESL, EFL, and NSHV students should never pressure students to perform any particular aspect of their identities, which might not only feel exploitative but would also only draw attention to students' diversity as the instructor perceives it. Rather, the written and oral requirements of this assignment are built to initiate conversations that encourage students to direct their partners' attention to whatever they feel to be relevant and safe.[7] The written requirements of the assignment can vary, adaptable to shifts in class sizes, scheduling, and grading support.[8]

Essential to any variation on this assignment, however, is the requirement that students share their original research with the class, and consequently that they are exposed to the original research of their fellow students. Thus, the various written components have always accompanied *student mini-lecture presentations* of original research, about five to seven minutes each. In lecture courses, two or three weeks into the semester, I set aside a small portion of every class meeting to accommodate these presentations, and thus to continually multiply the number of student voices (and varieties) that can take on a temporary role of instructor:

Starting in our third week of class, each of our course sessions will feature 3 or 4 student presentations of their *original fieldwork research*, which will likely cover material we haven't yet discussed, or, if not, will deepen and complicate the material we've already heard.[9] Mind your timing—each presentation must last no more than seven minutes, proceeding through the following steps:

1) You pre-circulate *a handout* to the class. Your handout must include an interlinear transcription, PDE and IPA, of about 250 words of your subject's spoken English (including whatever sample you play for us).
2) You play a *one-minute audio clip* of your case study speaking English, collected during an interview you will have conducted.[10] We follow along with the transcription (in PDE and IPA) on your handout.
3) You give us a *mini-lecture for 2-3 minutes*, analyzing and contextualizing one specific salient feature demonstrated in your sample. You must include any relevant information available to you about the historical contexts or sources of that feature.
4) In the time remaining, you answer your fellow scholars' questions, while making room for the next presenter to set up audio. You will be evaluated on the quality and engagement of the conversation you start, as well as on the quality of your engagement with other scholars' discussions. It is up to you to *choose an audio clip and lecture topic that will provoke an energetic discussion*.

Scheduling of student mini-lectures becomes more difficult with more students enrolled, but it is still quite manageable.[11]

The first time I assigned this exercise was at Berkeley, part of a "minority-majority" university known for the diversity of its student population; in 2015, meanwhile, over 16% of incoming first-years at the University of California were international students.[12] As a graduate student, I adapted the traditional HEL syllabus to fit the Berkeley composition workshop requirement—so that ESL, EFL, and NSHV students frustrated by language standards could hone their writing skills by historicizing and criticizing the mechanisms by which those standards are maintained.[13] By taking a fellow student as a subject of study, each participant in class could provisionally experience historical linguistics from the point of view of the subject and from that of the linguist. As subjects, students could experience just how contingent, incomplete, and sometimes troublingly biased any outsider's perspective on a variety—including those in our class readings—must be. As linguists, each student responded differently, some more creatively than others, to the challenge of identifying and observing the features that marked a fellow student's "linguistic community." That semester, I had the pleasure of reading a seasoned gamer's analysis of East Oakland hip-hop vernacular, alongside the Oaklander's critique of *World of Warcraft* slang; so too for a sorority sister and a Spanglish speaker; a first-generation Chinese-American student and a fashion designer; a leader of the campus Multicultural Center and a fraternity brother; a first-generation Indian-American student and a first-generation Filipina-American student; a Cal Bears football player and a resident of "Lothlorien Hall" (a progressive vegetarian co-op dormitory). A first-generation Polish-American student wrote about a surfer, who wrote about a raver. A student who enrolled late got paired with me, and researched, chillingly, the language patterns of UC-Berkeley graduate students.[14]

At the University of Toronto, approximately half of our students already "speak a language other than English at home," and 40% are the first in their families to attend a Canadian university.[15] In our larger courses, as oral presentations extend across the full term, each of my class lectures—which necessarily present a simplified narrative of HEL from a single perspective—is followed by students' mini-lectures, which continually unsettle that tidiness. I adjust my subsequent lectures in dialogue with those mini-lectures; the more ambitious students do well at adjusting their subsequent mini-lectures to respond to my responses. My last HEL curriculum thus included brief but thoughtful discussions of Persian English, Korean English/Konglish, Somali English, Dutch English, Afrikaans English, Greek English, Azerbaijani English, UK-Canada Naturalized English, Canadian Anglophile English, Physicist Jargon, Colloquial Debater English, Gay English, Straight Masculine English, Skater English, Californian English, Northern Ontario Summer Camp English, Poet English, Sports Journalism Jargon, and many more, each legitimizing *as a subject of study* a variety spoken by a student, or by someone close to a student.[16] Some varieties were visited twice: we compared one student-teacher's child-directed speech to another student-teacher's speech *about* children; we compared a Portuguese English variety originating in Baleal to another from São Miguel; we compared an online *League of Legends* gamer's English to that of a *World of Warcraft* gamer. In preparing my syllabus for this course, I had initially lamented my lack of room for readings on East Asian English varieties. By the end of the semester, our class had discussed Hong Kong English from four distinct and complementary perspectives—once focusing specifically on young female speakers, once on an older car mechanic (a student's father, and his code-switching when speaking to customers), once on an immigrant who had come to Toronto through Montreal, and once on a speaker who had first learned English in an Australian school.

In all the iterations of this exercise, most striking to students is the way that their data collection fails to conform to any tidy category, particularly to the standardized sets of salient features that linguists associate with recognized varieties. Students often found that their subjects had, consciously or otherwise, tried to assimilate to what they believed was proper English. Subjects who felt comfortable enough would often code-switch: I suggest to students that they meet their subjects in informal settings and ask them to retell funny stories from their childhood. Other subjects were fully naturalized: students who had learned English in Pakistan or Bermuda well into young adulthood now spoke varieties indistinguishable from classroom NAE/AmE, challenging linguists' distinctions between standards based on geographical origin.

My primary criteria for evaluation, which I explain repeatedly to the class, do not at all require the students' research to be successful. Students who do especially well on this assignment—though nearly all do impressive work, even students who underperform in other areas—are those who were able to think creatively and critically about the problems that arose in their research, presenting thoughtful analysis of what they did discover, and provoking subsequent conversation. Misalignments with what students expected, then, often produce the most interesting discussions, and the best grades. Above all, and particularly as they experience HEL from the uneasy point of view of the subject being studied, students are trained to understand the limitations that undergird HEL as a discipline: they realize that any generalized statement about English as spoken by a given group—at any moment in history—is contingent upon biased and incomplete reportage; their role as students must be, then, to think critically about, question, and supplement what they learn.

25.3. PRESENT-DAY ENGLISHES: CHALLENGING AUTHORITY, EMBRACING RAP

Like many other HEL instructors, I arrange topics in reverse-chronological order, so that students can face the most difficult OE material having garnered a semester's worth of training. PDE is our first topic, then, allowing students to practice HEL terms of art and IPA notation on examples from varieties that are relatively easy to understand, especially for ESL, EFL, and NSHV students. By the time we must move on to EMnE (Early Modern English), a quarter of the way through term, it becomes clear that three weeks are inadequate to cover the last two centuries' explosion of new varieties and features; thanks to students' ongoing in-class fieldwork presentations, woven into subsequent units, the present can continually reassert itself in relation to the past.

Reverse chronology, meanwhile, also makes it easier to read our class textbooks against the grain. Since I use Millward and Hayes's *A Biography of the English Language* for my course textbook and workbook, we thus discuss "English Around the World" (Millward-Hayes, Chapter 9) before approaching any paradigmatic "Present-Day English" readings (Millward-Hayes, Chapter 8).[17] Supplementary readings from Edgar Schneider's *English Around the World: An Introduction* and challenging articles from the journal *World Englishes*, in conjunction with the Fieldwork Assignment, have by then already destabilized the centrality and importance of any standard variety in our diverse classroom and made the limited "word-to-world fit" of standard PDE paradigms immediately apparent.[18] From there, discussion sessions transition easily into urgent critical inquiry, often student-driven: we determine that to present "global" varieties in the first place as a subject separate from "basic" PDE fundamentals is necessarily to affirm a center-and-margin model that perpetuates the postcolonial dominance of supranational acrolects. I remind students that the university classroom is, historically, a space that admits only acrolectal varieties, and suggest that it can, conversely, make a variety acrolectal by virtue of its admission. Without singling out anyone, I ask students to consider whether they have already code-switched away from their most familiar variety in order to participate in a class that ostensibly presents an objective view on global Englishes; I then ask them to think about what assumptions and pressures caused that switch.

I do not at all mean, here, to critique any particular textbook's approach—I prefer Millward-Hayes as my course textbook for many reasons, especially because of its deft, well-informed, and direct handling of politically sensitive material. Rather, my class introductions to PDE, augmented by a wide range of readings and student-generated research, make clear that *any* text offered in a university course—especially an undergraduate-oriented textbook, which must present an authoritative core curriculum as a coherent narrative—necessarily perpetuates the social dominance of certain varieties over others, even though the best textbooks' rhetoric tends toward a descriptivist ideal of objectivity and diversity. It is impossible to do otherwise; that impossibility can provide exciting opportunities for discussion. Two weeks into Toronto's HEL, after I began one class by inviting criticism of the Millward-Hayes Chapter 9's binary arrangement of global varieties into "native" and "nonnative," a student immediately countered me by energetically critiquing Schneider's attempts to present a less binary arrangement—an ostensibly even-handed approach which, as she argued, made postcolonial oppression seem less severe than it actually is.[19] Questions about co-option and cultural ownership are hot issues for twenty-first-century undergraduates; that early exchange helped to set a productively disputative tone for all subsequent discussions of readings from PDE to OE, in which students took a very active part.

Through composition-oriented syllabi at Berkeley, meanwhile, I was able to crystallize our ongoing debates into an essay assignment:

EXERCISE II: CHALLENGING THE "LANGUAGE GUIDE"

Choose any guide, handbook, or website that you have come across, in or out of class, that offers *instruction or correction on how to write, speak, or understand English*. Your assignment is to craft a *short argumentative critique* (3-5 pages) of your language guide of choice.

Aim for depth, not breadth: focus on one element of that guide in particular and suss out, using critical thinking and rigorous logic, the full implications and ramifications of that particular element of the guide.

For your subject, you can use any English-language text that presents itself as an authority on writing or speaking English. You may critique, for instance, any part of the *Oxford English Dictionary* online, any printed or online worksheet on "ESL Challenges," any class reading (including our textbook and websites that poke fun at English usage), and even Diana Hacker's *Rules for Writers* [then the Berkeley Department of English house style guide for undergraduates].[20]

That assignment also extended into optional blog posts, for extra credit, in which students could either identify and analyze everyday usage errors or critique the mechanisms by which they were identified as errors. Berkeley composition students—driven by their prior frustrations with grammar or usage instruction—produced surprisingly advanced and refreshingly energetic critical arguments. My ESL and EFL students in particular produced remarkable analyses, in essays and online, of Lynne Truss's *Eats, Shoots, and Leaves*, of the "ESL Challenges" worksheets they had been given in the past, and of offensive grammar-error parody websites like *Engrish.com*, which, as one student put it, presented "a simplicity and a rigidification of the English language" that discouraged "reading and analyzing."[21]

When HEL textbooks use PDE examples to demonstrate basic linguistic concepts, those examples—even when they simulate casually informal speech—tend to conform to NAE/AmE (North American English/American English) and BrE/RP (British English/Received Pronunciation) standards; the examples are sometimes drawn from canonical English and American works of literature. The PDE examples demonstrate basic concepts, though they range from highly formal writing to casually informal speech, tend to conform to NAE/AmE and BrE/RP standards, sometimes drawing on canonical English and American works.[22] In contrast, as we progress through the linguistic fundamentals of HEL alongside our PDE discussions, I choose diverse exempla strategically. During our first discussions of morphology and syntax, we refer to the section on Indian English (IE) at the online iteration of the *Electronic World Atlas of Varieties of English (EWAVE)*, alongside the Millward-Hayes workbook exercise on Indian English texts, revealing the practical utility of new terms like "zero article" or "copula" in attempts to isolate the elusively subtle features that make IE writing distinctive.[23] To introduce semantic change, I draw my examples from the many twentieth-century LGBTQ slang words that have recently shifted in meaning, particularly when borrowed into mainstream NAE/AmE: *closet[ed]* for generalization, *queer* for amelioration, *shade* for strengthening, and so forth.[24] Both Indian English and LGBTQ English provide examples that are generally recognizable to most of the class, but only personally familiar to a privileged few—but the privileged few shifts every time and does not align so easily with the usual proportions of privilege in the university classroom.

The primary source of demonstrative examples for my PDE classes—to which I refer throughout the semester—is hip-hop vernacular. I am, at best, a hip-hop dilettante, immediately identifiable as an outsider to most hip-hop communities. The effect is more pronounced with every passing year: I get older; most of my students remain young and far more in touch. To put hip-hop at the center of my HEL syllabus is thus to ensure that *some, if not most, of my students will always be more informed than I am.* Some students will be less informed than me: those students who have not heard of or do not often think about Drake or Nicki Minaj, however, tend to be the students most familiar with the privileged cultural canon that forms the background of most English classes.[25] NSHV students have, so far, tended to stand out as the best informed about hip-hop; ESL and EFL students, meanwhile, will quite likely have encountered global hip-hop or global media strongly influenced by hip-hop language, as one of their first and most familiar experiences of North American culture. Since my authority in speaking at all about hip-hop is so immediately suspicious, while the subject matter is so atypical for an academic setting, students often feel immediately entitled to speak up and correct me where I've gotten something wrong.[26] Rap is also decidedly an oral form, in which artists exploit the flexibility and range of English sound, offering a perfect opportunity to introduce the basics of phonology. In class, struggling with ways to represent in writing not only "what the rapper says" but the more crucial "how he says it," we turn to IPA; in order to demonstrate to my last class the IPA transcription required for the Fieldwork Assignment, for instance, I transcribed the bulk of Drake's "Used To"—a remarkably difficult task.[27] In some classes I've also discussed the limitations of graphics as records of sound by looking at controversies surrounding the transcriptions in the first edition of the *Yale Anthology of Rap*.[28]

Bringing hip-hop repeatedly into contact with HEL allows class material to resonate productively, in many ways, with what students consider to be real-world issues. Alongside computer-mediated discourse (CMD), hip-hop is generally the most productive source of linguistic innovation in the twenty-first century, but the legitimacy of language change and code-switching is continually in public contention among rappers. Unlike CMD, which tends to efface non-white, non-straight, and non-male

identity in its users, the most recent trends in hip-hop have framed identity politics as a visible and volatile point of contention.[29] Tobias Bernaisch's article in *World
Englishes* on Sri Lankan attitudes toward English varieties seems less remote, and
more useful, when considered alongside M.I.A.'s Sri Lankan activism—including her
support of the Tamil Tigers—as communicated through her distinctly British English
lyrics; the English that M.I.A. uses still registers with most Sri Lankans, according to
Bernaisch, as "educated" and "prestigious" but not "modern," "humble," or "friendly."[30]
The necessity of a post-varieties approach to HEL, already made apparent in student
presentations, is affirmed, meanwhile, by the fact that M.I.A.—easily the most globally famous Sri Lankan English speaker—raps in a variety much closer to standard
BrE than London's Dizzee Rascal, while South Africa's Die Antwoord code-switches
so drastically and quickly that a varieties-based model cannot keep up.[31]

To prepare for teaching HEL in Toronto, I hastily educated myself about Drake,
who has surely had more influence on global Englishes than any Torontonian to
date: he represents Toronto hip-hop, exerting considerable power over the way young
Torontonians speak. A master of lexicon, Drake is especially fond of neologisms, his
way of establishing "the 6ix" (his invented word for the city of Toronto) as culturally influential—and establishing himself as the steward of that influence.[32] Drake's
career thus provides a perfect practical lesson on language and power, undermining
textbook conceptions of what constitutes a prestige variety. A pluricentric model
of PDE prestige in hip-hop, especially in comparison to the various ways in which
privilege underlies the university classroom, leads to a frank in-class discussion of
the variety known as Black English (BE) or African-American Vernacular English
(AAVE).[33] Textbooks' sections on BE/AAVE tend to be their most cautious, controversial, and vulnerable to criticism; in lecture, I show that this caution resonates with
a lack of consensus among twentieth-century activists as to whether a distinctly
Black variety exists at all, depending on whether a given activist is more concerned
with equality or diversity—more evidence of the inherent bias of a varieties-based
model.[34] Here, as I acknowledge openly, necessary vulnerabilities in class readings
resonate with the inherent flaws in my own authority in the classroom: I am a white
HEL instructor who must either lecture on BE/AAVE or omit it; either choice enacts
my privilege troublingly. Humbling and unsettling as it may be for the instructor,
it is imperative to make those flaws conspicuously visible in a diverse classroom,
while yielding authority and actively facilitating a safe discussion, resisting the urge
to gloss quickly over politically sensitive material. The instructor's and textbook's
inadequacies on those topics, presented not as fact but as a subject for debate, may
provide the footholds that underrepresented students need to become authorities in
class discussion.

25.4. DIVERSE ENGLISHES BEFORE PDE

A diversity-oriented approach need not end with PDE: the present-day relevance
and relatability of historical English[es] relies on ESL, EFL, and NSHV students
being able to see their own concerns reflected in their historical predecessors. My

unit on EMnE, which I cannot describe at length here, emphasizes the role of post-colonial conflict and anti-authoritarianism in the early development of NAE/AmE, while pointing out the many "Global" varieties that were also beginning in Africa, South Asia, and the Caribbean at the same time. Via Matthew Giancarlo's "The Rise and Fall of the Great Vowel Shift," we transition from EMnE to ME; students are by now well-equipped, especially after our historicized approach to BE/AAVE paradigms, to understand Giancarlo's advanced critique of the way the very existence of the GVS fades unsettlingly in and out of linguists' view over time.[35] Meanwhile, we study the arrival of English into medieval Ireland, comparing the limited presence of English among other languages in the Pale as early as 1169 to the linguistic conquest enforced at Derry by James I's forces in 1607, suggesting that the sharpest shift from ME to EMnE occurs not in vowels but in the sudden emergence of English standardization as an instrument of colonial power.[36]

The students are thus primed to receive textbook ME paradigms, centered on Chaucer while marginalizing non-London varieties, as a somewhat misleadingly unified vision of linguistic history. For their first exposure to ME text, I hand out a randomized stack of twenty-five *different* samples. Then we step outside to conduct another exercise (if weather permits; if not, I reserve a large, flat indoor space):

EXERCISE III: MIDDLE ENGLISH DIALECTS

Once we've moved outside, I make this announcement: "Each of you has received one of twenty-five randomized samples of fifteenth-century English writing. First, find the other students who share the same sample as you, so that you form teams of two or three. For the next twenty minutes, your job is to arrange yourselves physically according to resemblance. I've circled key features on each text. Find matches, or close matches, in other teams' samples. If you share one feature with one team, but another feature with another team, then you should naturally stand between those two teams—but as far away as possible from teams with whom you share little or no resemblance. This will take a while, because each team will continually have to reposition itself as other teams adjust their position. Take your time and work together: remember that spelling is not fully standardized in ME, so try to figure out the phonology behind it!"

After ten minutes, I offer hints: "Let's clean up this picture: raise your hand if your team spells the word *should* or *shall* with the letter 'x'—it doesn't have to be every time. Make sure those groups are all standing close together. Okay: who has *should* or *shall* with a spelling that has a /s/ sound rather than a /ʃ/ sound?"

After about twenty minutes, I present new variables: "Is everyone happy with where they are standing? Will anyone who represents the word *church* as something like /kɪrk/ please raise their hand? Hands down. Now, try to find third-person plural forms of the verb "to be"—I've marked most of them. Now, if your team primarily uses words that start with /b/ for that third-person plural form, raise your hand. . . ."

After we explore the consistency of resemblances across the groups, I explain and make final adjustments: "You have just formed a rough dialect map of late medieval England. You guys, over here, are the East Midlands. This cluster is London. The range of samples across from me are the West Midlands. Over here is the North—and you, the outlier back here, are the one example I included from medieval Scotland. Central England got a little displaced this time—your group is standing in the Channel, I think—but you're all standing together, so it's close enough. . . ."

From there, we return to the lecture hall, where the *EWAVE* map has given way to samples from McIntosh's *A Linguistic Atlas of Late Mediaeval English*, which has very helpfully been uploaded to the internet by the University of Edinburgh as *eLALME*.[37] Students' first contact with ME allows them to see it as the disunified and pluricentric language that it was. Preceding the forcible uniformity (and resistances to that force) that characterized EMnE, the relative untidiness of ME looks liberating and exciting by comparison. Through continual resonance with present-day experiences, facilitated by the students' ongoing fieldwork presentations at the end of every class, I reaffirm that any centralized enforcement of language standards is a historically contingent and relatively new phenomenon in the history of the language, and that no standard is ever really enforced objectively or uniformly. I take care to repeat in lecture that the orthographic and phonetic idiosyncrasies that make standard classroom English so difficult for new speakers to master are not at all inherent to the language, nor to any consistent conception of correctness but, rather, are vestiges of power—power that is, in the present day, shifting.

25.5. CONCLUSION

Those speakers of English who regularly experience frustration with dominant language standards or whose limited facility with English-language writing can limit their attempts to communicate their ideas at university can thus understand their experience as a fundamental and normal part of HEL, from the end to the beginning. My last HEL lecture returns to lexicon and the politics of style: we compare the *average age of words* in our most difficult Academic English class reading to that of Drake's "Used To" lyrics. With reference to the differential descriptors offered by Bernaisch (outdated/modern, good English/bad English, unfriendly/friendly, etc.), the class agrees instinctively that the Drake text sounds "younger" and the Academic English "older." To everyone's surprise, we learn that Drake's words, even with his penchant for neologism, are on average *much older etymologically* than typical Academic English.[38] In the linguistic incubator of hip-hop, which in its purest form is an ephemeral medium better spoken than transcribed and which is usually more familiar to ESL, EFL, and NSHV students than any literary canon, an English-language tradition emerges that predates any of the academic readings that tend to frustrate those students.

PART SIX

Using Media and Performance in the History of English Classroom

CHAPTER 26

Approaching the History of English Through Material Culture

JONATHAN DAVIS-SECORD

Courses on the history of the English language (HEL) can easily slip into extreme abstraction. HEL courses do not primarily study language as a physical phenomenon, principally concerning themselves instead with the abstract forms of English as they morph over time. Discussions of the changes connecting one form of English to the next are then one further step abstracted from physicality, often appearing in almost mathematical expressions. I love these "language equations," which is my term for the dense linguistic descriptions often used to delineate sound changes, whether diachronic or synchronic. These equations seek to express the underlying features involved in a sound change, essentializing a myriad of individual examples into an abstract expression of constants and variables. Here is one of my favorites:

$$
\begin{array}{llll}
\text{drīf-} & \text{drāf-} & \text{drif-} & \text{drif-} \\
\text{-AXC-} & \text{-AXC-} & \text{-AXC-} & \text{-AXC-} \\
\text{-eiC-} & \text{-aiC-} & \text{-\O iC-} & \text{-\O iC-}^1
\end{array}
$$

This equation describes the ablaut series of strong class I verbs in Old English, exemplified by *drīfan* 'to drive': capital letters are mostly variables (A=Ablaut element, X=contextual element, C=consonant, Ø=null), and lowercase letters are specific components of the underlying pattern, which one might consider the constants of this particular equation. The equation illustrates that a single underlying contextual element appears throughout (/i/ in this case), with only the Ablaut element changing and subsequently affecting the surface realizations in actual, recorded language. Thus, what might be a confusing jumble of word forms in actual textual records linked by a difficult-to-identify pattern is reduced to a concise, abstract expression.

Students, however, rarely love language equations. Few students come to a HEL class with the linguistics background necessary to fully understand equations like the one earlier, especially when such equations address distant processes of a long-ago form of English. Rather, I have found that these equations alienate many students, leaving them glassy-eyed, disconnected from both the material and the class itself. Indeed, students in one of my early semesters teaching HEL were so alienated that they went beyond glassy-eyed-ness nearly to rebellion. They were so unable to comprehend abstract descriptions of the material—even much simpler equations than the previous one—that I risked losing them entirely. In order to save the semester and re-engage my students, I introduced exercises from the other end of the spectrum: material culture. If they had difficulty comprehending abstraction, I reasoned, then perhaps they would respond instead to concrete content.

Material reality in one form or another is of course never entirely absent from a HEL course. The "external history" of English figures in some way in almost every textbook, and professors are sure to assign primary readings at some point. Nonetheless, these features can feel barely more material than language equations. Cultural and political histories easily become exercises in data visualization through mapping, which risks losing the concrete through a different manner of abstraction. Primary texts in textbooks provide little visceral connection to the past with their modern punctuation, letter forms, lineations, editorial notes, and marginal glosses. Indeed, the many layers of editorial intervention can prevent students from connecting with original texts when they must dedicate much of their energy to reading notes and glosses rather than the text itself. On the other hand, original manuscripts, especially medieval manuscripts, confront students with an uncanny challenge. The visual format can be somewhat familiar—a block of text on a page of some sort—but even the appearance of that page, with its brownish color and deteriorating edges, undermines the students' assumptions of acquaintance. Closer examination provides additional alienating features, with the barely legible script making the "bizarre" characters even more derascinating than they appear in an orderly modern edition. That derascination, however, is counteracted by the inescapable physicality of the object itself, which reminds the students that actual people created and handled that item, that thing. In this way, even modern manuscripts—that is, original, handwritten copies of letters or literature in a more easily accessible form of English—can achieve a similar effect. A neatly typeset passage of *Jane Eyre* is one thing; Charlotte Brontë's original fair copy manuscript is another.[2] Thus, while a language equation certainly accurately describes a linguistic feature, a manuscript emphasizes the reality of that feature: actual people actually spoke that language. Although the language form, for medieval manuscripts at least, remains alien to most students, the context and reality of it ground the students. Manuscripts give the students something to hold onto—literally, conceptually, and metaphorically—which then helps them to process the linguistic abstractions necessary for understanding the history of English.

In two ways, then, incorporating material-based activities aligns with fundamental educational theories that call for grounding abstract concepts in physical reality. Both interacting with physical objects and also creating mental "hooks" for accruing subsequent knowledge figure prominently in important educational theory. In the early years of the twentieth century, Maria Montessori developed an educational method focused on child-directed learning and "practical play" that emphasizes both of those components.[3] Following her method, very young children in Montessori schools today still learn the first elements of math and language through manipulating physical objects, such as "golden beads" in various groupings (1, 10, 100) or sandpaper letters.[4] This practice lays foundations of material interaction which underlie the development of abstract concepts in later years. While this method is generally employed in educating the youngest students today, Montessori extended her theory through age twenty-four, supporting its application even at college age.[5] Recent theories of teaching and learning also call for similar pedagogical approaches, especially within the rubrics of "active learning" and "experiential learning," often associated with David Kolb.[6] Kolb's theory divides learning into four different types, two of which are Concrete Experience (CE) and Active Experimentation (AE), and for learners of these types actively engaging with material reality works best.[7] This theory covers learning any topic at any age and applies to college-level learners without difficulty.[8] The burgeoning study of material culture itself uses the concrete to understand the abstract without subjugating one to the other.[9] Setting students to work on (medieval) manuscripts puts a physical object at the forefront of their consciousness and necessitates an engagement with the material reality of records of old forms of English, fitting well the suggestions of educational theories and the methods of material culture studies.

Unfortunately, directly manipulating medieval manuscripts is an activity that is restricted and carefully guarded by the libraries that actually have such manuscripts, and very few do. Consequently, since I cannot give my students actual manuscripts, they must do with the next best thing: digital facsimiles. Printed facsimiles could also do the right work, but digital ones—especially online ones—have several advantages that make them preferable. Online versions are now much more accessible than printed ones ever were; while library reserves could hold one or even a few physical or disc facsimiles, every single student can access an online facsimile all at the same time, entirely removing the obstacle of limited access.[10] Moreover, accessing facsimiles on the internet makes the process both familiar yet uncannily unfamiliar for the students. Today's college students are fully at home on the internet, rendering the process of "navigating" to and accessing an online facsimile mundane. Nonetheless, online facsimiles resist and interrupt students' standard methods of reading, which have been shaped so powerfully by the multitasking, "browsing" method of textual consumption on the internet and electronic devices.[11] Almost all online facsimiles are plain images, set in sequence with sparse guiding information;[12] consequently, students must mix the familiar browsing of the internet with the linear, link-less format of the medieval book.

My favorite way of introducing medieval manuscripts mitigates the loss of actual material physicality entailed in using online facsimiles: I highlight the physicality of medieval books by describing in detail the process of creating one. Students take as given the easy availability, uniformity, and reproducibility of modern electronic and even paper books, and confronting the comparatively messy methods of creating parchment and books by hand resets their expectations. They usually find disturbing the fact that parchment—the material of the pages of medieval manuscripts—is made of animal skin, not plant matter. They usually find even more disturbing the detailed process of turning an animal into a page of a book: killing, skinning, scraping, washing, stretching, drying, shaping, and ruling.[13] Any remaining detachment from the materiality of manuscripts is generally wiped away by the facts that wet, bloody skin would make a poor writing surface and that hair or wool would further impede the writing process.

Even with these reminders of materiality, simply looking at images of a manuscript could easily slip into "looking at pretty pictures" and lose much of its impact and utility in teaching the history of English. A directed task requiring close examination of the manuscript and puzzling over its contents is necessary to maintain awareness of the material reality. For this reason, I set my students to transcribing part of a specific manuscript page in Old English—that is, the students must decipher the script of the manuscript and render it in modern letter forms but not translate or otherwise change the text. This task keeps the students focused on the text on a material level, working through the natural variation of handwritten copy, the imperfections of parchment, and other elements such as library stamps, all of which serve as reminders of the physical reality of the book, its creators, its readers, and its later owners. This assignment comes at a point in the semester before they can fully understand the content, but that is part of the point: their lack of understanding helps focus their attention on the physical page and the language's material context. Nonetheless, while the students do not need to understand Old English in order to produce a diplomatic transcription, their lack of familiarity with the script remains an obstacle. I therefore spend a portion of the class period introducing the basics of Anglo-Saxon paleography, concentrating on the "weird" letters—æsc <æ>, eth <ð>, thorn <þ>, wynn <ƿ>, and unfamiliar forms of modern letters, such as <g>, <r>, and <s>. This overview gives the students enough of a familiarity with the script that it will not fully alienate them while nonetheless remaining alien. That foreignness is again intentional: too much ease and familiarity could undermine the sense of physicality that I want the students to confront.

My standard page for this diplomatic transcription assignment is the Old English translation of the story of Abraham and Isaac in Genesis 22 as recorded beginning on folio 37v of the Illustrated Old English Hexateuch (London, British Library, MS Cotton Claudius B. iv; see Figure 26.1).[14] This choice of page serves several purposes, not the least of which is the further mitigation of the assignment's foreignness due to the general knowledge of the story and through the inclusion of an illustration filling approximately one-third of the page. Basic knowledge of the Abraham and Isaac story does not require deep familiarity with the Bible, and beginning the transcription with that knowledge gives the students another touchstone that helps ground them. Moreover, rather than overwhelm the students with a huge block of intimidating text in a difficult script, this page provides a visual break in the illustration that also subtly introduces medieval artistic styles.[15] The style of the illustration simultaneously reminds the students of the significant cultural gulf between modern and medieval, again both alienating and contextualizing the contents by taking the students out of the comfortable iconography of modern graphic style and reminding them that an individual created the illustration within a very different set of cultural and stylistic expectations. The presence of Latin in the top and bottom margins of

FIGURE 26.1. The story of Abraham and Isaac in *Genesis* 22 in *The Illustrated Old English Hexateuch* (London, British Library, MS Cotton Claudius B. iv), folio 37v

the page also prompts a discussion of the mutlilingual context of manuscript production and medieval Christian culture. While to a degree, any manuscript page of Old English could achieve the basic goals of the transcription assignment, pages like this one provide several features that make it preferable for the purposes of a HEL course interested in the variety of contexts informing early English and in the concretization of linguistic abstraction.

The activity of diplomatically transcribing a passage of Old English from an original manuscript source is certainly in and of itself a good way to promote the material reality of the history of English. The most effective pedagogy, however, builds connections between concrete assignments and other course material in a sequencing and scaffolding process—that is, following Montessori's and Kolb's suggestions that concrete interactions underlie later abstraction.[16] To this end, I view the transcription as simply the beginning of a series of assignments that progressively engage the students with historical forms of English at greater levels of abstraction. After my students complete their transcriptions and check them with me in class, I provide them with the official, correct transcription and set them to phonologically transcribing it in the International Phonetic Alphabet. This step grounds abstract pronunciation rules on the reality of the now-familiar materiality of the manuscript.

Rather than being faced with isolated Old English words chosen simply because they cover, say, the various pronunciations of <c> and <g>, the students work on material that retains a connection to the concrete record of Old English with which they have already worked. In this way, they develop their understanding of the pronunciation of Old English in a way that feels like building from the ground up rather than dropping in out of the blue. Again the Old English account of Abraham and Isaac provides good practice, as it covers nearly the entire array of thorny pronunciation questions for Old English.[17] The straightforward nature of the majority of the words allows the students to develop confidence, while the occasional challenging words retain rigor.

In the next step in this chain from concrete object to abstraction, I provide the students with a modern edition of the text and set them to translating it into Modern English. In particular, I direct the students to an online edition of the Abraham and Isaac passage rather than a printed one. As part of his Old English course at the University of Calgary, Murray McGillivray put together the online edition with each word hyperlinked to a glossary that, in one version, displays in a lower frame on the page.[18] This online version makes the Old English text as accessible as it can possibly be in ways that would be impossible or at the very least highly clunky in print. Navigating a webpage in a modern font returns the students to a familiar textual milieu, and the foreignness of the text is much less of an obstacle since they previously engaged with the text in two different ways. Moreover, parsing and defining every single word, as the online edition does, would prove most difficult in print, given the space restriction of a physical page. Such a print edition would probably have very little of the original Old English on each page, while the online edition displays a large portion of the passage without difficulty. This translation assignment then completes the connections between the exercises, and those connections are precisely the reasons that I assign this particular passage. Working with a text from its original material record through its pronunciation and translation provides a unique experience that grounds all of the levels of linguistic abstraction on a material foundation and demonstrates the interconnections of those levels. Thus, the assignment series teaches the standard abstract material of the Old English portion of a HEL course while involving a variety of cultural and linguistic contexts and emphasizing the materiality surrounding language which supports the comprehension of the abstractions.

This type of assignment remains relevant for later periods of English as well, although perhaps less necessary since later phases of the language are more accessible than Old English. I thus lead students through the same steps for Chaucer as I did for the Old English Abraham and Isaac: first examining and transcribing the beginning of Chaucer's *Knight's Tale* (from San Marino, CA, Huntington Library, MS Ellesmere 26.C.9, fol. 10r), then analyzing it phonetically, and ultimately translating it into Modern English. Discussions of William Caxton and the printing press and its linguistic and cultural effects orbit around exemplary images of early printed Bibles and Caxton's printing of *The Canterbury Tales*. Comparing the Ellesmere Chaucer to Caxton's print edition demonstrates the incremental changes in presentation—such as a decrease in colored, decorated initials—caused by the introduction of the printing press, which again grounds the students' thoughts in the material contexts of

English and its records. Keeping the pragmatic concerns of the printing press in mind, we then discuss other, substantive changes incurred by the move to print, such as replacing <þ> with <y> as in "Ye Olde Shoppe," and of course the fossilizing influence the press exerted on spelling and its unfortunate interaction with the Great Vowel Shift. I also lead the class in analyzing the title page of the first folio of Shakespeare's plays as part of teaching Early Modern English. This activity is one of the inflection points in my course, as it grounds Shakespeare, who often threatens to himself become an abstract personification of "English literature" for many students, in the material reality of his day. The analysis also displays for the students an important development in printing, since the frontis employs a font that is almost identical to modern letter forms but with important differences, such as ligatures, <vv> for <w>, and tall <s> forms. Moreover, the frontis includes an engraving, which underlines again the move from individual production of manuscripts to large-scale production of print books when compared to the illustrations from the Old English Hexateuch and the Ellesmere Chaucer.

Near the end of the semester, I continue emphasizing the material cultural contexts of English by requiring the students to produce a book description of the textbook assigned for the course. Throughout the semester, they examine exemplary moments in the history of the book, from early manuscript culture through the earliest English printed books to more mature print records. I do not present the assignments overtly as a study of the history of the book, but approaching the history of English through that paradigm—even without knowing it—prepares the students to explore the material contexts of contemporary English. The students look at their textbooks with fresh eyes, recognizing the amazing amount of meta-information they provide on their material production, such as place and date of publication, elements that they often note are absent from and contested concerning medieval manuscripts. Identifying the centralized, mass production of their textbooks also leads students to consider the centralization of authority: through the concrete things of their books they begin to recognize how control of the "rules" of language aligns with other types of control, such as monetary and political influence. Medieval scribes, at least in the early Middle Ages, felt the relative freedom to alter spelling and sometimes even wording to match their own pronunciation patterns and predilections, leading to variation between individual copies of the "same" text,[19] but modern books and the requirements of copyrighting to protect profits centrally concentrate the control over texts. In this way, directing students' attention to materiality again leads into abstraction and the examination of large systems, both linguistic and cultural. This final book description assignment thus quietly opens up students' awareness of the interconnections of language, money, power, and social status in the modern world.

To be sure, "material culture" encompasses much more than manuscripts and printed books: any concrete product of human activity that creates some type of meaning within human relationships should fall under the label. Finding material contexts for language, however, requires a much more restricted focus: the history of the language class, while not ignoring content, focuses most on linguistic systems of meaning. To study material culture, however, is generally to study different, non-linguistic systems for creating meaning.[20] Written records constitute the best intersection between the ephemera and abstraction of language and the materiality of lived experience. Retaining a focus on those records through an entire semester reminds students of the both living and historical reality of words, linguistic patterns, and even "language equations." Assignments exploring the material culture of language connect even with my nearly rebellious students who found linguistic abstraction so daunting. Ultimately those students found their way into my HEL class and into that abstraction through the assignments, and the concrete foundation created by the assignments continues to provide context in my classes.

CHAPTER 27

Teaching Original Pronunciation

DAVID CRYSTAL

27.1. INTRODUCTION

Serious interest in reconstructing the phonologies of earlier periods of literary English dates from the mid-nineteenth century, within the evolving study of comparative philology. The earliest reference I know to Shakespearean exploration is an essay by the American literary critic and lawyer Richard Grant White, whose many works on Shakespeare included two editions of the plays. He was also a music critic, and it was perhaps this joint interest which led him to pay special attention to pronunciation. In a "Memorandum on English Pronunciation in the Elizabethan Era" he analyses rhymes, puns, and spellings as evidence and anticipates the reaction of readers.[1] In Britain, at around the same time, Alexander Ellis was completing his thousand-page study, *On Early English Pronunciation* (1869–74), in which Chaucer and Shakespeare receive special attention. And soon after, in Europe, further interest was fostered by such scholars as Paul Passy, Wilhelm Viëtor, Henry Sweet, and Daniel Jones.[2]

The interest was purely scholarly. The academic tradition focused on the compilation and evaluation of the evidence, the listing of pronunciation variants, and (especially after the publication of the International Phonetic Alphabet, or IPA, in 1888) the choices now available for transcription. A great deal of teaching must have taken place through university lecture courses and in preparing readings and performances, but none of those involved give us information about how they worked in rehearsal or the problems they encountered. That there were problems is evident from the reviews of the (rare) performances in the first half of the twentieth century, both on stage and on the BBC, where critics mentioned uncertainties and inconsistencies in some actors' pronunciations, suggestive of under-rehearsal. British phonetician John Trim attended a production of *Macbeth*, starring Bernard Miles, at the Mermaid Theatre in 1952, and commented: "Miles himself was very enthusiastic and followed the reconstruction quite accurately, but I gained the impression (confirmed by the performance I attended) that others did not wish to spend time on detailed phonetic accuracy as opposed to giving a general impression."[3]

There was no further interest in stage performance in original pronunciation (OP) during the second half of the century. I put this down to several factors: the mixed critical reactions to the early experiments; the scholarly caution of the academics, who spent a great deal of time debating phonetic details but little time presenting the issues to a potentially interested general (and theatre-going) public; and, above all, to the total dominance of the classical stage by Received Pronunciation (RP). This was a period when RP was the dominant voice of British theatre, given resonant articulation by Laurence Olivier, John Gielgud, and other great Shakespearean actors. It was also the voice of the BBC, where broadcasts of Shakespeare and other early authors were always in RP. In the United States, actors struggled to acquire an RP accent for their Shakespeare performances. Putting on the plays in a regional accent was unimaginable; so a production which was perceived to be a mixture of regional accents—critics commented on the echoes of Irish, West Country, and other accents they heard in OP—was never likely to be well received.

Everything changed in 2004, when Shakespeare's Globe in London decided to mount an OP production of *Romeo and Juliet* as part of a commitment to introduce "original practices" into its reconstructed theatre. The experiment was sufficiently successful, in terms of audience reaction, to motivate the Globe to mount a second production the following year of *Troilus and Cressida*—this time with the whole run being presented in OP. American visitors to these events enthusiastically took the idea home with them, and the next decade saw several OP productions: *A Midsummer Night's Dream* (Kansas University, 2010), *Hamlet* (University of Nevada, Reno, 2011), *Cymbeline* (Portland Center Stage, Oregon, 2012), *Julius Caesar* (University of Houston, 2013), *Twelfth Night* (Classical Actors Ensemble, Minneapolis, 2014), *The Merchant of Venice* and *A Winter's Tale* (Shakespeare Factory, Baltimore, 2015–16), and *King Lear* (Indiana University, 2016). Europe saw productions of *As You Like It* (Bangor University, 2013), *Macbeth* (Shakespeare's Globe, 2014), *Henry V* (Shakespeare's Globe, 2015), and *Pericles* (Passion in Practice, Stockholm, 2015). In 2016, other writers began to receive an OP treatment, beginning with Marlowe's *Doctor Faustus* and an event based on Henslowe's Diary, both performed at the Globe. At the same time, interest was being shown in the expressive individuality of OP by other groups interested in the period, notably those involved in early vocal music, both secular and religious, as well as people working at heritage sites reconstructing life in the early seventeenth century, such as those at Stratford-upon-Avon (UK) and Plimouth Plantation (United States).

In all these cases, those involved had to be taught OP. Most had little or no general awareness of the history of English, and usually no training in phonetics. On the other hand, actors and singers have a good ear, are used to working with varying articulations, and—once they realize what is involved in OP—become hugely enthusiastic, willing to spend a great deal of time to get it right. The next section describes a teaching methodology that can be used for any OP project, based on my experience as consultant or dialect coach in almost all of the earlier mentioned productions.[4]

27.2. TEACHING OP: GENERAL CONSIDERATIONS

Although the concept of OP has an immediate intuitive appeal, it is essential to provide practitioners with some theoretical background about what they are about to learn, before going into the accent in detail. When the news breaks that there is to be an OP performance—whatever the period and genre, speech, or song—those involved will certainly be asked about it by family, friends, and colleagues, and they need to know how to respond. Two questions always arise. Everyone hears echoes of modern regional accents in OP ("We speak like that where I come from") and they want to know why. And everyone (other than historians of English) is intrigued by the process of reconstruction ("How do you know?"). I therefore always give a short introductory talk to the participants, putting OP into its historical setting, describing the evidence from rhymes, puns, spellings, and contemporary writers, and illustrating the impact of OP on performers and audience, based on the now substantial accumulation of events. The points would differ, according to the OP period being explored. For Old English, the focus would be entirely on the way missionaries first wrote English down and on the surviving dialect evidence. For Chaucer, more attention would be paid to the evidence of metre and rhyme. For Shakespeare, the writings of sixteenth- and seventeenth-century orthoepists would loom large.

The introductory talk also gives an account of what OP is, in order to dispel some of the myths and preconceptions that most practitioners will have. It is important to eliminate the idea that this is an individual accent: it is not "Shakespeare's pronunciation," about which we know nothing. Nor is OP a single accent, any more than present-day English is a single accent. Shakespearean OP is, technically, the phonological system of Early Modern English (as manifested around the year 1600). It is a phonology—the reconstruction of a sound system—and there is thus as much phonetic variability in the realisation of the abstract units (phonemes) as there would be in any modern accent. I like to point out the accent variations that would have been heard on the Globe stage in the early 1600s, given that we know a little about the regional backgrounds of several of the actors—such as Robert Armin from Norfolk, John Heminges from Worcestershire—and stress that present-day actors are no different, and need not be concerned about losing their accent identity. In the 2004 *Romeo*, for example, there was a Scots-tinged Juliet, a Cockney-tinged Nurse, an RP-tinged Romeo, and a Northern Irish-tinged Peter. In the U.S. productions of *A Midsummer Night's Dream* and *Hamlet* the OP was heard filtered through a range of American accents. Regional differences in intonation accounted for some of the effects, but vowels were affected too, with slight variations in tongue position causing slight variations of vowel quality that can signal regional or personal differences. Putting this in traditional linguistic terms: there can be several phonetic realizations of a vowel phoneme while preserving the status of that vowel within the sound system as a whole. With or without the terminology, the point needs to be appreciated that OP would have contained as much variation as any modern system.

In some ways, an introduction to OP is an introduction to basic linguistics. Not only do we need to draw attention to the existence of language variation, we also need to point out the nature of language change. With Shakespeare, writing over a period of twenty or so years, at a time when there was rapid linguistic change taking place in England, the co-existence of different pronunciation preferences needs to be recognized and taken into account in any production—just as it would today. I always remind people of the many variations in pronunciation that characterize present-day English as a result of language change and social variation (*schedule* vs. *skedule*, *often* pronounced with or without the /t/, *research* vs. *research*, etc.). There would have been many more in Early Modern English, which lacked the standardizing influence of dictionaries, and where there was no prestige accent, as in present-day RP. Shakespeare himself (in *Romeo and Juliet*) has a character referring to "the new tuners of accent" in society, and accent variation is mentioned several times in the plays. It was possible to rise to the top of the kingdom with a strong regional accent, as the Devonshire speech of Raleigh and Drake illustrate. And after 1603, when James I came to the throne, many in the court spoke with Scottish accents. British people without a knowledge of the history of English are usually surprised that there was ever a time when there was no RP, but that accent didn't evolve until the end of the eighteenth century. The actor playing the Prince in the *Romeo* company was especially confused when he discovered this: "'How can I play a Prince if I can't use a posh accent?' he asked the director, Tim Carroll. He received a one-word reply: 'Act.'"

All of this needs to be explained before beginning the training of the individual vowels, consonants, and syllabic features that make up OP. And the relevance of this for dramaturgical decisionmaking also has to be thought through; otherwise, a great deal of time will be wasted during rehearsal. For example, one of the important decisions affecting OP in performance is what to do with initial /h/ in such words as *house* and *hundred*. H-dropping has been a feature of the language since Middle English, and in Shakespeare's time it would have come and gone without notice, in much the same way as people today sometimes vary their pronunciations of *again*, *says*, and *often*. So it would be perfectly possible for an educated person to pronounce a word beginning with *h* in a stressed syllable either with or without the sound. If you were literate, and so knew that there was an *h* in the spelling, you might well pronounce it (Holofernes in *Love's Labour's Lost* certainly would), so *h*-retention would presumably have been available as a sign of an educated background, then as now. A directorial decision has thus to be made in relation to characters of different kinds. In the OP *A Midsummer Night's Dream*, for example, the decision was made to keep *h* for Theseus, Hippolyta, and the lovers, and to omit it for the mechanicals. But what do we do with the fairies? Do Oberon and Titania drop their *h*'s, as down-to-earth beings might do, or do they keep them, as might befit a well-brought-up Fairy King and Queen? And what about Puck, whose naughtiness might have a linguistic reflex in *h*-dropping? If he is an *h*-dropper, then he has an extra option, when mimicking the voices of Lysander and Demetrius in the forest, to add *h*'s as required.

Time has to be allowed early on in a production for a thorough discussion of questions of this kind, especially in cases (such as *h*) where people have been brought up to believe that a particular pronunciation is "wrong." The issues can be quite complex, as in *Henry V*, where decisions have to be made not only about educated English accents (and whether a king like Henry would have used one) but also about the regional accents of the Welsh, Scottish, and Irish captains, the accents of the French nobility speaking both English and French, and the accents of those characters who find themselves in language-learning situations (Katharine and Pistol). There are many OP variants here. The issues, moreover, go beyond plays, also affecting the voicing of poems and lyrics that are to be read aloud. Should the Sonnets be read in a colloquial or a formal style? Should *h*'s be dropped in a Dowland song? Would John Donne have dropped his *h*'s in a sermon? Directors, actors, and singers all need to "take a view," when they encounter variation, just as they do today.

It's not essential for practitioners to have the arguments at their fingertips, but their teachers should have some good examples to hand—which is partly why I compiled my *Dictionary of Original Shakespearean Pronunciation*.[5] Here is an illustration of the kind of issue we encounter in individual words. In *A Midsummer Night's Dream* we find that *gone* rhymes with *alone, anon, moan, none, on, Oberon*, and *upon*. We can divide these into three types. The rhymes with *on* and *upon*, which have always had short vowels in the history of English, along with *Oberon*, indicate the pronunciation that we still have today. The rhymes with *alone* and *moan* clearly indicate a long vowel. The rhymes with *anon* and *none* provide ambiguous evidence, as those words also had variant forms. This means that in any dictionary of Shakespearean pronunciation, both /gɒn/ and /goːn/ need to be represented. It also means that a choice is available when we encounter this word in a non-rhyming context. When Lucrece says, "O that is gone for which I sought to live" (line 1051), there is no way of knowing whether Elizabethans would have read this as /gɒn/ or /goːn/, or whether they would even have noticed the difference. We have a similar situation today with the vowel in *says*, which can be pronounced either short as /sez/ or long as /seɪz/. People switch from one to the other without a second thought, depending on such factors as euphony, emphasis, and speed of speaking—or singing. Early Modern English phonology will have been no different.

27.3. TEACHING OP: SPECIFIC CONSIDERATIONS

It would be perfectly possible to teach someone OP on a purely imitative basis: say what I say. No analysis, no transcription. Some actors prefer to work like that, in learning a character, and if they have a good ear their OP renditions can be excellent. Hilton McRae, for example, about to perform an extract from *King Lear* for a recording, listened to me saying his lines through once in OP and then repeated them with hardly an error. After two or three goes, he was perfect. The downside is that actors who have this ability are unable to transfer their OP skill to new parts without going through the same process. They have a brilliant ear, but no sense of the phonological system, so they do not generalize their learning.

At the opposite extreme there are those—the majority, in my experience—who learn best by working through the OP system, phoneme by phoneme, and who do end up being able to generalize. For this kind of workshop, it's useful to provide a handout with several examples of the distinctive vowels, diphthongs, consonants, and syllables, relating these to modern English. The focus of the examples will vary somewhat according to the properties of the learners' accents. If the learners are RP-speakers, for example, they will need to focus on the importance of post-vocalic /r/ in such words as *heart* and *car*, whereas most speakers of American English will not. If they come from some of the Celtic-speaking areas of Britain, they will automatically pronounce such words as *whales* with a voiceless *wh*, which is a feature of OP; if they normally make no difference between *whales* and *Wales*, as is the case in RP, then they will have to learn to make it. A similar listing, with copious examples, can also be provided online, as in Paul Meier's OP tutorials.[6] In face-to-face settings, the evidence that the system is being internalized comes when the participants begin to "play" with the accent, using it in non-literary contexts—wishing each other *good morning* with a postvocalic /r/ or saying *good night* with a centralized /əɪ/ diphthong in *night*. Having the teacher shout out a series of words in OP and the class repeat them in unison is also a useful technique: it boosts personal confidence and also introduces an element of accommodation within a group whose home accents might be very different from each other.

In providing examples, attention needs to be paid to the frequency of the sounds in OP. As with modern English, some vowels are much more common than others. Words like *day* and *way* are much more common than words like *boy* and *oil*, for instance. It is therefore important to spend a little more time ensuring that the *day* word-set is pronounced really well, with an open /ɛː/, as it will be heard many times in a Shakespeare speech, and provides an important element in the overall impression or "colour" of the accent. Similarly, resonant open long vowels, such as the /ɑː/ of *all* or *war*, with no lip-rounding, are going to be more noticeable, simply because of their sonority, than words with close short vowels, such as *cup* and *set*, and need a special focus. Inconsistency in such prominent vowels is one of the things that listeners do notice and conveys the impression of sloppiness that John Trim, among others, commented upon.

Because Shakespearean OP is the ancestor of many modern accents, there will be similarities, which of course fuels the impression that "we speak like that where I come from." It helps to draw attention to these points, as occasion arises. If participants know Canadian English, they will notice the centralized quality of the diphthong in words like *house* /həʊs/. Those who know Australian, New Zealand, or South African English will notice the /ɪ/ quality in words like *yet*. The /ɛː/ quality of such words as *day* will ring bells with anyone who is familiar with the accents of Lancashire and Yorkshire. The /ɐːɹ/ quality in words like *mercy* will remind people of many parts of the United States and Britain ("marcy me!"). The value of these associations is that they convey to the learner that OP is a "real" accent and not simply an arcane reconstruction by academic linguists.

It's important not to spend too long on the phoneme-by-phoneme stage. Actors in particular are impatient to hear their lines spoken in OP and to interact using it. It's impossible to listen to everyone saying all their lines in a group session, of course, so some element of one-to-one tuition is essential. I do this in two stages. First, I provide everyone with an audio version of the play in OP, read in what I call a "flat" recording—saying the lines as accurately as I can, respecting the metre and the sense, but avoiding emotion or idiosyncrasy of character. This can be made scene by scene or character by character.

If such a recording is made, we need to bear in mind that the director is likely to have cut the play, for a variety of reasons, and only wants to hear the lines that remain. In the case of Tim Carroll's *Romeo and Juliet*, some 600 lines were cut. If someone wants to bring *Hamlet* in within "two hours traffic on the stage," a third of the play will have to go. However, recording only the lines required by director A presents a long-term problem. The next time the same play is produced, director B will make a raft of different decisions. To avoid repeated recordings, it's therefore wise to record the whole of a play first, later providing the director with the required selection (or allowing others to edit it). This is easy enough to do if whole scenes or speeches have to be cut. It's trickier to edit when individual lines or half-lines have gone. If there are lots of these, it's quicker to record a scene twice: one version for the director; the other for posterity!

But even this is only a partial solution, as different directors may use different textual sources. There are often significant differences between the text of a play in the First Folio and one of the routinely available modern English versions. Choices also need to be made about the individual cruxes that have exercised editors over the years—whether it is *sullied* or *solid flesh* at *Hamlet 1.2.129*, for example. Because it's impossible to deal with all options, teachers need to note the decisions they make, so that a recording can be passed on to future users with appropriate commentary. I usually write a set of notes to accompany a recording so that people can see the choices made. For example, a text might be recorded in a colloquial reading with all the initial *h*'s and the final *g*'s (in verbs like *running*) dropped and unstressed pronouns shortened (such as *my* becoming /mɪ/), reflecting Hamlet's requirement that speech should come "trippingly upon the tongue." This would not suit a director who insisted on a more formal declamation.

An open question is whether it is helpful to accompany this recording with some sort of transcription. I learned early on that few actors and directors are able to interpret a full IPA transcription, so decided on a semi-phonetic system, in which only the phonemes that have realisations which differ from modern English are shown in a phonetic script. Everything else is in modern spelling. For example, the *Romeo* line "It is my lady. O it is my love. O that she knew she were" would look like this:

it is mɪ lɛːdəɪ. oː it is mɪ lʏve. oː that shɪ knew shɪ wɛːɹe

Having made such transcriptions[7] now of several plays, I remain in two minds about their usefulness. Some actors find them very helpful; others ignore them. Certainly they are extremely time-consuming to prepare, because each symbol has to be painstakingly added. Whereas a play might be audio-recorded in a day or so, a transcription of this kind can take several weeks to complete. From a linguistic point of view the exercise is valuable, as it forces the analyst to pay attention to the tiny points of detail that might be missed in a solely auditory version. Subtle alternatives in metrical phrasing become apparent, when one has to decide whether to transcribe a word with a short or a long vowel. Previously unnoticed puns and word nuances suggest themselves as one slowly transcribes. But these are bonuses. For the most part, I suspect, the bulk of a transcription remains unread by the actors it is intended to assist. Most tell me that they listen to the flat recording while reading their script in whatever modern edition has been chosen. These days I work far more with audio recordings than with transcripts.

The recordings are always greatly appreciated. Because the audio-files are large, I usually make them available to individuals using a file-transfer medium, such as Dropbox or WeTransfer. They are always accompanied by a health warning: actors should not be slavish in following my choices. Even though I am trying my best to avoid dramatic interpretations, these can't be completely avoided. A word that I emphasize might conflict with the way an actor or director sees the line. The recording, I stress, is an aid-memoire, not a template. I wouldn't advise listening to it more than once or twice, to avoid the risk of a particular reading getting stuck in someone's mind. Repeated listening can lead to nightmares (as the actor playing Romeo found, after falling asleep with his headphones still on, and my voice ringing in his dreams).

I ask individuals to practise their parts on their own, in their own time, before arranging to hear them one by one. Making academic and theatrical schedules coincide, to allow face-to-face interaction, is often impossible—it certainly was in 2004. If there is an in-house dialect coach (as there was for *Romeo*), this takes the pressure off the linguist, assuming the coach has taken the OP thoroughly on board; but the luxury of such expertise is often absent. As a result, these days I find online interactions, using such a medium as Skype, to be the best solution. A company of a dozen or so actors can be timetabled to call in for a session of fifteen minutes or so, at times to suit both actor and linguist.

As with all line-learning, the process of acquiring OP goes through three stages. An accurate enunciation can be achieved while "on-book," but as soon as the actor goes "off-book," performance deteriorates. It then takes time to build up to the previous level of accuracy. Actors need to be warned that this will happen. But that isn't the end of the story, for when they are on stage and beginning to move around, accuracy deteriorates again, and it takes yet more time to build up to the previous norm. If there is vigorous interaction, such as a Macbeth/Macduff fight, the energy devoted to the action can be at the expense of the articulation. Perhaps nobody (except a passing linguist) would notice, at such times. But I'm always impressed by the way the actors themselves, after getting their breath back, are the first to worry about the way their accent fluency dropped.

This is the point where it is essential to emphasize the most important principle of all: the play's the thing. Macbeth and Macduff need to have a convincing fight, however they speak. And if I heard members of the audience, after an OP production, talk only about the pronunciation, then in my view the exercise has failed. Anyone leaving a Shakespeare play should be on an emotional high as a result of what they have experienced, whether it was tragedy, comedy, or history. They should be bubbling about the drama, the acting, the production generally; they should be reflecting on what the play has "said" to them. And then, almost as an afterthought, they should be recalling how the OP added a new vitality to their experience. OP is a means to an end; it should never be thought of as an end in itself. The point needs to be emphasized, over and over, in rehearsal.

The OP adds to the theatrical experience in several ways. "Trippingly upon the tongue" means that lines are spoken faster than in many a traditional production. In the 2004 Romeo, which was presented both in OP and in modern English—the only time such a parallel process has happened—the OP performances were ten minutes shorter. The effect of using OP also immediately transfers to body posture and movement. As Glynn MacDonald, the master of movement at the Globe, commented the first time she saw her *Romeo* actors in rehearsal on stage: "They're holding themselves differently; they're moving differently." It was true: the centralized vowels seem to be giving the actors a different centre of gravity. Those who try to describe the feeling talk about the sounds coming from the gut rather than the head. And there are consequences for the way they interpret their characters. The actress playing Juliet found herself able to stand up to the nurse and her parents more in OP than in RP. The actor playing Mercutio found he could say his Queen Mab speech, with its allusions to the natural insect world, much more effectively in what he called the "earthiness" of OP. We have yet to explore all the interactions between OP and these other features of a production. As of 2016, only a third of Shakespeare's plays have been performed in this medium, and hardly any of other writers. We have yet to experience how OP would affect our appreciation of a Falstaff, a Coriolanus, or an Othello, or how the actors' characterisations would be influenced by it.

The OP movement, then, notwithstanding its origins in the nineteenth century, is still in its infancy. The conclusions I have arrived at, as a result of working almost exclusively with Shakespeare, need to be tested against a much larger corpus of contemporary material. The choices I have made about individual sounds and line-readings need to be compared with the views of other linguists interested in the relationship between historical phonology and theatre. We need more teaching experiences, to complement those outlined previously. We need more OP versions, from linguists with different backgrounds, to determine the maximum degree of plausibility we can achieve in reconstructing earlier sound systems. This to me is the supreme attraction, in working on such well-known texts as Shakespeare plays. It is sometimes said, after over two centuries of studies, that there is nothing more to be learned about Shakespeare. OP shows that this is not the case: any teacher who explores an old text for the first time will find something original to say about it, whatever the period and genre.

But at least historical phonology is now centre stage—a huge change from a generation ago. When I was first learning Old English, my tutor refused point-blank to read the texts aloud, on the grounds that all reconstructions are hypothetical and the best we can do is describe them in linguistic terms. So, for example, I was told that the first vowel in *cyning* ("king") was high, front, and rounded, but because we do not know just how much height, frontness, or rounding there would have been there was no justification for trying to articulate it, so rather than be given an inaccurate rendition I was given no rendition at all. As a result, Old English remained, for me, firmly on the page. For so many children today, their first encounters with Shakespeare have also remained on the page.

OP is one way of drawing attention to the way plays can be made to come alive, and in ways that are refreshing. Although there have been many wonderful performances of plays in RP, it is a fact that the majority of audiences around the world, who do not speak RP, find this accent introduces an auditory distance between what they hear on stage and what they hear in their everyday lives. OP helps to bridge that gap. As one inner-city London teenager told me, in a strong east London accent during the *Romeo* interval at the Globe: "Normally, when we go to the theatre, they speak all posh. But this lot, they're speakin' like us." It wasn't an accurate observation, as only a few features heard in present-day East London are found in OP, but that wasn't the point. From the teenager's point of view, the OP was reaching out to him in a way that RP had never been able to do. It is an experience I have since found to be widely shared—and not least in the United States, where actors are now realizing that in order to "own" Shakespeare, they no longer need to present him in a mock-British accent but can give him full rein in an accent that is actually much closer to the way they themselves speak.

It is this greater sense of ownership of a text that OP can provide, whether the listeners have English as a first or foreign language. And for teachers of historical phonology, it can be a revelation, for they learn that not only is their subject intrinsically fascinating—something they already knew—it also turns out to be popular and useful—something they never expected. No linguist teacher could ask for more.

27.4. RESOURCES FOR TEACHING

www.originalpronunciation.com. The site that provides information about past and future OP events around the world, as well as recordings of OP practice and further background on the OP movement.

David Crystal, *The Oxford Dictionary of Original Shakespearean Pronunciation* (Oxford: Oxford University Press, 2016), with an associated website containing a complete audio file and additional pages of rhyming and other data.

David and Ben Crystal, *The Oxford Illustrated Shakespeare Dictionary* (Oxford: Oxford University Press, 2015). A dictionary aimed specifically at young people, but with a broader student appeal, that includes all the words in the twelve most studied Shakespeare plays that display some difference of meaning with present-day vocabulary, with appendices on grammar and pronunciation.

Paul Meier, *Shakespeare and Original Pronunciation*, http://paulmeier.com/shakespeare.html. A website that includes a tutorial on learning OP and links to Meier's transcription and production of *A Midsummer Night's Dream*.

John Wall, "Virtual Paul's Cross Project," *Virtual St. Paul's Cathedral Project*, http://vpcp.chass.ncsu.edu. A virtual reconstruction of St Paul's Cathedral, used as a perspective for a John Donne sermon, read in OP.

CHAPTER 28

Engaging Multimedia in the HEL Classroom

NATALIE GERBER

28.1. INTRODUCTION

As a modernist teaching the History of the English Language (HEL) at a university without a linguistics department, I have learned to be fluid and inventive in my course design. Of all my experiments with different course texts, organizations of contents, and methods, I have found that incorporating podcasts and other multimedia sources into the course materials leads not only to the greatest student engagement but also to significantly richer learning experiences. This chapter reflects upon both what these materials are and why they should be so meaningful, as well as on what I find satisfying and engaging as a scholar and teacher in transforming my teaching in this way.

28.2. TEACHING HEL TO A GENERAL AUDIENCE

Many instructors of HEL find ourselves teaching in schools without linguistics departments or even the infrastructure of related courses. We also find ourselves teaching audiences enthusiastic about our subject matter but coming to it for a variety of reasons and from a variety of contexts and with no prior knowledge of historical or structural linguistics.

My experiences teaching HEL are situated in a midsized, rural state university with a fairly homogenous student demographic (77.8% Caucasian and 68.5% of students from a 150-mile radius[1]). Over the years, I have learned that I can't presume the kind of experiential knowledge that comes from frequent exposure to speakers of other American English dialects, let alone Global Englishes or foreign languages. I also can't assume common reference points since the course typically draws students as much for its satisfaction of a common-core requirement as for its subject matter.

The course instead has to find a way to create a meaningful experience for a student body whose broad-ranging interests, reference points, and needs can be indexed by their range of majors—which I've found to number as high as seventeen among a class of twenty-five to thirty-two students. These majors also tend to be spread fairly evenly across the university's pre-professional programs (e.g., education, social work, and speech pathology), liberal arts departments (e.g., art history, English, history, international studies, philosophy, and political science), social sciences (psychology and sociology), and visual and performing arts (music performance and photography); in short, there is no core audience or even, really, sizable cohorts toward whose interests one can reliably shape the course.

28.3. ENGAGING MULTIMEDIA: WHY AND WHEREFORE

As the experienced HEL instructor knows, working with students from such a wide range of academic backgrounds can be exhilarating since their multifaceted expertise can be brought to bear upon course materials through projects and debates. But designing a course that works for this population can be both daunting and time-consuming. The trial-and-error process that ultimately led me to a substantial engagement with multimedia began with years-long experiments with different course organizations (e.g., those organized by chronology, by internal language system, or by both), different course texts (e.g., those focused on external vs. internal history or a blend of the two), different instructional methodologies (e.g., lecture-driven, discussion-based, or project-based), and different assessment instruments (e.g., exams, detailed discussion-board posts and responses, and projects).

What I discovered fairly quickly from these only partially successful trials was that teaching many of the finer points of internal language change (e.g., learning in detail the different classes of strong verbs or analyzing the syntactic patterns of Old English and Middle English) was less likely to engage a class that either did not aspire to engage with medieval literature in its original textual form and/or, due to lack of opportunity, simply could not build upon the course's knowledge base through further classes.

Instead, what has worked well for this generalist population—as well as for my own limitations as a modernist with a strong interest in linguistics but no formal training and no prior experience in Anglo-Saxon or Middle English—is a blended course design: one that introduces students to internal language systems and to the notion of external history and that then connects the highlights of major changes in internal history to highlights of major changes in external history, with special emphasis upon Global Englishes today. This method, as it were, can be boiled down to the following four points:

• minimize jargon—and thoroughly and repeatedly explain necessary terminology;

- teach the basics of each language system (i.e., phonology, morphology, lexicon, syntax, semantics, and graphics), but limit coverage of internal language changes to the highlights, using apt examples and/or resources from contemporary media and pop culture to increase engagement;
- take a problem-based approach, inviting comparative engagement with "historical" and "contemporary" language debates while maximizing the use of new media to engage students in these debates; and
- focus on the status and changing fortunes of English as a global language, drawing attention to the impact of both explicit policies toward English as an official language and implicit attitudes toward English—and toward so-called Well-Edited English—as a de facto language, whether in coordination with or at the expense of local languages.

Admittedly, this approach in and of itself contains possibly tenuous factors since the interactions of internal and external history aren't always clearly demarcated.[2] However, bringing these questions to the forefront enlivens students' engagement with the difficulties inherent in reconstructing historical linguistics; it also demonstrates to students in terms they care about profoundly—equity, social class, and the politics of language—why they should care about the history of English and the stories we tell about it and thus about its speakers, including us.

This engagement is even greater when the course meaningfully taps into podcasts and other multimedia resources that engage students with questions of language change, then and now. In the rest of this chapter I will gather some of these examples, following the organization of my own course, to suggest how one can integrate multimedia and social-media resources in a variety of ways: to reinforce individual unfamiliar concepts in phonology and morphology; to demonstrate application of historical debates to contemporary issues, and vice versa; and, generally, to broaden, deepen, and inform the course experience. These examples won't come from online materials intended for instruction (e.g., International Phonetic Alphabet, or IPA, charts or audiovisual illustrations of the Great Vowel Shift), which I hope are known to you already, but rather from general resources that I've found—or that colleagues have generously shared—to leaven and enliven HEL.

28.4. LEAVENING HEL WITH MULTIMEDIA MATERIALS

Early in the semester, using multimedia resources even anecdotally, helps students overcome the steep learning curve—that is, the disconnect between their expectations that the course will be a historical narrative, organized around dates and events, and not what the course actually is in the first six weeks: a somewhat technical introduction to phonology, morphology, lexicon, and graphics, with cursory glances at syntax and semantics.

And while students certainly come to appreciate why they need this apparatus, this appreciation comes later in the semester—when we see the payoff, for example, through cognate words or pop-culture applications of morphology (the meme of the moment—*Brexit* and its many variants—is an especially poignant example, given its relevance to this volume[3]). But early on, the incorporation of media, especially comedic social and multimedia, can go a long way to build rapport and, frankly, trust that all of these *-ologies* may prove interesting.

28.4.1. Phonology

For example, in our unit on phonology, I use a clip from the 1990s sitcom *Friends* to illustrate the often elusive concept of allophonic variation—that is, the difference between a phoneme and an allophone or non-distinctive variant. In the clip in question, Joey, an aspiring actor, is performing a scene with a Shakespearean actor, who, to Joey's dismay, is spitting all over him. Joey attempts to shield himself from the spit until the actor tells him that great actors enunciate and when they enunciate they spit.

This particular bit of enunciation centers on the pronunciation of words and syllables beginning with a /p/, as in *picture, Paulette, pack,* and *personal*: for example, "*You went through my personal property?*" and "*Why do you have a picture of Paulette in your pack?*"[4] In such environments, the /p/ phoneme is pronounced with aspiration, that is, with a puff of breath accompanying a speech sound, and represented by the following diacritical mark: a tiny h above the phonetic symbol: [pʰ]. Aspiration does not occur, however, if *p* is not word- or syllable-initial; for example, there is no aspiration in the word *script* or *speech*. In English, the distinction between [p] and [pʰ] is not meaningful—that is, there are no minimal pairs differing in just these speech sounds in the way that /f/ and /v/ contrast and so comprise a minimal pair as in *fine/ vine*. Thus, the only difference is in the phonetic rendition of the same phoneme.

The scene is, of course, hilarious, and that hilarity—even in what is now a dated sitcom—reaps benefits that the use of traditional materials—for example, using the prosody of the three witches' chant in *Macbeth* to prove that sonorants like /r/ can be syllabic[5]—cannot; most notably, students themselves often start gathering and sharing examples they find in their daily social-media diets and pop-culture experiences (e.g., the very name, Tumblr, is itself a good example of syllabic /r/).

28.4.2. Morphology

As goes phonology, so goes morphology: Few students entering the HEL classroom have heard of morphology or are aware of the complex distinctions that hold between morphemes, syllables, and words. Yet a few simple video clips can, effectively and enjoyably, preview these concepts. For example, the song "Everywhere I Go" from the former children's cable TV channel Noggin is an especially felicitous resource for teaching morphology since it playfully demonstrates both correct and incorrect usage.

Here's how it works: before I play the YouTube video of the song (the first stanza of which I've transcribed is here, though I never provide a print version in class), I instruct students to write down all the words ending in *-iest*:

Days are the sunniest
Jokes are the funniest
Rabbits are the bunny-est
Hives are the honey-est
Elephants the ton-iest
Troubles—they're the none-iest
Everywhere I go![6]

When the song ends, I then ask students to work in a small group to decide not only which words are well formed or not but also why. Without fail, students quickly— and excitedly—deduce the underlying principles for appending the two morphemes (*-y* and *-est*) in question and express them quite clearly. As a result of this "gamification" (itself a great word to break into morphemes), we make much faster—and more intuitive—progress toward understanding both the general concept of a morpheme and the distinctions between derivational morphemes, like *-y*, and inflectional morphemes, like *-est*.

Students also enjoy puzzling through why a nonce word in the song like *bunny-est* does not work whereas another word, like *sunniest*, does. The recognition they arrive at—that words can have the same spelling or orthographic form but distinctive grammatical forms and functions—often leads to interesting conversations about what underlying rules constrain the attachment of suffixes that are derivational morphemes (e.g., that *-hood* may be appended to Anglo-Saxon but not to Latinate roots: priesthood, adulthood, falsehood, statehood...). It probably depends on when the Latin word was borrowed into English, no?

A classic *Saturday Night Live* character, the Richmeister, played by Rob Schneider, further illustrates these issues as he makes up irritating nicknames for office workers in lines like "The Tomster, makin' copies! Mr. Tom! Tommy!"; "Yeah, makin' friends with the Steveinator!"; "Steve-O, leavin' the room! Walkin' away with the Sandstress!"[7] Students—drawn into the skit for its comedy and its payoff (i.e., seeing a young Mike Myers "makin' copies") simultaneously take away the underlying morphological lesson (i.e., that appending *-ster* to *Tom* is nonstandard and thus funny). The explanation (that *-ster*, which is typically used as an agentive suffix that turns a common noun, such as *gang*, into an agent, i.e., *gangster*, can't be appended to a proper noun in so-called proper or Well-Edited English) may not be as funny, but the compelling and engaging lesson that motivates students is that while word formation may be rule-governed, the lexicon is a domain of invention that can be shaped as much by popular culture and slang as by what one might envision as an eighteenth-century lexicographer.

Multimedia resources also help enliven students' engagement with the formation and/or etymological origins, histories, and shifting usages of words in our lexicon. For instance, exemplification of back formations like the verb *to burgle* from the noun *burglar* may not excite student imaginations, but discussion of a very contemporary back formation like *snark*, "the glib finding fault with others,"[8] does, especially when that sophisticated discussion regarding etymology is also peppered with recognizable examples from pop-culture usage. Thus, the 2014 Lexicon Valley episode "Where Did the Word *Snark* Come From?" traces the nominal form's origin and explosion in the early 2000s back to the earlier adjectival form *snarky*, which itself dates to the nineteenth century. In the process, the episode disambiguates other false etymologies, like a possible connection to Lewis Carroll's poem "The Hunting of the Snark" (which did give rise to a prior but unrelated nominal lexeme, 'an imaginary animal') or *Urban Dictionary*'s characterization of *snark* as a portmanteau word or blend of *snide* and *remark*. In short, the episode models an exploration of lexical provenance in a manner that makes the stories of words compelling and energizes students' engagement, whether to conduct original research with words they choose or to continue their engagement with further examples from contemporary print resources: two of my favorite sources are *The Story of English in 100 Words*[9] and *Home Ground: Language for an American Landscape*.[10]

Also, returning to the *Saturday Night Live* skit, the generativity of nonce forms and lexical memes (The Disney channel is often a great source of ephemeral blends like *Monstober*[11]) can also be a great segue to learning more about the functions, resources, and implicit or explicit politics (see the next section) of dictionaries. For example, using a dictionary to look up affixes from the Richmeister skit (like *-ator*, *-stress*, *-meister*)—and from the additional current pop-culture references the students compile—becomes a more engaging way of leading students to discover that the contents of dictionaries include morphemes and roots as well as words.

This exercise can also lead to interesting discussions about dictionaries themselves and the significant role they have played in the politics of language—from nationalist distinctions like Noah Webster's famous differentiation between American and British English forms to prescriptivist versus descriptivist approaches (see the mentions about *Lexicon Valley* later in this chapter). Of course, many traditional resources make these points brilliantly, but integrating blogs, podcasts, and web-based media alongside discussions of readings by writers like Naomi Baron, David Crystal, Seth Lerer, and others, gives students new ways of engaging with lexical debates (and some typically continue to do so long after the course ends).

28.5. TAPPING PODCASTS AND MULTIMEDIA FOR COURSE ACTIVITIES, MINI-ASSIGNMENTS, AND DEBATES

These last few examples should suggest how web-based materials and multimedia can serve in the HEL classroom as far more than stand-alone instances that introduce or illustrate a concept. They can function as central resources that engage students in small- or large-scale reflections, activities, discussions, and debates.

28.5.1. Corpora of Present-Day English

Indeed, the HEL instructor is fortunate to have access to remarkable online resources on matters of direct relevance to the history and structure of English. These include corpora like the Yale Grammatical Diversity Project, an open-access site that maps the "syntactic diversity found in varieties of English spoken in North America."[12] Directing students to explore the phenomena noted in this or other corpora[13] and then to identify and to share and analyze examples from their own speech communities can lead to rich student-led discussions about prescriptive versus descriptive grammar; these informal conversations can, in turn, feed into structured, class-wide debates regarding, for example, what criteria should distinguish a language from a dialect, perhaps with reference to the grammatical richness of African American English, which has more present-tense options than so-called standard English.

28.5.2. Lexicographical Activities and Debates

Instructors can also design activities around the meticulous use of online dictionaries, which range from traditional print-based, established institutions with an online presence, like *Merriam-Webster's* and *American Heritage Dictionary* (*AHD*), and, by subscription, *The Oxford English Dictionary* (*OED*) or *The Dictionary of American Regional English* (*DARE*), to relatively recent crowd-sourced online enterprises like *Urban Dictionary*. Since a fair number of students are not aware of any fundamental distinction in contents or methodology among such dictionaries, designing small-group or independent projects that showcase their different features and areas of authoritative influence can be quite a useful enterprise. One exercise I've designed that students particularly like uses Heather McHugh's wickedly funny poem "Etymological Dirge" to engage students in using the etymological notes in a standard dictionary entry—as well as the distinctive appendices in the *AHD*—to explore the often startling discoveries of cognates (i.e., words derived from a common root). Students first read the poem, which deliciously points out words with divergent meanings that turn out to be cognate, such as *charity* and *whore* or *fear* and *lord*, as well as words with related surface forms that may appear to be cognates but in fact aren't (see, for example, *comely* and *come*); then, the students consult the etymological notes of both the *OED* and *AHD*, as well as the *AHD*'s invaluable appendix of Indo-European roots, to determine what common root exists and what other cognates there might be. Some wonderful outcomes of this exercise are deepening interests in the sound changes (like Grimm's Law) that underlie many of these cognates, as well as a deepening appreciation for poets' imaginative fascination with words, their etymologies, and political histories.[14]

Similar short and effective exercises can be designed around the distinctive feature(s) of any number of specific dictionaries: This could be *Merriam-Webster's* authoritative coverage of the latest spellings of compound forms (as open, closed, or hyphenated, as in *healthcare* or *health-care*) or the *OED's* meticulous documentation of historical usage through dated and attributed quotations. (This component of the *OED* is invaluable for not only asserting but even dating semantic shifts, which allows students to tie changes in language to sociohistorical contexts; such exercises can be tied to sociolinguistic topics, such as gender bias in relation to language and the tendency for pejoration of terms associated with women.[15])

Still other dictionary-based exercises with the potential to grow into final projects can begin with engaging pertinent Internet texts and multimedia resources (podcasts, YouTube videos, Internet memes, etc.) and then prompting students to engage in a comparative assessment of different dictionaries. I hope a sampling of such exercises, which follow, suggests a variety of entry points for discussions of lexicography and language politics, then and now:

1. Watch the original *The Wørd* sequence on *The Colbert Report*, which featured the "new" word, *truthiness*. Look up this word in the *OED*, *AHD*, and *Urban Dictionary*, plus one other source. Copy the entries exactly as they appear, if they appear; then analyze the differences and comment on what you might conclude about how each dictionary is compiled and vetted and by whom.

2. Use the online and print holdings of the library to compare entries discussed in Allan Metcalf's article "Death of a Dictionary? Or an Abduction?" (*The Chronicle*, March 21, 2012) and in the connected Lexicon Valley podcast "Untuning the String" about the outrage caused by *Webster's* third edition.[16] Use not only the second and third editions of *Webster's* from the library's print holdings but also select at least two other dictionaries (online or print). Note differences in definition, source and kind of quotation, and usage notes. Then write a 500-word response reflecting upon how this project changes your notion of dictionaries' objectivity as well as your thoughts about dictionaries as the language police.

3. Google "Word of the Year"[17] and check out choices from at least two sites with different selections and, if you can tell, different stances toward language. Consider the relationship suggested between a language's most popular words and the external history of its speakers. How long do you think these words will last and what factors will influence their longevity?

4. Audit Erin McKean's TED Talk "Redefining the Dictionary." Then, respond to McKean's vision of future dictionaries and lexicographers. Create at least two sample entries to demonstrate your notion of the ideal form for the transmission of information about language, thinking carefully not only about standard components of a dictionary entry but also medium, sourcing, dating, etc.

None of the exercises likely need glossing, but a comparison of the entries for *truthiness*[18]—especially when paired with further readings and podcasts on the nature of the dictionary—can become the foundation for an informed discussion or debate about changing forms of information structure in relation to the future of the dictionary, as well as changing aims and goals of lexicography and its functions, and radical changes in the identity and role of the lexicographer.

28.5.3. The Rise of Standards in Early Modern English

Similar shifts, of course, underlie each arena of institutionalized language use, from grammar, spelling, pronunciation, and handwriting to public speaking and rhetorical writing styles. Yet reading about the setting of standards—the names, dates, and so on, of different dictionaries, grammars, or orators—can be tedious. Students, I've found, are far more engaged if they are invited to connect the historical dates and debates relevant to standards in the Early Modern English era with the contemporary battles they witness (and are subject to) between standards upheld by today's educational, political, and economic institutions and their own preferences for individual and sometimes nonstandard practice.

In class, I invite small groups of students to report to their peers on one specific standard—be it orthoepy, the pronunciation of words; spelling; handwriting; or punctuation and grammar.[19] To do so, the group completes a handful of jigsaw readings and then collectively summarizes these readings and expresses to their peers what the standards were, why they were put into place, and by whom or how they were enforced. The most interesting part comes next: each group looks through email, social media, contemporary blogs on language, and other sources, for examples that do and don't comply with the historical standards and reflects upon what evidence they find, if any, that the shift from institutional-driven "publishing" to individual-driven "publishing" may eventually change individual entries in the lexicon or entire rules and paradigms (e.g., past-tense verbal endings) within any of the internal language systems. (We also discuss any evident shifting practices that they might miss: for example, the increasing disappearance of the serial comma and the shifting meanings of a period, that is, an end-stopped punctuation mark, in texts and social media.[20]) In short, we have a more meaningful conversation about what the standardization of language via the rise of Chancery English and the introduction of the printing press may have meant to "literature" and writing in the fifteenth century when we also bear in mind how the proliferation of web-based and social media today may be fostering shifts in authorship and publication, given the widespread dissemination of texts without a centralized authority or publisher.

28.5.4. Further Forums and Debates

Due to space limitations, I will have to gesture toward, rather than elaborate fully upon, other possibilities for structuring vibrant and meaningful student forums and debates around thoughtful uses of multimedia. Some of these forums might profitably incorporate broad, student-led investigations of web-based forums and discussions on hot-button topics, with the acknowledgment that these partisan websites and electronic email groups may not themselves be well-informed. Indeed, trusting students to fact check and assess the quality of information weighing in on either side of controversial issues like the English-Only movement; educational language policies for English-language learners (ELL); or the costs and benefits presented by choosing to use local versus global languages in specific or generalized contexts, can be remarkable proof for the entire class of just how much they have learned about the study of language and of language use.

Let me give one example. It's often fun to teach HEL in an election year since issues of language policy inevitably surface in political debates in one way or another. In 2012, for example, the year of a U.S. presidential election, my students examined Rick Santorum's insistence that Puerto Rico's bid for statehood should be contingent upon its acceptance of English as an official language just like the rest of the United States. They then contextualized these statements (and compiled and reacted to the responses Santorum received from different partisan communities) by researching in credible, discipline-specific sources what an official language is, whether the federal government in the United States had any official language policy (it did not), and which states, if any, had such policies. The discussion forum itself was dynamic; furthermore, it fostered a sense that the study of language use—and of language policy—has real-world application and makes us better-informed and more civically engaged citizens.[21] (The exercise, of course, can be repeated in, or regarding, any number of contexts involving public policies about language: in contemporary Quebec and Montreal; in Malta [see the next section]; etc.)

In closing, let me acknowledge that one particular web-based resource keeps coming up: Slate.com's podcast Lexicon Valley.[22] This podcast, with the tagline "A Show About the Mysteries of English," deserves special mention as a go-to resource that can enrich conversations throughout the semester. Its dozens of episodes offer brilliant and concise explorations of language issues covering a broad range of topics pertinent to the internal and/or external history of the language; with each core conversation lasting about twenty to thirty minutes, the podcast lends itself beautifully to a short listening assignment that can be coupled with a print reading and/or student-led blog responses. I have profitably used Lexicon Valley podcasts to introduce, discuss, or debate language questions ranging from the technical (i.e., diachronic and synchronic changes in syntax and the etymology of individual lexical items and of idioms); the sociolinguistic (i.e., debates over what counts as a language versus a dialect; the role that "language translation [and mistranslation] plays in our lives"; and the changing function of "so" to facilitate turn-taking in discourse); the aesthetic and innovative (i.e., the invention of new languages in literature and media, as well as the creation of new graphics systems for long-established spoken languages); and the moribund (the profound, albeit often unexamined, costs that the death of a language bears for all speakers). In short, if you wish to integrate podcasts and social media but have limited time for compiling materials from across the Web and various app platforms, you could do a lot worse than to incorporate episodes from Lexicon Valley as paired listening assignments and to encourage your students to alert you to other compelling programs.

28.6. TRANSFORMING MY TEACHING VIA MULTIMEDIA AND SOCIAL MEDIA

Integrating multimedia and social media into HEL has had a profound and unexpected influence on my teaching in general. While my initial goal was, as I suggested, simply to improve my course design and to better engage my students through materials that had immediate relevance to their interests, what I discovered was that incorporating new and social media transformed students' roles in and out of class. Because I had legitimized multimodal texts and experiences, students felt encouraged to connect their experiences in class with their experiences beyond it; they became thoughtful and conscientious informants, who actively compiled examples of synchronic difference from their everyday lives and media diet and then used our course discussion boards and structured debates to engage each other directly.

These experiences have also humanized the course and humanized our experiences of each other, joint venturers in a community of learners. Through our posts sharing pertinent examples from our own lives, and through online and in-class discussions elaborating upon these examples and, especially, the contexts in which they were encountered, we learned about some of the astonishing experiences members of our community brought to our subject. One student in particular—a veteran who had returned to school on the GI Bill to pursue her bachelor's in English Adolescence Education (she is now a school library media specialist)—shared materials that gave her and us a new perspective on the immediacy and relevance of questions regarding the politics of the English language. Her posts recounted many of her experiences as a member of the U.S. military stationed on overseas bases, having to find her way around in foreign territories. She says she didn't really register at the time that the maps or street signs in different locations reflected different languages (sometimes, the local language; sometimes, English) or different alphabets (sometimes the local language had been transliterated into the Latin alphabet). During our class a "lightbulb went off" in her head and she shared this post, which connected her experiences of street signs when she was traveling around Malta (and all the signs were in English) versus a change unfolding then, with street signs and maps being converted into Maltese in order to give greater prominence to the local language:

> The Times of Malta . . . reported this past summer that the island nation had begun putting up new road signs—but only in Maltese. Malta has two official languages, English and Maltese, but Maltese is considered the "national" language. The Malta Hotels and Restaurant Association (MHRA) objected to the change. They said that tourists—their clients—were having trouble finding their way around the island; the GPS systems and the maps were all in English and were incompatible with the new signage. . . .[23]

As she further reflected to me recently, our course prompted her now to ask, "[W]as this cultural imperialism or just practicality? What did speakers of other languages think about it? In Dhahran, there was a huge population of people from the Philippines and other countries of the not-'West.' What about them? The Malta article made me think of the kind of pride a population has about their language, and that's something that we Americans don't really have a problem with. The average American doesn't know how it feels to have his or her language threatened or diminished."[24] In short, her experiences helped us appreciate the often competing cultural, geopolitical, economic, and nationalist interests that underlie decisions regarding language use (and that these uses can themselves be both fluid and at odds with each other). Even more, her presence brought home to us the immediacy of language as both a site of affiliations and as a political, and politicized, instrument, one that we must both negotiate and negotiate by means of in a welter of "contact" situations.

Of course, humanizing a course is always a noteworthy goal, but it is a particularly apposite goal for a course whose subject goes to the heart of being human: our facility for language—the very nature of the language we use and of how we use—and choose to use—it, whether in compliance with local and/or global standards or actively seeking to refashion these standards—is inextricable from the intersections of the history of its speakers as individuals and as members of multiple, intersecting communities. As the great Polish poet and Nobel Laureate Czesław Miłosz once wrote that the goal of poetry is "to humanize time,"[25] a goal of HEL ought to be to humanize language—that is, to remind us, precisely through what cannot be found in encyclopedias or historical registers (i.e., the seemingly trivial details of an everyday life that we keenly observe) of the greater civic and global lessons that animate, and impart significance to, this enterprise. Integrating social and multimedia—where ephemeral memes can signal what are potentially seismic shifts in the language—and honoring one of our students' primary modes of engaging with language and with texts enables this transformation more than any other pedagogical device I've tried.

CHAPTER 29

Teaching the History of English Online

Open Education and Student Engagement

PHILIP SEARGEANT*

29.1. INTRODUCTION: AN ALTERED EDUCATIONAL LANDSCAPE

This chapter examines the teaching of the history of English on the interstices of two contemporary issues in higher education: the use of digital communication technology as a pedagogical tool and the use of open access materials to engage broad, often non-traditional audiences. In recent years the affordances of online communications have had a significant impact on pedagogy at all levels of education, offering new opportunities for student engagement, along with shifts in traditional patterns of learning and teaching. My focus in this chapter is specifically on the use of Open Educational Resources (OERs) and on how the development and delivery of these can be used effectively in the teaching of a topic such as the history of English and what they can add to subject area or sector. OERs are defined, in the words of the William and Flora Hewlett Foundation (funders for one of the earliest initiatives in the area) as "teaching, learning, and research resources that reside in the public domain or have been released under an intellectual property license that permits their free use and re-purposing by others."[1] Digital communications technology has been a key driver in the growth of OERs, facilitating their creation and dissemination in ways that were simply not possible (at least in terms of scale and reach) a few decades ago. Martin Weller writes that the successes of OERs in the relatively short space of time in which they have been a going concern are as follows:

> they have had a positive impact for learners, they have developed sustainable models of operation, there is a thriving global community . . . and . . . a resonance with

the social function of education, all wrapped up in a modern, 21st-century, digital approach.[2]

The evidence for this success is such that, in Weller's words, an OER approach has now entered "the mainstream in education," with studies showing that, for example, 71% of undergraduates in U.S. universities used OERs in 2013, and with institutions such as the Open University in the UK making over 10,000 hours of learning resources freely available in the public domain.[3]

Among the perceived advantages of OERs is the ability to reach broad, non-traditional student audiences, as well as the enhancement of the student learning experience and the promotion of personalized learning.[4] The OER Research Hub, which has been investigating the use of OERs by educators and learners around the globe, has drawn up a list of hypotheses about the aims and impact of such resources which motivate their use. Included among these are the beliefs that OER use leads to improvement in student performance and satisfaction, that they offer more equitable access to education thereby serving a larger base of learners than traditional means of educational provision, that they can function as a bridge to formal education, and that they offer an effective way for assisting with the retention of at-risk students. Evidence from the survey has, in broad terms, supported these hypotheses.[5] Data shows, for example, that a third of informal learners see OERs as a chance to try out university-level study before committing to a course,[6] and that over 90% of informal learners are likely to continue using OERs following their initial experience.[7] Furthermore, OERs can enhance student performance by means of factors such as increased confidence, satisfaction, and interest in and enthusiasm for the subject.[8]

Within the context of the changing educational landscape that initiatives of this sort are producing, this chapter addresses issues around the teaching of the history of English via online, multimedia platforms with an open education brief. It uses as a case study the video series "The History of English in Ten Minutes"—a ten-part animation series broadcast via YouTube and iTunesU—as a means of examining how pedagogical approaches which use new media resources can actively engage large, often non-traditional student audiences with English language studies. In reviewing the design, production, and dissemination of these teaching materials and looking at the implications of their reception and uptake for contemporary pedagogical approaches to the history of English, the chapter addresses the following issues: what challenges does pedagogy aimed at open, online audiences face, and how can new media resources be drawn upon to successfully meet these challenges? What were the aims and objectives of this series, and how were these achieved? And, what are the advantages of a focus on a topic such as the history of English for addressing different audiences and enhancing the appeal of English-language studies more generally? In order to answer these questions, the chapter gives a critical overview of the production of this resource, with a particular focus on the aims, approach, and techniques that were involved, along with the reflections of key personnel involved.

29.2. AIMS AND APPROACH

"The History of English in Ten Minutes" is a ten-part animation series exploring the development of the English language and the various roles it has played in social and cultural life around the world. It is introductory in approach, aimed at people with minimal if any prior knowledge of the topic. It was created by the Open University in the UK, as part of their provision of free-access educational materials, and made available on YouTube, iTunesU, and the Open University's own OpenLearn platform.[9] The overall rationale for the project was multifaceted, but key amongst its aims was to reach out to informal and non-traditional student audiences and create a learning experience able to prompt a curiosity and interest in the subject area of English-language studies—and in particular to explain the importance of the history of English for the language's current forms and status, as well as the diverse identities it has around the globe.

As noted above, the development of communications technologies—especially online ones—for the production and dissemination of OERs has offered great opportunities to be innovative with respect to aims such as these.[10] In the increasingly cluttered environment of the internet, however, a key challenge for projects with this type of open brief is finding ways to develop materials which have both a high-level of appeal (and can thus stand out within the wider environment) as well as content which is academically rigorous and able both to educate and prompt thought and reflection (and, in this way, it is hoped inspire interest and provide a pathway into further education). A solution to this challenge was the bite-sized video format, which introduced our key learning objectives by means of entertaining and visually dynamic content; this is a format that, as the development producer of the project, Catherine Chambers, explains, "has the potential—and indeed has been proven—to engage wider audiences in discussion and debate."[11] The style of approach, coupled with identification of suitable material, was therefore central to the distinctiveness of the project, and thus it is worth dwelling a little on these two issues.

To suit the online medium, the decision was made to keep the episodes succinct—each episode is only sixty to seventy seconds long—and to make them both educational and entertaining. The decision about timing was related to evidence of how audiences engage with this type of resource: "With the average YouTube video clocking in at four minutes and users often only staying for half of that, content should 'hook' the viewer in from the beginning."[12] As the intention was to offer an introduction to the topic generally, rather than a comprehensive treatment of particular issues or phenomena, this succinct format was not an especial limitation, though it did necessitate strict decisions about what to include and exclude. To best fulfill the dual education/entertainment brief, animation was chosen as the medium. As Catherine Chambers again explains, the vision was to take "a character driven visual storytelling approach,"[13] something which was initially inspired by the hand-drawn animated lectures that the RSA (the Royal Society for the Encouragement of Arts, Manufactures and Commerce) had pioneered as an online educational format[14]

Figure 29.1. "For the first time, when people were calling you 'a pickle herring,' a 'jobbernowl,' or a 'fopdoodle'—you could understand exactly what they meant." (The Age of the Dictionary, www.youtube.com/watch?v=c7W7UgFxri8)

but which, Catherine felt, "we could take . . . a step further [by] exploring concepts through comedic animations."[15]

Given the succinct nature of the format, the series gives a whistlestop tour of the history of the English language from its first development in the fifth century to its current status as a global force. The episodes are structured around simple narratives (another key component of their format) and include both a voice-over (which is a mixture of factual information and jokes) and animation. The advantages of animation for a project like this are that it not only offers a visually engaging element to the resource, but it can also provide a parallel or contrapuntal channel for the expression of ideas (Figures 29.1 and 29.2). This allows for the inclusion, for instance, of additional examples, factual information such as dates (which would clutter up the voice-over), and graphic information such as maps (which is communicated far more easily in visuals than in words).

The history was divided into the following episodes:

1. Anglo-Saxon;
2. The Norman Conquest;
3. Shakespeare;
4. The King James Bible;
5. The English of Science;
6. English and Empire;
7. The Age of the Dictionary;
8. American English;
9. Internet English; and
10. Global English.

Figure 29.2. "In 1857 a new book was started that would become the Oxford English Dictionary." (The Age of the Dictionary, www.youtube.com/watch?v=c7W7UgFxri8)

The motivation behind this division was to organise the history around concepts, figures, or events that would have pre-existing resonance for the target audience (thus, for example, using Shakespeare as an entry point for Early Modern English), at the same time doing so in way that reflected the development of the language into its current global variety and diversity (ensuring we included references and examples to World Englishes, the impact of technology, and dynamics such as globalization). Decisions regarding this structuring were also influenced by the medium. As Catherine Chambers notes, "Titles are very important for YouTube in terms of search engine optimisation. For example, focusing on themes rather than the chronological titling of videos—e.g., the King James Bible, Internet English—is more likely to result in higher searches."[16] While medium-related considerations did not determine the structure, they did therefore play a part in its organisation, with the intention being to generate interest by building on elements of the history that already have cultural recognition value and taking advantage of the affordances of the networked media through which they were disseminated. Given the introductory level and the desire to take a narrative approach, the focus was predominantly on the external history of English (the incidents, events, and personalities which have played a part in shaping the development) but with simple textual examples (predominantly in the form of lexis) included where possible.

The process of creating the episodes involved a great deal of collaboration, comprising producers, the academic writer, the script writer, illustrator, and animator. Once the relevant content had been identified and the structure decided upon, research was accumulated around each topic. This was then shaped into a short narrative for each episode, and the script for both the voice-over and the animation (which complement and play off each other) was written, at which point it was handed over to the animation team to create. As an example of the approach, here is the voice-over script for the seventh episode of the series, "The Age of the Dictionary" (subtitled "The definition of a hopeless task").

> With English expanding in all directions, along came a new breed of men called lexicographers, who wanted to put an end to this anarchy—a word they defined as "what happens when people spell words slightly differently from each other."
>
> One of the greatest was Doctor Johnson, whose *Dictionary of the English Language* took him 9 years to write.
>
> It was 18 inches tall—and contained 42,773 entries—meaning that even if you couldn't read, it was still pretty useful if you wanted to reach a high shelf.
>
> For the first time, when people were calling you 'a pickle herring,' a 'jobbernowl,' or a 'fopdoodle'—you could understand exactly what they meant—and you'd have the consolation of knowing they were all using the standard spelling.
>
> Try as he might to stop them, words kept being invented and in 1857 a new book was started that would become the *Oxford English Dictionary*. It took another 70 years to be finished after the first editor resigned to be an Archbishop, the second died of TB and the third was so boring that half his volunteers quit and one of the ended up in an asylum.
>
> It eventually appeared in 1928 and has continued to be revised ever since— proving the whole idea you can stop people making up words is complete snuffbumble.

As can be seen, the stylistic approach is for each point related to the history to be accompanied by a joke (or for each joke also to include some factual information) so that the humorous and educational components are inextricably interwoven (I will return to the rationale for this later). The learning points here are partially straight-forward factual information: the personnel involved in the development of diction-aries of the English language, their personal circumstances, and the details of their work. In addition, though, the script includes references to a selection of fundamen-tal theoretical concepts: the continuing evolution of the language, ideas about stan-dardisation, and prescriptivist attitudes to usage. The level is, of course, quite basic, but as a teaching tool it is able to introduce a number of foundational issues (and related facts), while also providing prompts which teachers are able to build upon should they wish to incorporate it into their lessons. And all this is done within a voice-over which lasts a mere sixty-two seconds.

In reflecting on the elements that make for a success with a project such as this, Jon Hunter, who wrote the text of the scripts, distinguishes between two issues. The first is ensuring that the episodes are initially able to attract attention to themselves, given the online context in which they will be discovered. As Catherine Chambers explains, "With a proliferation of content on social media channels [in 2015 YouTube reported that 300 hours of video were being uploaded every minute[17]] it is impor-tant to be distinctive," and this can be achieved by "a combination of well scripted comedy, factual references and a named narrator [in this case the British comedian Clive Anderson] . . . as [well as] entertaining visuals."[18]

The second, related issue is ensuring that the episodes work pedagogically within the context in which they are viewed. That is, people will most likely not be encountering them within a classroom setting, where they would be expecting to engage with a certain level of concentration, attentiveness, and so on. Instead, they will be coming across them in a public forum such as YouTube, where immediacy and salience in terms of communicative message is of greater importance. In order to do this, visual and aural style is key given the wealth of other content—most of it exclusively entertainment-based—with which it will be competing. As Jon Hunter says, "[T]he key element is definitely to make something that is simultaneously entertaining and informative—without letting one side outweigh the other. The initial thought when beginning a project like this is "how can we explain this topic in a funny and memorable way?"[19]

Of particular importance for this approach is the element of humour, which greatly adds to the effectiveness of the teaching, making the subject matter, in Catherine Chambers's words, "not only accessible but also memorable, in terms of [the] retention of complex information."[20] Jon Hunter, who also writes comedy scripts for BBC Radio 4, expands on this same issue, noting that humour is:

a way in to a topic that might otherwise be a bit dry or uninteresting—it's easier to remember a joke than it is a general point. Also people like to laugh, you tend to remember those teachers that entertained you at school/university and probably felt more of an affinity to their subject than you may otherwise have done. I also think that, when you laugh at something you automatically feel more relaxed / less intimidated by it—so more ready to listen/engage.[21]

It is for the reason that each learning point in the script is couched within, or accompanied by, a joke; it reflects a deliberate approach which is pedagogically motivated, with the form tailored to the format.

29.3. RECEPTION AND IMPACT

Hunter further notes that an entertaining asset is more likely to get shared via social media, which will mean a larger reach for the series and the opportunity for more people to engage with it. The impact of what a project such as this can achieve—especially in terms of reach—can be seen from a brief overview of its reception. Within the first three years of its release, combined viewing figures for the series on YouTube and iTunesU were over five million. The way the project is licenced by the Open University allows for it to be shared and used for non-profit purposes[22]; in addition to the direct views it has had via the Open University platforms, the project has also been reproduced on numerous other sites, such as Open Culture and the British Council, where it is embedded in their own teaching resources. It is the combination of medium, format, licence, and execution which produces this level of uptake and which thus fulfils one of the primary aims of the series in terms of introducing the topic to a broad audience beyond institutional education.

From a qualitative point of view, user comments from sites that have hosted the resource indicate the types of learner engagement that it achieved. The following quotes, from comments left on the YouTube posting, are indicative of the way it has provoked interest in the general subject and prompted a critical perspective on the role of language in society—another two of the key aims for the series.

"A witty and very good history of English and England. You'll pick up more from 10 minutes here, than you did in 6 months of high school."

"Whenever somebody says 'You're not speaking proper English' as if it's an intellectual hallmark, I kindly point out that there is no such thing as 'Proper English' by modern definition. . . .Bursting with fascinating facts, the series looks at how English grew from a small tongue into a major global language before reflecting on the future of English in the 21st century."[23]

This last quote brings me to the final point I wish to address, and that is the advantages of focusing on a topic such as the history of English for engaging with broad, non-traditional audiences and enhancing the appeal of English-language studies more generally. As noted earlier, one of the main objectives of the project was to raise awareness of English-language studies, and in doing so show how the English language is more than simply a means of communication but is also bound up with people's sense of identity and community, and with issues of social and cultural politics. Another key aim has been to illustrate the diversity and variety of English within the world today, where the language is used in some form or other by up to two billion people[24] and where proprietorial and prescriptivist attitudes are challenged by its identity as a global language. By opening these ideas up to students in ways which are at once engaging, arresting, and instructional, the hope was to prompt reflection on certain received beliefs about language that are often prevalent in mainstream discourse, and through this arouse an appetite for further exploration of issues that are fundamental to everyone's lives. The underlying belief on which this is based is that English Language Studies can be particularly useful for engaging students from all educational backgrounds and all walks of life precisely because the issues it covers have a direct and immediate relevance to their lives—language is a faculty that we all share, but with which we all have our own subtly distinctive and individual experience—and thus they already have an implicit investment in them.[25] The history of English, moreover, is an excellent entry point for such study because of the way it can be used to convey theoretical or abstract ideas by means of concrete examples and incident, providing the perfect source material for a pedagogical project of this sort.

APPENDIX

Resources for Teaching

COMPILED AND ANNOTATED BY MARY HAYES AND ALLISON BURKETTE

This annotated list of general resources speaks to their utility as main adoptions in a History of the English Language course. More specific resources are discussed in individual chapters.

Bailey, Richard W. *Images of English: A Cultural History of the Language*. Ann Arbor: Cambridge: Cambridge University Press, 2009.

> Bailey's book tracks social attitudes toward the English language with particular attention to understanding the received prestige of Standard English. Organized around various types of "Englishes," its chapters locate the language in dynamic relationships with its cultural influences (e.g. "English Discerned," "Emergent English," and "English Improved"). Especially interesting are Bailey's visual artefacts—advertisements and cartoons—that suggest how these conversations unfolded over various media.

Barber, Charles, Joan C. Beal and Philip Shaw. 2nd ed. *The English Language: A Historical Introduction*. Cambridge: Cambridge University Press, 2009.

> This book provides a solid introduction to linguistic concepts, especially in its initial chapters: "What is Language" and "The Flux of Language." Its coverage of lexicon, perhaps the most accessible system of language for beginning students, is especially good. The book models for students how to learn about the language's earlier phases from written texts. But an instructor would have to supplement the book with more examples to ground a course in philology. It ends with chapters on World Englishes and "English today and tomorrow," the latter of which focuses on general linguistic trends rather than influences particular to the twenty-first century (such as social media).

Bragg, Melvyn. *The Adventure of English: The Biography of a Language*. New York: Arcade Publishing, 2003.

This book is intended for general readers rather than academic audiences. It frames the language's story, as the title suggests, as an "adventure" driven by radical and exciting changes. It expands upon the author's television ("The Adventure of English") and radio ("The Routes of English") shows. It does not offer a general systemic treatment of the language. Rather, it focuses on features of the language whose salience at a given period contributes most to the excitement of the "adventure narrative." It is definitely a substantial book, but it does not drill paradigms or provide a consistently thorough treatment of linguistic concepts. An instructor would have to supplement this book with teaching apparatus.

Brinton, Laurel J., and Leslie Arnovick. *The English Language: A Linguistic History*. 3rd rev. ed. Don Mills, ONT: Oxford University Press, 2016.

This book is best used in a HEL class focused on linguistics and spoken Englishes. The authors' tacit focus on sociolinguistics brings a newer approach to a traditional subject. Additionally, they assess the language's relationship to changing media, such as radio and computers. The attention paid to Canadian English is a nice corrective to the usual tacit focus on British or American Englishes.

Burnley, David, ed. *The History of the English Language: A Sourcebook*. 2nd ed. Harlow, UK: Routledge, 2000.

Comprised of illustrative texts, Burnley's book is frequently used as a companion to more comprehensive textbooks. It is a very good alternative to workbooks that are too expensive, too prescriptive, or too focused on "inner history" to the neglect of philological and literary questions. Burnley's introductions to these illustrative texts work well. While the book attends to linguistic items in its annotations, it does not introduce them per se. This sourcebook is comprised mostly of HEL's "greatest hits," written texts that are familiar from textbooks. Furthermore, Burnley's latest example is from D. H. Lawrence's "Fanny and Annie," and he includes no World or American Englishes.

Burridge, Kate. *Blooming English: Observations on the Roots, Cultivations, and Hybrids of the English Language*. Cambridge: Cambridge University Press, 2002.

Intended as a book for laypeople, *Blooming English* could serve as a nice companion text in a HEL class. Its focus on word play and word trivia could be used as a bridge to technical discussions of topics like derivation and inflectional morphology, grammar, and language change. At the end of the book is a chapter on names, which HEL students would likely find interesting.

Cable, Thomas, and Albert C. Baugh. *A History of the English Language*. 6th ed. Boston: Pearson, 2013.

This classic text is known for its comprehensive account of English's "outer history." It does address "inner history" too; its treatment of foreign lexical borrowing is particularly strong. Its workbook, Cable's *A Companion to Baugh and Cable's*

A History of the English Language, includes language exercises that suggest its usefulness to various types of HEL classes. The textbook is accessible for students with no linguistics training, and the workbook would allow instructors to introduce or drill linguistic skills.

Crystal, David. *The Cambridge Encyclopedia of the English Language*. 2nd ed. 10th Printing. Cambridge: Cambridge University Press, 2014.
This book covers an exhaustive number of topics at an introductory level, making it adaptable to subjects other than HEL. Because of the text's wealth of topics, an instructor would have to navigate it purposefully in his or her course to keep students focused. Commonly adopted in HEL courses, this book tacitly focuses on more recent Englishes and current conversations about the language. In addition to traditional "HEL" material (Old English, Middle English, Early Modern English, Modern English, and World English), Crystal includes units on "English Vocabulary," "English Grammar," "Spoken and Written English," "Using English," and "Learning about English."

Crystal, David. *The Story of English in 100 Words*. New York: St. Martin's Press, 2012.
Crystal's trade paperback contains a series of word vignettes that together tell a chronological story of the language from the "first word" ("roe" from the fifth century) to "twittersphere" for present day. Crystal's choices highlight important HEL principles, such as major cultural developments (the consumption/production split evidenced by the borrowing of "pork" from French), linguistic concepts (such as doublets, which is explained in the entry for "skirt"), and important sources of loanwords. This would be a great book for a word-oriented HEL course. For any HEL course, an instructor could craft various assignments from it.

Culpepper, Jonathan. *History of English*. London: Routledge, 1997.
This text is a workbook; it is intended to teach the History of English through thoughtful exercises and investigative "tasks." Additionally, there are discussion questions and research prompts found throughout. This text would make an excellent companion text to a more literature- or history-based textbook.

Curran, S. Terrie. *From Cædmon to Chaucer: The Literary Development of English*. Prospect Heights, IL: Waveland Press, 2002.
This book is meant for students with "wide backgrounds" or "little or no linguistic knowledge." Driven by literary examples, it would indeed work best in HEL courses for literature students. Each chapter concludes with pedagogical apparatus. As the title suggests, however, the text only goes up to Chaucer. Instructors might use this title as a student-friendly workbook for the earliest part of the survey.

Fennell, Barbara. *A History of English: A Sociolinguistic Approach*. Oxford: Blackwell, 2001.
Fennell's book frames the external history of English in terms of "social and political history," which sets the stage for a section at the end of each time period dedicated to a "sociolinguistic focus," which introduces terms often used in

sociolinguistic analysis (language contact, prestige variety, social stratification, language variation, creolization, urbanization, etc.) and then applies them to linguistic phenomena discussed previously in the chapter. Generally speaking, this text has a more linguistics-based approach to the History of English, though it does include numerous literary examples and short excerpts from period texts.

Fisher, John H., and Diane D. Bornstein. *In Forme of Speche Is Chaunge: Readings in the History of the English Language*. 2nd ed. Lanham, MD: University Press of America, 1984.

This classic source text is composed of familiar selections, the latest of which dates from the nineteenth century. Yet it is worth looking at for the linguistic and philological notes that precede each selection as well as the "Questions and Assignments" that culminate each unit.

Freeborn, Dennis. *From Old to Standard English: A Course Book in Language Variations Across Time*. 3rd ed. New York: Palgrave Macmillan, 2006.

This book is driven by illustrative texts that speak to the diachronic and synchronic variety of early Englishes. Freeborn's substantial pedagogical apparatus is perhaps the best of any title's. The Text Commentary Book includes thorough analyses of the featured texts, and Word Book offers etymologies and lexical histories. These are available through the publisher's website, as are audiorecordings of the illustrative texts.

Gramley, Stephan. *The History of English: An Introduction*. Abingdon: Routledge, 2012.

This text has a companion website that includes chapter resources, texts, exercises, audio resources, and a "teacher's section" that contains project suggestions, a list of teaching points, and a list of study questions for each chapter. While the first few elements listed are available to anyone, the teacher's section must be accessed with a sign-in and password, though that also is free upon request. The audio section contains sentences with keyword vowel pronunciations from nine English varieties including "Shakespearean English."

Hogg, Richard, and David Denison, eds. *A History of the English Language*. Cambridge: Cambridge University Press, 2006.

This textbook is comprised of nine chapter-length essays by outstanding scholars. Its approach is different from other texts' in that it does not organize its chapters in a chronological sequence but rather discrete diachronic studies on the language's internal and external features. It is a great resource for instructors but is meant for advanced students.

Horobin, Simon. *How English Became English: A Short History of a Global Language*. Oxford: Oxford University Press, 2016.

This brief seven-chapter book includes only one chapter on the language's conventional history per se. Its other chapters on "Authorities," "Standards," and

"Varieties" critically examine this traditional story. For that, this title could well cooperate with a traditional HEL textbook as a meta-discursive corrective.

Lass, Roger. *The Shape of English: Structure and History*. London: J.M. Dent & Sons, 1987.

Lass's work is a linguistics-heavy account of the history of English. Lass provides sketches of English's external history, focusing more on descriptions of variation and change in the language's phonology and morphosyntax. This book also contains a lengthy chapter on the dialects of English, again with an eye toward both variation and change. Included at the end of each chapter are "Notes and References," which are themselves a rich resource.

Leith, Dick. *A Social History of English*. 2nd ed. New York: Routledge, 1997.

First published in 1983, this book tells the language's story informed by sociolinguistics. Traditional historical periods are treated as discursive examples; the late Middle English and Early Modern era is covered in a chapter on "Standardisation and Writing." Especially interesting is the book's penultimate chapter, "A critical linguistic history of English texts." In this diachronic selection of illustrative texts, the author not only annotates linguistic items but also offers commentary on the texts' importance to the field, such as the interpretative problems that they present along with their valuable information. Students would thus get a sense of scholars' practices and challenges.

Lerer, Seth. *Inventing English: A Portable History of the Language*. 2nd ed. New York: Columbia University Press, 2015.

For its philological approach, this book is both traditional and unique. Telling the history of English via the relationship between the author's "individual experience and literary culture" is a wonderful device. While this is not a textbook, it could serve as a main adoption, especially in English departments. Instructors would need a companion book with exercises or some other means for practicing the philological skills that Lerer demonstrates in his discussions.

Liberman, Anatoly. *Word Origins and How We Know Them: Etymology for Everyone*. Oxford: Oxford University Press, 2005.

Liberman's book explains not only the process behind the lexicographer's science but also how new words enter into a language and change over time. The book is organized around various types of word formation with diachronic examples (imitative words, folk etymology, reduplication, compounds, infixation). Lexical items often interest students the most, so this text would serve as a helpful resource for assignments and research projects.

McIntyre, Dan. *History of English: A Resource Book for Students*. Abingdon: Routledge, 2009.

This book follows the four-unit format used in this particular Routledge series. Section A includes English's "outer history," section B its "inner history," and section D critical debates on seminal issues such as the Great Vowel Shift and prescriptivist attempts to "fix" the language. Section C, "Exploring the History of English," is interactive, consisting of examples and activities. For instance, McIntyre presents English's multilingualism through analysis of place names and then includes exercises that ask students to do the same. After presenting a concept, he includes a section of "Comments" that acknowledges its difficult points or, in the case of "language family trees," why this conventional model is imperfect. This book has an accessible tone, especially in "Section C," that would engage students well.

McWhorter, John. *Our Magnificent Bastard Tongue: The Untold History of English.* New York: Gotham Books, 2009.

McWhorter's book views English through a creolist's lens, posing questions about the origins of aspects of English grammar (such as the use of "do" for question making and progressive *-ing*) and linking them to Celtic influence. This work is a good counterpoint to traditional stories of HEL (and their lack of attention to Celtic influence).

Millward, Celia M., and Mary Hayes, *A Biography of the English Language.* 3rd ed. Boston: Cengage Learning, 2011.

This text is known for nicely harmonizing the language's outer history with its inner history and then its internal subsystems (phonology, graphics, morphology, syntax, lexicon, semantics). Like any organizational device, this text's has been criticized for being too neat. Yet it explains these conventional categories clearly for beginning students with no prior linguistics. Its focus on linguistic matters requires reinforcement through workbook exercises.

Penhallurick, Rob. *Studying the English Language.* 2nd ed. Basingstoke, UK: Palgrave Macmillan, 2010.

This book is only about 350 pages long, yet it is expansive, covering not only the history of English but also topics from sociolinguistics, semantics, pragmatics, discourse studies, "slips of the tongue," Chomsky's generativism, and the origins of language. While it might not be the text to adopt for a HEL course, its first five chapters do provide solid descriptions of English's pre-history, Old English, Middle English, American English, and World Englishes, all of which is grounded in a discussion of diversity in language.

Pyles, Thomas, John Algeo, and Carmen Butcher, *The Origins and Development of the English Language.* 7th ed. Boston: Cengage Learning, 2013.

This classic text is best used in a HEL course offered in a linguistics department, a course that presumes students' prior knowledge of linguistics. For the text's focus on linguistics, its workbook would be an essential adoption.

Shay, Scott. *The History of English: A Linguistic Introduction.* San Francisco: Wardja Press, 2008.

The author's background is in German linguistics, so it's not surprising that this concise book offers a particularly strong treatment of Indo-European and its relationship to Germanic languages, including clear explanations of how "dead languages" are reconstructed.

Singh, Ishtla. *The History of English: A Student's Guide*. London: Hodder Arnold, 2005.
Singh's purpose is to intervene on the language's conventional story at key moments to attend to "updated and/or somewhat different perspectives." After an initial chapter that introduces students to linguistic terminology, Singh offers a chronological history of the language. Singh largely explains the language's history via scholarly conversations, such as those concerning the Indo-Europeans' homeland or Middle English's status as a creole. Thus, students taking this conventional subject would feel included in lively debates rather than passive learners of received ideas.

Strang, Barbara M. H. *A History of English*. London: Methuen, 1970.
Strang's textbook is famous for moving backward chronologically through the history of English, starting with "changes within living memory" (which are now themselves rather dated). It's a solid history, but like many older textbooks, relies entirely on prose (rather than a mixture of prose and charts/tables) to explicate grammatical and phonological principles.

Van Gelderen, Elly. *A History of the English Language*. 1st ed. Amsterdam: John Benjamins, 2006.
Van Gelderen's textbook is linguistics-oriented, which is where the detail of the text lies. The technical explanations are clear, the examples are wide-ranging, and the exercises are great. The text includes some "possible answers" to selected exercises along with an appendix of additional project/paper topic suggestions.

NOTES

CHAPTER 1

1. Francis A. March, "Recollections of Language Teaching," *PMLA* 8 (1893): 1738–41, reprinted in Gerald Graff and Michael Warner, eds., *The Origins of Literary Study in America: A Documentary Anthology* (New York: Routledge, 1989), 25–27, at 27.
2. Michael Adams, "Resources: Teaching Perspectives," in *English Historical Linguistics: An International Handbook*, edited by Alexander Bergs and Laurel Brinton (Berlin: Walter de Gruyter, 2012), 2:1163–78, at 1163.
3. Haruko Momma, "Afterword: HEL for the Monolingual Frame of Mind," *Studies in Medieval and Renaissance Teaching* 14 (2007): 109–15, at 112.
4. Jo Tyler, "Transforming a Syllabus from HEL," *Pedagogy* 5:3 (2005): 464–71, notes that "for many students 'hell' could well describe the netherworld experience they might expect upon entering the course" (464). She helpfully proposes framing a HEL course for prospective literature teachers around the linguistic subcategory of "grammar," whose history can enlist students in understanding the curricular obsession with standard English.
5. To give some indication of how often HEL is required of job candidates, we gathered information from the Modern Languages Association (MLA) job lists for the years 2000–2014. Of the ninety-five job ads that indicate the new hire will teach HEL, fewer than five were aimed at procuring someone to teach History of the English Language specifically. In fact, the vast majority of the MLA ads mention teaching HEL only as a "secondary" or "preferred" area of expertise. That being said, a startlingly wide variety of advertised positions included HEL among the courses a new hire would be expected to teach, including positions whose main focus would be a specific period of English literature. However, the ability to teach HEL was included in job ads for rhetoric and composition, general linguistics, English linguistics, and applied linguistics (including TESOL [Teaching English as a Second Language]). Ads for medievalist positions were clearly the most commonly attached to the teaching of HEL, followed by general English literature, linguistics, rhetoric and composition, and applied linguistics.
6. Albert C. Baugh, "Historical Linguistics and the Teacher of English," *College English* 24, no. 2 (1962): 106–10.
7. Richard Utz, "*Quo Vadis*, English Studies?" *Philologie im Netz* 69 (2014): 93–99.
8. Michael R. Dressman, "The History of the English Language Course: A Cross-Disciplinary Approach to the Humanities," *Arts & Humanities in Higher Education* 6 (2007): 107–13.
9. Tara Williams, "The Value of the History of the English Language Course for the Twenty-First Century," *Profession* 12 (2010): 165–76, at 167.
10. Momma, "Afterword," 111.
11. Adams, "Teaching Perspectives," 2:1164.
12. Thomas Cable, "A History of the English Language," *Studies in Medieval and Renaissance Teaching* 14 (2007): 17–25, at 17.

CHAPTER 3

* I am grateful to Natalie Gerber for her immensely helpful comments and suggestions.

1. A more technical way of saying it is that the suprasegmental phonology interacts with the segmental phonology, historically as well as synchronically.

2. Helen Gardner, "Auditory Imagination," in *The Art of T. S. Eliot: A Searching Evaluation of Eliot's Masterpiece*, Four Quartets (New York: Dutton, 1950).

3. Ibid., 4.

4. J. C. Wells, *Accents of English* (3 vols., with an accompanying tape) (Cambridge: Cambridge University Press, 1982). Cambridge University Press has kept the package in print, though finding a cassette player may be a challenge. The audio cassette bought directly from Cambridge University Press is currently $49.99.

5. Kenneth Pike, *The Intonation of American English* (Ann Arbor: University of Michigan Press, 1945).

6. Among many studies published since 2010, see Ee-Ling Low, "The Acoustic Reality of the Kachruvian Circles: A Rhythmic Perspective," *World Englishes* 29 (2010): 394–405; Ee-Ling Low, "The Rhythmic Patterning of English(es): Implications for Pronunciation Teaching," in *The Handbook of English Pronunciation*, edited by Marnie Reed and John M. Levis (Malden, MA: Wiley Blackwell, 2015), 125–38; Marina Nespor, Mohinish Shukla, and Jacques Mehler, "Stress-timed *vs.* Syllable-timed Languages," in *The Blackwell Companion to Phonology*, Vol. II, *Suprasegmental and Prosodic Phonology*, edited by Marc van Oostendorp et al. (Malden, MA: Wiley-Blackwell, 2011), 1147–59, and Rachel Siew Kuang Tan and Ee-Ling Low, "Rhythmic Patterning in Malaysian and Singapore English," *Language and Speech* 57 (2014): 196–214.

7. The idea was Bridget Drinka's, and it was put into action in her HEL class at the University of Texas at San Antonio, where I gave a guest lecture and laid out the basic assumptions.

8. See Thomas Cable, *The English Alliterative Tradition* (Philadelphia: University of Pennsylvania Press, 1991); and for a survey of recent scholarship, Thomas Cable, "Ictus as Stress or Length: The Effect of Tempo," in *Old English Philology: Studies in Honour of R. D. Fulk*, edited by Leonard Neidorf, Rafael J. Pascual, and Tom Shippey (Woodbridge, Suffolk, UK: Boydell & Brewer, 2016), 34–51. See also R. D. Fulk, *A History of Old English Meter* (Philadelphia: University of Pennsylvania Press, 1992), and Seiichi Suzuki, "Metrical Positions and Their Linguistic Realisations in Old Germanic Metre: A Typological Overview," *Studia Metrica et Poetica* 1, no. 2 (2014): 9–38.

9. John Dryden, *Essays*, edited by W. P. Ker (Oxford: Clarendon, 1926), II:258–59. It is interesting that Gardner identifies Dryden as superior even to Alexander Pope in auditory imagination ("Auditory Imagination," 5). However, Dryden imagined the possibilities for the language of his own day, not that of the fourteenth century.

10. See Cable, *English Alliterative*, 66–84. See also Ad Putter, Judith Jefferson, and Myra Stokes, *Studies in the Metre of Alliterative Verse* (Oxford: Society for the Study of Medieval Languages and Literature, 2007); Nicolay Yakovlev, "The Development of Alliterative Metre from Old to Middle English," PhD diss., University of Oxford, 2008; Nicolay Yakovlev, "On Final –e in the B-Verses of *Sir Gawain and the Green Knight*," in *Approaches to the Metres of Alliterative Verse*, edited by Judith Jefferson and Ad Putter (Leeds: Leeds Texts and Monographs, 2009), 135–57; Nicolay Yakovlev, "Prosodic Restrictions on the Short Dip in Late Middle English Alliterative Verse," *Yearbook of Langland Studies* 23 (2009): 217–42; Kristin Lynn Cole, "*The Destruction of Troy's* Different Rules: The Alliterative Revival and the Alliterative Tradition," *Journal of English and Germanic Philology* 109 (2010): 162–76; Kevin Psonak, "The Long Line of the Middle English Alliterative Revival: Rhythmically Coherent, Metrically Strict, Phonologically English" (PhD diss., University of Texas at Austin, 2012); Nicholas Myklebust, "Misreading English Meter: 1400–1514" (PhD, diss., University of Texas at Austin, 2012); Eric Weiskott, "Phantom Syllables in the English Alliterative Tradition," *Modern Philology* 110 (2013): 441–58; Eric Weiskott, *English Alliterative Verse: Poetic Tradition and Literary History* (Cambridge: Cambridge University Press, 2016); Ian

Cornelius, "The Accentual Paradigm in Early English Metrics," *Journal of English and Germanic Philology* 114 (2015): 459–81; Ian Cornelius, *Reconstructing Alliterative Verse: The Pursuit of a Medieval Meter* (Cambridge: Cambridge University Press, 2017); Noriko Inoue, "The Metrical Role of *-ly* and *-liche* Adverbs and Adjectives in Middle English Alliterative Verse: The A-Verse," *Modern Philology* 114 (2017): 773–92; Noriko Inoue, "Hiatus and Elision in the Poems of the Alliterative Revival: *-ly* and *-liche* Suffixes," *Yearbook of Langland Studies* (forthcoming). For a rejection of the idea that final *-e* was a part of the language and the meter, see H. N. Duggan, "Meter, Stanza, Vocabulary, Dialect," in *A Companion to the Gawain Poet*, edited by Derek Brewer and Jonathan Gibson (Cambridge: D.S. Brewer, 1997), 221–42, and articles by Duggan cited therein.

11. See Donka Minkova, *The History of Final Vowels in English: The Sound of Muting* (Berlin: Mouton de Gruyter, 1991).
12. For a recent discussion, see John H. McWhorter, *Language Interrupted: Signs of Non-native Acquisition in Standard Language Grammars* (Oxford: Oxford University Press, 2007), 59–103.
13. Braj B. Kachru, "Standards, Codification and Sociolinguistic Realism: The English Language in the Outer Circle," in *English in the World: Teaching and Learning the Language and Literatures*, edited by R. Quirk and H. Widdowson (Cambridge: Cambridge University Press, 1985), 11–30.
14. See Low, "Acoustic Reality," 395–96.
15. Phillip M. Carter, "Quantifying Rhythmic Differences between Spanish, English, and Hispanic English," in *Theoretical and Experimental Approaches to Romance Linguistics*, edited by Randall S. Gess and Edward J. Rubin (Amsterdam: Benjamins, 2005), 63–75.
16. Ibid., 400.
17. Natalie Gerber, "Global Englishes, Rhyme, and Rap: A Meditation Upon Shifts in Rhythm," in *On Rhyme*, edited by David Caplan (Liège, Belgium: Presses Universitaires de Liège, 2017), 221–36.

CHAPTER 4

1. Frank Palmer, *Grammar* (Harmondsworth, UK: Pelican, 1971).
2. David Crystal, *Linguistics* (Harmondsworth, UK: Pelican, 1971).
3. For the record, the ones who taught these courses were Ruth Boxall and Ailsa Stewart (Old English); Alan Lennox-Short and Brian Lee (Middle English); John van der Westhuizen (History of English; Old Icelandic); and J. M. Coetzee (Linguistics and Literature).
4. Roger Lass, *Old English: A Historical Linguistic Companion* (Cambridge: Cambridge University Press, 1994).
5. Braj B. Kachru, ed., *The Other Tongue: English Across Cultures* (Oxford: Pergamon, 1983), 31–57; Manfred Görlach, *Englishes* (Amsterdam: John Benjamins, 1991); Tom McArthur, "The English Languages?," *English Today* 3, no. 3 (July 1987): 9–11; David Crystal, *The Stories of English* (New York: Overlook Press, 2004).
6. Gwyn Jones and Thomas Jones, *The Mabinogion* (London: Golden Cockerel Press, 1949).
7. Barbara Fennel, *A History of English: A Sociolinguistic Approach* (Oxford: Blackwell, 2001).
8. Jean Branford, "New Germanic for Old: Afrikaans cognates and the translation of Old English," in *Seven Studies in English*, edited by Gildas Roberts (Cape Town: Purnell, 1971).
9. Fennel, *A History of English*.
10. Ibid., 60–4.
11. Thomas Cable, *A Companion to Baugh and Cable's* History of the English Language (London: Routledge, 2002).
12. Ibid., 62–7.
13. John Algeo and Thomas Pyles, *Problems in the Origins and Development of the English Language* (New York: Harcourt, Brace & World, 1966).
14. William Caxton, *Preface to the* Eneydos (New York: Harcourt, Brace & World, 1966 [1490]).

15. Cable, *Companion*, 105–17.
16. Crystal, *The Stories of English*, 5.
17. Daniel Schreier and Marianna Hundt, eds. *English as a Contact Language* (Cambridge: Cambridge University Press, 2013).
18. Mark Sebba, *Contact Languages: Pidgins and Creoles* (London: Palgrave, 1997).
19. Loreto Todd, *Modern Englishes: Pidgins and Creoles* (Oxford: Blackwell, 1984), 261–2.
20. Ibid., 263.
21. Rajend Mesthrie and Rakesh M. Bhatt, *World Englishes: The Study of New Linguistic Varieties* (Cambridge: Cambridge University Press, 2008).
22. Braj B. Kachru, "The Sacred Cows of English," *English Today* 4, no. 4 (October 1988): 3–8.
23. Edgar W. Schneider, "The Dynamics of New Englishes: From Identity Construction to Dialect Birth," *Language* 79, no. 2 (June 2003): 233–81.
24. Mesthrie and Bhatt, *World Englishes*.
25. Sebba, *Contact Languages*.
26. Mesthrie and Bhatt, *World Englishes*.
27. John C. Wells, *Accents of English*, 3 vols. (Cambridge: Cambridge University Press, 1982).
28. Alida Chevalier, "Globalization versus Internal Development: The Reverse Short Front Vowel Shift in South African English" (PhD diss., University of Cape Town, 2016).

CHAPTER 5

1. Barry J. Zimmerman, "From Cognitive Modeling to Self-Regulation: A Social Cognitive Career Path," *Educational Psychologist* 48, no. 3 (2013): 135–47.
2. See Paul A. Schutz, "Inquiry on Teachers' Emotion," *Educational Psychologist* 49, no. 1 (2014): 1–12, and Zimmerman, "From Cognitive Modeling to Self-Regulation."
3. Anita Woolfolk, *Educational Psychology: Active Learning Edition*, 13th ed. (Boston, MA: Allyn & Bacon, 2016).
4. Deborah J. Stipek, *Motivation to Learn: Integrating Theory and Practice* (Boston: Allyn & Bacon, 2002).
5. Carole Ames, "Conceptions of Motivation Within Competitive and Noncompetitive Goal Structures," in *Self-related Cognitions in Anxiety and Motivation*, edited by Ralf Schwarzer (Hillsdale, NJ: Erlbaum Associates, 1986), 229–46; Jere E. Brophy and Kathryn R. Wentzel, *Motivating Students to Learn* (New York: Routledge, 2013).
6. See Ames, "Conceptions of Motivation," 2013, and Brophy and Wentzel, *Motivating Students to Learn*, 2013.
7. See Ames, "Conceptions of Motivation," 2013; Mihaly Csikszentmihalyi, *Society, Culture, and Person: A Systems View of Creativity* (Dordrecht: Springer Netherlands, 2014); Edward L. Deci and Richard M. Ryan, "The 'What' and 'Why' of Goal Pursuits: Human Needs and the Self-Determination of Behavior," *Psychological Inquiry* 11, no. 4 (2000): 227–68.
8. See Csikszentmihalyi, *Society, Culture, and Person*, 2014.
9. See Ames, "Conceptions of Motivation," 2013, and Brophy and Wentzel, *Motivating Students to Learn*, 2013.
10. See Ames, Conceptions of Motivation," 2013; Dale H. Schunk, Judith R. Meece, and Paul R. Pintrich, *Motivation in Education: Theory, Research, and Applications*, 4th ed. (New York: Pearson Higher Education, 2014); Bernard Weiner, "The Development of an Attribution-Based Theory of Motivation: A History of Ideas," *Educational Psychologist* 45, no. 1 (2010): 28–36.
11. Ames, Conceptions of Motivation," 2013; Schunk, Meece, and Pintrich, *Motivation in Education*, 4th ed. 2014; and Wilbert McKeachie and Marilla Svinicki, *McKeachie's Teaching Tips* (Belmont, CA: Cengage Learning, 2013).
12. McKeachie and Svinicki, *Teaching Tips*; Schunk, Meece, and Pintrich, *Motivation in Education*, 2014.
13. Ames, Conceptions of Motivation," 2013; Weiner, "The Development of an Attribution-Based Theory of Motivation," 2010; David Scott Yeager and Carol S. Dweck, "Mindsets

That Promote Resilience: When Students Believe That Personal Characteristics Can Be Developed," *Educational Psychologist* 47, no. 4 (2012): 302–14.

14. McKeachie and Svinicki, *Teaching Tips*, 2013.

15. Julie Glover, "Gallagher and English Language," *YouTube*, accessed October 16, 2016, https://www.youtube.com/watch?v=Mfz3kFNVopk.

16. Claire Ellen Weinstein, "Executive Control Processes in Learning: Why Knowing How to Learn Is Not Enough," *Journal of College Reading and Learning* 21 (1988): 48–56.

17. McKeachie and Svinicki, *Teaching Tips*, 2013.

CHAPTER 6

1. The bibliography has grown in size and quality. For recent analyses and comprehensive bibliographies, see Haruko Momma, *From Philology to English Studies: Language and Culture in the Nineteenth Century* (Cambridge: Cambridge University Press, 2012); James Turner, *Philology: The Forgotten Origins of the Modern Humanities* (Princeton: Princeton University Press, 2014); Sidney Pollock and Ku-ming Kevin Chang, eds., *World Philology* (Cambridge: Harvard University Press, 2015); and most comprehensively, Suman Gupta, *Philology and Global English Studies: Retracings* (New York: Palgrave Macmillan, 2015).

2. Said's was later than, and drawn in contrast to, de Man's. See Paul de Man, "The Return to Philology," in *The Resistance to Theory* (Minneapolis: University of Minnesota, 1986), 21–26; Edward Said, "The Return to Philology," in *Humanism and Democratic Criticism* (New York: Columbia, 2004), 57–84. Both are discussed in depth in Gupta, *Philology and Global English Studies*, 123–49, 174–201; and for critical analysis, see Geoffrey Galt Harpham, "Roots, Races, and the Return to Philology," in *The Humanities and the Dream of America* (Chicago: University of Chicago, 2011),43–79; also Frances Ferguson, "Philology, Literature, Style," *ELH* 80 (2013): 323–41.

3. In addition to Momma's *From Philology to English Studies*, see Allen Frantzen, *Desire for Origins: New Language, Old English, and Teaching the Tradition* (New Brunswick: Rutgers University Press, 1990); the standard works by Hans Aarslef, *The Study of Language in England, 1780–1860* (Princeton, 1967); Gerald Graff, *Professing Literature: An Institutional History* (Chicago: University of Chicago, 1987 [2007]); John Guillory, *Cultural Capital: The Problem of Literary Canon Formation* (Chicago: University of Chicago, 1993); the essays collected in David Shumway and Craig Dionne, eds., *Disciplining English: Alternative Histories, Critical Perspectives* (Albany: State University of New York Press, 2002).

4. In what follows I use "literary theory" and "critical theory" largely as synonyms, eliding for present purposes the differences between them in focus and history. Students and instructors wishing to learn the basics of literary-critical theory can refer to several good guides and anthologies: Peter Barry, *Beginning Theory: An Introduction to Literary and Cultural Theory* (Manchester: Manchester University Press, 2009); Jonathan Culler, *Literary Theory: A Very Short Introduction* (Oxford, 2011); Terry Eagleton, *Literary Theory: An Introduction*, 2nd ed. (Minneapolis: University of Minnesota, 1996); Frank Lentricchia and Thomas McLaughlin, eds., *Critical Terms for Literary Study*, 2nd ed. (Chicago: University of Chicago, 1995); Lois Tyson, *Critical Theory Today: A User-Friendly Guide*, 2nd ed. (New York: Routledge, 2006); Irena Makaryk, ed., *Encyclopedia of Contemporary Literary Theory: Approaches, Scholars, Terms* (Toronto: University of Toronto, 1993); Michael Groden, ed., *The Johns Hopkins Guide to Literary Theory and Criticism*, 2nd ed. (Baltimore: Johns Hopkins, 2004); and others. For critical social theory, an excellent introduction and overview is Craig Calhoun, *Critical Social Theory: Culture, History, and the Challenge of Difference* (Cambridge: Blackwell, 1995).

5. Haruko Momma and Michael Matto, eds., *A Companion to the History of the English Language* (Oxford: Wiley-Blackwell, 2011).

6. Passage from Friedrich Nietzsche, "Homer und die classische Philologie," quoted and translated by Richard Utz, "Them Philologists: Philological Practices and Their

Discontents from Nietzsche to Cerquiglini," in *The Year's Work in Medievalism* 26 (2012): 4–12, at 8.

7. See Sheldon Pollock, "Philology in Three Dimensions," *postmedieval: a journal of medieval cultural studies* 5 (2014): 398–413; also Harpham, *The Humanities and the Dream of America*. A salutary level of critical self-awareness is evident in the HEL resources by David Crystal in particular: see David Crystal, *The Stories of English* (New York: Overlook Press, 2004); and several chapters from David Crystal, *The Cambridge Encyclopedia of the English Language* (Cambridge: Cambridge University Press, 2014).

8. On Saussure and structural linguistics, and early semiotics, see Jonathan Culler, *Ferdinand de Saussure*, revised ed. (Ithaca: Cornell University Press, 1986), and *Structuralist Poetics: Structuralism, Linguistics, and the Study of Literature* (Ithaca: Cornell University Press, 1975).

9. See particularly Calhoun, *Critical Social Theory*. These foci provide a strong point of contact between literary-critical theory and sociolinguistics in particular: see, e.g., Ronald Wardhaugh and Janet Fuller, *An Introduction to Sociolinguistics*, 7th ed. (Oxford: Wiley-Blackwell, 2014).

10. In addition to the studies already cited, see Michelle Warren, "Post-Philology," in *Postcolonial Moves: Medieval Through Modern*, edited by Patricia Ingham and Michelle Warren (New York: Palgrave Macmillan, 2003), 19–45.

11. Gupta, *Philology and Global English Studies*, 202–23; Matthew Giancarlo, "The Rise and Fall of the Great Vowel Shift? The Changing Ideological Intersections of Philology, Linguistics, and Literary History," *Representations* 76 (2001): 27–60. See also the chapters on English-language modelling and learning in *Cambridge Encyclopedia of the English Language*, 2–3, 436–56.

12. In various theoretical paradigms these metaphors invite exploration as expressions of systematic "metaphorical concepts" (Lakoff), discursive "themes" (Foucault) or narrative "tropes" (White): see George Lakoff and Mark Johnson, *Metaphors We Live By* (Chicago: University of Chicago, 1980); Michel Foucault, *The Archaeology of Knowledge and the Discourse on Language*, translated by A. M. Sheridan Smith (New York: Vintage, 1972 [2010]); Hayden White, *The Content of the Form: Narrative Discourse and Historical Representation* (Baltimore: Johns Hopkins Press, 1987).

13. See, for example, Saussure's radical re-use of the "wave" metaphor, and various pictorial representations throughout: Ferdinand de Saussure, *Cours de linguistique générale*, ed. Tullio de Mauro (Paris: Payot, 1984), at 155–69.

14. Related questions about "real" language or standard language, and the representative value of English language corpora, are also relevant: see Gupta on corpus linguistics, *Philology and Global English Studies*, 150–64; and an accessible classic essay by Stanley Fish, "How Ordinary is Ordinary Language?" in *Is There a Text in This Class? The Authority of Interpretive Communities* (Cambridge: Harvard University Press, 1980), 97–111.

15. Roman Jakobson, *Language in Literature* (Cambridge: Harvard Belknap Press, 1988); Emile Benveniste, *Problems in General Linguistics*, trans. Mary Elizabeth Meek (Coral Gables: University of Miami Press, 1971); Geoffrey Leech, *A Linguistic Guide to English Poetry* (London: Longman, 1969); and others.

16. Shelly Fisher Fishkin, *Was Huck Black? Mark Twain and African-American Voices* (Oxford: Oxford University Press, 1993); chapters on Chaucer, Shakespeare, Austen, Joyce, Faulkner, Twain, and Morrison in Momma and Matto, *A Companion to the History of the English Language*.

17. Gupta, *Philology and Global English Studies*, 1–42.

18. Ibid., 39–41.

19. Pollock, "Philology in Three Dimensions," 399; Pollock and Chang, *World Philology*, 22–23.

20. Richard Utz, "Quo Vadis, English Studies?" *Philologie im Netz* 69 (2014): 93–99.

21. One example among others is Warren, "Post-Philology," who asserts that "this kind of [post-philological] reading makes philology an active participant in the disruption

of hegemonic discourses, and thus of power . . .. [P]hilological, postmodern, and postcolonial criticisms all share engagements with history, methods for confronting relationships between universals and particulars, and challenges to hegemony" (23). See as well Pollock, "Philology in Three Dimensions." As a means to a method, (post) philology and HEL certainly have progressive engagements within the horizon of their possibilities. But strictly speaking, they are no more or less inherently "disruptive" than they are "reinforcing" of dominant discourses.

22. On this discourse-analysis perspective, see generally Foucault, *The Archaeology of Knowledge*.

23. Alastair Pennycook, *Global Englishes and Transcultural Flows*, new ed. (New York: Routledge, 2006), 7.

24. On a trans-theory approach to World Englishes, see also Suresh Canagarajah, *Translingual Practice: Global Englishes and Cosmopolitan Relations* (New York: Routledge, 2013). On code-meshing, see the essays collected in Vershawn Ashanti Young and Aja Y. Martinez, eds., *Code-Meshing as World English: Pedagogy, Policy, Performance* (Urbana, IL: National Council of Teachers of English, 2011).

25. For work on ANT, see Bruno Latour, *Reassembling the Social: An Introduction to Actor-Network-Theory* (Oxford: Oxford University Press, 2007), and related bibliography.

26. Gupta, *Philology and Global English Studies*, 167.

CHAPTER 7

1. Robert McCrum, William Cran, and Robert MacNeil, *The Story of English: A Companion to the PBS Television Series* (New York: Viking, 1986), 19. For a review of the various teleological narratives inherent in a history of English and their institutional consequences, see Richard J. Watts, *Language Myths and the History of English* (Oxford: Oxford University Press, 2011), especially 30–34.

2. Tim William Machan, *Language Anxiety: Conflict and Change in the History of English* (Oxford: Oxford University Press, 2009), these quotations from 23. Students and teachers may recall the unique approach of Barbara M. H. Strang, *A History of English* (London: Methuen, 1970), with its reverse chronological organization.

3. Among the many histories of the language that privilege canonical Old and Middle English literature in their narratives, A. C. Baugh and Thomas Cable, *A History of the English Language*, 6th ed. (Upper Saddle River, NJ: Longman, 2012) remains one of the most widely used classroom textbooks. For a provocative challenge to the scholarly and pedagogical tradition of canonical medieval literary works in the History of English, and for Chaucer's place in these narratives, see Tim William Machan, "Chaucer and the History of the English Language," *Speculum* 87 (2012): 147–75.

4. This sense of Shakespeare in original pronunciation may, however, change due to the ongoing work of David Crystal, whose advocacy of Shakespeare "OP" has stimulated a variety of performances, a detailed website, and a range of publications. See his website, http://www.originalpronunciation.com, and his recent *The Oxford Dictionary of Original Shakespearean Pronunciation* (Oxford: Oxford University Press, 2016), of which a notice in the *Times Literary Supplement* states: "we find ourselves among those who have 'dismissed the whole approach out of hand'" (April 6, 2016).

5. On the idiosyncrasies of Milton's spelling preferences, see Simon Horobin, *Does Spelling Matter?* (Oxford: Oxford University Press, 2013), 145. An intriguing example of such attentiveness is Milton's spelling of the word landscape as "lantskip" in Book IV of *Paradise Lost*—a spelling that explicitly associates Satan's initial view of Eden with the glossy surfaces of contemporary Dutch pastoral painting. See David Norbrook and Henry Woudhuysen, eds., *The Penguin Book of Renaissance Verse, 1509–1659* (London: Penguin, 1992), xxviii.

6. On Dickens, Eliot, and the relationships of Victorian fiction to developments in nineteenth-century philology and lexicography, see the overview and bibliography in Seth Lerer, *Error and the Academic Self* (New York: Columbia University Press, 2003), 103–174. On Henry James and the sound of the typewriter, see John Plotz,

"Henry James's Rat-tat-tat-ah: Insidious Loss, Disguised Recovery and Semi-Detached Subjects," *Henry James Review* 34 (2013): 232–44.

7. To be fair, there is a growing set of works on American English that have moved beyond the canon and vocabulary. See, in particular, David Simpson, *The Politics of American English, 1776-1865* (Oxford: Oxford University Press, 1986); Gavin Jones, *Strange Talk: The Politics of Dialect Literature in Gilded Age America* (Berkeley: University of California Press, 1999); John Algeo, *The Cambridge History of the English Language*, vol. 6, *English in North America* (Cambridge: Cambridge University Press, 2001). Still valuable for its anecdotal assemblies and its arresting critical tone is H. L. Mencken, *The American Language*, 4th ed., with supplements, revised and abridged by Raven I. McDavid, Jr. (New York: Knopf, 1977).

8. While not primarily a work of historical linguistics, Henry Louis Gates, Jr.'s landmark book, *The Signifying Monkey* (New York: Oxford University Press, 1988), called attention to the historical origins of African-American vernacular expression and its literary implications. The best technical description of African-American English, in its historical and social settings, remains that of Salikoko S. Mufwene, "African-American English," in Algeo, *Cambridge History of the English Language*, 291–324. A more popular approach by professional linguists is John Russell Rickford and Russell John Rickford, *Spoken Soul: The Story of Black English* (New York: Wiley, 2000). Broad sociological studies include Samy H. Alim and Geneva Smitherman, *Articulate While Black: Barack Obama, Language, and Race in the U.S.* (Oxford: Oxford University Press, 2012).

9. For the history of comparative philology in the late eighteenth and early nineteenth century, together with the discovery of Indo-European and the institutionalization of historical linguistics in American and European universities, see Hans Aarsleff, *The Study of Language in England, 1780–1860*, 2nd ed. (Minneapolis: University of Minnesota Press, 1983), and Haruko Momma, *From Philology to English Studies: Language and Culture in the Nineteenth Century* (Cambridge: Cambridge University Press, 2013).

10. Holger Pedersen, *Linguistic Science in the Nineteenth Century*, translated by J. W. Spargo (Cambridge, MA: Harvard University Press, 1931), 240.

11. Matthew Giancarlo, "The Rise and Fall of the Great Vowel Shift? The Changing Ideological Intersections of Philology, Historical Linguistics, and Literary History," *Representations* 76 (2001): 27–60, at 52.

12. Ibid., 42.

13. Ricardo Bermudez-Otero, "Prosodic Optimization: The Middle English Length Adjustment," *English Language and Linguistics* 2 (1998): 169–97, at 180.

14. James A. H. Murray, "President's Address," *Transactions of the Philological Society* (1884): 509. This quotation serves as the epigraph to Lynda Mugglestone's *Lexicography and the OED: Pioneers in an Untrodden Forest* (Oxford: Oxford University Press, 2000), at 1, though Mugglestone replaces the word "white" with an ellipsis.

15. Murray, "President's Address," 510.

16. Arnold Bennett's phrase comes from an essay in *The Evening Standard*, 5 January 1928. Among the many studies of the *OED*, its origins and impact, see K. M. Elisabeth Murray, *Caught in the Web of Words: James A. H. Murray and the Oxford English Dictionary* (New Haven: Yale University Press, 2001); Simon Winchester, *The Meaning of Everything* (Oxford: Oxford University Press, 2003); Linda Mugglestone, *Lost for Words: The Hidden History of the Oxford English Dictionary* (New Haven: Yale University Press, 2005).

17. I quote from the translation in Simon Keynes and Michael Lapidge, *Alfred the Great* (Harmondsworth: Penguin, 1983), 125. For the original Old English text, I have relied on the edition in which I first encountered it: Henry Sweet, *Anglo-Saxon Reader in Prose and Verse*, 15th ed., revised by Dorothy Whitelock (Oxford: Oxford University Press, 1977), 6.

18. David Wallace, ed., *The Cambridge History of Medieval English Literature* (Cambridge: Cambridge University Press, 1999). My chapter, "Old English and its Afterlife," appears at 7–34.

19. Jocelyn Wogan-Browne and Nicholas Watson, *The Idea of the Vernacular* (University Park: Penn State University Press, 1999).

20. This text appears with the title, "On Translating the Bible into English," in *The Idea of the Vernacular*, 146–48. The source is Cambridge, Trinity College MS B.14.50, fols. 27r-26v, dated c. 1401–7 from the South Midlands. The modern English translation is my own.

21. "And to those who say that the Gospel in English will make men err, know well that we find in Latin more heretics than in all other languages."

22. "Let them [that is, objectors to translation] know that, though a clerk or another man similarly learned can render his words into English better than a common man can, it does not follow from this that our language should be destroyed [by the latter]. To say this would be as much to say that those who cannot speak in as refined a manner [as the learned] should have their tongues cut out. But they should understand that 'grammatically' is nothing more than using correct speech, correct pronunciation, and correct writing."

23. I associate these changes with the work of the following scholars, each of whom has taken a distinctive approach to the question of vernacularity and literary history: Steven Justice, *Writing And Rebellion: England in 1381* (Berkeley: University of California Press, 1994) and *Adam Usk's Secret* (Philadelphia: University of Pennsylvania Press, 2015); James Simpson, *The Oxford English Literary History*, vol. 2, *1350–1547: Reform and Cultural Revolution* (Oxford: Oxford University Press, 2004); Paul Strohm, *England's Empty Throne: Usurpation and the Language of Legitimation, 1399–1422* (Notre Dame: University of Notre Dame Press, 2006); Nicholas Watson and Jacqueline Jenkins, *The Writings of Julian of Norwich* (University Park: Penn State University Press, 2006).

24. James Simpson, *Burning to Read: English Fundamentalism and its Reformation Opponents* (Cambridge, MA: Belknap Press of Harvard University, 2010); Sarah Beckwith, *Shakespeare and the Grammar of Forgiveness* (Ithaca: Cornell University Press, 2012).

25. I quote this poem from the online "Social Edition of the Devonshire Manuscript," at http://en.wikibooks.org/wiki/The_Devonshire_Manuscript, accessed March 27, 2016. The poem appears on fols. 81v-82r of the manuscript. There is no other manuscript witness. I discuss the textual and critical issues surrounding this poem, and the changing vernacular in the early sixteenth century, in "The Medieval Inheritance of Early Tudor Poetry," in Catherine Bates, ed., *The Blackwell Companion to Renaissance Poetry* (Oxford: Blackwell, forthcoming).

26. Material in this and the following paragraph adapts and qualifies a few sentences from my "Late Middle English (ca. 1380–1485)," in Haruko Momma and Michael Matto, eds., *A Companion to The History of the English Language* (Oxford: Wiley-Blackwell, 2008), 191–97, this material at 192–93. For the background on Chancery, standardization, and the claim for print in the regularization of English, see John Hurt Fisher, "Chancery and the Emergence of Standard Written English," *Speculum* 52 (1977): 870–89; John Hurt Fisher and Malcolm Richardson, *An Anthology of Chancery English* (Knoxville: University of Tennessee Press, 1984); John Hurt Fisher, *The Emergence of Standard English* (Lexington: University Press of Kentucky, 1996).

27. Fisher and Richardson, *An Anthology of Chancery English*, 26.

28. John Hart, *An Orthographie*, facsimile reprint in R. C. Alston, ed., *English Linguistics 1500–1800*, no. 209 (Menston: Scolar Press, 1969), 2.

29. Roger Ascham, *The Schoolmaster*, ed. Lawrence V. Ryan (Ithaca: Cornell University Press, 1967), 68.

CHAPTER 9

1. Laurel J. Brinton and Leslie K. Arnovick, *The English Language: A Linguistic History*. 3rd rev. ed. (Don Mills, ONT: Oxford University Press, 2017).

2. Andreas H. Jucker and Irma Taavitsainen, eds., *Historical Pragmatics* (Berlin: de Gruyter Mouton, 2010), xi.

3. Laurel J. Brinton, "Historical Discourse Analysis," in *Handbook of Discourse Analysis*, edited by Deborah Tannen, Heidi E. Hamilton, and Deborah Schiffrin (Maldon, MA: Blackwell Publishers: 2003), 222–43.

4. Laurel J. Brinton, ed., *English Historical Linguistics: Approaches and Perspectives* (Cambridge: Cambridge University Press, 2017), 224–5. Also see Elizabeth Closs Traugott "Historical Pragmatics," in *The Handbook of Pragmatics*, edited by Laurence R. Horn and Gregory Ward (Malden, MA: Blackwell, 2004), 538–61, 539.

5. Traugott, "Historical Pragmatics," 539.

6. Brinton, *English Historical Linguistics*, 237.

7. See further Juan Manuel Hernández-Campoy and Juan Camilo Conde-Silvestre, eds., *Handbook of Historical Sociolinguistics* (Malden, MA: Wiley Blackwell, 2012).

8. Leslie K. Arnovick and Laurel J. Brinton, "Historical Pragmatics and Historical Socio-pragmatics" (paper delivered at meeting of the Modern Language Association, Vancouver, British Columbia, January 8–11, 2015).

9. William Labov, *Sociolinguistic Patterns* (Philadelphia: University of Pennsylvania, 1972); Laurel J. Brinton and Leslie K. Arnovick, *The English Language: A Linguistic History*, 3rd ed. rev. (Don Mills, ON: Oxford University Press, 2016), 70.

10. Laurel J. Brinton and Leslie K. Arnovick, *The English Language: A Linguistic History*, 3rd ed. rev. (Don Mills, ON: Oxford University Press, 2016), 70.

11. Cf. Geoffrey N. Leech. *Principles of Pragmatics* (London: Longman, 1983), x, and Leslie K. Arnovick, *Written Reliquaries: The Resonance of Orality in Medieval English Texts* (Amsterdam: John Benjamins, 2006), 15.

12. Arnovick, *Written Reliquaries*, 15.

13. Stephen Levinson, *Pragmatics* (Cambridge: Cambridge University Press, 1983), 24.

14. Jacob Mey, *Pragmatics: An Introduction*, 2nd ed. (Malden, MA: Blackwell, 2001), 190.

15. Leech, *Principles of Pragmatics*, 13; and Arnovick, *Written Reliquaries*, 16.

16. Mey, *Pragmatics*, 10.

17. Andreas Jacobs and Andreas H. Jucker, "The Historical Perspective in Pragmatics," in *Historical Pragmatics: Pragmatic Developments in the History of English*, edited by Andreas H. Jucker (Amsterdam: John Benjamins, 1995), 3–33, 5.

18. Arnovick and Brinton, "Historical Pragmatics and Historical Socio-pragmatics."

19. Jacobs and Jucker, "The Historical Perspective in Pragmatics."

20. Traugott, "Historical Pragmatics," 548.

21. Jacobs and Jucker, "The Historical Perspective in Pragmatics," 6.

22. Ibid., 5.

23. Ibid., 11.

24. Ibid., 11.

25. Ibid., 13; Leslie K. Arnovick, *Journal of Pragmatics* 28 (1997): 383–412, review of Andreas H. Jucker (ed.), *Historical Pragmatics: Pragmatic Developments in the History of English* (Amsterdam: John Benjamins, 1995).

26. Traugott, "Historical Pragmatics," 539.

27. Ibid., 539.

28. Andreas H. Jucker and Irma Taavitsainen, eds. *Historical Pragmatics*, vol. 8, *Handbooks of Pragmatics* (Berlin: Mouton de Gruyter Mouton, 2010).

29. Arnovick and Brinton, "Historical Pragmatics and Historical Socio-pragmatics."

30. Cf. Brinton and Arnovick, *The English Language*, 18–19.

31. Andreas H. Jucker and Irma Taavitsainen, *Speech Acts in the History of English* (Amsterdam: John Benjamins, 2013), 28; Brinton and Arnovick, *The English Language*, 19.

32. Brinton and Arnovick, *The English Language*, 24.

33. Cf. Jucker and Taavitsainen, *Speech Acts*, 28.

34. Cf. Martin Spevack, ed., *A Complete and Systematic Concordance to the Works of Shakespeare* (Hildesheim, NY: Georg Olms, 1968-1994); Akio Oizumi, ed., *Complete Concordance to the Works of Geoffrey Chaucer* (Hildesheim, NY: Olms-Weidmann, 1991).

35. Guy Montgomery, ed., *Concordance to the Poetical Works of John Dryden* (Cambridge: Cambridge University Press, 1957); Weldon Thornton, ed., *Allusions in*

Ulysses: A Line-by-line Reference to Joyce's Complex Symbolism (Chapel Hill: University of North Carolina Press, 1968).

36. Jucker and Taavitsainen, *Speech Acts*, 44.
37. Leslie K. Arnovick and Laurel J. Brinton, "Historical Pragmatics and Historical Socio-pragmatics," (paper presented at the annual meeting of the Modern Language Association, Vancouver, British Columbia, January 8–11, 2015.
38. *Proceedings of the Old Bailey*, http://www.oldbaileyonline.org.
39. University of Michigan, *Corpus of Middle English Prose and Verse*, http://quod.lib.umich.edu/c/cme/about.html.
40. Jucker and Taavitsainen, *Speech Acts*, 45.
41. *Corpus of American Soap Operas*, http://corpus.byu.edu/soap/.
42. Brinton and Arnovick, *The English Language*, 19.
43. *Corpus of Historical American English*, http://corpus.byu.edu/coha/.
44. For an exercise using *COHA* to investigate the performative verb "warn," see Brinton, "Historical Pragmatics," in *English Historical Linguistics*, 2017, 274.
45. Brinton and Arnovick, *The English Language*, 87.
46. Ibid., 91.
47. Ibid., 91–92.
48. Ibid., 78.
49. Ibid., 86–87.
50. For additional case studies (e.g., genre and text types, speech acts, scientific and medical discourse, and narrative patterns) see Andreas Jucker and Irma Taavitsainen, *English Historical Pragmatics* (Ediburgh: Edinburgh University Press, 2013). See Jucker and Taavitsainen, *Speech Acts in the History of English* (Amsterdam: John Benjamins, 2008), for studies of speech acts in the history of English. See also the *Journal of Historical Pragmatics* (2000–) for scholarly research on English and other languages.
51. See Traugott 1982, 1985, 1989, 1995, 1997; Leslie K. Arnovick, *Diachronic Pragmatics: Seven Case Studies in English Illocutionary Development* (Amsterdam: John Benjamins , 1999), 12, 53, 64.
52. Brinton and Arnovick, *The English Language*, 77.
53. Arnovick, *Diachronic Pragmatics*, 58–71.
54. Elizabeth Closs Traugott, "On the Rise of Epistemic Meanings in English: An Example of Subjectification in Semantic Change," *Language* 65, no. 1 (1989): 49.
55. Elizabeth Closs Traugott and Ekkehard König, "The Semantics-pragmatics of Grammaticalization Revisited," in *Approaches to Grammaticalization*, edited by Elizabeth Closs Traugott and Bernd Heine, vol.1 (Amsterdam: John Benjamins, 1991), 192.
56. Elizabeth Closs Traugott, "Subjectification in Grammaticalisation," in *Subjectivity and Subjectivisation*, edited by Dieter Stein and Susan Wright (Cambridge: Cambridge University Press, 1995), 31–54, 47; Elizabeth Closs Traugott, "On the Rise of Epistemic Meanings in English," 31–55, 35; Elizabeth Closs Traugott, "Subjectification and the Development of Epistemic Meaning: The Case of *Promise* and *Threaten*," in *Modality in German Languages: Historical and Comparative Perspectives*, edited by Toril Swan and Olaf Jansen Westvik (Berlin: Mouton de Gruyter, 1997), 185.
57. Brinton and Arnovick, *The English Language*, 92.
58. Arnovick, *Diachronic Pragmatics*, 95–118.
59. Karen Aijmer, "*I think*—An English Modal Particle," in *Modality in Germanic Languages: Historical and Comparative Perspectives*, ed. Toril Swan and Olaf Jansen Westvik (Berlin: Mouton de Gruyter, 1997), 2.
60. Ibid., 2–3.
61. Arnovick, *Diachronic Pragmatics*, 95–118.
62. Thomas Kohnen, "Corpora and Speech Acts: The Study of Performatives," in *Corpus Linguistics and Linguistic Theory: Papers from the Twentieth International Conference of English Language Research on Computerized Corpora*, edited by Christian Mair and Marianne Hundt (Amsterdam: Rodopi, 2000), 177–86; Thomas Kohnen, "Explicit

Performatives in Old English: A Corpus-based Study of Directives," *Journal of Historical Pragmatics* 1, vol. 2 (2000): 301–321; Thomas Kohnen, "Directives in Old English: Beyond Politeness," in Jucker and Taavitsainen, *Speech Acts in the History of English*, 27–44; Thomas Kohnen, "Tracing Directives through Text and Time: Towards a Methodology of a Corpus-based Diachronic Speech Act Analysis," in Jucker and Taavitsainen, *Speech Acts in the History of English*, 295-310.

63. Kohnen, "Explicit Performatives in Old English," 301.
64. Brinton and Arnovick, *The English Language*, 90.
65. Ibid., 90.
66. Brinton, *English Historical Linguistics*, 245–74.
67. Macaulay, *Motel of the Mysteries*, 38.
68. Ibid., 32, 84.
69. Ibid., 32.
70. Ibid., 78.

CHAPTER 10

1. Thomas Hoffman and Graeme Trousdale, eds. *The Oxford Handbook of Construction Grammar* (New York: Oxford University Press, 2013). Additionally, see Adele E. Goldberg, *Constructions: A Construction Grammar Approach to Argument Structure* (Chicago: University of Chicago Press, 1995).
2. Geoffrey K. Pullum, "Slowcones: Lexicographical Dating to the Second," *Language Log*, January 16, 2004.
3. For an early discussion, see Charles J. Fillmore, Paul Kay, and Mary Catherine O'Connor, "Regularity and Idiomaticity in Grammatical Constructions," *Language* 64 (1998): 501–38.
4. See again Fillmore, Kay, and O'Connor "Regularity and Idiomaticity"; and Stefanie Wulff, "Words and Idioms," in *Oxford Handbook of Construction Grammar*, 274–89.
5. Timothy Colleman and Bernard De Clerck, "Constructional Semantics on the Move: On Semantic Specialization in the English Double Object Construction," *Cognitive Linguistics* 21, no. 1 (2011): 183–209.
6. Colleman and De Clerck, "Constructional Semantics," 194.
7. Elizabeth Closs Traugott, "'All that he endeavour'd to prove was . . .': On the Emergence of Grammatical Constructions in Dialogic Contexts," in *Language in Flux: Dialogue Co-ordination, Language Variation, Change and Evolution*, edited by Robin Cooper and Ruth Kempson (London: King's College Publications, 2008), 143–77.
8. For an overview, see Jóhanna Barðdal, "Construction-Based Comparative Historical Reconstruction," in *Oxford Handbook of Construction Grammar*, 438–57.
9. Recent monographs on this subject include Amanda L. Patten, *The English IT-Cleft: A Constructional Account and Diachronic Investigation* (Berlin: De Gruyter, 2012); Hendrik De Smet, *Spreading Patterns: Diffusional Change in the English System of Complementation* (Oxford: Oxford University Press, 2013); Martin Hilpert, *Constructional Change in English: Developments in Allomorphy, Word-formation and Syntax* (Cambridge: Cambridge University Press, 2013); and Peter Petré, *Constructions and Environments: Copular, Passive, and Related Constructions in Old and Middle English* (Oxford: Oxford University Press, 2013).
10. See Dirk Noël, "Diachronic Construction Grammar and Grammaticalization Theory," *Functions of Language* 14 (2007): 177–202, for an outline of the issues, and Elizabeth Closs Traugott and Graeme Trousdale, *Constructionalization and Constructional Changes* (Oxford: Oxford University Press, 2013), for a book-length treatment.
11. For a representative study, see Joybrato Mukherjee and Stefan Th. Gries, "Collostructional Nativisation in New Englishes: Verb-construction Associations in the International Corpus of English," *English World Wide* 30 (2009): 27–51.
12. E.g., Hilpert, *Constructional Change in English*; Martin Hilpert, "From *Hand-Carved* to *Computer-Based*: Noun-participle Compounding and the Upward-Strengthening Hypothesis," *Cognitive Linguistics* 26 (2015): 1–36; and Petré, *Constructions and Environments*.

13. Martin Hilpert, "Diachronic Collostructional Analysis Meets the Noun Phrase: Studying Many a Noun in COHA," in *The Oxford Handbook of the History of English*, edited by Elizabeth Closs Traugott and Terttu Nevalainen (New York: Oxford University Press, 2012), 233–44.

14. Hilpert, "Diachronic Collostructional Analysis Meets the Noun Phrase."

15. Ibid., 240.

16. Ibid.

17. See Martin Hilpert, *Germanic Future Constructions: A Usage-based Approach to Language Change* (Amsterdam: John Benjamins, 2008) on collocational differences between *will* V and *be going to* V in the history of English.

18. Traugott and Trousdale, *Constructionalization and Constructional Changes*, 180.

19. Ibid., 179.

20. Ibid., 178.

21. See further David Denison, "Category Change in English With and Without Structural Change," in *Gradience, Gradualness and Grammaticalization*, edited by Elizabeth Closs Traugott and Graeme Trousdale (Amsterdam: John Benjamins), 105–28; David Denison, "Parts of Speech: Solid Citizens or Slippery Customers?," *Journal of the British Academy* 1 (2013): 151–85; and David Denison, "Word Classes in the History of English," (Chapter 13, this volume).

22. See the debate between Bas Aarts, "In Defence of Distributional Analysis, Pace Croft," *Studies in Language* 31 (2007): 431–43, and William Croft, "Beyond Aristotle and Gradience: A Reply to Aarts," *Studies in Language* 31 (2007): 409–30, which is not of direct relevance to the teaching of the history of English, but might provide useful background reading for work on category change.

23. Anne Curzan, "Revisiting the Reduplicative Copula with Corpus-based Evidence," in *Oxford Handbook of the History of English*, 211–22.

24. Paul J. Hopper and Sandra A. Thompson, "Projectability and Clause-Combining in Interaction," in *Cross-linguistic Studies of Clause Combining: The Multifunctionality of Conjunctions*, edited by Ritva Laury (Amsterdam: Benjamins, 2008), 99–123.

25. Graeme Trousdale, "Words and Constructions in Grammaticalization: The End of the English Impersonal Construction," in *Studies in the History of the English Language IV: Empirical and Analytical Advances in the Study of English Language Change*, edited by Susan Fitzmaurice and Donka Minkova (Berlin: De Gruyter, 2008), 301–26.

26. Trousdale, "Words and Constructions in Grammaticalization," 310.

27. Willem Hollman, "Constructions in Cognitive Sociolinguistics," in *Oxford Handbook of Construction Grammar*, 491–509.

CHAPTER 11

1. William A. Kretzschmar, Jr. *The Linguistics of Speech* (Cambridge: Cambridge University Press, 2009); William A. Kretzschmar, Jr. *Language and Complex Systems* (Cambridge: Cambridge University Press, 2015).

2. Now in its seventh edition, with Carmen Butcher as an additional editor. Thomas Pyles, John Algeo, and Carmen Butcher, *The Origins and Development of the English Language*. 7th ed. (Boston: Cengage Learning, 2013).

3. Santa Fe Institute, www.santafe.edu.

4. James Milroy, *Linguistic Variation and Change* (Oxford: Blackwell, 1992).

5. All LAMSAS data discussed here may be recovered from http://www.lap.uga.edu.

6. See Kretzschmar, *Language and Complex Systems*, 81–104.

7. Such as, for example, the mathematical discussion of curves in Kretzschmar, *Language and Complex Systems*, 155–200.

8. Jules Gilliéron and J. Mongin, *Scier dans la Gaule romance* (Paris: Champion, 1905).

9. E.g., Walt Wolfram and Eric Thomas, *The Development of African American English* (Oxford: Wiley-Blackwell, 2002).

10. Joycelyn Wilson, "Outkast'd and Claimin' True: The Language of Schooling and Education in the Southern Hip-Hop Community of Practice" (PhD diss., University of Georgia, 2007).

11. Richard W. Bailey, *Nineteenth-Century English* (Ann Arbor: University of Michigan Press, 1996), 215.

CHAPTER 12

1. For an introduction to historical corpus linguistics, see, e.g., Merja Kytö, "Corpora and historical linguistics," *Revista Brasileira de Linguística Aplicada* 11, no. 2 (2011): 417–57.
2. See Suzanne Romaine, "The Variationist Approach," in *Cambridge Handbook of English Historical Linguistics*, edited by Merja Kytö and Päivi Pahta (Cambridge: Cambridge University Press, 2016), 19–35.
3. See Martin Hilpert and Stefan Gries, "Quantitative Approaches to Diachronic Corpus Linguistics," in *Cambridge Handbook of English Historical Linguistics*, edited by Merja Kytö and Päivi Pahta (Cambridge: Cambridge University Press, 2016), 36–53.
4. Tim Johns, "Should You Be Persuaded: Two Examples of Data-Driven Learning," *English Language Research Journal* 4 (1991): 1–16, 3; see also Tim Johns, "Whence and Whither Classroom Concordancing?" in *Computer Applications in Language Learning*, edited by Theo Bongaerts et al. (Dordrecht: Foris, 1988): 9–33; and Gerald Knowles, "Using Corpora for the Diachronic Study of English," in *Teaching and Language Corpora*, edited by Anne Wichmann et al. (London: Longman, 1990), 195–210.
5. See Geoffrey N. Leech, "Teaching and Language Corpora: A Convergence," in *Teaching and Language Corpora*, 1–23; Randi Reppen, "Corpus Linguistics and Language Teaching," in *English Corpus Studies* 8 (2001): 19–31; Tim Johns, "Data-Driven Learning: The Perpetual Challenge," in *Teaching and Learning by Doing Corpus Analysis*, edited by Bernhard Kettemann and Georg Marko, *Proceedings of the Fourth International Conference on Teaching and Language Corpora*, Graz 19, July 24, 2000 (Amsterdam: Rodopi, 2002), 107–17; Silvia Bernardini, "Exploring New Directions for Discovery Learning," in *Teaching and Learning by Doing Corpus Analysis*, 165–82; John Sinclair, *How to Use Corpora in Language Teaching* (Amsterdam: John Benjamins, 2004); Angela Chambers, "Integrating Corpus Consulation in Language Studies," *Language Learning and Technology* 9(2): 111–25; Joybrato Mukherjee, "Corpus Linguistics and Language Pedagogy: The State of the Art-and Beyond," in *Corpus Technology and Language Pedagogy*, edited by Sabine Braun, Kurt Kohn, and Joybrato Mukherjee (Frankfurt am Main: Peter Lang, 2006), 5–24; Lynne Flowerdew, "Applying Corpus Linguistics to Pedagogy: A Critical Evaluation," *International Journal of Corpus Linguistics* 14:3 (2009), 393–417; Ute Römer "Corpora and Language Teaching," in *Corpus Linguistics: An International Handbook*, edited by Anke Lüdeling and Merja Kytö (Berlin: de Gruyter Mouton, 2009), 112–31; Randi Reppen, "Using Corpora in the Language Classroom, " in *Materials Development in Language Teaching*, edited by Tomlinson, Brian (Cambridge: Cambridge University Press, 2011), 35–50.
6. See Kate Donley and Randi Reppen, "Using Corpus Tools to Highlight Academic Vocabulary in Sustained Content Language Teaching," *TESOL Journal* 10 (2001): 7–12; Ken Hyland, *Teaching and Researching Writing* (Harlow, Essex: Longman, 2002); Gena R. Bennett, *Using Corpora in the Language Learning Classroom* (Ann Arbor: University of Michigan Press, 2011).
7. There are some textbooks that do provide corpus evidence and frequency information. For example, see Terttu Nevalainen, *An Introduction to Early Modern English* (Oxford: Oxford University Press, 2006); and Ingrid Tieken-Boon van Ostade, *An Introduction to Late Modern English* (Edinburgh: Edinburgh University Press, 2009).
8. Tony McEnery and Andrew Wilson, *Corpus Linguistics*, 2nd ed. (Edinburgh: Edinburgh University Press, 2001), 123.
9. Andreas Jucker and Irma Taavitsainen, *English Historical Pragmatics* (Edinburgh: Edinburgh University Press, 2013), 41.
10. Ondřej Tichý, "Lexical Obsolescence and Loss in English: 1700–2000," in *Patterns in Text: Corpus-driven Methods and Applications*, edited by Joanna Kopaczyk and Jukka Tyrkkö (Amsterdam: John Benjamins, accepted).
11. Kytö, "Corpora and Historical Linguistics," 417–57, at 421.

12. Matti Rissanen, "Three Problems Associated with the Use of Diachronic Corpora," *ICAME Journal* 13 (1989): 16–19.
13. Anne Curzan, "English Historical Corpora in the Classroom: The Intersection of Teaching and Research," *Journal of English Linguistics* 28 (2000): 77–89, 81.
14. Leech, "Teaching and Language Corpora: A Convergence."
15. Römer, "Corpora and Language Teaching," 113.
16. See also Daniel Krieger, "Corpus Linguistics: What It Is and How It Can Be Applied to Teaching," in *The Internet TESL Journal*, IX, no. 3 (2003), n.p., iteslj.org/Articles/Krieger-Corpus.html.
17. Martin Warren, "Introduction to Data-Driven Learning," in *The Routledge Handbook of Language Learning and Technology*, edited by Fiona Farr and Liam Murray (London: Routledge, 2016), 339.
18. For historical corpora of English, see, e.g., Corpus Resource Database, University of Helsinki, http://www.helsinki.fi/varieng/CoRD/index.html.
19. Perhaps the most widely used corpus tools include the freeware Antconc and associated tools developed by Lawrence Anthony, WordSmith Tools developed by Mike Smith, and CasualConc developed by Yasu Imao. All three are easy to find online. Advanced students should be encouraged to familiarise themselves with programming languages such as R, Python, and Livecode. Web-based corpora incorporating query tools include The Brigham Young corpora developed by Mark Davies and the UCREL CQPweb corpora developed by Andrew Hardie.
20. Examples include *Oxford Dictionary of National Biography*, *Oxford English Dictionary*, and the *Historical Thesaurus of the Oxford English Dictionary*.
21. Judgment sampling is also known as *purposive sampling* or *selective sampling*.
22. The corpus was released in 2010. It was compiled by the Scientific thought-styles project lead by Prof. Irma Taavitsainen at the VARIENG research unit at the University of Helsinki.
23. Marianne Hundt, "Colonial Lag, Colonial Innovation or Simply Language Change,?" in *One Language-Two Grammars? Differences Between British and American English*, edited by Günter Rohdenburg and Julia Schlüter (Cambridge: Cambridge University Press, 2009), 13–37.
24. Lieselotte Anderwald, "*Throve, Pled, Shrunk*: The Evolution of American English in the 19th Century Between Language Change and Prescriptive Norms," in *Outposts of Historical Corpus Linguistics: From the Helsinki Corpus to a Proliferation of Resources*, edited by Jukka Tyrkkö et. al. (Helsinki: Varieng, 2012).
25. Access to CQPweb and a variety of corpora hosted by UCREL can be arranged by contacting the UCREL centre.
26. For discussion of non-linear distributions, Zipfian distributions and so-called asymptotic hyperbolic curves, see William A. Kretzschmar, Jr., "Language Variation and Complex Systems," *American Speech* 85 (2010): 263–86.

CHAPTER 13

1. Arnold Zwicky, "Just between Dr. Language and I," *Language Log*, 2005, accessed May 4, 2006, http://itre.cis.upenn.edu/~myl/languagelog/archives/002386.html.
2. Sebastian Hoffman et al., *Corpus Linguistics with BNCweb—A Practical Guide* (English Corpus Linguistics 6) (Frankfurt am Main: Peter Lang, 2006).
3. See, for instance, Frank Keller, Maria Lapata, and Olga Ourioupina, "Using the Web to Overcome Data Sparseness," in *Proceedings of the Conference on Empirical Methods in Natural Language Processing*, edited by J. Hajič & Y. Matsumoto (New Brunswick: Association for Computational Linguistics: 2002), 230–7; Adam Kilgarriff and Gregory Grefenstette, "Introduction to the Special Issue on the Web as Corpus," *Computational Linguistics* 29.3 (2003): 333–47; Jean Véronis, "Google's Counts Faked?," *Technologies du Langage*, accessed January 26, 2005, http://aixtal.blogspot.com/2005/01/web-googles-counts-faked.html; Marianne Hundt, Nadja Nesselhauf, and Carolin Biewer, eds., *Corpus Linguistics and the Web* (Language and Computers: Studies in Practical Linguistics no. 59) (Amsterdam: Rodopi, 2006), 59.

4. David Denison, "Ambiguity and Vagueness in Historical Change," in *The Changing English Language: Psycholinguistic Perspectives* (Studies in English Language), edited by Marianne Hundt, Sandra Mollin, and Simone E. Pfenninger (Cambridge: Cambridge University Press, 2017), 292–318.

5. David Denison. "Patterns and Productivity," in *Studies in the History of the English Language,* vol. 4, *Empirical and Analytical Advances in the Study of English Language Change,* Topics in English Linguistics 61, edited by Susan M. Fitzmaurice and Donka Minkova (Berlin: Mouton de Gruyter, 2008), 208–10.

6. See Terttu Nevalainen, "Lexis and Semantics," in *The Cambridge History of the English language,* vol. 3, *1476–1776,* edited by Roger Lass (Cambridge: Cambridge University Press, 1999), 424–30.

7. See, for example, "Invite vs. Invitation," English Grammar and Usage: Prescriptive Grammar and Standard English, https://grammarusage.wordpress.com/2012/04/03/invite-vs-invitation/.

8. For a nice example of how the *human* parser can go astray with a word that is ambiguously verb or noun, see Mark Liberman, "Nounification of the week," *Language Log,* 2016, accessed March 16, 2016, http://languagelog.ldc.upenn.edu/nll/?p=24726.

9. David Denison, "Parts of Speech: Solid Citizens or Slippery Customers?" *Journal of the British Academy* 1 (2013): 151–85; Denison, "Ambiguity and Vagueness in Historical Change."

10. Denison, "Ambiguity and Vagueness in Historical Change."

11. See Geoffrey Leech and Lu Li, "Indeterminacy Between Noun Phrases and Adjective Phrases as complements of the English verb," in *The Verb in Contemporary English: Theory and Description,* edited by Bas Aarts and Charles F. Meyer (Cambridge: Cambridge University Press: 1995), 183–202; Hendrik De Smet, "The Course of Actualization," *Language* 88, no. 3 (2012): 601–33, 621–8; and Paul Kiparsky, "New Perspectives in Historical Linguistics," in *The Routledge Handbook of Historical Linguistics,* edited by Claire Bowern and Bethwyn Evans, *Routledge Handbooks in Linguistics* (London: Routledge, 2014).

12. See David Denison, "Syntax," in *The Cambridge History of the English Language,* vol. 4, *1776–1997,* edited by Suzanne Romaine, 92–329 (Cambridge: Cambridge University Press, 1998), 229–30.

13. See Douglas Biber et al., *Longman Grammar of Spoken and Written English* (Harlow: Pearson, 1999), 867–71. For a fuller discussion of the range of SKT constructions than I have space for here, see among many other works David Denison, "History of the *sort of* Construction Family," paper presented at ICCG2: Second International Conference on Construction Grammar, Helsinki, 2002; Evelien Keizer, *The English Noun Phrase: The Nature of Linguistic Categorization,* Studies in English Language (Cambridge: Cambridge University Press, 2007); Lieselotte Brems and Kristin Davidse, "The Grammaticalisation of Nominal Type Noun Constructions with *kind/sort of:* Chronology and Paths of Change," *English Studies* 91, no. 2 (2010): 180–202.

14. For some discussion, see David Denison, "Non-inflecting Verbs in Modern English," paper presented at Autour du verbe/Around the verb: Colloque en l'honneur de Claude Delmas, Paris, 2012, §4.4; and Denison, "Syntax," 140–2, 210–2.

CHAPTER 14

1. See Philip Durkin, *Borrowed Words: A History of Loanwords in English* (Oxford: Oxford University Press, 2014).

2. C. T. Onions, *Oxford Dictionary of English Etymology* (Oxford: Clarendon Press, 1966); *Oxford English Dictionary,* edited by J. A. H. Murray et al., 13 vols. (Oxford: Oxford University Press, 1933). Available by subscription in a digital edition at http://www.oed.com/.

3. W. W. Skeat, *Etymological Dictionary of the English Language,* 4th ed. (Oxford: Clarendon Press, 1909).

4. Robert K. Barnhart and Sol Steinmetz, *Barnhart Dictionary of Etymology* (New York: H. W. Wilson, 1988).

5. Clarence Barnhart, "American Lexicography, 1947–1973," *American Speech* 53 (1978): 113.

6. Anatoly Liberman, *An Analytic Dictionary of English Etymology: An Introduction* (Minneapolis: University of Minnesota Press, 2008).

7. Ibid.

8. See Michael Adams, "Review of Anatoly Liberman, *A Bibliography of English Etymology: Sources and Word List*," *NOWELE* 60/61 (2011): 231–244.

9. I should reveal here, in the interest of transparency, that I was a Consulting Editor on *AHD4* and a Contributing Editor to *Word Histories and Mysteries: Abracadabra to Zeus*, and that I was Editor of *American Speech* for a decade, from 2006 through 2015.

10. Michael Adams, "Resources: Teaching Perspectives," in *English Historical Linguistics: An International Handbook*, edited by Alexander Bergs and Laurel J. Brinton (Berlin: Mouton de Gruyter, 2012), 1173–1174.

11. Fred W. Householder, for instance, once mused, "I don't know whether anyone else [interviewed for the Oral Archive of for the History of American Linguistics] has mentioned this—but I used to go to the library and read dictionaries, just browse through them. I found them fascinating" ("A Sketch of How I Came to Be a Linguist," in *First Person Singular: Papers from the Conference on an Oral Archive for the History of American Linguistics*, edited by Boyd H. Davis and Raymond O'Cain [Amsterdam: John Benjamins, 1980], 193), as do some history of English students.

12. John Considine, "Why Do Large Historical Dictionaries Give So Much Pleasure to Their Owners and Users?" *EURALEX '98 Proceedings*, edited by Thierry Fontanelle (Liège: Université de Liège, 1998); Michael Adams, "Historical Dictionaries and the History of Reading," in *Reading in History: New Methodologies from the Anglo-American Tradition*, edited by Bonnie Gunzenhauser (London: Pickering & Chatto, 2010), 56–62.

13. For instance, see Michael Adams, "*DARE*, History, and the Texture of the Entry," *American Speech* 77 (2002): 370–82; Michael Adams, "The Lexical Ride of a Lifetime," *American Speech* 88 (2013): 168–195, 170–78.

14. T. K. Pratt, *Dictionary of Prince Edward Island English* (Toronto: University of Toronto Press, 1988).

15. The foundational account of enregisterment is Asif Agha, "The Social Life of Cultural Value," *Language and Communication* 23 (2003): 231–73. But since it was published, several sociolinguists have put it into practice, led by Barbara Johnstone, in too many works to mention here. For the briefest possible, student-friendly account of enregisterment, see Michael Adams, "Enregisterment: A Special Issue," *American Speech* 84 (2009): 115–117; the special issue of *American Speech* it introduces illustrates in several fine contributions—including one by Johnstone—enregisterment's explanatory value.

16. Sidney Landau, *Dictionaries: The Art and Craft of Lexicography* (New York: Charles Scribner's Sons, 1984), 4.

17. Pratt, *Dictionary of Prince Edward Island English*.

18. *Dictionary of American English*, 4 vols., edited by William A. Craigie et al. (Chicago: University of Chicago Press, 1938–1944).

19. *Dictionary of American Regional English*, 6 vols., edited by Frederic G. Cassidy et al. (Cambridge: Belknap Press of the Harvard University Press, 1985–2013). Available in a digital edition by subscription at http://www.daredictionary.com/.

20. J. E. Lighter, *Historical Dictionary of American Slang* (New York: Random House, 1994 and 1997). To date, two volumes have been published.

21. Bryan A. Garner, *Garner's Modern American Usage*, 1st ed., titled *A Dictionary of Modern American Usage*, 1998; 2nd ed., 2003; 3rd ed., 2009; 4th ed., 2016 (New York: Oxford University Press).

22. *American Heritage Dictionary of the English Language*, 1st ed., edited by William Morris et al., published in New York by American Heritage, 1969; 2nd College ed., edited by

Pamela B. De Vinne et al., published in Boston by Houghton Mifflin; 4th ed., edited by Joseph P. Pickett et al., published in Boston by Houghton Mifflin, 2000; and 5th ed., edited by Joseph P. Pickett et al., published in Boston by Houghton Mifflin Harcourt, 2011.

23. Michael Adams, "Language Ideologies and the *American Heritage Dictionary of the English Language*: Evidence from Motive, Structure, and Design," *Dictionaries* 36 (2015): 17–46.

24. Deborah Cameron, *Verbal Hygiene* (New York: Routledge, 1995), 32.

25. Ibid., 32.

26. Wilson Follett, *Modern American Usage* (New York: Hill & Wang, 1966).

27. *Merriam-Webster's Concise Dictionary of English Usage* (Springfield, MA: Merriam-Webster, 2002).

28. Constance Hale and Jessie Scanlon, *Wired Style: Principles of English Usage in the Digital Age*, 2nd ed. (New York: Broadway, 1999).

29. *American Heritage Book of English Usage* (Boston: Houghton Mifflin, 1996).

30. Robert Cawdrey, 1604, *A Table Alphabeticall of Hard usual English Words*, rpt. Scholar's Facsimiles and Reprints (Gainesville, FL: 1966, and Delmar, NY: 1976).

31. Charles Richardson, *A New Dictionary of the English Language*, 2 vols. (London: Pickèring, 1837).

32. W. S. Ramson, ed., *The Australian National Dictionary* (Melbourne: Oxford University Press, 1989)

33. Dorothy Jauncey, *Bardi Grubs and Frog Cakes: South Australian Words* (South Melbourne, Australia: Oxford University Press, 2004).

34. For an explanation, see Arnold Zwicky, "Libfixes," *Arnold Zwicky's Blog*, accessed April 3, 2016, http:// arnoldzwicky.org/ 2010/ 01/ 23/ libfixes/. For further examples, see Liberman, "Whatpocalypse Now?," *Language Log*, accessed October 16, 2016, http:// languagelog.ldc.upenn.edu/ nll/ ?p=3209.

35. See Michael Manis, *The "Magic: The Gathering" Lexicon* (MA thesis, Indiana University, 2012).

36. See Aaron Dinin, *The Krzyzewskiville Tales* (Durham, NC: Duke University Press, 2005), 225–49.

37. See Wayne Glowka et al., "Among the New Words," *American Speech* 82 (2007): 420–437; and Wayne Glowka et al., "Among the New Words," *American Speech* 83 (2008): 85–98.

38. Grant Barrett, *The Official Dictionary of Unofficial English* (New York: McGraw-Hill, 2006).

39. Mark Peters, *Wordlustitude*, 2004–2012, last accessed April 3, 2016, http://wordlust. blogspot.com/.

40. See Wayne Glowka et al., "*Among the New Words* as an Editing Project in a Methods of Research Class," *Dictionaries* 21: (2000): 100–108.

41. William Labov, *Principles of Linguistic Change: Internal Factors* (Oxford and Cambridge, MA: Blackwell, 1994), 11.

42. Jesse Sheidlower, "How Quotation Paragraphs in Historical Dictionaries Work: *The Oxford English Dictionary*," in *Contours of English and English Language Studies*, ed. Michael Adams and Anne Curzan (Ann Arbor: University of Michigan Press, 2011), 204–05.

43. See Michael Adams, *Slayer Slang: A Buffy the Vampire Slayer Lexicon* (New York: Oxford University Press, 2003), 87–111.

44. Cecily Clark, "Historical Linguistics—Linguistic Archaeology," in *Papers from the 5th International Conference on English Historical Linguistics*, edited by Sylvia Adamson et al. (Amsterdam and Philadelphia: John Benjamins, 1990), 65.

45. Adams, "Historical Dictionaries and the History of Reading," 48–54.

46. For a thorough map of the process, including potential quagmires, practical advice, and further project ideas, see Michael Adams, "Vocabulary Analysis in Sociolinguistic Research," in *Research Methods in Sociolinguistics: A Practical Guide*, edited by Janet Holmes and Kirk Hazen (Malden, MA: Wiley-Blackwell, 2014), 163–76.

47. Adams, "Resources: Teaching Perspectives," 1175–76.

48. Most recently in Erik Blanco et al., *U.C.L.A. Slang 6* (UCLA Occasional Papers in Linguistics no. 24), edited by Pamela Munro (Los Angeles: Department of Linguistics, University of California, 2009).
49. Glowka et al., "*Among the New Words* as an Editing Project."
50. John Considine, *Dictionaries in Early Modern Europe: Lexicography and the Making of Heritage* (Cambridge: Cambridge University Press, 2008); John Considine, *Academy Dictionaries 1600–1800* (Cambridge: Cambridge University Press, 2014).
51. Adams, "Resources: Teaching Perspectives," 1164.

CHAPTER 15

1. E.g., John Algeo and Carmen Butcher, *The Origins and Development of the English Language*, 7th ed. (Boston: Cengage Learning, 2013), 76–78; Celia M. Millward and Mary Hayes, *A Biography of the English Language*, 3rd ed. (Boston: Cengage Learning, 2011), 65–67.
2. Don Ringe, *A Linguistic History of English*, vol. 1, *From Proto-Indo-European to Proto-Germanic* (New York: Oxford University Press, 2006), 90–93, 105–12, gives copious detail on the development of labiovelars.
3. This formulation of Verner's Law is deliberately vague about some details that are best ignored in an introductory course. For example, "voiced environments" does not just mean between voiced sounds. Rather, it includes (1) word-final position, and (2) word-initial position in unstressed clitics, such as the OE prefix *ge-* < PIE **kom-*. Guus Kroonen, *Etymological Dictionary of Proto-Germanic* (Leiden: Brill, 2013), xxiv, offers a brief and clear exposition of Verner's Law; Joseph Wright and Elizabeth M. Wright, *Old English Grammar*, 3rd ed. (New York: Oxford University Press, 1925), 125–28, provide numerous examples of its consequences in Old English.
4. Benjamin W. Fortson, *Indo-European Language and Culture: An Introduction* (Malden, MA: Blackwell), 2004, 73–75, gives a good overview of ablaut. For a much longer discussion, see Andrew Sihler, *New Comparative Grammar of Greek and Latin* (New York: Oxford University Press, 1995), 108–34.
5. Fortson, *IE Language and Culture*, 74; Sihler, *Comparative Grammar*, 129–31.
6. For a concise explication, see Richard M. Hogg and R. D. Fulk, *A Grammar of Old English*, vol. 2, *Morphology* (Malden, MA: Wiley-Blackwell, 2011), 225–30. The origins of a few forms, such as the preterite plurals of Class IV–V, are disputed, as are the exact histories of Classes VI and VII.
7. The list of ModE words derived from **(s)teg-* goes well beyond these four; see Calvert Watkins, *The American Heritage Dictionary of IE Roots*, 2nd ed. (Boston: Houghton Mifflin, 2000), s.v. *(s)teg-²*, for a full list.
8. For additional cognates, see Watkins, *Dictionary of IE Roots*, s.v. *sed-¹*.
9. Marianne Mithun, "Active/Agentive Case Marking and Its Motivations," *Language* 67 (1991): 510–46.
10. The case for seeing the late PIE perfect as descending from an earlier stative is laid out convincingly by Sihler, *Comparative Grammar*, 445, 564–68; an interesting parallel development in modern Mohawk is described in Mithun, "Active/Agentive Case Marking," 528–33. However, some scholars, e.g., Hogg and Fulk, *Grammar of Old English*, 2:299, hold that the perfect meaning was the original one and that some verbs "for semantic reasons developed in such a way that their preterites came to be used in present contexts." For an introductory history of English course, the disagreement isn't particularly important. Both sides agree that the late PIE perfect and stative, whichever is assigned diachronic priority, descend from a single early PIE verb category that was distinct from the active/eventive present.
11. Many specialists, e.g., Ringe, *From PIE to Proto-Germanic*, 153, 157, hold that the aorist was lost entirely (i.e., that all strong preterite forms descend from perfects). I follow Eduard Prokosch, *A Comparative Germanic Grammar* (Philadelphia: Linguistic Society of America, 1939), 160–64, in regarding some forms, such as the OE second singular preterite indicative suffix *-e*, as reflexes of the PIE aorist.

12. For the details of the Latin development, see Sihler, *Comparative Grammar*, 579–90. The French development is self-evident in the present-day language.

13. Most of the works named in the following paragraphs are cited in notes 1 through 12, rendering detailed citation here superfluous. Those not cited previously are Richard M. Hogg, *A Grammar of Old English, Volume 1: Phonology* (Oxford, Blackwell: 1992); Don Ringe and Ann Taylor, *A Linguistic History of English*, vol. 2, *The Development of Old English* (New York: Oxford University Press, 2006). Citations noted previously from Fortson, *IE Language and Culture*, reference the first edition, published in 2004; a second edition was published by Wiley-Blackwell in 2010.

14. Algeo and Butcher, *The Origins and Development of the English Language*; Celia M. Millward and Mary Hayes, *A Biography of the English Language*. 3rd ed. (Boston: Cengage Learning, 2011).

15. Benjamin W. Fortson, *Indo-European Language and Culture: An Introduction* (Malden, MA: Blackwell, 2004).

16. Andrew Sihler, *New Comparative Grammar of Greek and Latin* (New York: Oxford University Press, 1995).

17. Eduard Prokosch, *A Comparative Germanic Grammar* (Philadelphia: Linguistic Society of America, 1939).

18. Joseph Wright and Elizabeth M. Wright, *Old English Grammar*. 3rd ed. (New York: Oxford University Press, 1925).

19. Richard M. Hogg, *A Grammar of Old English*, vol. 1, *Phonology* (Malden, MA: Wiley-Blackwell, 1992); Richard M. Hogg and R. D. Fulk, *A Grammar of Old English*, vol. 2, *Morphology* (Malden, MA: Wiley-Blackwell, 2011).

20. Don Ringe, *A Linguistic History of English*, vol. 1, *From Proto-Indo-European to Proto-Germanic* (New York: Oxford University Press, 2006); Don Ringe and Ann Taylor, *A Linguistic History of English*, vol. 2, *The Development of Old English* (New York: Oxford University Press, 2014).

21. Calvert Watkins, *The American Heritage Dictionary of IE Roots*, 2nd ed. (Boston: Houghton Mifflin, 2000).

22. I believe that the phrase "relief from puzzlement," which I picked up from somewhere a long time ago and used for years without knowing its source, originated with the philosopher Michael Polanyi; see his "Logic and Psychology," *American Psychologist* 21, no. 1 (1968): 36–37, for a brief explication.

CHAPTER 16

1. Thomas Cable, "A History of the English Language," in *Studies in Medieval and Renaissance* Teaching 14 (2007): 17–25, rightly wonders how to cover HEL's basic material while complicating the "succinct story" (17).

2. See James Turner, *Philology: The Forgotten Origins of the Modern Humanities* (Princeton University Press, 2014); and Haruko Momma, *From Philology to English Studies: Language and Culture in the Nineteenth Century* (New York: Cambridge University Press, 2012).

3. Geoffrey Russom, "Literary Form as an Independent Domain of Validation in HEL Pedagogy," in *Studies in Medieval and Renaissance Teaching* 14 (2007): 46–54, speaks to the value of addressing meter in a HEL course; Seth Lerer, *Inventing English: A Portable History of the Language* (New York: Columbia University Press, 2007) has served me well as a main text in HEL courses for literature students.

4. James Andrew Johnston, "Interdisciplinarity and Historiography: Literature," in *English Historical Linguistics: An International Handbook*, vol. 2, ed. Alex Bergs and Laurel Brinton (Boston: de Gruyter, 2012), 1201–13, 1201.

5. Ted Underwood, *Why Literary Periods Mattered: Historical Contrast and the Prestige of English Studies* (Stanford, CA: Stanford University Press, 2013), 84.

6. Ibid., 2.

7. Ibid., 164.

8. Ibid., 6.

9. See Richard J. Watts, "English Historical Linguistics: Myths of the English Language," in *English Historical Linguistics: An International Handbook*, vol. 2, ed. Alex Bergs and Laurel Brinton (Boston: de Gruyter, 2012), 1256–73, for a "funnel view" of language in which any heterogeneity is ultimately homogenized.

10. Anne Curzan, "Periodization in the History of the English Language," in *English Historical Linguistics: An International Handbook*, vol 2, ed. Alex Bergs and Laurel Brinton (Boston: de Gruyter, 2012), 1232–56, 1234.

11. Richard Harris, *A Chorus of Grammars: The Correspondence of George Hickes and His Collaborators on the Thesaurus linguarum septentrionalium* (Toronto: Pontifical Institute of Medieval Studies, 1992), 79.

12. Curzan, "Periodization in the History of the English Language," cites Kemp Malone, "When Did Middle English Begin?" *Language* 6, no. 4 (1930): 110–17, as the earliest critical commentary on period boundaries.

13. Curzan, "Periodization in the History of the English Language," 1236.

14. Adam Nicolson, *God's Secretaries: The Making of the King James Bible* (New York: HarperCollins, 2003), offers an accessible take on the KJV that contextualizes it in its political climate.

15. *The Psalter or Psalms of David and Certain Canticles by Richard Rolle of Hampole*, ed. H. R. Bramley (Oxford: Clarendon Press, 1884), ix.

16. Curzan, "Periodization in the History of the English Language," 1235.

17. David Burnley, "Alfred's Preface to the *Pastoral Care*," in *The History of the English Language: A Source Book*, 2nd ed. (New York: Routledge, 2000), 20–28.

18. Turner, *Philology*, 256.

19. Haruko Momma, "Afterword: HEL for the Monolingual Frame of Mind," in *Studies in Medieval and Renaissance Teaching* 14 (2007): 110–7, at 113.

20. Francis A. March, "Recollections of Language Teaching," *PMLA* 8 (1893): 1738–41, 1741.

21. Barbara M. H. Strang, *A History of English* (London: Methuen, 1970), is a well-respected text that uses a reverse-chronological approach.

22. Francis March, qtd. in Turner, *Philology*, 258.

23. Christopher Cannon, *The Making of Chaucer's English: A Study of Words* (Cambridge: Cambridge University Press, 1998).

24. Comparative diachronic translations are found in several HEL textbooks. Celia M. Millward and Mary Hayes, *A Biography of the English Language*, 3rd ed. (Boston: Cengage Learning, 2011), includes diachronic translations from Boethius's *Consolation of Philosophy* (429–37). A nice brace of diachronic exercises is found in Dennis Freeborn, *From Old to Standard English: A Coursebook in Language Variation Across Time*, 3rd ed. (New York: Palgrave, 2006). One sequence centers on Genesis 3:1, which tells of the serpent's seduction of Eve (416–19). For instructors looking to interject some humor into their HEL courses, use the diachronic translations of Matthew 26:69–75, in which Peter is told, "Your accent gives you away!" (Freeborn, *From Old to Standard English*, 419–27). Burnley, *A History of the English Language*, has sequences from Mark 18–30 (389–93) and Matthew 7: 13–29 (393–98). The rest of the book has notes, but these appendices do not. Alister McGrath, *In the Beginning: The Story of the King James Bible and How It Changed a Nation, a Language, and a Culture* (New York: Doubleday, 2001), has diachronic translations of the Shepherd Psalm in modernized spelling (311–13).

25. Turner, *Philology*, 357.

26. March, *Method of Philological Study of the English Language*, iv.

27. Turner, *Philology*, 357.

28. Patrick P. O'Neill, ed. and trans., *Old English Psalms*, Dumbarton Oaks Medieval Library no. 42 (Cambridge: Harvard University Press, 2016), vii.

29. *Old English Psalms*, vii–viii.

30. *Old English Psalms*, 72–4. The text is also available at http://www.medievalacademy.org/resource/resmgr/maa_books_online/oneill_0104.htm.

31. Lerer, *Inventing English*, 33–7.

32. Josiah Forshall and Frederic Madden, eds., *The Holy Bible, containing the Old and New Testaments, with the Apocryphal books, in the earliest English versions made from the Latin Vulgate by John Wycliffe and His Followers* (Oxford: Oxford University Press, 1850), 2: 758–9.

33. Patrick P. O'Neill, ed. and trans., *King Alfred's Old English Prose Translation of the First Fifty Psalms*, Medieval Academy Books no. 104 (Cambridge, MA: Medieval Academy of America, 2001), 10.

34. A student-friendly chart that compares ME dialectal forms can be found in Celia M. Millward and Mary Hayes, *Workbook to Accompany A Biography of the English Language* (Cengage Learning: Boston, 2011), 158.

35. *The Psalter or Psalms of David*, ix.

36. *The Preface to a Wycliffite Biblical Concordance*, in *The History of the English Language: A Source Book*, 2nd ed., edited by David Burnley (New York: Routledge, 2000), 175–81, line 67.

37. "Prologue to Wycliffite Bible," in *Sections from English Wycliffite Writings*, edited by Anne Hudson, Medieval Academy Reprints for Teaching (Cambridge: Medieval Academy of America, 1997), 67–72.

38. William Allen, *Holy Bible Faithfvlly Translated into English: Ovt of the Authentical Latin, Diligently Conferred with the Hebrew, Greek, and Other Editions in Diuers Languages* (Rheims: Printed by Iohn Cousturier, 1635), 2:5. This text is available in several online formats including Google Books.

39. George Zarnecki, Janet Holt, and Tristam Holland, eds., *English Romanesque Art 1066–1200* (London: Weidenfeld and Nicolson, 1984), 119.

CHAPTER 17

1. R. D. Fulk, Robert E. Bjork, and John D. Niles, eds., *Klaeber's Beowulf and The Fight at Finnburg*, 4th ed. (Toronto: University of Toronto Press, 2008), li.

2. M. M. Bakhtin, *The Dialogic Imagination* (Austin: University of Texas Press, 1981), 13.

3. Fulk et al., *Klaeber's Beowulf*, xxvii.

4. Elliott van Kirk Dobbie, ed., *Beowulf and Judith*, Anglo-Saxon Poetic Records no. 4. (New York: Columbia University Press, 1953).

5. J. R. R. Tolkien, *Beowulf: A Translation and Commentary together with Sellic Spell*, ed. Christopher Tolkien (Boston: Houghton Mifflin Harcourt, 2014); R. M. Liuzza, *Beowulf: A New Verse Translation* (Peterborough, ONT: Broadview, 2000); Seamus Heaney, *Beowulf: A New Verse Translation*, bilingual edn. (New York: W. W. Norton, 2000).

6. Alistair Campbell, *Old English Grammar* (Oxford: Clarendon Press, 1959), 223.

7. See Campbell, *Old English Grammar*, 173–4. Another consonant subjected to palatalization is /k/ (< c >), which becomes /tʃ/ in the same context (see ibid.). Some editions, including *Klaeber's Beowulf* (Fulk et al., *Klaeber's Beowulf*), indicate palatalization with a dot above the letter: i.e., ġ, ċ. Other examples of palatalization include ġeong ('young') and ċild ('child').

8. Campbell, *Old English Grammar*, 321.

9. Peter Goolden, *The Old English Apollonius of Tyre* (Oxford: Oxford University Press, 1958), ix–xii.

10. Ibid. 42.

11. Samuel Johnson, "The History of the English Language," in *A Dictionary of the English Language: In Which the Words Are Deduced from Their Originals, and Illustrated in Their Different Significations by Examples from the Best Writers*, 2 vols. (London: Strahan, 1755a), K2ʳ.

12. E.g., Raymond Wiley, *John Mitchell Kemble and Jacob Grimm: A Correspondence, 1832–1852* (Leiden: Brill, 1971), 57.

13. Samuel Johnson, "Preface," in *A Dictionary of the English Language: In Which the Words Are Deduced from Their Originals, and Illustrated in Their Different Significations by Examples from the Best Writers*, 2 vols. (London: Strahan, 1755b), C1ʳ.

14. Richard Harris, *A Chorus of Grammars: The Correspondence of George Hickes and His Collaborators on the Thesaurus linguarum septentrionalium* (Toronto: Pontifical Institute of Medieval Studies, 1992), 79.
15. Henry Sweet, *A History of English Sounds* (London: Trübner, 1874), 158.
16. Elaine Treharne, *Living Through Conquest: The Politics of Early English, 1020–1220* (Oxford: Oxford University Press, 2012), 91–146.
17. Johnson, "The History of the English Language," D1ʳ.
18. John M. Kemble, *History of the English Language: First, or Anglo-Saxon Period* (Cambridge: J. & J. J. Deighton, 1834), 4.
19. Ibid., 5.
20. William Jones, "On the Hindus," in *The Collected Works of Sir William Jones*, ed. Garland Cannon, 13 vols. (New York: New York University Press, 1993), 35, [italics in the original].
21. Johnson, "The History of the English Language," D1ʳ [italics in the original].
22. Ibid., K2ʳ.
23. Ibid., D1ʳ.
24. John M. Kemble, ed., *The Anglo-Saxon Poems of Beowulf, The Travellers Song and the Battle of Finnes-burh* (London: Pickering, 1833), 3.
25. Ibid., 11.
26. See further Haruko Momma, "The *Brut* as Saxon Literature: The New Philologists Read Lawman," in *Reading Laȝamon's Brut: Approaches and Explorations*, edited by Rosamund Allen, Jane Roberts, and Carole Weinberg (Amsterdam: Rodopi, 2013), 53–68.
27. Kemble. *The Anglo-Saxon Poems of Beowulf*, 35–6.
28. Ibid., xii, xix.
29. Henirich Leo, *Bëówulf: das älteste deutsche, in angelsächsischer mundart erhaltene, heldengedicht* (Halle: Anton, 1839).
30. Johnson, "The History of the English Language," D1ʳ˒ᵛ [italics in the original].
31. Malcolm Godden and Susan Irvine, eds., *The Old English Boethius: An Edition of the Old English Versions of Boethius's De Consolatione Philosophiae*, 2 vols. (Oxford: Oxford University Press, 2009), 1:243.
32. Ibid., 2, 4.
33. Kemble, *History of the English Language*, 8.
34. Ibid., 9.
35. Ibid., 4.
36. Johnson, "The History of the English Language," E1ʳ, F1ᵛ [italics in the original].
37. Ibid., E1ʳ.
38. Kemble, *History of the English Language*, 6–7.
39. Kemble, *The Anglo-Saxon Poems of Beowulf*.
40. Fulk et al., *Klaeber's Beowulf*.
41. Wiley, *John Mitchell Kemble and Jacob Grimm*, 48–9, 57 n. 4.
42. See Momma, *From Philology to English Studies*, esp. 60–136.
43. I have used Bullough's interpretation in Bullough, "What Has Ingeld to Do with Lindisfarne?," 93–125, 124.
44. Bullough, "What Has Ingeld to Do with Lindisfarne?," 93–125.
45. *Beowulf*, ll. 102–14.
46. Kemble, *History of the English Language*, 15.
47. Bullough, "What Has Ingeld to Do with Lindisfarne?"
48. Kemble, *History of the English Language*, ix.
49. London, British Library, MS Cotton Vitellius. A. xv, c. 1000, fol. 132ʳ.
50. Cf. Michael Matto, "Remainders: Reading an Old English Poem through Multiple Translations," *Studies in Medieval and Renaissance Teaching* 22, no. 2 (2015): 81–9.
51. George Jack, ed., *Beowulf: A Student Edition* (Oxford: Clarendon Press, 1994); Michael Alexander, *Beowulf* (London: Penguin, 1995).
52. Oswald Cockayne, *Leechdoms, Wortcunning and Starcraft of Early England*, 3 vols. (London: Longman, 1864–66), 1, 378.

53. Take betony and boil well in wine or in old ale and wash the head with the infusion and afterwards place the herb, as warm, around the head and wrap with cloth, and let it be so all night. (Translated by author)

54. Johnson, "The History of the English Language," D1ʳ.

55. Janet Bately, ed., *The Anglo-Saxon Chronicle: A Collaborative Edition*, vol. 3, *MS A: A Semi-diplomatic Edition with Introduction and Indices* (Cambridge: Brewer, 1986), 19.

56. Johnson, "The History of the English Language," G2ᵛ.

57. Richard Sylvester, ed., *The Complete Works of St Thomas More*, vol. 2 (New Haven: Yale University Press, 1963), 8.

58. Johnson, "The History of the English Language," G2ᵛ.

CHAPTER 18

1. Barbara M. H. Strang, *A History of English* (London: Methuen, 1970), xv.

2. Late Modern English is generally agreed to cover the period 1700-1900.

3. Capitalization and italics are original. Richard W. Bailey, *Nineteenth-Century English* (Ann Arbor: University of Michigan Press, 1996), 89.

4. William Labov, *Sociolinguistic Patterns* (Oxford: Blackwell, 1978), 114.

5. Defined in the *Oxford English Dictionary* (*OED*) online as "flabbergasted, astounded; speechless or incoherent with amazement."

6. Charles Jones, *A History of English Phonology* (London: Longman, 1989), 279.

7. Manfred Görlach, *English in Nineteenth-Century England* (Cambridge: Cambridge University Press, 1999), and *Eighteenth-Century English* (Heidelberg: C. Winter, 2001).

8. Joan C. Beal, *English Pronunciation in the Eighteenth Century* (Oxford: Clarendon Press, 1999).

9. Joan C. Beal, *English in Modern Times 1700–1945* (London: Arnold, 2004).

10. Suzanne Romaine (ed.), *The Cambridge History of the English Language*, vol. IV, *1776–1997* (Cambridge: Cambridge University Press, 1998).

11. Ingrid Tieken-Boon van Ostade, *An Introduction to Late Modern English* (Edinburgh: Edinburgh University Press, 2009).

12. Samuel Johnson, *A Dictionary of the English Language: In Which the Words Are Deduced from Their Originals, and Illustrated in Their Different Significations by Examples from the Best Writers*, 2 vols. (London, Strahan, 1755a).

13. Robert Lowth, *A Short Introduction to English Grammar* (London: Miller and Dodsby, 1762).

14. John Walker, *A Critical Pronouncing Dictionary and Expositor of the English Language* (London: G. G. J. and J. Robinson and T. Cadell, 1791).

15. Jane Hodson, "The Problem of Joseph Priestley's (1733–1804) Descriptivism," *Historiographia Linguistica* 33 (2006): 57–84.

16. This colloquium and the research project from which it sprang were supported by the Association of Commonwealth Universities and the British Academy (International Collaboration Grant CADF 2001-20).

17. Einar Haugen, "Dialect, Language, Nation," *American Anthropologist* 68 (1966): 922–35.

18. James Milroy and Lesley Milroy, *Authority in Language*, 2nd ed. (London: Routledge, 1991).

19. Terttu Nevalainen and Ingrid Tieken-Boon van Ostade, "Standardisation," in *A History of the English Language*, edited by Richard Hogg and David Denison (Cambridge: Cambridge University Press, 2006), 271–311.

20. Stirling A. Leonard, *The Doctrine of Correctness in English Usage, 1700–1800* (Madison, WI: Russell & Russell, 1929), 13.

21. Ibid., 129.

22. Geoffrey K. Pullum, "Lowth's Grammar: A Re-Evaluation," *Linguistics* 137 (1974): 63.

23. There is no mention of the split infinitive in Lowth's or any other eighteenth-century grammar. This issue is first raised in the *New England Magazine* in 1834.

1. The idea that Old English is learned like a foreign language can be seen in standard textbooks, such as Bruce Mitchell and Fred C. Robinson, *A Guide to Old English*, 6th ed. (Malden, MA: Blackwell, 2001), which notes that the syntax often resembles that of Modern English, but "at other times, we seem to be wrestling with a foreign language," at once quelling the student's fear of its unintelligibility, but taunting him or her with the promise of a good challenge. The claim is also made in more public, but less reputable venues, such as the WikiHow webpage on "How to Learn Old English," which advises students to "Treat Old English as a foreign language." Perhaps now most pervasively and positively, the claim has been used to make Old English satisfy foreign language requirements in many American graduate programs. In my opinion, this is a good development, since it encourages English doctoral students to learn Old English, once a standard requirement in many programs, and in turn reduces its marginalization within English departments. But at the same time, classifying it as a foreign language (and the departmental debates that precede such classification) necessarily raises questions of whether it properly counts as "foreign"; the response points out its differences from Modern English, the pedagogical methods used in teaching it, and the fact that learning it opens the student up to a new and wide body of literature previously inaccessible in its original form. In Chapter 2 in this volume, John McWhorter captures this foreignness of Old English best when he comments that many of his HEL students "might as well have been seeing Turkish in my slides" (15).

2. See Haruko Momma, Chapter 17, in this volume. Or as Carl T. Berkhout explains in "Laurence Nowell (1530–ca. 1570)," in *Medieval Scholarship: Biographical Studies on the Formation of a Discipline*, vol. 2, *Literature and Philology*, edited by Helen Damico (New York: Garland, 1998), 1–17, at 3, "By the mid-sixteenth century Old English had become virtually a foreign language in a country whose scholars and antiquaries were slow to accept even Modern English as a language of learning" (3).

3. See Seth Lerer, Chapter 7, in this volume, "The History of the English Language and the Medievalist" (72).

4. Strang, *A History of English*, is a rare textbook that takes a reverse chronological approach.

5. Johnson, *Dictionary of the English Language*.

6. The model was first proposed in Kachru, "Standards, Codification and Sociolinguistic Realism," 11–30. For a history of other models, see McArthur, "Models of English," 78–101. Graddol, "English Next," 101, has suggested that Kachru's model should be replaced with a model of "functional nativeness" based on proficiency level. The inner circle is thus classified as highly proficient (which entails skilled communication at an international level rather than a highly local level), and as we move outward, international proficiency decreases and becomes more localized. This model is certainly problematic in the way elides the variety and autonomy of Englishes (and to some degree that is Graddol's vision for the future). For further discussion, see Jenkins, *Global Englishes*, 19.

7. An exception is van Gelderen, *History of the English Language*, 253.

8. Yasukata Yano, "The Future of English and the Kachruvian Three Circle Model," in *World Englishes - Problems, Properties and Prospects: Selected Papers from the 13th IAWE Conference*, ed. Thomas Hoffman and Lucia Siebers (Amsterdam: John Benjamins, 2009), 379–84, at 381.

9. It should be noted that there are also numerous other textbooks with less traditional approaches that focus on diversity and non-standard forms of the language (though many of these are collections of scholarly essays rather than introductory textbooks). See, for example, Graddol, Leith, and Swann, *English: History, Diversity and Change*, which contains one chapter on English manuscripts, one chapter on the origins of English (from OE to the late Middle Ages), one chapter on modern English as a

national language, one chapter on colonial and postcolonial Englishes, and then four chapters on features of variety in English (grammar, accents, style, and the judgment of good and bad English).

10. Albert C. Baugh, *A History of the English Language*, 1st ed. (New York: D. Appleton-Century Company), 1935; Albert C. Baugh and Thomas Cable, *A History of the English Language*, 6th ed. (Upper Saddle River, NJ: Longman, 2012).

11. Thomas Pyles and John Algeo, *The Origins and Development of the English Language*, 1st ed. (Boston: Cengage Learning, 1964); Thomas Pyles and John Algeo, *The Origins and Development of the English Language*, 6th ed. (Boston: Cengage Learning, 2010).

12. Celia M. Millward, *A Biography of the English Language*, 1st ed. (Ft. Worth, TX: Harcourt Brace Jovanovich, 1989); Celia M. Millward and Mary Hayes, *A Biography of the English Language*, 3rd ed. (Boston: Cengage Learning, 2011).

13. Elly van Gelderen, *A History of the English Language*, 1st ed. (Amsterdam: John Benjamins, 2006); Elly van Gelderen, *A History of the English Language*, rev. ed. (Amsterdam: John Benjamins, 2014).

14. For example, Rajend Mesthrie and Rakesh M. Bhatt, *World Englishes: The Study of New Linguistic Varieties* (Cambridge: Cambridge University Press, 2008).

15. John Algeo, "In Memoriam: Thomas Pyles (1905–1980)," *Names: A Journal of Onomastics* 28, no. 4 (1980): 291–92.

16. Baugh, *History of the English Language*, 1st ed., §7, 9–11; *History of the English Language*, 2nd ed., §7, 7–8.

17. Baugh and Cable, *History of the English Language*, 3rd ed., §7, 6–8.

18. Baugh and Cable, *History of the English Language*, 4th ed., §7, 7–8.

19. Baugh and Cable, *History of the English Language*, 6th ed. , §§257–64, 397–407.

20. Baugh, *History of the English Language*, 1st ed., §229, 394–98.

21. Baugh, *History of the English Language*, 2nd ed., §229, 384–88.

22. Baugh and Cable, *History of the English Language*, 3rd ed.,§229, 318–24.

23. Baugh and Cable, *History of the English Language*, 4th ed., §229, pp. 313–25, §230, 325–28.

24. This influence can also be seen in volumes such as Richard Hogg and David Denison, eds., *A History of the English Language* (Cambridge: Cambridge University Press, 2008). However, in the six-volume *Cambridge History of the English Language*, the essays on World Englishes are contained in the fifth volume, which precedes the final volume on English in North America; see Robert Burchfield, ed., *The Cambridge History of the English Language*, vol. 5, *English in Britain and Overseas: Origins and Development* (Cambridge: Cambridge University Press, 1994).

25. Randolph Quirk, *The Use of English* (London: Longman, 1962), 17–18. For his argument that non-native Englishes were deficient, see "Language Varieties and Standard Language," *English Today* 6, no. 1 (1990): 3–10.

26. Millward, *Biography*.

27. Though she also wrote on American English; for example, Celia Millward, "Benewell Kemler's Black English," *American Speech* 69, no. 2 (1994): 155–67.

28. This rhetoric is surprising given her sensitive handling of African American Vernacular English (AAVE) a few pages earlier, noting, for instance, that "BE is just as grammatical—in the sense that a grammar is a set of rules—as standard English. For example, the omission of the copula is far from random sloppiness; in fact, it is dropped only when standard English can contract it, and not otherwise" (Millward, *Biography*, 331).

29. In the 1960s, some textbooks included sections on "the future of English" and English around the world; e.g., Mario Pei, *The Story of the English Language* (Philadelphia: Lippincott, 1967).

30. van Gelderen, *History of the English Language*, 269.

31. Salman Rushdie, *Imaginary Homelands: Essays and Criticism 1981–1991* (London: Granta Books, 1991), 64, quoted in David Crystal, *English as a Global Language* (Cambridge: Cambridge University Press, 2003), 184.

32. For example, Arundhati Roy's political writings in English (e.g., "The End of Imagination") apparently "angered many in her upper-caste, urban, English-speaking audience, even as it attracted another. Most of her new fans had never heard of her novel; they often spoke languages other than English and felt marginalized because of their religion, caste, or ethnicity, left behind by India's economic rise. They devoured the essays Roy began writing, which were distributed in unauthorized translations, and flocked to rallies to hear her speak;" Siddhartha Deb, "Arundhati Roy, the Not-So-Reluctant Renegade," *New York Times Magazine*, March 5, 2014.

33. For a sense of the complexity involved in handling this topic, see the debate around Robert Phillipson's influential book, *Linguistic Imperialism* (Oxford: Oxford University Press, 1992). Several of Phillipson's articles on the topic along with the reviews of his book and his responses are printed in volume 5 of Kingsley Bolton and Braj B. Kachru, eds., *World Englishes: Critical Concepts in Linguistics*, 6 vols. (London: Routledge, 2006), 286–336.

34. See Robert J. Baumgardner and Kimberly Brown, "World Englishes: Ethics and Pedagogy," *World Englishes* 22, no. 3 (2003): 245–51.

35. Quirk, "Language Varieties and Standard Language," 3–10; and Braj B. Kachru, "Liberation Linguistics and the Quirk Concern," *English Today* 7, no. 1 (1991): 3–13.

36. E.g., Robert Phillipson, "Voice in Global English: Unheard Chords in Crystal Loud and Clear," *Applied Linguistics* 20, no. 2 (1999): 265–76; and David Crystal, "On Trying to Be Crystal-Clear: A Response to Phillipson," *Applied Linguistics* 21, no. 3 (2000): 415–21, who strongly defends his book against Phillipson's critique.

37. Whereas a more journalistic survey dedicated to World Englishes, like Crystal's *English as a Global Language,* can present a dynamic and less teleological picture.

38. Millward, *Biography*, 1st ed., 341.

39. Ibid., 341.

40. Kachru, "Liberation Linguistics and the Quirk Concern," 12.

41. Tom McArthur, "English World-wide in the Twentieth Century," in *The Oxford History of English*, edited by Lynda Mugglestone (Oxford: Oxford University Press, 2012), 446–87.

42. In Chapter 25 in this volume, Matthew Sergi outlines a similar reverse-chronological plan and its numerous benefits. I'm grateful for my friendship with Sergi and the many conversations we've shared, which have profoundly shaped my approach to HEL pedagogy. I particularly admire the design of his course, but I would have trouble reversing the chronology completely, since I like to show my students how one change opens up the possibility of subsequent changes, and I find it hard to avoid teleological assumptions when working backward from PDE.

43. Burchfield, *English in Britain and Overseas*, 98–99.

44. Rajend Mesthrie, "World Englishes and the Multilingual History of English," *World Englishes* 25, no. 3–4 (2006): 381–90.

CHAPTER 20

1. I am not a historian of the English language, though I have often been invited to write essays on the subject matter. What I do in this chapter, as in the others before, is put my experience as a genetic creolist to advantage by re-examining provocatively the received doctrine on the emergence and evolution of English. I discuss especially the actuating ecology, which involves what historians of English have called "external history." I focus on population movements and the ensuing language contacts that influenced the emergence of English in southern and eastern England and, repeatedly, its spread and its appropriation by populations speaking other languages characterized as substrate. I invite the reader to engage in a comparative examination of whether the ecological factors that influenced the evolution of English in the British Isles (e.g., population structure, modes of transmission, patterns of interaction, languages previously spoken by the new speakers, and time of language shift) are different from those that have played a role in its speciation in other parts of the world.

2. Salikoko S. Mufwene, *The Ecology of Language Evolution* (Cambridge: Cambridge University Press, 2001).
3. Salikoko S. Mufwene, *Language Evolution: Contact, Competition and Change* (London: Continuum Press, 2008); Mufwene, *Ecology of Language Evolution*.
4. Alfred W. Crosby, *Ecological Imperialism: The Biological Expansion of Europe, 900-1900* (Cambridge: Cambridge University Press, 1986).
5. Dick Leith, "English—Colonial to Postcolonial," in *Changing English*, edited by David Graddol, Dick Leith, Joan Swann, Martin Rhys, and Julia Gillen (Abingdon, UK: Routledge, 2007), 117–52.
6. See among others, Markku Filppula, "Contact and the Early History of English," in *The Handbook of Language Contact*, edited by Raymond Hickey (Malden, MA: Wiley-Blackwell, 2010), 432–53.
7. For a more detailed explanation, see Mufwene, *Ecology of Language Evolution*.
8. Jeff Siegel, *Language Contact in a Plantation Environment: A Sociolinguistic History of Fiji* (New York: Cambridge University Press, 1987).
9. Mufwene, *Ecology of Language Evolution*.
10. Ibid.
11. It should actually be quite informative to investigate the extent to which the names of particular languages are correlated with the construction of the polities or ethnicities they are historically associated with, although we learn in the case of creole vernaculars that they emerged later than the locally born individuals identified as Creoles in the European settlement colonies (Robert Chaudenson, *Creolization of Language and Culture* [London: Routledge, 2001] and there are Creole populations that are not associated with a creole vernacular (Virginia Domínguez, *White by Definition: Social Classification in Creole Louisiana* [New Brunswick, NJ: Rutgers University Press, 1986]; Charles Stewart, ed., *Creolization: History, Ethnography, Theory* [Walnut Creek, CA: Left Coast Press, 2007]).
12. Joseph Embley Emonds and Jan Terje Faarlund. *English: The Language of the Vikings* (Olomouc, Czech: Palacký University, 2014), 155. This phrase suggests that Old English emerged somehow before, as they claim, the Anglo-Saxons shifted to Norse as their vernacular. On the other hand, according to Emonds and Faarlund (23, note 6),

> Just as the Germanic etymological root of "French" [viz., *Frankish*] does not suggest that this language is Germanic, so the etymological root of "English" does not suggest it derives from Anglo-Saxon. There is no a priori burden of proof on disputing this widespread belief

This flat denial is debatable regarding Old English, which is actually not covered by their hypothesis.
13. See Mufwene, *Ecology of Language Evolution*, 106–26.
14. David Crystal, *The Cambridge Encyclopedia of the English Language* (Cambridge: Cambridge University Press, 1995).
15. Crosby, *Ecological Imperialism*.
16. Mufwene, *Ecology of Language Evolution*.
17. Emonds and Faarlund, *English: The Language of the Vikings*, 55, note 36.
18. According to Emonds and Faarlund, *English: The Language of the Vikings*.
19. Raymond Hickey, "Arguments for Creolisation in Irish English," in *Language History and Linguistic Modelling: A Festschrift for Jacek Fisiak on his 60th Birthday*, edited by Raymond Hickey and Stanisław Puppel (Berlin: Mouton de Gruyter, 1997), 969–1038, characterizes the process, instead, as a case of koinéization, which underscores the fact that the languages in contact were both Germanic.
20. Emonds and Faarlund, *English: The Language of the Vikings*.
21. Ibid. 44, note 24.
22. Mufwene, *Ecology of Language Evolution*.
23. According to Emonds and Faarlund, *English: The Language of the Vikings*.
24. Hickey, "Arguments for Creolisation in Irish English."

25. Elizabeth Traugott, *A History of English Syntax: A Transformational Approach to the History of English Sentence Structure* (New York, Chicago: Holt, Rinehart, and Winston, 1972).
26. Population structure is often invoked in Mufwene, *Ecology of Language Evolution*, to account for differential evolution.
27. According to Hickey, "Arguments for Creolisation in Irish English."
28. Nancy Dorian, *Investigating Variation: The Effects of Social Organization and Social Setting* (Oxford: Oxford University Press, 2010).
29. This observation should not be construed as denying cases obvious African substrate influence as the serial construction *fly go a Miami* 'fly/flew to Miami' in Jamaican Creole compared to the ambiguous case of *swim cross di riba* 'swim/swam across the river.' The point is that in many cases it is also (partial) congruence between the lexifier and some substrate languages that drove the divergence away from the acrolectal varieties of the lexifiers, on which genetic creolistics has typically focused, misguidedly. Mufwene, *Ecology of Language Evolution* and Mufwene, *Language Evolution*.
30. Chaudenson, *Creolization of Language and Culture*; Mufwene, *Ecology of Language Evolution*.
31. According to Hickey, "Arguments for Creolisation in Irish English."
32. Ibid., 976, 977.
33. According to Karen Corrigan, *Irish English*, vol. 1, *Northern Ireland* (Edinburgh: Edinburgh University Press, 2010).
34. This is according to an interpretation of this ecological factor provided by Salikoko S. Mufwene, "Driving Forces in English Contact Linguistics," in *English as a Contact Language*, edited by by Daniel Schreier and Marianne Hundt (Cambridge: Cambridge University Press, 2012), 204–21.
35. Salikoko S. Mufwene, "The Universalist and Substrate Hypotheses Complement One Another," in *Substrata versus Universals in Creole Genesis*, edited by Pieter Muysken and Norval Smith (Amsterdam: John Benjamins, 1986); John Singler, "The Homogeneity of the Substrate as a Factor in Pidgin/Creole Genesis," *Language* 64 (1988): 27–51.
36. Roger Keesing, *Melanesian Pidgin and the Oceanic Substrate* (Stanford: Stanford University Press, 1988).
37. Edgar Schneider and Michael B. Montgomery, "On the Trail of Early Nonstandard Grammar: An Electronic Corpus of Southern U.S. Antebellum Overseers' Letters," *American Speech* 76, no. 4 (2001): 388–410.
38. "Compulsory Education," *Wikipedia*, accessed March 21, 2016, https://en.wikipedia.org/wiki/Compulsory_education.
39. Mufwene, *Ecology of Language Evolution*.
40. Salikoko S. Mufwene, "Globalisation économique mondiale des XVIIe-XVIIIe siècles, émergence des créoles, et vitalité langagière," in *Langues créoles, mondialisation, éducation*, edited by Arnaud Carpooran (Vacoas, Mauritius: Editions le Printemps, 2014).
41. According to Philip Baker and Peter Mühlhäusler, "From Business to Pidgin," *Journal of Asian Pacific Communication* 1 (1990): 87-115.
42. Salikoko S. Mufwene, "The Emergence of African American English: Monogenetic or Polygenetic? Under How Much Substrate Influence?" in *The Oxford Handbook of African American language*, edited by Sonja Lanehart (Oxford: Oxford University Press, 2015).
43. Mufwene, "Globalisation économique mondiale des XVIIe-XVIIIe siècles.
44. This term is from Emanuel J. Drechsel, *Language Contact in the Early Colonial Pacific: Maritime Polynesian Pidgin before Pidgin English* (Cambridge: Cambridge University Press, 2014).
45. Discussed in detail in Marianne Mithun, "The Substratum in Grammar and Discourse," in *Language Contact: Theoretical and Empirical Studies*, edited by Ernst Håkon Jahr, 103–15 (Berlin: Mouton de Gruyter, 2012).
46. Mufwene, *Ecology of Language Evolution*.
47. Formal education certainly played a role in the case of children of immigrant Europeans, especially in facilitating the learning process but also in fostering environments where

there have been regular interactions with native-speaking children. We must also make a distinction between, on the one hand, the standard varieties taught in school, for specialized functions, and, on the other, the vernacular varieties spoken naturally during socialization. Even for native speakers, the standard variety is an L2 variety, although having a genetically related mother tongue facilitates its acquisition.

48. Mufwene, *Ecology of Language Evolution;* Salikoko S. Mufwene. "The Indigenization of English in North America," in *World Englishes: Problems, Properties, Prospects,* edited by Thomas Hoffmann and Lucia Siebers (Amsterdam: Benjamins, 2009).

49. Thomas Babington Macaulay, "Minute on Indian Education, February 1835," in *Sketches of Some Distinguished Anglo-Indians: (Second series) Including Lord Macaulay's Great Minute on Education in India,* compiled by William Ferguson Beatson Laurie (London: J. B. Day, 1875), 170–85.

50. Mufwene, "The Indigenization of English in North America."

51. Edgar W. Schneider, *Postcolonial English: Varieties Around the World* (Cambridge: Cambridge University Press, 2007).

52. Braj B. Kachru, "Standards, Codification, and Sociolinguistic Realism: The English Language in the Outer Circle," in *English in the World: Teaching and Learning the Language and Literatures,* edited by Randolph Quirk and Henry Widdowson (Cambridge: Cambridge University Press, 1985); Braj B. Kachru, *World Englishes and Culture Wars* (Cambridge: Cambridge University Press, 2017).

53. For the purposes of this chapter, I will ignore the Expanding Circle, consisting of other polities such as Japan and Western European countries, where English has been accepted as an important international language, its speakers are typically non-native, and they do not use it as a lingua franca among themselves.

54. This is what Mufwene, *Ecology of Language Evolution,* characterizes as changes in the external ecology of the language.

CHAPTER 21

1. David Burnley, ed., *The History of the English Language: A Source Book,* 2nd ed. (Harlow, Essex: Pearson, 2000), 388–93; Bible Society of the West Indies, "Maak 6," *Di Jamiekan Nyuu Testiment (JNT),* 2012, https://www.bible.com/bible/476/mrk.6.jnt.

2. D. H. Lawrence, "Fanny and Annie," in Burnley, *The History of the English Language,* 368–73.

3. Terttu Nevalainen, *An Introduction to Early Modern English* (Edinburgh: Edinburgh University Press, 2006), 51–52.

4. "chocolate, n. and adj. B1b," *OED Online,* accessed March 12, 2016, http://www.oed.com.myaccess.library.utoronto.ca/view/Entry/32100?rskey=t3eyMt&result=1&isAdvanced=false.

5. Phil Benson, *Ethnocentrism and the English Dictionary* (New York: Routledge, 2001); Lynda Mugglestone, "Patriotism, Empire and Cultural Prescriptivism: Images of Anglicity in the *OED,*" in *Languages of Nation: Attitudes and Norms,* ed. Carol Percy and Mary Catherine Davidson (Bristol: Multilingual Matters, 2012), 175–91; Sarah Ogilvie, "Rethinking Burchfield and World Englishes," *International Journal of Lexicography* 21 (2008): 23–59, and *Words of the World: A Global History of the* Oxford English Dictionary (Cambridge: Cambridge University Press, 2013).

6. Suzanne Romaine, "Contact with Other Languages," in *English in North America,* vol. 6, *The Cambridge History of the English Language,* edited by John Algeo (Cambridge: Cambridge University Press, 2001), 154–83; Keren Rice, "112: English in Contact: Native American Languages," in *English Historical Linguistics: An International Handbook,* edited by Alexander Bergs and Laurel Brinton (Berlin: Mouton de Gruyter, 2012), 2: 1753–67.

7. Stefan Dollinger, Laurel J. Brinton, and Margery Fee, eds. *DCHP-1 Online: A Dictionary of Canadianisms on Historical Principles Online,* 2013. First published 1967 by Gage Press. http://dchp.ca/DCHP-1/.

8. Mark Davies, *Corpus of Global Web-Based English: 1.9 Billion Words from Speakers in 20 Countries* [*GloWbE*] 2013. http://corpus.byu.edu/glowbe/

9. Mario Saraceni, *World Englishes: A Critical Analysis* (London: Bloomsbury, 2015).

10. Online Newspaper Directory for the World, accessed March 11, 2016, www.onlinenewspapers.com; Factiva, accessed March 11, 2016, https://www.dowjones.com/products/factiva/.

11. D.H. Lawrence, "Fanny and Annie," in Burnley, *The History of the English Language*, 369.

12. Susan L. Ferguson, "Drawing Fictional Lines: Dialect and Narrative in the Victorian Novel," *Style* 32, no. 1 (1998): 4–7.

13. Jane Hodson, *Dialect in Film and Literature* (Houndmills: Palgrave Macmillan, 2014): 171–82.

14. Asif Agha, "The Social Life of Cultural Value," *Language & Communication* 23, no. 3 (2003): 231–73.

15. Victor J. Ramraj, ed. *Concert of Voices: an Anthology of World Writing in English*, 2nd ed. (Peterborough: Broadview Press, 2009).

16. Dohra Ahmad, ed. *Rotten English: a Literary Anthology* (New York and London: W.W. Norton & Company, 2007).

17. Carol Percy, ed. *The English Language(s): Cultural & Linguistic Perspectives*, 2000–2008, http://homes.chass.utoronto.ca/~cpercy/courses/HELEncyclopedia.htm; David Zok, "Turkey's Language Revolution and the Status of English Today," *The English Languages: History, Diaspora, Culture* 1 (2010), http://jps.library.utoronto.ca/index.php/elhdc/article/view/14300; Alexander Eastwood, "A Fantastic Failure: Displaced Nationalism and the Intralingual Translation of Harry Potter," *Papers of the Bibliographical Society of Canada* 49, no. 2 (2012): 167–88.

CHAPTER 22

1. Braj B. Kachru, "The Second Diaspora of English," in *English in its Social Contexts: Essays in Historical Sociolinguistics*, ed. Tim William Machan and Charles T. Scott, 230–52 (New York: Oxford University Press, 1992).

2. See Kachru, "The Second Diaspora of English," 234, for a full list of regions and countries.

3. Ibid.

4. David Crystal, *English as a Global Language*, 2nd ed. (Cambridge: Cambridge University Press, 2003), 69.

5. Edgar Schneider, "Colonization, Globalization, and the Sociolinguistics of World Englishes," in *The Cambridge Handbook of Sociolinguistics*, edited by Rajend Mesthrie, 335–54 (Cambridge: Cambridge University Press, 2011), at 335.

6. Rajend Mesthrie and Rakesh M. Bhatt, *World Englishes: The Study of New Linguistic Varieties* (Cambridge: Cambridge University Press, 2008).

7. Braj B. Kachru, *The Alchemy of English: The Spread, Functions and Models of Non-native Englishes* (London: Pergamon, 1986).

8. Tom McArthur, *The English Languages* (Cambridge: Cambridge University Press, 1998).

9. Kachru, "The Second Diaspora of English."

10. Kachru, *The Alchemy of English*.

11. Cf. Rakesh M. Bhatt, "World Englishes," *Annual Review of Anthropology* 30 (2001): 527–50; A. Suresh Canagarajah, *Resisting Linguistic Imperialism in English Teaching* (Oxford: Oxford University Press, 1999); Kachru, *The Alchemy of English*.

12. William Bright, "Toward a Cultural Grammar," *Indian Linguistics* 29 (1968): 20–29.

13. Allison Henry, *Belfast English and Standard English: Dialect Variation and Parameter Setting* (Oxford: Oxford University Press, 1996).

14. Braj B. Kachru, *The Indianization of English: The English Language in India* (Delhi: Oxford University Press, 1983); Peter Trudgill and Jean Hannah, *International English* (London: Edward Arnold, 1985).

15. Rakesh M. Bhatt, "Optimal Expressions in Indian English," *English Language and Linguistics* 4 (2000): 69–95.

16. Anthea Fraser Gupta, "The Pragmatic Particles of Singapore Colloquial English," *Journal of Pragmatics* 18 (1992): 31–57; Jock Wong, "The Particles of Singapore English: A Semantic and Cultural Interpretation," *Journal of Pragmatics* 36 (2004): 739–93.

17. See Bright, "Toward a Cultural Grammar," 29; Dell Hymes, *Foundations of Sociolinguistics: An Ethnographic Approach* (Philadelphia: University of Pennsylvania Press, 1974); Jean D'souza, "Interactional Strategies in South Asian languages: Their Implications for Teaching English Internationally," *World Englishes* 7 (1988): 159–71; Rakesh M. Bhatt, "World Englishes," *Annual Review of Anthropology* 30 (2001): 527–50; Rakesh M. Bhatt, "Expert Discourses, Local Practices, and Hybridity: The Case of Indian Englishes," in *Reclaiming the Local in Language Policy and Practice*, edited by A. Suresh Canagarajah, 25–54 (Mahwah, NJ: Lawrence Erlbaum, 2005).

18. Cf. Bhatt, "World Englishes"; and Bhatt "Expert Discourses, Local Practices, and Hybridity."

19. Penelope Brown and Steven C. Levinson, *Politeness: Some Universals in Language* (Cambridge: Cambridge University Press, 1987).

20. Rakesh M. Bhatt, "Prescriptivism, Creativity, and World Englishes," *World Englishes* 14 (1995): 247–60; Bhatt, "World Englishes;" and Bhatt, "Expert Discourses, Local Practices, and Hybridity."

21. See Winnie Cheng and Martin Warren, "'She Knows More about Hong Kong Than You Do Isn't It': Tags in Hong Kong Conversational English," *Journal of Pragmatics* 33 (2001): 1419–39.

22. Anne Pakir, "English in Singapore: The Codification of Competing Norms," in *Language, Society and Education in Singapore: Issues and Trends*, ed. Saravanan Gopinathan et al., 92–118 (Singapore: Times Academic Press, 1994); Lubna Alsagoff and Ho Chee Lick, "The Grammar of Singapore English," in *English in New Cultural Contexts: Reflections from Singapore*, edited by Joseph A. Foley et al., 127–51 (Oxford: Oxford University Press, 1998).

23. Edmund O. Bamiro, "Syntactic Variation in West African English," *World Englishes* 17:2 (1995): 189–204; Eyamba G. Bokamba, "The Africanization of English," in *The Other Tongue: English Across Cultures*, edited by Braj B. Kachru, 125–47 (Urbana: University of Illinois Press, 1992).

24. See Bhatt, "World Englishes"; and Bhatt, "Expert Discourses, Local Practices, and Hybridity: The Case of Indian Englishes."

25. Rajend Mesthrie and Rakesh M. Bhatt, *World Englishes: The Study of New Linguistic Varieties* (Cambridge: Cambridge University Press, 2008).

26. Alsagoff and Lick, "The Grammar of Singapore English."

27. Chinua Achebe, *Arrow of God* (New York: Doubleday, 1969), 29.

28. Ibid.

29. Kachru, *The Alchemy of English: The Spread, Functions and Models of Non-native Englishes.*

30. Cf. Mesthrie and Bhatt, *World Englishes: The Study of New Linguistic Varieties.*

31. Ron Scollon and Suzanne Wong Scollon, "Topic Confusion in English-Asian Discourse," *World Englishes* 10, no. 2 (1991): 113–25.

32. Ayo Bamgbose, "Corpus Planning in Yoruba: The Radio as a Case Study," *Research in Yoruba Language and Literature* 2 (1992): 1–13.

33. Cf. Dhanesh K. Jain, *Pronominal Usage in Hindi: A Sociolinguistic Study* (PhD diss., University of Pennsylvania, 1973); and Jean D'souza, "Speech Acts in Indian English Fiction," *World Englishes* 10, no. 3 (1991): 307–16.

34. Erica Britt, "Doing Being Black," Unpublished manuscript, University of Illinois, Urbana, 2012.

35. Rajend Mesthrie, *English in Language Shift* (Cambridge: Cambridge University Press, 1992), 219.

36. Rakesh M. Bhatt, "In Other Words: Language Mixing, Identity Representations, and Third Space," *Journal of Sociolinguistics* 12, no. 2 (2008): 177–200.

37. The contextually appropriate translations of the code-switched items are:

saat pheraas: the term refers to the ritual in which the bride and the groom walk around the fire together, pledging commitment to each other for seven births.

agni: the sacred fire in the wedding ritual. Fire is believed to be the messenger (or priest) who operates on behalf of the people who perform the sacrificial ritual. Agni takes the prayers of the people to gods in the heaven, and brings back their blessings to the people.

lakshmana rekha: refers to the line of protection drawn by Lakshmana (in the epic *Ramayana*) around Sita's hut to protect her from dangers of the external world. Maricha, the demon (in the form of the deer) disguised his voice as Rama's, and called for Lakshmana's help. This was a trick to lure Lakshmana away from Sita and give an opportunity to Ravana to approach Sita who would be left unprotected. Lakshmana, however, draws a line around the hut and tells Sita not to cross it lest she will encounter a danger. Thus the term *Lakshmana rekha* (literally, a line), has become a symbol of protection, and transgressing it has acquired the meaning of allowing undesirable results to occur.

38. *Times of India news-brief*, www.timesofindia.com, October 12, 2001.
39. Bill Ashcroft, Gareth Griffiths, and Helen Tiffin, *The Empire Writes Back: Theory and Practice in Post-Colonial Literatures* (London: Routledge, 1989), 53.
40. Cf. Harris Berger and Michael Carroll, eds., *Global Pop, Local Languages* (Jackson: University of Mississippi Press, 2003); Jamie S. Lee and Yamuna Kachru, eds., *World Englishes Special Issue: Symposium on World Englishes in Pop Culture* 25, no. 2 (2006): 191–311; and Rakesh M. Bhatt, "World Englishes, Globalization and the Politics of Conformity," in *Contending with World Englishes in Globalization*, edited by Mukul Saxena and Tope Ominiyi (London: Multilingual Matters, 2010), 93–112.
41. Alastair Pennycook, "Global English, Rip Slyme, and Performativity," *Journal of Sociolinguistics* 7, no. 4 (2003): 513–33.
42. Cf. Russel A. Potter, *Spectacular Vernaculars: Hip-Hop and the Politics of Postmodernism* (Albany: State University of New York Press, 1995).
43. Alex Perullo and John Fenn, "Language Ideologies, Choices, and Practices in Eastern African Hip Hop," in *Global Pop, Local Language*, edited by Harris M. Berger and Michael Thomas Carroll (Jackson: University Press of Mississippi, 2003), 19–33.
44. Tope Omoniyi, "Hip Hop Through the World Englishes Lens: A Response to Globalization," *World Englishes* 25, no. 2 (2006): 195–208.
45. Ian Condry, "The Social Production of Difference: Imitation and Authenticity in Japanese Rap Music," in *Transactions, Transgressions, and Transformations*, edited by Heide Fehrenbach and Uta G. Polger (New York: Berghan Books, 2000), 166–84; and Jamie S. Lee, "Crossing and Crossers in East Asian Pop Music: Korea and Japan," *World Englishes* 25, no. 2 (2006): 235–50.
46. Omoniyi, "Hip Hop Through the World Englishes Lens"; cf. also Perullo and Fenn, "Language Ideologies, Choices, and Practices in Eastern African Hip Hop."
47. Cf. Omoniyi, "Hip Hop Through the World Englishes Lens."
48. Gurcharan Das, "Inescapably English," *The Times of India*, October 21, 2001, 14.
49. Jonathan Green, "English in India—The Grandmother Tongue," *Critical Quarterly* 40, no. 1 (1998): 107–11, 111.
50. Rakesh M. Bhatt, "Expert Discourses, Local Practices, and Hybridity: The Case of Indian Englishes."
51. Cf. Jean-Francois Lyotard, *The Postmodern Condition: A Report on Knowledge* (Manchester: Manchester University Press, 1984).
52. Cf. Rakesh M. Bhatt, "Experts, Dialects, and Discourse," *International Journal of Applied Linguistics* 12, no. 1 (2002): 74–109; and Bhatt, "Expert Discourses, Local Practices, and Hybridity: The Case of Indian Englishes."
53. Cf. Bhatt, "Expert Discourses, Local Practices, and Hybridity."
54. Canagarajah, *Resisting Linguistic Imperialism in English Teaching*; Randolph Quirk, "The English Language in a Global Context," in *English in the World: Teaching and Learning the Language and Literatures*, edited by Randolph Quirk and H. G. Widdowson (Cambridge: Cambridge University Press, 1985), 1–6.

55. Kachru, *The Alchemy of English*.

CHAPTER 23

1. See Stephen Jay Gould and Niles Eldredge, "Punctuated Equilibrium Comes of Age," *Nature* 366 (1993): 233–37, for more on "punctuated equilibrium." Also note that this chapter echoes themes of emergence found within the chapters by Kretzschmar (Chapter 11) and Mufwene (Chapter 20) in this volume.
2. Raven McDavid, "The Dialects of American English," in *The Structure of American English*, edited by W. Nelson Francis (New York: Ronald Publisher, 1958), 500.
3. Hans Kurath, *A Word Geography of the Eastern United States* (Ann Arbor: University of Michigan Press, 1949).
4. For more background information on the larger project along with details about the Linguistic Atlas of the Middle and South Atlantic States (LAMSAS), see William A. Kretzschmar Jr., Virginia G. McDavid, Theodore K. Lerud, and Ellen Johnson, eds., *Handbook of the Linguistic Atlas of the Middle and South Atlantic States* (Chicago: University of Chicago Press, 1993).
5. Kurath, *Word Geography of the Eastern United States*.
6. William Labov, Sharon Ash, and Charles Boberg, *Phonological Atlas of North American English: Phonetics, Phonology and Sound Change* (Berlin: Mouton de Gruyter, 2006).
7. John McWhorter via Language Log, "On American r-lessness": http://languagelog.ldc.upenn.edu/nll/?p=19486, n.p.
8. Ibid.
9. Ibid.
10. The colonial Massachusetts inventories are available on the Plymouth Colony Archive website: http://www.histarch.illinois.edu/plymouth/probates.html. The Virginia inventories are available from Colonial Williamsburg's Digital Library: http://research.history.org/DigitalLibrary/inventories/.
11. H[enry] L[ouis] Mencken, "American and English Today," in *The American Language: A Preliminary Inquiry into the Development of English in the United States* (New York: Knopf, 1919), 97–130.
12. "American Dictionary of the English Language" online edition: webstersdictionary1828.com/Preface.
13. Richard Whelan, "The American Spelling Reform Movement," *Verbatim* 27, no. 4 (2002): 1–7.
14. John R. Rickford, a proponent of the creolist viewpoint, outlines the debate (and his position) in "The Creole Origins of African-American Vernacular English: Evidence from Copula Absences," in *African-American English: Structure, History and Use*, eds. Salikoko S. Mufwene, John R. Rickford, Guy Bailey and John Baugh (New York: Routledge, 1998), 154–200, which can also be found online: http://web.stanford.edu/~rickford/papers/CreoleOriginsOfAAVE.html.
15. Rosina Lippi-Green, *English with an Accent* (New York: Routledge, 1997).
16. Linguistic Atlas Project: www.lap.uga.edu.
17. Nina Porzucki, "A Hidden History of Spanglish in California," *Public Radio International*, last modified February 12, 2015, http://www.pri.org/stories/2015-02-11/hidden-history-spanglish-california.
18. See also Kretzschmar, Chapter 11, this volume.
19. See Dennis Preston, "The South: The Touchstone," in *Language Variety in the South Revisited*, edited by C. Bernstein, T. Nunnally, and R. Sabino (Tuscaloosa: University of Alabama Press, 1997), 311–51.
20. Dennis Preston, "A Language Attitude Approach to the Perception of Regional Variety," in *Handbook of Perceptual Dialectology*, edited by D. R. Preston (Amsterdam: Benjamins, 1999).
21. J. K. Chambers, "Vernacular Universals," in *ICLaVE 1: Proceedings of the First International Conference on Language Variation in Europe*, edited by Josep M. Fontana et al. (Barcelona: Universitat Pompeu Fabra, 2001).

22. Thomas Pyles and John Algeo, *The Origins and Development of the English Language* 4th ed. (Fort Worth: Harcourt Brace, 1993), 159.

CHAPTER 24

1. Uriel Weinreich, William Labov, and Marvin I. Herzog, "Empirical Foundations for a Theory of Language Change," in *Directions for Historical Linguistics: A Symposium*, edited by Winfred P. Lehmann and Yakov Malkiel (Austin: University of Texas Press), 95–195.
2. Weinreich et al., "Empirical Foundations for a Theory of Language Change," 188.
3. Rob Penhallurick, *Studying the English Language*, 1st ed. (Basingstoke: Palgrave Macmillan, 2003); Rob Penhallurick, *Studying the English Language*, 2nd ed. (Basingstoke: Palgrave Macmillan, 2010).
4. David R. Parry, "Courses in English Language for First-Year Intending Honours Students" (unpublished handout, Department of English Language and Literature, University College, Swansea, 1975), 4.
5. Ferdinand de Saussure, *Cours de linguistique générale*, edited by Charles Bally and Albert Sechehaye, in collaboration with Albert Riedlinger (Paris: Éditions Payot). English translations (*Course in General Linguistics*) by Wade Baskin (New York: The Philosophical Library, 1960) and Roy Harris (London: Duckworth, 1983). I used Baskin's translation here (pp. 71–8) and throughout.
6. Ibid., 74.
7. Weinreich et al., 188.
8. Krine Boelens, *The Frisian Language* (Leeuwarden, Netherlands: Information Service of the Province of Friesland and Fryske Akademy, 1979), 29.
9. Salikoko S. Mufwene, "Is Gullah Decreolizing? A Comparison of a Speech Sample of the 1930s with a Sample of the 1980s," in *The Emergence of Black English: Text and Commentary*, edited by Guy Bailey, Natalie Maynor, and Patricia Cukor-Avila (Amsterdam: John Benjamins, 1991), 213–30, at 223.
10. de Saussure, *Cours de linguistique générale*, 193.
11. Salikoko S. Mufwene, "Gullah: Morphology and Syntax," in *Varieties of English 2: The Americas and the Caribbean*, edited by Edgar W. Schneider (Berlin: Mouton de Gruyter), 551–71, at 551.
12. J. C. Wells, "Accents of English," *UCL Division of Psychology and Language Sciences*, accessed October 15, 2016, http://www.phon.ucl.ac.uk/home/wells/accentsanddialects/.
13. "Frisian, Western Language," *Global Recordings Network*, accessed October 15, 2016, http://globalrecordings.net/en/language/3033.
14. Wolfgang Viereck, *Regionale und soziale Erscheinungsformen des britischen und amerikanischen Englisch,* Anglistische Arbeitshefte 4 (Tübingen: Niemeyer, 1975).
15. "Sounds," *The British Library*, accessed October 15, 2016, http://sounds.bl.uk/Accents-and-dialects.
16. "Hear and Read Gullah," *Gullah Tours*, accessed October 15, 2016, http://gullahtours.com/gullah/hear-and-read-gullah.
17. "Learning English Timeline," *The British Library*, accessed October 15, 2016, http://www.bl.uk/learning/langlit/evolvingenglish/accessvers/index.html.
18. University of Texas at Austin Linguistics Research Center, accessed October 15, 2016, http://liberalarts.utexas.edu/lrc/.
19. Warren Maguire, "An Atlas of Alexander J. Ellis's *The Existing Phonology of English Dialects*," accessed October 15, 2016, http://www.lel.ed.ac.uk/EllisAtlas/Index.html.
20. The Leeds Archive of Vernacular Culture, accessed October 15, 2016, https://library.leeds.ac.uk/special-collections/collection/61/the_leeds_archive_of_vernacular_culture.
21. Digitaler Wenker-Atlas, accessed October 15, 2016, http://www.diwa.info/.

CHAPTER 25

1. See Celia M. Millward and Mary Hayes, *A Biography of the English Language*, 3rd ed. (Boston: Cengage Learning, 2011), 1.

2. See Anne Curzan and Michael Adams, *How English Works: A Linguistic Introduction* (Indianapolis: Pearson Education, 2012), xxxi. Curzan and Adams describe that defamiliarization process at length in the prefatory material to their undergraduate textbook: "As native speakers of language, we all come to the study of language with strong prior understandings, some of which are accurate and some of which are not. Sometimes it can be difficult to accept the findings of linguists, particularly if these findings, presented as 'facts' about language, run counter to what we think we already know . . .. We use the language so much, we hardly notice it—[and we] tend to take it for granted. Language can seem mundane because we learn it as children and use it every day without having to think consciously about it. In fact, one of the fundamental properties of spoken (or signed) human language is that we learn it without explicit instruction as long as we are exposed to it."

3. Paul Stephens, "International Students: Separate but Profitable," *Washington Monthly*, September/October 2013, washingtonmonthly.com/magazine/september_october_2013/features/ international_students_separat046454.php; Karin Fischer, "International-Student Numbers Continue Record-Breaking Growth," *The Chronicle of Higher Education*, last modified November 17, 2014, chronicle.com.myaccess. library.utoronto.ca/article/International-Student-Numbers/150049. See also Ian Wilhelm, "Where the International Students Are, State by State," *The Chronicle of Higher Education*, last modified November 12, 2014, chronicle.com.myaccess.library. utoronto.ca/article/Where-the-International/135634. Statistics measuring the enrollment increase are difficult to calculate and to verify; what's clear is that the rate of change is very steep. According to Stephens, the "total number of international students at U.S. colleges and universities" between 2006 and 2013 "ballooned by roughly 200,000—growing to more than 764,000 in less than six years," a sudden influx of 35%. Wilhelm puts the full count at 764,495 in the United States in 2011–12, which at that point makes up "3.7 percent of the total student population." According to Fischer, the figure in 2013–14 had leapt to "a record 886,052 foreign students" in the United States, which Fischer reports as an 8% increase. (It is an over 16% increase over Stephens's figure for the prior year.)

4. Karin Fischer provides an example: "The English classes bored her. The assignments, she thought, were simplistic. The students were given basic tasks, like looking up words and identifying parts of speech. They had several days to write and revise a single paragraph." See Karin Fischer, "A Freshman Year, Far From Home," *The Chronicle of Higher Education*, last modified May 29, 2014, chronicle.com/article/A-Freshman-Year-Far-From-Home/141303.

5. As a new professor, my experience in HEL teaching is considerably more limited than many of the contributors to this volume. While undergoing Katherine O'Brien O'Keeffe's "certification" in teaching HEL, I adapted UC Berkeley's open-ended R1A composition course as "A People's History of the English Language," on which more later; I repeated that course again in 2010. At Wellesley College, where I held my first permanent faculty position, I reprised "A People's History" as a composition course and also took on their standard History of the English Language lecture course. Now, at the University of Toronto, I have the honor of being the junior faculty "pinch-hitter" supporting Carol Percy (whose work on HEL diversity is also featured in this section of the volume); I periodically take on Toronto's undergraduate course in HEL or the HEL-based "The English Language in the World." (I have taught each of those courses once so far in my short time at Toronto.) Since the tools and methods I'll discuss here are primarily geared toward large university settings, I'll focus primarily on Toronto and Berkeley for this study. The Fieldwork Exercise, importantly, was not successful at Wellesley, where my students in English classes tended to be less diverse.

6. All attempts to bypass ESL, EFL, and NSHV students' challenges and exploit their strengths are still experimental. I haven't yet garnered the funding or years of experience teaching HEL that I'd need to systematically determine whether and how

much these methods have affected the performance of the ESL, EFL, and NSHV speakers in my classes.

7. For the University of Toronto's "English Language in the World," I tested a version of this assignment without the partnering element, instead encouraging students to direct their attention away from campus: "To complete this assignment, you must seek out an interview subject who lives in Toronto (or the Greater Toronto Area). Choose a subject with whom you can meet easily, with whom you have met and spoken at least once before, who speaks English well enough to tell a complex story in it, and—most important—who is a member of a linguistic community in which you are not a member." The results were equally compelling, and the assignment generally successful, but the variation did not provide students the important experience of *being* the linguistic subject.

8. For a more linguistics-oriented class, I have required students to follow up on their in-class discussion with a long-form research report, which includes all of the data they found, followed by an IPA transcription of part of their interview, a summary of prior linguists' work on comparable varieties, and then a discussion of the implications of their study. In more humanities-oriented classes, I have required students to write short argumentative essays that unpack the sociopolitical stakes of the features they observed. Most recently, in an HEL course condensed for a summer term, I simply required students to attach to their IPA transcription a chart showing a comparative breakdown of six to eight salient features of the sample, arranged in comparison to an already-researched variety, with endnotes where necessary.

9. Students request their first and second choice of presentation date using an in-class worksheet; compiling a master list is relatively painless. In large classes, I do not ask students to establish ahead of time the variety or feature that they will be discussing. If a student finds that her variety (or something close to it) has already been presented on by someone else in a prior class, I make clear that it is that student's responsibility to present her work in dialogue with the earlier presentation, as a response and alternate perspective, focusing on other features.

10. This assignment benefits from the fact that most of my university students now walk around with high-quality recording and playback devices at all times (easily downloadable on most smartphones). For cases in which students might not have easy access to those devices, I encourage the student to share with a partner, or to borrow one of three spare blank-cassette hand-held dictaphones I now keep in my office (which can now be purchased cheaply online). For in-class playback, I either bring my own compact portable speaker to class or, where available, use the standard audiovisual classroom equipment, which a student can easily attach to a handheld device's headphone jack by means of a "male-to-male" audio cable (easy to find at any electronics store).

11. The exercise consumes class time that could otherwise be used for lecture—again, my emphasis is on *yielding authority* in the classroom—but need not use up too much. For instance, for a recent class with a cap of fifty students, meeting twice per week in twelve weeks, I set aside an average of seventeen and a half minutes per class across twenty of my twenty-four class sessions (sometimes longer, sometimes shorter or absent)—giving each student seven minutes of presentation and transition time, while securing enough time to accommodate my own lectures. In the HEL lecture class I taught at Wellesley College, I was able to replace some of my usual office hours with a series of conference-style special sessions, of which students were required to attend at least one (though most showed up voluntarily at more than one). Larger courses that provide teaching assistants might already have recitation sessions built in that would handily accommodate student presentations. As for classes whose size would make individual student presentations entirely prohibitive, it would be necessary to arrange for students to read some or all of each other's written work outside class, a less desirable variation, but one which could be easily done through

an online forum; my HEL-based classes at the University of California-Berkeley used blogging successfully for similar collaborative readings.

12. That percentage that has increased quickly enough to cause controversy (especially since admission rates for Californian students are declining). See Larry Gordon, "Fewer Californians got into UC, while offers to foreign students rose," *Los Angeles Times*, last modified July 2, 2015, latimes.com/local/education/la-me-ln-uc-admit-20150702-story.html. Among the United States, California boasts "the largest number of international students" in total, though the highest percentage of international students is in Massachusetts and Wellesley College, where I honed many of these approaches, reported in 2015 an excellent range of ethnic diversity, while 11% of its most recent incoming class were international students though that diversity was not (in my experience) reflected in enrollments in English classes (see Note 5). See Ian Wilhelm, "Where the International Students Are, State by State," *The Chronicle of Higher Education*, last modified November 12, 2014, chronicle.com.myaccess.library.utoronto.ca/article/Where-the-International/135634, as well as Wellesley College's "Behold! Just the Facts and Class of 2018 Statistics," last modified September 1, 2016, wellesley.edu/admission/facts.

13. For this earliest iteration of the exercise and its underlying pedagogy, much of which is reproduced in the current chapter, see Matthew Sergi, "A People's History of the English Language: Dialect Communities" (Teaching Effectiveness Award Essay, 2010), Berkeley Graduate Division: Graduate Student Instructor Teaching and Resources Center, accessed June 30, 2017, gsi.berkeley.edu/sergim-2010.

14. See Sergi, "A People's History of the English Language."

15. See "Ways to Help Your ESL Students," The Centre for Teaching Support and Innovation, teaching.utoronto.ca/teaching-support/strategies/inclusive-teaching/diversity-in-the-classroom/ways-to-help-your-esl-students. See also the University of Toronto's "First in the Family" program at studentlife.utoronto.ca/mpp/fitf/program.

16. I make good on my promise to include material from students' oral presentations on the final exam. About an eighth of the questions are based on students' original research, often using student-generated transcripts as examples to demonstrate core HEL concepts. For instance, I adapted one question from the mini-lecture presented by the student who had left Hong Kong to study at an Australian school, who had been partnered with a student who identified his variety as Gay English:

Which of the following most accurately describes the development of the word "twunk" from our class presentation on Toronto Gay English?

a. "Twink" is usually a Gay English verb. However, by conjugating "twink" like a weak noun in the past participle form, speakers can refer to a "past tense" twink, i.e., a man too old to be a twink.

b. "Twink" is usually a Gay English noun. However, by conjugating "twink" like a strong verb in the past participle form, speakers can refer to a "past tense" twink, i.e., a man too old to be a twink.

c. "Twink" is usually a Gay English noun. However, by conjugating "twink" like a weak verb in the past participle form, speakers can refer to a "past tense" twink, i.e., a man too old to be a twink.

d. "Twink" is usually a Gay English verb. However, by conjugating "twink" like a strong noun in the past participle form, speakers can refer to a "past tense" twink, i.e., a man too old to be a twink.

[The correct answer is B.]

17. Since Millward and Hayes's first three chapters are non-chronological, introducing core concepts, my syllabus starts with Chapter 9, then proceeds through Chapters 2, 8, 1, 7, 6, 3, 5, then (if time allows) 4. See Celia M. Millward and Mary Hayes, *A Biography of the English Language*, 3rd ed. (Boston: Cengage Learning, 2011).

18. Edgar W. Schneider, *English Around the World: An Introduction* (New York: Cambridge University Press, 2011), is the core text for my version of the Toronto "English

Language in the World" course. From *World Englishes*, Tobias Bernaisch, "Attitudes toward Englishes in Sri Lanka," *World Englishes* 31, no. 3 (2012): 279–91, describes the process of discovering (or inventing) an emerging variety, Sri Lankan English, through the controversy that surrounded the publication of Michael Meyler's 2007 *A Dictionary of Sri Lankan English*. Philip Seargeant and Caroline Tagg, "English on the internet and a 'post-varieties' approach to language," *World Englishes* 30, no. 44 (2011): 496–514, suggests that a varieties-based paradigm has always been a function of nationalism, which has never had an adequate "word-to-world fit" and which is especially ill-equipped to understand computer-mediated discourse. I emphasize very recent work, to show that the field of global Englishes is active and changing. These advanced readings are often difficult for undergraduates to parse, especially for ESL, EFL, and NSHV students—a strategically deployed difficulty that can, via open-ended and slow-paced discussions, not only demand that we suss out the difficult theories in the articles as a collaborative effort but also invite critiques of Academic English as an acrolect in itself. *World Englishes* provides tough material to begin a semester with, but as long as the subsequent discussions are well-facilitated, the concepts resound productively throughout the semester.

19. The student drew attention to Schneider's discussion of Filipino English, when he refers to the call center industry as "a new, subtle type of dependence and quasi-colonialism"; the student was concerned that Schneider's description elides the more insidious and severe manifestations of full-on colonialism in the Philippines that are not mentioned in the chapter. See Schneider, *English Around the World*, 156. It is important to note, too, that the student who identified the concern was not Filipino herself; while ESL, EFL, and NSHV students are increasingly visible, they are usually hesitant at first to talk back or speak out. Usually, the first students to jump on the opportunity to critique class texts are not ESL, EFL, or NSHV themselves but rather historically privileged, politically correct students advocating on behalf of others: with care, those interventions can themselves be reframed as subjects of critique ("Who are you, though, to speak up for someone else?"), always with emphasis that the classroom is a safe space in which conscious disagreement can occur. So far, by the end of term, the playing field has become considerably more level.

20. I have since considered adding, in the language of the prompt, the direction that students should only write on guides or handbooks to which they have *legal access*. One of my Berkeley students, the daughter of a military employee, tried to use a document with guidelines on what was acceptable to write or say about the military in public forums. According to the student, her essay-in-progress—and the computer she was using to write it—was confiscated by military officers. When she told me this, I laughed, saying that this was the most impressive "my dog ate it" excuse I'd ever heard; the student, who was an excellent student otherwise, burst into very real tears; chillingly, I think she may have been telling the truth.

21. See Sergi, "A People's History of the English Language," for further context on this assignment. Some of my students' blog posts are still online, though most of these isolate proofreading issues without reference to ESL, EFL, and NSHV issues. My favorite, and the most relevant to this discussion, is the thoughtful critique posted by a Chinese EFL student about an entry on *Engrish.com*, followed in the comments area by equally thoughtful meta-critique by a native English-speaking Asian-American student. See the thought-provoking work of then-undergraduate Tory Li, "Tory's Post: Think Twice Before You Judge," *A People's History of the English Language*, last modified April 6, 2009, at goodwise.blogspot.com/2009/04/torys-post-think-twice-before-you-judge.html.

22. In its "Grammar Review," for instance, Millward and Hayes, *Biography of the English Language*, uses "My mistress' eyes are nothing like the sun" (at 416), "Parsley, sage, rosemary, and thyme" (at 418), and "Grandma, what big teeth you have!" (at 423), three examples clearly chosen to add familiarity and color, but all referring to a cultural background shared primarily by native speakers of English. Otherwise, Millward

and Hayes use *ad hoc* examples crafted to fit, which generally conform to classroom-standard grammar ("The soldiers are stalwart and strong," at 416; "Chastened by his teacher's reprimand, the boy sat quietly at his desk," at 423; "The dog will have been being bathed," at 414) or offer colloquial but still relatively polite variations still representative of present-day NAE/AmE and RP/BrE ("Oh my God! What have you done?" at 419; "Being a jerk will get you nowhere," at 423). These examples, by implying the existence of a "default" shared English from which fundamentals are always demonstrated, implicitly affirm an exclusionary idea that standard supranational varieties in the HEL classroom are stable, central, and universally accessible, in contrast to global varieties.

23. Devyani Sharma, "Indian English," in *The Electronic World Atlas of Varieties of English*, edited by Bernd Kortmann and Kerstin Lunkenheimer (Leipzig: Max Planck Institute for Evolutionary Anthropology, 2013), available online at http://ewave-atlas.org/languages/52. See also Celia M. Millward and Mary Hayes, "9.7. Written Indian English," in *Workbook to Accompany A Biography of the English Language*, 3rd edition (Boston: Wadsworth, 2011): 249–52.

24. Compare the accessibility of these terms with Millward-Hayes, who use sample words *farina, mead, croon, fool, blast, drown, soon, quell, heathen, bedlam*, and *elf* (from IE *albho-*, for whiteness) at 4–5. *Closet[ed]* (as *adj*), in contrast to OED definition 10b, in conversational English now often means any identity kept secret out of embarrassment (e.g., "I'm a closet Red Sox fan"). *Queer* is among the quintessential "reclaimed" terms, once derogatory, now a badge of pride. *Shade*, in 1980s ball-culture slang, referred to an understated or subtle insult (as Dorian Corey defines it in 1990s *Paris Is Burning*, shade-throwers "don't have to tell you you're ugly, because you know you're ugly"); in present-day mainstream culture (frequently on *Buzzfeed.com*) the term is used frequently to refer to very direct, scathing insults. Other examples I use in class: *straight* for narrowing, *fierce* for weakening, *lesbian* for abstraction, *vogueing* for concretization, and (provocatively, and not unproblematically) *positive* for pejoration.

25. So far, the only broad demographic of students I think I've encountered who consistently do not feel at least somewhat familiar with hip-hop *and* who have not had privileged access to English-language canons are students whose age is above the average for undergraduates by about ten years or more. In the cases where these students feel excluded by hip-hop culture, however, I express *my* solidarity with them, and my desperation in trying to keep up—a strategy that becomes more effective every year.

26. In my first HEL-based class at Berkeley, I introduced Snoop Dogg's putative claim (in his appearance on *Martha Stewart Living*, which I often show to classes) that he invented certain slang terms; the East Oakland hip-hop aficionado in my class was immediately incensed, seeing this as one of many cases in which Southern Californian hip-hop culture claims ownership over innovations that began in Northern California. The student, who had previously been rather quiet, was suddenly one of the most enthusiastic contributors in class, and remained that way for the duration of the semester. See "Snoop Dogg on *Martha Stewart* Part 1," uploaded to YouTube.com by user "CashmereAgency," November 21, 2008, youtube.com/watch?v=kXhnCCLPjQA.

27. Drake, "Used To," on his independent mix-tape album "If You're Reading This It's Too Late" (OVO Records, 2015). On this track (and many others), Drake uses distinctive variations in intonation, pronunciation, and vowel length that cannot be represented with standard English graphics.

28. As Paul Devlin puts it, "[N]ot all of the [transcription] mistakes are small. Some stem not just from mishearing but from an apparent lack of understanding of the cultural context." See Paul Devlin, "Fact-Check the Rhyme," *Slate.com*, last modified November 4, 2010, slate.com/articles/arts/culturebox/2010/11/factcheck_the_rhyme.html.

29. The recent feud between Azealia Banks and Iggy Azalea, for instance, and then the subsequent counterpoints offered by male rappers, gets at the heart of the way identity and power are bound up with different varieties of PDE. Students this year

piped up immediately when I brought up that feud, which I had looked into only briefly for the express purpose of bringing it up in class. A brief look at *Buzzfeed* or any rapper's Twitter feed (particularly Banks) before future classes will be enough for a basic update on whatever sociolinguistic conflict is most recognizably current.

30. Bernaisch, "Attitudes Toward Englishes," 288.

31. We consider the prelude to Die Antwoord's "Zars," in which white South African rapper Ninja provocatively and defensively announces: "*Tjekkit*. A lot of people ask me why I sometimes speak with an Afrikaans accent. *Tjek*, the cool thing about South Africa is that you got 11 national languages to choose from. So, if I'm speaking to an Afrikaans person, I can speak in an Afrikaans accent. And if I'm speaking to an English person, I can speak with a fucking English accent. And when I'm speaking to my brothas, we like to speak with a black accent, *nè*?" In subsequent discussions, we consider whether Dizzee Rascal's Multicultural London English (MLE), known in British slang as "Jafaican" (i.e., "fake Jamaican") is a sign that British hip-hop artists consider Jamaican English as a prestige variety. I pick up the question of Jamaican prestige in later discussions. See also Emine Sinmaz, "Is This The End of Cockney? Hybrid Dialect Dubbed 'Multicultural London English' Sweeps Across the Country," *Daily Mail* Online, last modified November 10, 2013, dailymail.co.uk/news/article-2498152/Is-end-Cockney-Hybrid-dialect-dubbed-Multicultural-London-English-sweeps-country.html.

32. About half of my students were able to identify the meaning of "the 6ix," though Drake had only started using the term in public a year earlier. See Josh McConnell, "We The 6: Why the Name Drake Gave Us Is Here to Stay," *The Globe and Mail*, last modified July 10, 2015, theglobeandmail.com/news/toronto/we-the-6-why-the-name-drake-gave-us-is-here-to-stay/article25421112/.

33. For a helpful list of nearly every title that linguists have tried to apply to the variety, see Lisa J. Green, *African American English: A Linguistic Introduction* (Cambridge University Press, 2002), 5–6.

34. Millward-Hayes takes care to tread carefully here—there are considerable changes from the second edition to the third in its sections on BE as a source of PDE loanwords (at 329, provocatively suggesting that BE is a *non*-PDE variety) and on AAVE as an "ethnic and socioeconomic variety" (at 358–61, in a chapter otherwise entirely devoted to "dialects whose boundaries are geographical"). Students in my classes generally still chafe at statements that establish a racial binary that leaves out non-white and non-black people ("often exaggerated—by blacks and whites alike") or that imply that whiteness provides the assumed context for every other variety discussed in the book ("Like many non-Black dialects of English, AAVE is nonrhotic . . . "). Still, again, the given understanding in our classes is that our course text is doing the very best work, if necessarily flawed work, that a textbook can do in presenting this material—excellent for igniting critical thinking and class debate, and certainly a superior choice to leaving it out.

35. Matthew Giancarlo, "The Rise and Fall of the Great Vowel Shift? The Changing Ideological Intersections of Philology, Historical Linguistics, and Literary History," *Representations* 76.1 (Fall 2001): 27–60. Students must still learn a paradigm of vowel shifts, but it is adapted from Giancarlo's varied source texts to present each vowel's progress (in London alone) from 1300 to 1800.

36. Raymond Hickey's work provides useful historical and linguistic material here to augment standard textbook offerings on ME. See Raymond Hickey, "Development and Diffusion of Irish English," in *Legacies of Colonial English*, edited by Raymond Hickey, 82–118 (Cambridge University Press, 2005), esp. 83–85.

37. Michael Benskin and Margaret Laing, "An Electronic Version of A Linguistic Atlas of Late Mediaeval English (*eLALME*)," *Angus McIntosh Centre for Historical Linguistics at the University of Edinburgh*, accessed June 30, 2017, lel.ed.ac.uk/ihd/elalme/elalme.html.

38. Using *Oxford English Dictionary* (*OED*) etymological data, my estimated average "date of birth" for the first fifty-two words in Drake's "Used To" (on *If You're Reading This It's*

Too Late, 2015)—a number I calculated very roughly (assigning each word to a century of origin, then averaging those numbers together) and also very conservatively (dating basic Old English words to the year 900, though most certainly predate that year)— was the year 1120. Using the same method, the first fifty-two words of our sample Academic English reading, which I will not mention directly here because we chose it for its obscure language (nor is it cited elsewhere in this chapter), had an average "date of birth" in the year 1277. Considering that Drake's fifty-two words included an array of words distinctly later than any used in the academic piece ("airwaves," "Gs," "sickos," and the neologism "6-side,"), we found it quite remarkable that his lyrics' average "date of birth" was still 157 years older.

CHAPTER 26

1. Richard Hogg, *An Introduction to Old English* (Edinburgh: Edinburgh University Press, 2002), 59.
2. "Fair Copy Manuscript of Charlotte Bronte's *Jane Eyre*," British Library, accessed June 30, 2017, https://www.bl.uk/collection-items/fair-copy-manuscript-of-charlotte-bronts-jane-eyre.
3. Maria Montessori, *The Montessori Method*, translated by Anne E. George (New York: Frederick A. Stokes, 1912).
4. See full explanations and sample work for these materials at "Introduction to Quantity," *Montessori Primary Guide*, accessed June 30, 2017, http://www.infomontessori.com/mathematics/decimal-system-intoduction-to-quantity.htm and "Sandpaper Letters," *Montessori Primary Guide*, accessed June 30, 2017, http://www.infomontessori.com/language/written-language-sandpaper-letters.htm.
5. Maria Montessori, "The Four Planes of Education," *AMI Communications* 4 (1971): 4–10, and Camillo Grazzini, "The Four Planes of Development," *NAMTA Journal* 21, no. 2 (1996): 208–41. For a recent study of the application of Montessori methods at the college level, see Norman Lorenz, "Montessori on the Move: A Case Study of the Montessori Pedagogical Instructional Principles and Implications for Community College Course Graduates and their Career Paths," (PhD diss., University of California, Davis, 2015).
6. David A. Kolb. *Experiential Learning: Experience as the Source of Learning and Development*, 2nd ed. (New York: Pearson Education, 2014).
7. Kolb, *Experiential Learning*, 42. See also the idea of "bodily-kinesthetic intelligence" in Howard Gardner, *Frames of Mind: The Theory of Multiple Intelligences* (London: Fontana Press, 1983 [Reprint, New York: Basic Books, 2011]), 217–50.
8. Laurie Richlin, *Blueprint for Learning: Constructing College Courses to Facilitate, Assess, and Document Learning* (Sterling, VA: Stylus, 2006).
9. Henry Glassie, *Material Culture* (Bloomington: Indiana University Press, 1999), 41, describes the term "material culture" as a "conjunction of the abstract and the concrete," concluding that "[w]e have things to study, and we must record them dutifully and examine them lovingly if the abstraction called culture is to be compassed."
10. The pragmatics of using disc-based digital facsimiles often undermines their utility and makes them more difficult to use than print facsimiles. Many disc-based facsimiles use old coding/scripting environments and are thus difficult to get working in new operating systems and web browsers, effectively making them outdated only a few years after their release. Moreover, many require prior installation to work properly and simply would not work smoothly from a library's reserves.
11. See, for example, Ziming Liu, "Reading Behavior in the Digital Environment: Changes in Reading Behavior over the Past Ten Years," *Journal of Documentation* 61, no. 6 (2005): 700–12, and Ziming Lui, *Paper to Digital: Documents in the Information Age* (Westport, CT: Libraries Unlimited, 2008).
12. Some digital facsimiles on disc embed links to editorial materials in the images, but such practice is relatively rare, as far as I know. Most online facsimiles that I know of present plain images.

13. For a detailed account of this process, see Raymond Clemens and Timothy Graham, *Introduction to Manuscript Studies* (Ithaca, NY: Cornell University Press, 2007), 10–17.

14. The full manuscript can be found in digital facsimile under "Cotton MS Claudius B IV," *British Library*, accessed June 30, 2017, http://www.bl.uk/manuscripts/FullDisplay. aspx?ref=Cotton_MS_Claudius_B_IV and in print facsimile in C. R. Dodwell and Peter Clemoes, eds., *The Old English Illustrated Hexateuch: British Museum Cotton Claudius B. IV,* Early English Manuscripts in Facsimile no. 18, (Copenhagen: Rosenkilde and Bagger, 1974).

15. For analyses of the illustrations in Cotton Claudius B. IV, see David F. Johnson, "A Program of Illumination in the Old English Illustrated Hexateuch: 'Visual Typology'?," 165–99, and Catherine E. Karkov, "The Anglo-Saxon Genesis: Text, Illustration, and Audience," 201–37, both in *The Old English Hexateuch: Aspects and Approaches*, edited by Rebecca Barnhouse and Benjamin C. Withers (Kalamazoo, MI: Medieval Institute Publications, 2000).

16. On scaffolding and sequencing, see R. Keith Sawyer, *The Cambridge Handbook of the Learning Sciences* (Cambridge: Cambridge University Press, 2006), 51 and 51–2. "Scaffolding" as a term was first introduced in David Wood, Jerome Bruner, and Gail Ross, "The Role of Tutoring in Problem Solving," *Journal of Child Psychology and Psychiatry* 17 (1976): 89–100. "Sequencing" first appeared in Richard R. Burton, John Seely Brown, and Gerhard Fischer, "Skiing as a Model of Instruction," in *Everyday Cognition: Its Developmental and Social Context*, edited by Barbara Rogoff and Jean Lave (Cambridge, MA: Harvard University Press, 1984), 139–50, and Barbara White, "Designing Computer Games to Help Physics Students Understand Newton's Laws of Motion," *Cognition and Instruction* 1 (1984): 69–108.

17. For example, <c> and <g> (*God* [god], *cumað* [kumaθ], *gelogode* [jeloɣode], *ic* [itʃ], *sceoldon* [ʃeoldon]), voicing of fricatives (*fandian* [fandian], *lufast* [luvast], *ðus* [θus], *hraðe* [hraðe]), and nasals (*unc* [uŋk]).

18. "The Story of Abraham and Issac," *Old English Grammar*, accessed June 30, 2017, http://www.oegrammar.ca/texts/abraham-and-isaac/.

19. See, for example, Katherine O'Brien O'Keeffe, *Visible Song: Transitional Literacy in Old English Verse* (Cambridge: University of Cambridge Press, 1990).

20. See, for example, the "Disciplinary Perspectives" section in Dan Hicks and Mary C. Beaudry, eds., *The Oxford Handbook of Material Culture Studies* (Oxford: Oxford University Press, 2010), 25–188.

CHAPTER 27

1. Richard G. White, "Memorandum on English Pronunciation in the Elizabethan Era," *Appendix to vol. 12 of The Works of William Shakespeare* (Boston: Little, Brown, 1865).

2. I review the history in detail in David Crystal, "Early Interest in Shakespearean Original Pronunciation," *Language and History* (2013): 5–17.

3. Personal communication, July 2012.

4. David Crystal, *Pronouncing Shakespeare* (Cambridge: Cambridge University Press, 2005) provides an account of the procedures used for the 2004 *Romeo and Juliet* production.

5. David Crystal, *The Oxford Dictionary of Original Shakespearean Pronunciation* (Oxford: Oxford University Press, 2016).

6. "Shakespeare and Original Pronunciation,". *Paul Meier Dialect Services*, http://www.paulmeier.com/shakespeare/.

7. Other examples can be seen in Crystal, *Pronouncing Shakespeare*, and a complete semi-phonetic transcription made for Paul Meier's *A Midsummer Night's Dream* is viewable on his website.

CHAPTER 28

1. The data regarding ethnicity derives from my university's online *University Fact Book* Fall 2015, p. 9. The data regarding geographic distances was generated for me based on Fall 2015 enrollment figures by the Office of Institutional Research, Planning, and

Assessment. This figure includes both undergraduate and graduate students; it also excludes any student records without a valid zip code. This office has my thanks for running this query for me.

2. As one exemplary model of debate, consider the question of whether the Great Vowel Shift should be regarded as a matter of internal history, that is, prompted entirely by a so-called chain shift or whether the GVS ought to be understood in connection with external history—that is, as Seth Lerer posits, as "part of a larger, social process of replacing a lost prestige *language* with a prestige *dialect*—a dialect not keyed to region but to social class, to education, or to wealth." *Inventing English: A Portable History of the Language* (New York: Columbia University Press, 2007), 111.

3. As of late June 2016, there are many examples in blogs, Facebook posts, Twitter. See for example *Elle* team, "The Most Hilarious Brexit Memes," *Elle India blog*, http://elle.in/blog/the-most-hilarious-brexit-memes. See also John Kelly, "Brexit. Debression. Oexit. Zumxit. Why Did Brexit Trigger a Brexplosion of Wordplay?" Lexicon Valley (blog), June 29, 2016, accessed June 30, 2016, http://www.slate.com/blogs/lexicon_valley/2016/06/29/why_has_brexit_sparked_an_explosion_of_wordplay.html.

4. "Enunciate by Spitting," YouTube video of *Friends* episode "The One with Monica and Chandler's Wedding (Part I)," 2:58, posted by SNA Gilbert, March 2, 2008, https://www.youtube.com/watch?v=0ISJS4gSBh0.

5. The trochaic tetrameter necessitates that the word *fire* in "Fire burn, and cauldron bubble" be realized as a disyllable, making the /r/ syllabic, and not consonantal. See William Shakespeare, *The Tragedy of Macbeth*, 4.1.10–11, *The Complete Works of William Shakespeare*, http://shakespeare.mit.edu/macbeth/macbeth.4.1.html, accessed June 30, 2016.

6. *Noggin*, "Everywhere I Go," YouTube video, 1:26, posted by 24fpsfan, January 2, 2016, https://www.youtube.com/watch?v=j4MASJ7sLQA; transcription of lyrics is my approximation.

7. "The Richmeister," *Saturday Night Live* Transcripts, January 19, 1991, accessed June 30, 2016, http://snltranscripts.jt.org/90/90krichmeister.phtml.

8. Bob Garfield and Mike Vuolo, "Where Did the Word *Snark* Come From? (podcast)," *Lexicon Valley* episode 45: LinguaFile IV, 41:35, October 20, 2014, accessed June 30, 2016, http://www.slate.com/articles/podcasts/lexicon_valley/2014/10/lexicon_valley_the_etymology_and_history_of_the_word_snark_with_lexicographer.html.

9. David Crystal. *The Story of English in 100 Words* (New York: St. Martin's Press, 2012).

10. Barry Lopez and Debra Gwartney, eds., *Home Ground: Language for an American Landscape* (San Antonio, TX: Trinity University Press, 2006). A recent successful lesson paired a brief social history of lawns, as discussed in the *OED* and Lopez, *Homeground* with *New York Times* articles discussing the socioeconomic divide between those communities that can afford to "shower their lush lawns" with water, imitating the romantic parks of well-to-do homeowners of the past, and those who cannot afford the water bills required to create green lawns in the midst of a desert. See Scott Russell Sanders, "Lawn," in Lopez and Gwartney, *Homeground*, 211. See also Adam Nagourney and Jack Healy, "Drought Frames Economic Divide of Californians," *The New York Times* online, April 26, 2015, accessed June 30, 2016, http://www.nytimes.com/2015/04/27/us/drought-widens-economic-divide-for-californians.html?_r=0.

11. See, for example, "Disney Channel Monstober Zap," *Disney Channel*, accessed June 30, 2016, http://lol.disney.com/games/disney-channel-monstober-zap.

12. *Yale Grammatical Diversity Project: English in North America*, Yale University, accessed June 30, 2016, http://microsyntax.sites.yale.edu/.

13. Additional collections of texts and corpora of spoken and written English reflecting diversity based on place of origin, original language, age, and other dialectal factors can be found on The Linguist List, an invaluable international community of linguists.

14. For attention to the etymological origins of English words and idioms in relation to the external, political histories of English-language speakers, including English-language learners, you might use Robert Hass's brilliant and excoriating poem "English: An Ode"

and Linda Gregerson's related essay "Ode and Empire." Or for an uncomfortable and important dialogue on the politics of English as a "mother tongue" and/or "foreign anguish," have classes read M. NourbeSe Philip's "Discourse on the Logic of Language"; for bendings of the language by speakers with rhythms and perspectives based on their own language histories, try Tato Laviera's "AmeRícan." Robert Hass, "English: An Ode," in *Sun Under Wood* (New York: Ecco Press, 1996), 62–70; Linda Gregerson, "Ode and Empire," *Triquarterly* 129 (2007): 9–19. Rpt. in *Radiant Lyre: Essays on Lyric Poetry*, ed. David Baker and Ann Townsend (St. Paul: Graywolf Press, 2007), 117–28, and in *Poetry Daily* (January 29, 2008); M. NourbeSe Philip, "Discourse on the Logic of Language," in *She Tries Her Tongue—Her Silence Softly Breaks*, new ed. (Middletown, Conn.: Wesleyan UP, 2015), 29–34; Tato Laviera, *AmeRícan*, 2nd ed. (Houston, Tex.: Arte Publico Press, 2003), 94–95.

15. As one example, consider Lexicon Valley's episode "A Bundle of Faggots," which traces the semantic shift of this term from "a bundle of sticks, twigs, or small branches of trees bound together" to its contemporary derogatory uses based on a person's sexual orientation or contemptibility. "Faggot," *Oxford English Dictionary* online, accessed June 30, 2016, http://www.oed.com.dbsearch.fredonia.edu:2048/view/Entry/67623?isAdvanced=false&result=1&rskey=cn0ATY&. See also Mike Vuolo, "A Bundle of Faggots," 30:12, *Lexicon Valley* (podcast), *Slate*, February 13, 2012, accessed June 30, 2016, http://www.slate.com/articles/podcasts/lexicon_valley/2012/02/lexicon_valley_the_history_future_and_reclamation_of_the_word_faggot_.html.

16. Some other helpful readings pertinent to the discussion of lexicography then and now include Seth Lerer's book chapters "A Harmless Drudge: Samuel Johnson and the Making of the Dictionary" and "Horrid, Hooting Stanzas, Lexicography and Literature in American English" from *Inventing English: A Portable History of the Language*, 2nd ed. (New York: Columbia University Press, 2015); Naomi Baron's discussion of "Hard Words to Usage Panels" in her chapter "Setting Standards" in *Alphabet to Email: How Written English Evolved and Where It's Heading* (New York: Routledge, 2000); and James Gleick's chapter "Two Wordbooks" in *The Information: A History, a Theory, a Flood* (New York: Pantheon, 2011).

17. It is also interesting to note how the election of an emoji as the Word of the Year for 2015 by *Oxford Dictionaries* has led to productive conversations about what is a word, the nature of graphic representations of language, and the relationship between emoticons, emojis, and pictograms. See Mike Ayers, "Oxford Dictionaries Selects an Emoji as Word of the Year" (blog post), *Speakeasy, Wall Street Journal* online, November 16, 2015, accessed June 30, 2016, http://blogs.wsj.com/speakeasy/2015/11/16/oxford-dictionaries-word-of-the-year-emoji/. See also David Crystal, "What Makes Texting Distinctive?" *Txtng: The gr8 db8* (Oxford: Oxford University Press, 2008), 35–62, and David Crystal, "Punctuating the Internet," in David Crystal, *Making a Point: The Persnickety Story of English Punctuation* (New York: St. Martin's Press, 2015), 327–341.

18. The lack of an entry for "truthiness" even today—more than ten years after *truthiness* became a cultural phenomenon—in either *American Heritage Dictionary* or *Merriam-Webster's Online* offers weight to Colbert's send-up of dictionaries and reference works as "elitist" and of *Webster's* in particular as the "word police." Yet the *OED* online entry, which until December 2015 noted "This entry has not yet been fully updated (first published 1915)," reveals that the word has in fact existed for more than 200 years, albeit with a now obsolete usage/meaning "characterized by truth; truthful, true" as in this circa 1800 quotation from J. H. Colls *Theodore* i: 'You are afraid Theodore your sweetheart shouldn't prove truthy.'" *Oxford English Dictionary* online, s.v. "truthiness," accessed June 30, 2016. Indeed, to find *truthiness* as Colbert defines it, one must consult *Urban Dictionary*: its "top definition" (there are multiple ones) defines the term as "[t]he quality of stating concepts one wishes or believes to be true, rather than the facts"; reports its origin as "Stephen Colbert, 'The Colbert Report,' 2005"; and provides a source quotation from the broadcast as well as the hyperlinked name of the person creating the entry and the date the entry was created. *Urban Dictionary*,

s.v. "truthiness," accessed June 30, 2016, http://www.urbandictionary.com/define.php?term=truthiness.

19. While readings tend to vary from semester to semester, students have enjoyed jigsaw readings they have done from Naomi Baron's "Setting Standards" (*From Alphabet to Email*), Seth Lerer's "Visible Speech: The Orthoepists and the Origins of Standard English" (*Inventing English*), Francis Katamba, "Should English be spelt as she is spoke?," in *English Words: Structure, History, and Usage* (New York: Routledge, 2005) and (especially apt for future English teachers) selections from Edgar H. Schuster, *Breaking the Rules: Liberating Writers Through Innovative Grammar Instruction* (London: Heinemann, 2003). For the future, I plan to add discussion of serial commas (see next note) and periods (which are being associated with a negative emotional valence and so disfavored in texts and social media).

20. Carol Leth Stone, email to Copyediting-L List, copyediting-l@list.indiana.edu, June 28, 2016. Carol, who signs herself "devotee of the serial comma," reports of the disappearance of the serial comma in yet another traditional print-based publication, *National Parks Magazine*. Crystal's book *Making a Point* gives further examples of serial commas disappearing from exams.

21. I also bring in colleagues from my university who can address practical issues; for example, Dr. Kate Mahoney has visited my course to discuss her research regarding the impact of English-only education on the learning outcomes of ELL students in Arizona. In my HEL course's most recent iteration, I also had students read *English as a Global Language* by Crystal and bring in multimedia examples addressing the changing nature of World Englishes. One of the more interesting debates we had centered on President Obama's comment that U.S.-China relations would be one of the most important issues of our century and looked at shifting powers between the nations and the shifting potentials of English versus Mandarin to be the pre-eminent global language.

22. My friend, Laura Mitchell Woolson, has my tremendous thanks for introducing me to Lexicon Valley.

23. Lisa Carlson, course blog post for ENGL 352: History of the English Language, December 4, 2012, State University of New York at Fredonia; used with permission of author.

24. Lisa Carlson, personal email to author, July 1, 2016.

25. Czesław Miłosz, *A Treatise on Poetry*, translated by Czesław Miłosz and Robert Hass (New York: Ecco Press, 2001), 116, note 51.

CHAPTER 29

* I am grateful to the Open University for allowing me to reproduce sections from the script for the series, as well as visuals from one of the episodes. I would like to thank Catherine Chambers and Jon Hunter for agreeing to be interviewed about the production of the series. Full credits of those involved in the series are as follows: Development producer, Catherine Chambers; Executive producer, Richard Osborne; Producer, Seb Barwell; Academic writer, Philip Seargeant; Script writer, Jon Hunter; Illustrator, Henry Paker; Animator, Victoria Kitchingman.

1. M. Weller, *Battle for Open: How Openness Won and Why It Doesn't Feel Like Victory* (London: Ubiquity Press, 2012); "Open Educational Resources," Hewlett Foundation, http://www.hewlett.org/programs/education/open-educational-resources, n.d.

2. Weller, *The Battle for Open*, 87.

3. Ibid., 75.

4. Ibid.

5. "OER Impact Map," *OER Research Hub*, http://oermap.org/.

6. Robert Farrow et al., "Impact of OER Use on Teaching and Learning: Data from OER Research Hub (2013–2014)," *British Journal of Educational Technology* 46, no. 5 (2015): 972–76.

7. "Data Report 2013-2015: Informal Learners," *OER Research Hub*, http://oerresearchhub.org/2015/09/07/data-report-2013-2015-informal-learners/.

8. Farrow et. al., "Impact of OER Use."

9. "The History of English in Ten Minutes," *ouLearn on YouTube*, https://www.youtube.com/playlist?p=PLA03075BAD88B909E; https://itunes.apple.com/us/itunes-u/history-english-in-ten-minutes/id446082239?mt=10; "The History of English in Ten Minutes," *The Open University*, www.open.edu/openlearn/languages/english-language/the-history-english-ten-minutes.

10. Weller, *Battle for Open*.

11. Catherine Chambers, personal communication with author.

12. Catherine Chambers, "Think Visual," *Viewfinder Online*, http://bufvc.ac.uk/articles/think-visual.

13. Ibid., n.p.

14. These consist of the audio from public lectures, with animation added as a means of visualising the content: https://www.thersa.org/discover/videos/rsa-animate/.

15. Catherine Chambers, "Think Visual," *Viewfinder Online*, http://bufvc.ac.uk/articles/think-visual.

16. Catherine Chambers, personal communication with author.

17. "Statistics," YouTube, accessed 21 December 2015, https://www.youtube.com/yt/press/statistics.html.

18. Catherine Chambers, personal communication with author.

19. John Hunter, personal communication with author.

20. Catherine Chambers, personal communication with author.

21. John Hunter, personal communication with author.

22. "Frequently Asked Questions," *OpenLearn*, accessed 18 January 2016, http://www.open.edu/openlearn/about-openlearn/frequently-asked-questions-on-openlearn.

23. John Hunter, personal communication with author.

24. Philip Seargeant, *Exploring World Englishes: Language in a Global Context* (Abingdon: Routledge, 2012).

25. Ann Hewings and Philip Seargeant, "English Language Studies: A Critical Appraisal," in *Futures for English Studies: Teaching Language, Literature and Creative Writing in Higher Education*, edited by Ann Hewings, Lynda Prescott, and Philip Seargeant (Hounslow: Palgrave Macmillan, 2016).

BIBLIOGRAPHY

Aarslef, Hans. *The Study of Language in England, 1780–1860*. Princeton: Princeton
  University Press, 1967.
———. *The Study of Language in England, 1780–1860*. 2nd ed. Minneapolis: Minneapolis
  University Press, 1983.
Aarts, Bas. "In Defence of Distributional Analysis." *Studies in Language* 31 (2007): 431–43.
Achebe, Chinua. *Arrow of God*. New York: Doubleday, 1969.
Adams, Michael. "*DARE*, History, and the Texture of the Entry." *American Speech* 77
  (2002): 370–82.
———. *Slayer Slang: A Buffy the Vampire Slayer Lexicon*. New York: Oxford University
  Press, 2003.
———. "Review of Anatoly Liberman." *A Bibliography of English Etymology: Sources and
  Word List*. NOWELE 60/61 (2011): 231–44.
———. "Enregisterment: A Special Issue." *American Speech* 84 (2009): 115–17.
———. "Historical Dictionaries and the History of Reading." In *Reading in History: New
  Methodologies from the Anglo-American Tradition*, edited by Bonnie Gunzenhauser,
  47–62 and 143–45. London: Pickering & Chatto, 2010.
———. "Resources: Teaching Perspectives." In *English Historical Linguistics: An
  International Handbook*, edited by Alexander Bergs and Laurel J. Brinton, 1163–78.
  Berlin: Mouton de Gruyter, 2012.
———. "The Lexical Ride of a Lifetime." *American Speech* 88 (2013): 168–95.
———. "Vocabulary Analysis in Sociolinguistic Research." In *Research Methods in
  Sociolinguistics: A Practical Guide*, edited by Janet Holmes and Kirk Hazen, 163–76.
  Oxford: Wiley-Blackwell, 2014.
———. "Language Ideologies and the *American Heritage Dictionary of the English
  Language*: Evidence from Motive, Structure, and Design." *Dictionaries* 36
  (2015): 17–46.
Agha, Asif. "The Social Life of Cultural Value." *Language & Communication* 23, no. 3
  (2003): 231–73.
Ahmad, Dohra, ed. *Rotten English: A Literary Anthology*. New York: W. W. Norton, 2007.
Aijmer, Karen. "*I think*—An English Modal Particle." In *Modality in Germanic
  Languages: Historical and Comparative Perspectives*, edited by Toril Swan and Olaf
  Jansen Westvik, 1–47. Berlin: Mouton de Gruyter, 1997.
Alexander, Michael. *Beowulf*. London: Penguin, 1995.
Algeo, John. "In Memoriam: Thomas Pyles (1905–1980)." *Names: A Journal of Onomastics*
  28, no. 4 (1980): 291–92.
———. *The Cambridge History of the English Language*, vol. 6, *English in North America*.
  Cambridge: Cambridge University Press, 2001.
———. *The Origins and Development of the English Language*. 6th ed. Boston: Cengage
  Learning, 2009.
Algeo, John, and Carmen Butcher. *The Origins and Development of the English Language*.
  7th ed. Boston: Cengage Learning, 2013.

Algeo, John, and Thomas Pyles. *Problems in the Origins and Development of the English Language*. New York: Harcourt, Brace, & World, 1966.

Alim, Samy H., and Geneva Smitherman. *Articulate While Black: Barack Obama, Language, and Race in the U.S.* Oxford: Oxford University Press, 2012.

Allen, William. *Holy Bible Faithfully Translated into English: Ovt of the Authentical Latin, Diligently Conferred with the Hebrew, Greek, and Other Editions in Diuers Languages*. Rheims: Iohn Cousturier, 1635.

Alsagoff, Lubna, and Ho Chee Lick. "The Grammar of Singapore English." In *English in New Cultural Contexts: Reflections from Singapore*, edited by Joseph A. Foley et al., 127–51. Oxford: Oxford University Press, 1998.

American Heritage Book of English Usage. Boston: Houghton Mifflin, 1996.

American Heritage Dictionary of the English Language. 1st ed. Edited by William Morris et al. New York: American Heritage, 1969.

———. 2nd College ed. Edited by Pamela B. De Vinne et al. Boston: Houghton Mifflin, 1982.

———. 4th ed. Edited by Joseph P. Pickett et al. Boston: Houghton Mifflin, 2000.

———. 5th ed. Edited by Joseph P. Pickett et al. Boston: Houghton Mifflin Harcourt, 2011.

Ames, Carole. "Conceptions of Motivation Within Competitive and Noncompetitive Goal Structures." In *Self-Related Cognitions in Anxiety and Motivation*, edited by Ralf Schwarzer, 229–46. Hillsdale, NJ: Lawrence Earlbaum Associates, Inc., 1986.

Anderwald, Lieselotte. "Throve, Pled, Shrunk: The Evolution of American English in the 19th Century Between Language Change and Prescriptive Norms." In *Outposts of Historical Corpus Linguistics: From the Helsinki Corpus to a Proliferation of Resources*, edited by Jukka Tyrkkö et al. Studies in Variation, Contacts and Change in English no. 10. Helsinki: Research Unit for Variation, Contacts, and Change in Language, 2012.

Arnovick, Leslie K. *Diachronic Pragmatics: Seven Case Studies in English Illocutionary Development*. Amsterdam: John Benjamins, 1999.

———. Review of Andreas H. Jucker, ed., *Historical Pragmatics: Pragmatic Developments in the History of English* (Amsterdam: John Benjamins, 1995). In *Journal of Pragmatics* 28 (1997): 383–412.

———. *Written Reliquaries: The Resonance of Orality in Medieval English Texts*. Amsterdam: John Benjamins, 2006.

Arnovick, Leslie K., and Laurel J. Brinton. "Historical Pragmatics and Historical Socio-pragmatics." Paper presented at the annual meeting of the Modern Language Association, Vancouver, British Columbia, January 8–11, 2015.

Ascham, Roger. *The Schoolmaster*. Edited by Lawrence V. Ryan. Ithaca, NY: Cornell University Press, 1967.

Ashcroft, Bill, Gareth Griffiths, and Helen Tiffin. *The Empire Writes Back: Theory and Practice in Post-Colonial Literatures*. London: Routledge, 1989.

Ayers, Mike. "Oxford Dictionaries Selects an Emoji as Word of the Year" (blog post). *Speakeasy, Wall Street Journal* online, November 16, 2015, accessed June 30, 2016, https://blogs.wsj.com/speakeasy/2015/11/16/oxford-dictionaries-word-of-the-year-emoji/.

Bailey, Richard W. *Images of English: A Cultural History of the Language*. Ann Arbor: University of Michigan, 1991 [Reprint, Cambridge: Cambridge University Press, 2009].

———. *Nineteenth-Century English*. Ann Arbor: University of Michigan Press, 1996.

Baker, Philip, and Peter Mühlhäusler. "From Business to Pidgin." *Journal of Asian Pacific Communication* 1 (1990): 87–115.

Bakhtin, M. M. *The Dialogic Imagination*. Edited by Michael Holquist. Translated by Caryl Emerson and Michael Holquist. Austin: University of Texas Press, 1981.

Bamgbose, Ayo. "Corpus Planning in Yoruba: The Radio as a Case Study." *Research in Yoruba Language and Literature* 2 (1992): 1–13.

Bamiro, Edmund O. "Syntactic Variation in West African English." *World Englishes* 17, no. 2 (1995): 189–204.

Barber, Charles, Joan C. Beal and Philip Shaw. 2nd ed. *The English Language: A Historical Introduction*. Cambridge: Cambridge University Press, 2009.

Barnhart, Clarence L. "American Lexicography, 1947–1973." *American Speech* 53 (1978): 83–140.

Barnhart, Robert K., and Sol Steinmetz. *Barnhart Dictionary of Etymology*. New York: H. W. Wilson, 1988.

Barðdal, Jóhanna. "Construction-Based Comparative Historical Reconstruction." In *The Oxford Handbook of Construction Grammar*, edited by Thomas Hoffmann and Graeme Trousdale, 438–57. Oxford: Oxford University Press, 2013.

Baron, Naomi. "Setting Standards." In *Alphabet to Email: How Written English Evolved and Where It's Heading*. New York: Routledge, 2000.

Barrett, Grant. *The Official Dictionary of Unofficial English*. New York: McGraw-Hill, 2006.

———. "Double-Tongued Dictionary." *A Way with Words*, July 18, 2012. http://www.waywordradio.org/double-tongued-dictionary/.

Barry, Peter. *Beginning Theory: An Introduction to Literary and Cultural Theory*. Manchester: Manchester University Press, 2009.

Bately, Janet M., ed. *The Anglo-Saxon Chronicle: A Collaborative Edition*, vol. 3, *MS A: A Semi-diplomatic Edition with Introduction* and *Indices*. Cambridge: Brewer, 1986.

Baugh, Albert C. *A History of the English Language*. 1st ed. New York: D. Appleton-Century Company, 1935.

———. *A History of the English Language*. 2nd ed. New York: Appleton-Century-Crofts, 1957.

———. "Historical Linguistics and the Teacher of English." *College English* 24, no. 2 (1962): 106–10.

Baugh, Albert C., and Thomas Cable. *A History of the English Language*. 3rd ed. Englewood Cliffs, NJ: Prentice-Hall, 1978.

———. *A History of the English Language*. 4th ed. Englewood Cliffs, NJ: Prentice-Hall, 1993.

———. *A History of the English Language*, 6th ed. Upper Saddle River, NJ: Longman, 2012.

Baumgardner, Robert J., and Kimberly Brown. "World Englishes: Ethics and Pedagogy." *World Englishes* 22, no. 3 (2003): 245–51.

Beal, Joan C. *English Pronunciation in the Eighteenth Century: Thomas Spence's "Grand Repository of the English Language" (1775)*. Oxford: Clarendon Press, 1999.

———. *English in Modern Times 1700–1945*. London: Hodder Arnold, 2004.

Beckwith, Sarah. *Shakespeare and the Grammar of Forgiveness*. Ithaca: Cornell University Press, 2012.

Bennett, Arnold. "Books and Persons." *The Evening Standard*. January 5, 1928.

Bennett, Gena R. *Using Corpora in the Language Learning Classroom*. Ann Arbor: University of Michigan Press, 2011.

Benson, Phil. *Ethnocentrism and the English Dictionary*. New York: Routledge, 2001.

Benveniste, Emile. *Problems in General Linguistics*. Translated by Mary Elizabeth Meek. Coral Gables: University of Miami Press, 1971.

Berger, Harris, and Michael Carroll, eds. *Global Pop, Local Languages*. Jackson: University of Mississippi Press, 2003.

Berkhout, Carl T. "Laurence Nowell (1530–ca.1570)." In *Medieval Scholarship: Biographical Studies on the Formation of a Discipline*, vol. 2, *Literature and Philology*, edited by Helen Damico. 1–17. New York: Garland, 1998.

Bermudez-Otero, Ricardo. "Prosodic Optimization: The Middle English Length Adjustment." *English Language and Linguistics* 2 (1998): 169–97.

Bernaisch, Tobias. "Attitudes Toward Englishes in Sri Lanka." *World Englishes* 31, no. 3 (2012): 279–91.

Bernardini, Silvia. Exploring New Directions for Discovery Learning. In *Teaching and Learning by Doing Corpus Analysis*, edited by Bernhard Ketteman and Georg Marko. *Proceedings of the Fourth International Conference on Teaching and Language Corpora*, Graz no. 19, July 24, 2000, 165–82.

Bhatt, Rakesh M. "Prescriptivism, Creativity, and World Englishes." *World Englishes* 14 (1995): 247–60.

———. "Optimal Expressions in Indian English." *English Language and Linguistics* 4 (2000): 69–95.

———. "World Englishes." *Annual Review of Anthropology* 30 (2001): 527–50.

———. "Experts, Dialects, and Discourse." *International Journal of Applied Linguistics* 12, no. 1 (2002): 74–109.

———. "Expert Discourses, Local Practices, and Hybridity: The Case of Indian Englishes." In *Reclaiming the Local in Language Policy and Practice*, edited by A. Suresh Canagarajah, 25–54. Mahwah, NJ: Lawrence Erlbaum, 2005).

———. "In Other Words: Language Mixing, Identity Representations, and Third Space." *Journal of Sociolinguistics* 12, no. 2 (2008): 177–200.

———. "World Englishes, Globalization and the Politics of Conformity." In *Contending with World Englishes in Globalization*, edited by Mukul Saxena and Tope Ominiyi, 93–112. London: Multilingual Matters, 2010.

Biber, Douglas, et al. *Longman Grammar of Spoken and Written English*. Harlow, Essex: Pearson, 1999.

Bible Society of the West Indies. "Maak 6." In *Di Jamiekan Nyuu Testiment (JNT)*, 2012. YouVersion. https://www.bible.com/bible/476/mrk.6.jnt.

Blanco, Erik, et al. *U.C.L.A. Slang 6* UCLA Occasional Papers in Linguistics no. 24, edited by Pamela Munro. Los Angeles: Department of Linguistics, University of California, 2009.

Boelens, Krine. *The Frisian Language*. Leeuwarden, Netherlands: Information Service of the Province of Friesland and Fryske Akademy, 1979.

Bokamba, Eyamba G. "The Africanization of English." In *The Other Tongue: English Across Cultures*, edited by Braj B. Kachru, 125–47. Urbana: University of Illinois Press, 1992.

Bolton, Kingsley, and Braj B. Kachru, eds. *World Englishes: Critical Concepts in Linguistics*. 6 vols. London: Routledge, 2006.

Boult, Adam. "#YouAintNoMuslimBruv: A 'Very London' Response to Leytonstone Tube Terror Attack." *The Guardian*. December 6, 2015.

Bragg, Melvyn. *The Adventure of English: The Biography of a Language*. New York: Arcade, 2003.

Branford, Jean. "New Germanic for Old: Afrikaans Cognates and the Translation of Old English." In *Seven Studies in English*, edited by Gildas Roberts. Cape Town: Purnell, 1971.

Brems, Lieselotte, and Kristin Davidse. "The Grammaticalisation of Nominal Type Noun Constructions with kind/sort of: Chronology and Paths of Change." *English Studies* 91, no. 2 (2010): 180–202.

Bright, William. "Toward a Cultural Grammar." *Indian Linguistics* 29 (1968): 20–29.

Brinton, Laurel J. "Historical Discourse Analysis." In *Handbook of Discourse Analysis*, edited by Deborah Tannen, Heidi E. Hamilton, and Deborah Schiffrin, 222–43. Malden, MA: Blackwell, 2003.

———, ed. *English Historical Linguistics: Approaches and Perspectives*, 245–74. Cambridge: Cambridge University Press, 2016.

———. "Historical Pragmatics." In *English Historical Linguistics: Approaches and Perspectives*, edited by Laurel Brinton. Cambridge: Cambridge University Press, 2017.

Brinton, Laurel J., and Leslie K. Arnovick. *The English Language: A Linguistic History*. 3rd rev. ed. Don Mills, ONT: Oxford University Press, 2017.

The British Library. "Learning English Timeline," accessed October 15, 2016, http://www.bl.uk/learning/langlit/evolvingenglish/accessvers/index.html.

———. "Sounds: Accents and Dialects," accessed October 15, 2016, http://sounds.bl.uk/Accents-and-dialects.

Brophy, Jere E. and Kathryn R. Wentzel, *Motivating Students to Learn*. New York: Routledge, 2013.

Brown, Penelope, and Steven C. Levinson, *Politeness: Some Universals in Language*. Cambridge: Cambridge University Press, 1987.

Buck, Carl Darling. *A Dictionary of Selected Synonyms in the Principal Indo-European Languages: A Contribution to the History of Ideas*. Chicago: University of Chicago Press, 1949.

Bullough, D. A. "What Has Ingeld to Do with Lindisfarne?" *Anglo-Saxon England* 22 (1993): 93–125.

———. "Alcuin (*c*.740–804)." In *Oxford Dictionary of National Biography*. Oxford: Oxford University Press, 2004; online edition, accessed August 26, 2016, http://www.oxforddnb.com/view/article/298.

Burchfield, Robert, ed. *The Cambridge History of the English Language*, vol. 5, *English in Britain and Overseas: Origins and Development*. Cambridge: Cambridge University Press, 1994.

Burnley, David, ed. *The History of the English Language: A Source Book*, 2nd ed. New York: Routledge, 2000.

Burridge, Kate. *Blooming English: Observations on the Roots, Cultivations, and Hybrids of the English Language*. Cambridge: Cambridge University Press, 2002.

Burton, Richard R., John Seely Brown, and Gerhard Fischer. "Skiing as a Model of Instruction." In *Everyday Cognition: Its Developmental and Social Context,* edited by Barbara Rogoff and Jean Lave, 139–50. Cambridge, MA: Harvard University Press, 1984.

Cable, Thomas. *The English Alliterative Tradition*. Philadelphia: University of Pennsylvania Press, 1991.

———. *A Companion to Baugh and Cable's History of the English Language*. 3rd ed. London: Routledge, 2002.

———. "A History of the English Language." *Studies in Medieval and Renaissance Teaching* 14 (2007): 17–25.

———. "Ictus as Stress or Length: The Effect of Tempo." In *Old English Philology*, edited by Leonard Neidorf, Rafael J. Pascual, and Tom Shippey, 34–51. Woodbridge, Suffolk, UK: Boydell & Brewer, 2016.

Cable, Thomas, and Albert C. Baugh. *A History of the English Language*. 6th ed. Boston: Pearson, 2012.

Calhoun, Craig. *Critical Social Theory: Culture, History, and the Challenge of Difference*. Cambridge: Blackwell, 1995.

Cameron, Deborah. *Verbal Hygiene*. New York: Routledge, 1995.

Campbell, Alistair. *Old English Grammar*. Oxford: Clarendon Press, 1959.

Canagarajah, A. Suresh. *Resisting Linguistic Imperialism in English Teaching*. Oxford: Oxford University Press, 1999.

Canagarajah, Susan. *Translingual Practice: Global Englishes and Cosmopolitan Relations*. New York: Routledge, 2013.

Cannon, Christopher. *The Making of Chaucer's English: A Study of Words*. Cambridge: Cambridge University Press, 1998.

Carter, Phillip M. "Quantifying Rhythmic Differences between Spanish, English, and Hispanic English." In *Theoretical and Experimental Approaches to Romance Linguistics,* edited by Randall S. Gess and Edward J. Rubin, 63–75. Amsterdam: Benjamins, 2005.

Cawdrey, Robert. *A Table Alphabeticall of Hard Usual English Words*. Rpt. Scholar's Facsimiles and Reprints. Gainesville, FL: 1966; Delmar, NY: 1976.

Caxton, William. Preface to the *Eneydos*. In *Problems in the Origins and Development of the English Language*, edited by John Algeo and Thomas Pyles, 179. New York: Harcourt, Brace & World, 1966 [1490].

Chambers, Angela. "Integrating Corpus Consulation in Language Studies." *Language Learning and Technology* 9(2): 111–25.

Chambers, C. Think Visual. *Viewfinder Online*. Accessed January 6, 2016. http://bufvc.ac.uk/articles/think-visual.

Chambers, J. K. "Vernacular Universals." In *ICLaVE 1: Proceedings of the First International Conference on Language Variation in Europe*, edited by Josep M. Fontana et al. Barcelona: Universitat Pompeu Fabra, 2001.

Chaudenson, Robert. *Creolization of Language and Culture*. London: Routledge, 2001.

Cheng, Winnie, and Martin Warren. "'She Knows More About Hong Kong Than You Do Isn't It': Tags in Hong Kong Conversational English." *Journal of Pragmatics* 33 (2001): 1419–39.

Chevalier, Alida. *Globalisation versus Internal Development: The Reverse Short Front Vowel Shift in South African English*. Unpublished PhD diss., University of Cape Town, 2016.

Clark, Cecily. "Historical Linguistics-Linguistic Archaeology." In *Papers from the 5th International Conference on English Historical Linguistics*, edited by Sylvia Adamson et al., 55–68. Amsterdam: John Benjamins, 1990.

Clemens, Raymond, and Timothy Graham. *Introduction to Manuscript Studies*. Ithaca, NY: Cornell University Press, 2007.

Cockayne, Oswald. *Leechdoms, Wortcunning and Starcraft of Early England*. 3 vols. London: Longman, 1864.

Cole, Kristin Lynn. "The Destruction of Troy's Different Rules: The Alliterative Revival and the Alliterative Tradition." *Journal of English and Germanic Philology* 109 (2010): 162–76.

Colleman, Timothy, and Bernard De Clerck. "Constructional Semantics on the Move: On Semantic Specialization in the English Double Object Construction." *Cognitive Linguistics* 21, no. 1 (2011): 183–209.

Condry, Ian. "The Social Production of Difference: Imitation and Authenticity in Japanese Rap Music." In *Transactions, Transgressions, and Transformations*, edited by Heide Fehrenbach and Uta G. Polger, 166–84. New York: Berghan Books, 2000.

Considine, John. "Why Do Large Historical Dictionaries Give So Much Pleasure to Their Owners and Users?" *EURALEX '98 Proceedings*, edited by Thierry Fontanelle, 579–87. Liège, Belgium: Université de Liège, 1998.

———. *Dictionaries in Early Modern Europe: Lexicography and the Making of Heritage*. Cambridge: Cambridge University Press, 2008.

———. *Academy Dictionaries 1600–1800*. Cambridge: Cambridge University Press, 2014.

Cooper, Jilly. *Wicked!: A Tale of Two Schools*. London: Bantam Press, 2006.

Cornelius, Ian. "The Accentual Paradigm in Early English Metrics." *Journal of English and Germanic Philology* 114 (2015): 459–81.

———. *Reconstructing Alliterative Verse: The Pursuit of a Medieval Meter*. Cambridge: Cambridge University Press, 2017.

Corrigan, Karen P. *Irish English*, vol. 1, *Northern Ireland*. Edinburgh: Edinburgh University Press, 2010.

Croft, William. "Beyond Aristotle and Gradience: A Reply to Aarts." *Studies in Language* 31 (2007): 409–30.

Crosby, Alfred W. *Ecological Imperialism: The Biological Expansion of Europe, 900-1900*. Cambridge: Cambridge University Press, 1986.

Crystal, David. *Linguistics*. Harmondsworth, UK: Pelican, 1971.

———. *The Cambridge Encyclopedia of the English Language*. 1st ed. Cambridge: Cambridge University Press, 1995.

———. "On Trying to Be Crystal-Clear: A Response to Phillipson." *Applied Linguistics* 21, no. 3 (2000): 415–21.

———. *English as a Global Language*. 2nd ed. Cambridge: Cambridge University Press, 2003.

———. *The Stories of English*. New York: Overlook Press, 2004.

———. *Pronouncing Shakespeare*. Cambridge: Cambridge University Press, 2005.

———. *Txtng: The gr8 bd8*. Oxford: Oxford University Press, 2008.

———. *The Story of English in 100 Words*. New York: St. Martin's Press, 2012.

———. "Early Interest in Shakespearean Original Pronunciation." *Language and History* 56 (2013): 5–17.

————. *The Cambridge Encyclopedia of the English Language*. 2nd ed. 10th Printing. Cambridge: Cambridge University Press, 2014.

————. *Making a Point: The Persnickety Story of English Punctuation*. New York: St. Martin's Press, 2015.

————. *The Oxford Dictionary of Original Shakespearean Pronunciation*. Oxford: Oxford University Press, 2016.

Crystal, David, and Ben Crystal. *The Oxford Illustrated Shakespeare Dictionary*. Oxford: Oxford University Press, 2015.

Csikszentmihalyi, Mihaly. *Society, Culture, and Person: A Systems View of Creativity*. Dordrecht: Springer Netherlands, 2014.

Culler, Jonathan. *Structuralist Poetics: Structuralism, Linguistics, and the Study of Literature*. Ithaca, NY: Cornell University Press, 1975.

————. *Ferdinand de Saussure*, rev. ed. Ithaca, NY: Cornell University Press, 1986.

————. *Literary Theory: A Very Short Introduction*. Oxford: Oxford University Press, 2011.

Culpepper, Jonathan. *History of English*. London: Routledge, 1997.

Curran, S. Terrie. *From Cædmon to Chaucer: The Literary Development of English*. Prospect Heights, IL: Waveland Press, 2002.

Curzan, Anne. "English Historical Corpora in the Classroom. The Intersection of Teaching and Research." In *Journal of English Linguistics* 28, no. 1 (March 2000): 77–89.

————. "Periodization in the History of the English Language." In *English Historical Linguistics: An International Handbook*. Vol. 2, edited by Alex Bergs and Laurel Brinton, 1232–56. Boston: Mouton de Gruyter, 2012.

————. "Revisiting the Reduplicative Copula with Corpus-based Evidence." In *The Oxford Handbook of the History of English*, edited by Elizabeth C. Traugott and Terttu Nevalainen, 211–22. New York: Oxford University Press, 2012.

Curzan, Anne, and Michael Adams. *How English Works: A Linguistic Introduction*. Indianapolis, IN: Pearson Education, 2012.

Das, Gurcharan. "Inescapably English." *The Times of India*. October 21, 2001.

Davies, Mark. *Corpus of Global Web-Based English: 1.9 Billion Words from Speakers in 20 Countries, [GloWbE]* 2013. Available online at http://corpus.byu.edu/glowbe/.

Deb, Siddhartha. "Arundhati Roy, the Not-So-Reluctant Renegade." *New York Times Magazine*, March 2014.

Deci, Edward L., and Richard M. Ryan. "The 'What' and 'Why' of Goal Pursuits: Human Needs and the Self-Determination of Behavior." *Psychological Inquiry* 11, no. 4 (2000): 227–68.

de Man, Paul. "The Return to Philology." In *The Resistance to Theory*, edited by Paul de Man, 21–26. Minneapolis: University of Minnesota, 1986.

de Saussure, Ferdinand. *Cours de linguistique générale*. Translated by Wade Baskin. New York: The Philosophical Library, 1960.

————. *Cours de linguistique générale*. Translated by Roy Harris, London: Duckworth, 1983.

————. *Cours de linguistique générale*. Edited by Tullio de Mauro. Paris: Payot, 1984.

De Smet, Hendrik. "The Course of Actualization." *Language* 88, no. 3 (2012): 601–33.

————. *Spreading Patterns: Diffusional Change in the English System of Complementation*. Oxford: Oxford University Press, 2013.

Denison, David. "Syntax." In *The Cambridge History of the English Language*, vol. 4, 1776–1997, edited by Suzanne Romaine, 92–329. Cambridge: Cambridge University Press, 1998.

————. "History of the *sort of* Construction Family." Paper presented at ICCG2: Second International Conference on Construction Grammar, Helsinki, 2002.

————. "Patterns and Productivity." In *Studies in the History of the English Language*, vol. 4, *Empirical and Analytical Advances in the Study of English Language Change*. Topics in English Linguistics no. 61, edited by Susan M. Fitzmaurice and Donka Minkova, 207–30. Berlin: Mouton de Gruyter, 2008.

————. "Category Change in English With and Without Structural Change." In *Gradience, Gradualness and Grammaticalization*, edited by Elizabeth C. Traugott and Graeme Trousdale, 105–28. Amsterdam: John Benjamins, 2010.

———. "Non-inflecting verbs in Modern English." Paper presented at Autour du verbe/ Around the Verb: Colloque en l'honneur de Claude Delmas. Paris, 2012.

———. "Parts of Speech: Solid Citizens or Slippery Customers?" *Journal of the British Academy* 1 (2013): 151–85.

———. "Ambiguity and Vagueness in Historical Change." In *The Changing English Language: Psycholinguistic Perspectives*. Studies in English Language, edited by Marianne Hundt, Sandra Mollin, and Simone Pfenninger. Cambridge: Cambridge University Press, submitted.

Dictionary of American English. 4 vols., edited by William A. Craigie et al. Chicago: University of Chicago Press, 1938–44.

Dictionary of American Regional English. 6 vols., edited by Frederic G. Cassidy et al. Cambridge: Cambridge, MA: Belknap Press of the Harvard University Press, 1985– 2013. Available in a digital edition by subscription at http://www.daredictionary. com/.

Dictionary of the Older Scottish Tongue. Edited by W. A. Craigie, A. J. Aitken, J. M. Templeton, and J. A. C. Stevenson. Aberdeen: Aberdeen University Press, 1931.

Dinin, Aaron. *The Krzyzewskiville Tales*. Durham, NC: Duke University Press, 2005.

"Disney Channel Monstober Zap." *Disney Channel*, accessed June 30, 2016, http://lol. disney.com/games/disney-channel-monstober-zap.

Dobbie, Elliott van Kirk, ed. *Beowulf and Judith*. Anglo-Saxon Poetic Records no. 4. New York: Columbia University Press, 1953.

Dodwell, C. R., and Peter Clemoes, eds. *The Old English Illustrated Hexateuch: British Museum Cotton Claudius B. IV*. Early English Manuscripts in Facsimile no. 18. Copenhagen: Rosenkilde and Bagger, 1974.

Dollinger, Stefan, Laurel J. Brinton, and Margery Fee, eds. *DCHP-1 Online: A Dictionary of Canadianisms on Historical Principles Online*, 2013. First published by Gage Press, 1967. Available at http://dchp.ca/DCHP-1/.

Domínguez, Virginia R. *White by Definition: Social Classification in Creole Louisiana*. New Brunswick, NJ: Rutgers University Press, 1986.

Donley, Kate, and Randi Reppen. "Using Corpus Tools to Highlight Academic Vocabulary in Sustained Content Language Teaching." In *TESOL Journal* 10, nos. 2/3 (2001): 7–12.

Dorian, Nancy. *Investigating Variation: The Effects of Social Organization and Social Setting*. Oxford: Oxford University Press, 2010.

Drechsel, Emanuel J. *Language Contact in the Early Colonial Pacific: Maritime Polynesian Pidgin Before Pidgin English*. Cambridge: Cambridge University Press, 2014.

Dressman, Michael R. "The History of the English Language Course: A Cross-Disciplinary Approach to the Humanities." *Arts & Humanities in Higher Education* 6 (2007): 107–13.

Dryden, John. *Essays*, Edited by W. P. Ker. 2 volumes. Oxford: Clarendon, 1926.

D'souza, Jean. "Interactional Strategies in South Asian Languages: Their Implications for Teaching English Internationally." *World Englishes* 7 (1988): 159–71.

———. "Speech Acts in Indian English Fiction." *World Englishes* 10, no. 3 (1991): 307–16.

Duffy, Eamon. *The Stripping of the Altars: Traditional Religion in England, 1400-1580*. London: Yale University Press, 1992.

Duggan, H. N. "Meter, Stanza, Vocabulary, Dialect." In *A Companion to the Gawain Poet*, edited by Derek Brewer and Jonathan Gibson, 221–42. Cambridge: D.S. Brewer, 1997.

Durkin, Philip. *Borrowed Words: A History of Loanwords in English*. Oxford: Oxford University Press, 2014.

Eagleton, Terry. *Literary Theory: An Introduction*, 2nd ed. Minneapolis: University of Minnesota, 1996.

Eastwood, Alexander. "A Fantastic Failure: Displaced Nationalism and the Intralingual Translation of Harry Potter." *The English Languages: History, Diaspora, Culture* 1 (2010), http://jps.library.utoronto.ca/index.php/elhdc/article/view/14365.

Elle team. "The Most Hilarious Brexit Memes." *Elle India blog*, accessed June 30, 2016, http://elle.in/blog/the-most-hilarious-brexit-memes.

Emonds, Joseph Embley, and Jan Terje Faarlund. *English: The Language of the Vikings*. Olomouc, Czech Republic: Palacký University, 2014.

"Enunciate by Spitting." YouTube video excerpted from *Friends* episode "The One with Monica and Chandler's Wedding (Part 1)," 2:58. Posted by SNA Gilbert, March 2, 2008, https://www.youtube.com/watch?v=0ISJS4gSBh0.

Factiva. https://global-factivacom.myaccess.library.utoronto.ca/sb/default.aspx?lnep=hp.

Farrow, Robert, et al. "Impact of OER Use on Teaching and Learning: Data from OER Research Hub (2013–2014)." *British Journal of Educational Technology*, 46, no. 5 (2015): 972–76.

Fennell, Barbara. *A History of English: A Sociolinguistic Approach*. Oxford: Blackwell Publishers, 2001.

Ferguson, Frances. "Philology, Literature, Style." *ELH* 80 (2013): 323–41.

Ferguson, Susan L. "Drawing Fictional Lines: Dialect and Narrative in the Victorian Novel." *Style* 32, no. 1 (1998): 1–17.

Fillmore, Charles J., Paul Kay, and Mary Catherine O'Connor. "Regularity and Idiomaticity in Grammatical Constructions." *Language* 64 (1988): 501–38.

Filppula, Markku. "Contact and the Early History of English." In *The Handbook of Language Contact*, edited by Raymond Hickey, 432–53. Malden, MA: Wiley-Blackwell, 2010.

Fischer, Karin. "International-Student Numbers Continue Record-Breaking Growth." *The Chronicle of Higher Education*. Last modified November 17, 2014. chronicle.com. myaccess.library.utoronto.ca/article/International-Student-Numbers/150049.

———. "A Freshman Year, Far From Home." *The Chronicle of Higher Education*. Last modified May 29, 2014. chronicle.com/article/A-Freshman-Year-Far-From-Home/141303.

Fish, Stanley. *Is There a Text in This Class? The Authority of Interpretive Communities*. Cambridge, MA: Harvard University Press, 1980.

Fisher, John Hurt. "Chancery and the Emergence of Standard Written English." *Speculum* 52 (1977): 870–89.

———. *The Emergence of Standard English*. Lexington: University of Kentucky Press, 1996.

Fisher, John Hurt, and Diane D. Bornstein. *In Forme of Speche Is Chaunge: Readings in the History of the English Language*. 2nd ed. Lanham, MD: University Press of America, 1984.

Fisher, John Hurt, and Malcolm Richardson. *An Anthology of Chancery English*. Knoxville: University of Tennessee Press, 1984.

Fishkin, Shelly Fisher. *Was Huck Black? Mark Twain and African-American Voices*. Oxford: Oxford University Press, 1993.

Flowerdew, Lynne. "Applying Corpus Linguistics to Pedagogy: A Critical Evaluation." In *International Journal of Corpus Linguistics* 14, no. 3 (2009): 393–417.

Follett, Wilson. *Modern American Usage*. New York: Hill & Wang, 1966.

Forshall, Josiah, and Frederic Madden. *The Holy Bible, containing the Old and New Testaments, with the Apocryphal books, in the earliest English versions made from the Latin Vulgate by John Wycliffe and His Followers*. Vol 2. Oxford: Oxford University Press, 1850.

Fortson, Benjamin W. *Indo-European Language and Culture: An Introduction*. Malden, MA: Blackwell, 2004.

Foucault, Michel. *The Archaeology of Knowledge and the Discourse on Language*. Translated by A. M. Sheridan Smith. New York: Vintage, 1972 [Reprint, 2010].

Fought, Carmen. *Chicano English in Context*. New York: Palgrave, Macmillan, 2003.

Fowler, H. W. *A Dictionary of Modern English Usage*. 1st ed. Oxford: Oxford University Press, 1926.

———. *A Dictionary of Modern English Usage*. 2nd ed., revised by Ernest Gowers. Oxford: Oxford University Press, 1965.

———. *A Dictionary of Modern English Usage*. 3rd ed., under the title *The New Fowler's Modern English Usage*, edited by R. W. Burchfield. Oxford: Oxford University Press, 1996.

———. *A Dictionary of Modern English Usage*. 4th ed., under the title *Fowler's Dictionary of Modern English Usage*, edited by Jeremy Butterfield, Oxford: Oxford University Press, 2015.

Frantzen, Allen. *Desire for Origins: New Language, Old English, and Teaching the Tradition*. New Brunswick, NJ: Rutgers University Press, 1990.

Freeborn, Dennis. *From Old to Standard English: A Coursebook in Language Variation Across Time*. 3rd ed. New York: Palgrave Macmillan, 2006.

Fry, Stephen. "Kinetic Typography-Language." *YouTube*, 6:33. Posted by Matthew Rogers on September 30, 2010, accessed June 30, 2016, https://www.youtube.com/watch?v=J7E-aoXLZGY.

Fulk, R. D. *A History of Old English Meter*. Philadelphia: University of Pennsylvania Press, 1992.

Fulk, R. D., Robert E. Bjork, and John D. Niles, eds. *Klaeber's Beowulf and The Fight at Finnburg*. 4th ed. Toronto: University of Toronto Press, 2008.

Gardner, Helen. "Auditory Imagination." In *The Art of T. S. Eliot: A Searching Evaluation of Eliot's Masterpiece, Four Quartets*. New York: Dutton, 1950.

Gardner, Howard. *Frames of Mind: The Theory of Multiple Intelligences*. London: Fontana Press, 1983. [Reprint, New York: Basic Books, 2011.]

Garfield, Bob, and Mike Vuolo. "Where Did the Word *Snark* Come From?" *Lexicon Valley* podcast, 41:35, *Slate*, October 20, 2014, accessed June 30, 2016. Available at http://www.slate.com/articles/podcasts/lexicon_valley/2014/10/lexicon_valley_the_etymology_and_history_of_the_word_snark_with_lexicographer.html.

Garner, Bryan A. *Garner's Modern American Usage*. 1st ed., titled *A Dictionary of Modern American Usage*. New York, Oxford University Press, 1998.

———. *Garner's Modern American Usage*. 2nd ed. New York, Oxford University Press, 2003.

———. *Garner's Modern American Usage*. 3rd ed. New York, Oxford University Press, 2009.

———. *Garner's Modern American Usage*. 4th ed. New York: Oxford University Press, 2016.

Gates, Henry Louis Jr.,. *The Signifying Monkey*. New York: Oxford University Press, 1988.

Gerber, Natalie. "Global Englishes, Rhyme, and Rap: A Meditation Upon Shifts in Rhythm." In *On Rhyme*, edited by David Caplan, 221–36. Liège, Belgium: Presses Universitaires de Liège, 2017.

Giancarlo, Matthew. "The Rise and Fall of the Great Vowel Shift? The Changing Ideological Intersections of Philology, Linguistics, and Literary History." *Representations* 76 (2001): 27–60.

Gilliéron, Jules, and J. Mongin. *Scier dans la Gaule romance*. Paris: Champion, 1905.

Glassie, Henry. *Material Culture*. Bloomington: Indiana University Press, 1999.

Gleick, James. "Cyber-Neologoliferation." *New York Times Magazine* online, November 5, 2006, accessed June 30, 2016. http://www.nytimes.com/2006/11/05/magazine/05cyber.html.

Gleick, James. *The Information: A History, a Theory, a Flood*. New York: Pantheon, 2011.

Gleick, James. "Two Wordbooks." In *The Information: A History, a Theory, a Flood*. New York: Pantheon, 2011.

Global Recordings Network. "Frisian, Western Language," accessed October 15, 2016, http://globalrecordings.net/en/language/3033.

Glover, Julie. "Gallagher and English Language," *YouTube*, accessed October 16, 2016, https://www.youtube.com/watch?v=Mfz3kFNVopk.

Glowka, Wayne, et al. "*Among the New Words* as an Editing Project in a Methods of Research Class." *Dictionaries* 21 (2000): 100–8.

Glowka, Wayne, et al. "Among the New Words." *American Speech* 82 (2007): 420–37.

———. "Among the New Words." *American Speech* 83 (2008): 85–98.

Godden, Malcolm, and Susan Irvine, eds. *The Old English Boethius: An Edition of the Old English Versions of Boethius's De Consolatione Philosophiae*. 2 vols. Oxford: Oxford University Press, 2009.

Goldberg, Adele E. *Constructions: A Construction Grammar Approach to Argument Structure*. Chicago: University of Chicago Press, 1995.

Goldberg, Adele E. "Constructionist Approaches." In *The Oxford Handbook of Construction Grammar*, edited by Thomas Hoffmann and Graeme Trousdale, 15–31. New York: Oxford University Press, 2013.

Goolden, Peter, ed. *The Old English Apollonius of Tyre*. Oxford: Oxford University Press, 1958.

Gordon, Larry. "Fewer Californians Got into UC, While Offers to Foreign Students Rose." *Los Angeles Times*. Last modified July 2, 2015. latimes.com/local/education/la-me-ln-uc-admit-20150702-story.html.

Görlach, Manfred. *Englishes*. Amsterdam: John Benjamins, 1991.

———. *English in Nineteenth-Century England*. Cambridge: Cambridge University Press, 1999.

———. *Eighteenth-Century English*. Heidelberg: C. Winter, 2001.

Gould, Stephen Jay, and Niles Eldredge. "Punctuated Equilibrium Comes of Age." *Nature* 366 (1993): 233–37.

Graddol, David. "English Next: Why Global English May Mean the End of 'English as a Foreign Language.'" London: British Council, 2006.

Graddol, David, Dick Leith, and Joan Swann, eds. *English: History, Diversity and Change*. London: Routledge, 1996.

Graff, Gerald. *Professing Literature: An Institutional History*. Chicago: University of Chicago, 1987. [Reprint, 2007.]

Gramley, Stephan. *The History of English: An Introduction*. Abingdon: Routledge, 2012.

Grazzini, Camillo. "The Four Planes of Development." *NAMTA Journal* 21, no. 2 (1996): 208–41.

Green, Jonathan. "English in India—The Grandmother Tongue." *Critical Quarterly* 40, no. 1 (1998): 107–11.

Green, Lisa J. *African American English: A Linguistic Introduction*. Cambridge: Cambridge University Press, 2002.

Gregerson, Linda. "Ode and Empire." *TriQuarterly* 129 (2007): 9–19.

Groden, Michael, ed. *The Johns Hopkins Guide to Literary Theory and Criticism*. 2nd ed. Baltimore: Johns Hopkins University Press, 2004.

Guillory, John. *Cultural Capital: The Problem of Literary Canon Formation*. Chicago: University of Chicago, 1993.

Gullah Tours. "Hear and Read Gullah," accessed October 15, 2016, http://gullahtours.com/gullah/hear-and-read-gullah.

Gupta, Anthea Fraser. "The Pragmatic Particles of Singapore Colloquial English." *Journal of Pragmatics* 18 (1992): 31–57.

Gupta, Suman. *Philology and Global English Studies: Retracings*. New York: Palgrave Macmillan, 2015.

Hale, Constance, and Jessie Scanlon. *Wired Style: Principles of English Usage in the Digital Age*. 2nd ed. New York: Broadway, 1999.

Harpham, Geoffrey Galt. "Roots, Races, and the Return to Philology." In *The Humanities and the Dream of America*, 43–79. Chicago: University of Chicago, 2011.

Harris, Richard L., ed. *A Chorus of Grammars: The Correspondence of George Hickes and His Collaborators on the Thesaurus linguarum septentrionalium*. Toronto: Pontifical Institute of Medieval Studies, 1992.

Hart, John. *An Orthographie*. Facsimile reprint in R. C. Alston, ed., *English Linguistics 1500–1800*, no. 209. Menston: Scholar Press, 1969.

Hass, Robert. "English: An Ode." *Sun Under Wood*. New York: Ecco Press, 1996. 62–70.

Haugen, Einar. "Dialect, Language, Nation." *American Anthropologist* 68 (1966): 922–35.

Heaney, Seamus. *Beowulf: A New Verse Translation*, bilingual ed. New York: W.W. Norton, 2000.

Hebel, William, Hoyt Hudson, Francis Johnson, and Wigfall Green, eds. *Prose of the English Renaissance*. New York: Appleton-Century-Crofts, 1952.

Helsinki Corpus TEI XML Edition. 1st ed. Designed by Alpo Honkapohja, Samuli Kaislaniemi, Henri Kauhanen, Matti Kilpiö, Ville Marttila, Terttu Nevalainen, Arja

Nurmi, Matti Rissanen and Jukka Tyrkkö. Implemented by Henri Kauhanen and Ville Marttila. Based on *The Helsinki Corpus of English Texts,* 1991. Helsinki: The Research Unit for Variation, Contacts and Change in English (VARIENG), University of Helsinki, 2011.

Hernández-Campoy, Juan Manuel, and Juan Camilo Conde-Silvestre, eds. *Handbook of Historical Sociolinguistics.* Malden, MA: Wiley-Blackwell, 2012.

Henry, Allison. *Belfast English and Standard English: Dialect Variation and Parameter Setting.* Oxford: Oxford University Press, 1996.

"Heroes and Demons." *Star Trek: Voyager.* CBS. April 24, 1995.

Hewlett Foundation. "Open Educational Resources," accessed January 6, 2016, http://www. hewlett.org/programs/education/open-educational-resources.

Hewings, Ann, and Philip Seargeant. "English Language Studies: A Critical Appraisal." In *Futures for English Studies: Teaching Language, Literature and Creative Writing in Higher Education,* edited by Ann Hewings, Lynda Prescott, and Philip Seargeant. Hounslow: Palgrave, Macmillan, 2016.

Hickes, George. *Linguarum Vett. Septentrionalium Thesauri Grammatico-Critici et Archæologici.* 2 vols. Oxoniæ: E Theatro Sheldoniano, 1705.

Hickey, Raymond. "Arguments for Creolisation in Irish English." In *Language History and Linguistic Modelling: A Festschrift for Jacek Fisiak on his 60th Birthday,* edited by Raymond Hickey and Stanisław Puppel, 969–1038. Berlin: Mouton de Gruyter, 1997.

———. "Early English and the Celtic Hypothesis." In *The Oxford Handbook of the History of English,* edited by Terttu Nevalainen and Elizabeth Traugott. New York: Oxford University Press, 2012.

Hicks, Dan, and Mary C. Beaudry, eds. "Disciplinary Perspectives." In *The Oxford Handbook of Material Culture Studies,* 25–188. Oxford: Oxford University Press, 2010.

Hilpert, Martin. *Germanic Future Constructions: A Usage-based Approach to Language Change.* Amsterdam: John Benjamins, 2008.

———. "Diachronic Collostructional Analysis Meets the Noun Phrase: Studying *Many a* Noun in COHA." In *The Oxford Handbook of the History of English,* edited by Elizabeth Closs Traugott and Terttu Nevalainen, 233–44. New York: Oxford University Press, 2012.

———. *Constructional Change in English: Developments in Allomorphy, Word-Formation and Syntax.* Cambridge: Cambridge University Press, 2013.

———. "From *Hand-Carved* to *Computer-Based*: Noun-Participle Compounding and the Upward-Strengthening Hypothesis." *Cognitive Linguistics* 26 (2015): 1–36.

Hilpert, Martin, and Stefan Gries. "Quantitative Approaches to Diachronic Corpus Linguistics." In *Cambridge Handbook of English Historical Linguistics,* edited by Merja Kytö and Päivi Pahta, 36–53. Cambridge: Cambridge University Press, 2016.

Hodson, Jane. "The Problem of Joseph Priestley's (1733-1804) Descriptivism." *Historiographia Linguistica* 33 (2006): 57–84.

———. *Dialect in Film and Literature.* Houndmills: Palgrave Macmillan, 2014.

Hoffmann, Sebastian, et al. *Corpus Linguistics with BNCweb—A Practical Guide.* English Corpus Linguistics no. 6. Frankfurt am Main: Peter Lang, 2008.

Hoffmann, Thomas, and Graeme Trousdale, eds. *The Oxford Handbook of Construction Grammar.* New York: Oxford University Press, 2013.

Hogg, Richard M. *An Introduction to Old English.* Edinburgh: Edinburgh University Press, 2002.

———. *A Grammar of Old English,* vol. 1, *Phonology.* Malden, MA: Wiley-Blackwell, 1992.

Hogg, Richard M., and David Denison, eds. *A History of the English Language.* Cambridge: Cambridge University Press, 2008.

Hogg, Richard M., and R. D. Fulk. *A Grammar of Old English,* vol. 2, *Morphology.* Malden, MA: Wiley-Blackwell, 2011.

Hollman, Willem. "Constructions in Cognitive Sociolinguistics." In *The Oxford Handbook of Construction Grammar,* edited by Thomas Hoffmann and Graeme Trousdale, 491–509. New York: Oxford University Press, 2013.

Hopper, Paul J. and Sandra A. Thompson. "Projectability and Clause-Combining in Interaction." In *Cross-linguistic Studies of Clause Combining: The Multifunctionality of Conjunctions,* edited by Ritva Laury, 99–123. Amsterdam: Benjamins, 2008.

Horobin, Simon. *Does Spelling Matter?* Oxford: Oxford University Press, 2013.

———. *How English Became English: A Short History of a Global Language.* Oxford: Oxford University Press, 2016.

Householder, Fred W. "A Sketch of How I Came to Be a Linguist." In *First Person Singular: Papers from the Conference on an Oral Archive for the History of American Linguistics,* edited by Boyd H. Davis and Raymond O'Cain, 193–99. Amsterdam: John Benjamins, 1980.

Hymes, Dell. *Foundations of Sociolinguistics: An Ethnographic Approach.* Philadelphia: University of Pennsylvania Press, 1974.

Hundt, Marianne, Nadja Nesselhauf, and Carolin Biewer, eds. "Corpus Linguistics and the Web." *Language and Computers—Studies in Practical Linguistics* 59. Amsterdam: Rodopi, 2007.

Hundt, Marianne. "Colonial Lag, Colonial Innovation or Simply Language Change?" In *One Language—Two Grammars? Differences Between British and American English,* edited by Rohdenburg Günter and Julia Schlüter, 13–37. Cambridge: Cambridge University Press, 2009.

Hyland, Ken. *Teaching and Researching Writing.* Harlow, Essex: Longman, 2002.

Inoue, Noriko. "Hiatus and Elision in the Poems of the Alliterative Revival: *-ly* and *–liche* Suffixes." *Yearbook of Langland Studies,* forthcoming.

———. "The Metrical Role of *–ly* and *–liche* Adverbs and Adjectives in Middle English Alliterative Verse: The A-Verse." *Modern Philology* 114 (2017): 773–92.

Jack, George, ed. *Beowulf: A Student Edition.* Oxford: Clarendon Press, 1994.

Jacobs, Andreas, and Andreas H. Jucker. "The Historical Perspective in Pragmatics." In *Historical Pragmatics: Pragmatic Developments in the History of English,* edited by Andreas H. Jucker, 3–33. Amsterdam: John Benjamins, 1995.

Jain, Dhanesh K. "Pronominal Usage in Hindi: A Sociolinguistic Study." PhD diss., University of Pennsylvania, 1973.

Jakobson, Roman. *Language in Literature.* Cambridge, MA: Harvard Belknap Press, 1988.

Jauncey, Dorothy. *Bardi Grubs and Frog Cakes: South Australian Words.* South Melbourne, Australia: Oxford University Press, 2004.

Jenkins, Jennifer. *Global Englishes: A Resource Book for Students.* 3rd ed. New York: Routledge, 2015.

Johns, Tim. "Whence and Whither Classroom Concordancing?" In *Computer Applications in Language Learning,* edited by Theo Bongaerts et al. Dordrecht, The Netherlands: Foris, 1988.

———. "Should You Be Persuaded: Two Examples of Data-Driven Learning." In *Classroom Concordancing.* Edited by Johns Tim and Philip King. Special issue *English Language Research Journal* 4 (1991): 1–16.

———. "Data-Driven Learning: The Perpetual Challenge." In *Teaching and Learning by Doing Corpus Analysis,* edited by Bernhard Kettemann and Georg Marko. *Proceedings of the Fourth International Conference on Teaching and Language Corpora,* Graz 19, 107–17. Amsterdam: Rodopi, 2002.

Johnson, David F. "A Program of Illumination in the Old English Illustrated Hexateuch: 'Visual Typology'?" In *The Old English Hexateuch: Aspects and Approaches,* edited by Rebecca Barnhouse and Benjamin C. Withers, 165–99. Kalamazoo, MI: Medieval Institute Publications, 2000.

Johnson, Samuel. *A Dictionary of the English Language: In Which the Words Are Deduced from Their Originals, and Illustrated in Their Different Significations by Examples from the Best Writers.* 2 vols., 1: D1^r–K2^r. London, Strahan, 1755.

———. "Preface." In *A Dictionary of the English Language: In Which the Words Are Deduced from Their Originals, and Illustrated in Their Different Significations by Examples from the Best Writers.* 2 vols. 1: A2^r–C2^v. London: Strahan, 1755.

Johnston, James Andrew. "Interdisciplinarity and Historiography: Literature." In *English Historical Linguistics: An International Handbook*. Vol. 2, edited by Alex Bergs and Laurel Brinton, 1201–13. Boston: Mouton de Gruyter, 2012.

Jones, Charles. *A History of English Phonology*. London: Longman, 1989.

Jones, Gavin. *Strange Talk: The Politics of Dialect Literature in Gilded Age America*. Berkeley: University of California Press, 1999.

Jones, Gwyn, and Thomas Jones. *The Mabinogion*. London: Golden Cockerel Press, 1949.

Jones, William. "The Third Anniversary Discourse, Delivered 2nd February, 1786." *Asiatic Researches; or, Transactions of the Society, Instituted in Bengal, for Inquiring into the History and Antiquities, the Arts, Sciences, and Literature of Asia*, Vol. I (1799): 415–31.

———. "On the Hindus." *The Collected Works of Sir William Jones*. 13 vols., edited by Garland Cannon, 24–46. New York: New York University Press, 1993.

Jucker, Andreas H., ed. *Historical Pragmatics: Pragmatic Developments in the History of English*. Amsterdam: John Benjamins, 1995.

Jucker, Andreas H., and Irma Taavitsainen, eds. *Speech Acts in the History of English*. Amsterdam: John Benjamins, 2008.

———, eds. *Historical Pragmatics*, vol. 8, *Handbooks of Pragmatics*. Berlin: Mouton de Gruyter, 2010.

———. *English Historical Pragmatics*. Edinburgh: Edinburgh University Press, 2013.

Justice, Steven. *Writing and Rebellion: England in 1381*. Berkeley: University of California Press, 1994.

———. *Adam Usk's Secret*. Philadelphia: University of Pennsylvania Press, 2015.

Kachru, Braj B. *The Indianization of English: The English Language in India*. Delhi: Oxford University Press, 1983.

———, ed. *The Other Tongue: English Across Cultures*. Oxford: Pergamon, 1983.

———. "The Sacred Cows of English." *English Today* 4, no. 4 (1988): 3–8.

———. "Standards, Codification, and Sociolinguistic Realism: The English Language in the Outer Circle." In *English in the World: Teaching and Learning the Language and Literatures*, edited by Randolph Quirk and Henry Widdowson, 11–30. Cambridge: Cambridge University Press, 1985.

———. *The Alchemy of English: The Spread, Functions and Models of Non-native Englishes*. London: Pergamon, 1986.

———. "Liberation Linguistics and the Quirk Concern." *English Today* 7, no. 1 (1991): 3–13.

———. "The Second Diaspora of English." In *English in Its Social Contexts: Essays in Historical Sociolinguistics*, edited by Tim William Machan and Charles T. Scott, 230–52. New York: Oxford University Press, 1992.

———. *World Englishes and Culture Wars*. Cambridge: Cambridge University Press, 2017.

Kachru, Braj, Yamuna Kachru, and Cecil Nelson, eds. *The Handbook of World Englishes*. Malden, MA: Wiley-Blackwell, 2009.

Karkov, Catherine E. "The Anglo-Saxon Genesis: Text, Illustration, and Audience." In *The Old English Hexateuch: Aspects and Approaches*, edited by Rebecca Barnhouse and Benjamin C. Withers, 201–37. Kalamazoo, MI: Medieval Institute Publications, 2000.

Katamba, Francis. "Should English Be Spelt as She Is Spoke?" In *English Words: Structure, History, and Usage*, 2nd ed., 197–232. New York: Routledge, 2005.

Keesing, Roger M. *Melanesian Pidgin and the Oceanic Substrate*. Stanford, CA: Stanford University Press, 1988.

Keizer, Evelien. *The English Noun Phrase: The Nature of Linguistic Categorization* (Studies in English Language). Cambridge: Cambridge University Press, 2007.

Keller, Frank, Maria Lapata, and Olga Ourioupina. "Using the Web to Overcome Data Sparseness." In *Proceedings of the Conference on Empirical Methods in Natural Language Processing*, edited by J. Hajic and Y. Matsumoto, 230–37. New Brunswick: Association for Computational Linguistics, 2002.

Kelly, John. "Brexit. Debression. Oexit. Zumxit. Why Did Brexit Trigger a Brexplosion of Wordplay?" June 29, 2016, http://www.slate.com/blogs/lexicon_valley/2016/06/29/why_has_brexit_sparked_an_explosion_of_wordplay.html.

Kemble, John M., ed. *The Anglo-Saxon Poems of Beowulf, The Travellers Song and the Battle of Finnes-burh*. London: Pickering, 1833.

———. *History of the English Language: First, or Anglo-Saxon Period*. Cambridge: J. & J. J. Deighton, 1934.

Keynes, Simon, and Michael Lapidge. *Alfred the Great*. Harmondsworth: Penguin, 1983.

Kilgarriff, Adam and Gregory Grefenstette. "Introduction to the Special Issue on the Web as Corpus." *Computational Linguistics* 29, no. 3 (2003): 333–47.

Kiparsky, Paul. "New Perspectives in Historical Linguistics." In *The Routledge Handbook of Historical Linguistics*. Routledge Handbooks in Linguistics, edited by Claire Bowern and Bethwyn Evans. New York: Routledge, 2014.

Knowles, Gerald. 1997. "Using Corpora for the Diachronic Study of English." In *Teaching and Language Corpora*, edited by Anne Wichmann et al., 195–210. London: Longman, 1997.

Kohnen, Thomas. "Corpora and Speech Acts: The Study of Performatives." In *Corpus Linguistics and Linguistic Theory. Papers from the Twentieth International Conference of English Language Research on Computerized Corpora (ICAME)*, edited by Christian Mair and Marianne Hundt, 177–86. Amsterdam: Rodopi, 2000.

———. "Explicit Performatives in Old English: A Corpus-based Study of Directives." *Journal of Historical Pragmatics* 1, no. 2 (2000): 301–21.

———. "Directives in Old English: Beyond Politeness." In *Speech Acts in the History of English*, edited by Andreas Jucker and Irma Taavitsainen, 27–44. Amsterdam: John Benjamins, 2008.

———. "Tracing Directives through Text and Time: Towards a Methodology of a Corpus-Based Diachronic Speech Act Analysis." In *Speech Acts in the History of English*, edited by Andreas Jucker and Irma Taavitsainen, 295–310. Amsterdam: John Benjamins, 2008.

Kolb, David A. *Experiential Learning: Experience as the Source of Learning and Development*. 2nd ed. New York: Pearson Education, 2014.

Kortmann, Bernd, and Kerstin Lunkenheimer. "The Electronic World Atlas of Varieties of English (eWAVE)." Leipzig: Max Planck Institute for Evolutionary Anthropology, 2013.

Kretzschmar, William A. Jr., *The Linguistics of Speech*. Cambridge: Cambridge University Press, 2009.

———. "Language Variation and Complex Systems." In *American Speech* 85 (2010): 263–86.

———. *Language and Complex Systems*. Cambridge: Cambridge University Press, 2015.

Kretzschmar Jr., William A., Virginia G. McDavid, Theodore K. Lerud, and Ellen Johnson, eds. Handbook of the Linguistic Atlas of the Middle and South Atlantic States. Chicago: University of Chicago Press, 1993.

Krieger, Daniel. "Corpus Linguistics: What It Is and How It Can Be Applied to Teaching." In *The Internet TESL Journal*, IX, no. 3 (2003). Available online at iteslj.org/Articles/Krieger-Corpus.html.

Kroonen, Guus. *Etymological Dictionary of Proto-Germanic*. Leiden: Brill, 2013.

Kučera, Henry, and W. Nelson Francis. *Computational Analysis of Present-Day American English*. Providence, RI: Brown University Press, 1967.

Kurath, Hans. *Word Geography of the Eastern United States*. Ann Arbor: University of Michigan Press, 1949.

Kytö, Merja. "Corpora and Historical Linguistics." *Revista Brasileira de Linguística Aplicada*, 11, no 2. (2011): 417–57.

Labov, William. *Sociolinguistic Patterns*. Philadelphia: University of Pennsylvania Press, 1972.

———. *Principles of Linguistic Change: Internal Factors*. Oxford and Cambridge, MA: Blackwell, 1994.

Labov, William, Sharon Ash, and Charles Boberg. *Phonological Atlas of North American English: Phonetics, Phonology and Sound Change*. Berlin: Mouton de Gruyter, 2006.

Lakoff, George, and Mark Johnson. *Metaphors We Live By*. Chicago: University of Chicago, 1980.

Landau, Sidney I. *Dictionaries: The Art and Craft of Lexicography*. New York: Charles Scribner's Sons, 1984

Lass, Roger. *The Shape of English: Structure and History*. London: J.M. Dent & Sons, 1987.

———. *Old English: A Historical Linguistic Companion*. Cambridge: Cambridge University Press, 1994.

Latour, Bruno. *Reassembling the Social: An Introduction to Actor-Network-Theory*. Oxford: Oxford University Press, 2007.

Laviera, Tato. *AmeRícan*. 2nd ed, 94–95. Houston, Tex.: Arte Publico Press, 2003.

Lawrence, D. H. "Fanny and Annie." In *The History of the English Language: A Source Book*. 2nd ed., edited by David Burnley, 368–73. Harlow, Essex: Pearson, 2000.

Lee, Jamie S. "Crossing and Crossers in East Asian Pop Music: Korea and Japan." *World Englishes* 25, no. 2 (2006): 235–50.

Lee, Jamie S., and Yamuna Kachru, eds. *World Englishes* (Special Issue: Symposium on World Englishes in Pop Culture) 25, no. 2 (2006): 191–311.

Leech, Geoffrey N. *A Linguistic Guide to English Poetry*. London: Longman, 1969. [Reprint, Oxford University Press, 2007.]

———. *Principles of Pragmatics*. London: Longman, 1983.

———. "Teaching and Language Corpora: A Convergence." In *Teaching and Language Corpora,* edited by Anne Wichmann et al., 1–23. London: Longman, 1997.

Leech, Geoffrey N., and Lu Li. "Indeterminacy Between Noun Phrases and Adjective Phrases as Complements of the English Verb." In *The Verb in Contemporary English: Theory and Description*, edited by Bas Aarts and Charles F. Meyer, 183–202. Cambridge: Cambridge University Press, 1995.

Lehmann, Winfred P., ed. *A Reader in Nineteenth Century Historical Indo-European Linguistics*. 1st ed. Bloomington: Indiana University Press. Austin, TX: Linguistics Research Center of the University of Texas at Austin, 1967 (online edition, 2006).

Leith, Dick. *A Social History of English*. 2nd ed. New York: Routledge, 1997.

———. "The Origins of English." In *Changing English*, edited by David Graddol et al., 39–77. New York: Routledge, 2003.

———."English—Colonial to Postcolonial." In *Changing English*, edited by David Graddol, Dick Leith, Joan Swann, Martin Rhys, and Julia Gillen, 117–52. Abingdon, UK: Routledge, 2007.

Lentricchia, Frank, and Thomas McLaughlin, eds., *Critical Terms for Literary Study*. 2nd ed. Chicago: University of Chicago, 1995.

Leo, Heinrich. *Bëówulf: das älteste deutsche, in angelsächsischer mundart erhaltene, heldengedicht*. Halle: Anton, 1838.

Leonard, Stirling A. *The Doctrine of Correctness in English Usage 1700-1800*. Wisconsin: Madison, 1929.

Lerer, Seth. *Error and the Academic Self*. New York: Columbia University Press, 2003.

———. "A Harmless Drudge: Samuel Johnson and the Making of the Dictionary." In *Inventing English: A Portable History of the Language*, 167–80. New York: Columbia University Press, 2007.

———. "Horrid, Hooting Stanzas, Lexicography and Literature in American English." In *Inventing English: A Portable History of the Language*, 180–91. New York: Columbia University Press, 2007.

———. "Visible Speech: The Orthoepists and the Origins of Standard English." In *Inventing English: A Portable History of the Language*, 153–66. New York: Columbia University Press, 2007.

———. "Late Middle English (ca. 1380–1485)." In *A Companion to The History of the English Language,* edited by Haruko Momma and Michael Matto, 191–97. Oxford: Wiley-Blackwell, 2008.

———. *Inventing English: A Portable History of the Language*. 1st ed. New York: Columbia University Press, 2007.

———. *Inventing English: A Portable History of the Language*. 2nd ed. New York: Columbia University Press, 2015.

———. "The Medieval Inheritance of Early Tudor Poetry." In *The Blackwell Companion to Renaissance Poetry*, edited by Catherine Bates. Oxford: Blackwell, forthcoming.

———. "Old English and its Afterlife." In *The Cambridge History of Medieval English Literature*, edited by David Wallace, 7–34. Cambridge: Cambridge University Press, 1999.

Levinson, Stephen. *Pragmatics*. Cambridge: Cambridge University Press, 1983.

Liberman, Anatoly. *Word Origins and How We Know Them: Etymology for Everyone*. Oxford: Oxford University Press, 2005.

———. *An Analytic Dictionary of English Etymology: An Introduction*. Minneapolis: University of Minnesota Press, 2008.

———. *A Bibliography of English Etymology: Sources and Word List*. Minneapolis: University of Minnesota Press, 2010.

Liberman, Mark. "Nounification of the Week." *Language Log*, last accessed April 3, 2016, http://languagelog.ldc.upenn.edu/nll/?p=24726.age.

———. "Whatpocalypse Now?" *Language Log*. Accessed October 16, 2016. http://languagelog.ldc.upenn.edu/nll/?p=3209.

Lighter, J. E. *Historical Dictionary of American Slang*. 2 vols. to date. New York: Random House, 1994 and 1997.

Lippi-Green, Rosina. *English with an Accent*. New York: Routledge, 1997.

Liu, Ziming. "Reading Behavior in the Digital Environment: Changes in Reading Behavior over the Past Ten Years." *Journal of Documentation* 61, no. 6 (2005): 700–12.

———. *Paper to Digital: Documents in the Information Age*. Westport, CT: Libraries Unlimited, 2008.

Liuzza, R. M. *Beowulf: A New Verse Translation*. Peterborough, ONT: Broadview, 2000.

Lopez, Barry, and Debra Gwartney, eds. *Home Ground: Language for an American Landscape*. San Antonio, TX: Trinity University Press, 2006.

Lorenz, Norman. "Montessori on the Move: A Case Study of the Montessori Pedagogical Instructional Principles and Implications for Community College Course Graduates and their Career Paths." PhD diss., University of California, Davis, 2015.

Low, Ee-Ling. "The Acoustic Reality of the Kachruvian Circles: A Rhythmic Perspective." *World Englishes* 29 (2010): 394–405.

———. "The Rhythmic Patterning of English(es): Implications for Pronunciation Teaching." In *The Handbook of English Pronunciation*, edited by Marnie Reed and John M. Levis, 125–38. Malden, MA: Wiley-Blackwell, 2015.

Lowth, Robert. *A Short Introduction to English Grammar*. London: Miller and Dodsby, 1762.

Lyotard, Jean-Francois. *The Postmodern Condition: A Report on Knowledge*. Manchester: Manchester University Press, 1984.

Macaulay, David. *Motel of the Mysteries*. Boston: Houghton Mifflin, 1979.

Macaulay, Thomas Babington. "Minute on Indian Education, February 1835." In *Sketches of Some Distinguished Anglo-Indians: (Second series) Including Lord Macaulay's Great Minute on Education in India*, compiled by William Ferguson Beatson Laurie, 170–85. London: J. B. Day, 1875.

Machan, Tim William. *Language Anxiety: Conflict and Change in the History of English*. Oxford: Oxford University Press, 2009.

———. "Chaucer and the History of the English Language." *Speculum* 87 (2012): 147–75.

Maguire, Warren. "An Atlas of Alexander J. Ellis's *The Existing Phonology of English Dialects*," accessed October 15, 2016, http://www.lel.ed.ac.uk/EllisAtlas/Index.html.

Makaryk, Irena, ed. *Encyclopedia of Contemporary Literary Theory: Approaches, Scholars, Terms*. Toronto: University of Toronto, 1993.

Malone, Kemp. "When Did Middle English Begin?" *Language* 6, no. 4 (1930): 110–17.

Manis, Michael. *The "Magic: The Gathering" Lexicon*. MA thesis, Indiana University, 2012.

March, Francis A. *Method of Philological Study of the English Language*. New York: Harper and Brothers Publishers, 1865.

————. "Recollections of Language Teaching." *PMLA* 8 (1893): 1738–41.

Matto, Michael. "Remainders: Reading an Old English Poem through Multiple Translations." *Studies in Medieval and Renaissance Teaching*, 22.2 (2015): 81–89.

McArthur, Tom. "The English Languages?" *English Today* 3, no. 3 (1987): 9–11.

————. *The English Languages*. Cambridge: Cambridge University Press, 1998.

————. "English World-wide in the Twentieth Century." In *The Oxford History of English*, edited by Lynda Mugglestone, 446–87. Oxford: Oxford University Press, 2012.

McConnell, Josh. "We The 6: Why the Name Drake Gave Us Is Here to Stay." *The Globe and Mail*. Last modified July 10, 2015. theglobeandmail.com/news/toronto/we-the-6-why-the-name-drake-gave-us-is-here-to-stay/article25421112/.

McCreary, Don R. *"Dawgspeak!* The Slanguage Dictionary of the University of Georgia." *Dictionaries* 33 (2012): 137–55.

McCrum, Robert, William Cran, and Robert MacNeil. *The Story of English: A Companion to the PBS Television Series*. New York: Viking, 1986.

McDavid, Raven. "The Dialects of American English." In *The Structure of American English*, edited by W. Nelson Francis. New York: Ronald Publisher, 1958.

McEnery, Tony, and Andrew Wilson. *Corpus Linguistics*, 2nd ed. Edinburgh: Edinburgh University Press, 2001.

McGrath, Alister. *In the Beginning: The Story of the King James Bible and How It Changed a Nation, a Language, and a Culture*. New York: Doubleday, 2001.

McIntyre, Dan. *History of English: A Resource Book for Students*. New York: Routledge, 2009.

McKeachie, Wilbert J. "Learning, Thinking, and Thorndike." *Educational Psychologist* 25 (1990): 127–41.

McKeachie, Wilbert, and Marilla Svinicki. *McKeachie's Teaching Tips*. Boston: Cengage Learning, 2013.

McWhorter, John. *Language Interrupted: Signs of Non-Native Acquisition in Standard Language Grammars*. Oxford: Oxford University Press, 2007.

————. *Our Magnificent Bastard Tongue: The Untold History of English*. New York: Gotham Books, 2009.

————. "On American r-lessness." *Language Log*, accessed October 16, 2016, http://languagelog.ldc.upenn.edu/nll/?p=19486.

Mencken, H[enry] L[ouis]. *The American Language: A Preliminary Inquiry into the Development of English in the United States*. New York: Knopf, 1919.

Merriam-Webster's Concise Dictionary of English Usage. Springfield, MA: Merriam-Webster, 2002.

Mesthrie, Rajend. *English in Language Shift*. Cambridge: Cambridge University Press, 1992.

————. "The World Englishes Paradigm and Contact Linguistics: Refurbishing the Foundations." *World Englishes* 22, no. 4 (2003): 449–62.

————. "World Englishes and the Multilingual History of English." *World Englishes* 25, no. 3–4 (2006): 381–90.

Mesthrie, Rajend, and Rakesh M. Bhatt. *World Englishes: The Study of New Linguistic Varieties*. Cambridge: Cambridge University Press, 2008.

Mey, Jacob. *Pragmatics: An Introduction*. 2nd ed. Malden, MA: Blackwell, 2001.

Middle English Dictionary, edited by Hans Kurath et al. Ann Arbor: University of Michigan Press, 1952–2001.

Millward, Celia M. *A Biography of the English Language*. 1st ed. Fort Worth, TX: Harcourt Brace Jovanovich, 1989.

————. "Benewell Kemler's Black English." *American Speech* 69, no. 2 (1994): 155–67.

————. *A Biography of the English Language*. 2nd ed. Thomson Learning, 1996.

Millward, Celia M., and Mary Hayes. *A Biography of the English Language*. 3rd ed. Boston: Cengage Learning, 2011.

————. *Workbook to Accompany A Biography of the English Language*. 3rd ed. Boston: Cengage Learning, 2011.

Miłosz, Czesław. *A Treatise on Poetry*. Translated by Czesław Miłosz and Robert Hass. New York: Ecco Press, 2001.

Milroy, James. *Linguistic Variation and Change*. Oxford: Blackwell, 1992.

Milroy, James, and Lesley Milroy. *Authority in Language*. London: Routledge, 1991.

Minkova, Donka. *The History of Final Vowels in English: The Sound of Muting*. Berlin: Mouton de Gruyter, 1991.

Mitchell, Bruce, and Fred C. Robinson. *A Guide to Old English*. 6th ed. Malden, MA: Blackwell, 2001.

Mithun, Marianne. "Active/Agentive Case Marking and Its Motivations." *Language* 67 (1991): 510–46.

———. "The Substratum in Grammar and Discourse." In *Language Contact: Theoretical and Empirical Studies,* edited by Ernst Håkon Jahr, 103–15. Berlin: Mouton de Gruyter, 1992.

Momma, Haruko. *From Philology to English Studies: Language and Culture in the Nineteenth Century*. Cambridge: Cambridge University Press, 2013.

———. "The *Brut* as Saxon Literature: The New Philologists Read Lawman." In *Reading Laʒamon's Brut: Approaches and Explorations,* edited by Rosamund Allen, Jane Roberts, and Carole Weinberg, 53–68. Amsterdam: Rodopi, 2013.

———. "Afterword: HEL for the Monolingual Frame of Mind." In *Studies in Medieval and Renaissance* Teaching 14 (2007): 110–17.

Momma, Haruko, and Michael Matto, eds. *A Companion to the History of the English Language*. Oxford: Wiley-Blackwell, 2011.

Montessori, Maria. *The Montessori Method*. Translated by Anne E. George. New York: Frederick A. Stokes, 1912.

———. "The Four Planes of Education." *AMI Communications* 4 (1971): 4–10.

Montgomery, Guy, ed. *Concordance to the Poetical Works of John Dryden*. Cambridge: Cambridge University Press, 1957.

More, Thomas St. *Utopia*. Translation by Raphe Robynson (1551). In *Prose of the English Renaissance,* edited by William Hebel et al., 1–24. New York: Appleton-Century-Crofts, 1952.

Mufwene, Salikoko S. "The Universalist and Substrate Hypotheses Complement One Another." In *Substrata Versus Universals in Creole Genesis*, edited by Pieter Muysken and Norval Smith, 129–62. Amsterdam: John Benjamins, 1986.

———. "Is Gullah Decreolizing? A Comparison of a Speech Sample of the 1930s with a Sample of the 1980s." In *The Emergence of Black English: Text and Commentary*, edited by Guy Bailey, Natalie Maynor, and Patricia Cukor-Avila, 213–30. Amsterdam: John Benjamins: 1991.

———. "African-American English." In *The Cambridge History of the English Language*, vol. 6, edited by John Algeo, 291–324. Cambridge: Cambridge University Press, 2001.

———. *The Ecology of Language Evolution*. Cambridge: Cambridge University Press, 2001.

———. "Gullah: Morphology and Syntax." In *Varieties of English 2: The Americas and the Caribbean*, edited by Edgar W. Schneider, 551–71. Berlin: Mouton de Gruyter, 2008.

———. "The Indigenization of English in North America." In *World Englishes: Problems, Properties, Prospects*, edited by Thomas Hoffmann and Lucia Siebers, 353–68. Amsterdam: Benjamins, 2008.

———. *Language Evolution: Contact, Competition, and Change*. London: Continuum Press, 2008.

———. "Driving Forces in English Contact Linguistics." In *English as a Contact Language*, edited by Daniel Schreier and Marianne Hundt, 204–21. Cambridge: Cambridge University Press, 2012.

———. "Globalisation économique mondiale des XVIIe–XVIIIe siècles, émergence des créoles, et vitalité langagière." In *Langues créoles, mondialisation, éducation*, edited by Arnaud Carpooran, 23–79. Vacoas, Mauritius: Editions le Printemps, 2014.

———. "The Emergence of African American English: Monogenetic or Polygenetic? Under How Much Substrate Influence?" In *The Oxford Handbook of African*

American Language, edited by Sonja Lanehart, 57–84. Oxford: Oxford University Press, 2015.

Mufwene, Salikoko, and Charles Gillman. "How African Is Gullah and Why?" American Speech 62 (1987): 120–39.

Mufwene, Salikoko S., John R. Rickford, Guy Bailey and John Baugh, editors. African-American English: Structure, History and Use. New York: Routledge, 1998.

Mugglestone, Lynda. Lexicography and the OED: Pioneers in an Untrodden Forest. Oxford: Oxford University Press, 2000.

———. Lost for Words: The Hidden History of the Oxford English Dictionary. New Haven, CT: Yale University Press, 2005.

———. "Patriotism, Empire and Cultural Prescriptivism: Images of Anglicity in the OED." In Languages of Nation: Attitudes and Norms, edited by Carol Percy and Mary Catherine Davidson, 175–91. Bristol, UK: Multilingual Matters, 2012.

Mukherjee, Joybrato. "Corpus Linguistics and Language Pedagogy: The State of the Art-and Beyond." In Corpus Technology and Language Pedagogy, edited by Sabine Braun, Kurt Kohn, and Joybrato Mukherjee, 5–24. Frankfurt am Main: Peter Lang, 2006.

Mukherjee, Joybrato, and Stefan Th. Gries. "Collostructional Nativisation in New Englishes: Verb-construction Associations in the International Corpus of English." English World Wide 30 (2009): 27–51.

Murray, James A.H. "President's Address." Transactions of the Philological Society (1884): 509.

Murray, K. M. Elisabeth. Caught in the Web of Words: James A. H. Murray and the Oxford English Dictionary. New Haven, CT: Yale University Press, 2001.

Myklebust, Nicholas. "Misreading English Meter: 1400–1514." PhD diss., University of Texas at Austin, 2012.

Nespor, Marina, Mohinish Shukla, and Jacques Mehler. "Stress-timed vs. Syllable-timed Languages." In The Blackwell Companion to Phonology, edited by Marc van Oostendorp et al. Vol. II, Suprasegmental and Prosodic Phonology, 1147–59. Malden, MA: Wiley-Blackwell, 2011.

Nevalainen, Terttu. "Lexis and Semantics." In The Cambridge History of the English Language, vol. 3, 1476–1776, edited by Roger Lass, 332–458. Cambridge: Cambridge University Press, 1999.

———. An Introduction to Early Modern English. Edinburgh: Edinburgh University Press, 2006.

Nevalainen, Terttu, and Ingrid Tieken-Boon van Ostade. "Standardisation." In A History of the English Language, edited by Richard Hogg and David Denison, 271–311. Cambridge: Cambridge University Press, 2006.

Nicolson, Adam. God's Secretaries: The Making of the King James Bible. New York: Harper Collins, 2003.

Noël, Dirk. "Diachronic Construction Grammar and Grammaticalization Theory." Functions of Language 14 (2007): 177–202.

Norbrook, David, and Henry Woudhuysen, eds. The Penguin Book of Renaissance Verse, 1509-1659. London: Penguin, 1992.

OER Research Hub. 2014. OER Impact Map, accessed January 6, 2016, http://oermap. org/.

OER Research Hub. 2015. Data Report 2013–2015: Informal Learners, accessed January 6, 2016, https://oerhub.net/data/data-report-2013-2015-informal-learners/.

Ogilvie, Sarah. "Rethinking Burchfield and World Englishes." International Journal of Lexicography 21 (2008): 23–59.

———. Words of the World: A Global History of the Oxford English Dictionary. Cambridge: Cambridge University Press, 2013.

Oizumi, Akio, ed. Complete Concordance to the Works of Geoffrey Chaucer. Hildesheim, NY: Olms-Weidmann, 1991.

O'Keeffe, Katherine O'Brien. Visible Song: Transitional Literacy in Old English Verse. Cambridge: University of Cambridge Press, 1990.

Omoniyi, Tope. "Hip Hop Through the World Englishes Lens: A Response to Globalization." *World Englishes* 25, no. 2 (2006): 195–208.

Onlinenewspapers.com, accessed September 22, 2016, http://www.onlinenewspapers.com.

OpenLearn. *Frequently asked questions*, accessed January 18, 2016. http://www.open.edu/openlearn/about-openlearn/frequently-asked-questions-on-openlearn.

O'Neill, Patrick P., ed. and trans. *King Alfred's Old English Prose Translation of the First Fifty Psalms*. Medieval Academy Books no. 104. Cambridge, MA: Medieval Academy of America, 2001.

———. *Old English Psalms*, Dumbarton Oaks Medieval Library no. 42. Cambridge, MA: Harvard University Press, 2016.

Onions, C. T. *Oxford Dictionary of English Etymology*. Oxford: Clarendon Press, 1966.

Otheguy, Ricardo, and Nancy Stern. "On So-Called Spanglish." *International Journal of Bilingualism* 15 (1): 85–100.

Oxford English Dictionary. 13 vols. Edited by J. A. H. Murray et al. Oxford: Oxford University Press, 1933.

Pakir, Ann. "English in Singapore: The Codification of Competing Norms." In *Language, Society and Education in Singapore: Issues and Trends*, edited by Saravanan Gopinathan et al., 92–118. Singapore: Times Academic Press, 1994.

Palmer, Frank. *Grammar*. Harmondsworth, UK: Pelican, 1971.

Parry, David R. "Courses in English Language for First-year Intending Honours Students." Unpublished handout, Department of English Language and Literature, University College, Swansea, 1975.

Patten, Amanda L. *The English IT-Cleft: A Constructional Account and Diachronic Investigation*. Berlin: Mouton de Gruyter, 2012.

Pedersen, Holger. *Linguistic Science in the Nineteenth Century*. Translated by J. W. Spargo. Cambridge, MA: Harvard University Press, 1931.

Pei, Mario. *The Story of the English Language*. Philadelphia: Lippincott, 1967.

Penhallurick, Rob. *Studying the English Language*. 1st ed. Basingstoke, UK: Palgrave Macmillan, 2003.

———. *Studying the English Language*. 2nd ed. Basingstoke, UK: Palgrave Macmillan, 2010.

Pennycook, Alastair. "Global Englishes, Rip Slyme, and Performativity." *Journal of Sociolinguistics* 7, no. 4 (2003): 513–33.

———. *Global Englishes and Transcultural Flows*. 2nd ed. New York: Routledge, 2006.

Percy, Carol, ed. *The English Language(s): Cultural & Linguistic Perspectives*. 2000–08, http://homes.chass.utoronto.ca/~cpercy/courses/HELEncyclopedia.htm.

———. *The English Languages: History, Diaspora, Culture*. 2010–13, http://jps.library.utoronto.ca/index.php/elhdc/index.

Perullo, Alex, and John Fenn. "Language Ideologies, Choices, and Practices in Eastern African Hip Hop." In *Global Pop, Local Language*, edited by Harris M. Berger and Michael Thomas Carroll, 19–33. Jackson: University of Mississippi Press, 2003.

Peters, Mark. *Wordlustitude*, accessed April 3, 2016, http://wordlust.blogspot.com/.

Petré, Peter. *Constructions and Environments: Copular, Passive, and Related Constructions in Old and Middle English*. Oxford: Oxford University Press, 2013.

Phillipson, Robert. *Linguistic Imperialism*. Oxford: Oxford University Press, 1992.

———. "Voice in Global English: Unheard Chords in Crystal Loud and Clear." *Applied Linguistics* 20, no. 2 (1999): 265–76. [Reprinted in *World Englishes*, vol. 5, *Critical Concepts in Linguistics*, edited by Kingsley Bolton and Braj B. Kachru, 337–49. New York: Routledge, 2006.]

Philip, M. NourbeSe. "Discourse on the Logic of Language." In *She Tries Her Tongue— Her Silence Softly Breaks*, new ed., 29–34. Middletown, Connecticut: Wesleyan University Press, 2015.

Pike, Kenneth L. *The Intonation of American English*. Ann Arbor: University of Michigan Press, 1945.

Plotz, John. "Henry James's Rat-tat-tat-ah: Insidious Loss, Disguised Recovery and Semi-Detached Subjects." *Henry James Review* 34 (2013): 232–44.

Polanyi, Michael. "Logic and Psychology." In *American Psychologist* 21, no. 1 (1968): 36–37.

Pollock, Sheldon. "Philology in Three Dimensions." *postmedieval: a journal of medieval cultural studies* 5 (2014): 398–413.

Pollock, Sidney, and Ku-ming Kevin Chang, eds. *World Philology*. Cambridge, MA: Harvard University Press, 2015.

Porzucki, Nina. "A Hidden History of Spanglish in California." *Public Radio International*. Last modified February 12, 2015. https://www.pri.org/stories/2015-02-11/hidden-history-spanglish-california.

Potter, Russel A. *Spectacular Vernaculars: Hip-Hop and the Politics of Postmodernism*. Albany: State University of New York Press, 1995.

Pratt, T. K. *Dictionary of Prince Edward Island English*. Toronto: University of Toronto Press, 1988.

The Preface to a Wycliffite Biblical Concordance. In *The History of the English Language: A Source Book*, 2nd ed., edited by David Burnley, 175–81. New York: Routledge, 2000.

Preston, Dennis. "The South: The Touchstone." In *Language Variety in the South Revisited*, edited by C. Bernstein, T. Nunnally, and R. Sabino, 311–51. Tuscaloosa: University of Alabama Press, 1997.

———. "A Language Attitude Approach to the Perception of Regional Variety." In *Handbook of Perceptual Dialectology*, edited by D. R. Preston. Amsterdam: John Benjamins, 1999.

"Prologue to Wycliffite Bible." In *Sections from English Wycliffite Writings*, edited by Anne Hudson. Medieval Academy Reprints for Teaching. 67–72. Cambridge: Medieval Academy of America, 1997.

Prokosch, Eduard. *A Comparative Germanic Grammar*. Philadelphia: Linguistic Society of America, 1939.

The Psalter or Psalms of David and Certain Canticles by Richard Rolle of Hampole, edited by H. R. Bramley. Oxford: Clarendon Press, 1884.

Psonak, Kevin. "The Long Line of the Middle English Alliterative Revival: Rhythmically Coherent, Metrically Strict, Phonologically English." PhD diss., University of Texas at Austin, 2012.

Pullum, Geoffrey K. "Lowth's Grammar: A Re-Evaluation." *Linguistics* 137 (1974): 63–78.

———. Snowclones: Lexicographical Dating to the Second. *Language Log*, January 16, 2004, http://itre.cis.upenn.edu/~myl/languagelog/archives/000350.html.

Putter, Ad, Judith Jefferson, and Myra Stokes, eds. *Studies in the Metre of Alliterative Verse*. Oxford: Society for the Study of Medieval Languages and Literature, 2007.

Pyles, Thomas, and John Algeo, *The Origins and Development of the English Language*, 1st ed. Boston: Cengage Learning, 1964.

———. *The Origins and Development of the English Language*. 4th ed. Fort Worth, TX: Harcourt Brace, 1993.

———. *The Origins and Development of the English Language*, 6th ed. Boston: Cengage Learning, 2010.

Quirk, Randolph. *The Use of English*. London: Longman, 1962.

———. "The English Language in a Global Context." In *English in the World: Teaching and Learning the Language and Literatures*, edited by Randolph Quirk and H. G. Widdowson, 1–6. Cambridge: Cambridge University Press, 1985.

———. "Language Varieties and Standard Language." *English Today* 6, no. 1 (1990): 3–10.

Ramraj, Victor J, ed. *Concert of Voices: An Anthology of World Writing in English*. 2nd ed. Peterborough: Broadview Press, 2009.

Ramson, W. S., ed. *The Australian National Dictionary*. Melbourne, Australia: Oxford University Press, 1989.

Reppen, Randi. "Corpus Linguistics and Language Teaching." In *English Corpus Studies* 8 (2001): 19–31.

———. "Using Corpora in the Language Classroom." In *Materials Development in Language Teaching*, edited by Brian Tomlinson, 35–50. Cambridge: Cambridge University Press, 2011.

Rice, Keren. "112: English in Contact: Native American Languages." In *English Historical Linguistics: An International Handbook*. Vol. 2, edited by Alexander Bergs and Laurel Brinton, 1753–67. Berlin: Mouton de Gruyter, 2012.

Richardson, Charles. *A New Dictionary of the English Language*. 2 vols. London: Pickering, 1837.

Richlin, Laurie. *Blueprint for Learning: Constructing College Courses to Facilitate, Assess, and Document Learning*. Sterling, VA: Stylus, 2006.

Rickford, John R. "The Creole Origins of African-American Vernacular English: Evidence from Copula Absences." In African-American English: Structure, History and Use, edited by Salikoko S. Mufwene, John R. Rickford, Guy Bailey and John Baugh, 154–200. New York: Routledge, 1998.

Rickford, John Russell, and Russell John Rickford. *Spoken Soul: The Story of Black English*. New York: Wiley, 2000.

Ringe, Don. *A Linguistic History of English*, vol. 1, *From Proto-Indo-European to Proto-Germanic*. New York: Oxford University Press, 2006.

Ringe, Don, and Ann Taylor. *A Linguistic History of English*, vol. 2, *The Development of Old English*. New York: Oxford University Press, 2014.

Rissanen, Matti. "Three Problems Associated with the Use of Diachronic Corpora." *ICAME Journal* 13 (1989): 16–19.

Rissanen, Matti. "Corpora and the Study of the History of English." In *English Corpus Linguistics: Crossing Paths,* edited by Merja Kytö. Amsterdam: Rodopi, 2012.

Romaine, Suzanne, ed. *The Cambridge History of the English Language*, vol. 4, *1776-1997*. Cambridge: Cambridge University Press, 1998.

———. "Contact with Other Languages." In *The Cambridge History of the English Language*, vol. 6, *English in North America*, edited by John Algeo, 154–83. Cambridge: Cambridge University Press, 2001.

———. "The Variationist Approach." In *Cambridge Handbook of English Historical Linguistics,* edited by Merja Kytö and Päivi Pahta, 19–35. Cambridge: Cambridge University Press, 2016.

Römer, Ute. "Corpora and Language Teaching." In *Corpus Linguistics: An International Handbook*, edited by Anke Lüdeling and Merja Kytö, 112–31. Berlin: Mouton de Gruyter, 2009.

Römer, Ute, and Stefanie Wulff. "Applying Corpus Methods to Written Academic Texts: Explorations of MICUSP." In *Journal of Writing Research* 2, no. 2 (2010): 99–127.

Rushdie, Salman. *Imaginary Homelands: Essays and Criticism 1981–1991*. London: Granta Books, 1991.

Russom, Geoffrey. "Literary Form as an Independent Domain of Validation in HEL Pedagogy." *Studies in Medieval and Renaissance Teaching* 14 (2007): 46–54.

Said, Edward W. "The Return to Philology." In *Humanism and Democratic Criticism*, edited by Edward W. Said, 57–84. New York: Columbia University Press, 2004.

Salmons, Joseph, and Thomas Purnell. "Contact and the Development of American English." In *Handbook of Language Contact*, edited by Ray Hickey, 454–78. London: Blackwell, 2012.

Sankoff, Gillian. "Linguistic Outcomes of Language Contact." In *Handbook of Language Variation and Change*, edited by Peter Trudgill, J. Chambers, and N. Schilling-Estes, 638–68. Oxford: Wiley-Blackwell, 2004.

Saraceni, Mario. *World Englishes: A Critical Analysis*. London: Bloomsbury, 2015.

Sawyer, R. Keith. *The Cambridge Handbook of the Learning Sciences*. Cambridge: Cambridge University Press, 2006.

Schmidt, Jürgen Erich and Joachim Herrgen, eds. *Digitaler Wenker-Atlas*, 2001–2009. Accessed October 15, 2016. http://www.diwa.info/.

Schneider, Edgar W. "The Dynamics of New Englishes: From Identity Construction to Dialect Birth." *Language* 79, no. 2 (2003): 233–81.

———. *Postcolonial English: Varieties Around the World*. Cambridge: Cambridge University Press, 2007.

———. "Colonization, Globalization, and the Sociolinguistics of World Englishes." In *The Cambridge Handbook of Sociolinguistics*, edited by Rajend Mesthrie, 335–54. Cambridge: Cambridge University Press, 2011.

———. *English Around the World: An Introduction*. New York: Cambridge University Press, 2011.

Schneider, Edgar W., and Michael B. Montgomery. "On the Trail of Early Nonstandard Grammar: An Electronic Corpus of Southern U.S. Antebellum Overseers' Letters." *American Speech* 76, no. 4 (2001): 388–410.

Schreier, Daniel, and Marianna Hundt, eds. *English as a Contact Language*. Cambridge: Cambridge University Press, 2013.

Schunk, Dale H., Judith R. Meece, and Paul R. Pintrich. *Motivation in Education: Theory, Research, and Applications*, 4th ed. New York: Pearson Higher Education, 2014.

Schuster, Edgar H. *Breaking the Rules: Liberating Writers Through Innovative Grammar Instruction*. London: Heinemann, 2003.

Schutz, Paul A. "Inquiry on Teachers' Emotion." *Educational Psychologist* 49, no. 1 (2014): 1–12.

Schwarzer, Ralf, ed. *Self-related Cognitions in Anxiety and Motivation*. Hillsdale, NJ: Lawrence Earlbaum Associates, Inc., 1986.

Scollon, Ron, and Suzanne Wong Scollon. "Topic Confusion in English-Asian Discourse." *World Englishes* 10, no. 2 (1991): 113–25.

Seargeant, Philip. *Exploring World Englishes: Language in a Global Context*. Abingdon: Routledge, 2012.

Seargeant, Philip, and Caroline Tagg. "English on the Internet and a 'Post-Varieties' Approach to Language." *World Englishes* 30, no. 4 (2011): 496–514.

Sebba, Mark. *Contact Languages: Pidgins and Creoles*. London: Palgrave, 1997.

Sharma, Devyani. "Indian English." In *The Electronic World Atlas of Varieties of English*, edited by Bernd Kortmann and Kerstin Lunkenheimer. Leipzig: Max Planck Institute for Evolutionary Anthropology, 2013.

Shay, Scott. *The History of English: A Linguistic Introduction*. San Francisco: Wardja Press, 2008.

Sheidlower, Jesse. "How Quotation Paragraphs in Historical Dictionaries Work: *The Oxford English Dictionary*." In *Contours of English and English Language Studies*, edited by Michael Adams and Anne Curzan, 191–212. Ann Arbor: University of Michigan Press, 2011.

Shumway, David and Craig Dionne, eds. *Disciplining English: Alternative Histories, Critical Perspectives*. Albany: State University of New York Press, 2002.

Siegel, Jeff. *Language Contact in a Plantation Environment: A Sociolinguistic History of Fiji*. New York: Cambridge University Press, 1987.

Sievers, Eduard. *Altgermanische Metrik*. Halle: Max Niemeyer, 1893.

Sihler, Andrew. *New Comparative Grammar of Greek and Latin*. New York: Oxford University Press, 1995.

Simpson, David. *The Politics of American English, 1776-1865*. Oxford: Oxford University Press, 1986.

Simpson, James. *The Oxford English Literary History*, vol. 2, *1350–1547: Reform and Cultural Revolution*. Oxford: Oxford University Press, 2004.

———. *Burning to Read: English Fundamentalism and its Reformation Opponents*. Cambridge, MA: Belknap Press of Harvard University, 2010.

Sinclair, John. *How to Use Corpora in Language Teaching*. Amsterdam: John Benjamins, 2004.

Singh, Ishtla. *The History of English: A Student's Guide*. London: Hodder Arnold, 2005.

Singler, John. "The Homogeneity of the Substrate as a Factor in Pidgin/Creole Genesis." *Language* 64 (1988): 27–51.

Sinmaz, Emine. "Is This the End of Cockney? Hybrid Dialect Dubbed 'Multicultural London English' Sweeps Across the Country." *Daily Mail*. Last modified November 10, 2013. dailymail.co.uk/news/article-2498152/

Is-end-Cockney-Hybrid-dialect-dubbed-Multicultural-London-English-sweeps-country.html.

Skeat, W. W. *Etymological Dictionary of the English Language.* 4th ed. Oxford: Clarendon Press, 1909.

Smith, Jeremy. *An Historical Study of English.* London: Routledge, 1996.

Smitherman, Geneva. *Black Talk: Words and Phrases from the Hood to the Amen Corner.* Rev. ed. New York: Mariner Books, 2000.

Spevack, Martin, ed. *A Complete and Systematic Concordance to the Works of Shakespeare.* Hildesheim, NY: Georg Olms, 1968–1994.

Stephens, Paul. "International Students: Separate but Profitable." *Washington Monthly.* September/October 2013. washingtonmonthly.com/magazine/september_october_2013/features/international_students_separat046454.php.

Sterne, Laurence, and Harold H. Kollmeier, eds. *A Concordance to the English Prose of John Milton.* Binghamton, NY: Medieval & Renaissance Texts & Studies, 1985.

Stewart, Charles, ed. *Creolization: History, Ethnography, Theory.* Walnut Creek, CA: Left Coast Press, 2007.

Stipek, Deborah J. *Motivation to Learn: Integrating Theory and Practice.* Boston: Allyn & Bacon, 2002.

Strang, Barbara M. H. *A History of English.* London: Methuen, 1970.

Strohm, Paul. *England's Empty Throne: Usurpation and the Language of Legitimation, 1399–1422.* Notre Dame, IN: University of Notre Dame Press, 2006.

Suzuki, Seiichi. "Metrical Positions and Their Linguistic Realisations in Old Germanic Metre: A Typological Overview." *Studia Metrica et Poetica* 1, no. 2 (2014): 9–38.

Sweet, Henry. *A History of English Sounds.* London: Trübner, 1874.

——. *Anglo-Saxon Reader in Prose and Verse,* 15th ed., revised by Dorothy Whitelock. Oxford: Oxford University Press, 1977.

Sylvester, Richard S., ed. *The Complete Works of St. Thomas More.* Vol. 2. New Haven, CT: Yale University Press, 1963.

Taavitsainen, Irma, and Andreas H. Jucker. "Twenty Years of Historical Pragmatics. Origins, Developments and Changing Thought Styles." *Journal of Historical Pragmatics* 16, no. 1 (2015): 1–24.

Tan, Rachel Siew Kuang, and Ee-Ling Low. "Rhythmic Patterning in Malaysia and Singapore English." *Language and Speech* 57 (2014): 196–214.

Thomas, Erik. "Prosodic Features of African American English." In *The Oxford Handbook of African American Language,* edited by Jennifer Bloomquist, Lisa J. Green, and Sonja L. Lanehart. Oxford: Oxford University Press, 2015.

Thornton, Weldon, ed. *Allusions in Ulysses: A Line-by-line Reference to Joyce's Complex Symbolism.* Chapel Hill: University of North Carolina Press, 1968.

Tichý, Ondřej. "Lexical Obsolescence and Loss in English: 1700–2000." In *Patterns in Text: Corpus-driven Methods and Applications,* edited by Joanna Kopaczyk and Jukka Tyrkkö. Amsterdam: John Benjamins, forthcoming.

Tieken-Boon van Ostade, Ingrid. *An Introduction to Late Modern English.* Edinburgh: Edinburgh University Press, 2009.

Times of India news-brief, October 12, 2001, www.timesofindia.com.

Todd, Loreto. *Modern Englishes: Pidgins and Creoles.* Oxford: Blackwell, 1984.

Tolkien, J. R. R. *Beowulf: A Translation and Commentary together with Sellic Spell,* edited by Christopher Tolkien. Boston: Houghton Mifflin Harcourt, 2014.

Traugott, Elizabeth. *A History of English Syntax: A Transformational Approach to the History of English Sentence Structure.* New York: Holt, Rinehart, and Winston, 1972.

——. "From Propositional to Textual and Expressive Meanings: Some Semantic-pragmatic Aspects of Grammaticalization." In *Perspectives on Historical Linguistics,* edited by Winfred P. Lehmann and Yakov Malkiel, 45–271. Amsterdam: John Benjamins, 1982.

——. "On Regularity of Semantic Change." *Journal of Literary Semantics* 14, no. 3 (1985): 155–73.

———. "On the Rise of Epistemic Meanings in English: An Example of Subjectification in Semantic Change." *Language* 65, no. 1 (1989): 31–55.

———. "Subjectification in Grammaticalisation." In *Subjectivity and Subjectivisation,* edited by Dieter Stein and Susan Wright, 31–54. Cambridge: Cambridge University Press, 1995.

———. "Subjectification and the Development of Epistemic Meaning: The Case of *Promise* and *Threaten*." In *Modality in German Languages: Historical and Comparative Perspectives,* edited by Toril Swan and Olaf Jansen Westvik, 185–210. Berlin: Mouton de Gruyter, 1997.

———. "Historical Pragmatics." In *The Handbook of Pragmatics,* edited by Laurence R. Horn and Gregory Ward, 538–61 Malden, MA: Blackwell, 2004.

———. "'All that he endeavour'd to prove was . . .': On the Emergence of Grammatical Constructions in Dialogic Contexts." In *Language in Flux: Dialogue Co-ordination, Language Variation, Change and Evolution,* edited by Robin Cooper and Ruth Kempson, 143–77. London: King's College Publications, 2008.

Traugott, Elizabeth Closs, and Ekkehard König. "The Semantics-Pragmatics of Grammaticalization Revisited." In *Approaches to Grammaticalization,* vol.1, edited by Elizabeth Closs Traugott and Bernd Heine, 189–218. Amsterdam: John Benjamins, 1991.

Traugott, Elizabeth Closs, and Terttu Nevalainen, eds. *The Oxford Handbook of the History of English.* New York: Oxford University Press, 2012.

Traugott, Elizabeth Closs, and Graeme Trousdale. *Constructionalization and Constructional Changes.* Oxford: Oxford University Press, 2013.

Treharne, Elaine. *Living Through Conquest: The Politics of Early English, 1020–1220.* Oxford: Oxford University Press, 2012.

Tristram, Hildegard. "Diglossia in Anglo-Saxon England, or What Was Spoken Old English Like?" *Studia Anglica Posnaniensa* 40 (2004): 79–110.

Trousdale, Graeme. "Words and Constructions in Grammaticalization: The End of the English Impersonal Construction." In *Studies in the History of the English Language,* vol. 4, *Empirical and Analytical Advances in the Study of English Language Change,* edited by Susan Fitzmaurice and Donka Minkova, 301–26. Berlin: Mouton de Gruyter, 2008.

Trudgill, Peter, and Jean Hannah. *International English.* London: Edward Arnold, 1985.

Turner, Lorenzo Dow, Katherine Wyly Mille, and Michael B. Montgomery. *Africanisms in the Gullah Dialect.* Columbia: University of South Carolina Press, 2002.

Turner, James. *Philology: The Forgotten Origins of the Modern Humanities.* Princeton, NJ: Princeton University Press, 2014.

Tyler, Jo. "Transforming a Syllabus from HEL." *Pedagogy* 5, no. 3 (2005): 464–71.

Tyson, Lois. *Critical Theory Today: A User-Friendly Guide,* 2nd ed. New York: Routledge, 2006.

Underwood, Ted. *Why Literary Periods Mattered: Historical Contrast and the Prestige of English Studies.* Stanford, CA: Stanford University Press, 2013.

University of Texas at Austin Linguistics Research Center, accessed October 15, 2016, http://liberalarts.utexas.edu/lrc/.

Utz, Richard. "Them Philologists: Philological Practices and Their Discontents from Nietzsche to Cerquiglini." *The Year's Work in Medievalism* 26 (2012): 4–12.

———. "*Quo Vadis,* English Studies?" *Philologie im Netz* 69 (2014): 93–99.

van Gelderen, Elly. *A History of the English Language.* 1st ed. Amsterdam: John Benjamins, 2006.

———. *A History of the English Language.* Rev. ed. Amsterdam: John Benjamins, 2014.

Véronis, Jean. "Web: Google's Counts Faked?" *Technologies du Langage,* accessed January 26, 2005, http://aixtal.blogspot.com/2005/01/web-googles-counts-faked.html.

Viereck, Wolfgang. *Regionale und Soziale Erscheinungsformen des Britischen und Amerikanischen Englisch*. Tübingen: Niemeyer, 1975.

Walker, John. *A Critical Pronouncing Dictionary and Expositor of the English Language*. London: G. G. J. and J. Robinson and T. Cadell, 1791.

Wallace, David, ed. *The Cambridge History of Medieval English Literature*. Cambridge: Cambridge University Press, 1999.

Wardhaugh, Ronald and Janet Fuller. *An Introduction to Sociolinguistics*, 7th ed. Oxford: Wiley-Blackwell, 2014.

Warren, Michelle. "Post-Philology." In *Postcolonial Moves: Medieval Through Modern*, edited by Patricia Ingham and Michelle Warren, 19–45. New York: Palgrave, Macmillan, 2003.

Warren, Martin. "Introduction to Data-Driven Learning." In *The Routledge Handbook of Language Learning and Technology*, edited by Fiona Farr and Liam Murray, 337–48. London: Routledge, 2016.

Watkins, Calvert. *The American Heritage Dictionary of IE Roots*. 2nd ed. Boston: Houghton Mifflin, 2000.

Watson, Nicholas, and Jacqueline Jenkins. *The Writings of Julian of Norwich*. University Park: Penn State University Press, 2006.

Watts, Richard J. *Language Myths and the History of English*. Oxford: Oxford University Press, 2011.

———. "English Historical Linguistics: Myths of the English Language." In *English Historical Linguistics: An International Handbook*. Vol. 2, edited by Alex Bergs and Laurel Brinton, 1256–73. Boston: Mouton de Gruyter, 2012.

Webster's New International Dictionary of the English Language. 3rd ed., edited by Philip B. Gove et al. Springfield, MA: Merriam-Webster, 1961.

Webster, Noah. *Preface to American Dictionary of the English Language*. Accessed October 16, 2016. webstersdictionary1828.com/Preface.

Weiner, Bernard. "The Development of an Attribution-based Theory of Motivation: A History of Ideas." *Educational Psychologist* 45, no. 1 (2010): 28–36.

Weinreich, Uriel, William Labov, and Marvin I. Herzog. "Empirical Foundations for a Theory of Language Change." In *Directions for Historical Linguistics: A Symposium*, edited by Winfred P. Lehmann and Yakov Malkiel, 95–195. Austin: University of Texas Press, 1968.

Weinstein, Claire Ellen. "Executive Control Processes in Learning: Why Knowing How to Learn Is Not Enough." *Journal of College Reading and Learning* 21 (1988): 48–56.

Weiskott, Eric. "Phantom Syllables in the English Alliterative Tradition." *Modern Philology* 110 (2013): 441–58.

———. *English Alliterative Verse: Poetic Tradition and Literary History*. Cambridge: Cambridge University Press, 2016.

Weller, M. "The Openness-Creativity Cycle in Education." *Journal of Interactive Media in Education* 1 (2012): p.Art. 2.

———. *Battle for Open: How Openness Won and Why It Doesn't Feel like Victory*. London: Ubiquity Press, accessed January 6, 2016, http://dx.doi.org/10.5334/bam.

Wells, John C. *Accents of English*. 3 vols. Cambridge: Cambridge University Press, 1982.

———. "Accents of English." *UCL Division of Psychology and Language Sciences*, accessed October 15, 2016, http://www.phon.ucl.ac.uk/home/wells/accentsanddialects/.

Whelan, Richard. "The American Spelling Reform Movement." *Verbatim* 27, no. 4 (2002): 1–7.

White, Barbara. "Designing Computer Games to Help Physics Students Understand Newton's Laws of Motion." *Cognition and Instruction* 1 (1984): 69–108.

White, Hayden. *The Content of the Form: Narrative Discourse and Historical Representation*. Baltimore: Johns Hopkins University Press, 1987.

White, Richard G. "Memorandum on English Pronunciation in the Elizabethan Era." *Appendix to Vol. 12 of The Works of William Shakespeare*. Boston: Little, Brown, 1865.

Wiley, Raymond A. *John Mitchell Kemble and Jacob Grimm: A Correspondence, 1832-1852*. Leiden: Brill, 1971.

Wilhelm, Ian. "Where the International Students Are, State by State." *The Chronicle of Higher Education*. Last modified November 12, 2014. chronicle.com.myaccess.library.utoronto.ca/article/Where-the-International/135634.

Williams, Tara. "The Value of the History of the English Language Course for the Twenty-First Century." *Profession* 12 (2010): 165–76.

Wilson, Joycelyn. "Outkast'd and Claimin' True: The Language of Schooling and Education in the Southern Hip-Hop Community of Practice." PhD diss., University of Georgia, 2007.

Winchester, Simon. *The Meaning of Everything*. Oxford: Oxford University Press, 2003.

Wogan-Browne, Jocelyn, and Nicholas Watson. *The Idea of the Vernacular*. University Park: Penn State University Press, 1999.

Wolfram, Walt, and Erik Thomas. *The Development of African American English*. Oxford: Wiley-Blackwell, 2002.

Wong, Jock. "The Particles of Singapore English: A Semantic and Cultural Interpretation." *Journal of Pragmatics* 36 (2004): 739–93.

Wood, David, Jerome Bruner, and Gail Ross. "The Role of Tutoring in Problem Solving." *Journal of Child Psychology and Psychiatry* 17 (1976): 89–100.

Woolfolk, Anita. *Educational Psychology: Active Learning Edition*. 13th ed. Boston, MA: Allyn & Bacon, 2016.

Wright, Joseph, and Elizabeth M. Wright. *Old English Grammar*. 3rd ed. New York: Oxford University Press, 1925.

Word Histories and Mysteries: From Abracadabra to Zeus. Boston: Houghton Mifflin, 2004.

Wulff, Stefanie. "Words and Idioms." In *The Oxford Handbook of Construction Grammar*, edited by Thomas Hoffmann and Graeme Trousdale, 274–89. Oxford: Oxford University Press, 2013.

Yakovlev, Nicolay. "The Development of Alliterative Metre from Old to Middle English." Ph.D. diss., University of Oxford, 2008.

———. "On Final –e in the B-Verses of *Sir Gawain and the Green Knight*." In *Approaches to the Metres of Alliterative Verse*, edited by Judith Jefferson and Ad Putter, 135–57. Leeds: Leeds Texts and Monographs, 2009.

———. "Prosodic Restrictions on the Short Dip in Late Middle English Alliterative Verse." *Yearbook of Langland Studies* 23 (2009): 217–42.

Yano, Yasukata. "The Future of English and the Kachruvian Three Circle Model." In *World Englishes-Problems, Properties and Prospects: Selected Papers from the 13th IAWE Conference*, edited by Thomas Hoffman and Lucia Siebers, 379–84. Amsterdam: John Benjamins, 2009.

Yeager, David Scott, and Carol S. Dweck. "Mindsets That Promote Resilience: When Students Believe That Personal Characteristics Can Be Developed." *Educational Psychologist* 47, no. 4 (2012): 302–14.

Young, Vershawn Ashanti, and Aja Y. Martinez, eds. *Code-Meshing as World English: Pedagogy, Policy, Performance*. Urbana, IL: National Council of Teachers of English, 2011.

YouTube. *Statistics*, accessed December 21, 2015. https://www.youtube.com/yt/press/statistics.html.

Zarnecki, George, Janet Holt, and Tristam Holland. *English Romanesque Art 1066–1200*. London: Weidenfeld and Nicolson, 1984.

Zimmerman, Barry J. "From Cognitive Modeling to Self-Regulation: A Social Cognitive Career Path." *Educational Psychologist* 48, no. 3 (2013): 135–47.

Zok, David. "Turkey's Language Revolution and the Status of English Today." *The English Languages: History, Diaspora, Culture* 1 (2010), http://jps.library.utoronto.ca/index.php/elhdc/article/view/14300.

Zwicky, Arnold. "Just Between Dr. Language and I." *Language Log*, accessed May 4, 2006, http://itre.cis.upenn.edu/~myl/languagelog/archives/002386.html.

Zwicky, Arnold. "Libfixes." *Arnold Zwicky's Blog*, accessed April 3, 2016, http://arnoldzwicky.org/2010/01/23/libfixes/.

INDEX

corpora (*contd.*)

Parsed Spoken English (DCPSE), 160; *Dictionary of Old English Web Corpus*, 98; *Helsinki Corpus (of English Texts)*, 98, 103, 141, 144, 148, 171, 387n18, 387n22, 387n24; *International Computer Archive of Modern and Medieval English (ICAME)*, 98; *International Corpus of English (ICE)*, 249, 385n11; *Lampeter Corpus of Early Modern English Tracts*, 99; *Lancaster-Oslo/ Bergen (LOB) Corpus*, 98; *The Old Bailey Corpus*, 99, 100, 161, 170; *Old English Dictionary Corpus*, 99; *A Representative Corpus of Historical English* Registers 3.2 (*ARCHER*), 161, 170; *See also* Linguistic Atlas Project

corpus linguistics. *See* linguistics

creoles, 8, 13, 18–19, 36–37, 51, 86, 241–42, 243, 245, 250, 253–54, 255–62, 266, 267–68, 295, 310, 376n18, 376n19, 400n11, 401n35, 401n40, 406n14; Gullah, 262, 295, 298, 309–11, 407n9, 407n11, 407n16; Jamaican, 261, 272, 401n29, 413n31; *See also* English (varieties of); pidgins; postcolonialism

creolist perspective, 38, 254, 296, 370, 399n1, 401n29, 406n14

derivation, 102–3, 161–64, 349, 366

diachronic change, 7, 8, 29–31, 35, 61, 64, 74, 94, 96–97, 108–16, 142, 149–54, 195–209, 239, 368, 369, 383n51, 384n62, 384n9, 384n10, 385n13, 386n3, 386n4, 387n12, 393–94n24

dialects. *See* English (varieties of); regional dialects and varieties

dialectology, 311–12, 407n20

dictionaries, 7, 64–65, 73–74, 98–99, 107–8, 159–62, 173–84, 202, 213, 219, 225–26, 228, 267–68, 292, 339, 344, 350–53, 360–62, 389n12, 389n16, 390n42, 391n50, 402–3n5, 417n16, 417n17, 417–18n18. *See also* Oxford English Dictionary

digital communication, 9, 97–100, 141–42, 176–77, 225–26, 267–71, 289, 291–94, 310–12, 329, 332, 351–52, 357–64. *See also* multimedia; pedagogical resources

education (as an academic program), 2, 41, 82, 117–18

Early Modern English, 9, 18, 31, 35-6, 49, 51, 54, 66, 78, 79, 82, 94, 99, 102, 141, 148-9, 151, 153, 164, 171, 181, 183, 197, 198, 199, 205–8, 217, 231, 266, 267, 319, 323, 324, 333, 337-9, 353, 361, 369

Eliot, George, 72–73

Emergence, 6–7, 8, 117–39, 253–63, 381n26, 399–400n1

English (varieties of), 136–37, 239–40, 242, 261–63, 273–75; African American Vernacular (AAVE/AAE), 38, 72, 86–87, 138, 241, 280–82, 295–99, 302, 304, 322–23, 351, 378n16, 380n8, 386n9, 398–99n28, 401n42, 406n14, 413n33, 413n34; American (AmE), 8, 19, 27, 138, 149–51, 153–55, 159–60, 162, 168–70, 272, 280, 285–304, 340, 366, 370, 374n5, 380n7, 387n23, 387n24, 390n18, 406n2, 406n6, 417n16; Australian, 26, 36, 39, 99, 179, 228–29, 233, 240–42, 243, 245, 257–58, 260, 340, 390n32, 390n33; Canadian, 36, 117, 136–37, 241–42, 243, 258, 268, 272, 340, 366, 403n7, 403n17; Chicano, 299–300; English as a Second (Foreign) Language (EFL/ESL), 9, 26, 27, 142, 242, 243–44, 247, 273, 313–24; Indian (IE), 38, 99, 241, 247, 261, 275–78, 281, 282, 321, 404n14, 404n15, 404n17, 405n33, 406n50, 412n2 (*see also* India); Nigerian, 22, 261, 269, 272, 278, 280; non-standard home variety (NSHV), 313–34, 316–17, 319, 321, 324; Present-Day English (PDE), 22, 26–27, 29, 38, 47, 54, 98–100, 102–4, 143, 151–53, 187–88, 192, 202, 204, 208, 238, 241–42, 293, 300–3, 315–17, 319–22, 338, 351, 412n22, 413n29, 413n34; Singapore, 276–78, 374n6, 404n16; South African, 30, 38–39, 243, 278, 340, 376n28; Southern American (SAE), 291, 296–97, 301–3 (*see also* Early Modern English; Late Modern English; Middle English; New Englishes; Old English; World Englishes); *See also* creoles; pidgins; regional dialects and varieties